How to Start, Finance
and Operate
YOUR OWN BUSINESS

How to Start, Finance and Operate
YOUR OWN BUSINESS

By James L. Silvester

Foreword by former United States Senator Paul S. Trible, Jr.

A Birch Lane Press Book
Published by Carol Publishing Group

A Birch Lane Press Book
Published by Carol Publishing Group
Birch Lane Press is a registered trademark of Carol Communications,
   Inc.
Editorial Offices: 600 Madison Avenue, New York, N.Y. 10022
Sales & Distribution Offices: 120 Enterprise Avenue, Secaucus,
   N.J. 07094
In Canada: Canadian Manda Group, One Atlantic Avenue, Suite 105,
   Toronto, Ontario M6K 3E7
Queries regarding rights and permissions should be addressed to
Carol Publishing Group, 600 Madison Avenue, New York, N.Y. 10022

Carol Publishing Group books are available at special discounts for
bulk purchases, sales promotions, fund-raising, or educational
purposes. Special editions can be created to specifications. For
details contact: Special Sales Department, Carol Publishing
Group, 120 Enterprise Avenue, Secaucus, N.J. 07094

Manufactured in the United States of America
10 9 8 7 6 5 4 3 2 1

Library of Congress Cataloging-in-Publication Data

Silvester, James L.
   How to start, finance and operate your own business / by James L.
Silvester. — [New ed.]
      p. cm.
   "A Birch Lane Press Book."
   Includes index.
   ISBN 1-55972-287-8
1. New business enterprises.   I. Title.
HD62.5.S56   1995
658.1′1—dc20   94–44301
                                                              CIP

3 2280 00518 5848

CONTENTS

FOREWORD

Do you want to start your own business?

Then you need the information this book can provide. As someone who participates daily in the representative process that is the hallmark of our national government, I am keenly aware of the limits to what government can do. While we can in some cases provide information and in certain limited cases take direct action, we cannot create.

Only you can do that. I fervently hope you do. We all know that it is so-called "small businesses" that create jobs, provide services, strengthen communities, and are a critical element of the mysterious condition called "prosperity."

Yet I think we need to go a step beyond the phrase "small business" and think in terms of a particular type of small business—what I would call "infant business." The moment an idea moves from the dream stage in your mind to the planning stage, then I think you are an infant business. Now the challenge is to bring you forth into a productive small business.

James Silvester gives you the tools to help move you from being an infant business to a small business. In our society, each of us has the opportunity to create a small business. If you've picked up this book, you no doubt have the motivation. This book will help provide the third element you need—the knowledge to do so.

The combination of the opportunity our society provides and your motivation and knowledge will be what determines if our nation prospers. As George Gilder said about the processes of our economy:

> This is a drama most essentially not of measurable money and machines, aggregates and distributions, but of mind and morale. Above the vast architecture of production, and surrounding it, is a statistically invisible atmosphere of moods and ideas, a phantasmagoria of images and visions of the future, which either

admit, or eclipse, the sustaining light and power of the sun: the life-giving faith in the possibility that free enterprises can prevail among the unpredictable forms of wealth in the unknown world to come.

Paul S. Trible, Jr.
Former United States Senator from Virginia

PREFACE

This book is designed as a guide for those individuals seeking to be in business for themselves and those existing enterprises searching for new opportunities. Chapter 1 specifically deals with people who have not yet started their own businesses. It attempts to convey to prospective entrepreneurs the characteristics needed to be successfully self-employed.

Chapter 2 shows how an individual or existing firm may evaluate business opportunities so as to avoid potentially dangerous mistakes commonly made because sufficient analysis is lacking.

Chapter 3 deals with different sources of managerial assistance available to the small business community.

Chapter 4 explains the importance of proper legal structure in fulfilling the objectives of owners and managers.

The nature of business funding arrangements in different situations is described in Chapter 5. It also outlines the use of capital relative to the profit-making function and shows how to determine funding needs.

Chapter 6 specifically reviews the nature of business funding and the various types of capital involved. In addition, traditional and non-traditional financial outlets are broadly described.

The details concerning the construction of the "all important" business plan is discussed in Chapter 7. An inadequate plan will be rejected without question. There are standards that must be considered.

Chapter 8 reviews the particulars in dealing with funding sources. Producing an excellent business plan isn't enough. The plan must be presented verbally in a confident and convincing manner keeping in mind that hard give-and-take negotiations will occur.

Chapter 9 explains the need for sound management practices when operating a business in today's tough environment. Certain managerial techniques are identified and reviewed.

Chapter 10 explains some of the important elements to consider when starting and funding a service, retail, wholesale, or manufacturing business.

Part II expands on the sources listed in Chapter 6 by homing in on specific government programs directed at small firms and the individual investment preferences of many private funding outlets.

Appendixes A–K offer additional sources of help and information to entrepreneurs.

NOTE: Neither the author nor the publisher will be held liable for any transactions with any person, proprietorship, partnership, corporation, or association listed in this book. It is believed that all names, addresses, and telephone numbers listed in this book are accurate as of the time of printing, although no guarantee can or will be made.

ACKNOWLEDGMENTS

I dedicate this book to my deceased parents. Without their support and encouragement throughout life, this project would not have been possible.

Acknowledgment must also be given to my two friends who helped in gathering the pertinent information contained herein:

Todd M. McConville
and
Sherri L. Renner

INTRODUCTION
A NEW EMPHASIS

It's a relief to note that a large contingent of public and private economists, academicians, and journalists are currently acknowledging the vital role of small businesses in the total economy. Many of these experts believe that government should do more to foster small business vitality and growth. In fact, some call it our economic salvation. Many a futurist has proclaimed that small business entrepreneurs will lead us to continuing economic prosperity in the 90's and beyond. There is reason to believe this is true.

Recent studies conducted by major universities, think tanks, congressional committees, and the U.S. Small Business Administration have revealed that most of the economic growth over the last twenty years can be traced to the small business community. The same studies concluded that small firms are accountable for about 50 percent of the country's output and most of the growth in employment over the same period. To illustrate this point, one can turn to a research study conducted by MIT Professor David Birch, which concluded that between 1969 and 1976 approximately 82 percent of all the new jobs created in the United States were the result of small business activity. To top all this off is the fact that most innovations over the last century originated in the research departments of small businesses or by individual entrepreneurs. These facts have given reason to call the small business sector, which comprises nearly 95 percent of all private firms in the country, the "vital majority."

For too many years small firms were looked upon as an insignificant part of our economic life and largely ignored by representative governments. Two decades ago the catch phrase was "bigger is better" and much of the country's tax policies and resources were shifted in favor of giant corporations at the expense of small businesses and prospective entrepreneurs. Society has paid the price of this approach. It is safe to say that a strong correlation exists between the nation's emphasis on large corporate organizations and its general economic decline. Without a doubt, many giant firms are stagnant and drifting without focus or resolve. Most cannot compete in the international marketplace and are severe drags on the U.S. economy.

Many of these large concerns are attempting to maintain the status quo against enlightened politicians who would emphasize free trade and shift the country's resources, either wholly or partially, back to the more productive small business sector. If they are successful in their lobbying efforts and reverse this new direction, it would condemn the United States to continued economic stagnation and compromise our standing as a world leader. In addition, it must never be forgotten that American political freedoms are directly linked to the survival of the entrepreneur as a vital force in society.

Part I
EVERYTHING YOU NEED TO KNOW

1

ARE YOU THE TYPE?
It's Important to Know

The New Wave

The 1990s have been called the "era of the entrepreneur" for good reason. Despite severe economic conditions and the highest level of business failure since the Great Depression, more people are pursuing self-employment than at any time in our country's history, as evidenced in Table 1. Self-satisfaction, desire for independence, limited job opportunities, and layoffs seem to be the main reasons why individuals are seeking to be their own bosses.

Know Your Limitations

The lure of self-employment should be tempered with a keen sense of reality based on some facts. Most new businesses fail within the first three years of operation, according to numerous studies conducted by private groups and the Small Business Administration. Researchers have concluded that most of these failures were due to poor business practices on the part of the entrepreneur. In addition, the studies found that many individuals seeking the self-employment option were not cut out for the task. Some people think they can beat the odds by buying an established business that has been in operation for some time or by purchasing a franchise. True, it will increase your chances somewhat in the beginning, but if you fail to use sound business techniques, and/ or lack the necessary personality traits, then the possibility of success in any business endeavor is greatly diminished.

TABLE 1

New Business Incorporations

1965	203,897	1980	533,520
1966	200,010	1981	581,661
1967	206,569	1982	566,942
1968	233,635	1983	600,400
1969	274,267	1984	634,991
1970	264,209	1985	668,904
1971	287,577	1986	702,101
1972	316,601	1987	685,377
1973	329,358	1988	683,808
1974	319,149	1989	678,653
1975	326,345	1990	646,702
1976	357,766	1991	629,886
1977	436,170	1992	669,519
1978	478,019	1993	707,413
1979	524,565		

Note: These figures do not include new businesses that were started as sole proprietorships or partnerships. If they did, the numbers would exceed 1 million.

Source: By permission of Dun & Bradstreet Credit Services, a company of The Dun & Bradstreet Corporation and U.S. Small Business Administration.

Whether you are starting a new business or buying an existing operation, asking yourself the following question could reveal potential problem areas: Do I have what it takes? Most small businesses are risky at best, but your chances of success are improved if you realistically understand the difficulties involved and work out as many of them as you can before jumping in with both feet.

Studies by the U.S. Small Business Administration have concluded that most successful entrepreneurs display common characteristics. They are as follows:

Drive

- *Responsibility*—ability to make sure things get done
- *Persistence*—willingness to see things finalized
- *Health*—having physical and mental stamina

- *Initiative*—ability to take charge when necessary and be the first to act
- *Vigor*—having the limitless vitality needed to succeed

Thinking Ability

- *Originality*—ability to create new ideas and approaches
- *Creativity*—ability to think and explore in unorthodox ways; also initiative
- *Critical Sense*—ability to make intelligent comparison and comment
- *Analytical Sense*—ability to reason in practical, theoretical and abstract terms

Human Relations Ability

- *Sociability*—ability to get along with others, including peers, in a number of settings (home, work, politics, international relations, etc.)
- *Cooperation*—willingness to work with others in a constructive manner
- *Tactfulness*—ability to hold or water down discomforting comments or actions
- *Cheerfulness*—willingness to laugh and smile even when the going gets rough
- *Consideration*—ability to appreciate the value of other people's time and money
- *Personal Relations*—ability to get along with people who are close
- *Ascendancy*—ability to govern and control wisely without excessive ego involvement
- *Emotional Stability*—having appropriate maturity level for the task
- *Cautiousness*—ability to give serious evaluation before taking risk; successful entrepreneurs avoid gambling; they are moderate risk takers

Communications Ability

- *Oral Communications*—ability to speak in a clear, concise, and logical manner

- *Verbal Comprehension*—ability to listen, absorb, and understand others' conversation
- *Written Communication*—ability to write in a clear, concise, and logical way

Technical Knowledge

- *Information*—expertise about the physical process of producing the goods or services.

If it can be determined that you possess most of the above-mentioned traits or can acquire them if deficiencies exist, then your chance of success in a small business is greatly enhanced. In your comparison, try to avoid overly optimistic estimates of yourself. Be candid about your personality traits and abilities. It is better to learn now that you are not suited for self-employment before investing time, money, and hard work in something that is doomed to fail from the beginning. Economic and emotional scares can be avoided if you heed the warning signals.

Additional insight into self-evaluation can be gained by answering the questions in Table 2. Again, honest appraisal is called for to ensure accuracy in defining yourself. Remember, you are risking your time and hard-earned dollars.

If most of the checks are on the left-hand side of the table, then your chances of small business success are reasonable. Make sure that these positive answers were not a result of wishful thinking. Checks found in the center or on the right-hand side of the table should be carefully examined to determine if these weaknesses can be overcome. Perhaps in the short term you should hire associates and/or consultants whose strong points compensate your weak areas. Many of your weaknesses can probably be corrected through education and training. But that is a long-term consideration. If you are weak in too many areas, it is in your best interest not to pursue self-employment any further.

Unorthodox Characteristics

A. David Silver, a noted venture capitalist and author, who manages various venture-related firms in New Mexico, contends in his book *The Entrepreneurial Life: How to Go for It and Get It* (New York: John Wiley and Sons) that many successful entrepreneurs experience a

TABLE 2

RATING SCALE FOR PERSONAL TRAITS IMPORTANT TO A BUSINESS PROPRIETOR

INSTRUCTIONS: After each question place a check mark on the line at the point closest to your answer. The check mark need not be placed directly over one of the suggested answers because your rating may lie somewhere between two answers. Be honest with yourself.

ARE YOU A SELF-STARTER? _____

I do things my own way. Nobody needs to tell me to get going.	If someone gets me started, I keep going all right.	Easy does it. I don't put myself out until I have to.

HOW DO YOU FEEL ABOUT OTHER PEOPLE? _____

I like people. I can get along with just about anybody.	I have plenty of friends. I don't need anyone else.	Most people bug me.

CAN YOU LEAD OTHERS? _____

I can get most people to go along without much difficulty.	I can get people to do things if I drive them.	I let someone else get things moving.

CAN YOU TAKE RESPONSIBILITY? _____

I like to take charge and see things through.	I'll take over if I have to, but I'd rather let someone else be responsible.	There's always some eager beaver around wanting to show off. I say let him.

HOW GOOD AN ORGANIZER ARE YOU? _____

I like to have a plan before I start. I'm usually the one to get things lined up.	I do all right unless things get too goofed up. Then I cop out.	I just take things as they come.

HOW GOOD A WORKER ARE YOU? _____

| I can keep going as long as necessary. I don't mind working hard. | I'll work hard for a while, but when I've had enough, that's it! | I can't see that hard work gets you anywhere. |

CAN YOU MAKE DECISIONS? _____

| I can make up my mind in a hurry if necessary, and my decision is usually o.k. | I can if I have plenty of time. If I have to make up my mind fast, I usually regret it. | I don't like to be the one who decides things. I'd probably blow it. |

CAN PEOPLE TRUST WHAT YOU SAY? _____

| They sure can. I don't say things I don't mean. | I try to be on the level, but sometimes I just say what's easiest. | What's the sweat if the other fellow doesn't know the difference. |

CAN YOU STICK WITH IT? _____

| If I make up my mind to do something, I don't let anything stop me. | I usually finish what I start. | If a job doesn't go right, I turn off. Why beat your brains out? |

HOW GOOD IS YOUR HEALTH? _____

| I never run down. | I have enough energy for most things I want to do. | I run out of juice sooner than most of my friends seem to. |

SOURCE: U.S. Small Business Administration.

number of common difficulties in early life that may account for their later achievements. These difficulties include "educational arrest, lack of social interaction or motivation, sickly in nature, less wealth than peers, and small physical build." In addition, Silver suggests that venture capitalists prefer adult entrepreneurs who suffer from "guilt," especially the kind of guilt derived from "divorce." They feel it is a highly "motivating" factor. Also, individuals experiencing guilt in their "marriages" are considered good prospects. Silver also implied in an April 19, 1978, article published by the periodical *Chicago Business*, that successful entrepreneurs tended to be dominated by "achievement oriented mothers" and have "extraordinary sex drives."

It should not be implied that the aforementioned characteristics are necessary in order to be successful in your own business. It is obvious that many people have made a go of their businesses without having a single characteristic mentioned in this section. What should be remembered is that some who have made it through self-employment had experienced stumbling blocks in earlier years, thereby providing a foundation to face the difficult choices encountered in starting and managing a business.

In addition, keep in mind that Mr. Silver was referring to venture capitalists, who tend to be a unique breed unlike other funding sources. These financiers pursue people and opportunities who are quite different from the typical Joe or Jane running the average small business. Generally, venture capitalists will invest only in firms and entrepreneurs that are geared for fast growth. They want to make big bucks and feel it takes a certain type of individual to accomplish this task. Chapter 6 provides more discussion about venture capitalists.

Not a Bed of Roses

Once it is determined that you possess most of the necessary traits to run a small business and can deal with deficiencies that exist, you must consider the pros and cons of self-employment before committing time and energy beyond this point. There are some distinct negative aspects of running your own business. They are highlighted below:

- *Insecurity*—Rapid inflation and disinflation, compressed economic cycles, unanticipated trends, and other factors can cause business to fluctuate dramatically for a small firm throughout one year or from one year to the next.
- *Number of Business Failures*—The failure rate for small businesses is at an all-time high, obviously reflecting the current severity of the recession.

- *Possibility of Losing Money*—Where you find potential reward the possibility of risk is always present. An individual can lose a considerable amount of money if the business is a losing proposition and he fails to bail out in time to cut large losses.
- *Long Hours*—Contrary to popular belief, most successful entrepreneurs put in 12-hour days. Most work as hard as corporate executives.
- *Medium Income*—Successful small business people make, on the average, about the same as a mid-level manager in a large corporation.
- *Income Variation*—Income derived from your own business will be less regular than the receipt of a salary or wage from an employer. If you are starting a new business, the first six to twelve months might be bad because the operation is normally functioning at a loss. Even after business income is generated, variations in profits can be expected because of many factors (seasonal business, slow accounts receivables, heavy inventories, etc.).

On the other hand, there are also advantages to self-employment.

- *Independence*—Self-employment provides a degree of personal and economic freedom not found when working for somebody else.
- *Job Security*—Many individuals feel that given the frequency of employee cutbacks in large and medium-sized firms, self-employment actually gives someone a degree of job security that corporate employees lack. Consequently, many business executives and hourly workers are seriously pursuing small business opportunities. Many are already running sideline businesses hoping to someday generate a full-time operation.
- *Potential Profit*—Where you find the potential for risk, profit opportunities also exist. With the recession almost over and economic expansion under way, it is an ideal time to be starting a small business. This is even more true of service enterprises, which comprise most of the nation's small firms. The service field is expected to be the fastest growing sector of the economy. For the time being, inflation is under control and that is a positive note to investors, managers, and consumers.
- *Quality of Life*—Many individuals find a high degree of fulfillment in self-employment. Some successful entrepreneurs have reported

an enhanced self-image and positive attitude along with other psychological rewards.

- *New Emphasis on Small Firms*—As mentioned in the introduction, governments are starting to realize the importance of the small business sector to the whole economy. Consequently, more governmental resources and favorable tax legislation will be directed to the small business community. Someday in the near future the entrepreneur will be seen, not as an enemy to be wiped out, but as our economic salvation.

2

EVALUATING BUSINESS OPPORTUNITIES
Protection Against Disaster

Take Time to Investigate

When seeking to start a business or buy an existing operation, investigation and analysis should be given high priority. It is surprising to note the many well-intentioned opportunity seekers, both individuals and companies pursuing expansion, who fail to properly examine prospective investment possibilities. The consequence of this inadequate investigation is generally financial hardship. In some cases, horror would be a better term to use.

There are many reasons why people fail to make proper evaluations before jumping in with both feet. The primary ones are quite obvious. Would-be entrepreneurs often lack the knowledge to conduct proper investigation and analysis and/or are unable to pay for professional help to do the necessary work. Sometimes people are impulsive and lack the patience to perform an adequate examination. Inappropriate or insufficient investigation will lead to predictable outcomes that include but are not limited to the following:

— Underestimation of capital needs
— Overestimation of market potential
— Underestimation of competition
— Inappropriate location

— Acquisition of obsolete equipment
— Acquisition of unanticipated business debts and claims
— Questionable business reputation that may take years to correct

Spend the time to investigate and analyze all possible aspects of a business proposition. Failure to do so could result in financial disaster, not to mention the negative psychological effects that can leave an individual or organization scarred for a long time to come.

Which Way to Go

What business opportunity should I pursue? This is a question generally answered before you know your suitability for self-employment. It is something that should be carefully examined up to the very minute before committing yourself to any course of action.

A good starting point would be an evaluation of your experience and background. This would include your education, employment history, and hobbies. Compare your achievements with what you like to do. The more knowledge and experience you possess that can be used in operating a business, the greater are your chances of success.

So it is wise to pick a field that you know something about. Make sure you like operating in that area. Dislike or lack of enthusiasm for the business you choose will probably lead to failure. You might consider working for another small business, in your area of interest, in order to learn the ropes.

Your road to business ownership can lead in four directions, each having unique pros and cons. You can purchase a firm already in business or start from scratch. Acquiring a franchise is another possibility; it incorporates the features of both a start-up and an existing operation. When you purchase a franchise you are basically paying for the right to market an already established product or service owned by somebody else (the franchisor). Under your franchise agreement, you (the franchisee) are expected to market the product/service successfully. The fourth road to ownership is limited to a few individuals. Someday you might be lucky enough to inherit a business. Since this possibility is remote for most people, its advantages and disadvantages will not be discussed.

Purchasing an Existing Operation

There are some advantages to buying an existing business. Occasionally a going concern may be available at a bargain price because the owner is anxious to sell. Investigation by you and your attorney or accountant should determine the owner's exact reasons for selling. Even though the price seems low, other factors might make the deal a costly endeavor.

Buying an existing operation reduces the time and cost associated with establishing a new business. Your customer base is already established and much of the legwork associated with starting out is already completed. In addition, the previous owner might convey some helpful tips and experiences in operating the business, thereby reducing the time involved in the learning process. You might consider hiring the former owner full or part time. The biggest advantage to buying an existing firm is the fact that the business already has a proven track record. Research shows that the longer a business has been around the less likely it is to fail. Table 3 illustrates this fact.

However, buying an existing operation can also provide pitfalls to potential entrepreneurs. You may pay too much for the business because of inflated estimates of worth. Current inventories and accounts receivables (customer accounts) may be dated. The firm's equipment might be in poor condition. Customer relations (goodwill) might be in bad shape, and the firm's present location may not be the best. Refer to Table 4 for causes of business failure.

TABLE 3

AGE OF BUSINESS FAILURE

Age in Years	Percentage of Total Failures
Five Years or Less	49.1
Six to Ten Years	30.7
Over Ten Years	20.2

SOURCE: "The Business Failure Record." By permission of Dun & Bradstreet Credit Services, a company of The Dun & Bradstreet Corporation.

TABLE 4

Apparent Causes 1981	Percent	Manufacturers	Wholesalers	Retailers	Construction	Commercial Services	All
NEGLECT Due to	Bad Habits	0.1	0.4	0.1	0.2	0.1	0.2
	Poor Health	0.1	0.4	0.2	0.2	0.2	0.2
	Marital Difficulties	0.1	—	0.1	0.1	—	0.1
	Other	0.1	0.1	0.3	0.1	0.1	0.2
FRAUD On the part of the principals, reflected by	Misleading Name	—	0.1	0.0	—	0.1	0.0
	False Financial Statement	0.1	0.3	0.1	0.0	0.1	0.1
	Premeditated Overbuy	0.1	0.1	0.0	—	—	0.0
	Irregular Disposal of Assets	0.2	0.3	0.0	0.0	0.1	0.1
	Other	—	—	0.0	0.0	0.1	0.0
LACK OF EXPERIENCE IN THE LINE	Inadequate Sales	58.2	58.9	60.9	63.6	50.4	59.4
LACK OF MANAGERIAL EXPERIENCE	Heavy Operating Expenses	32.5	25.6	21.9	21.5	29.9	24.7
	Receivables Difficulties	11.9	12.1	2.4	9.1	5.0	6.4
UNBALANCED EXPERIENCE	Inventory Difficulties	5.4	10.9	11.6	1.0	0.8	6.9
INCOMPETENCE	Excessive Fixed Assets	4.7	1.9	2.7	1.9	5.6	3.1
	Poor Location	0.5	0.7	4.2	0.5	1.5	2.2
Evidenced by inability to avoid conditions which resulted in	Competitive Weakness	14.7	16.9	17.9	14.7	15.7	16.3
	Other	3.5	2.3	1.8	8.0	2.4	3.5
DISASTER	Fire	0.3	0.1	0.2	0.0	0.2	0.2
Some of these occurrences could have	Flood	0.1	—	0.0	—	0.0	0.0
been provided against through insurance	Burglary	0.1	0.1	0.0	—	0.1	0.0
	Employees' Fraud		0.1	0.0	—	—	0.0
	Strike	0.1	0.2	0.0	0.0	0.0	0.1
	Other	0.1	0.1	0.2	0.2	0.0	0.1
REASON UNKNOWN		8.1	7.5	9.3	9.9	16.5	10.1
	Percent Of Total Failures	13.2	10.2	41.0	21.5	14.1	100.0

Because some failures are attributed to a combination of apparent causes, the totals of these columns exceed the totals of the corresponding columns on the left.

SOURCE: "The Business Failure Record." By permission of Dun & Bradstreet Credit Services, a company of The Dun & Bradstreet Corporation.

15

Your lawyer and accountant should assist you in identifying negative conditions that may exist before purchasing an existing enterprise. An independent financial audit by a CPA of your choice should be mandatory. After the audit is completed, ask the CPA to analyze the financial statements carefully. In addition, request that the assets listed by the seller be verified to determine true worth. These services will cost you several hundred dollars, but the cost is minimal compared to what you could lose in a bad deal. Talking to former, present, and potential customers of the business in question might give you some insights. Table 5 outlines most of the pros and cons in buying an existing business.

Starting a New Business

The advantages in starting your own business from scratch are many. You can avoid unpleasant precedents that might be established by another owner relating to vendors, customers, bankers, and creditors.

TABLE 5

BUYING AN ESTABLISHED BUSINESS

ADVANTAGES
Suppliers already established
Existing community goodwill
Established customer base
Location known to be adequate
Facilities are existent
Regulatory requirements have already been met
Credit relationships have already been established
Some inventories and supplies may be on hand
Many growing pains have been overcome
Proven employees

DISADVANTAGES
Ownership changes can result in loss of community goodwill and customers
Current policies may be difficult to break because of precedents established by former owners
Existing employees may resist change
Equipment may be in poor condition and/or obsolete
Present location may not be the best and moving is or will be required

Starting anew will insure some discretion over the location of the new enterprise, product/services to be marketed, employees hired, accounting and tax procedures used, etc. A new firm, with a unique product or service, may be the first to exploit a market in an area, thereby gaining a strong foothold against potential competitors.

A start-up situation can prove to be equally discouraging for a number of reasons. A lot of groundwork is involved in acquiring business licenses and permits, establishing relations with suppliers, buying equipment/supplies, etc. Also, new firms generally lack a customer base to support operations initially, and confidence and goodwill take time to build. In addition, credit by suppliers and banks may be slow in coming until you become established and prove your ability to pay. Finally, most new enterprises fail within the first three years of operation due to business and managerial incompetence on the part of the entrepreneur (refer to Table 4). Also, Table 6 lists most of the advantages and disadvantages in starting a small business from scratch.

TABLE 6

STARTING A BUSINESS

Many entrepreneurs prefer to start a small business and build it themselves from the ground floor up. There are unique advantages to this approach, but pitfalls also exist. Careful examination is warranted before moving in this direction.

ADVANTAGES

Suppliers can be evaluated and chosen fresh.
Credit connections are new and can be nurtured from the beginning.
The latest equipment, supplies, and inventories can be picked according to exact requirements and specifications.
Client contacts and relationships are new. Negative precedents can be avoided from the beginning.
The development of community goodwill is wide open, with the possibility of developing a unique image.
The optimum location can be identified and acquired or leased.
Financial records can be tailored to exact needs.

DISADVANTAGES

Starting a business entails a greater risk than buying an existing operation.

Capital and credit may be more difficult to obtain, given the lack of operating histories and/or the inexperience of the people involved.
Starting and organizing will require time and energy.
Positive customer and community reaction may be slow in coming.
Supplemental income may be needed until the business begins to turn profits.
Needed employees may be difficult to lure initially, given financial constraints in the early years of operation.

The Franchising Route

Franchising, another road to business ownership, has distinct pluses worth noting. The product/service is established and, in some cases, customer goodwill has already been achieved. Many franchise organizations will provide partial start-up funding and credit after operations begin as well as local, regional, and national promotion assistance. In addition, your limited experience and/or education can be supplemented with the franchisor's extensive knowledge in a product or service area if management training and follow-up assistance is provided. Also, affiliation with some franchisors will allow for cost savings in purchasing supplies and equipment due to combined buying power of the franchisees through the franchise organization. The more reputable franchisors will recommend or require certain layouts, displays, facilities, property, business techniques, etc. It is wise to adopt these since most have proven successful in actual operation by other franchisees.

Taking the franchise route can cause you some headaches. Freedom to set your own prices and change or alter the product/service line may be limited. The degree of limitation will depend upon the franchisor. You will have to split your sales revenues with the franchise organization, and payments vary anywhere between 1 and 20 percent of gross sales, with 4 percent being the average. Also, many franchisors require a lot of paperwork from their franchisees. If the above-mentioned situations haven't scared you yet, the franchise contracts might. They tend to be long, complex, and, in some cases, vague. Many questionable points may be diluted or hidden in legal terminology. See that your attorney reads the contract document to ensure that the franchisor cannot evade its promises and responsibilities under the terms of the franchise agreement. Make sure that the organization is not expecting unreasonable demands in the form of up-front fees, percentage paybacks, limiting controls, etc.

High front fees can be discouraging for anyone pursuing the franchise alternative. Many of the better-known franchisors require that you have a couple of hundred thousand dollars before getting the franchise. That's only half the cost. They will lend you the rest. But don't be fooled by low fees either. It may mean that the franchise organization is not providing adequate support functions after operations commence.

Once you have narrowed your choice down to a particular franchise, additional evaluation is needed. The federal government and many states require franchise organizations to provide detailed information about their operations to prospective franchisees. This data is provided to assist you in making your decision. Even though the federal government has gone to extreme lengths to ensure credibility within the franchise industry through disclosure requirements, indiscretions still exist. Question the franchisor concerning costs, business policies, contract terms, etc. Verify the answers with current franchisees. Talking to individuals associated with the franchise organization (as franchisees) will provide a valuable source of information. Don't ask the franchisor for references. Seek out the franchisees yourself so as to ensure unbiased comments.

Find out if the franchise organization is reputable and delivers what is promised. Make sure that the franchisor is really on your side. In addition, call or write the National Better Business Bureau, 230 Park Avenue, New York, NY 10017, and the Better Business Bureau in the city where the franchise headquarters is located. Ask for a report on the company.

It is wise to consider a few questions before spending countless hours on a serious franchise evaluation. The following questions are designed to help you determine if you are looking at a reputable franchise organization or not. The answers you receive may save you time, money, and grief.

1. Were promises made concerning enormous profits?
2. Were promises made concerning minimal effort?
3. Were promises made concerning getting rich quick?
4. Was the franchisor more interested in making a sale than making the franchisee successful?
5. Was pressure exerted to sign a purchase contract?

6. Was pressure exerted to sign a purchase contract based upon the franchisor's threat that the "so-called" opportunity would not be available tomorrow?
7. Does the franchisor constantly pursue in order to make a sale (telephone, mail, showing up without an appointment, etc.)?
8. Did the franchisor refuse or evade any direct questions?
9. Were the franchisor's answers to questions stated in vague terms?
10. Did the franchisor hedge on questions relating to references (other franchisees that can be asked for their opinions)?
11. Did the franchisor hedge on questions concerning training and assistance programs made available to franchisees? Did the answers lack specifics in reference to dates, length of assistance, trainers, etc.?
12. Did the franchisor hesitate to agree on having the franchisee's attorney available to ask questions and/or review the franchise contract?

If the answer to any of these questions is "yes," serious consideration should be given before doing business with the franchisor. Once the differences are resolved to your satisfaction, if possible, and the initial research facts are in order, proceed by conducting a comprehensive evaluation of the franchise deal by answering the questions that appear on pages 22 through 25. This should assist you in determining whether the franchise organization and agreement is right for you. In addition, several good books have been published by private and government organizations on the subject of franchising. Drop a note and ask for information. Several of these provide extensive information on franchise organization:

Franchise Opportunities Handbook
Superintendent of Documents
U.S. Government Printing Office
Washington, DC 20402

Franchise Index/Profile
Superintendent of Documents
U.S. Government Printing Office
Washington, DC 20402

Directory of Franchising Organization
Pilot Industries
103 Cooper Street
Babylon, NY 11702

The Franchise Annual Handbook and Directory
Info Press Inc.
728 Center Street
Lewiston, NY 14092

IFA Membership Directory
International Franchise Association
1350 New York Avenue NW
Suite 900
Washington, DC 20005
(202) 628-8000

Investigate Before Investing: Guidance for Prospective Franchisees
International Franchise Association
1350 New York Avenue NW
Suite 900
Washington, DC 20005
(202) 628-8000

Franchise firms that are not acting appropriately should be reported to a number of private and public organizations. They are:

International Franchise Association
1350 New York Avenue NW
Suite 900
Washington, DC 20005
(202) 628-8000

Franchise and Business Opportunities Program
Federal Trade Commission
Federal Trade Commission Building
6th & Pennsylvania Avenue, NW
Washington, DC 20580

Council of Better Business Bureaus
4200 Wilson Boulevard
Suite 800
Arlington, VA 22203
(703) 276-0100

National Better Business Bureau
230 Park Avenue
New York, NY 10017

Better Business Bureau in the city where the franchise headquarters
is located.

In addition, many states maintain agencies that monitor franchise organizations. If you have problems, write to the State Corporation Commission in your state capital.

Questions to Answer Affirmatively
Before Going Into Franchising

Check if answer is "yes"

The Franchisor

1. Has the franchisor been in business long enough (five years or more) to have established a good reputation? _____

2. Have you checked Better Business Bureaus, chambers of commerce, Dun and Bradstreet, or bankers to find out about the franchisor's business reputation and credit rating? _____

3. Did the above investigations reveal that the franchisor has a good reputation and credit rating? _____

4. Does the franchising firm appear to be financed adequately so that it can carry out its stated plan of financial assistance and expansion? _____

5. Have you found out how many franchisees are now operating? _____

6. Have you found out the "mortality" or failure rate among franchisees? _____

7. Is the failure rate small? _____

8. Have you checked with some franchisees and found that the franchisor has a reputation for honesty and fair dealing among those who currently hold franchises? _____

9. Has the franchisor shown you certified figures indicating exact net profits of one or more going operations which you have personally checked? _____

10. Has the franchisor given you a specimen contract to study with the advice of your legal counsel? _____

11. Will the franchisor assist you with:
    a. A management training program? _____
    b. An employee training program? _____
    c. A public relations program? _____
    d. Obtaining capital? _____
    e. Good credit terms? _____
    f. Merchandising ideas? _____
    g. Designing store layout and displays? _____
    h. Inventory control methods? _____
    i. Analyzing financial statements? _____

12. Does the franchisor provide continuing assistance for franchisees through supervisors who visit regularly? _____

13. Does the franchising firm have an experienced management trained in depth? _____

14. Will the franchisor assist you in finding a good location for your business? _____

15. Has the franchising company investigated you carefully enough to assure itself that you can successfully operate one of its franchises at a profit both to it and to you? _____

16. Have you determined exactly what the franchisor can do for you that you cannot do for yourself? _____

The Product or Service

17. Has the product or service been on the market long enough to gain good consumer acceptance? _____

18. Is it priced competitively? _____

19. Is it the type of item or service which the same consumer customarily buys more than once? _____

20. Is it an all-year seller in contrast to a seasonal one? _____

21. Is it a staple item, in contrast to a fad? _____

22. Does it sell well elsewhere? _____

23. Would you buy it on its merits? _____

24. Will it be in greater demand five years from now? _____

25. If it is a product rather than a service:
    a. Is it packaged attractively? _____
    b. Does it stand up well in use? _____
    c. Is it easy and safe to use? _____
    d. Is it patented? _____
    e. Does it comply with all applicable laws? _____
    f. Is it manufactured under certain quality standards? _____
    g. Do these standards compare favorably with similar products on the market? _____
    h. If the product must be purchased exclusively from the franchisor or a designated supplier, are the prices to you, as the franchisee, competitive? _____

26. Does the franchise fee seem reasonable? _____

The Franchise Contract

27. Do continuing royalties or percent of gross sales payment appear reasonable? _____

28. Are the total cash investment required and the terms for financing the balance satisfactory? _____

29. Does the cash investment include payment for fixtures and equipment? _____

30. If you will be required to participate in company-sponsored promotion and publicity by contributing to an "advertising fund," will you have the right to veto any increase in contributions to the fund? _____

Check if
answer
is "yes"

31. If the parent company's product or service is protected by patent or liability insurance, is the same protection extended to you? _____

32. Are you required to purchase a minimum amount of merchandise or can you buy only what you believe you need? _____

33. Can you, as the franchisee, return merchandise for credit? _____

34. Can you engage in other business activities? _____

35. If there is an annual sales quota, can you retain your franchise if it is not met? _____

36. Does the contract give you an exclusive territory for the length of the franchise? _____

37. Is your territory protected? _____

38. Is the franchise agreement renewable? _____

39. Can you terminate your agreement if you are not happy for some reason? _____

40. Is the franchisor prohibited from selling the franchise out from under you? _____

41. May you sell the business to whomever you please? _____

42. If you sell your franchise, will you be compensated for the goodwill you have built into the business? _____

43. Does the contract obligate the franchisor to give you continuing assistance after you are operating the business? _____

44. Are you permitted a choice in determining whether you will sell any new product or service introduced by the franchisor after you have opened your business? _____

45. Is there anything with respect to the franchise or its operation which would make you ineligible for special financial assistance or other benefits accorded to small business concerns by federal, state, or local governments? _____

46. Did your lawyer approve the franchise contract after he studied it paragraph by paragraph? _____

47. Is the contract free and clear of requirements which would call upon you to take any steps which are, according to your lawyer, unwise or illegal in your state, county, or city? _____

48. Does the contract cover all aspects of your agreement with the franchisor? _____

49. Does it really benefit both you and the franchisor? _____

Your Market

50. Are the territorial boundaries of your market completely, accurately, and understandably defined? _____

51. Have you made any study to determine whether the product or service you propose to sell has a market in your territory at the prices you will have to charge? _____

52. Does the territory provide an adequate sales potential? _____

53. Will the population in the territory given you increase over the next 5 years? _____

54. Will the average per capita income in the territory remain the same or increase over the next 5 years? _____

55. Is existing competition in your territory for the product or service not too well entrenched? _____

YOU—The Franchisee

56. Do you know where you are going to get the equity capital you will need? _____

57. Have you compared what it would take to start your own similar business with the price you must pay for the franchise? _____

58. Have you made a business plan—for example:
    a. Have you worked out what income from sales or services you can reasonably expect in the first 6 months? The first year? The second year?
    b. Have you made a forecast of expenses, including a regular salary for yourself? _____

59. Are you prepared to give up some independence of action to secure the advantages offered by the franchise? _____

60. Are you capable of accepting supervision, even though you will presumably be your own boss? _____

61. Are you prepared to accept rules and regulations with which you may not agree? _____

62. Can you afford the period of training involved? _____

63. Are you ready to spend much or all of the remainder of your business life with this franchisor, offering his product or service to the public? _____

SOURCE: U.S. Small Business Administration.

Franchising has created opportunities for thousands of American entrepreneurs. Many of these individuals could not have pursued self-employment without the introduction and growth of the franchise concept. But the franchise route does not guarantee success by any means. Even with the backing of a strong and reputable franchisor, success can only be achieved by hard work and the intelligent use of time and money.

Look Before You Leap

Before venturing into self-employment, an individual must conduct adequate investigation to ensure that a business being started or purchased stands a chance of success. Information concerning various aspects of internal and external conditions facing a prospective owner must be sought and candidly scrutinized. Lack of data or the unwillingness to pursue questions can lead to disaster.

Below are described the more common considerations that should be addressed when contemplating entrepreneurship. Approach each one with an open mind and try to avoid personal bias that may cloud the facts.

MARKET

Determine the ability of the market to carry all existing businesses serving it and prospective firms considering an introduction. There are occasions where a new or existing business can be so efficient and well managed, relative to its competitors, that it can survive in an overly competitive or declining market and, in some cases, even prosper. When analyzing the market as the only seller with a new product or service, make sure a real need is present before committing resources. Only through the use of statistical analysis can these conclusions be reached. Examining data in reference to community growth patterns, levels of economic activity, traffic counts, etc., may reveal some interesting facts. Opinion surveys may also prove useful. Part of Chapter 7 deals with estimating market conditions relative to sales forecasting.

COMPETITIVE CONDITIONS

Evaluate the degree of competition within the marketplace in question. How many competitors exist? Who are they? Where are they located? What are their strengths and weaknesses? Who is growing, stagnating, declining, and why?

REGULATORY ENVIRONMENT

In some cases, fortunes are made or lost depending upon the actions of local government officials. Changes in zoning regulations and patterns, alterations of traffic flows, changes in building codes, decisions concerning public transportation and parking, etc., can have a significant effect on any business. Many motels and restaurants have met with demise due to the redirection of traffic flows. Most local communities have short- and long-range growth plans. It is wise to study these plans carefully and ask local officials questions regarding the existing or potential location.

Also, keep in mind the impact of existing and potential state and federal government regulations. Examination of these is of paramount importance. Seeking the advice of officials representing agencies charged with any regulatory responsibilities may be wise.

HUMAN RELATIONS

Before purchasing an existing operation, look into the current state of employee relations. Negative attitudes on the part of needed and hard-to-replace workers may be compromising the firm's existence. If starting a business, it would be wise to examine the general nature of employee relationships which may be common within local areas. Many business owners interact and establish informal standards. It is amazing how consistent these standards can be from business to business in the same community.

PRIOR CLAIMS

In reference to buying a business, always have an attorney investigate any legal claims that may exist against the operation before purchasing. Unpaid taxes, wages, bills, and/or mortgage liabilities can exist and are usually passed on to the new owner upon acquisition.

PHYSICAL FACILITIES

Physical condition of all buildings and equipment should be given careful consideration before purchasing a business. Professional appraisers can determine the fair value of tangible assets. Obsolete and inefficient facilities are normally expensive to replace, especially if an exorbitant price was paid initially for these assets.

PRODUCTS/SERVICES

Evaluate existing or future product/service lines. Determine the positive and negative features in relation to price, promotion, distribution, and competition.

ENVIRONMENTAL RISKS

Is the proposition in question susceptible to external uncontrollable events? If so, which ones and to what extent? For example, governmental actions, international events, or reactions by competitors may cause difficulties. Evaluate all facets of the environment and determine how the business in question will be affected. External threats are listed on page 151.

Buyer Beware

A seller always has a motivation for disposing of property. It may or may not be candidly revealed to prospective purchasers. This is why it's important that proper investigation be conducted into the reasons for selling. Hiring a competent consultant, accountant, or attorney can help in identifying and analyzing various aspects of the proposition. Surprising situations may be discovered that are not apparent to the untrained observer.

Below are listed some of the more common explanations for someone's selling out. Make sure the truth is known before committing time and money.

— Wants to retire
— Too old to pursue
— Not interested anymore
— Going back to the corporate world
— Not making enough money
— Loss of profits, sales, and/or markets
— Sickness
— Desires to relocate outside the immediate area
— Wants to pursue other business endeavors
— Competitive pressures
— Tired of the problems and headaches associated with business ownership

Watch Out for the Lemon

A failing business can be easily detected if the right elements are examined and understood. Generally, an operation ceases to be viable for more than one specific reason, although it centers around a single broad deficiency—managerial incompetence on the part of owners and managers. Dun and Bradstreet, the well-known financial reporting firm, states that 92.1 percent of small firms that fail do so because of managerial ineptness. They further break down statistics to account for exact causes of demise, all relating to management deficiencies, which can be found by referring to Table 4 in this chapter.

Below are mentioned some of the more specific reasons attributed to small business failure. If one or more of these conditions exists, it should be quite obvious to the professionally trained eye and may even be apparent to anyone taking a close look.

LACK OF MARKET POTENTIAL

Many businesses fail due to the lack of an adequate market for their products or services. Also, the total existing market may be contracting at a rate faster than the ability or willingness of the firm to react and shift emphasis. Only through sufficient market examination and evaluation can these threats be revealed. Chapter 7 goes into detail about determining market potential.

CAPITAL STARVATION

Many new businesses and existing enterprises tend to underestimate their capital requirements, thereby creating a capital squeeze somewhere down the pike, generally at an inopportune time. In many cases, adequate capital is present, but mismanagement of funds causes difficulties. These factors will affect the firm's ability to generate sales, thus adversely affecting profits. Many lenders and investors will simply be reluctant to advance and risk their money if these conditions prevail, probably forcing the closing or scaling back of operations.

HEAVY COMPETITION

Many entrepreneurs, before purchasing or starting a business, fail to account for competitive factors in the market to be served by their new operation. Severe competition both domestic and foreign can have a detrimental effect on any organization, forcing it to close, in many cases, before it gets off the ground. Consequently, a comprehensive examination is necessary to determine if existing and potential demand can support all firms currently serving the market and projected newcomers.

UNCONTROLLED GROWTH

Many businesses expand too quickly, thereby causing strains on their financial and/or managerial structures. Both large and small organizations fall victim to this deadly sin. Several large corporations have recently gone bankrupt because of expansion beyond their resource capabilities. Once profits begin to decline or evaporate, lenders and investors run for the hills. Growth should be planned well in advance, making sure that adequate resources are available to support endeavors before committing to expansion goals.

Inappropriate Location

A bad location can be difficult to spot initially. Therefore, adequate investigation is necessary to determine the history of the location and whether it is suitable. How many businesses have been at the location in the part twenty years? What types of businesses were there? Why did they leave? Always conduct research concerning the location of an existing business being contemplated for purchase or the suitability of placing a business in a particular locale. Collecting information such as opinion surveys and analyzing data in reference to traffic counts and parking facilities will reveal considerable information about the viability of any location whether new or old.

Disastrous Events

Is the business subject to catastrophic events that can drain its vitality and resources to the point where it cannot recover? Has it occurred before?

Unusual Agreements

Examine the existence of any agreements the business has with present owners, employees, and third parties. Do these contracts compromise the present or future profitability of the enterprise? Can they be broken if the firm is purchased? Always have an attorney evaluate and comment on any agreements that may exist to ensure flexibility in business operations. On some occasions, owners who are selling out may attempt to lock in favored employees with contractual agreements whereby the new owners cannot replace those workers for a given period of time.

What to Expect

If one or more of the conditions mentioned in the preceding section exists, expect any number of the following situations to prevail within a business.

- Uncontrolled Expenses—Costs may be increasing faster on a proportionate basis than sales revenues, thus eating into or eliminating profits and creating losses. Many business operations fail to maintain adequate accounting procedures that would alert management to excessive cost increases.
- Falling Profits—Consistently falling profits are due to either deteriorating sales revenues or expenses increasing faster than sales.
- Accelerated Debt Service—If indebtedness becomes too great, the ability of the businesses to serve its debts becomes questionable. It may spell trouble in the near future. If this condition exists, the business will probably attempt to pay debts by borrowing additional funds (borrow from Peter to pay Paul), which is only a quick fix in most cases. Eventually, both Peter and Paul come collecting at the same time.
- Falling Sales—A steady trend of falling sales can produce negative consequences for any business. Normally, expenses do not decline relative to sales, thereby squeezing or eliminating profit margins. In addition to the conditions reviewed in the previous section that could cause a decline in sales revenues, poor internal management in reference to product/service planning, market research, promotion efforts, and distribution can also result in declining sales.

If one or more of the just-mentioned conditions prevail within a business enterprise, the firm may have some degree of difficulty meeting its current obligations. Its liquid position, also known as working capital, may be deteriorated to the point where current bills can't be paid on time.

What Is the Fair Price?

There are two basic approaches used to determine the fair price for a business. The methods are described below.

Book Value/Goodwill Method

This approach is simple to compute. Subtract the liabilities of the business (debts) from its assets. What's left over is called book value. It is assumed that if the assets of a business were sold and the debts paid in full, what would remain in the form of cash is the true monetary worth of an operation. In addition to computing this figure when selling a business, an intangible asset called goodwill is taken into account and given a dollar value. Goodwill is simply described as the reputation or positive condition achieved by a business because of sound management or, in some cases, just good fortune. Once goodwill is financially evaluated, the value established will be added to the book value in order to determine the selling price.

Anticipated Profit Method

Many experts feel that using the book value and goodwill approach is inadequate and not a reliable indicator of true business worth. In fact, they support the contention that expected profits should dictate the selling price for a business. For example, in the real estate business, a house's value is not based upon the cost of materials (tangibles) and labor (intangibles) but is determined by what the market will pay for the structure.

When using this method, an estimation of future profits will need to be made. This can be done by examining past and current performance, present and anticipated market conditions, and environmental threats facing the business. After profits are projected, they can be compared against the selling price (potential investment) in order to determine an adequate value. To illustrate, suppose a buyer is interested in purchasing a business priced at $150,000. The potential buyer also wants to return his investment in 10 years, not counting salary draw. It has been determined that an average annual net profit of $14,000 can be generated by the business over the next decade. By using the simple formula shown below, the following conclusion can be determined.

$$\frac{\text{Purchasing Price}}{\text{Average Annual Net Profits}} = \frac{\$150,000}{14,000} = 10.7 \text{ years to return investment}$$

Obviously, the buyer must either accept a longer pay-back period or negotiate a lower price. Another factor that may enter into the discussion about price is the degree of risk inherent in the business proposition. A greater risk generally demands a faster pay-back and if average net income is set at $14,000 per year, the price of the business should come down to reflect those uncertainties. For example, a purchase price of $125,000 will be returned in 8.9 years as the following calculation shows:

$$\frac{\text{Purchase Price}}{\text{Average Annual Net Profits}} = \frac{\$125,000}{14,000} = 8.9 \text{ years}$$

Conversely, a lesser risk may demand a longer pay-back period because of the higher price demanded.

When using the net tangible asset/goodwill or anticipated profit methods, also seek the assistance of competent accountants and attorneys to help in assigning values and making projections. Profit estimation is reviewed in Chapter 7.

Using Financial Information

When analyzing business opportunities, serious consideration must be given to the "nuts and bolts" aspects. Financial information, when used and presented in proper format, can weed out the losers from the winners in short order. In addition, it may help to reveal the "right price" to pay for a business if acquisition is contemplated. When starting a business from the ground floor, financial data can be obtained to assist in determining the necessary capital base needed to begin and support operation until profits are generated. Once in operation, the information provided by financial statements can help ensure sound fiscal management.

FINANCIAL STATEMENTS

Financial statements can say a whole lot about a firm's viability. Consequently, it is imperative to know the major financial statements generally available for evaluation purposes. First, the balance sheet is used to list a firm's assets and liabilities. These two major elements are further divided into sub-classifications (Current Assets, Non-Current Assets, Current Liabilities, Non-Current Liabilities, and Owners Equity). Second, the profit and loss statement, also known as the income statement, is used in listing and analyzing revenue and expense accounts to determine the firm's profitability. Third, a cash-flow statement is sometimes used as a supplement to the two major elements just mentioned. Its purpose is to get a closer look at how a firm manages liquid (cash) resources. Segments of Chapter 7, including tables 20, 21, and 22, describe and illustrate these financial statements and discuss their functional purpose.

Financial information is useless without a means of comparison. A firm's financial statement should be compared to those of similar businesses and against the industry as a whole before attempts are made to analyze its performance. To accomplish this task, various accounts within the balance sheet and income statement can be divided into each other to determine what are called financial ratios. Since ratios are compiled and published on many firms and industries by several research organizations, standards of comparison are easy to make for existing businesses. Some research outlets maintain ratios and cost information dealing with starting a new business.

Most trade associations maintain comparative ratio data on the industries they represent. Write to them for the ratio information.

Ratio Analysis for Small Business
Handbook of Small Business Finance

TABLE 7

COMMON RATIOS USED TODAY

Ratio	*Used to Determine*
Current Assets / Current Liabilities	Cash position (ability to pay short-term debts)
Quick Assets / Current Liabilities	Cash position (ability to pay short-term debts)
Current Liabilities / Net Worth	Relationship between capital invested and short-term (year to year) debt obligations
Net Sales / Net Worth	How often capital is being recycled
Net Sales / Inventory	How many times inventory is turned over to generate sales
Fixed Assets / Net Worth	Relationship between invested capital and hard assets such as plant and equipment
Total Debt / Net Worth	Relationship between invested capital and all debt obligations
Net Profit / Net Sales	Rate of return on sales generated

$\dfrac{\text{Net Profit}}{\text{Net Worth}}$	Efficient use of invested capital
$\dfrac{\text{Net Sales}}{\text{Working Capital}}$	How much working capital should be maintained in relation to a given level of sales
$\dfrac{\text{Accounts Receivables}}{\text{Daily Credit Sales}}$	If customer accounts are being paid according to terms

Appendix A contains a list of research organizations (names and addresses) offering financial ratios and other useful data to prospective entrepreneurs and current business owners. Information about specific types of businesses is available from these outlets and listed under each address.

Additional Insight

You might want to make some final considerations before pressing ahead with your plans. Answering the following questions might provide additional insights into your readiness for business ownership. If you have already decided to purchase a franchise, many of the following questions will be answered automatically by the franchise organization and/or previous series of questions. But it wouldn't hurt to go ahead and answer the questions for your own protection, just in case something was overlooked.

Consider these questions carefully before answering. Be honest and fair with yourself because it's your time and money at stake. Answer all that apply to your situation. Obviously, some will not. If you respond to most in a favorable way (yes) and feel comfortable with the rest, then the next step in the actualization of your business involves obtaining capital.

Check if answer is yes

ARE YOU THE TYPE?
Have you rated your personal qualifications using a scale similar to that presented earlier in this section? _____

*Check if
answer
is yes*

Have you had some objective evaluators rate you on such scales?

_____

Have you carefully considered your weak points and taken steps to improve them or to find an associate whose strong points will compensate for them?

_____

WHAT BUSINESS SHOULD YOU CHOOSE?

Have you written a summary of your background and experience to help you in making this decision?

_____

Have you considered your hobbies and what you would like to do?

_____

Does anyone want the service you can perform?

_____

Have you studied surveys and/or sought advice and counsel to find out what fields of business may be expected to expand?

_____

Have you considered working for someone else to gain more experience?

_____

WHAT ARE YOUR CHANCES FOR SUCCESS?

Are general business conditions good?

_____

Are business conditions good in the city and neighborhood where you plan to locate?

_____

Are current conditions good in the line of business you plan to start?

_____

WHAT WILL BE YOUR RETURN ON INVESTMENT?

Do you know the typical return on investment in the line of business you plan to start?

_____

Have you determined how much you will have to invest in your business?

_____

Are you satisfied that the rate of return on the money you invest in the business will be greater than the rate you would probably receive if you invested the money elsewhere?

_____

HOW MUCH MONEY WILL YOU NEED?

Have your filled out worksheets similar to those shown in Chapter 5 of this book?

_____

In filling out the worksheets, have you taken care not to overestimate income? _____

Have you obtained quoted prices for equipment and supplies you will need? _____

Do you know the costs of goods which must be in your inventory? _____

Have you estimated expenses only after checking rents, wage scales, utility and other pertinent costs in the area where you plan to locate? _____

Have you found what percentage of your estimated sales your projected inventory and each expense item is and compared each percentage with the typical percentage for your line of business? _____

Have you added an additional amount of money to your estimates to allow for unexpected contingencies? _____

WHERE CAN YOU GET THE MONEY?

Have you counted up how much money of your own you can put into the business? _____

Do you know how much credit you can get from your suppliers—the people you will buy from? _____

Do you know where you can borrow the rest of the money you need to start your business? _____

Have you selected a progressive bank with the credit services you may need? _____

Have you talked to a banker about your plans? _____

Does the banker have an interested, helpful attitude toward your problems? _____

SHOULD YOU SHARE OWNERSHIP WITH OTHERS?

If you need a partner with money or know-how that you don't have, do you know someone who will fit— someone you can get along with? _____

Do you know the good and bad points about going it alone, having a partner, and incorporating your business? _____

Have you talked to a lawyer about it? _____

WHERE SHOULD YOU LOCATE?

Check if answer is yes

Have you studied the makeup of the population in the city or town where you plan to locate? _____

Do you know what kind of people will want to buy what you plan to sell? _____

Do people like that live in the area where you want to locate? _____

Have you checked the number, type, and size of competitors in the area? _____

Does the area need another business like the one you plan to open? _____

Are employees available? _____

Have you checked and found adequate: utilities, parking facilities, police and fire protection, available housing, schools and other cultural and community activities? _____

Do you consider costs of the location reasonable in terms of taxes and average rents? _____

Is there sufficient opportunity for growth and expansion? _____

Have you checked the relative merits of the various shopping areas within the city, including shopping centers? _____

In selecting the actual site, have you compared it with others? _____

Have you had a lawyer check the lease and zoning? _____

SHOULD YOU BUY A GOING BUSINESS?

Have you considered the advantages and disadvantages of buying a going business? _____

Have you compared what it would cost to equip and stock a new business with the price asked for the business you are considering buying? _____

HOW MUCH SHOULD YOU PAY FOR IT?

Have you estimated future sales and profits of the going business for the next few years? _____

Are your estimated future profits satisfactory? _____

Have you looked at past financial statements of the business to find the return on investment, sales, and profit trends? _____

Have you verified the owner's claims about the business with reports from an independent accountant's analysis of the figures? _____

Is the inventory you will purchase a good buy? _____

Are equipment and fixtures fairly valued? _____

If you plan to buy the accounts receivable, are they worth the asking price? _____

Have you been careful in your appraisal of the company's goodwill? _____

Are you prepared to assume the company's liabilities and are the creditors agreeable? _____

Have you learned why the present owner wants to sell? _____

Have you found out about the present owner's reputation with his employees and suppliers? _____

Have you consulted a lawyer to be sure that the title is good? _____

Has your lawyer checked to find out if there is any lien against the assets you are buying? _____

Has your lawyer drawn up an agreement covering all essential points, including a seller's warranty for your protection against false statements? _____

SHOULD YOU INVEST IN A FRANCHISE?

Have you considered how the advantages and disadvantages of franchising apply to you? _____

Have you made a thorough search to find the right franchise opportunity? _____

Have you evaluated the franchise by answering the questions asked earlier in this section? _____

HAVE YOU WORKED OUT PLANS FOR BUYING?

Have you estimated what share of the market you think you can get? _____

Do you know how much or how many of each item of merchandise you will buy to open your business? _____

Have you found suppliers who will sell you what you need at a good price? _____

Do you have a plan for finding out what your customers want? _____

Check if
answer
is yes

Have you set up a model stock assortment to follow in your buying? _____

Have you worked out stock control plans to avoid over-stocks, under-stocks, and out-of-stocks? _____

Do you plan to buy most of your stock from a few suppliers rather than a little from many, so that those you buy from will want to help you succeed? _____

HOW WILL YOU PRICE YOUR PRODUCTS AND SERVICES?

Have you decided upon your price ranges? _____

Do you know how to figure what you should charge to cover your costs? _____

Do you know what your competitors charge? _____

WHAT SELLING METHODS WILL YOU USE?

Have you studied the selling and sales promotion methods of competitors? _____

Have you studied why customers buy your type of product or service? _____

Have you thought about why you like to buy from some salesmen while others turn you off? _____

Have you decided what your methods of selling will be? _____

Have you outlined your sales promotion policy? _____

HOW WILL YOU SELECT AND TRAIN PERSONNEL?

If you need to hire someone to help you, do you know where to look? _____

Do you know what kind of person you need? _____

Have you written a job description for each person you will need? _____

Do you know the prevailing wage scales? _____

Do you have a plan for training new employees? _____

Will you continue training through good supervision? _____

WHAT OTHER MANAGEMENT PROBLEMS WILL YOU FACE?

Do you plan to sell for credit? _____

If you do, do you have the extra capital necessary to carry accounts receivable? _____

Have you made a policy for returned goods? _____

Have you planned how you will make deliveries? _____

Have you considered other policies which must be made in your particular business? _____

Have you made a plan to guide yourself in making the best use of your time and effort? _____

WHAT RECORDS WILL YOU KEEP?

Have you planned a system of records that will keep track of your income and expenses, what you owe other people, and what other people owe you? _____

Have you worked out a way to keep track of your inventory so that you will always have enough on hand for your customers but not more than you can sell? _____

Have you planned on how to keep your payroll records and take care of tax reports and payments? _____

Do you know what financial statements you should prepare? _____

Do you know how to use these financial statements? _____

Have you obtained standard operating ratios for your type of business which you plan to use as guides? _____

Do you know an accountant who will help you with your records and financial statements? _____

WHAT LAWS WILL AFFECT YOU?

Have you checked with the proper authorities to find out what, if any, licenses to do business are necessary? _____

Do you know what police and health regulations apply to your business? _____

Will your operations be subject to interstate commerce regulations? If so, do you know to which ones? _____

Check if
answer
is yes

Have you received advice from your lawyer regarding your responsibilities under federal and state laws and local ordinances?   _____

HOW WILL YOU HANDLE TAXES AND INSURANCE?

Have you worked out a system for handling the withholding tax for your employees?   _____

Have you worked out a system for handling sales taxes? Excise taxes?   _____

Have you planned an adequate record system for the efficient preparation of income tax forms?   _____

Have you prepared a worksheet for meeting tax obligations?   _____

Have you talked with an insurance agent about what kinds of insurance you will need and how much it will cost?   _____

WILL YOU SET MEASURABLE GOALS FOR YOURSELF?

Have you set goals and sub-goals for yourself?   _____

Have you specified dates when each goal is to be achieved?   _____

Are these realistic goals; that is, will they challenge you but at the same time not call for unreasonable accomplishments?   _____

Are the goals specific so that you can measure performance?   _____

Have you developed a business plan, using one of the SBA Aids to record your ideas, facts, and figures?   _____

Have you allowed for obstacles?   _____

WILL YOU KEEP UP-TO-DATE?

Have you made plans to keep up with improvements in your trade or industry?   _____

Have you prepared a business plan which will be amended as circumstances demand?   _____

Source: U.S. Small Business Administration.

3

SOURCES OF HELP
Ripe for the Picking

Few individuals are aware of the reservoir of assistance available from public and private organizations directed to the small business community. Taking advantage of these services may mean the difference between success and failure for many struggling businesses and entrepreneurs. Many of these informational outlets will help when evaluating business opportunities and specific propositions.

Help Galore

U.S. SMALL BUSINESS ADMINISTRATION (SBA)

One of the primary objectives of the U.S. Small Business Administration is to promote the economic well-being of small firms and entrepreneurs. This is partly accomplished by providing an array of business and managerial assistance programs that are available upon request. The next several pages will be devoted to describing these non-financial services. Information concerning SBA financial assistance programs can be found later in the book.

* SCORE (Service Corps of Retired Executives)—Retired business executives within this program offer advice to the small-business community on a free basis. The combined experience of SCORE counselors spans the entire spectrum of American business. Volunteers meet with small-business owners and prospective entrepreneurs to determine and discuss their difficulties. After careful consideration and evaluation, the counselor will formulate a plan of action designed to help minimize or eliminate the problem

areas. In addition, the individual(s) requesting assistance will be guided through this sometimes difficult process. If the problem is extremely difficult or complex, several SCORE representatives may be asked to assist. Sometimes, other SBA and outside resources may be brought to bear. Currently, there are over 6,000 SCORE advisors located throughout the country.

- University Business Development Centers (UBDCs)—These organizations are established in tandem with the U.S. Small Business Administration to provide additional counseling services to the small-business community. UBDCs are simply college- or university-based counseling centers utilizing institutional resources, including faculty and students. In addition, these centers muster community involvement and volunteers to accomplish their task of providing help to small firms and people wanting to start businesses. Small Business Development Centers are listed in Appendix C.

- Small Business Institutes (SBIs)—The U.S. Small Business Administration has contracted with hundreds of colleges and universities to establish small business institutes. This program, although similar to the UBDC approach, does have distinct differences. Counseling services provided by SBIs are limited in one respect but more extensive in others. SBI student and faculty counselors are assigned to certain projects with the objective of providing detailed verbal and written recommendations to specific problem areas that a prospective entrepreneur or business owner may face. This approach enables students to experience real-life business situations. The cost for this service is free to individuals or businesses seeking assistance. The UBDCs listed in Appendix C can direct you to existing SBIs.

- Call Contracting Program—This SBA-financed program is designed to give free professional advice and expertise to small firms and individuals who qualify. The agency contracts with reputable and reliable accounting and/or consulting firms to carry out the objectives of this program. Generally, problems of a very difficult or technical nature are handled under call contracting.

- Management Training—The SBA co-sponsors several types of training functions. Working in unison with private experts, the SBA provides courses, conferences, problem clinics, and workshops designed to deliver counseling services to local communities throughout the country. Checking with the regional SBA office can yield a schedule of events in particular areas served.

In addition, when seeking SBA managerial assistance services, call or write the field offices maintained by the agency. They are listed in Appendix B. They will send an assistance form that is to be completed and returned to the field office.

DEPARTMENT OF COMMERCE

The U.S. Department of Commerce maintains an array of informational resources that are available to anyone. This department is constantly collecting economic, financial, and business data relating to the economy, different industries, states, and, in some cases, individual firms. Over the last decade, the Commerce Department has been heavily involved in the promotion of American products abroad. It has enormous amounts of data that can be used by domestic exporters when studying overseas markets. In addition, the department gets actively involved in setting up channels of distribution for any business (new or existing) wanting to exploit foreign market potentials. Department of Commerce field offices can be contacted for details concerning their publications and assistance programs. Refer to Appendix B for a listing of these offices.

The Minority Business Development Agency (MBDA), which is part of the Commerce Department, provides basic services to minority-owned firms. Call the local U.S. Commerce Department field office concerning this agency.

U.S. FEDERAL TRADE COMMISSION (FTC)

The FTC was set up to protect consumers and businesses against firms that would promote restraint of trade and use unfair competitive methods. It publishes material on what constitutes illegal practices when conducting business. Write to the address below and request the publications concerning these matters. Knowing what to avoid initially may save many headaches later. Also, the publications might provide some insights into whether competitors are acting appropriately or not.

Federal Trade Commission
6th & Pennsylvania Avenue, NW
Washington, DC 20580

GOVERNMENT PROCUREMENT ASSISTANCE

The U.S. Small Business Administration provides help to small firms wishing to do business with the federal government through the SBA's procurement automated source system (PASS); a small firm's capabilities are matched to those government agencies requiring what the firm has to offer. Also, PASS will identify large companies that have obtained government procurement contracts and are in need of small sub-contractors to fulfill requirements in the agreements. Table 8 illustrates the PASS application form used by the SBA.

In addition, the U.S. Superintendent of Documents publishes the *Commerce Business Daily*, which reports most procurement opportunities available from Uncle Sam. Most of the PASS information received by the SBA is also contained in this publication. Therefore, subscribing to this daily report may be unnecessary. However, it does provide information on other opportunities that can be examined for potential exploitation. A subscription can be obtained by writing to:

> Superintendent of Documents
> Government Printing Office
> Washington, DC 20402

The cost for the publication is $316.25 per year. Allow six weeks for delivery of the first issue.

Many state and local governments actively encourage small businesses to bid on their purchasing requirements. Contact their procurement offices for additional details. Also, foreign governments are always seeking American products and services. SBA and Department of Commerce field offices, listed in Appendix B, can provide assistance in reaching foreign government procurement offices located in the United States. Contacting their embassies in Washington or consulate offices in major cities may also help.

Reading these publications will be of great help to you in understanding governmental procurement procedures and may open up opportunities not apparent before.

U.S. INTERNAL REVENUE SERVICE

The IRS can provide information related to business taxation. It publishes many useful and free reports concerning the tax obligation of business enterprises. Some of the publications will assist in establishing the necessary accounting procedures for the proper handling and payment of taxes. Write or call the nearest IRS office and request a list of the booklets.

GOVERNMENT PUBLICATIONS

The federal government publishes and sells a list of valuable business-related publications, periodicals, and electronic products. The list can be obtained by writing to the U.S. Government Printing Office, Superintendent of Documents, Washington, DC 20402. Ask for the United States Government Publications for Business.

STATE GOVERNMENTS

Most state governments are realizing the importance of small-business activity to their local economy. Many have developed assistance programs aimed at helping prospective entrepreneurs and existing small firms. Services may include managerial, procurement, and/or funding help. The degree of assistance varies from state to state. To find out what may be available, write or call the offices listed in Appendix B for more information.

LOCAL GOVERNMENTS

Most municipalities maintain records in reference to local economic activity. Statistics dealing with retail sales, personal income, construction permits, traffic counts, and growth patterns can be obtained and are useful when analyzing general business prospects or specific propositions. For example, when evaluating several possible store locations, traffic counts and area growth patterns should be carefully reviewed.

ACCOUNTANTS

In addition to their traditional role as bookkeeper and auditor, many accountants provide invaluable information and assistance relative to decisions concerning business propositions. Included below are some of the more common services that can be expected from most accountants.

— Record keeping and auditing
— Corporate and individual tax planning

**Increase your business opportunities!
List your company in SBA's Automated
Directory of Small Businesses...PASS**

Complete and Return this Form To:
U.S. Small Business Administration
P.O. BOX 9000
Melbourne, FL 32902-9919

Instructions: Complete all items on this form as accurately as possible. Key items are defined on the reverse side of the form. The form must be signed by a principal of the company as distinguished from an agent, however constituted. The completed form will constitute official self certification as to size, minority, and/or woman owned status. See certification statement at signature block. Write N/A in boxes if not applicable.

What Happens: We will notify you as soon as your company is listed in the Procurement Automated Source System (PASS). Your company's capabilities are then available to many Government agencies and major corporations when they request potential bidders for contracts and subcontracts. Remember - although PASS increases your exposure, it does NOT guarantee solicitations or contracts. PASS should be just one element of your regular marketing efforts.

PASS is Free! You have nothing to lose and possibly new contracts to gain. Don't delay...Return this applicatiion today!

The following company profile is ☐ a new listing or ☐ an updated listing.

PROCUREMENT AUTOMATED SOURCE SYSTEM (PASS) - COMPANY PROFILE

Identification Section

Company Name_____

_____

Mailing Address_____

_____

City_____ State _____ ZIP _____

Phone Number (   )   FAX Number (   )

Contact _____ Title _____

Employer Id Number_____
(EIN, Tax Id, or SS#)
DUNS Number_____
(DUN & Bradstreet)
Year Business Established_____
Average Gross Revenues_____
(Last Three Years)
Average Number of Employees_____
(Last Twelve Months)

Organizational Data

Type of Organization   ☐ Corporation   ☐ S. Corporation   ☐ Sole Proprietorship   ☐ Partnership

Parent Company Name_____
Average Gross Revenue (Last Three Years)_____
Average No. Employees (Last Twelve Months)_____

Affiliate Name_____
Average Gross Revenue (Last Three Years)_____
Average No. Employees (Last Twelve Months)_____

Affiliate Name_____
Average Gross Revenue (Last Three Years)_____
Average No. Employees (Last Twelve Months)_____

Affiliate Name_____
Average Gross Revenue (Last Three Years)_____
Average No. Employees (Last Twelve Months)_____

Ownership Data

Check boxes appropriately if company is at least 51% owned, controlled and actively managed by any of the following. (Note: Minority Person includes Black, Hispanic, Native American, Asian Indian, or Asian Pacific)

☐ U.S. Citizen   ☐ Minority Person   ☐ Woman/Women   ☐ Veteran   ☐ Disabled Veteran   ☐ Vietnam Vet. (1964-1975)
If you checked Minority Person, check one of the following.

☐ Black American   ☐ Hispanic American   ☐ Native American   ☐ Subcontinent Asian American   ☐ Asian Pacific American

Native American includes American Indian, Eskimo, Aleut, and Hawaiian - Subcontinent Asian American includes India, Pakistan, Bangladesh, etc.* - Asian Pacific American includes Orientals, Pacific Islands, Philippines, etc.*   *For complete list, refer to 13 CFR 124.105b

Business Types

PASS is divided into 4 types of business. Please estimate the percentage of your business allocated to the following (total must equal 100) and complete the appropriate Section(s).

Manufacturing/Supplies [____]%

Check Applicable Box(es)

☐ Manufacturer   ☐ Dealer   ☐ Wholesale Distributor

Manufacturing Facility Size _____SQ. FT.

Construction [____]%

Current Aggregate Bonding Level $_____
Current Bonding Level Per Contract $_____
Maximum Operating Radius _____(miles)
-Anywhere in the U.S., enter 3999 above.
-Anywhere in the World, enter 9999 above.

Research and Development [____]%

Number of Engineers and Scientists_____
Expertise of Key Personnel (Limit 150 Characters)_____
_____
_____

Services [____]%

Current Aggregate Bonding Level $_____
Current Bonding Level Per Contract $_____
Maximum Operating Radius _____(miles)
-Anywhere in the U.S., enter 3999 above.
-Anywhere in the World, enter 9999 above.

Capabilities Section (Limit 350 characters; be concise and avoid abbreviations and generalities)

List products, services, special capabilities, and important categories under which you want your business listed. The system searches businesses based on the capabilities you list in this section.

_____
_____
_____
_____
_____
_____
_____

Standard Industrial Classification (SIC) Code(s)

If unknown, leave blank. Appropriate codes will be assigned.

☐☐☐☐☐☐☐☐☐☐☐☐☐☐☐☐☐☐☐☐☐☐☐☐☐☐☐☐

Special Equipment/Materials (Limit 50 characters)

List_____

CAGE Code	Manufacturing Quality Assurance	Miscellaneous		
☐☐☐☐☐☐	☐ MIL-I-45208 ☐ MIL-Q-9858 ☐ Other_____	Metric Capability	☐ Yes	☐ No
		Accept VISA Credit Card	☐ Yes	☐ No

Security Clearance   **Export Activity**

	Top Secret	Secret	Confidential	Other
Key Personnel	☐	☐	☐	☐
Site	☐	☐	☐	☐

If other provide description_____

☐ Active Experienced Exporter
☐ Interested And/Or New to Exporting
☐ Not Interested

If you checked Active or Interested, please check one or more of the following geographic areas.

☐ Western Europe   ☐ Middle East
☐ Eastern Europe/NIS   ☐ Asian Pacific
☐ The Americas   ☐ Africa

Performance History (Contract References)

Contract Start Date_____   Contract Start Date_____
Dollar Value_____   Dollar Value_____
Product/Service Desc._____   Product/Service Desc._____

Contact Name_____   Contact Name_____
Contact Phone No._____   Contact Phone No._____

Contract Start Date_____   Contract Start Date_____
Dollar Value_____   Dollar Value_____
Product/Service Desc._____   Product/Service Desc._____

Contact Name_____   Contact Name_____
Contact Phone No._____   Contact Phone No._____

Definitions

SIZE OF BUSINESS - A small business concern for the purpose of Government procurement is a concern, including its affiliates, which is independently owned and operated, is not dominant in the field of operation in which it is competing for government contracts and can further qualify under the criteria concerning number of employees, average annual receipts, and other criteria as prescribed by the U.S. Small Business Administration. (See Code of Federal Regulations, Title 13, Part 121, as appended, which contains detailed industry definitions and related procedures.)

MINORITY/WOMEN/VETERAN OWNED STATUS - Qualifying firms must be at least 51% owned, controlled, and actively managed by such individuals.

CAGE Code (Commercial and Government Entity Code) This is a code assigned to contractors providing goods and services to the Federal Government. For information about CAGE codes, call (616) 961-4955

DISASTER RESPONSE - Firm's capacity for disaster response (if any) should be included in the capability statement. Required information includes 24 hour-a-day contact and the ability to ship manufactured goods within 24 hours of receiving order.

QUALITY ASSURANCE - Information applies to manufacturing processes for the Department of Defense.

CERTIFICATION - I certify 1) that this is a small business as defined in the DEFINITION section; 2) that the characteristics of the firms ownership are accurately reflected in the OWNERSHIP section; 3) that all information supplied herein (including all attachments) is correct; and 4) that neither the applicant nor any person (or concern) in any connection with the applicant as principal or officer, so far as known, is now debarred or otherwise declared ineligible by any agency of the Federal Government from making offers for furnishing materials, supplies, or services to the Government or any agency thereof.

INFORMATION IN THIS PROFILE MAY BE DISCLOSED AT THE DISCRETION OF THE U.S. SMALL BUSINESS ADMINISTRATION

Signature of Company Officer_____   Title_____   Date_____

Please Note: The estimated burden hours for the completion of this form is 15 minutes per response. If you have any questions or comments concerning this estimate or any other aspect of this information collection please contact, Chief Administrative Information Branch, U.S. Small Business Administration, 409 3rd St., SW, Washington, D.C. 20416, or Gary Waxman, Clearance Officer, Paperwork Reduction Project (3245-0024), Office of Management and Budget, Washington, D.C. 20503

SBA Form 1167 (3/93)
OMB Approved: 3245-0024 Exp: (3/31/96)
*U.S. GPO: 1993-358-240/89139

TABLE 8

— Sales and income projection
— Budget construction
— Identification and exploitation of capital sources
— Construction of past, present, and pro forma (future) financial statements
— Cost containment analysis and procedures
— Determination and projection of working capital requirements
— Overall financial analysis

Although most are listed in the phone book, it is wise to consult a banker, attorney, or business consultant when seeking a suitable accountant. Bankers and lawyers are in constant contact with the accounting profession and they generally know the accountants that can provide adequate help at reasonable cost. A good approach is to seek out owners in similar lines of business and ask for advice. This can be the best source of reference available because of the direct contact between accountant and owner. In addition, there are two national, professional accounting associations that may provide referrals upon request. They are listed below. Also, try state associations. Many of them are more familiar with their membership than are the national groups.

American Institute of Certified Public Accountants
1211 Avenue of the Americas
New York, NY 10036-8775
(212) 596-6200
1-800-862-4272

National Society of Public Accountants
1010 North Fairfax Street
Alexandria, VA 22314-1574
(703) 549-6400

Accountants can save you a tremendous amount of pain and expense if you use them wisely. Always have an accountant explore a prospective business proposition before you make a purchase, for obvious reasons cited earlier in the book. If already in business, you need accountants to evaluate any large investment decision you are contemplating. Even if a business has an internal accountant, outside opinion should be sought. It can be helpful in spotting difficulties that may not be apparent from the inside. The small price paid for the information is an investment if it helps avoid a bad deal which potentially could cause severe losses. Remember, it's better to pay a little now than a whole lot later.

ADVERTISING FIRMS

Advertising agencies are potential sources of marketing assistance often overlooked by existing firms and prospective entrepreneurs. Many agencies provide services over and above their traditional function of selling media. These include:

— Evaluation of marketing objectives
— Planning of advertising strategy and tactics
— Selection of correct media outlets
— Production of ad layouts and commercials
— Coordination and execution of strategy and tactics
— Evaluation of advertising results

Generally, small advertising accounts will have to pay for the additional services rendered over and above the cost of media purchased from the agency. However, larger accounts can expect some, if not all, of the aforementioned services to be included as a part of the media fee paid. In other words, these services may be performed free of charge if large amounts of media are purchased.

Advertising agencies are located in the yellow pages of most phone books. In addition, various media and other businesses may provide information concerning the services and reputation of various agencies. Also, several professional advertising associations might provide referrals upon request. Some names and addresses are listed below.

American Advertising Federation
1101 Vermont Avenue NW, Suite 500
Washington, DC 20005
(202) 898-0089

American Association of Advertising Agencies
666 Third Avenue, 13th Floor
New York, NY 10017
(212) 682-2500

Mutual Advertising Agency Network
25700 Science Park Drive
Cleveland, OH 44122
(216) 292-6609

North American Advertising Agency Network
245 Fifth Avenue, Suite 2103
New York, NY 10016
(212) 481-3022

The publication entitled *Standard Directory of Advertising Agencies* will provide comprehensive information on most agencies, including their areas of specialty. This work can normally be found in a library. If not, write to the publisher and request the three-volume set. It may seem expensive to purchase but consider the time and money associated with an extensive search.

National Register Publishing Company, Inc.
121 Chanlon Road
New Providence, NJ 07974
(908) 464-6800

Associations (Trade and Professional)

Trade and professional associations represent a specific group of businesses or individuals that find themselves in the same or similar line of business. Many trade associations maintain assistance programs designed to help and serve the firms they represent. Newsletters, seminars, toll-free hotlines, etc., are but a few services offered by many of these trade organizations. In addition, quite a few associations collect and analyze financial data in reference to the whole industry they serve as well as individual firms. This information is organized and in many cases made available to members and prospective entrepreneurs wishing to enter the industry through a start-up operation or by purchasing an existing firm.

A list of trade and professional associations can be found by referring to the two publications given below. One or both should be found in most libraries. If not found, write or call the publishers for details.

Encyclopedia of Associations
Publisher—Gale Research Company
835 Penobscot Building
Detroit, MI 48226
(313) 961-2242

National Trade and Professional Associations of the United States
Publisher—Columbia Books, Inc.
1212 New York Avenue, NW, Suite 330
Washington, DC 20005
(202) 898-0662

There are many associations that represent the interests of the small business community in general. Some will provide useful information that could be utilized by an entrepreneur or existing firm when evaluating overall business conditions and trends and, in some cases, specific opportunities. These organizations are listed in Appendix E.

CHAMBERS OF COMMERCE

Local chambers of commerce can provide valuable assistance to prospective entrepreneurs and existing small businesses. Besides facilitating interaction between local business people, civic groups, and professionals, CCs can be an important source of community contacts that could help any business. In addition, many chambers of commerce maintain small-business committees that promote and/or assist small firms within the area they serve. Also, some chambers have strong ties to the U.S. Small Business Administration and other governmental bodies, including state and local agencies that represent the interests of small enterprises.

Some chambers collect statistical data on the communities they serve and make this information publicly available. Facts concerning sales, income structure, growth patterns, etc., may be acquired so as to assist in the planning function. A listing of all chambers of commerce in the world can be obtained by referring to a publication entitled *World Wide Chamber of Commerce Directory*. If it cannot be found in a library, write the publisher mentioned below. The book costs less than $29, at last word.

WCCD
P.O. Box 1029
Loveland, CO 80539

COMPETITION

Competitors are almost always looked upon as "the enemy." However, with a little creative thinking, competitors can be viewed as a source of vital information. Some will candidly provide useful data upon request, while others will not. Even if some competitors are tightlipped about conveying ideas and information, their actions in the marketplace can reveal interesting particulars worth noting. For example, an unanticipated price hike may indicate that a competitor is experiencing unusually strong demand, falling profit margins, or increasing cost pressures. It may also signal a shift in marketing strategy or tactics. So, always ask questions, listen, and observe.

CUSTOMERS

Customers can yield valuable tips about the firm's image to the public at large. Many small-business entrepreneurs have been shocked to hear the comments about their business from their clientele. Before starting a small business, it is wise to speak with potential customers. They might reveal some pros and cons that may not have been apparent upon initial or later evaluation. In reference to buying a going concern, seeking out current and potential customers could be an excellent way to gauge the viability of the enterprise being considered for acquisition.

FINANCIAL INSTITUTIONS

Local financial institutions have an intimate knowledge of the community they serve. Therefore, they can be an important source of information concerning business prospects. Many will help in analyzing financial data concerning the local economy and specific business opportunities. Most know what businesses can work in the community and which ones have a high chance of failure. Some even know which locations are good or bad for particular types of businesses.

FRIENDS, FAMILY, AND ASSOCIATES

Personal and professional relationships can yield valuable information even though extensive research is being conducted. Drawing on the combined experiences of friends, relatives, and associates can augment existing research efforts and in some cases fill knowledge vacuums that may exist. Asking for advice can also bring some interesting insights often underemphasized or overlooked in the research endeavor. In some cases, it may provide profit opportunities, and in other situations, help avoid financial disaster.

U.S. presidents have been known to call on family members and friends when delineating major policy directions. John Kennedy constantly consulted his father on civil rights issues and Jimmy Carter drew on his mother and Southern friends for advice. Even his daughter, Amy, was consulted on nuclear arms questions.

Soliciting advice can be like picking peaches. Generally, a yield of good, average, and rotten fruit is collected. Therefore, when absorbing advice from friends, family, and/or associates, consider the source very carefully. Was previous advice and information solid and sound? If so, to what degree? If not, watch out.

INSURANCE COMPANIES

Insurance companies and their local agents can provide useful information relating to the reduction of liability under a number of conditions. Besides providing the traditional business insurance services such as casualty, health, and life protection, many are involved in the reduction of risks relating to defective products or services, nonpayment of client accounts, international transactions, etc.

To find out which companies are involved in comprehensive risk reduction programs may require some time and energy. It may take time to find the right kind of insurance combination required at a good price. Generally, calling local agents will reveal vital and necessary information. Again, talking to bankers, attorneys, accountants, and consultants will usually provide insight into the types of insurance required and where to find it.

Some insurance companies provide additional services to small firms and prospective entrepreneurs. These services can range anywhere from setting up pension and profit-sharing plans to providing in-house consulting services on such things as cash-flow and resource management.

LEGAL COMMUNITY

Attorneys are important in the business process and should be utilized when there are any doubts or unanswered questions when examining situations that can have legal ramifications either now or in the future. Start-up firms need to seek out legal assistance on matters such as legal structure, personal and business liabilities, permits, licenses, etc. Besides the items just mentioned, attorneys can help in the following areas:

— Analysis and evaluation of contracts
— Negotiation with investors, lenders, and suppliers
— Compliance with legal statutes and codes
— Defense in legal matters
— Identification of capital sources

Attorneys are listed in the yellow pages of the phone book. In addition, you may call or write the state bar association, which is usually located in the capital city of a particular state, to obtain a list of lawyers located in a given area of that state. However, the best source of contact information concerning competent legal help will come from bankers, accountants, and business consultants. Most work with legal expertise on a regular basis and are in a position to know the best lawyer for a given situation. Also, try other businesses in a related field. Some good legal contacts may surface.

Consulting the publication entitled *The Lawyer's Register By Specialties and Fields of Law* may provide some helpful sources. If not located in a library, the book may be obtained by contacting the publisher at the address below.

Lawyer's Register Publishing Company
28790 Chagrin Boulevard, Suite 140
Cleveland, OH 44122

The cost is $119.00.

LIBRARIES (PUBLIC, PRIVATE, AND COLLEGE)

Most large and medium-sized libraries maintain an array of business books and periodicals that can be helpful to any existing or prospective entrepreneur. In addition, some have learning resource centers with the latest in business-related audio and visual aids. Normally, a city with a population of around 5,000 has at least one library, although it may lack adequate materials and facilities. There is an exception to this rule. Small towns harboring universities or colleges may have the advantage of the institution's library resources. Libraries within population centers exceeding 100,000 are more sophisticated and detailed in their information-delivery capabilities. All things being equal, college and university libraries tend to be the best for business research purposes.

Many of the large state universities collect, assimilate, and publish an array of economic information on local areas within the state they serve. The quality of this data tends to be very high and can provide a small firm or prospective entrepreneur with valuable information when planning or analyzing opportunities.

PLANNING DISTRICTS
(Economic Development Centers)

Many localities belong to planning districts. These districts maintain offices and are funded by one or more communities for the purpose of coordinating growth objectives. They gather, disseminate, organize, and publish an array of data about the areas they serve. The information tends to be somewhat technical, but it can prove helpful to any firm or individual examining potentials within a locality. Market trends, population shifts, income patterns, and activity in certain lines of business are but a few of the types of information available from the office of a good planning district. Call the municipal manager of the local government to find out if such an organization exists and how to make contact if it does.

Some local governments call planning districts, economic development companies or centers.

MANAGEMENT CONSULTANTS

Every business occasionally finds itself in a management situation that it cannot directly control or correct. When this condition prevails, a management consultant can be hired to help with the difficulties. In addition, a prospective entrepreneur may want to use a consultant to assist in the start-up phase of a new enterprise. Keep in mind that most of these consultants specialized in particular segments of management, although some generalists remain.

The management consulting profession is an unregulated industry requiring no certification. Consequently, many calling themselves consultants actually lack the necessary education and expertise needed to be a good advisor. Given these circumstances, carefully examine the educational background and experience of any consultant before signing a service contract. Ask for client references and check them out thoroughly to ensure the credibility and capability of the consultant.

Bankers, lawyers, and accountants might be able to recommend good management consultants. Also, potential or existing competitors may tell you about consultants willing to provide services in your area of business.

Another source of referrals are the professional associations that represent management consultants. Some maintain codes of ethics to enhance the credibility of their membership. These organizations are listed below.

Association of Managing Consultants
521 Fifth Avenue, 35th Floor
New York, NY 10175
(212)697-8262

The Association of Management Consulting Firms
521 Fifth Avenue
New York, NY 10175
(212) 697-9693

Council of Consulting Organizations
521 Fifth Avenue, 35th Floor
New York, NY 10175
(212) 697-9693

Institute of Management Consultants
19 West 44th Street
New York, NY 10036
(212) 921-2885

Society of Professional Management Consultants
16 West 56th Street
New York, NY 10019
(212) 586-2041

MARKETING CONSULTANTS

Like management problems, marketing difficulties can also surface that demand the attention of outside expertise. Marketing consultants should possess the same combination of education and experience as management advisors, except in different fields, of course. The types of assistance to expect from a marketing consultant include but are not limited to the following:

— Market research
— Market planning
— Mail order
— Direct mail
— Distribution
— Market testing
— Merchandising

Keep in mind that marketing consultants also tend to specialize in a particular field, thus a generalist may be difficult to locate. The yellow pages of the phone books in larger cities will list some prospects. In addition, bankers, accountants, and attorneys may provide good contacts. The best leads are generally given by firms that are currently using or have employed a marketing consultant. When initially talking to consultants, always ask for background information and client references. Check the information out carefully to ensure credibility. A bad consultant can be costly in terms of lost time, markets, and money.

PERIODICALS

There are several excellent periodicals that serve the small business community. Reading and studying the contents contained within their covers can prove to be helpful to the individual wishing to start or buy a business. Also, existing enterprises can find useful material relating to the operational matters. Information to be found in these publications includes but is not limited to the following:

— Successful management techniques
— Dealing with lenders and investors
— Sources of capital
— Government assistance programs
— Marketing techniques and tips
— Bartering of goods and services
— Exporting

Below are two of the best small-business oriented periodicals.

Entrepreneur magazine
2311 Pontius Avenue
Los Angeles, CA 90064

Inc. magazine
38 Commercial Wharf
Boston, MA 02110

Public Relations Firms and Consultants

These organizations and consultants provide publicity services to firms or individuals wishing to exploit the news value of particular business happenings. Publicity is usually an inexpensive means of creating an image and/or generating sales. However, the public relations (PR) function does have limits and it should never be viewed as a substitute for advertising. In fact, PR is normally seen as an extension of the marketing effort.

Public relations firms and consultants are listed in the yellow pages of phone books in large and medium-sized cities. However, the best sources of contacts include business consultants, bankers, accountants, lawyers, and other businesses who have used PR services. In addition, contacting the professional association listed below might provide some referrals. When talking to potential firms or consultants, always ask for background information and investigate thoroughly.

Public Relations Society of America
33 Irving Place
New York, NY 10003
(212) 995-2230

Also, it is important to remember that many advertising agencies perform public relations services. When searching for advertising expertise, ask about PR functions as well.

Suppliers

Some vendors provide a wealth of information and help to new or existing businesses in the field they serve. A few suppliers will even go so far as to set up an entrepreneur in business by providing location, inventory, and financial assistance. Most do not go to those extremes, but many will help in one or more vital areas.

Constantly search for new suppliers. Evaluate their services and credit terms carefully. It is not unethical to play them against each other. In fact, it makes good business sense. Tell one or more suppliers that a better deal can be obtained elsewhere. Watch for their reactions. Some will bend and others will not.

Suppliers can be located in a set of publications known as *The Thomas Registers*. Most libraries have the volumes. If not available otherwise, they can be obtained by writing to the publisher whose address and phone number appears below. Inquire concerning information and the cost involved.

Thomas Publishing Company
One Penn Plaza
New York, NY 10119
(212) 695-0500

UNIVERSITIES AND COLLEGES

Many institutions of higher education have resources available for use by the small-business community. Most college and universities maintain large numbers of books, magazines, and newsletters in the fields of business and economics that can be used for research or other related purposes. In addition, these institutions offer numerous classes that may provide helpful information. Currently, over 300 business schools offer courses in "small-business management" and/or "entrepreneurism." The U.S. Small Business Administration is compiling a list of these colleges, which should be available soon. Call your regional SBA office to get the list. Also, many business professors moonlight as free-lance consultants offering their expertise at rates normally below those charged by established consulting firms. They can be a source of valuable information.

Some business schools want their students to work on outside projects so as to allow them real-life experiences. Many schools make it a requirement. These colleges are always looking for challenging situations that can be used as a proving ground for their students. Generally, no fee is charged to the entrepreneur or small firm, and these students can provide valuable talent in most problem situations.

Seminars and workshops are additional services provided by some institutes of higher education to existing businesses of all sizes and to prospective entrepreneurs. Topics can cover the entire business spectrum, and the fees are normally low. Many of these interaction meetings are held in unison with the U.S. Small Business Administration, U.S. Department of Commerce, state or local chamber of commerce, or other bodies representing business interests.

Call the local college or university for details.

Incubators

Small-business and entrepreneurial incubators are small vestibules of opportunity for any new start-up or other embryonic concept. Usually set up and funded by colleges, universities, chambers of commerce, and local or regional economic development authorities, both public and private, these organizations can provide much assistance to entrepreneurs.

Not only do incubators provide free or low-cost managerial assistance, they can also provide office and plant space at a reduced price in addition to clerical support. Also, the individuals or organizations that run the incubators will help in securing needed funding to help launch and/or expand the enterprise.

Generally, the stay in the incubator is for a limited time, no more than two or three years, after which time the enterprise must relocate and attempt to survive under normal business conditions.

Still, incubators can provide that extra edge and opportunity that many young businesses need in order to make it past the critical first years of business life.

A list of incubators is located in Appendix D.

There are many more than are represented in this list. Call or write the one nearest to you and ask if there is one that is even closer to you. Also, you may want to write the International Venture Capital Institute, P.O. Box 1333, Stamford, CT 06904, or call them at (203) 323-3143. They have the most complete listing of incubators in the country. At this printing the price of their list was $9.95. But a new list is reportedly in the works and it may cost more.

4

CORRECT LEGAL STRUCTURE
Evaluation Is Necessary

Legal Forms of Organization

It is vitally important that entrepreneurs select the correct form of legal structure. Whether it is a new business just starting out or an existing operation, the legal form will determine to a great extent the way in which business is conducted, not to mention tax affairs. It will also affect the degree of freedom to operate within the total business environment.

Selecting the most appropriate form of legal organization is easier said than done. Many aspects must be examined, taking into account both personal and business considerations.

Six kinds of legal structure are in general use today. They are as follows: sole proprietorship, general partnership, limited partnership, corporation, subchapter S corporation, and limited liability company. Each has unique characteristics with certain advantages and disadvantages that need to be evaluated. Only the form that maximizes the interests of the entrepreneur and business should be selected.

SOLE PROPRIETORSHIP

Over 95 percent of all businesses in the country are classified as proprietorships. It is the simplest form of legal structure, generally requiring only a local business license to operate. Normally, the owner also serves as manager. The primary advantages of this structure are as follows:

- *They are easy to form.* Establishing a sole proprietorship is simple and inexpensive, requiring little or no government approval. Check with the local court clerk to determine if there are any licensing requirements.
- *The owner keeps all profit.* There are no partners to share it with.
- *Government regulation is minimal.* Most government agencies direct their regulatory efforts toward large corporate entities, although the government paperwork requirement for small businesses has increased somewhat over the last decade. Whatever the case, small firms are expected to comply with all local, state, and federal regulations.
- *Taxes are low.* The owner of a sole proprietorship is taxed as an individual, at a rate normally lower than the corporate tax rate.
- *The owner has complete control.* The owner makes all of the decisions and determines management policy. Generally, one person can make decisions more quickly than a number of individuals can.
- *Little working capital is needed.* In many cases, sole proprietorship can be operated with limited capital requirements.
- *They are easy to terminate.* A sole proprietorship can quickly and easily cease operations without red tape.

Disadvantages of the sole proprietorship form of legal organization are listed below.

- *There may be a lack of continuity.* If the owner becomes ill or dies, the business may terminate.
- *Liability is unlimited.* The owner is legally responsible for all debts of the business without question. If the business fails and there are debts outstanding, creditors may sue the owner to satisfy their claims. The owner's personal assets could be at risk. Certain types of loss (physical, personal injury, theft, etc.) can be prevented by maintaining adequate insurance programs.
- *Capital may be hard to find.* Some proprietorships have difficulty raising money because of the limited funding alternatives available to the legal form (only one owner, can't sell stock, etc.).

- *The owner may be spread too thin.* The owner has to wear many hats, performing a number of diverse business functions (marketing, purchasing, bookkeeping, etc.). Such a "one person" show with limited experience in many facets of business operations may be unable to attract needed expertise because of its small size and/or little growth potential.
- *It may be difficult to transfer ownership.* Selling all or part of a sole proprietorship can be equated to the difficulty in transacting real estate. In fact, many times real estate is involved.

GENERAL PARTNERSHIP

A partnership is defined by the Uniform Partnership Act as "an association of two or more persons to carry on as co-owners of a business for profit." Most general partnerships are evidenced by a written agreement called "Articles of Partnership." Though these articles are not required by law, most individuals involved in partnerships agree it is in the best interest of all to have a written agreement. In addition, the articles should be recorded with the clerk of the local court as a matter of public record for the protection of all individuals associated with the partnership. Articles of Partnership are designed mainly to spell out the contributions made by each partner to the business, whether by money or property, and the responsibilities of the partners in the firm. Table 9 lists the different types of partners that may be involved in partnership activities.

TABLE 9

TYPES OF PARTNERS

Ostensible (General) Partner—Active in the business and publicly known as a partner.

Active Partner—Active in the business and may or may not be publicly associated with the firm.

Secret Partner—Active in the firm but not presented publicly as a partner.

Dormant Partner—Inactive in the firm and not presented publicly as a partner.

Silent Partner—Inactive in the firm and not presented as being associated with the partnership.

Nominal Partner—Not a partner in the firm but held out publicly to be a partner, usually for prestige reasons. In some cases, these partners can be held liable for partnership activity if their names are used to represent the firm.

Subpartner—Not a partner but contracts with an active partner so as to participate in the partner's business and profits.

Limited Partner—Is not involved in managing the partnership, therefore his/her liability is limited to the amount invested and no more.

Below are some of the more common components of a general partnership agreement:

— Name, address, and purpose of the partnership
— Date of formation and duration of the partnership
— Names and addresses of partners
— Contributions made by each partner
— How business expenses are handled
— Division of profits and losses among partners
— Duties and responsibilities of each partner
— Salary and/or draw of each partner
— Procedure for selling partnership interest
— Method of accounting and record keeping
— How to change the partnership agreement
— How to handle disagreements
— How to deal with absence and disability
— Required and prohibited actions
— Protection of remaining partners if a partner dies
— Provisions for the retirement of partners

Advantages to the general partnership form of legal organization include:

- *They are easy to form.* Procedures and expenses are minimal.
- *Capital may be easier to raise.* Two or more people will be providing and searching for capital. In addition, funding sources are more likely to entertain financing requests because of the broader capital base.
- *Taxes are low.* General partners are taxed as individuals. The individual tax rate is normally lower than that of a corporation.
- *There is a broader management base.* Two or more heads are better than one.

- *Better quality employees might be hired.* Partnerships tend to attract good employees because of the possibility of becoming a principal in the firm.
- *There is managerial flexibility.* Generally, important decisions can be made quickly, although not as fast as in a sole proprietorship.
- *Government interference is minimal.* Like sole proprietorships, partnerships are normally free of extensive governmental scrutiny, although compliance with regulations is a must.

Disadvantages inherent in the general partnership include the following:

- *Liability is unlimited.* The general partners are personally liable for the debts of the partnership. General partners can legally bind each other. This is why it is extremely important to know intimately the partners involved in the firm. Make sure all general partners are credible.
- *There may be a lack of continuity.* Normally, a general partnership has a limited life and is terminated on the date specified in the Articles of Partnership or upon the death of a general partner. Termination can be avoided by stating in the articles that the partnership is perpetual.
- *Authority may be divided.* General partners may disagree, causing organization disharmony.
- *Profits are shared.* They are divided up among all the general partners.
- *Appropriate partners can be difficult to locate.*

LIMITED PARTNERSHIP

Basically, limited and general partnerships share the same characteristics, with a few distinct differences worth noting. A limited partnership is defined as an association of at least one general partner and one limited partner. The limited partner is an individual who only invests capital and does not participate in managing the firm. In fact, the limited partnership form of business organization is viewed by many as a capital-generating mechanism used quite frequently in real estate, oil and gas development, and mining deals. Very attractive tax benefits can be passed on to investors involved in a limited partnership agreement.

The main thing to remember is that the general partner(s) in a limited partnership has unlimited liability for the debts of the business without question. On the other hand, limited partners are not liable for partnership debts if they do not participate in managing the business. Their personal assets are not at stake if the limited partnership incurs debts. They can lose only the amount invested and nothing more. Recent court rulings have determined that limited partners who actively get involved in management functions and affairs are not, in fact, limited partners and should be considered general partners, thereby assuming unlimited risk for the debts of the partnership.

If the limited partnership generates profits, the general partners are normally rewarded by receiving between 1 and 20 percent of all income produced after expenses are paid. The remaining 80 to 99 percent is divided among the limited partners. Percentages vary among different propositions.

CORPORATION

The corporation is the most complex legal structure discussed thus far. In 1819, Chief Justice Marshall defined a corporation as an "artificial being, invisible, intangible, and existing only in contemplation of the law." Consequently, the corporation is a legal entity separate from the people who own or operate it.

The formation of a corporation is normally subject to the approval of the state government in the state in which the corporation will reside. If doing business in a number of states, the corporation needs to get the approval of each state and will be classified as a "foreign corporation" within those borders.

In order to form a corporation, an organizational meeting must take place. The organizer(s) must draft a corporate charter, also known as "Articles of Incorporation," which outline the powers and limitations of the proposed corporation. Table 10 shows an example of actual articles of incorporation that can be used by a Virginia corporation. The charter is then submitted to the secretary of state in the domicile state for approval. If the charter is disapproved, the secretary's office will probably recommend changes in the articles of incorporation so as to facilitate a positive decision. Table 10 illustrates an approved charter issued after articles of incorporation were submitted and accepted by the State of Virginia.

Typical articles of incorporation would include the following elements:

- *Name of corporation*—Most states will not allow a corporation to pick a name similar to a corporate name already in existence, in order to avoid confusion. In addition, the name chosen may not be offensive or deceptive to the public. It is wise to call the State Corporation Commission or secretary of state before submitting the articles of incorporation to determine if the name selected can be used. Time and energy may be saved by avoiding disapproval and return of the articles. Some states will allow corporate organizers to reserve a name until the articles of incorporation are sent to the appropriate agency. Normally, there is a small fee for this service.

- *Purpose*—The purpose for which the corporation was formed must be stated in precise terminology. Some states allow the use of broad language when stating corporate purpose, such as, "The purpose of the corporation is to engage in any lawful act or activity for which a corporation may be organized." However, most states want exact purposes clearly stated. Many corporate organizers use both approaches, for good reason. Making a specific statement of purpose will satisfy most states without question. In addition, others (such as funding sources) may look more favorably on the corporation if specific purposes are stated. Also, other states will be more willing to let the corporation do business within its borders without changing the corporate charter (articles of incorporation). A broad statement of purpose will give the corporation maneuvering room to expand into other profitable areas when opportunities arise.

- *Life of the business*—A statement of how long the corporation is to remain in business. It may be for months, years, or perpetuity. Some states will not require that this be answered, but will assume that the life is perpetual unless otherwise stated.

- *Location*—The address of the corporation's registered office must be stated. If the corporation wishes to incorporate in a state other than the one in which it resides, an office may be required in the other state. However, the establishment of the office can be avoided if the corporation appoints a "registered agent" in the state to act on behalf of its interests. The agent will be required to maintain certain corporate records and to accept communications between the state of incorporation and the corporation. Some states will require the agent representing the corporation to maintain an office. Some agents offer their services to many corporations wanting to incorporate in other states. Their fees for agent services are very reasonable. Call the State Corporation Commission or secretary of state in the state where incorporation is desired and ask for a list of registered agents.

- *Incorporator(s)*—The names and addresses of the incorporator(s) (organizers) need to be stated. Most states require that at least one incorporator be a resident of the state in which incorporation will take place.
- *Capital Structure*—The type of capital stock and the maximum amount authorized to be issued must be stated. The corporation must promulgate the number and class of shares to be offered. In addition, the privileges and limitations of each class of shares must be detailed in some states.
- *Capital Requirement*—Many states require a minimum capital infusion before the corporate charter (articles of incorporation) is approved.
- *Preemptive Rights*—There must be a statement detailing the rights or restrictions of existing stockholders to purchase additional shares if issued by the corporation in proportion to their existing ownership interest before offering the new stock to prospective shareholders. Allowing preemptive rights gives existing shareholders the right to maintain their percentage control of the business.
- *Initial Directors*—The names and addresses of the individuals who will serve as initial directors must be given. These people serve until the first stockholders' meeting, after which they will either continue to serve or be replaced.
- *Internal Affairs*—There must be a statement of how the corporation will be regulated. In most cases, by-laws are acknowledged as being the internal law of the corporation and will be discussed below.
- *Charter Changes*—Procedures for changing the articles of incorporation should be stated even though they are defined in state law.

After the charter is approved by the state, stockholders need to have a meeting to adopt corporate by-laws and elect the board of directors. The board will in turn appoint the corporate officers. The by-laws are designed to serve as internal regulations that govern the operation of the corporation by establishing rights and limitations. Some by-laws

TABLE 10

ARTICLES OF INCORPORATION
of
Telemedia, Inc.

FIRST.—The name of this corporation is Telemedia, Inc.

SECOND.—Its registered office in the State of Virginia is located at *100 Anywhere Drive* in the City of *Winchester*. The registered agent in charge thereof is James L. Silvester who is a resident of the State of Virginia and who is a director of the corporation and whose business office is the same as the registered office of the corporation.

THIRD.—The purposes for which the corporation is organized are as follows:

A. To contract for and fund the development and production of television programs for distribution to cable television networks, on a syndicated basis to independent and major network owned and affiliated commercial television stations, to pay television systems, to public television stations and systems, and to such additional outlets as become available for programming. The Company intends to develop the ancillary marketing potential of these projects, and other projects independent of the television market, for distribution to the video disk and video cassette markets, audiocassette markets, records, radio, books, newspapers, and other print media, so as to enhance merchandising opportunities.

B. To do all other things lawful, necessary, or incident to the accomplishment of the purposes set forth above; to exercise all lawful powers now possessed by Virginia corporations of similar character; and to engage in any business in which a corporation organized under the laws of Virginia may engage except any business that is required to be specifically set forth in the articles of incorporation.

FOURTH.—The amount of the total authorized capital stock of this corporation is 10,000 common shares—par value five ($5.00) dollars per share, which equals fifty thousand dollars ($50,000).

FIFTH.—The number of directors constituting the initial board of directors is *three*, and the names and addresses of the persons who are to serve as the initial directors are: (names and addresses are listed here).

SIXTH.—The directors shall have power to make and to alter or amend the By-Laws; subject to stockholders' rights under Section 13.1–24 of the codes of the State of Virginia; to fix the amount to be reserved as working capital, and to authorize and cause to be executed, mortgages and liens without limit as to the amount, upon the property and franchise of the corporation.

The By-Laws shall determine whether and to what extent the accounts and books of this corporation, or any of them shall be open to the inspection of the stockholders; and no stockholder shall have any right of inspecting any account, or book or document of this corporation, except as conferred by the law or the By-Laws, or by resolution of the stockholders.

The stockholders and directors shall have power to hold their meetings and keep the books, documents and papers of the corporation outside the State of Virginia, at such places as may be from time to time designated by the By-Laws or by resolutions of the stockholders or directors, except as otherwise required by the laws of the State of Virginia.

The object, powers, and purposes specified in any clause or paragraph herein above contained shall be construed as general powers conferred by the laws of the State of Virginia; and it is hereby expressly provided that the foregoing enumeration of specific powers shall in no wise limit or restrict any other power, object, or purpose of the corporation, or in any matter affect any general powers or authority of the corporation.

I, the UNDERSIGNED, for the purpose of forming a corporation under the laws of the State of Virginia, do make, file, and record these articles, and do certify that the facts herein are true; and I have accordingly hereunto set my hand.

DATED: _____   SIGNED: _____
                                                Incorporator

---

will duplicate provisions of the articles of incorporation (charter) and state law. The most common by-laws used in corporation include, but are not limited to, the following:

- Address of the principal office. If preferred, all offices can be listed.
- Time, place, and required notification of annual stockholder meeting.
- Procedure for calling special stockholders' meetings.
- Required quorum and voting rights and limitations of stockholders.
- Number of corporate directors involved along with their compensation, if any. Lengths of terms of office, methods for electing and reelecting, and procedures for creating or dealing with vacancies on the board.
- Time, place, and required notification of regular board meetings.
- Procedures for calling special board meetings.
- Required quorum and voting rights and limitations of directors.
- Method of selecting corporate officers.

- Statement of major corporate officers (titles such as chairman of the board, vice chairman of the board, president, vice president, treasurer, secretary, etc.), including responsibilities and term of office.
- Procedures for creating new corporate positions and dealing with vacancies.
- Procedures for the issuance of stock.
- Form of stock certificate to use, including the terminology on the certificate.
- Procedures for handling stock transfers and record keeping.
- Procedure for the approval and issuance of dividends on a regular or irregular basis.
- Statement of the fiscal year.
- Sample of the corporate seal.
- Authorization to open financial accounts and sign checks.
- Procedures for issuing the annual statement and other periodic reports to the stockholders.
- Steps and procedures for changing the by-laws.

The corporate form of legal structure has definite pros and cons. Advantages are listed below:

- *Limited Liability*—Stockholders are liable only for the amount of their investment, in most cases. In rare situations, stockholders may be at risk for more than the amount invested if the stock they purchase is assessable. Check the stock certificate. If it says "fully paid and assessable," liability may be greater than investment. However, most certificates read "fully paid and non-assessable" which means the risk is limited. Also, if the corporation is sued, stockholders are normally free of liability. However, managers may be subject to suit.
- *Ease of Transferability*—Ownership can be easily transferred by signing the stock certificate(s).
- *Legal Entity*—A corporation is a separate entity standing by itself, divorced from its owners and managers in the eyes of the law.
- *Diversified Management*—Some corporations have the ability to attract and draw on the skills of several individuals.
- *Continuous Life*—Corporations are generally perpetual in nature and can only be terminated by a vote of the stockholders. The state may revoke a corporate charter if laws are being broken by the

corporation. Rarely, a corporation will elect to limit its life. This limitation must be stated in the articles of incorporation. If the corporation decides at a later date to be perpetual, the articles may be changed to reflect that wish.

- *Ease in Raising Capital*—Money can be generated by issuing shares of stocks and/or issuing bonds, in addition to the same funding methods available to other legal structures.

The corporate structure can present a number of difficulties to its owners and managers. Below are listed the most common:

- *Government Interference*—Corporations are more regulated than the other forms of legal organizations.
- *Double Taxation*—Corporations are taxed twice, in that they pay taxes on business income and then the stockholders must pay tax on their dividends. In addition, many states require corporations to pay a tax on their total capital.
- *Corporate Formation*—Starting a corporation is more difficult and usually more expensive than other legal forms.
- *Charter Restrictions*—The activities of a corporation may be limited by its articles of incorporation and laws not affecting other legal forms.
- *Records*—Normally, corporations require more bookkeeping responsibilities than do sole proprietorships or partnerships.
- *Possible Liability*—Many lenders will require the managers and major stockholders of a small corporation to endorse and guarantee loan agreements. This procedure may extend to other contractual agreements as well. This situation puts the personal assets of the managers and stockholders at risk.

It is not really difficult to form a corporation in most states. In fact, many entrepreneurs form their own without legal assistance, thereby saving hundreds or even thousands of dollars. Generally, states will assist in incorporation by providing booklets, forms, and samples to use in the process. Table 11 shows the sample "articles of incorporation" provided by the State of Virginia to prospective incorporators. Some states actually promote individuals to incorporate within their boundaries by using incentives. For example, Delaware, Nevada, and Wyoming are very popular incorporation states because of low capital taxes and a friendly attitude toward corporations. Also, these states

TABLE 11

MODEL FORM FOR ARTICLES OF INCORPORATION

For a Virginia stock corporation for general business purposes

NOTE: This is designed as a model of the shortest permissible form of articles of incorporation; it contains all the required provisions. Other provisions may be added as desired in accordance with specific Sections of the Act to which reference should be made.

ARTICLES OF INCORPORATION
OF

_____

We hereby associate to form a stock corporation under the provisions of Chapter 1 of Title 13.1 of the Code of Virginia and to that end set forth the following:

(a) The name of the corporation is

(b) The purpose or purposes for which the corporation is organized are:

(c) The aggregate number of shares which the corporation shall have authority to issue and the par value per share are as follows:

CLASS AND SERIES	NUMBER OF SHARES	PAR VALUE PER SHARE OR NO PAR VALUE

NOTE: If there is to be more than one class of stock, the preferences, limitations and relative rights of the different classes should be set forth in this article.

(d) The post-office address of the initial registered office:

_____, Virginia.
(Number)   (Street)   (Post Office)   (Zone)

The name of the city or the name of the county in which the initial registered

office is located is _____

of _____. The name of its registered agent is _____,

who is a resident of Virginia and who is a director of the corporation or who is

a member of Virginia State Bar, and whose business office is the same as the

registered office of the corporation.

(e) The number of directors constituting the initial board of directors is

_____ and the names and addresses of the persons who are to

serve as the initial directors are:

        Name   *Address*

Dated _____, 19_____.

_____

_____

_____

                                      Incorporators

FEES ARE ON THE BACK OF THIS FORM

---

have no corporate income taxes. Following are the addresses of the offices to contact in these three states:

> Secretary of State
> State of Delaware
> Dover, DE 19901
>
> Secretary of State
> State of Nevada
> Carson City, NV 89710
>
> Secretary of State
> State of Wyoming
> Capitol Building
> Cheyenne, WY 82002

Normally, individuals can incorporate their businesses and expect no legal problems. There are instances in which the complexities of the business might necessitate an attorney being involved in the incorporation process. For example, a firm with many investors and/or engaged in interstate commerce might consider using legal assistance in putting the corporation together. The entrepreneur will have to decide for himself/herself if an attorney is needed. Whatever the case, most small business people should never pay over $300 in legal fees for incorporation services unless the business affairs of the business are complex. If self-incorporation is the desired approach, get a copy of the book *How to Form Your Own Corporation Without a Lawyer for Under $50* by Ted Nicholas (Wilmington, Del.: Enterprise Publishing). This publication is considered the bible of self-incorporators, with over 1 million copies in print. It includes ready-made forms to use along with the names, addresses, and fees for all state agencies involved in the incorporation process.

SUBCHAPTER S CORPORATION

A number of years ago, Congress recognized the need to increase the flexibility of small firms that use the corporate form of legal structure. Therefore, the subchapter S corporation was created and designed to permit closely held "small-business corporations" to be treated as partnerships from a tax perspective, thereby eliminating double taxation. A standard corporation is taxed on two occasions. It must pay tax on its business income and then shareholders (owners) are taxed on the portion of net profits distributed and paid as dividends. Subchapter S provisions allow shareholders to absorb all corporate income or losses as partners and report it as individual taxpayers. In essence, the subchapter S corporation is not affected by corporate income taxes, thereby eliminating the double taxation feature of standard corporations. Aside from being treated as a partnership from a tax standpoint, the subchapter S and standard corporation share most of the same pros and cons, with a few exceptions.

A corporation must meet certain requirements before the subchapter S alternative becomes feasible. They are:

— The corporation must be a domestic entity (incorporated within the United States).
— The corporation can only have one class of stock.
— Only individuals or estates can be shareholders.
— The corporation cannot be part of another organization.
— The number of shareholders may not exceed 40.
— The corporation cannot have any non-resident alien shareholders.
— 20 percent or more of its revenue must be domestically generated.
— Dividends, interests, royalties, rents, annuities, and securities transactions cannot account for more than 20 percent of total revenues.

If the corporation meets all of the above requirements and wants to adopt the subchapter S option, it must do so within 75 days of starting business activity. In the case of an existing firm, adoption must be executed sometime within the initial 75 days of the firm's fiscal year. All shareholders in the business must give consent to electing the subchapter S structure. Their willingness will be evidenced by signing IRS Form 2553, which can be obtained by writing the local or regional IRS office. Table 12 illustrates this document. The adoption will remain effective until the corporation decides to cancel the status or the IRS revokes it because the firm has failed to maintain the required conditions. Cancellation will prevent the firm from adopting the subchapter S structure a second time in the near future. There is a waiting period of several years before the status can be renewed.

Subchapter S corporations do provide a few very attractive benefits to family corporations. Recent tax legislation has made it extremely advantageous to establish retirement programs under subchapter S provisions. In addition, family members who are shareholders can shift income from one member to another in order to minimize the tax bite. For example, a father in a high tax bracket can shift income to his son whose tax rate is lower, thereby reducing the tax burden on the whole family.

The major negative aspect of the subchapter S legal structure is its limitation on the number of shareholders it can assume (40 maximum). If the corporation is in an expansion mode and needs to raise additional funds over and above the financial capabilities of its present shareholders, the subchapter S status may have to be forfeited. The firm's management will need to evaluate the benefits or receiving the additional capital versus the cost of dropping the subchapter S form of legal organization. In addition, many states refuse to officially acknowledge the subchapter S form; therefore, corporate income or loss is not given preferential treatment under the income tax codes of the hostile state, although federal income tax advantages still exist.

Limited Liability Company

This relatively new organizational structure, also known as an LLC, incorporates the best of the five traditional forms of legal organization. It gives you the opportunity to avoid double taxation; income and losses flow through to the owners' personal tax returns, thus eliminating corporate taxation.

TABLE 12

Form **2553** Rev. September 1993) Department of the Treasury Internal Revenue Service	**Election by a Small Business Corporation** (Under section 1362 of the Internal Revenue Code) ▶ For Paperwork Reduction Act Notice, see page 1 of instructions. ▶ See separate instructions.	OMB No. 1545-0146 Expires 8-31-96

Notes: 1. *This election, to be an "S corporation," can be accepted only if all the tests are met under Who May Elect on page 1 of the instructions; all signatures in Parts I and III are originals (no photocopies); and the exact name and address of the corporation and other required form information are provided.*

2. *Do not file Form 1120S, U.S. Income Tax Return for an S Corporation, until you are notified that your election is accepted.*

Part I **Election Information**

Please Type or Print	Name of corporation (see instructions)	A Employer identification number (EIN)
	Number, street, and room or suite no. (If a P.O. box, see instructions.)	B Date incorporated
	City or town, state, and ZIP code	C State of incorporation

Election is to be effective for tax year beginning (month, day, year) . . . . ▶ / /

Name and title of officer or legal representative who the IRS may call for more information | F Telephone number of officer or legal representative ( )

If the corporation changed its name or address after applying for the EIN shown in A, check this box . . . . ▶ ☐

If this election takes effect for the first tax year the corporation exists, enter month, day, and year of the **earliest** of the following: (1) date the corporation first had shareholders, (2) date the corporation first had assets, or (3) date the corporation began doing business . . . . ▶ / /

Selected tax year: Annual return will be filed for tax year ending (month and day) ▶ ....

If the tax year ends on any date other than December 31, except for an automatic 52-53-week tax year ending with reference to the month of December, you **must** complete Part II on the back. If the date you enter is the ending date of an automatic 52-53-week tax year, write "52-53-week year" to the right of the date. See Temporary Regulations section 1.441-2T(e)(3).

J Name and address of each shareholder, shareholder's spouse having a community property interest in the corporation's stock, and each tenant in common, joint tenant, and tenant by the entirety. (A husband and wife (and their estates) are counted as one shareholder in determining the number of shareholders without regard to the manner in which the stock is owned.)	K Shareholders' Consent Statement. Under penalties of perjury, we declare that we consent to the election of the above-named corporation to be an "S corporation" under section 1362(a) and that we have examined this consent statement, including accompanying schedules and statements, and to the best of our knowledge and belief, it is true, correct, and complete. (Shareholders sign and date below.)		L Stock owned		M Social security number or employer identification number (see instructions)	N Share-holder's tax year ends (month and day)
	Signature	Date	Number of shares	Dates acquired		

For this election to be valid, the consent of each shareholder, shareholder's spouse having a community property interest in the corporation's stock, and each tenant in common, joint tenant, and tenant by the entirety must either appear above or be attached to this form. (See instructions for Column K if a continuation sheet or a separate consent statement is needed.)

Under penalties of perjury, I declare that I have examined this election, including accompanying schedules and statements, and to the best of my knowledge and belief, is true, correct, and complete.

Signature of officer ▶ | Title ▶ | Date ▶

See Parts II and III on back. | Cat. No. 18629R | Form **2553** (Rev. 9-93)

Also, there are no restrictions on the number of owners and their nationality as is the case with subchapter S corporations. And there is ease of transferability of ownership. Also, an LLC eliminates the need for a general partner, which a limited partnership must have. No one within the LLC structure has to sustain personal liability.

In fact, that is its greatest feature. Most of the 48 states that have enacted LLC statutes have made it impossible for the owners of the LLC to be held personally liable for the actions of the LLC. In other words, the owners cannot be personally sued if something goes haywire with the LLC.

A limited liability company is formed by applying to the state in which you want to conduct business. Soon there will be the Uniform Limited Liability Company Act, in which all of the states with limited liability company codes will agree to general standards of application. This will allow a limited liability company to transact business in another state without having to form an LLC in that state, but will still provide its owners the same degree of legal protection afforded any LLC.

Table 13 illustrates the form needed to start a limited liability company in the State of Virginia. The procedure is nearly the same in every state. Write to or call your state corporation commission and ask for the necessary documents and explanation booklet. (In some states the proper authority might be the Office of Secretary of State.)

However, it is advisable to read up on this new form of legal structure. Also, have your attorney look things over.

Section 1244 Stock

Before forming a corporation it is wise to remember that certain tax incentives are available to make a business an attractive investment to prospective investors who may want to purchase stock (ownership) in the enterprise. When the directors have the first board meeting, they should consider the election of a section under the Internal Revenue Code (Number 1244) that allows an investor to treat a loss in "small-business stock" as an ordinary instead of a capital loss, thereby enhancing its positive tax impact. In order for a corporation to qualify its shares as "section 1244 stock," it must approve the concept at the first director's meeting and before the issuances of any equity. Also, the shares issued can only be common stock and must be sold by the firm in exchange for money or property subject to a promulgated plan,

TABLE 13

LLC-1011 (2/93)

COMMONWEALTH OF VIRGINIA
STATE CORPORATION COMMISSION
ARTICLES OF ORGANIZATION

Pursuant to Chapter 12 of Title 13.1 of the Code of Virginia the undersigned states as follows:

1. The name of the limited liability company is

_____

(The name must contain the words "limited company" or "limited liability company" or their abbreviations "L.C." or "L.L.C.")

2. The address of the initial registered office in Virginia is

_____

(number/street)   (city/state/zip)

located in the [ ] City or [ ] County of _____ .

3. A. The registered agent's name is _____
whose business address is identical with the registered office.

   B. The registered agent is (mark appropriate box)
       (1) an INDIVIDUAL who is a resident of Virginia and
           [ ] a manager of the limited liability company
           [ ] a member of the limited liability company
           [ ] a member of the Virginia State Bar
                   OR
       (2) [·] a professional corporation of attorneys registered
           under Virginia Code Section 54.1-3902

4. The post office address of the principal office where the records will be maintained pursuant to Virginia Code Section 13.1-1028 is

_____

(number/street)   (city/state/zip)

5. The latest date on which the limited liability company is to be dissolved and its affairs wound up is

_____ .

6. Signature:

_____   _____
     (organizer)   (date)

_____
     (printed name)

SEE INSTRUCTIONS ON THE REVERSE

with a few restrictions. Another legal limitation states that the amount of capital received for the shares may not exceed certain dollar limits that have been established.

Question Thyself

Before deciding what legal form to select, consider the following questions very carefully.

- What is the nature of liability from a personal standpoint?
- Would the business continue if the entrepreneur or other key principals of the firm became ill and/or died? Is it important that it does continue?
- Which legal structure would allow the greatest flexibility in management?
- Can additional capital be easily sought if needed?
- Can additional expertise be attracted if needed?
- Does the degree of regulation hamper business activity?
- What legal form can best fulfill the goals of the entrepreneur and business?

Many people lack the legal and accounting expertise needed to make a sound judgment about legal structure. Therefore, it is advisable to seek out the help of a competent tax attorney or certified public accountant (CPA) to ensure the correct selection.

5

SMALL-BUSINESS FINANCING
Be Prepared

Capital and the Small Business

That old maxim that suggests its takes money to make money is as true today as it was a century ago. Both new and existing businesses must have access to financial resources in order to take advantage of profitable situations that may arise. Funds are needed to market new products, pay vendors, meet payrolls, buy equipment, and extend credit to customers, just to mention a few business activities.

Money alone will not ensure you a successful operation. Capital, like any resource, must be managed efficiently in order to maximize profits. Many cash-rich firms have failed to turn profits because of poor or inadequate financial management. For example, a company that has large cash deposits on hand in a checking account, earning nominal interest income, may feel secure in the short term. But these are idle funds, not being used to generate revenues, which are vital in creating adequate profits.

Many new small businesses suffer from undercapitalization and/or funds mismanagement. These afflictions are major causes of business failures. Generally, the end result is a capital squeeze forcing the owners to close down. The trick is to recognize the problem, early in the ball game, before it becomes unmanageable, thereby avoiding the squeeze altogether.

Capital and the New Business

The capital requirements to start a new business will vary depending upon many factors. These need to be analyzed and investigated with great care so as to avoid underestimating financial resources needed to start and carry the business until profits are generated internally to support operations. For example, the type of operation you are starting will determine, to a great extent, your initial capital needs. A manufacturing operation will require more funds than service firms. Other items that need to be considered include location of the enterprise, current and projected economic climate, product/service to be offered, credit policies, etc.

A lot of thought and consideration should be given when studying your initial capital requirements. Many entrepreneurs, with good products and services, fail in their business attempts because of underestimating capital requirements in the beginning.

Tables 14 and 15 are provided courtesy of the Small Business Administration. If used correctly, they will provide you with estimates of capital needs to start any small business. It is advisable to have your lawyer and/or accountant assist you in completing the sheets. This will help in making accurate estimates. Once capital needs have been determined, the next step is to obtain the necessary funds to commence operation. These procedures will be discussed in chapters 6 through 8.

Capital and the Existing Business

Many entrepreneurs fail to anticipate capital needs for present and future operations. Eventually, cash flow problems develop because of the undercapitalization, and existing funds will prove inadequate in paying current obligations. This situation is not reserved exclusively for the small-business person. Some large firms have met their demise because of failing to project funding needs. W. T. Grant, the giant discount chain, collapsed because it grew too quickly before uncovering sources of funds to finance the expansion. Cash flow problems developed that could not be reversed, and the rest is history.

As a business expands, so do its capital needs. If growth increases faster than capital availability, a cash squeeze will occur causing financial hardship. Likewise, if the business is stagnant due to economic conditions and the availability of capital contracts, cash flow difficulties will ensue.

TABLE 14

ESTIMATED MONTHLY EXPENSES			What to put in column 2 (These figures are typical for one kind of business. you will have to decide how many months to allow for in your business.)
Item	Your estimate of monthly expenses based on sales of $_____ per year	Your estimate of how much cash you need to start your business (See column 3.)	
	Column 1	Column 2	Column 3
Salary of owner-manager	$	$	2 times column 1
All other salaries and wages			3 times column 1
Rent			3 times column 1
Advertising			3 times column 1
Delivery expense			3 times column 1
Supplies			3 times column 1
Telephone and telegraph			3 times column 1
Other utilities			3 times column 1
Insurance			Payment required by insurance company
Taxes, including Social Security			4 times column 1
Interest			3 times column 1
Maintenance			3 times column 1
Legal and other professional fees			3 times column 1
Miscellaneous			3 times column 1
STARTING COSTS YOU ONLY HAVE TO PAY ONCE			Leave column 2 blank
Fixtures and equipment			Fill in table 15 and put the total here
Decorating and remodeling			Talk it over with a contractor
Installation of fixtures and equipment			Talk to suppliers from whom you buy these
Starting inventory			Suppliers will probably help you estimate this
Deposits with public utilities			Find out from utilities companies
Legal and other professional fees			Lawyer, accountant, and so on
Licenses and permits			Find out from city offices what you have to have
Advertising and promotion for opening			Estimate what you'll use
Accounts receivable			What you need to buy more stock until credit customers pay
Cash			For unexpected expenses or losses, special purchases, etc.
Other			Make a separate list and enter total
TOTAL ESTIMATED CASH YOU NEED TO START WITH	$		Add up all the numbers in column 2

SOURCE: U.S. Small Business Administration

TABLE 15

LIST OF FURNITURE, FIXTURES, AND EQUIPMENT

Leave out or add items to suit your business. Use separate sheets to list exactly what you need for each of the items below.	If you plan to pay cash in full, enter the full amount below and in the last column.	If you are going to pay by installments, fill out the columns below. Enter in the last column your down payment plus at least one installment.		Estimate of the cash you need for furniture, fixtures, and equipment
		Price	Down payment	Amount of each installment	
Counters	$	$	$	$	$
Storage shelves, cabinets					
Display stands, shelves, tables					
Cash register					
Safe					
Window display fixtures					
Special lighting					
Outside sign					
Delivery equipment if needed					
TOTAL FURNITURE, FIXTURES, AND EQUIPMENT (Enter this figure also in table 13 under "Starting Costs You Only Have To Pay Once.")					$

SOURCE: U.S. Small Business Administration.

86

Capital needs arise because of many factors. Economic conditions on the local, state, or national level can cause revenues to temporarily decline, thereby making it difficult to meet obligations. Abnormal increases in accounts receivable (customer accounts) due to asset mismanagement and/or unexpected growth can cause a need for financial resources. Increasing inventory levels to support revenue growth and the purchase of new equipment to increase productivity will call for additional capital input. Purchasing merchandise before suppliers increase their prices and seasonal factors will increase the need to finance these inventories until sales are made and receivables collected. In addition, the exploitation of unexpected profit opportunities as they arise will call for capital over and above that which is normally available. Also, excessive withdrawal of earnings from the business and a reduction in credit or payment terms by suppliers will also increase capital needs.

TABLE 16

Cash Budget
(For three months, ending March 31, 19 _____)

	January		February		March	
	Budget	Actual	Budget	Actual	Budget	Actual
Expected Cash Receipts:						
1. Cash sales						
2. Collections on accounts receivable						
3. Other income						
4. Total cash receipts						
Expected Cash Payments:						
5. Raw materials						
6. Payroll						
7. Other factory expenses (including maintenance)						
8. Advertising						
9. Selling expense						
10. Administrative expenses (including salary of owner-manager)						

	January		February		March	
	Budget	Actual	Budget	Actual	Budget	Actual
11. New plant and equipment	___	___	___	___	___	___
12. Other payments (taxes, including estimated income tax; repayment of loans; interest; etc.)	___	___	___	___	___	___
13. Total cash payments	___	___	___	___	___	___
14. Expected Cash Balance at beginning of the month	___	___	___	___	___	___
15. Cash increase or decrease (item 4 minus item 13)	___	___	___	___	___	___
16. Expected cash balance at end of month (item 14 plus item 15)	___	___	___	___	___	___
17. Desired working cash balance	___	___	___	___	___	___
18. Short-term loans needed (item 17 minus item 16, if item 17 is larger)	___	___	___	___	___	___
19. Cash available for dividends, capital cash expenditures, and/or short investments (item 16 minus item 17, if item 16 is larger than item 17)	___	___	___	___	___	___
Capital Cash:						
20. Cash available (item 19 after deducting dividends, etc.)	___	___	___	___	___	___
21. Desired capital cash (item 11, new plant equipment)	___	___	___	___	___	___
22. Long-term loans needed (item 21 less item 20, if item 21 is larger than item 20)	___	___	___	___	___	___

Source: U.S. Small Business Administration.

Causes of capital shortages cannot be traced to any single event. There is a combination of factors that create the problems. Identification and positive reaction to these anticipated funding problems will insure proper cash flow and help avoid a potentially injurious capital squeeze. The cash budget in Table 16 will help project the capital needs for a business already in operation. The table, listing only three months, should be expanded to include an entire year, taking into consideration yearly objectives.

An accountant should assist when recording the projections. If expense records are maintained and posted to the table on a monthly basis, a comparison between budget estimates and actual expenditures can be made. Any variances that exist (differences between what was budgeted and actually spent) can be analyzed to determine the effects upon the financial structure of the business.

6

UNDERSTANDING MONEY SOURCES
The Bank Isn't the Final Stop

Never Enough Money

Once you start or buy a small business, your need for capital is constant. Money is needed to finance current operations, expansion, seasonal inventories, and, in some cases, just to stay afloat. Unfortunately, traditional sources of funding for entrepreneurs have been less accommodating lately. Commercial banks, which supply over 65 percent of small-business capital requirements, have downgraded their commitment to small firms. Many banks are raising service fees to small businesses above that which is charged their larger business customers. What's more, small firms usually are charged higher interest rates on loans than are larger businesses. Aspiring entrepreneurs, wishing to start their own businesses, have been left out in the cold almost completely. Banks claim that financing new, unproven enterprises is just too risky. To make matters worse, the U.S. Small Business Administration, which has come to be known as the lender of last resort, and other government funding outlets, have fallen victim to the federal budget ax.

Individuals wishing to start new businesses or expand existing operations do have alternatives when seeking capital beyond the traditional avenues of friends, family, self, and banks. Many of these are overlooked by entrepreneurs in the search process.

Capital Evolution

The capital needs of a business will be determined, to a great extent, by its stage of evolution. Each stage will have different funding requirements. An understanding of these stages will help you to project your business's need for financial resources.

- Seed Stage—This is capital to formulate an idea. The product or service is still being developed on the drawing board. At this stage market feasibility studies are conducted and examined. Most of this funding is provided by the entrepreneur and/or close associates, although it should be pointed out that some financial organizations have begun to fund businesses in the seed stage.
- Start-up Stage—This type of financing is used to get the new company off the ground. Product/service development is being completed and it has been determined that a market exists. Major emphasis is placed on developing managerial expertise, completing final market studies, projecting financial resources, etc. Generally, the product or service is not being marketed at this point.
- First Stage—This funding is provided to launch production of the product or service and to initiate marketing efforts.
- Second Stage—Capital is made available to finance initial cash flow and facilitate expansion of the new company. At this point, the company is not usually showing a profit. Money is needed to support inventories and accounts receivable (customer accounts) until sufficient profits are generated to support operations.
- Third Stage—Normally this money is provided to expand the business on a large scale. Sales are growing very rapidly and profits are being generated. Very little of the market for the firm's product or service has been exploited and funds are needed to support additional marketing endeavors, production, and working capital.
- Fourth Stage (also referred to as bridge financing)—This capital is used as interim financing until financial resources are obtained through a public offering of stock. At times, the bridge money is repaid out of the proceeds of the stock offering once executed. In this stage the company is attempting to make the transition from small firm to a medium-size business. Subsequent public offerings can be made in order to continue expansion and growth.

- Acquisition Funding—Resources made available to allow a company to expand by purchasing other firms is an example of acquisition financing. Mergers and consolidations are common results of using this method of funding.
- Leveraged Buyout—This financing technique can be used when the existing net assets of a company exceed its selling price. Since most companies are sold based upon a multiple of earnings, and that multiple has been decreasing over the last decade due to economic conditions, companies can be purchased by third parties utilizing assets as collateral for loans provided to these parties by financial outlets and/or previous owners. Management and employees can use this method to purchase their company. There have been cases reported where management teams have bought entire firms, using leverage techniques, without investing a penny of their own funds.

Capital Generation—Two Forms

Profits generated within a business can be used to finance various aspects of a firm's operation. This is referred to as *internal funding* and is an inexpensive source of money. Internal capital generation can be achieved in several ways. Cutting costs, selling surplus inventories and equipment, speeding up collection of accounts receivable, and retaining more profits in the business are a number of ways to augment internal capital.

In contrast, capital generated outside the business is called *external financing*. Outlets such as banks, suppliers, commercial finance companies, and investment bankers would be examples of sources external to the firm. Generally there are costs associated with this form of financing and they will be discussed later in this chapter.

Before utilizing external sources, a company should determine if its capital requirements can be met internally. Even though this may not generate all capital requirements needed, it will reduce dependency on external funding, thereby reducing interest costs and/or loss of control. Furthermore, the demonstrated capability to maximize internal capital will enhance the confidence of lenders and investors in the company and its management. This will increase their incentive to commit financial resources on a reasonable basis.

Utilizing internal funding can be costly at times. For example, selling assets to generate cash may have to be done at a loss; unloading certain fixed assets now may force the business to pursue costly sources of materials later on down the road; rigorous inventory reductions may cause stock shortages needed to generate production and/or sales; and the tightening of credit policies may result in loss of customers.

Generally speaking, a business that uses internal financing to the maximum will benefit from the approach. However, this policy may have to be altered if at some point in the future external funding is needed, especially equity capital. Many equity investors are interested in dividend income. These investors may be discouraged if the firm's policies mandate reinvesting all net income in the business without rewarding investors in the form of dividends. Some speculative investors may be interested only in the capital gain potential of an investment (increase in the value of their investment) without expecting dividend income. Normally, investors expect both dividend yield and capital gains.

What Kind of Capital

When seeking funding alternatives for your small business, it is important to analyze carefully the purpose for which the capital will be used. This will determine the kinds of funds needed to carry out your objectives. Deciding what type of capital to employ can be a difficult task since many of the kinds of capital available, although different in name, can be used at the same time and for similar or identical purposes.

In general terms, there are two ways to fund a new or existing business. Many firms use a combination of these to finance operations. *Debt financing* is simply money borrowed from a lender, where you promise to repay the principal amount of the loan plus interest on agreed-upon terms, usually evidenced by a contract (loan agreement). *Equity financing* is somewhat different. This technique allows a business owner to exchange ownership in the firm for capital resources. These funds do not have to be repaid like a loan, but the equity investor will expect a return on investment in the form of stock dividends and/or capital gains selling the stock back to your or a third party. The major disadvantage to this form of financing is your loss of some control over the business because of the new owners.

Debt comes in several forms. A loan can be *unsecured*, in which no collateral is used to back the note. Your credit reputation is the only security available to the lender in this agreement. On the other hand, the *secured* loan is backed by some form of asset to insure the lender against loss due to nonrepayment. Even borrowers with good credit histories may be required to pledge assets occasionally due to economic conditions, bank policy changes, and industry shifts. Generally, it depends on the lender's perception of your financial condition. For example, if a prospective borrower's financial statements are in question as to ability to support a loan, the lender will be inclined to ask for collateral. The more common types of loan security are:

- Guarantor—This individual or firm guarantees payment of an obligation as evidenced by signing a contract (guarantor agreement).
- Endorsers—An endorser signs the obligation agreement and in some cases may have to post collateral. If the principal borrower defaults, the endorser is expected to pay.
- Comaker—A comaker is a principal in an obligation agreement. The borrower and comaker share joint responsibility.
- Accounts Receivable (Customer Accounts)—These are commonly used as collateral on short-term loans. Repayment is made when customers pay on their accounts.
- Equipment—A lender will consider making loans against equipment that has been paid in full. The lender will determine the fair market value of the equipment and will lend up to a certain percentage (usually 60 percent) of that value.
- Marketable Securities (Stocks and Bonds)—Lenders will accept securities as collateral if they are readily marketable. Generally, financial sources will advance no more than 70 percent of the market value so as to protect against price declines. If the security prices drop below what the lender considers acceptable, then the borrower might have to post additional assets. These terms are spelled out in the loan contract.
- Real Estate—Most financial outlets consider real estate excellent collateral and will normally lend up to 90 percent of market value of the property.
- Savings Accounts—Certificates of deposit and saving accounts can be used to secure loans. The lender will hold the certificate or

passbook as collateral with the right to the funds if default occurs. In most cases, lower rates of interest are offered on these loans because of the liquid nature of the pledged assets. These are commonly referred to as passbook or certificate loans.

- Chattel Mortgage—This instrument is somewhat like a real estate mortgage in that they both secure loans with property. In this case equipment is being used for collateral purposes. The lender will evaluate the present and future market value of the equipment and then advance funds amounting to something less than the present value. The business will be expected to make up the difference through a down payment and/or trade-in. If default occurs, the lender can foreclose on the equipment. The business must maintain the equipment and insure it against accidental loss.
- Insurance Policies—Lenders will accept life insurance policies as collateral for loans. They will advance up to the cash value of the policy and it must be assigned to them. When the terms of the loan contract are fulfilled, the policy can be reassigned back to its original status.
- Warehouse Merchandise—Financial institutions will lend up to a certain percentage of the market value of merchandise being stored in a bonded warehouse. The goods must be marketable and evidenced by a warehouse receipt, which is the collateral document used to secure the loan.
- Display Merchandise—Cars, appliances, furniture, etc., can be financed through a technique known as floor planning by using trust receipts as collateral. Lenders will advance funds against display merchandise, held in trust by the borrower, to be repaid when the items are sold.
- Leases—A lender holding a mortgage on property involved in a lease transaction may demand assignment of the lease such that rent payments are made directly to the lender. This will help insure loan repayments.

Collateral requirements and lender demands can place limitations upon your business activities. If the company is considered a good credit risk, limitations will be minimized. Conversely, a bad risk will be met with stiff conditions. Knowing the kinds of restrictions which a lender may demand will help you understand their possible effect on your business. Below are some of the more common loan restrictions used in lending transactions.

— Restriction of your ability to take on additional debt
— Limitation of the selling of accounts receivable and/or excess inventories to raise cash
— Prevention of dividend (earnings) pay-out beyond a certain level to ensure that enough funds are left in the business to retire debt
— Maintenance of certain levels of working capital
— Obligation to supply the lender with appropriate financial statements on a periodic basis

All lending restrictions are known as covenants and appear in the loan contract. Negative covenants limit the borrower's ability to act in certain areas without the permission of the lender. In contrast, positive covenants outline specifically the things which the borrower must do. The first three aforementioned loan restrictions are examples of negative covenants and the last two are positive.

When negotiating with lenders, keep in mind that they have three primary objectives. First and foremost on their minds is repayment of the loan. Lenders will evaluate a prospective borrower's ability to repay by analyzing the loan application and supporting documentation required to be completed. This will be explained in more detail in Chapter 8. These forms will determine the ability to generate adequate cash to make loan payments without adversely affecting other organizational needs, such as working capital. Second, lenders are concerned with protecting their lending position. It is the nature of financial outlets to insure the money they lend with collateral agreements and loan restrictions (some were mentioned earlier). Third, lenders will attempt to charge the highest interest rate possible so as to maximize profits. Keep in mind that they are subject to market forces and must compete with other financial institutions. Letting them know that you have other alternatives might help in achieving a lower rate.

Before signing a loan agreement, make sure you and your attorney and/or accountant read the documentation carefully. No matter how desperate you are for the funds, make sure your interests are represented and protected. Attempt to negotiate terms that limit your restrictions. You will find that lenders will bargain on certain loan conditions. Also, keep in mind that after the loan is made, many financial outlets will amend loan restrictions, on a periodic basis, depending upon the financial health of your business at the time. For example, if after a year into the loan your business is expanding and profits growing, some loan restrictions may be removed by the lender.

You might be able to assume additional debt or sell your accounts receivable to generate cash. On the other hand, if your business deteriorates, additional security and limitations could be called for under the terms of the loan agreement. The point to remember is that lenders are flexible and will negotiate loan conditions.

Time factors are also important in understanding debt financing. In many cases these factors will determine the interest rate to be charged on a loan and whether collateral should be used.

Short-term borrowings are used to finance inventories and accounts receivable. When inventories are sold and outstanding accounts paid by customers, the loans are expected to be repaid. Many lenders will do this on either a secured or unsecured basis depending upon the business. Firms that have seasonal needs will generally have to operate on a secured basis. Some financial outlets offer borrowers *lines of credit*. These give you access to funds for short-term demands without having to apply for a loan every time the need arises. There is an upper limit that can be borrowed, established by the lender, based on the firm's ability to repay. Lines of credit, like all short-term credit, are expected to be paid in full within a period of one year.

Intermediate loans run longer than one year but less than five. These loans can be secured with collateral or can be unsecured, and are used to finance equipment purchases. *Long-term borrowings* extend beyond five years. They are collateralized and used to finance acquisitions, leveraged buyouts, and major plant expansions.

The specific kind of money used can also be distinguished by the source of repayment. As we mentioned earlier, short-term notes are paid from funds generated by retiring customer accounts and inventory turnover. Intermediate and long-term loans are repaid out of business earnings.

Evaluation of Capital Alternatives

In considering your funding situation, you must evaluate the implications of choosing a course of action. This can be accomplished by studying the factors listed below. Your reactions to these will determine, to some extent, the kinds of capital sources you pursue.

- Risk—Lenders are always exposed to some degree of risk when they invest their funds. Likewise, the recipient of the capital is also at risk. Debt funds must be repaid in the form of principal and interest. This can place strains upon the cash flow of the company. If debt burden becomes too great, default is a possibility and with it a host of other problems such as credit denial, foreclosure, and maybe even bankruptcy. Even if you recover, your ability to raise funds in the future could be impaired. Lenders will either refuse to do business with you or will charge exceptionally high interest rates because they perceive you to be a questionable credit risk.

- Maneuverability—Many lenders will require that you place restrictions on the firm's assets. They may ask that you refrain from selling or borrowing against accounts receivable, equipment, and/or inventories. These limitations will be written into the loan contract. If you break the agreement, the lender may have the right to call in the loan or charge a higher rate of interest.

  Another example of reduced flexibility is the reliance on just a few sources of capital. Avail yourself of as many financial outlets as possible. This will enhance your access to funding.

  In addition, relying too much on internal financing as opposed to external, and vice versa, could also prove to be restricting. Capital that is available but is not being utilized to generate sales will result in loss of growth and profits.

- Cost—Capital costs are determined by their effects on business profits and the current owners. There are situations in which business profits could be higher if equity financing were used instead of debt. But since the current owners' profit participation would be diluted by taking on new stockholders, the equity alternative is rejected. For example, consider a firm that is comparing the cost of debt with that of equity financing. The company has the option of borrowing $50,000 at 16 percent interest or selling 20 percent of the stock to equity investors. Net income is expected to reach $100,000 this year and the company's effective income tax rate is 30 percent. The cost of debt in this case can be determined by using the following formula:

Cost of Debt to the Present Owners
$$= \text{Interest Rate} \times (1 - \text{Effective Income Tax Rate})$$
$$= 16 \times (1 - .30)$$
$$= 16 \times (.70)$$
$$= 11.2\%$$

Assuming a one-year loan to be repaid in one installment, the interest expense would equal $5,600, reducing net income to $94,400. Since debt is used, the present owners are entitled to all profits. If the equity alternative is used by the firm, net income would be $100,000 because no interest expense would be incurred. However, only $80.000 could be claimed by the present investors, since $20,000 would be directed to the new owners for their investment. This is generally viewed by the current owner as a cost of doing business and can be determined in the formula below:

Cost of Equity to the Present Owners

$$= \frac{\text{Earnings Directed to New Investors}}{\text{Investment}}$$
$$= \frac{\$20,000}{\$50,000}$$
$$= .40 \text{ or } 40\%$$

Even though the equity alternative produces higher net income, it will probably be rejected due to the loss of control and earnings on the part of the current owners. The losses are a cost to them as shown in the computation above.

- Availability—A business may find that its preferred sources of capital have dried up for any number of reasons (economic conditions, industry status, international events, company factors, etc.). At this point, the firm must pursue other funding alternatives. For example, a company may be using retained earnings (internal financing) and short-term debt to finance operations. If a recessions sets in and profits contract, internal funds will become strained. In addition, high interest rates, which usually accompany economic downturns, will discourage borrowing. The business might be forced to seek equity funding despite loss of control and earnings in order to survive.

- Control—Using debt and internal financing will not compromise control of the present ownership in most cases. If lenders do get nervous, they might demand a representation in the firm's management structure which could affect control somewhat. The use of equity financing will reduce the control of present owners. The degree of loss will depend on the amount of equity exchanged for capital. New firms will need to give more equity (ownership) for the same amount of funds than the more established companies with track records. Normally, equity investors are entitled to managerial voting rights in proportion to the stock they own in the business.

Where to Turn—Private and Government Outlets

The capital sources outlines in this section represent only a broad overview of what is available to small businesses and prospective entrepreneurs. Specific and detailed information regarding these financial outlets can be found in Chapter 11.

SELF

In the early stages of your business endeavors, capital may be hard to find. If this is the case, you might have to rely on personal resources to finance operations until you gain the trust of creditors.

There are a number of ways to tap your hidden wealth. You might consider using the money in your savings accounts and/or certificates of deposit. This prospect may be disquieting to you, but there is a way to borrow against these accounts without disturbing the finds. It's called "passbook borrowing." Bankers don't like to talk about it, but you can borrow up to the amount that is on deposit using savings accounts and certificates of deposit as collateral. The unique feature to this alternative is the interest rate. According to current regulations, financial institutions can charge between 1 and 5 percentage points above the rate being paid on the accounts. Most charge 2 or 3 percentage points above.

Let's say you want to borrow $25,000 to finance a start-up business. You have $12,000 in your savings account paying 5½ percent and $20,000 in a certificate of deposit drawing 13 percent. You can borrow the $12,000 from your savings account for approximately 8 percent with the additional $13,000 coming from your certificate account costing in the neighborhood of 16 percent. Your total cost of capital, about 13 percent, is well below what is currently charged by financial outlets for small-business lending purposes. Your savings and certificate accounts will remain intact, earning interest income. In fact, some or all or that interest income can be used to offset the interest charges against the passbook loan. If you use this approach the cost of the loan can be reduced to below 13 percent, depending upon the amount of interest income used. Of course, the money in your savings and certificate accounts will fail to grow in proportion to the amount of interest income utilized to reduce loan cost.

Another possibility you might want to consider is the cash value of your life insurance policies. This money can be borrowed and repaid over a long period of time. Loan rates vary among insurance companies, but generally run between 6 and 8 percent. You might wonder if this affects your life insurance coverage. It does to a degree. For example, if $10,000 is borrowed from your $50,000 life insurance policy and soon after something happens to you, those policies will only pay $40,000, minus interest charges incurred, to your estate. This assumes that you do not make any principal or interest payments. If you did, the amount paid would increase accordingly. So in essence, your insurance is reduced by the amount owed against the policy. It would be wise to purchase inexpensive term life insurance to cover the amount you borrow so as not to adversely affect your beneficiaries.

The house in which you live is another source of financing worth exploring. Equity you have built in your home can be borrowed by getting a second mortgage. Many lenders will advance up to 80 or 90 percent of the value of your home minus the first mortgage. Some will go as high as 95 and a few will lend up to 100 percent, although this is very rare. Lenders want to protect themselves against a dip in housing prices that could negatively affect their collateral position. These loans can run as long as fifteen years, but most lenders prefer a seven- to ten-year payback period.

To illustrate how a second mortgage can be used, let's say that you purchased a house in 1972 for $30,000. Currently, its fair market value, as determined by a certified appraiser, is $70,000. The first mortgage amounts to $22,000. Your borrowing ability based upon the above information is calculated as follows:

$$85\% \text{ of } \$70,000 = \$59,500$$
$$- \quad 22,000 \text{ first mortgage}$$
$$= \$37,500 \text{ equity available for borrowing}$$

FAMILY AND FRIENDS

Relatives and acquaintances might be willing to help in financing your business venture. They can raise funds in the manner just described. Keep in mind that these individuals expect to be repaid with interest and/or profits, which can reduce your future earnings. Some may want the business to post collateral in the form of plant and equipment, inventories, accounts receivable, etc. Many will demand a "piece of the action," thereby diluting your control, although if investors do buy in, specific collateral does not have to be offered. Their investment is secured by the stock they own.

If you face any of the above situations, be ready with some answers. Offer your friends and relatives a reasonable interest rate on loans. A few may seek a chunk of the profits generated. Make sure that your future interest is protected. Agree that profits should reward their investment with an adequate return, but only up to a limited point. After that has been achieved, attempt to get their hands out of your pockets. If some want ownership, don't panic. Try to negotiate an agreement whereby you have the right to buy them out, at a profit, of course, sometime in the future when you and the business can afford to do so.

Management can also become a problem. Some of your friends and relatives, upon advancing funds, might feel compelled to help you run the business whether you like it or not. In some cases this cannot be avoided. If they own stock in the business, certain voting rights are guaranteed, in proportion to their investment, under state laws. Of course, if more than 50 percent of the stock is owned by you, control is in your hands. To avoid hard feelings, make sure it is made clear up front that you are the boss and interference in running the business will not be tolerated. A legal agreement outlining that requirement may be appropriate. Check with your attorney.

If at all possible, it is advisable to steer clear of family and friends for funding purposes. These sources can be less than amiable at times, creating more ill will than happy endings. In fact, these individuals can become adversaries very quickly, especially when it comes to money. They tend to do so more frequently than lenders/investors who are not acquainted with you on a personal basis. If no other financing alternative exists, the answer becomes academic. Take their money.

BANKS

Many large banks, located in metropolitan areas, are severing relationships with their small-business clients. They cite risk factors and increasing costs of servicing small accounts as the primary reasons for the shift in emphasis. Most are at least raising service fees to small firms above what is charged to larger businesses. In addition, small businesses are charged higher interest rates on loans than are larger businesses. These changes will adversely affect entrepreneurs located in these areas, not to mention the whole American economy, although some banks, especially those found in smaller cities and rural areas, continue to provide financial services to small businesses, and many are actively seeking new accounts.

Banks active in small-business funding will either lend on a conventional basis or in tandem with a government agency. With conventional financing the bank utilizes its own funds without government involvement. Lending programs, including local, state, or federal entities, are normally in the form of loan participations involving direct government funds or loan guarantees. When an agency participates in a lending situation, part of the funds are advanced by the government and the remainder is supplied by the bank. Under guaranteed programs, banks that provide funds to businesses are protected against non-repayment to a certain percent of the loan amount (usually 90 percent). Banks like government-backed loans because the guaranteed portion can be sold to investors in the secondary markets for handsome profits. In addition, this frees capital to be used to make additional guaranteed loans to be sold at a profit. The lending process can be repeated continuously.

Banks offering conventional or government-sponsored loans to existing firms or start-ups will demand stiff collateral requirements in most cases. Business assets, such as customer accounts, inventories, equipment, and land, will have to be pledged in order to secure capital. Security in the form of personal assets might also be requested. Savings accounts, cars, residential property, jewelry, etc., can be used as collateral for business loans. Of course, tying up too many assets can adversely affect your business operations as was described earlier in the chapter. Keep in mind that bankers have to compete among themselves for loans. Letting them know that other alternatives exist will probably bring you collateral terms that can be tolerated.

Even though banks are among the most conservative sources of capital available, they still supply 60 percent of small-business funding needs. In the future, some of this burden will be shifted to other financial outlets more amiable to small firms. But for now, those seeking funds should locate banks actively involved with helping small enterprises and prospective entrepreneurs. In Chapter 14 there is a comprehensive list (over 940) of banks that specialize in U.S. Small Business Administration financing programs.

VENTURE CAPITAL COMPANIES

Venture capital firms are private concerns that pool the financial resources of wealthy individuals and organizations interested in making investments in small businesses. Some are subsidiaries of major corporations. Exxon and General Electric own venture capital companies. Recent federal legislation has provided tax benefits for venture capital outlets involved in funding projects. Consequently, this form of financing has increased dramatically, augmenting the money available to small enterprises and prospective entrepreneurs.

These firms will invest their capital in a number of ways. They might make loans, buy bonds (debt), or invest in companies by purchasing equity through stock ownership. A combination of the above may be used. Generally, their preferred approach is an equity purchase. Also, they might acquire bonds with equity kickers. In other words the bond can be converted to stock ownership at the option of the investor.

Venture capital firms expect to receive an average of five times their original investment within five to seven years. This is why loans are not favored by venture capitalists. Loans to small business seldom give a return of more than 20 percent a year, somewhat less than is considered normal for the venture capital industry. At this point one might question the advantages of seeking out venture firms if they require such a large return. It must be remembered that a business receiving equity funds does not have to worry about principal and interest payments, which can make life easier in the early years of operation. The investor is expecting the business to grow rapidly and someday return a handsome profit. In most cases, before selling out, the venture firm will give the entrepreneur the option to purchase its interest in the business before offering it to a third party. The right of first refusal can be stipulated in the venture capital agreement.

Conversely, the disadvantage of equity participation is the loss of control. When ownership is exchanged for capital resources, the entrepreneur's ability to influence business affairs will be diluted. Investor input must be taken into consideration. The degree of loss will depend on several factors. Firms that have been in operation showing track records can normally convince venture capital firms to take less equity than if it was a start-up situation. Also, entrepreneurs providing a large portion of the money required for a start-up company can strike a better deal with venture capital organizations than entrepreneurs supplying little of their own personal funds. In any case, most of these financial outlets will not acquire more than 50 percent of the company receiving assistance. Therefore, ultimate control is left to the entrepreneur and managing team. Many venture firms will require that they be represented in management, but will make waves only if they feel it's in their best interest. Besides, these firms can provide valuable insight into running an operation successfully.

Venture capital companies will invest only in prospects that have bright futures and the potential for rapid growth. Small businesses such as gas stations, corner grocery stores, dry cleaners, etc., will not be able to pursue this alternative unless they plan to expand through chain operations.

The professional association representing the venture capital industry is listed in Appendix I. It may provide valuable information concerning finding appropriate funding sources.

SMALL BUSINESS INVESTMENT COMPANIES (SBICs)

SBICs are private profit-making concerns created under the Small Business Investment Act of 1958. Their primary goal is to provide financial resources to existing small businesses and prospective entrepreneurs. All SBICs that fall under the above act are licensed, regulated, and partially funded by the U.S. Small Business Administration. Some financial organizations call themselves small business investment companies but prefer not to fall under the jurisdiction of the SBA. They generally operate on the same basis as do licensed SBICs with one exception. Low-interest government money, provided by the SBA, will not be available to them for relending purposes, thereby reducing their funding flexibility.

Like venture capital companies, these financial outlets will invest in equity (stock), make loans, or buy bonds. They prefer to acquire debt as opposed to making equity investments because of their capital structure. Many SBICs borrow from the government and then relend to small businesses. If they make stock purchases, returns on their investment may be a long time coming. On the other hand, making loans and buying bonds will generate immediate income to pay the government for the funds borrowed.

SBICs prefer to finance small businesses with track records of at least six months or more. They will consider start-up situations in some cases. Only those prospects or firms that have promising futures are given consideration by small business investment companies.

Minority Enterprise Small Business Investment Companies

(MESBICs) provide funding specifically to businesses owned by members of a minority group. In addition, capital is made available to minorities interested in starting a new business or purchasing an existing operation. MESBICs are basically the same as SBICs. They are regulated and licensed by the U.S. Small Business Administration and receive part of their capital from the agency.

Appendix J contains a list of professional associations representing small-business investment companies. Contacting them may result in funding contracts.

Commercial Finance Companies

Many small businesses snubbed by banks can turn to commercial finance companies for help in certain areas. Even businesses experiencing financial difficulties can turn to these sources for assistance. Since these financial outlets tend to charge higher interest rates than do banks, it is wise to try the banks first. If unsuccessful in that regard, a firm has the option of pursuing over 2,500 commercial finance companies now operating in this country.

Commercial finance companies will lend on a short- and/or inter-mediate-term basis with collateral always being required. For example, these companies will grant short-term (less than a year) loans using accounts receivable and inventories as collateral. Generally you can borrow up to 90 percent of the value of good receivables and 60 percent of inventory value. In addition, intermediate loans (one to five years) can be granted for equipment purchase. The finance company will collateralize the equipment for security purposes.

Leasing is another service offered by many commercial finance organizations. If a business is in need of some new equipment but lacks the necessary financial resources to purchase, leasing is an alternative. The finance company will buy the equipment and lease it to the business. Monthly rental payments must be made that usually last three to seven years. The advantages to leasing are many. Little or no down payment is required; the equipment can be bought at the end of the lease agreement for a fraction of original cost; the business is protected against obsolescence; leases do not appear as liabilities on the financial statements of the business, thus not reducing its ability to borrow for other reasons; and lease payments are fully deductible as expenses. Other advantages are pointed out in Table 17.

TABLE 17

LEASING ADVANTAGES

• Leasing generally requires little or no down payment.

• Working capital is preserved that can be used for other revenue-generating projects.

• Leasing does not compromise control of the business.

• Leasing does not disrupt existing financing arrangements.

• You make lease payments out of pre-tax revenues, thereby creating a tax write-off as opposed to purchasing capital equipment out of retained earnings (net income-dividends paid to investors, if any) and thereby losing important tax advantages. Lease payments are entirely deductible as business expenses.

• Lease liabilities are not generally reported on the firm's financial statements, thereby preserving its financial position.

• You can lease the latest and most efficient equipment, which might not otherwise be available due to financial constraints.

• Leasing provides protection against inflation, since lease payments are made in current money.

• Leasing provides protection against rapid obsolescence—if property becomes obsolete before the end of the lease period, it is generally possible to trade up without much difficulty or cost.

• After the lease term is completed, it is the responsibility of the leasing firm to dispose of the equipment.

• While the cost of leasing is higher than that of most other financing methods, earnings on the capital that would otherwise be used outweigh the cost.

• Leasing can be used as an alternative or supplement to bank credit when borrowing conditions become too restrictive or uneconomical.

Commercial finance companies can also factor (buy) accounts receivable. They will purchase your receivables at a discount of between 1 and 15 percent. Their fees are determined by a number of considerations, including volume of sales, general quality of the firm's customers, credit policies within the firm, and average size of an account. The factoring procedure can be conducted on a nonnotification basis, which means customers are not aware that their accounts have been sold. Factoring is a costly financial tool to be utilized only if bank credit is unattractive or not available. There are some reasons to believe this may not be true. When evaluating expenses associated with factoring, you should carefully analyze the services being rendered. If receivables, bookkeeping, collection, and credit risks are being assumed, either partially or wholly by the factor, internal costs associated with these functions will decrease in proportion to the increased participation of the factor. In addition, factoring service frees up cash, otherwise tied up in receivables, that can be used to generate revenues. So the elimination or reduction of the credit function within the business plus the profits created from unencumbered cash may make the factoring decision an attractive alternative or supplement to existing bank relationships. Table 18 outlines the advantages in dealing with a factor.

TABLE 18

Advantages to Factoring

- Factors will collect accounts receivable.

- Factors will do all the bookkeeping relative to the credit function.

- Factoring can be used as a supplement or substitute to bank credit when borrowing conditions become too restrictive or uneconomical.

- Factors will conduct credit investigations on the firm's existing and prospective accounts. In fact, factors are experts in credit analysis. This will establish confidence in the ability to collect the accounts receivable.

- Factors assume all the credit risks associated with accounts receivable.

- Factors allow firms to utilize all available cash for revenue generation. Banks may require that a business maintain compensating balances on hand (ranging between 5 and 15 percent of the loan amount). In addition, certain factoring arrangements can free cash that would otherwise be set aside to meet projected current obligations.

- Factoring can actually enhance a firm's relationship with banks and other funding outlets. If lenders and investors are confident that a factoring organization will purchase the accounts receivable of a firm if the cash is needed, they will be more willing to provide assistance.

In addition, these commercial finance companies will advance funds for leveraged buyouts and acquisitions if sufficient collateral is made available. For example, a business might be interested in purchasing another firm but lacks the immediate financial resources to do so. A commercial finance company will fund all or part of the acquisition if enough collateral in the form of non-pledged (clean) assets is available in the firm to be acquired.

The two major associations representing the commercial finance industry are listed in Appendix K. They may provide information about funding outlets.

LIFE INSURANCE COMPANIES

Traditionally, life insurance companies have been an unlikely source of small-business funding. In fact, most of these firms prefer to invest in amounts of $1 million or more per business deal. Obviously, this is beyond the financial requirements of most small enterprises. This is not to suggest that insurance companies should be written off as a source. Many of these insurers are starting to realize the profit potential in financing small businesses, and some are currently active in providing funding programs. Most insurance companies will not entertain start-up situations. They prefer going concerns with profitable track records that have potential for future growth. Long-term lending is their favorite form of financing. The loans are expected to finance internal expansion. Funds can also be used for external growth through acquisition and leveraged buyouts.

PENSION FUNDS

Like insurance companies, pension funds prefer to finance only existing operations with attractive growth prospects. In fact, many insurers are partially pension funds. Start-up funding is avoided, with most consideration being given to long-term loans. Historically, these financial outlets have favored large businesses, but some are looking in the direction of small firms.

INVESTMENT BANKERS (UNDERWRITERS)

There are some investment banking houses that specialize in raising capital for small businesses with growth potential. They will make a *public offering* of securities in the business to the investment community. What happens, in fact, is that the underwriter (investment banker) sells stock and/or bonds for the small firm to individual investors willing to buy. Start-ups and existing firms can use this funding alternative to raise needed capital.

Underwriters will demand to be paid a minimum commission of 10 percent on the gross dollar amount they sell. In addition, fees called accountable and non-accountable expenses are charged, and they can be substantial. After everything is considered, the cost of raising capital through a public offering can exceed 35 percent of the amount sought. In other words, raising $300,000 can cost in excess of $100,000. If the offering is unsuccessful (not enough money raised), any stock purchased must be returned to the investor for a refund. The underwriter will not charge you for those sales, but some expenses incurred will be passed on to the small firm or entrepreneur. All conditions of a public offering are normally covered in an underwriting agreement between the investment banker and the business to be financed. Attorneys for both parties should review this contract to determine if it suits the requirements of all involved.

In addition, an interstate public offering must be approved by the Securities Exchange Commission in Washington, DC, and every state in which securities are sold. If the offering is intrastate (located within the confines of a particular state), only approval from that state is needed. The underwriter will take care of the details involved in notifying and registering with the appropriate government agencies.

Small Business Administration (SBA)

The U.S. Small Business Administration has been called the lender of last resort by small-business advocates. One of its primary objectives is to help entrepreneurs secure financial resources to start businesses or expand existing operations. It is authorized to make participation loans and provide loan guarantees and in some cases make direct loans to those firms classified as small by the agency. Consequently, many small businesses and prospective owners, frustrated by strained relations with their local bankers and economic conditions, have turned to the SBA for lending support.

To be considered for a loan, an individual or business firm must meet certain conditions, such as the following:

—It must have adequate credentials.

—It must not be dominant in its field.

—It must comply with all federal employment laws.

—It must pursue traditional lending sources (only upon rejection by private lenders does the SBA alternative become a possibility).

—It must be classified as small business by SBA size standards (these classifications are based on number of employees or the value of sales stated in dollars).

The criteria for determining whether a business is small will vary depending upon the type of business. The specific criteria and other information concerning the SBA funding guidelines are included in Table 19.

TABLE 19

U.S. SMALL BUSINESS ADMINISTRATION
"LENDING THE SBA WAY"

The Program

HOW IT WORKS

- SBA guarantees up to 90 percent of a loan made by a lender.

- Lender checks with SBA prior to formal application for "ballpark" feasibility of project.

- Lender submits letter of intent to SBA if interim financing is to be supplied prior to formal consideration of the loan request.

- Lender forwards application and deals directly with SBA officers.

- Completed applications are processed by SBA in 20 or fewer working days.

- Guaranty fee of 2 percent is paid by the lender and may be passed on to the borrower.

A LONGER TERM

- Usually five to seven years for working capital

- Up to 25 years for real estate or equipment

INTEREST RATE

- Both fixed and variable rates

- Rate pegged to the lowest prime rate as listed in the *Wall Street Journal*

- Pegged at up to 2.25 percent over the lowest prime rate for loans of less than seven years

- Pegged at up to 2.75 percent over the lowest prime rate for loans of seven years or longer

WHO QUALIFIES?

- Independently owned and operated for-profit businesses not dominant in their fields

- Businesses unable to obtain private financing on reasonable terms, but with a good chance of succeeding

MAXIMUM SIZE STANDARDS (VARIES BY INDUSTRY)

- Manufacturing—from 500-1,500 employees

- Wholesaling—100 employees

- Services—from $2.5 million to $14.5 million in annual receipts

- Retailing—from $3.5 million to $17.0 million in annual receipts

- General construction—from $13.5 million to $17.0 million in annual receipts

- Special trade construction—average annual receipts not to exceed $7.0 million

- Agriculture—from $0.5 million to $7.0 million

LOAN PURPOSES

- To expand or renovate facilities

- To purchase machinery, equipment, fixtures and leasehold improvements

- To finance increased receivables and augment working capital

- To refinance existing debt for compelling credit reason of benefit to borrower

- To provide seasonal lines of credit

- To construct new commercial buildings
- To purchase existing land or buildings

MAXIMUM AMOUNT, REPAYMENT, COLLATERAL

- Guarantee(s) totaling a maximum of $750,000
- More than one loan is possible
- A 90 percent guarantee for loans up to $155,000
- An 85 percent guarantee for loans of $155,000 and over
- Monthly installments of principal and interest
- No balloons, no penalty for prepayment, no application fee, no points
- May delay first payment up to six months
- Take all collateral available; may include personal property

WHAT WE LOOK FOR

- Management ability and experience in the field
- Feasible business plan
- Adequate investment (generally 20 percent to 30 percent equity) by the owner in the new business starts
- Ability to repay the loan from the projected cash flow and profits

WHAT THE APPLICANT NEEDS TO TAKE TO THE LENDER

- Purpose of loan
- History of the business
- Financial statements for three years (balance sheet and income statements) for existing businesses
- Schedule of term debts (for existing businesses)
- Aging of accounts receivable and payable (for existing businesses)
- Lease details (if available)
- Amount of investment in the business by the owner
- Projections of income, expenses and cash flow
- Signed personal financial statements
- Personal résumés

SOURCE: U.S. Small Business Administration

The SBA has offices around the country. For the one nearest you, consult the "U.S. Government" section of your telephone directory, or call the SBA Answer Desk at 1-800-8-ASK-SBA. For specific information write: Office of Financial Institutions, U.S. Small Business Administration, 409 Third Street SW, 8th Floor, Washington, DC 20416.

These fundamental criteria are only the beginning. Many exceptions are allowed in specific businesses and industries. The local SBA field office can help determine which criteria apply to a particular business.

Assuming all SBA conditions are met, an entrepreneur can submit a business proposal to the agency for consideration. It will be carefully evaluated, and if the project is found to have merit (adequate market, good management, sufficient collateral, possibility of loan repayment, etc.), the SBA will offer a loan guarantee. It must be kept in mind that this is not a loan. The agency simply guarantees that a lender will be protected against default if funds are advanced to a small business concern. Up to 85 percent of the principal loan amount is covered for non-repayment to a maximum of $500,000; in other words, risk exposure is minimized. In addition, interest charges on these loans generally run a couple of points above the prime rate. It is hoped that the guarantees will induce lenders to advance the necessary financial resources to initiate and carry out the business project. Using the maximum guarantee limit, a loan for $588,235 can be granted with an 85 percent guarantee to the lender. A larger loan will reduce the guarantee below 85 percent and may increase lender resistance.

The SBA does provide direct loans to Vietnam era and disabled veterans as well as to handicapped individuals.

The U.S. Small Business Adminstration (SBA) also has a new loan program called the FASTRAK. It requires less documentation than a regular SBA loan and gives more power to make funding decisions to local and regional lenders and investors, and less to government officials. However, lending cannot exceed $100,000. Information about this program can be obtained by writing or calling the SBA offices listed in Appendix B.

Farmers Home Administration (FmHA)

This agency falls under the jurisdiction of the U.S. Department of Agriculture. Its primary goal is to enhance the quality of rural life through upgrading the economic environment. This is accomplished by an array of funding programs designed to promote industrial, business, and agricultural development. It is the intention of the agency to provide supplemental financial support, augmenting the efforts of private lending sources rather than competing with them. Under most FmHA programs, borrowers are required to pursue private funding when financially able to do so. The programs directed to agriculture are designed to build the family farm system, which is the economic base of many rural areas. Borrowers must be family-size operators, living on and operating the farm, at least on a part-time basis. Funding is available also for any type of agricultural activity. Business and industrial loans are made available to large and small businesses to promote economic development in communities with a population base below 50,000. Preference is given to applications for projects in open country, rural communities, and in towns of 25,000 people or fewer. These funds can be used to develop and finance business or industry, increase employment, and control or abate pollution. Within this broad framework, uses include, but are not limited to, the following:

— Business and industrial acquisition, construction, conversion, enlargement, repair, and modernization
— Purchase and development of land, easements, rights-of-way, buildings, facilities, leases, materials, and custom feed lots
— Purchase of equipment, lease-hold improvements, machinery, and supplies
— Start-up costs and working capital

FmHA will provide loan guarantees to private lenders who advance funds under its programs. The agency guarantees to limit any loss due to loan default to a certain percentage of the total amount involved (usually 90 percent). Interest rates are negotiated between the borrower and private lender unless the rate is mandated by statute. Insured loans are also offered. These funds are originated and made by the Farmers Home Administration directly. The agency sells the loans to private investors and insures repayment. Interest rates on insured funds are about the same as the current cost of federal borrowing. Some rates may be established by law.

Certain programs provide grants (which do not have to be repaid) and low interest loans to individuals and organizations involved in certain agricultural pursuits. In addition, the FmHA provides emergency and disaster loan assistance to the farming community at very attractive interest rates.

Farm Credit Administration (FCA)

The Farm Credit Administration is an independent federal organization that oversees the nationwide farmer-owned and -managed farm credit system. This network provides funding to the U.S. agricultural community through a number of programs. Federal Land Banks, located in most communities, supply long-term mortgage credit to purchase, enlarge, and improve farms. These banks will also finance mortgages on farm property and lend for other farming endeavors. Production Credit Associations, which are also supervised by FCA, make short- and intermediate-term loans for farm production, farm home, and/or farm family purposes. In addition, Cooperative Banks provide loan services to cooperatives supplying agricultural needs.

Department of Energy (DOE)

The U.S. Department of Energy maintains funding programs directed to all businesses, regardless of size, operating in certain energy areas. In the past, the agency tended to favor large corporations. Recent evidence has shown that small firms are much more innovative than large ones, forcing the DOE to redirect some of its financial resources.

Most DOE programs provide grants to firms exploring ways to enhance domestic energy efficiency through conservation, new methods of energy utilization, and the development of alternative energy sources. This money does not have to be repaid. In addition, the department is providing loan guarantees to financial outlets lending to companies that develop new and old sources of coal. Guarantees run as high as $30 million. DOE also has a similar program available to firms operating in the geothermal energy field. Up to $200 million can be guaranteed.

Maritime Administration

The Maritime Administration falls under control of the U.S. Department of Commerce. It provides an array of programs designed to aid large and small firms in the construction, reconstruction, or reconditioning of vessels in the American Merchant Marine. Most programs give direct payments to private ship owners. In one case, $45 million was given just for a single ship. In addition, loan guarantees up to $126 million per ship are offered to commercial lenders willing to provide funding.

NATIONAL OCEANIC AND ATMOSPHERIC ADMINISTRATION

Under the U.S. Department of Interior, this agency provides funding to assist in strengthening the domestic fishing industry. Loans are made to finance and refinance the cost of purchasing, constructing, equipping, maintaining, repairing, or operating new or used commercial fishing vessels or gear. Only U.S. citizens with experience in the fishing trade are advised to apply.

BUREAU OF INDIAN AFFAIRS

This bureau, which falls under the jurisdiction of the U.S. Department of Interior, offers programs to encourage the economic development of federal Indian reservations. Grants, direct government loans, and loan guarantees (up to $1 million) are made available to Native Americans for this purpose.

EXPORT-IMPORT BANK (EXIMBANK)

The Export-Import Bank is an independent government agency established to promote U.S. exports overseas. This is accomplished through a number of programs directed to firms involved in exporting and to commercial banks.

The Eximbank can authorize the Foreign Credit Insurance Association (FCIA) to issue policies insuring exporters against political and/or commercial risks on short- and medium-term credit extended to foreign buyers. Insurance can be bought from banks participating in FCIA programs or directly from the Association. In addition, the Eximbank itself will offer guarantees to U.S. businesses covering political and commercial risks involved in the performance of services overseas and in the leasing, consignment, or exhibition of U.S. goods abroad. The agency will also guarantee payment of medium-term export loans held by commercial banks. The aforementioned programs are designed to help U.S. exporters compete in the international marketplace. Without Eximbank-sponsored guarantees, many exporters would not offer foreign customers credit terms, thereby placing them at a competitive disadvantage with suppliers in other nations offering attractive terms. In short, Eximbank insurance programs provide reimbursement coverage to U.S. exporters and bankers should foreign customers fail to pay.

Some lenders will advance only a certain amount of funds to finance exports. After this limit is reached, export money will be cut off or higher interest rates will be charged to international firms. Now, Eximbank will purchase export loans from commercial banks to provide additional capital, at reasonable interest rates, to firms wishing to sell overseas. Another program designed to facilitate U.S. exports provides direct loans to overseas buyers of American goods and services.

Overseas Private Investment Corporation (OPIC)

The Overseas Private Investment Corporation is an independent federal agency that promotes U.S. investment abroad. It offers an array of programs that can benefit American firms wishing to start new operations or expand existing facilities in less developed nations. The agency provides loan guarantees (up to 100 percent) to lenders that assist organizations in exploiting international opportunities. Direct loans are also made available. All funding programs are long term (exceeding five years) in nature and charge commercial interest rates. Capital advanced under OPIC cannot finance more than 50 percent of the foreign venture. Therefore, additional money must be obtained from other sources.

Insurance programs are also offered to protect companies against certain investment losses arising from operations in other countries. The coverage reduces the risk associated with nationalization, war, revolution, insurrection, civil strife, and currency inconvertibility.

Federal Reserve Board (FRB)

The Federal Reserve Board will offer loan guarantees to lenders who financially assist firms engaged in producing goods or services for national defense purposes. Specifically, its intention is to facilitate and expedite the funding of contractors, subcontractors, and others engaged in operations deemed necessary for defense of the United States. The interest rates on these loans are low and 100 percent loan guarantees are provided.

SMALL BUSINESS INNOVATION RESEARCH (SBIR) PROGRAM

Various government agencies provide grant money to assist small firms conducting scientific research in the areas of new product/ process development. Some grants have exceeded $1 million. The money, which does not have to be repaid, is designed for basic research and is not to be used to commercially market anything created. After research and testing is conducted utilizing SBIR sources, the firm is expected to have private funding available in order to execute any marketing endeavors.

Given the scientific emphasis of SBIR funding, only those small companies that are technical in nature should seek this funding option.

The SBIR is administered by the U.S. Small Business Administration. Appendix G highlights the program in more detail.

STATE DEVELOPMENT COMPANIES (SDCs)

An SDC is sanctioned by state law to provide financial and managerial assistance to all businesses located within the state it serves. These development companies receive their capital from traditional funding outlets such as banks, pension funds, insurance companies, etc. In addition, SDCs can borrow from the U.S. Small Business Administration to provide loans to qualified small firms located in the state. Call the state office of the U.S. Small Business Administration, listed in Appendix B, to find out the name, address, and telephone number of the SDC that would serve your needs.

STATE GOVERNMENTS

Most state governments maintain programs to promote the economic well-being of small businesses located within their jurisdiction. In many cases, assistance is also provided to individuals wishing to start a new business or purchase an existing operation. Appendix B contains a listing of state agencies.

LOCAL GOVERNMENTS

Some local governments are actively involved in providing managerial and/or financial assistance to prospective entrepreneurs and existing small firms located within the municipality. Contact the city or county administrator's office to determine which agencies are responsible for this function.

Many local governments are providing help to firms of all sizes through the use of a relatively new financing mechanism referred to as industrial revenue bonds. A business may get approval from a local government to raise funds through the sale of tax-exempt bonds if the project provides direct benefits to the locality in the form of increased revenues, taxes, and employment. The project must also fit into the overall growth plan of the municipality. The principal advantage to this form of financing is its low cost. Generally, interest rates on the bonds sold run one to two percentage points below those of other conventional funding sources. Investors like these bonds because the interest income paid to them is free from federal, state, and local income taxes.

There are two major drawbacks with industrial revenue bonds. Start-up firms are normally discouraged from pursuing this funding option due to the lack of operating history. It may be difficult to convince local officials and investors that a new business just starting out deserves consideration. In addition, using industrial revenue bonds may disqualify a business from utilizing other attractive government funding programs.

Some states allow their local municipalities to use this funding technique more than others. Check with the municipal manager to determine what kinds of projects may be funded. It is also wise to talk with officials of any state or federal government agency from which assistance may be forthcoming. See if the bonds will disturb anticipated help from this direction.

CERTIFIED DEVELOPMENT COMPANIES (CDC)

Local development companies (LDCs) and certified development companies (CDCs) are profit or non-profit corporations started by local business people with the intention of stimulating economic development within their immediate community. They are a little-known source of small-business funding and assistance and are often overlooked by many existing businesses and prospective entrepreneurs. LDCs/CDCs do not see profit as their objective. Primary consideration is given to positive economic impact on the community they serve. Like state development companies, LDCs/CDCs receive a large portion of their funding capability from the U.S. Small Business

Administration for relending purposes to qualified small firms and entrepreneurs. SBA money passing through LDCs/CDCs may be loaned for up to 25 years at prevailing interest rates.

These organizations can provide valuable help because of their local nature. Many have established contacts within the immediate area allowing opportunity seekers access to conventional funding and managerial assistance. These firms are listed in Chapter 13.

APPLICATION PROCEDURES

All private and government financial outlets require initial application forms to be completed. The forms are elementary and easy to answer. But don't be fooled: The real work is just beginning. Additional documentation will be required. Most lenders and investors will request a detailed report outlining all particulars of a prospective business proposal. It's used in the funding decision to evaluate the soundness of the project and is called a business plan. Its construction can be a long, difficult, and tedious process. Some exceed 100 pages in duration. Length and detail depend on the amount of money requested, use of funds, type of business or industry, and whether the funding is used for a start-up or existing operation. Generally the more capital requested, the greater the amount of information needed. Likewise, start-ups will require more data than firms already conducting business because of the increased uncertainty involved.

There are some exceptions to the above rules. For example, a business that has an established relationship with lenders may not have to go through the pains of constructing a business plan every time capital needs arise. Many lenders, acquainted with their clients, will request only a completed application form, business and personal financial statements, tax returns, and owner guarantees.

The business plan is discussed in the next chapter. The information provided is appropriate for most private and government funding requests.

7

THE BUSINESS PLAN
Roadmap to Success

Design

Most individuals seeking capital to finance a business proposition fail to realize the importance of a properly structured business plan. One entrepreneur recently asked, "Why do I need to spend the time developing a business plan when it's the greatest idea in the world—everybody will invest." Because of this kind of thinking, over 90 percent of all plans requesting funds are rejected by financial outlets.

A business plan is essentially a sales tool used to stimulate investor interest. It must be packaged correctly in order to attract the necessary money sources. The design and construction can be a major undertaking challenging the most astute business person.

An adequate business plan should run between 40 and 60 pages (typed and double spaced) with an adequate number of appendixes for purposes of illustration and detail. Hundreds of hours and many months will be consumed putting it together and perfecting the final document. In some cases, it may be costly. Entrepreneurs who lack business experience and expertise in one or more areas may have to pay professionals to research and/or write part or all of it.

The plan's importance in the funding decision cannot be overstated. Prospective capital sources use it to evaluate the merits of a proposal before risking their money. In addition, the plan lets potential investors know that the entrepreneur/managing team has given thoughtful and serious consideration to the business proposition and that they are capable of managing profitably. A well-documented and convincing business plan showing the potential for future profits is what capital sources are seeking. It should touch on all pertinent areas without being detailed to the point where investors get bored reading it.

The business plan should never be viewed as being solely for the use of financial outlets. Indeed, it can be utilized by businesses as a guide pointing to the most profitable and least hazardous way to carry out an idea. It allows for careful consideration of different objectives, alternatives, strategies and tactics, and analyzes available resources before committing funds. These initial evaluations will prevent many costly mistakes from being made. In fact, the plan gives a five-year path to follow by forcing entrepreneurs to set realistic goals, predict resource allocation, and project future earnings. Also, problems concerning competitive conditions, promotional opportunities, industry trends, etc., are addressed. Such a practice over a period of time will enhance the decision-making ability of the entrepreneur and others involved in the enterprise.

In the final analysis, the business plan is the roadmap directing energies in a coherent fashion. It outlines what must be accomplished and how to carry it out. Developing a plan that can stand up to critical evaluation and the extreme scrutiny of investors is the initial hurdle that must be cleared.

The next major section of this chapter deals with the proper construction of an appropriate business plan. It should be reviewed and studied very carefully. The following outline is from a pamphlet published by Institute for New Enterprise Development, Cambridge, Massachusetts. This material is a most useful guide when preparing a business plan.

TABLE OF CONTENTS

C. Sales Tactics
D. Service and Warranty Policies
E. Advertising and Promotion

4. DESIGN AND DEVELOPMENT PLANS
   A. Development Status and Tasks
   B. Difficulties and Risks
   C. Product Improvement and New Products
   D. Costs

5. MANUFACTURING AND OPERATIONS PLAN
   A. Geographic Location
   B. Facilities and Improvements
   C. Strategy and Plans
   D. Labor Force

6. MANAGEMENT TEAM
   A. Organization
   B. Key Management Personnel
   C. Management Compensation and Ownership
   D. Board of Directors
   E. Management Assistance and Training Needs
   F. Supporting Professional Services

7. OVERALL SCHEDULE

8. CRITICAL RISKS AND PROBLEMS

9. COMMUNITY BENEFITS
   A. Economic Development
   B. Human Development
   C. Community Development

10. THE FINANCIAL PLAN
    A. Profit and Loss Forecast
    B. Pro Forma Cash Flows Analysis
    C. Pro Forma Balance Sheets
    D. Breakeven Chart
    E. Cost Control

    PRO FORMA INCOME STATEMENTS
    PRO FORMA CASH FLOWS STATEMENTS
    PRO FORMA BALANCE SHEETS
    BREAKEVEN CHART

11. PROPOSED COMPANY OFFERING
    A. Desired Financing
    B. Securities Offering

    C. Capitalization
    D. Use of Funds

THE SUMMARY

Many investors like to read through a one- or two-page summary of a business plan that highlights its important features and opportunities, and allows them to determine quickly whether or not the venture described is of interest.

Do not write your summary until you have written your plan. As you draft each section, circle one or two sentences that you think are important enough to be included in a summary.

Allow plenty of time to write an appealing and convincing summary, remembering that the summary is the first thing about you and your venture that the prospective investor is going to read. Unless it is appealing and convincing, it will also be the last. You may have spent many weeks on the rest of your plan and it may be very good. However, if that quality does not come through in your summary, you may not get a chance to make a presentation at which you can convincingly rebut criticism and clear up misunderstandings.

It is recommended that, at a minimum, your summary should contain brief statements about the following features of your venture.

The Company and Its Founders: You should indicate when the company was formed, what it will do, and what is special or unique about its product or technology. Also indicate what in the backgrounds of the entrepreneurs makes them particularly qualified to pursue the business opportunity.

If your company has been in business for a few years, indicate what its sales and profits were in its most recent fiscal year and the trend of sales and profits.

Market Opportunity: Identify and briefly explain the market opportunity. This explanation should include information on the size and growth rate of the market for your company's product or service, and a statement indicating the percentage of that market that will be captured. A brief statement about industry-wide trends is useful. You might also indicate any plans for expanding the initial product line.

Products and Technology: Identify any proprietary technology, trade secrets, or unique skills that give you a competitive edge in the marketplace.

Financial Projections: State your sales and profit projections for the first and second years of operation after obtaining the necessary financing.

Proposed Financing: Briefly indicate how much equity financing you want, how much of your company you are prepared to offer for that financing, and what use will be made of the capital raised.

1. THE INDUSTRY, THE COMPANY, AND ITS PRODUCTS

The purpose of this section is to give the investor some context in which to fit all that you are about to say concerning your product and its market. This section should clearly present the business that you are in, the product you will offer, the nature of your industry, and the opportunities available to market your product.

The Industry

Present the current status and prospects for the industry in which the proposed business will operate. Discuss any new products or developments, new markets and customers, new requirements, new companies, and any other national or economic trends and factors that could affect the venture's business positively or negatively. Identify the source of all information used to describe industry trends.

The Company

Describe briefly what business area your company is in or intends to enter; what products or services it will offer; and who are or will be its principal customers.

As background give the date your venture was incorporated and describe the identification and development of its products and the involvement of the company's principals in that development.

If your company has been in business for several years and is seeking expansion financing, review its history and cite its prior sales and profit performance. If your company has had setbacks or losses in prior years, discuss these and emphasize what has and will be done to prevent a recurrence of these difficulties and to improve your company's performance.

The Products or Services

The potential investor will be vitally interested in exactly what you are going to sell, what kind of product protection you have, and the opportunities and possible drawbacks to your product or service.

A. *Description:* Describe in detail the products or services to be sold. Discuss the application of your product or service. Describe the primary end-use as well as any significant secondary applications. Emphasize any unique features of your product or service, and highlight any differences between what is currently on the market and what you will offer that will account for your market penetration.

Define the present state of development of the product or service. For products, provide a summary of the functional specifications. Include photographs when available.

B. *Proprietary Position:* Describe any patents, trade secrets, or other proprietary features. Discuss any head start that you might have that would enable you to achieve a favored or entrenched position in your industry.

C. *Potential:* Describe any features of your product or service that give it an advantage over the competition. Discuss any opportunities for the expansion of the product line or the development of related products or services. Emphasize your opportunities and explain how you will take advantage of them.

Discuss any product disadvantage or the possibilities of rapid obsolescence because of technological or styling changes, or marketing fads.

2. *MARKET RESEARCH AND ANALYSIS*

The purpose of this section of the plan is to present enough facts to convince the investor that your venture's product or service has a substantial market in a growing industry and can achieve sales despite the competition. The discussion and the guidelines given below should help you do this.

This section of the plan is one of the most difficult to prepare and also one of the most important. Almost all subsequent sections of the business plan depend on the sales estimates that are developed in this section. The sales levels you project based on the market research and analysis directly influence the size of the manufacturing operation, the marketing plan, and the amount of debt and equity capital you will require. Yet most entrepreneurs seem to have great difficulty preparing and presenting market research and analyses that will convince potential investors that the venture's sales estimates are sound and attainable.

Because of the importance of market analysis and the dependence of other parts of the plan on the sales projections, we generally advise entrepreneurs to prepare this section of the business plan before they do any other. We also advise entrepreneurs to take enough time to do this section very well and to check alternate sources of market data for key numbers such as "market size" and "market growth rates."

A. *Customers:* Discuss who the customers are for the anticipated application of the product or service. Classify potential customers into relatively homogeneous groups (major market segment) having common, identifiable characteristics. For example, an automotive part might be sold to automotive manufacturers or to parts distributors supplying the replacement market.

Who and where are the major purchasers for the product or service in each market segment? What is the basis for their purchase decisions: price, quality, service, personal contacts, political pressures, or some combination of these factors?

List any potential customers who have expressed an interest in the product or service and indicate why. List any potential customers who have shown no interest in the proposed product or service and explain why this is so. Explain what you will do to overcome negative customer reaction. If you have an existing business, list your current principal customers and discuss the trend in your sales to them.

B. *Market Size and Trends:* What is the total size of the current market for the product or service offered? This market size should be determined from available market data sources and from a knowledge of the purchases of competing products by potential customers in each major market segment. Discussions with potential distributors, dealers, sales representatives, and customers can be particularly useful in establishing the market size and trends. Describe the size of the total market in both units and dollars. If you intend to sell regionally, show the regional market size. Indicate the sources of data and methods used to establish current market size. Also state the credentials of people doing market research.

Describe the potential annual growth of the total market for your product or service for each major customer group. Total market projections should be made for at least three future years. Discuss the major factors affecting market growth (industry trends, socio-economic trends, government policy, population shifts). Also review previous trends in the market. Any differences between past and projected annual growth rates should be explained. Indicate the sources of all data and methods used to make projections.

C. *Competition:* Make a realistic assessment of the strengths and weaknesses of competitive products and services and name the companies that supply them. State the data sources used to determine which products are competitive and the strengths of the competition.

Compare competing products or services on the basis of price, performance, service, warranties, and other pertinent features. A table can be an effective way of presenting these data. Present a short discussion of the current advantages and disadvantages of competing products and services and say why they are not meeting customer needs. Indicate any knowledge of competitors' actions that could lead you to new or improved products and an advantageous position.

Review the strengths and weaknesses of the competing companies. Determine and discuss each competitor's share of the market, sales, distribution, and production capabilities. Also review the profitability of the competition, and their profit trend. Who is the pricing leader; quality leader? Discuss why any companies have entered or dropped out of the market in recent years.

Discuss your three or four key competitors and why the customer buys from them. From what you know about their operations, explain why you think you can capture a share of their business. Discuss what makes you think it will be easy or difficult to compete with them.

D. *Estimated Market Share and Sales:* Summarize what it is about your product or service that will make it saleable in the face of current and potential competition.

Identify any major customers who are willing to make purchase commitments. Indicate the extent of those commitments and why they are made. Discuss which customers could be major purchasers in future years and why.

Based upon your assessment of the advantages of your product or service; the market size and trends; customers; the competition and their products, and the sales trends in prior years; estimate your share of the market, and your sales in units and dollars for each of the next three years. The growth of the company's sales and its estimated market share should be related to the growth of its industry, the customers, and the strengths and weaknesses of competitors. This data can be presented in a table:

Sales and Market Share Data

| | | \multicolumn{4}{c|}{1st Year} | \multicolumn{2}{c|}{Year} |
		1Q	2Q	3Q	4Q	2	3
Estimated Total	Units						
Market	Dollars						
Estimated Sales	Units						
	Dollars						
Estimated Market	Units						
Share, %	Dollars						

The assumptions used to estimate market share and sales should be clearly stated. If yours is an existing business, indicate the total market and your market share and sales for two prior years.

E. *Ongoing Market Evaluation:* Explain how you will evaluate your target markets on a continuing basis to assess customer needs; to guide product improvement and new product programs; to plan for expansions of your production facility; and to guide product/service pricing.

3. MARKETING PLAN

The marketing plan describes how the sales projections will be attained. It should detail the overall marketing strategy, sales and service policies, pricing, distribution, and advertising strategies that will be used to achieve the estimated market share and sales projections. It should describe specifically *what* is to be done, *how* it will be done, and *who* will do it.

A. *Overall Marketing Strategy:* Describe the general marketing philosophy and strategy of the company. This should be derived partly from the market research and evaluation. It should include a discussion of: What kinds of customer groups will be targeted for initial intensive selling effort? What customer groups for later selling efforts? How will specific potential customers in these groups be identified and how will they be contacted? What features of the product or service—e.g., quality, price, delivery, warranty—will be emphasized to generate sales? Are there any innovative or unusual marketing concepts that will enhance customer acceptance—e.g., leasing where only sales were previously attempted?

Indicate whether the product or service will be introduced initially, nationally, or on a regional level. If on a regional level, explain why and indicate if and when you plan to extend sales to other sections of the country. Discuss any seasonal trends and what can be done to promote sales out of season.

Describe any plans to obtain government contracts to support product development costs and overhead.

B. *Pricing:* Many entrepreneurs have told us that they have a superior product that they plan to sell for a lower price than their competitors' product. This makes a bad impression for two reasons. First, if their product is as good as they say it is, they must think they are very poor salespeople to have to offer it at a lower price than the competition. Second, costs tend to be underestimated. If you start out with low costs and prices, there is little room to maneuver; and price hikes will be tougher to implement than price cuts.

The pricing policy is one of the most important decisions you will have to make. The "price must be right" to penetrate the market, maintain a market position, and produce profits. Devote ample time to considering a number of pricing strategies and convincingly present the one you select.

Discuss the prices to be charged for your products or services and compare your pricing policy with those of your major competitors. Discuss the gross profit margin between manufacturing and ultimate sales costs. Indicate whether this margin is large enough to allow you a profit and also allow for distribution and sales; warranty; service; amortization of development and equipment costs; and price competition.

Explain how the price you set will enable you to:

- Get the product or service accepted
- Maintain and profitably increase your market share in the face of competition
- Produce profits.

Justify any price increases over competitive items on the basis of newness, quality, warranty, and service.

If your product is to be priced lower than your competition's, explain how you will do this and maintain profitability—e.g., greater effectiveness in manufacturing and distributing the product, lower labor costs, lower overhead, or lower material costs.

Discuss the relationship of price, market share, and profits. For example, a higher price may reduce volume but result in a higher gross profit. Describe any discount allowance for prompt payment of volume purchases.

C. *Sales Tactics:* Describe the methods that will be used to make sales and distribute the product or service. Will the company use its own sales force; sales representatives; distributors? Can you use manufacturers' sales organizations already selling related products? Describe both the initial plans and longer-range plans for a sales force. Discuss the margins to be given to retailers, wholesalers, and salesmen and compare them to those given by your competition.

If distributors or sales representatives are to be used, describe how they have been selected, when they will start to represent you, and the areas they will cover. Show a table that indicates the buildup of dealers and representatives by month and the expected sales to be made by each dealer. Describe any special policies regarding discounts, exclusive distribution rights, etc.

If a direct sales force is to be used, indicate how it will be structured and at what rate it will be built up. If it is to replace a dealer or representative organization, indicate when and how. Show the sales expected per salesperson per year, what commission incentive and/or salary they are slated to receive, and compare these figures to the average for your industry.

Present as an exhibit a selling schedule and a sales budget that includes all marketing, promotion, and service costs. This sales expense exhibit should also indicate when sales will commence and the lapse between a sale and a delivery.

D. *Service and Warranty Policies:* If your company will offer a product that will require service and warranties, indicate the importance of these to the customers' purchasing decision and discuss your method of handling service problems. Describe the kind and term of any warranties to be offered, whether service will be handled by a company service organization, agencies, dealers and distributors, or factory return. Indicate the proposed charge for service calls and whether service will be a profitable or breakeven operation. Compare your service and warranty policies and practices to those of your principal competitors.

E. *Advertising and Promotion:* Describe the approaches the company will use to bring its product to the attention of prospective purchasers. For OEM and industrial products indicate the plans for trade show participation, trade magazine advertisements, direct mailings, the preparation of product sheets and promotional literature, and the use of advertising agencies. For consumer products indicate what kind of advertising and promotional campaign is contemplated to introduce the product and what kind of sales aids will be provided to dealers. The schedule and cost of promotion and advertising should be presented. If advertising will be a significant part of company expenses, an exhibit showing how and when these costs will be incurred should be included.

4. DESIGN AND DEVELOPMENT PLANS

If the product, process, or service of the proposed venture requires any design and development before it is ready to be placed on the market, the nature and extent of this work should be fully discussed. The investor will want to know the extent and nature of any design and development and the costs and time required to achieve a marketable product. Such design and development might be the engineering work necessary to convert a laboratory prototype to a finished product; or the design of special tooling; or the work of an industrial designer to make a product more attractive and saleable; or the identification and organization of manpower, equipment, and special techniques to implement a service business—e.g., the equipment, new computer software, and skills required for computerized credit checking.

A. *Development Status and Tasks:* Describe the current status of the product or service and explain what remains to be done to make it marketable. Describe briefly the competence or expertise that your company has or will acquire to complete this development. Indicate the type and extent of technical assistance that will be required, state who will supervise this activity within your organization and his experience in related development work.

B. *Difficulties and Risks:* Identify any major anticipated design and development problems and approaches to their solution. Discuss their possible effect on the schedule, cost of design and development, and time of market introduction.

C. *Product Improvement and New Products:* In addition to describing the development of the initial products, discuss any ongoing design and development work that is planned to keep your product or service competitive and to develop new related products that can be sold to the same group of customers.

D. *Costs:* Present and discuss a design and development budget. The costs should include labor, materials, consulting fees, etc. Design and development costs are often underestimated. This can seriously impact cash flow projections. Accordingly, consider and perhaps show a 10%-20% cost contingency. These cost data will become an integral part of the financial plan.

5. *MANUFACTURING AND OPERATIONS PLAN*

The manufacturing and operations plan should describe the kind of facilities, plant location, space requirements, capital equipment, and labor force (part- and full-time) that are required to provide the company's product or service. For a manufacturing business, discuss your policies regarding inventory control, purchasing, production control, and "make or buy decisions" (i.e., which parts of the product will be purchased and which operations will be performed by your work force). A service business may require particular attention and focus on an appropriate location, an ability to minimize overhead, lease the required equipment, and obtain competitive productivity from a highly skilled or a trained labor force.

The discussion guidelines given below are general enough to cover both product and service businesses. Only those that are relevant to your venture—be it product or service—should be addressed in the business plan.

A. *Geographic Location:* Describe the planned location of the business and discuss any advantages or disadvantages of the site in terms of wage rates, labor unions, labor availability, closeness to customers or suppliers, access to transportation, state and local taxes and laws, utilities, and zoning. For a service business, proximity to customers is generally a "must."

B. *Facilities and Improvements:* If yours is an existing business, describe the facilities currently used to conduct the company's business. This should include plant and office space; storage and land areas; machinery, special tooling, and other capital equipment.

If your venture is a start-up, describe how and when the necessary facilities to *start* production will be acquired. Discuss whether equipment and space will be leased or acquired (new or used) and indicate the costs and timing of such actions. Indicate how much of the proposed financing will be devoted to plant and equipment. (These cost data will become part of the financial plan.)

Discuss how and when plant space and equipment will be expanded to the capacities required for future sales projections. Discuss any plans to improve or add to existing plant space or move the facility. Explain future equipment needs and indicate the timing and cost of such acquisitions. A three-year planning period should be used for these projections.

C. *Strategy and Plans:* Describe the manufacturing processes involved in your product's production and any decisions with respect to subcontracting component parts rather than manufacturing in-house. The "make or buy" strategy adopted should consider inventory financing, available labor skills, and other non-technical questions as well as purely production, cost, and capability issues. Justify your proposed "make or buy" policy. Discuss any surveys you have completed of potential subcontractors and suppliers, and who these are likely to be.

Present a production plan that shows cost-volume information at various sales levels of operation with breakdowns of applicable material, labor, purchased components, and factory overhead. Discuss the inventory required at various sales levels. These data will be incorporated into cash flow projections. Explain how any seasonal production loads will be handled without severe dislocation—e.g., by building inventory or using part-time help in peak periods.

Briefly, describe your approach to quality control, production control, inventory control. Explain what quality control and inspection procedures the company will use to minimize service problems and associated customer dissatisfaction.

Discuss how you will organize and operate your purchasing function to ensure that adequate materials are on hand for production, the best price has been obtained, and that raw materials and in-process inventory, and hence, working capital, have been minimized.

D. *Labor Force:* Exclusive of management functions (discussed later), does the local labor force have the necessary skills in sufficient quantity and quality (lack of absenteeism, productivity), to manufacture the products or supply the services of your company? If the skills of the labor force are inadequate to the needs of the company, describe the kinds of training that you will use to upgrade their skills. Discuss whether the business can provide training and still offer a competitive product both in the short-term (first year) and longer-term (two to five years).

6. MANAGEMENT TEAM

The management team is the key to turning a good idea into a successful business. Investors look for a committed management team with a balance of technical, managerial, and business skills, and experience in doing what is proposed.

Accordingly, this section of the business plan will be of primary interest to potential investors and will significantly influence their investment decisions. It should include a description of the key management personnel and their primary duties; the organizational structure; and the board of directors.

A. *Organization:* In a table, present the key management roles in the company and the individual who will fill each position.

Discuss any current or past situations where the key management people have worked together that indicate how their skills complement each other and result in an effective management team. If any key individuals will not be on hand at the start of the venture, indicate when they will join the company.

In a new business, it may not be possible to fill each executive role with a full-time person without excessively burdening the overhead of the venture. One solution is to use part-time specialists or consultants to perform some functions. If this is your plan, discuss it and indicate who will be used and when they will be replaced by a full-time staff member.

If the company is established and of sufficient size, an organization chart can be appended as an exhibit.

B. *Key Management Personnel:* Describe the exact duties and responsibilities of each of the key members of the management team. Include a brief (three- or four-sentence) statement of the career highlights of each individual that focuses on accomplishments that demonstrate his or her ability to perform the assigned role.

Complete resumés for each key management member should be included here or as an exhibit to the business plan. These resumés should stress training, experience, and accomplishments of each person in performing functions similar to that person's role in the venture. Accomplishments should be discussed in such concrete terms as profit and sales improvement; labor management; manufacturing or technical achievements; and ability to meet budgets and schedules. Where possible it should be noted who can attest to accomplishments and what recognition or rewards were received—e.g., pay increases, promotions, etc.

C. *Management Compensation and Ownership:* The likelihood of obtaining financing for a start-up is small when the founding management team is not prepared to accept initial modest salaries. If the founders demand substantial salaries in excess of what they received at their prior employment, the potential investor will conclude that their psychological commitment to the venture is a good deal less than it should be.

State the salary that is to be paid to each key person and compare it to the salary received at his/her last independent job. Set forth the stock ownership planned for the key personnel, the amount of their equity investment (if any), and any performance-dependent stock option or bonus plans that are contemplated.

D. *Board of Directors:* Discuss the company's philosophy as to the size and composition of the board. Identify any proposed board members and include a one- or two-sentence statement of the member's background that shows how he or she can benefit the company.

E. *Management Assistance and Training Needs:* Describe, candidly, the strengths and weaknesses of your management team and board of directors. Discuss the kind, extent, and timing of any management training that will be required to overcome the weaknesses and obtain effective venture operation. Also discuss the need for technical and management assistance during the first three years of your venture. Be as specific as you can as to the kind, extent, and cost of such assistance and how it will be obtained.

F. *Supporting Professional Services:* State the legal (including patent), accounting, advertising, and banking organizations that you have selected for your venture. Capable, reputable and well-known supporting service organizations can not only provide significant direct, professional assistance, but can also add to the credibility to your venture. In addition, properly selected professional organizations can help you establish good contacts in the business community, identify potential investors, and help you secure financing.

7. OVERALL SCHEDULE

A schedule that shows the timing and interrelationship of the major events necessary to launch the venture and realize its objectives is an essential part of a business plan. In addition to being a planning aid and showing deadlines critical to a venture's success, a well-prepared schedule can be an extremely effective sales tool in raising money from potential investors. A well-prepared and realistic schedule demonstrates the ability of the management team to plan for venture growth in a way that recognizes obstacles and minimizes risk.

Prepare, as a part of this section, a month-by-month schedule that shows the timing of activities such as product development, market planning, sales programs, and production and operations. Sufficient detail should be included to show the timing of the primary tasks required to accomplish an activity.

Show on the schedule the deadlines or milestones critical to the venture's success. This should include events such as:

- Incorporation of the venture (for a new business)

- Completion of design and development

- Completion of prototypes (a key date; its achievement is a tangible measure of the company's ability to perform)

- When sales representatives are obtained

- Displays at trade shows

- When distributors and dealers are signed up

- Order of materials in production quantities

- Start of production or operation (another key date because it is related to the production of income)

- Receipt of first orders

- First sales and deliveries (a date of maximum interest because it relates directly to the company's credibility and need for capital)

- Payment of first accounts receivable (cash in)

The schedule should also show the following and their relation to the development of the business:

- Number of management personnel

- Number of production and operations personnel

- Additions to plant or equipment

Discuss in a general way the activities most likely to cause a schedule slippage, and what steps you would take to correct such slippages. Discuss the impact of schedule slippages on the venture's operation, especially its potential viability and capital needs. Keep in mind that the time to do things tends to be underestimated—even more than financing requirements. So be realistic about your schedule.

8. CRITICAL RISKS AND PROBLEMS

The development of a business has risks and problems, and the business plan invariably contains some implicit assumptions about them. The discovery of any unstated negative factors by potential investors can undermine the credibility of the venture and endanger its financing.

On the other hand, identifying and discussing the risks in your venture demonstrates your skills as a manager and increases your credibility with a venture capital investor. Taking the initiative to identify and discuss risks helps you demonstrate to the investor that you have thought about them and can handle them. Risks then tend not to loom as large black clouds in the investor's thinking about your venture.

Accordingly, identify and discuss the major problems and risks that you think you will have to deal with to develop the venture. This should include a description of the risks relating to your industry, your company and its personnel, your product's market appeal, and the timing and financing of your start-up. Among the risks that might require discussion are:

- Price cutting by competitors

- Any potentially unfavorable industry-wide trends

- Design or manufacturing costs in excess of estimates

- Sales projections not achieved

- Product development schedule not met

- Difficulties or long lead times encountered in the procurement of parts or raw materials

- Difficulties encountered in obtaining bank credit lines because of tight money

- Larger than expected innovation and development costs to stay competitive

- Availability of trained labor

This list is not meant to be complete but only indicative of the kinds of risks and assumptions that might be discussed.

Indicate which of your assumptions or potential problems are most critical to the success of the venture. Describe your plans for minimizing the impact of unfavorable developments in each risk area on the success of your venture.

9. COMMUNITY BENEFITS

The proposed venture should be an instrument of community and human development as well as economic development, and it should be responsive to the expressed desires of the community.

Describe and discuss the potential economic and non-economic benefits to members of the community that could result from your venture.

Among the potential benefits that may merit discussion are:

Economic Development

- Number of jobs generated in each of the first three years of the venture
- Number and kind of new employment opportunities for previously unemployed or underemployed individuals
- Number of skilled and higher paying jobs
- Ownership and control of venture assets by community residents
- Purchase of goods and services from local suppliers

Human Development

- New technical skills development and associated career opportunities for community residents
- Management development and training
- Employment of unique skills within the community that are now unused

Community Development

- Development of community's physical assets
- Improved perception of CDC responsiveness and their role in the community
- Provision of needed, but unsupplied, services or products to the community
- Improvements in the living environment
- Community support, participation, and pride in the venture.
- Development of community-owned economic structure and decreased absentee business ownership

Describe any compromises or time lags in venture profitability that may result from trying to achieve some or all of the kinds of benefits cited above. Any such compromises or lags in profitability should be justified in the context of all the benefits achieved and the role of the venture in a total, planned program of economic, human, and community development.

10. *THE FINANCIAL PLAN*

The financial plan is basic to the evaluation of an investment opportunity and should represent the entrepreneur's best estimates of future operations. Its purpose is to indicate the venture's potential and the timetable for financial viability. It can also serve as an operating plan for financial management of the venture.

In developing the financial plan, three basic forecasts must be prepared:

a. Profit and loss forecasts for three years

b. Cash-flow projections for three years

c. Pro forma balance sheets at start-up, semiannually in the first year and at the end of each of the first three years of operation

In the case of an existing venture seeking expansion capital, balance sheets and income statements for the current and two prior years should be presented in addition to these financial projections.

Sample forms for preparing financial projections have been provided as tables 20–22.* It is recommended that the venture's financial and marketing personnel prepare them, with assistance from an accountant if required. In addition to these three basic financial exhibits, a breakeven chart (Table 23) should be presented that shows the level of sales required to cover all operating costs.

After you have completed the preparation of the financial exhibits, briefly highlight in writing the important conclusions that can be drawn. This might include the maximum cash requirement, the amount to be supplied by equity and debt; the level of profits as a percent of sales; how fast any debts are repaid; etc.

---

*Robert Morris Associates (The National Association of Bank Loan Officers and Credit Men) also publishes forms for preparing financial projections as well as instructions for preparing supporting worksheets for Accounts Payable Disbursements, Accounts Receivables Collections, Material Flow and Purchases, etc. These instructions and forms are: Charles G. Zimmerman, "Projection of Financial Statements— And the Preparatory Use of Work Sheet Schedules for Budgets" and RMA Form C-117, "Projection of Financial Statements," (Philadelphia, PA: 1961).

A. *Profit and Loss Forecast (Table 20)*

The preparation of pro forma income statements is the profit planning part of financial management. Crucial to the earnings forecasts—as well as other projections—is the sales forecast. You have already developed sales forecasts while completing your Market Research and Analysis section. The sales data projected should be used here.

Once the sales forecasts are in hand, production costs (or operations costs for a service business) should be budgeted. The level of production or operation that is required to meet the sales forecasts and also to fulfill inventory requirements must be determined. The material, labor, service, and manufacturing overhead requirements must be developed and translated into cost data. A separation of the fixed and variable elements of these costs is desirable, and the effect of sales volume on inventory, equipment acquisitions, and manufacturing costs should be taken into account.

Sales expense should include the costs of selling the distribution, storage, discounts, advertising, and promotion. General and administrative expense should include management salaries, secretarial costs, and legal and accounting expenses. Manufacturing or operations overhead includes rent, utilities, fringe benefits, telephone, etc.

Earnings projections should be prepared monthly in the first year of operation and quarterly for the second and third years.

If these earnings projections are to be useful they must represent management's realistic, best estimates of probable operating results. Sales or operating cost projections that are either too conservative or too optimistic have little value as aids to policy formulation and decision-making.

Discussion of Assumptions: Because of the importance of profit and loss projections as an indication of the potential financial feasibility of a new venture to potential investors, it is extremely important that any assumptions made in its preparation be fully explained and documented. Such assumptions could include the amount allowed for bad debts and discounts, and any assumptions made with respect to sales expenses or general and administrative costs which are fixed percentages of costs or sales.

Risks and Sensitivity: Once the income statements have been prepared, draw on Section 8 of these guidelines to highlight any major risks that could prevent the venture's sales and profit goals from being attained, and the sensitivity of profits to these risks.

TABLE 20

Pro Forma Income Statements

	1st Year – Months												2nd Year Quarters				3rd Year Quarters			
	1	2	3	4	5	6	7	8	9	10	11	12	1Q	2Q	3Q	4Q	1Q	2Q	3Q	4Q
Sales																				
Less: Discounts																				
Less: Bad Debt Provision																				
Less: Materials Used																				
Direct Labor																				
Manufacturing Overhead[1]																				
Other Manufacturing Expense (Leased Equipment)																				
Total Cost of Goods Sold																				
Gross Profit (or Loss)																				
Less: Sales Expense																				
Engineering Expense																				
General and Administrative Expense[2]																				
Operating Profit (or Loss)																				
Less: Other Expense (e. g., interest, depreciation)																				
Profit (Loss) Before Taxes																				
Income Tax Provision																				
Profit (Loss) After Taxes																				

(1) Includes rent, utilities, fringe benefits, telephone.
(2) Includes office supplies, accounting and legal services, management, etc.

This discussion should reflect the entrepreneur's thinking about the risks that might be encountered in the firm itself, the industry, and the environment. This could include such things as the effect of a 20% reduction in sales projections, or the impact over time of a learning curve on the level of productivity.

B. *Pro Forma Cash Flows Analysis (Table 21)*

For a new venture the cash flows forecast can be more important than the forecasts of profits because it details the amount and timing of expected cash inflows and outflows. Usually the level of profits, particularly during the start-up years of a venture, will not be sufficient to finance operating asset needs. Moreover, cash inflows do not match the outflows on a short-term basis. The cash flows forecast will indicate these conditions and allow management to plan cash needs.

Given a level of projected sales and capital expenditures over a specific period, the cash forecast will highlight the need for and timing of additional financing and indicate peak requirements for working capital. Management must decide how this additional financing is to be obtained, on what terms, and how it is to be repaid. Part of the needed financing will be supplied by the equity financing (that is sought by this business plan), part by bank loans for one to five years, and the balance by short-term lines of credit from banks. This information becomes part of the final cash flows forecast.

If the venture is in a seasonal or cyclical industry, or is in an industry in which suppliers require a new firm to pay cash, or if an inventory buildup occurs before the product can be sold and produce revenues, the cash flows forecast is crucial to the continuing solvency of the business. A detailed cash flows forecast which is understood and used by management can help them direct their attention to operating problems without distractions caused by periodic cash crises that should have been anticipated. Cash flows projections should be made for each month of the first year of operation and quarterly for the second and third years.

Discussion of Assumptions: This should include assumptions made about the timing of collections receivables, trade discounts given, terms of payments to vendors, planned salary and wage increases, anticipated increases in any operating expenses, seasonality of the business as it affects inventory requirements, inventory turnovers per year, and capital equipment purchases. Thinking about such assumptions when planning your venture is useful for identifying issues which may later require attention if they are not to become significant problems.

TABLE 21

Pro Forma Cash Flows

	1st Year - Months												2nd Year Quarters				3rd Year Quarters			
	1	2	3	4	5	6	7	8	9	10	11	12	1Q	2Q	3Q	4Q	1Q	2Q	3Q	4Q
Cash Balance: Opening																				
Add: Cash Receipts																				
Collection of Accounts Receivable																				
Miscellaneous Receipts																				
Bank Loan Proceeds																				
Sale of Stock																				
Total Receipts																				
Less: Disbursements																				
Trade Payables																				
Direct Labor																				
Manufacturing Overhead																				
Leased Equipment																				
Sales Expense																				
Warranty Expense																				
General and Administrative Expense																				
Fixed Asset Additions																				
Income Tax																				
Loan Interest @ _____ %																				
Loan Repayments																				
Other Payments																				
Total Disbursements																				
Cash Increase (Decrease)																				
Cash Balance: Closing																				

Cash Flow Sensitivity: Once the cash flow has been completed, discuss the impact on cash needs that possible changes in some of the crucial assumptions would have; e.g., slower receivables collection or scales below forecasts. This will enable you to test the sensitivity of the cash budget based on differing assumptions about business factors, and to view several possible outcomes. Investors are vitally interested in this because it helps them estimate the possibility that you will need more cash sooner than planned.

C. *Pro Forma Balance Sheets (Table 22)*

The balance sheets detail the assets required to support the projected level of operations and show how these assets are to be financed (liabilities and equity). Investors and bankers look at the projected balance sheets to determine if debt to equity ratios, working capital, current ratios, inventory turnover, etc., are within the acceptable limits required to justify future financings projected for the venture.

Pro forma balance sheets should be prepared at start-up, semi-annually for the first year, and at the end of each of the first three years of operation.

D. *Breakeven Chart (Table 23)*

A breakeven chart shows the level of sales (and hence, production) needed to cover all your costs. This includes those costs that vary with the production level (manufacturing labor, material, sales costs) and those that do not change with production (rent, interest charges, executive salaries, etc.). The sales level that exactly equals all costs is the breakeven level for your venture.

It is very useful for the investor and the management to know what the breakeven point is and whether it will be easy or difficult to attain. It is very desirable for your projected sales to be sufficiently larger than the breakeven sales so that small changes in your performance do not produce losses. You should prepare a breakeven chart and discuss how your breakeven point might be lowered in case you start to fall short of your sales projections. You should also discuss the effect on your breakeven point of lower production capacity requirements.

E. *Cost Control*

Your ability to meet your income and cash flows projections will depend on your ability to monitor and control costs. For this reason many investors like to know what type of accounting and cost control system you have or will use in your business. Accordingly, the financial plan should include a brief description of how you will obtain and report costs, who will be responsible

TABLE 22

PRO FORMA BALANCE SHEET

	Start-up	End of 6 Months	End of First Year	End of Second Year	End of Third Year
ASSETS					
<u>Current</u>					
Cash					
Marketable Securities					
Accounts Receivable					
Inventories					
Raw Materials and Supplies					
Work in Process					
Finished Goods					
Total Inventory					
Prepaid Items					
Total Current Assets					
Plant and Equipment					
Less: Accumulated Depreciation					
Net Plant and Equipment					
Deferred Charges					
Other Assets (Identify)					
TOTAL ASSETS					
LIABILITIES AND STOCKHOLDERS'					
<u>EQUITY</u>					
Notes Payable to Banks					
Accounts Payable					
Accruals					
Federal and State Taxes					
Other					
TOTAL CURRENT LIABILITIES					
Long Term Notes					
Other Liabilities					
Common Stock					
Capital Surplus					
Retained Earnings					
<u>**TOTAL LIABILITIES AND STOCKHOLDERS' EQUITY**</u>					

TABLE 23

SAMPLE BREAKEVEN CHART

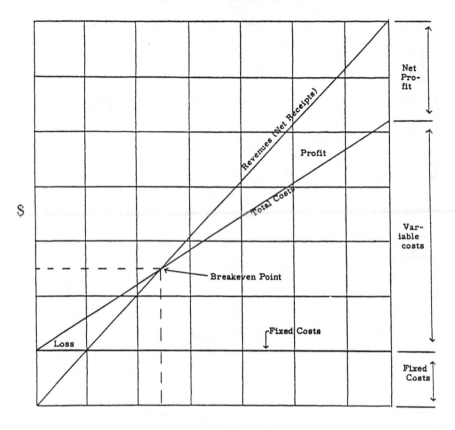

Units Produced

for controlling various cost elements, how often he or she will obtain cost data, and how you will take action on budget overruns.

11. *PROPOSED COMPANY OFFERING*

The purpose of this section of the plan is to indicate the amount of money that is being sought, the nature and amount of the securities offered to the investor, and a brief description of the uses that will be made of the capital raised. The discussion and guidelines given below should help you do this.

You should realize that the financing terms you propose here are the first step in a negotiation process with a venture capital investor who is interested in your "deal." It is very possible that when you close your financing, you will be selling a different kind of security (e.g., convertible debt instead of common stock) for a different price than you originally proposed.

A. *Desired Financing:* Summarize from your cash flows projections how much money is required over the next three years to carry out the development and expansion of your business as described. Indicate how much of the capital requirement will be obtained by this offering and how much will be obtained from term loans, lines of credit, or other sources.

B. *Securities Offering:* Describe the kind (common stock, convertible debenture, etc.), unit price, and total amount of securities to be sold in this offering. For securities other than common stock (e.g., debt with warrants, debt plus stock) indicate interest, maturity, and conversion conditions. Also show the percentage of the company that the investors of this offering will hold after it is completed, or after exercise of any stock conversion or purchase rights in the case of convertible debentures or warrants.

If the securities are being sold as a "private placement" (that is, exempt from SEC registration), you should include the following statement in this part of the plan:

"The shares being sold pursuant to this offering are restricted securities and may not be resold readily. The prospective investor should recognize that such securities might be restricted as to resale for an indefinite period of time. Each purchaser will be required to execute a Non-Distribution Agreement satisfactory in form to corporate counsel."

C. *Capitalization:* Present in tabular form the current and proposed (post-offering) number of outstanding shares of common stock. Indicate any shares offered by key management people and show the number of shares that they will hold after completion of the proposed financing.

Indicate how many shares of your company's common stock will remain authorized but unissued after the offering and how many of these will be reserved for stock options for future key employees.

D. *Use of Funds:* Investors like to know how their money is going to be spent. Provide a description of how the capital raised will be used. Summarize, as specifically as possible, what amount will be used for such things as product design and development; capital equipment; marketing; and general working capital needs.

The main body of the business plan ends here. Appendixes begin at this point.

Final Note

All projections within a business plan must be based on realistic projections of future outcomes. In addition, projections will be the basis for critical decisions relating to all aspects of the firm's operation. Unreasonable expectations can cause resources to be spent unwisely and create suspicion among potential lenders and investors.

Every projection stated must be firmly documented, giving reasonable evidence that it can be achieved. A plan of action must be detailed, discussing strategy and tactics. For example, in a market forecast a firm must undertake an analysis of market opportunities and the capability of the firm to exploit those potentials. Once the sales projection is made, it should be backed up by reasonable assurances of an expanding market. After this is accomplished, specific marketing steps to achieve the stated objective must be discussed. These endeavors might include the opening of new offices; introduction of new or modified products/services; addition of new sales personnel; new customer identification; expanding needs of existing customers; and/or enhanced promotion effort.

Whether it is sales projections, profit and loss estimates, cash flow forecasts, or other financial predictions, realistic appraisals and approaches are mandatory in order to prevent unwise application of resources and disappointment among managers, creditors, and investors.

An entrepreneur should also consider and evaluate internal and external forces that affect the business in question and report their impact in the business plan under the section entitled "Critical Risks and Problems."

Examples of internal factors include:

— Expansion Plans
— Pricing Structure
— Operational Limitations
— Financial Limitations
— Research and Development
— Introduction of New Product/Services

— Marketing Dynamics
— Revenue and Earnings Projections
— Market Expansion

Examples of external (environmental) factors include:

— Economic Cycles
— Business Trends
— Government Regulations
— State of Technology
— Domestic Competitive Conditions
— Changing Demand Patterns
— Industry Trends
— Unions
— Inflation
— Changes in Population Profile
— International Political Events
— International Business Competition

It is the opinion of many small-business experts that entrepreneurs/ managing teams should not attempt to construct statements or attempt forecasting. Most simply lack the marketing, financial, and accounting expertise to accomplish these feats adequately and to the satisfaction of funding outlets. Therefore, competent business consultants and/ or accountants should be sought out to complete this laborious and tedious task. Chapter 3 provides information on individuals and/or organizations that may provide assistance.

8

APPROACHING THE INVESTOR
What Is Expected

Beefing Up the Business Plan

The success of any business endeavor will hinge on the decisions made by the entrepreneur and managers involved. A comprehensive business plan will assist in the decision-making function by allocating the firm's limited resources and evaluating managerial decisions. In addition, it forces the business to establish reasonable objectives and make logical choices. The plan should be viewed and conveyed as a path to follow. It allows the business to guide itself through anticipated and unexpected economic environments by forcing the entrepreneur to identify and deal with real and potential problems before they threaten the business.

As was mentioned earlier, the business plan should run between 40 and 60 pages (typed and double spaced), with an adequate number of appendixes for purposes of illustration and detail. There are exceptions to this rule. Some plans can get by with fewer pages and others take more. It depends on many factors, some of which include product/service being marketed, age of the firm, type of industry, nature of funding, etc. Whatever the case, the business plan must be detailed enough to tell the whole story without being so long and drawn out as to bore the reader.

Copies of the finished plan must be made for prospective investors. All reproductions should have nice-looking protective covers so as to project a professional image. Do an adequate job, but don't go overboard. Too much attention to cosmetics will give investors the immediate impression that substance is being compromised for image purposes, even though this may not be the case. If it is apparent that lots of time and money was spent to produce an "attention getter" cover, investors will feel that extravagance is the name of the game. Recently, an entrepreneur and managing team of a small wholesale business submitted a business plan with an expensive gold-embossed cover to a New York venture capital firm. To make matters worse, the first page of the business plan contained a smiling photograph of the entrepreneur. Well, it was good for a couple of laughs before being returned with a rejection letter.

Keep in mind that certain aspects of the business plan are more important than others. Quality and capability of management is generally given the highest consideration and must be emphasized accordingly. "Good managers can sell anything. Look at the pet rock, it was really nothing, but they made it sell," quoted an investor. He went on to say that "management is given approximately 60 percent weight in a funding decision, with the rest divided among the various components of the business plan." In addition, the marketing research segment of the plan is of great importance because it attempts to convey the marketability of the firm's product or service. Therefore, this section should be given added emphasis.

Initial Contacts With Money Sources

Most financial outlets have specific investment preferences. Many will invest only in selected geographic areas and in certain types of businesses. Also, they limit themselves as to the amount invested. Many will entertain proposals only for existing firms while others welcome start-up situations. Some do both. Studying these particulars will save countless hours pursuing the wrong funding sources. Most of the investors mentioned in Chapter 11 have been listed with their preferences. After matching proposition with correct source, the next step involves contact.

Financial outlets generally don't like phone calls. They prefer that entrepreneurs mail them a cover letter and a two- or three-page summary of the business plan for initial consideration. The summary section of the completed plan can be used for this purpose. Make sure a competent business consultant, attorney, or accountant has reviewed the summary before you send it to investors. In fact, several people should evaluate the summation to determine its merits. Their recommendation should be carefully considered. Just remember that the summary must never exceed three pages. It is strictly an attention getter designed to spark investors' interest in reading the entire business plan. If they are pleased with what they see, the whole plan will be requested for additional consideration. Don't get discouraged if this process takes some time. An excellent way to determine an investor's interest in the proposition is the amount of time he or she spends looking over the plan. Extensive evaluation is a positive signal, without question.

While the business plan is being examined, the entrepreneur should be making a background investigation of the investor. This must be done to protect the business from hooking up with an unethical or otherwise difficult capital source. Ask for references. Contacting firms that have received funds from the prospective funding outlet is an ideal way to learn about the investor. Checking with the U.S. Small Business Administration in Washington might prove to be helpful, and speaking with the local chamber of commerce in the city where the investor resides should also yield some information. Some investors belong to professional trade organizations. Give them a call to check the credentials of the funding source. Pay particular attention to potential investors' relationships with affiliated entrepreneurs and how much initial and ongoing managerial assistance they provide. Taking these inexpensive and cautious measures in the beginning may eliminate costly headaches down the road.

After the investors have critically evaluated and scrutinized the business plan, the entrepreneur will be informed of the decision by letter or phone. If the response is negative, ask why and what can be done to improve the chances of successful funding. Perhaps they know another source that may be interested. A positive answer will invoke an invitation to meet the money source personally.

The procedure just outlined applies to most financial outlets. The exceptions are banks and governmental sources of funding. These outlets will normally meet with entrepreneurs beforehand to discuss the proposal. They may even request that a simple application form be completed. Ultimately, these sources will also demand a comprehensive business plan.

Presentation of the Business Plan

When a financial outlet requests a verbal presentation of the business plan, respond at once to set an appointment. Go to the meeting dressed appropriately. Appear mildly confident and poised. Avoid excessive zeal. In addition, conducting oneself in a polite, professional, and dignified manner is a must. Many entrepreneurs with good business plans have failed to obtain capital because they didn't project a solid image to investors.

The presentation is used to evaluate the entrepreneur and/or management team more than the business plan. After all, the investors have already read the plan at this point. The entrepreneur and others involved must be prepared to discuss all facets of the proposal in an intelligent and convincing manner with a command of the facts. Below are some observations that will probably be made during the presentation state:

— Does the entrepreneur and/or managing team appear structured and systematic?
— Is there enough business and technical expertise involved in the proposition? Can it be obtained if lacking?
— Are the entrepreneur and others involved realistic in their estimates of projections, risks, time, resources, etc.?
— How is criticism handled? Can helpful comments be accepted?
— Is forthrightness displayed? Are inconsistencies admitted frankly or evaded?
— Does the entrepreneur and/or managing team communicate effectively?

Specific questions will be asked. Even though most have been covered extensively in the business plan, a verbal response will be expected. Remember, the investors are searching for weaknesses. They will attempt to detect contradictions between the verbal presentation and what is stated in the plan. The most common questions put to entrepreneurs during the presentation are as follows:

— How much capital is requested?
— For what purposes will it be used?

— How will it be repaid?
— What security is being offered?
— Describe the product or service to be marketed.
— Who are the customers?
— Why will they buy?
— Who are the competitors?
— Why is this product/service better than the competition?
— By how much is the total market for the product/service growing?
— How long will it take to gear up for marketing?
— When will marketing endeavors begin?
— What are the background and track record of the company's management relative to the product/service industry?
— What are their relevant management and business skills?
— What are the risks involved in this venture?
— What are the strengths of the proposal?
— What are the weaknesses of the proposal?
— What is the credit history of the principals involved in the project?
— How much capital do the principals intend to invest in the project?
— Has all the appropriate personal and business insurance been considered?
— Does the business have a competent attorney? Accountant?

The responses received from the aforementioned questions will determine to a great extent whether funding is approved. A good presentation will substantially enhance the chances of getting funds.

Give and Take in Final Funding Negotiations

If the entrepreneur and business plan live up to investor expectations, the next barrier to overcome regards funding terms. This is a major bone of contention between investor and management which demands careful consideration. Many good deals have fallen apart during this stage of discussion. In a lending situation, the point of confrontation centers around the interest rate to be charged. Most businesses feel that financial outlets are demanding too much while the lenders contend it's not enough. When equity (ownership) is involved in the discussions, the argument rages over how much ownership the entrepreneur and others involved must forfeit to investors in exchange for their capital. The question of who controls what takes center stage.

It all boils down to perceived risks by the investors. Greater risks will force the entrepreneur to give up a larger portion of ownership in an equity deal or pay higher interest rates if lending is the financing vehicle. There is no steadfast rule used by investors to determine the pitfalls in prospective business propositions. Each financial outlet sees things differently and will act accordingly, although there are some general guidelines used in analyzing risks. Knowing these before going into negotiations will reduce frustration from the outset. They are:

- The less capital invested by the entrepreneur and others involved in the business, the more ownership demanded by investors in an equity arrangement. If loans are contemplated, higher rates of interest will be required. Most investors prefer that management invest in the business proposition to the maximum degree possible. One venture capitalist recently commented that he sleeps better knowing individuals running the business have invested money. "If their money is on the line, you can bet they will try harder to make things work."

- A start-up company will need to give up more ownership and/or pay higher interest rates than does a going operation. This reasoning is quite obvious. An existing concern has a greater chance of survival.

- A business that operates in a high-growth industry (computers, medical technology, alternative energy, information transfer, etc.) will be able to negotiate better equity terms or lower interest rates on loans than can a firm in a less promising sector of the economy.

- The general economic climate will affect investor attitude. Periods of recession and stagnation will make financial outlets wary and extremely cautious, probably demanding more equity or higher interest rates than would be the case in an expanding economy.

- Anticipated earnings growth will also affect investor reactions. If the prospects for continued profits are good, a better equity or lending deal can be arranged with the funding outlets.

Before entering into negotiations with investors, do some homework. Study similar funding arrangements. Know what to expect.

Consult attorneys, accountants, and consultants in reference to the business proposition. Being well informed will impress the investors and help ensure a fair funding agreement. When negotiating, keep in mind that both parties must give and take. Try to establish a candid and friendly rapport with the investor. Disagreements will happen, but it is critically important to maintain a positive and professional posture at all times. Communication is an absolute necessity during the negotiation process. Each party must clearly state their goals and let the other know if changes in position occur. Without this interaction, negotiation will eventually come to a halt.

The entrepreneur/managing team should be keen negotiators. Investors will respect shrewdness. If a loan is being discussed, tell the lender that a high interest rate will retard earnings and adversely affect the firm's rate of growth. Attempt to prove this with hard figures. In an equity situation, mention that giving up too much ownership will have a negative impact on managerial incentive. Throw the investors a "highball." Tell them that a high percentage of ownership must be retained by management. Use this as a starting point in the discussions.

Always appear willing to negotiate. Investors expect to give and take. Above all, don't get greedy: that's a turnoff to serious funding sources. Recently, an inventor created a number of ingenious energy-efficient products, and several investors expressed interest in providing capital to finance marketing endeavors. The inventor refused to give up more than 75 percent ownership in the business for what he called "control purposes." Because the products were new and unproven the investors refused to provide funding under his conditions. They made a counteroffer to hold 60 percent of ownership and would further reduce it to 40 percent once earnings were generated, thereby giving the inventor control down the road. He still declined the offer and the deal broke apart. Realizing his mistake, the inventor decided to accept the offer, but it was too late. The investors wouldn't have anything to do with the proposition.

Too much emphasis on the idea of control can kill a good deal as it did in the case mentioned above. Remember, it's better to have 20 percent of a watermelon than 80 percent of a raisin. A properly structured deal can ensure the entrepreneur and others involved eventual control of the business. Many investors will negotiate incentive/equity deals. This is where the entrepreneurs are given a smaller percentage of ownership in the beginning, which will increase as the business grows.

Whatever the case, don't get desperate and accept anything that comes along, even though the money is desperately needed. Most businesses would be wise not to accept poor or inadequate funding offers. The ideal scenario would be teaming up with reputable investors who are willing to assist in making the proposition operate and function successfully. Investors willing to help rather than hinder should be sought out. Appendix F provides an outline of a typical investment agreement.

Twenty-one Reasons Why Funds Requests Are Rejected

Listed below are some of the more common reasons why financial outlets refuse funding requests. The problems stem from deficiencies within the business and/or because of difficulties with the entrepreneur/managing team.

- *Lack of Continuity*—The business plan must demonstrate that the firm will continue uninterrupted if key employees of the firm leave or die.
- *Unwillingness to Part With Equity*—Too many entrepreneurs are unduly concerned over giving up ownership and/or control of the business.
- *Inability to Take Criticism*—Many investors will make helpful suggestions concerning the proposal. Defensive reactions on the part of the entrepreneur/managing team will leave a bad impression. It denotes immaturity.
- *Underestimating Capital Needs*—Many entrepreneurs tend to underestimate capital requirements for the business. In some cases, it is a deliberate attempt to impress investors that something can be accomplished with less. Well, it doesn't. In fact, it displays a lack of good business sense. One of the major reasons for business failure is lack of adequate capitalization.
- *Lack of a Total Plan*—Most business plans that are submitted to funding outlets are strictly financial in nature. They fail to consider non-financial aspects such as production considerations.
- *Unrealistic, Low-Expense Forecasts*—Reasonable expense projections must be made in order to accurately predict earnings flow.

Overstated profit expectations based on erroneous expense data will only give investors the impression that numbers are being "churned" in order to create an attractive picture.

- *Overstated Revenue Projections*—If revenues fail in living up to expectation, the chances are that profits will do the same. Since the technical aspects of funding deals rely heavily on projected revenues and profits, realistic projections need to be made. In fact, investors will not allow overstated forecasts. They will use their financial expertise to adjust the figures appearing in the business plan. It's nice to have it done right the first time around. It shows that the entrepreneur/managing team know what they are doing.

- *Little or No Experience in the Area of Operation*—Investors will feel uncomfortable knowing that the firm's management is weak in the product/service area. The firm can compensate for this by hiring a consultant and/or managers with experience and knowledge in the product/service and industry.

- *Inability to Delegate*—Many entrepreneurs don't like delegating authority to others when it needs to be done. They tend to be egocentric and think everything must evolve around them. Most fear losing control. Entrepreneurs who fail to recognize the need for a team effort are naïve. Today's business environment demands it.

- *Too Much Show*—Trying to impress investors with fancy offices and cars will have only a negative impact. They will feel that too much is being spent on cosmetics and not enough on substance. Normally it gives the impression of extravagance.

- *Seeking More Than Is Needed*—This is called "fudging" and is considered a no-no. It is easy to detect, and invokes the question, why is the extra money needed? The entrepreneur will find that it's an embarrassing situation and could weaken the relationship with the investor.

- *Using Investors Against Each Other*—Don't try to pit money sources against each other to enhance the bargaining position. It's a turnoff to investors and will not work. Many will refuse to talk after being exposed to this tactic. Now don't get the wrong idea. It is okay to have other funding alternatives. Just don't use them as bait to squeeze out what might be considered a better deal. It shows lack of tact.

- *Inability to Learn*—The ability to learn rapidly is essential in today's business environment. Entrepreneurs must convince investors that they are capable to catching on quickly. Formal and informal discussion between investor and entrepreneur will reveal this quality. Learn from what the investor has to say. If learning ability is not shown to investors, funding may not be forthcoming.

- *Sweet Talk*—Don't butter up the investors. It's obvious and they do not like it one bit. Being too sweet and nice could kill a deal in short order. The investors know something is up and it creates suspicion from the very beginning, and that is "strike one" against the entrepreneur.

- *Lack of Managerial Depth*—Management is the most important consideration in the funding decision. Without the proper breadth of management and business experience to run the operation with a good chance of success, the probability of securing funds is nil.

- *Wrong Timing*—The product or service may not be ready for the market at this time, or the right time has already passed and there are too many existing competitors.

- *Inability to Communicate*—Entrepreneurs who can't convey their ideas clearly and concisely in written or verbal form stand little chance of being funded. If the entrepreneur and managing team can't explain and answer questions about the proposal in a clear and logical fashion, investors will wonder how they are going to market their service or product.

- *Lack of Trust*—Many entrepreneurs feel that funding outlets can't be trusted and are cheats. It becomes obvious very quickly. Information is withheld, former relationships are criticized, and complaints are made about rotten terms they got from other funding sources. One investor recently remarked that "When a paranoid entrepreneur comes down the pike, we run for the hills. It's trouble from the start."

- *Defensiveness*—Information about personality and background will be sought by the prospective investors. Entrepreneurs who get insulted and upset when probing questions are asked leave a bad impression.

- *Lack of Appreciation for a Buck*—If the entrepreneur/managing team fail to show investors that their money is going to be treated with a lot of consideration and prudence, the deal will come apart. One of the biggest fears on the part of investors is that once their money is given to the entrepreneurs, it will be spent indiscriminately and recklessly. Entrepreneurs need to dispel this fear by showing the investor exactly how funds will be employed. Studies have shown that most successful entrepreneurs are moderate risk takers and not the "high stakes rollers" they are publicized to be.

- *Lack of Testing*—A product or service should be tested on a small scale to evaluate results before attempting large distribution efforts. Testing reveals potentially costly faults that can be corrected before large efforts are executed. Telling investors that the product/service is ready to be marketed on a large scale without appropriate testing because "it's the greatest thing ever developed" is giving the wrong impression and will scare off serious investors. The business plan should make reference to testing procedures. If testing has already taken place, the results should be revealed.

9

MAKE IT SUCCESSFUL
Sweat and Money Are At Stake

Aim Toward the Future

Setting long-term goals and objectives can prove to be a roadmap guiding the business along a path to future profits and success. One of the foremost reasons for America's lack of competitive success in the international marketplace is the unwillingness of domestic business leaders to plan for the future. U.S. managers have been criticized throughout the industrial world for being "short termers," exploiting only immediate opportunities and therefore compromising long-term considerations that could prove to be more profitable. In reality, it is not the fault of the managers but of society at large. American business leaders are rewarded by shareholders for their yearly performance. Consequently, they will do their best to look good on a short-term basis in order to enhance their immediate compensation and position. This problem is cultural and needs to be addressed by the country's political, business, and academic leadership.

Whatever the case, when looking to the future, an entrepreneur must also consider the past and present. By analyzing past and current business performance, insight can be gained into the forecasting function. Evaluating the firm's strengths and weaknesses relative to financial performance will set the stage for accurate projections. In addition, knowing the environmental conditions besetting the marketplace should play a significant role in the process of establishing forecasts.

Always plan at least five years into the future. Be flexible enough to allow for emergency situations that may or may not be anticipated (this is called "crisis planning"). For example, prior to the predicted gasoline crunch of 1979, Mayor Kelley of Ocean City, Maryland, which is a large eastern summer resort, stockpiled gas supplies and promised every visitor that he would have enough gas to get home. He saved the resort from financial disaster that year.

Failure to plan for the long haul will result in short-term adventurism, thereby misallocating the firm's limited resources and compromising greater profit potentials.

It is important to know every aspect of the business inside and out. Knowledge of what makes the firm tick and move can be valuable in successfully overcoming present and future problems. Good information resources and personal experiences can be used to gain this valuable insight.

Managing for Success

Management is a broad topic covering many different disciplines. It is impossible to discuss all facets of the subject in the confines of this book. However, the important managerial elements of running a small business must be highlighted.

MANAGING CASH AND CREDIT

Always remember that money is a commodity that is bought and sold for a price (interest rates). It is one of the most precious resources available to a business and requires effective management if the firm is to survive and prosper.

Send out invoices consistently and promptly at about the same time each month. The bills should contain all relevant information about the sale (date purchased, cost, account balance, terms, etc.). When income is received from receivables or cash sales, deposit it promptly in interest-bearing checking accounts or other insured accounts that can be drawn on readily. After paying obligations due, put the remaining cash back into the operation immediately so as to generate additional sales and profits. Having idle cash or money sitting in low-yielding accounts is ineffective money management.

Make sure that accounts receivable are current and take steps to keep them that way. Past dues can be costly if money must be borrowed or existing funds used to finance operations until accounts are collected. Therefore, credit and collection control procedures are critical to successful operation. Grant credit based upon certain conditions that may vary depending on the customer. This can be accomplished by evaluating potential accounts relative to their ability to pay. After that, payment terms and credit limits can be established. Also, existing accounts should be reviewed periodically in order to determine if changes in credit arrangements are necessary.

All prospective and existing accounts must be required to fill out a credit application form. The form should include a promise to pay according to the terms of the credit agreement and it can be used to investigate customers' credit history. Make sure the application has a release statement allowing permission to conduct a credit investigation.

If accounts are offered to customers, expect some problems to surface, especially during periods of economic recession. Normally, it is advisable and advantageous to work with slow payers instead of being overly rigid and maybe losing business as a result. Set up procedures for dealing with slow or delinquent accounts. Degrees of slowness should be established with the objective of applying increasing measures of pressure the longer the overdue remains unpaid. Extreme cases may have to be pursued legally. Many of these delinquent situations can be avoided if standards are developed and instituted to disallow existing or prospective customers from billing beyond their ability to repay.

When the business decides to use credit, always exercise conservatism and precedence. Pay bills on or before due dates so as to maintain a healthy credit history. A bad payment record can be expensive in terms of loss of credit privilege and higher interest charged by worried lenders. Take advantage of early payment discounts if they are economically favorable from a cash float standpoint (savings generated from the payment discount must be greater than the income that could be created by using the money in another way before the invoice is due).

In addition, maintaining good relations with all creditors, including bankers, can prove to be beneficial in the long run. Keep them informed as to what is happening with the business. Below are some tips that may help to accomplish this objective.

- Be candid about positive and negative situations. Many creditors will work with a business in a difficult environment if they are aware of the problems besetting the enterprise and its industry.

- Help the creditors to understand the business and industry. Sometimes ignorance is the biggest stumbling block to effective relationships.
- Provide some insight into management and control functions. This will gain the creditor's confidence and faith because it shows a willingness to make things operate smoothly and efficiently.
- Be specific about short-term, intermediate-term, long-term, and crisis planning. Creditors dislike unanticipated disruptions. Tell them when things are going to take place.

It is not necessary to incorporate the aforementioned tips into creditor relationships, but they will help relieve some of the natural and obvious tensions that exist between borrowers and creditors. An atmosphere of mutual trust and respect will also be fostered, leading to a lasting and growing relationship.

Managing Other Finances

Existing and prospective small-business owners should attempt to understand the financial complexities involved in business operations. A thorough understanding of financial statements (balance sheet, profit and loss statement, cash flow statement) will provide a solid foundation for making good business decisions. These statements, showing all revenue, expense, asset, and liability accounts, should be prepared and examined once a month by a competent accountant and reviewed by the firm's owner(s). Each account within the statements should be shown for the current period and the same period for last year. In addition, current year-to-date totals can be given for financial control purposes.

Good financial statements will also serve to contain costs. Studying past and present information concerning cost accounts may provide valuable insight into the conditions affecting expense figures. Also, an examination of revenue accounts may indicate the degree of product/service markup or markdown required to maintain adequate levels of sales and profits. It may show a need to alter existing lines through modification, new introductions, and/or phase-out.

Financial statements are discussed extensively in Chapter 7.

Managing Growth

Growing too fast can be as hazardous as a no-growth situation, if not more so. Growth must be implemented and managed carefully to ensure that the business does not expand beyond its ability to control and/or finance operations. Many firms have met with demise because of uncontrollable expansion. The giant W. T. Grant failed because it grew beyond its capability to finance expansion internally and externally. The result was bankruptcy.

Growth should be mapped out well in advance. Within these plans a reasonable estimation of resources necessary to carry out objectives must be evaluated and scrutinized to determine the feasibility of expansion. If resources will be lacking because of internal constraints and/or environmental factors, expansion objectives should be altered to meet with the realities of the situation.

Managing Inventory

Proper inventory management can mean the difference between profit or loss and in some cases survival. Excessive inventories will lock up needed cash that would otherwise be used to generate sales and profits.

If an inventory system is to be effective, its main objectives should be cost containment and efficient delivery. A study of purchase activity relative to finished goods and raw materials will need to be performed in order to accomplish these goals. Once the study and evaluation is completed, a minimum amount of inventory within each item and raw material classification can be stored to satisfy short-term customer orders. In addition, production can be maintained.

Below are some additional tips for addressing the inventory problem.

— Compare prices among suppliers.
— Purchasing should be controlled by one individual or department. Duplication of effort is a waste of time and money.
— All finished goods or raw material orders should be confirmed in writing, outlining every cost and condition, to avoid misunderstandings.
— When goods are delivered, check to make sure that everything is received in proper condition.
— Cross-reference the supplier's invoice with the written quotation. This will avoid overcharges.

Whatever inventory procedure is implemented, the cost of the endeavor must be less than its potential savings. Excessive inventory control can inflict the same harm as too little. A balance must be struck. The optimum solution is hard to find, but it is imperative if the business is to manage resources correctly.

There are complex statistical methods used to determine optimum inventory levels. Discussion of these is beyond the scope of this book. Therefore, seek out a competent business consultant when faced with inventory problems. Talking with other business owners who have faced similar difficulties may provide a wealth of helpful information. Also, seeking out college professors with specialties in the field of information sciences may prove to be useful in solving problems related to inventory control.

MANAGING MARKETS

All businesses survive based upon their ability to react to changes in market conditions and consumer tastes. If a business expects to prosper, it should be constantly monitoring trends that may provide opportunities if exploited or that may help avoid costly disasters. Expanding markets must be carefully evaluated against available resources to determine the possibility of further penetration or introduction. Stagnating markets require serious review if the business is involved. Can existing sales be maintained profitably? Is there any room for new sales? If so, why and how can they be achieved? Does the firm possess unique advantages allowing it to beat competition in stagnant markets? Declining markets are equally important to understand, especially when existing sales are at stake. Are sales holding firm or declining slower than the total market? Can further profits be squeezed out? When should market exit take place?

Addressing the reality of changing markets will help ensure continual existence and profitable operation. Constantly be aware of trends and try to determine how the business may be affected.

Exporting provides some of the greatest business opportunities over the next fifty years for all types of enterprises, both large and small. The United States has for the last eighty years been the largest market on the planet. And it still is at the moment. Many a nation of the world built its economy according to the tastes of the American consumer and industrial market.

Historically, this huge market has provided enough opportunity for U.S.–based businesses not to entertain exporting as a serious business opportunity, especially among small firms.

Even though the United States is the world's largest exporter in dollar terms, on a proportional economic size basis compared to other nations it is not the largest exporter. For example, Germany, with an economy approximately one-third the size of the U.S. economy, exports almost as much as the U.S. in absolute dollar amounts. In other words, exports impact their economy three times more than the U.S. economy.

What we do know is the following. Domestic market growth within the industrialized world (first world nations) is starting to slow in relation to other second and third world nations. Also, profit margins across a broad industrial and consumer scale within the first nations are beginning to shrink due to enhanced competitive pressures and slowing productivity.

Of course, we have not even addressed the more favorable tax and wage environment of these second and third world countries. That is why we have many U.S. businesses relocating to Latin America.

Business opportunities in other nations are beginning to look more promising than here in the domestic marketplace.

Simply put, export means employment to any nation. Consequently, many countries, including the United States, attempt to assist all types of firms, both large and small, to enter and succeed within the export market.

Appendix H provides a good brief on the mechanics of exporting, provided courtesy of the U.S. Department of Commerce. Also, the listing of various government agencies and authorities in Appendix B can assist you with exporting. Call or write. And do not overlook the state agencies. Although they differ in intent and intensity of assistance, many states have export programs that are as good as if not better than what is provided by the federal government, especially within certain industrial groupings.

For example, the State of Virginia has an excellent program for the export of agricultural commodities.

Managing People

Many business experts contend that people are a firm's most important resource. This reasoning revolves around the fact that labor is generally the largest expenditure faced by most businesses. Therefore, it would make economic sense to manage labor resources efficiently.

Periodically analyze and evaluate personnel requirements. Make sure there are enough people to get the job done. Failure to operate at demand capacity will result in lost opportunities and increased costs. If too many workers are employed, expenses will increase faster than sales or profits on a percentage basis, thereby suggesting a reduction in force. In addition, all positions within the business should be reviewed regularly to determine their relative importance and worth to the business. Time will constantly change perceptions. This job analysis may reveal such things as redundant effort, reduced work load, downtime, etc., that would justify employment cuts. It may be discovered that full-time positions should be reduced to part-time status. Generally, it is less costly to maintain two part-timers than one full-timer doing the same job, although there are hazards to this approach. Small businesses have enough problems attracting good help because of financial constraints. Emphasizing part-time positions too heavily may turn good employees or prospective candidates away.

Employment cutback decisions are difficult to make because of the human element involved. But remember, "It is better to rule from the head than to be dominated by the heart in a business situation." Employees singled out for cuts should be given ample warning. Try to assist them in finding new jobs. In addition, explaining the reasons for cuts to terminated and remaining employees will lessen the negative impact on morale.

It is also wise to develop a plan for absenteeism, which can be costly in terms of lost efficiency and the paying of overtime to someone else to perform the necessary work. For example, most absenteeism occurs on Monday which, of course, follows the weekend. One large company adopted a policy of distributing paychecks on Monday, and no-shows were reduced by 50 percent within two weeks of the decision. Another illustration explaining the effectiveness of a policy directed toward controlling absenteeism can be found in the Small Business Administration's management aid number 206, written by Jack H. Feller. It states that an owner/manager of one small company eliminated vacations and sick leave. Instead, this owner/manager gave each employee thirty days' annual leave to use as the employee saw fit. At the end of the year, the employees were paid at their regular rates for the leave they didn't use. To qualify for the year-end pay, the employee had to prove that sick leave was taken only for that purpose. Non-sick leave had to be applied for in advance. As a result, unscheduled absences and overtime pay were reduced significantly. In addition, employees were happier and more productive than they had been under the old system.

When approaching worker incentives, always recognize and compensate exceptional work and effort. Both monetary (money and fringes) and psychological (non-monetary benefits) rewards should be used to stimulate interest, productivity, and satisfaction. In addition, always try to involve employees in the management of the business. Seek out their advice and counsel. Many employees have ideas that may not be apparent to the owners and/or managers. Giving them a feeling of worth and allowing their input into the decision-making function will usually provide positive reinforcement for all concerned.

Keeping good records is also an important part of people management. It can also protect the business from unwarranted legal actions taken by disgruntled employees or governmental bodies. The firm should make all employees fill out applications that conform to federal government standards. Asking the wrong questions on the form can bring legal suit, but the procedure is necessary to ensure accurate information on employees. In addition, records concerning work history (absenteeism, sick leave, vacation time, promotion, demotion, salary/wage increases or decreases) should be verified by appropriate documentation. For example, use written appraisal forms when evaluating employees. Review the contents of the forms with workers and then ask them to sign the final appraisal documents. This will protect the firm in the event that certain employees pursue legal action because of the firm's reactions due to the results appearing on the appraisal form. Also, interviewing and asking exiting employees to sign an exit document outlining their reason for leaving can save the firm expenses incurred because of unjust unemployment insurance claims.

Businesses employing workers must have an in-depth knowledge of every job within the firm. First, a job analysis needs to be completed that attempts to identify the specific tasks within each position and how the particular jobs relate to their immediate environment. Table 24 contains a checklist for conducting a job analysis. Second, after the job analysis is performed, a description of each position must be written detailing the responsibilities and conditions of each position in the business. This job description, as it is called, is utilized for purposes of promoting, demoting, selecting, transferring, and training

TABLE 24

Summary/Review Checklist for Conducting a Job Analysis

____ 1. Gather data concerning the duties and qualifications of the job:
　　 ____ a. Think about the various duties, responsibilities, and qualifications of the job and write them down.
　　 ____ b. Utilize the job analysis outline form to help you organize your thoughts.
　　 ____ c. Ask an employee who now holds the job to list the duties and responsibilities of the job as well as the qualifications which he or she believes are needed.
　　 ____ d. Review the duties, responsibilities, and qualifications for the job with the person who supervises the job, if you are not doing that yourself directly.
　　 ____ e. Combine all job analysis notes to create a clear picture of the job.
____ 2. Keep in mind the ultimate goals of the analysis: to simplify and improve employee recruitment, training, and development; to evaluate jobs so that appropriate salary and wage rates can be set.

Source: U.S. Small Business Administration

existing or prospective employees. An outline of a job description appears in Table 25.

Third, job specifications must be developed and used to identify and describe the physical and mental qualifications needed to perform the tasks in question. Generally, this document will also outline the hazards inherent in these positions. Test requirements may also be included in order to evaluate the capabilities of existing or potential employees. The job specification procedure will protect the firm against legitimate discrimination decision. For example, the specification document might state that individuals over six feet tall are unsuitable for a particular task. Therefore, people exceeding six feet in height will probably be hard-pressed to bring suit unless they can prove that the job specification itself is flawed. An outline for writing a job specification is shown in Table 26. Fourth, a job classification system is needed to show how valuable various positions are to a business. This is determined by examining job complexities, duties, and contribution to the firm. Once this procedure is completed, pay scales are developed.

TABLE 25

Outline for Writing a Job Description

INSTRUCTIONS: Determine the positions for which you would like to write job descriptions. Remember that job descriptions are particularly useful in areas where job turnover is high, since they aid in recruitment, selection, and training of new employees. Now, complete the information below.

Job Description

Date: _____

JOB TITLE:

STATEMENT OF THE JOB
(A brief summary of the job, stating its general nature)

MAJOR DUTIES
(Including responsibilities for quantity and quality of work, safety of others, equipment, decisions to be made, and schedules to be met. Most jobs can be described in outline form with three to eight duties)

MINOR DUTIES
(Include those duties only performed occasionally)

RELATIONSHIPS
(Whom does a person in this position supervise? report to? work with?)

SOURCE: U.S. Small Business Administration

TABLE 26

Outline for Writing a Job Specification

INSTRUCTIONS: Determine the positions for which you would like to write job specifications. Remember that job specifications are particularly useful in areas where job turnover is high, since they aid recruitment, selection, and training of new employees. Now, complete the information below.

Job Specification

JOB TITLE: *Date:_____*

Education (List only that which is really necessary for the job, e.g., high school, college, trade schools, or other special training.)

Experience (The amount of previous and related experience which a new employee should have.)

Knowledge/Skills (List the specific knowledge and skills which the job may require.)

Physical and Mental Requirements (Mention any special physical or mental abilities required for the job, e.g., 20/20 eyesight, ability to lift 80 lb, bags, availability for irregular work hours, ability to work under time pressure, etc.)

SOURCE: U.S. Small Business Administration

Many employers are learning the benefits of conducting orientation programs for new employees. Their purpose should be to familiarize new workers with the firm and their work environment. The objective is to reduce early turnovers, which can be a costly business expense. Generally, most firms do not begin to recover their cost of maintaining new inexperienced employees until after the first six months of employment. Unfortunately, this is when the greatest amount of turnover takes place. Most is due to misunderstandings or lack of communication between the firm and new workers. It may result in employees feeling out of place and/or overwhelmed. Involuntary termination or voluntary departure normally follows suit. Table 27 contains a checklist for establishing a job orientation program.

TABLE 27

JOB ORIENTATION CHECKLIST

____ Explain:
    ____ company purpose
    ____ company image
    ____ kind of clients catered to
____ Introduce to other employees and positions
____ Explain relationship between new employee's position and other positions
____ Tour the building:
    ____ working areas
    ____ management office
    ____ rest facilities
    ____ records
    ____ employee locker room or closet
    ____ other relevant areas
____ Explain facilities and equipment
____ Review the duties and responsibilities of the job from the job description

____ Introduce to emergency equipment and safety procedures
____ Questions and answers

SOURCE: U.S. Small Business Administration

MANAGING PRODUCTS/SERVICES

Those products or services offering the greatest potential for sales and/or profits should be given highest priority in the marketing effort. Individual items or services being sold should have enough markup to cover all costs associated with it, including handling, warranties, and servicing arrangements, plus an adequate profit margin.

Products and services travel through "life cycles" and most will become less appealing to the marketplace as time passes on. Therefore, it is essential that business owners be constantly aware of changing conditions and customer tastes. Modify existing lines when necessary and move into new product or service areas when market forces demand to shift. Look at insurance companies today. A decade ago "whole life" policies were in style and now they won't sell. Inflation made them obsolete because of their low dividend yields on the cash values built into the policies. Consequently, the insurance industry has replaced the "whole life" concept with what is called "universal life," which pays higher yields on the cash values. Incidentally, "whole life" policies can still be purchased, but the primary marketing thrust, on the part of many insurance companies, has been directed to "universal life."

MANAGING RISK

Understanding risk is an important aspect of running any business. Some experts contend that an adequate insurance program designed to reduce risk is just as vital to the success of a firm as are other business functions. Without question, assets left unprotected could compromise the future existence of the business if loss occurred. Therefore, a sound risk-reduction plan should be implemented and carefully managed to ensure economic viability in the event of loss due to unanticipated events.

The items listed below should be considered by all existing business owners and prospective entrepreneurs thinking about purchasing a small enterprise.

- Determine how loss may occur—Recognizing the probability of loss is the initial step in understanding risk. Realistic appraisal is a must in order to protect the firm's assets and livelihood.
- Seek professional advice—Talk to agents employed by insurance companies and independent agents representing different companies. Ask for their assistance in determining insurance needs. To determine the credibility of the agents, request references and check them out. In addition, talking to other business owners may provide reliable agent contacts.
- Shop around for the best buy—Insurance products are subject to competitive forces; therefore, prices will differ among companies. Following a few simple rules will help to reduce the cost of carrying insurance coverage.
- Identify risks and the potential for loss.
- Structure an insurance program—A formalized plan outlining all aspects of the insurance program should be set forth for management purposes.

Cost

Following a few simple rules will help reduce the cost of carrying insurance coverage.

- Identify risks and the potential for loss.
- Insure the largest risk factor initially.
- Try to use deductibles. High deductibles will reduce insurance costs.
- Eliminate all overlapping insurance coverage. It is a waste of money, since most companies share the burden of loss as opposed to the owner getting extra coverage.
- Purchase insurance in large units, if possible. Avoid many small policies, since they tend to be more expensive for the same coverage.
- Some insurance companies sell consolidated policies incorporating all coverage into one central agreement. In addition, many professional and trade associations have insurance products at discount group rates.
- Always evaluate the firm's risk exposure on a timely and regular basis for purposes of upgrading or downgrading. This will give you

adequate coverage at reasonable cost, and, in some cases, phase out protection that has become unnecessary.

Structuring Your Insurance Plan

Your insurance plan may include, but is not limited to, the following procedures:

- State the objective of the insurance plan.
- Try to deal with only one agent, if possible. Dealing with several may create confusion and disinformation.
- Assign responsibility for the program to one individual.
- Prevent or minimize losses through safety and inspection procedures.
- State the potential for loss candidly. Failure to acquire needed coverage because of disinformation can be a threat to the viability of the firm.
- All risks should be covered no matter how small the chance for loss. Avoid underestimation of asset value to save money. If loss does occur, the firm may not recover its investment.
- Periodically, evaluate the insurance program to determine the need for modification. Some risk programs have automatic cost-of-living increases built in to protect against loss caused by increasing asset value due to inflation. All assets should be appraised occasionally to determine insurance requirements.
- Always maintain adequate records concerning the risk-reduction program. This information may be helpful later when attempting to change or modify coverage.

The following insurance checklist is provided courtesy of the U.S. Small Business Administration; it was written by Professor Mark R. Greene. It is designed to provide insight into the insurance needs of small businesses.

Points reviewed in the checklist are classified into three groups. They are as follows: essential coverage, desirable but nonessential coverage, and employee coverage. After reading each statement, place a check under the column entitled "No action needed" if the statement and how it affects the insurance plan is understood. If it isn't, check the column entitled "Look into this." After completing the study, evaluate existing and/or prospective insurance coverage, keeping in mind the points covered in the checklist. Discuss any problems or concerns with an agent.

ESSENTIAL COVERAGE

Four kinds of insurance are essential: fire, liability, automobile, and workers' compensation. In some areas and in some kinds of businesses, crime insurance, which is discussed under "Desirable Coverages," is also essential.

Are you certain that all the following points have been given full consideration in your insurance program?

	No Action Needed	Look Into This
Fire Insurance		
1. You can add other perils—such as windstorm, hail, smoke, explosion, vandalism, and malicious mischief—to your basic fire insurance at a relatively small additional cost.	—	—
2. If you need comprehensive coverage, your best buy may be one of the all-risk contracts that offer the broadest available protection for the money.	—	—
3. The insurance company may indemnify you—that is, compensate you for your losses—in any one of several ways: (1) It may pay actual cash value of the property at the time of loss. (2) It may repair or replace the property with material of like kind and quality. (3) It may take all the property at the agreed or appraised value and reimburse you for your loss.	—	—
4. You can insure property you don't own. You must have an insurable interest—a financial interest—in the property when a loss occurs but not necessarily at the time the insurance contract is made. For instance, a repair shop or dry cleaning plant may carry insurance on customers' property in the shop, or a person holding a mortgage on a building may insure the building although he or she doesn't own it.	—	—

5. When you sell property, you cannot assign the insurance policy along with the property unless you have permission from the insurance company.   ____   ____

6. Even if you have several policies on your property, you can still collect only the amount of your actual cash loss. All the insurers share the payment proportionately. Suppose, for example, that you are carrying two policies—one for $20,000 and one for $30,000—on a $40,000 building, and fire causes damage to the building amounting to $12,000. The $20,000 policy will pay $4,800; that is   ____   ____

$\frac{20,000}{50,000}$, or $\frac{2}{5}$, of $12,000. The $30,000 policy will pay $7,200; which is $\frac{30,000}{50,000}$ or $\frac{3}{5}$, of $12,000.

7. Special protection other than the standard fire policy is needed to cover the loss by fire of accounts, bills, currency, deeds, evidences of debt, and money and securities.   ____   ____

8. If an insured building is vacant or unoccupied for more than 60 consecutive days, coverage is suspended unless you have a special endorsement to your policy canceling this provision.   ____   ____

9. If, either before or after a loss, you conceal or misrepresent to the insurer any material fact or circumstance concerning your insurance or the interest of the insured, the policy may be voided.   ____   ____

10. If you increase the hazard of fire, the insurance company may suspend your coverage even for losses not originating from the increased hazard. (An example of such a hazard might be renting part of your building to a dry cleaning plant.)   ____   ____

11. After a loss, you must use all reasonable means to protect the property from further loss or run the risk of having your coverage canceled.

12. To recover your loss, you must furnish within 60 days (unless an extension is granted by the insurance company) a complete inventory of the damaged, destroyed, and undamaged property, showing in detail quantities, costs, actual cash value, and amount of loss claimed.

13. If you and the insurer disagree on the amount of loss, the question may be resolved through special appraisal procedures provided for in the fire-insurance policy.

14. You may cancel your policy without notice at any time and get part of the premium returned. The insurance company also may cancel at any time with a 5-day written notice to you.

15. By accepting a coinsurance clause in your policy, you get a substantial reduction in premiums. A coinsurance clause states that you must carry insurance equal to 80 or 90 percent of the value of the insured property. If you carry less than this, you cannot collect the full amount of your loss, even if the loss is small. What percent of your loss you can collect will depend on what percent of the full value of the property you have insured it for.

16. If your loss is caused by someone else's negligence, the insurer has the right to sue this negligent third party for the amount it has paid you under the policy. This is known as the insurer's right of subrogation. However, the insurer will usually waive this right upon request. For example, if you have leased your insured building to someone and have waived your right to recover from the tenant for any insured damages to your property,

	No	*Look*
	Action	*Into*
	Needed	*This*

you should have your agent request the insurer to waive the subrogation clause in the fire policy on your leased building. ___ ___

17. A building under construction can be insured for fire, lightning, extended coverage, vandalism, and malicious mischief. ___ ___

Liability Insurance

1. Legal liability limits of $1 million are no longer considered high or unreasonable even for a small business. ___ ___

2. Most liability policies require you to notify the insurer immediately after an incident on your property that might cause a future claim. This holds true no matter how unimportant the incident may seem at the time it happens. ___ ___

3. Most liability policies, in addition to covering bodily injuries, may now cover personal injuries (libel, slander, and so on), if these are specifically insured. ___ ___

4. Under certain conditions, your business may be subject to damage claims even from trespassers. ___ ___

5. You may be legally liable for damages even in cases where you used "reasonable care." ___ ___

6. Even if the suit against you is false or fraudulent, the liability insurer pays court costs, legal fees, and interest on judgments in addition to the liability judgments themselves. ___ ___

7. You can be liable for the acts of others under contracts you have signed with them. This liability is insurable. ___ ___

8. In some cases you may be held liable for fire loss to property of others in your care. Yet, this property would normally not be covered by your fire or general

liability insurance. This risk can be covered by fire
legal liability insurance or through requesting subrogation waivers from insurers of owners of the property.   ____   ____

Automobile Insurance

1. When an employee or a subcontractor uses his own
car on your behalf, you can be legally liable even if you
don't own a car or truck yourself.   ____   ____

2. Five or more automobiles or motorcycles under one
ownership and operated as a fleet for business purposes
can generally be insured under a low-cost fleet policy
against both material damage to your vehicle and
liability to others for property damage or personal
injury.   ____   ____

3. You can often get deductibles of almost any
amount—say $250 or $500—and thereby reduce your
premiums.   ____   ____

4. Automobile medical-payments insurance pays for
medical claims, including your own, arising from
automobile accidents regardless of the question of
negligence.   ____   ____

5. In most states, you must carry liability insurance or
be prepared to provide other proof (surety bond) of
financial responsibility when you are involved in an
accident.   ____   ____

6. You can purchase uninsured-motorist protection to
cover your own bodily-injury claims from someone
who has no insurance.   ____   ____

7. Personal property stored in an automobile and not
attached to it (for example, merchandise being delivered) is not covered under an automobile policy.   ____   ____

Workers' Compensation

1. Common law requires that an employer (1) provide
his employees a safe place to work, (2) hire competent

	No Action Needed	Look Into This

fellow employees, (3) provide safe tools, and (4) warn his employees of an existing danger. ___ ___

2. If an employer fails to provide the above, under both common law and workers' compensation laws he is liable for damage suits brought by an employee. ___ ___

3. State law determines the level or types of benefits payable under workers' compensation policies. ___ ___

4. Not all employees are covered by workers' compensation laws. The exceptions are determined by state law and therefore vary from state to state. ___ ___

5. In nearly all states, you are not legally required to cover your workers under workers' compensation. ___ ___

6. You can save money on workers' compensation insurance by seeing that your employees are properly classified. ___ ___

7. Rates for workers' compensation insurance vary from 0.1 percent of the payroll for "safe" occupations to about 25 percent or more of the payroll for very hazardous occupations. ___ ___

8. Most employers in most states can reduce their workers' compensation premium cost by reducing their accident rates below the average. They do this by using safety and loss-prevention measures. ___ ___

DESIRABLE COVERAGES

Some types of insurance coverage, while not absolutely essential, will add greatly to the security of your business. These coverages include business interruption insurance, crime insurance, glass insurance, and rent insurance.

Business Interruption Insurance

1. You can purchase insurance to cover fixed expenses that would continue if a fire shut down your business— such as salaries to key employees, taxes, interest,

| | *No Action Needed* | *Look Into This* |

depreciation, and utilities—as well as the profits you would lose.   ___   ___

2. Under properly written contingent business interruption insurance, you can also collect if fire or other peril closes down the business of a supplier or customer and this interrupts your business.   ___   ___

3. The business interruption policy provides payments for amounts you spend to hasten the reopening of your business after a fire or other insured peril.   ___   ___

4. You can get coverage for the extra expenses you suffer if an insured peril, while not actually closing your business down, seriously disrupts it.   ___   ___

5. When the policy is properly endorsed, you can get business interruption insurance to indemnify you if your operations are suspended because of failure or interruption of the supply of power, light, heat, gas, or water furnished by a public utility company.   ___   ___

Crime Insurance

1. Burglary insurance excludes such property as accounts, articles in a showcase window, and manuscripts.   ___   ___

2. Coverage is granted under burglary insurance only if there are visible marks of the burglar's forced entry.   ___   ___

3. Burglary insurance can be written to cover, in addition to money in a safe, inventoried merchandise and damage incurred in the course of a burglary.   ___   ___

4. Robbery insurance protects you from loss of property, money, and securities by force, trickery, or threat of violence on or off your premises.   ___   ___

5. A comprehensive crime policy written just for small businesses is available. In addition to burglary and robbery, it covers other types of loss by theft, destruc-

	No Action Needed	*Look Into This*

tion, and disappearance of money and securities. It also covers thefts by your employees. ___ ___

6. If you are in a high-risk area and cannot get insurance through normal channels without paying excessive rates, you may be able to get help through the federal crime insurance plan. Your agent or state insurance commissioner can tell you where to get information about these plans. ___ ___

Glass Insurance

1. You can purchase a special glass insurance policy that covers all risk to plate-glass windows, glass signs, motion-picture screens, glass brick, glass doors, show-cases, countertops, and insulated glass panels. ___ ___

2. The glass insurance policy covers not only the glass itself, but also its lettering and ornamentation, if these are specifically insured, and the costs of temporary plates or boarding up when necessary. ___ ___

3. After the glass has been replaced, full coverage is continued without any additional premium for the period covered. ___ ___

Rent Insurance

1. You can buy rent insurance that will pay your rent if the property you lease becomes unusable because of fire or other insured perils and your lease calls for continued payments in such a situation. ___ ___

2. If you own property and lease it to others, you can insure against loss if the lease is canceled because of fire and you have to rent the property again at a reduced rental. ___ ___

EMPLOYEE BENEFIT COVERAGES

Insurance coverages that can be used to provide employee benefits include group life insurance, group health insurance, disability insurance, and retirement income. Key-man insurance protects the company against financial loss caused by the death of a valuable employee or partner.

	No Action Needed	Look Into This

Group Life Insurance

1. If you pay group-insurance premiums and cover all employees up to $50,000, the cost to you is deductible for federal income-tax purposes, and yet the value of the benefit is not taxable income to your employees.   ——   ——

2. Most insurers will provide group coverages at low rates even if there are 10 or fewer employees in your group.   ——   ——

3. If the employees pay part of the cost of the group insurance, state laws require that 75 percent of them must elect coverage for the plan to qualify as group insurance.   ——   ——

4. Group plans permit an employee leaving the company to convert the group-insurance coverage to a private plan, at the rate for his or her age, without a medical exam if he or she does so within 30 days after leaving the job.   ——   ——

Group Health Insurance

1. Group health insurance costs much less and provides more generous benefits for the worker than individual contracts would.   ——   ——

2. If you pay the entire cost, individual employees cannot be dropped from a group plan unless the entire group policy is canceled.   ——   ——

3. Generous programs of employee benefits, such as group health insurance, tend to reduce labor turnover.   ——   ——

Disability Insurance

1. Workers' compensation insurance pays an employee only for time lost because of work injuries and work-related sickness, not for time lost because of disabilities incurred off the job. But you can purchase, at a low

	No Action Needed	Look Into This

premium, insurance to replace the lost income of workers who suffer short-term or long-term disability not related to their work. ___ ___

2. You can get coverage that provides employees with an income for life in case of permanent disability resulting from work-related sickness or accident. ___ ___

Retirement Income

1. If you are self-employed, you can get an income tax deduction for funds used for retirement for you and your employees through plans of insurance or annuities approved for use under the Employees Retirement Income Security Act of 1974 (ERISA). ___ ___

2. Annuity contracts may provide for variable payments in the hope of giving the annuitants some protection against the effects of inflation. Whether fixed or variable, an annuity can provide retirement income that is guaranteed for life. ___ ___

Key-Man Insurance

1. One of the most serious setbacks that can come to a small company is the loss of a key man or woman. But your key person can be insured with life insurance and disability insurance owned by and payable to your company. ___ ___

2. Proceeds of a key-man policy are not subject to income tax, but premiums are not a deductible business expense. ___ ___

3. The cash value of key-man insurance, which accumulates as an asset of the business, can be borrowed against, and the interest and dividends are not subject to income tax as long as the policy remains in force. ___ ___

MANAGING TAXES

Prospective entrepreneurs and existing business owners must realize the importance of paying and managing their tax liabilities. Improper use of taxes due can be costly in terms of penalties imposed by state, local, and federal revenue agencies, not to mention the time involved in audits that will surely ensue. Effective management of tax obligations entails the following major points.

— Know the degree of tax liability in reference to the taxes imposed, their dollar amounts, and when they are due.
— Make sure that funds are available to pay the tax obligations.
— Always pay on or before the due date to avoid costly late-payment charges, which can exceed 25 percent of the amount due in some cases.
— Seek competent tax advice from an expert in the field (CPA or tax attorney).

Below is a list of taxes that a business owner may expect to face when running an operation.

— Federal income tax
— State income tax
— Local income tax
— Social Security tax
— Federal unemployment tax
— State unemployment tax
— Excise taxes
— State sales tax
— Local sales tax

Types and amounts of taxes will vary depending upon many factors such as line of business, state residency, and profitability, to mention but a few. For example, five state governments do not have income taxes imposed on business profits.

Taxes are normally paid on a periodic basis to the various government agencies. Payments are accompanied with a form supplied by the governing body. Check with the agency responsible for the collection of taxes to determine payment procedures. Table 28 contains a worksheet that can be used by a business when analyzing and computing tax obligations.

TABLE 28

Kind of Tax	Due Date	Amount Due	Pay To	Date For Writing The Check
FEDERAL TAXES				
Employee Income Tax and Social Security Tax	_____	_____	_____	_____
	_____	_____	_____	_____
	_____	_____	_____	_____
	_____	_____	_____	_____
Excise Tax	_____	_____	_____	_____
Owner-Manager's and/or Corporation's Income Tax	_____	_____	_____	_____
	_____	_____	_____	_____
	_____	_____	_____	_____
	_____	_____	_____	_____
Unemployment Tax	_____	_____	_____	_____
	_____	_____	_____	_____
	_____	_____	_____	_____
	_____	_____	_____	_____
STATE TAXES				
Unemployment Taxes	_____	_____	_____	_____
	_____	_____	_____	_____
	_____	_____	_____	_____
	_____	_____	_____	_____
Income Taxes	_____	_____	_____	_____
Sales Taxes	_____	_____	_____	_____
	_____	_____	_____	_____
	_____	_____	_____	_____
	_____	_____	_____	_____
Franchise Tax	_____	_____	_____	_____
Other	_____	_____	_____	_____
	_____	_____	_____	_____
	_____	_____	_____	_____
	_____	_____	_____	_____
LOCAL TAXES				
Sales Tax	_____	_____	_____	_____
	_____	_____	_____	_____
	_____	_____	_____	_____
	_____	_____	_____	_____
Real Estate Tax	_____	_____	_____	_____
Personal Property Tax	_____	_____	_____	_____
Licenses (retail, vending machine, etc.)	_____	_____	_____	_____
Other	_____	_____	_____	_____
	_____	_____	_____	_____

MANAGING PROBLEMS

A good manager has been defined as an individual with the ability to solve potential problems before they become real problems and threaten the business. Most management experts agree that solving difficulties should be a sequential process involving a number of specific procedures. They are listed below.

- *Define the problem.* The problem must be clearly stated and understood. An evaluation concerning the direct and indirect effects of the difficulty must be made. Problem identification is the single largest stumbling block to effective decision making. Also, the unwillingness or inability to deal with difficulties once apparent will greatly impede progress toward goal attainment.
- *Make an initial investigation.* This stage attempts to obtain a concise definition of the problem and its potential ramifications.
- *Identify and select alternative courses of action.* Several plans should be developed with the objective of defusing the problem or minimizing its impact.
- *Collect relevant data.* Information in relation to each course of action must be collected, organized, and evaluated to determine which one is the suitable solution. Statistical analysis is often used in this stage.
- *Select the Alternative.* Once the optimum alternative is identified it should be officially adopted as the solution to the problem.
- *Implement the course of action.* Put the solution into effect.
- *Evaluate the course of action taken.* Periodic examination of the action implemented is needed in order to determine its effectiveness. Evaluation may reveal a need for modification of the existing alternative or the employment of a new course of action.

The experiences gained and recorded by using problem-solving procedures and solutions will help to develop and refine the decision-making abilities of owners/managers.

Decision Making Is Necessary

When the time comes for decision making, business owners and managers should not procrastinate. Hesitation is one of the foremost reasons for missed opportunities and the assumption of unreasonable costs. This is not to say that an owner should react without due consideration. On the contrary, when lacking appropriate information, it may be a good idea to delay a decision, but dangers and opportunities may still present themselves. The delayed decision must be weighed against the potential losses due to inaction.

The optimum solution is to have reliable and accurate information available at all times. This will help to avoid the unpleasant situation of making decisions using inadequate data or taking no action at all.

Knowing When to Seek Advice

When the need for outside assistance becomes apparent, get it immediately without hesitation. Delay can be costly, especially if problems grow to the point of unmanageability. Also, avoid being egotistical and trying to solve insurmountable problems without assistance or by utilizing limited in-house staff. Businesses that are both large and small occasionally need the help of outside expertise when facing environmental or internal problems. Sources of professional assistance are discussed in Chapter 3.

10

IMPORTANT CONSIDERATIONS
Before Venturing

Cover the Bases

Every prospective or practicing entrepreneur must consider and evaluate certain critical elements before starting or, in some cases, relocating operations. Failure to do so could lead to disastrous consequences. It is impossible to discuss all the different small businesses relative to these important features within the confines of this book. Therefore, the four major categories of business classification (retail, wholesale, service, and manufacturing) will be used as a means of broad comparison.

Table 29 shows which elements should be considered by the various business categories. An asterisk (*) means evaluation is definitely necessary while an (X) means some critical analysis is needed. Blanks indicate little or no relationship.

CAPITAL

All businesses must be concerned that an adequate amount of capital is available to begin and support operations. Service firms, by their very nature, are generally less capital intensive than other types of businesses. Therefore, they can operate on the proverbial shoestring.

Capital needs are discussed extensively in Chapter 5.

Table 29

ELEMENTS TO CONSIDER BEFORE VENTURING

	Retail	Wholesale	Service	Manufacturing
1. Capital	*	*	X	*
2. Channels of Distribution		X		*
3. Climate	X			*
4. Competition	*	*	*	*
5. Credit Policies	*	*	*	*
6. Delivery	X	*		*
7. Demographics	*	*	*	*
8. Economic Climate	*	*	*	*
9. Financial Control	*	*	*	*
10. Government Regulation	X	*	X	*
11. Industry Trends	*	*	*	*
12. Inflation	*	*	*	*
13. International Events	X	X		*
14. Labor	*	*	*	*
15. Licenses	X	*	X	*
16. Location	*	*		*
17. Market Research	*	*	*	*
18. Operations Policy	*	*	*	*
19. Pricing	*	*	*	*
20. Product/Service	*	*	*	*
21. Raw Materials				*
22. Research & Development				*
23. Service	*	*	X	*
24. State of Technology	X	X	X	*
25. Storage	X	*		*
26. Topography	X	*	X	*
27. Trade Credit	*	*		*
28. Vendors (Suppliers)	*	*	X	*
29. Warranties	*	*	*	*

CHANNELS OF DISTRIBUTION

Most manufacturers must worry about getting their products in the hands of consumers. In many cases, this is accomplished through the use of intermediaries, which are commonly referred to as "middlemen." These intermediaries are links in a channel of distribution and help move the product to its destination. Wholesalers must also be concerned with this matter because many employ middlemen known as agents and brokers to facilitate the flow of their products to retailers. Service businesses should not be overly concerned with channels of distribution since most services are performed by the originator. Some businesses franchise their operations to achieve growth. In these cases, the franchisee would serve as the distributor for the franchisor.

Below are listed the more common channels of distribution:

— Manufacturer-Wholesaler-Retailer-Customer
— Manufacturer-Broker-Wholesaler-Retailer-Customer
— Manufacturer-Broker-Agent-Wholesaler-Retailer-Customer
— Manufacturer-Broker-Jobber-Wholesaler-Retailer-Customer
— Manufacturer-Broker-Retailer-Customer
— Manufacturer-Jobber-Retailer-Customer
— Service Originator-Customer
— Service Originator-Agent-Customer

Many products and industries have standardized channels of distribution that have been used for years. Some companies mistakenly think they can reduce costs and increase profits by eliminating middlemen. Most firms that attempt to do this fail in their efforts. Always remember that intermediaries are specialists in their fields and they know the ropes. Consequently, they are cost effective to use even though they charge commissions and represent an added link in the channel. The only way a company can make money by eliminating these organizations is to gain the necessary expertise and apply it better than the middlemen being replaced. A few large discount chains have accomplished this feat.

CLIMATE

Some manufacturing and retailing establishments must consider the effects of climatic conditions on their business. Failure to do so could be detrimental to profitable operations. For example, some years ago the Del Monte Corporation built a large pineapple cannery in Mexico on a river. The fruit groves were located upriver. During picking season the fruit was to be barged downriver to the cannery for processing and shipment. Management failed to consider one very important point and it was a costly mistake. The river's flood stage and picking season just so happened at the same time. Consequently, the river could not support barge movement and the factory was never used. Millions of dollars were lost due to failure to consider the climate's effect on operations.

Retail firms can also be affected by climate. Stores and shops located along coastal resorts can be adversely affected if unseasonably cold weather grips their areas for a season or two. Likewise, retail businesses in winter resorts can experience the same fate if a warmer than normal winter occurs.

Wholesaling and servicing enterprises are not affected by weather as compared to the aforementioned. Wholesalers sell to retailers and, therefore, it is the retailer's responsibility to get the product to the ultimate customer. Service firms normally take the product directly to the customer, thereby minimizing the impact of weather on a potential customer. For example, an electrician or plumber will work rain or shine. Of course, extreme weather conditions can stymie any operation.

COMPETITION

The impact of competition is important to any business operation. The degree and strength of competitive forces within a particular market should be considered and evaluated very carefully to determine the effects on existing or prospective endeavors. Is there room for another seller? If the market is crowded with competitors, can an enterprise with exceptional management skills survive or prosper, forcing other, less efficient firms to concede market share?

More details concerning competitive factors can be found in Chapter 7.

CREDIT POLICIES

Most businesses are forced to give customers credit privileges because of competitive forces within most markets. A standardized credit policy is a must in order to establish uniformity and minimize the possibility of credit discrimination. In addition, it will establish procedures for granting credit and collecting past dues. A good policy will facilitate the entire credit function. More insight about credit can be gained by referring to Chapter 9.

Delivery

Product delivery is a primary concern for wholesale and manufacturing operations. These organizations must deliver their products to the appropriate link in the channel of distribution in order to ultimately sell the goods. Some retail firms, such as mail order companies, are also involved in the process of delivery, although to a much lesser extent than the previously mentioned types of business. Service companies normally do not worry about delivery, since services are delivered when performed. There are exceptions. For example, consulting firms, research firms, photocopy centers, etc., may be involved in the delivery of various papers and reports.

Demographics

All businesses must be concerned with the characteristics of the marketplace they are trying to exploit. An understanding of demographics will help accomplish this by classifying the total market into various segments. This is called market segmentation. The most common classifications are listed below:

— Age
— Income
— Geographic Area
— Marital Status
— Religion
— Sex
— Occupation

Economic Climate

The systematic risk inherent in the overall economy will affect all businesses. Having an idea when recessions will occur can help ensure proper preparation and thus defense against the impact of economic downturns. It is interesting to note the number of companies that fail to take heed of a recession's warning signals and fall victim. Businesses that are on guard normally weather the storm, and some even prosper.

Below are listed the most common recession signals:

— Interest rates steadily rising. (When short-term rates exceed long-term rates it is called an "inversion" and a recession will generally follow suit.)

—Economic output falling
—Corporate profits falling
—Leading economic indicators constantly down
—Consumer and business confidence constantly negative
—Business inventories consistently rising

Most of these statistics are reported monthly in a government publication known as *The Survey of Current Business*, available at many libraries or directly from the Department of Commerce. Their addresses are listed in Appendix B.

FINANCIAL CONTROL

Maintaining financial control of a business is contingent upon managing resources so as to generate adequate profit levels. The management of physical, financial, and intangible assets would fall in this category. Chapter 9 deals with this subject in depth.

GOVERNMENT REGULATION

Local, state, and federal government regulations affect all businesses, both large and small, costing the U.S. business community approximately $175 billion per year. Even though the larger firms tend to be watched more closely, small firms are expected to abide by all codes and statutes. Writing to government agencies and requesting information on laws affecting a particular line of business would be wise.

INDUSTRY TRENDS

All businesses must be concerned with events taking place within their industries. Even though the overall economy is recovering from the recession, many industries are failing to respond. Some will never regain their former strength, and a few will slowly die. The service industries have, for the most part, been unaffected by economic downturns. In fact, services, which now account for 60 percent of the nation's output, will climb to 80 percent of economic activity by the end of the 1990s.

Checking activities with a particular industry in question will help gain insight into the dynamic forces working to strengthen, stagnate, or weaken performance in that area.

Inflation

Inflation affects all businesses. Initially, the results of rising inflation are quite positive, with sales and profits increasing, although much of the increase is artificial. For example, if a business achieves a 10 percent return on investment (ROI) one year and inflation for that same period runs at 8 percent, the firm has only realized a 2 percent gain on its investment, although most companies would report a 10 percent increase. Many establishments actually base expansion plans on inflated figures and later down the pike experience a capital squeeze because (inflation-adjusted) accounting records were not used to make the decision.

All financial and accounting records should reflect the damage caused by inflation. Failure to do so could lead to disaster. In addition, high levels of inflation (exceeding 10 percent per year) generally cause recessions. So inflation can be viewed as an indicator of future economic vitality. Conversely, lower levels of inflation (2 to 4 percent) are considered good for the economy. An economic system experiencing either no inflation or deflation (declining price levels) is thought to be in serious trouble.

International Events

Whether or not it is a popular nation, the United States has joined the world economic community out of necessity because of resource dependency. Consequently, the American economy is subject to forces beyond the immediate control of domestic leaders. Some lines of business are more affected than others. A knowledge of international forces that may do harm to particular industries and firms will help to ensure survivability if negative events occur. For example, what should petroleum retailers and wholesalers do if war in the Middle East causes a major disruption in oil supplies? How can American automobile manufacturers and dealers respond to the ever-increasing tide of foreign competition?

Much has been said about the inability of American manufacturers to compete with more efficient and productive foreign counterparts. This is largely true, and domestic producers will have to respond in order to survive. On the other hand, retailers and wholesalers may be affected only temporarily due to overseas competition, because they can always change to more marketable foreign competition since most nations haven't concentrated upon exporting services as of this date. In fact, the service sector is considered an area where American firms could compete successfully in the international marketplace.

LABOR

All firms must have adequate human resources available to support operations. A manufacturing firm should be concerned that a particular location has enough skilled, semiskilled, and managerial talent. Businesses offering technical services may be interested in the number of qualified technical personnel who could be hired in a given location.

Firms failing to consider the implications of inadequate labor supply before starting or relocating operations will suffer the additional cost of attracting needed individuals located outside the immediate area of operation.

LICENSES

Most local and state agencies require business establishments to apply for any number of licenses. In addition, many want payment of a flat and/or percentage of estimated sales fee before granting permits. Requirements vary from one area to another. Larger concerns may need federal permits. For example, a license must be acquired from the U.S. Department of Commerce before a firm may engage in export activities.

Small firms should check with the local clerk of the court. He/she will have information concerning any local, state, or federal licensing requirements for particular types of businesses.

LOCATION

It is important for manufacturing businesses to be located near their markets. Transportation costs can be minimized. Some manufacturers may also decide to locate in the vicinity of their needed raw materials. For example, steel mills in Pennsylvania are located near large coal deposits which are critical to the steel-making process. Transportation charges for coal are astronomical, thereby necessitating a location near the source of the raw material. Wholesaling firms normally attempt to spread out their distribution facilities to be near as many of their retail customers as possible. Retail establishments want to locate where traffic flow is adequate to support operations. Specialty retail stores need not worry to the same degree because customers will make special efforts to obtain items of specific characteristics and quality. Finally, only those service firms that provide in-house services need not worry about location. When the customer must come to the place of business, location can be of prime importance.

Market Research

Market research is necessary to determine whether a product or service can be successfully sold. This research, if conducted properly, will reveal the threats inherent in the marketplace as well as any opportunities that may exist. Many small businesses fail because managers failed to consider the impact of competitive forces and overestimated customer base. Market research will address these weaknesses.

Chapter 7 addresses the topic of market research extensively.

Operations Policy

An operations policy explains the procedures to follow in maintaining effective operations. Generally, the need for operations policy increases as a firm grows. It is not surprising to find many small retail or service businesses operating efficiently without an operations policy, although they probably maintain at least an employee policy to ensure compliance with employment laws.

The standard operations policy should include a description of key functions within the business and who is in charge of each. An organizational chart would normally be part of the policy manual, along with a description of responsibilities and spans of control to reduce administrative overlap. Standard operating procedures (SOPs) would be established for each function. A statement relating to events not covered by SOPs is generally incorporated with policy to reduce confusion if an exceptional situation were to occur.

Pricing

All businesses must worry about pricing their products and services. After all, the prices chosen will affect a firm's ability to successfully compete. Price setting can be a complicated task. Many things need to be considered carefully. For example, if the product/ service is new, a higher price can normally be set. Conversely, strong competitive forces within the market would force a lower price. Pricing strategy should also be integrated with long-term goals. A "skimming" price policy means that a firm is setting a high price in order to achieve large profit margins. However, a lower market share is achieved. Consequently, when competitors enter the field, the ability to survive will be in question due to a thin customer base. On the other hand, a "penetration" policy sets a lower price to achieve a wider market acceptance, which helps to fight off competitive threats.

An interesting illustration of these two pricing policies can be found in analyzing the battle between Texas Instruments and Bomar Corporation. Bomar introduced one of the first hand-held calculators and chose a skimming price policy. Therefore, only a small market share was gained. Texas Instruments came out with their calculator (basically the same product), but adopted a penetration policy to achieve a wider market share. The rest is history. Bomar went out of business because its market share was too small to support operations after competition set in.

Pricing is discussed in Chapter 7.

PRODUCT/SERVICE

The product or service offered will determine business success. Obviously, many products and services are widely available today from many different sources. Some will continue to be in demand while others will stagnate or die. New ones will come and go. The trick is to find a line that has achieved some degree of success in the marketplace with a lot of growth potential left and yet only a few competitors. Chapter 7 contains information about product development.

Franchising is staged to make a comeback, but a franchise is only as good as the product or service it represents. Details concerning franchise ownership are discussed in Chapter 2.

Below is a list of some good and bad business prospects that exist today. Keep in mind that changing economic conditions could alter what constitutes a positive or negative proposition.

Good Prospects:
— Information Services
— Computer Software and Hardware
— Medical Instruments, Services, and Supplies

— Aerospace and Defense-Related Products and Services
— Entertainment Products and Services
— Sports Products and Services
— Educational Products and Services
— Specialty Retailing
— Financial and Tax Services
— Convenience Stores
— Fast-Food Outlets
— Precision Instruments
— Do-It-Yourself Stores
— Consulting Services

Bad Prospects:
— Domestic Car Dealers
— Gasoline Service Stations
— Conventional Grocery Stores
— General Department Stores
— Residential Construction
— Steel-Related Businesses
— Textile-Related Businesses

Raw Materials

The location of raw materials is of primary concern to manufacturing outfits. Some will locate their operations near sources of raw materials in order to minimize the cost of transportation that is usually passed on to the manufacturer. This is usually the case where raw materials are extremely heavy and bulky. For example, many steel mills will locate near coal mines. In addition, availability is a major consideration. Manufacturers must be sure that adequate raw materials and/or components are available to keep production flowing. Failure to deliver finished goods to customers on time may result in a loss of goodwill.

Some manufacturers may attempt to optimize their location between major customers and sources of materials needed for production. In some cases, it may be more advantageous to locate near markets as opposed to suppliers. It could be that both market and raw material locations are minimized in favor of a location that is more favorable because of wages, taxes and/or climate.

RESEARCH AND DEVELOPMENT (R&D)

Research and development is a primary concern for manufacturing firms for survival reasons. Without the new products or processes initially created through R&D efforts, a company's ability to compete effectively would be compromised. In fact, many economists feel that U.S. manufacturers are becoming less competitive than foreign firms because industry as a whole is spending much less on R&D in real terms (inflation adjusted) than it did a decade ago. At the same time foreign manufacturers have been increasing their R&D emphasis. This situation underscores the necessity of maintaining an adequate R&D program if the future is to be met with success.

Retail, wholesale, and service businesses should concern themselves with research and development to the extent that trends affect their marketing endeavors. Obviously, existing products and services will give way to new ones. The trick is to know when these events will happen and how they can be exploited. Research will tell how.

SERVICE

Some products need periodic servicing. The work can be done by the retailer, wholesaler, or manufacturer. Generally, there exist cooperative agreements between the aforementioned to decide who will handle what and when. In any case, the need to service products sold must be taken into account. Proper service capability is of primary importance to potential customers. Even a service business should be concerned. For example, let's say a management consultant performs a market study for a firm. Six or seven weeks after the study is finished the consultant should call or visit the firm to determine if the study had indeed been of assistance. This is called "servicing the service." If everybody is happy with the previous work, it would be an ideal time to push additional services.

STATE OF TECHNOLOGY

Technology is changing the way all firms conduct themselves in the marketplace. Failure to acknowledge and use the latest in technical innovations will mean demise. To illustrate, many U.S. manufacturers have failed to innovate to the same degree as their foreign counterparts. Consequently, international markets have been losing to the more productive foreign producers. Even on a smaller scale, those retailers and service firms failing to consider the impact of technology on their existing lines will fall victim to changing demand patterns.

Determine which emerging technologies will affect existing and/or prospective lines and to what degree. Outline how these changes may be exploited profitably.

Storage

A retail business must store inventory in order to fulfill customer wants when immediate demand occurs. Some retail outlets succeed or fail based on their ability to provide a quick and adequate supply of their product, especially in a competitive market. Wholesalers and manufacturers generally need larger storage facilities to accommodate the enormous volume of finished and unfinished material that must be stored until production or shipment is made. Storage is not a big problem for service firms, since services are intangibles and cannot be warehoused.

The right amount of storage space is important. Too little might cause production and delivery delays, thereby resulting in a loss of customer goodwill. On the other hand, underutilized space is wasteful and is an overhead expense not covered by revenues.

Topography

Many areas are not conducive to manufacturing facilities because of land contour. There is one county in the state of Virginia where 85 percent of the land has an incline exceeding 15 degrees, which is considered restrictive for manufacturing and large wholesaling purposes. Normally, this situation would not affect retail or service establishments, which tend to be smaller by nature, although any area that is largely inaccessible would be bad for businesses dependent on traffic flow. Another thing to be considered is the impact of no industrial growth. Opportunities for any type of business may be restricted if growth is stymied. To illustrate, the seat of the aforementioned county is a town of 8,000 people. It has one of the highest failure rates for small businesses in the state. Main Street is littered with empty storefronts and many existing operations are barely afloat.

Trade Credit

It is wise to check with prospective suppliers about their credit arrangements. If the business is new it can expect to pay cash on delivery for merchandise and supplies during the first few months of operation. This obstacle can be overcome if the owner has a good credit rating and is willing to personally guarantee payment. Then immediate credit terms are normally available.

Many businesses fail to follow through in getting better terms with a supplier after a relationship has been established. One small motorcycle and repair shop in Virginia was dealing with four different suppliers for 18 months, and all were demanding cash on delivery. A consultant advised the owners to write and demand favorable credit terms or other vendors would be found. Three graciously gave credit while one refused. Luckily, the one that resisted was the smallest and least important of the four. In addition, ask suppliers for a discount upon making early payments. Many will grant a 1 or 2 percent reduction for paying bills within ten days. Evaluate the cost of paying cash, taking into consideration the discount against the advantage of using the float (suppliers' credit). The answer will be determined by analyzing the rate of return on utilized dollars. For example, if the average annual rate of return on invested capital exceeds the annual adjusted rate of the suppliers' discount, it would not be wise to make early payments because the business can make more return by using the suppliers' float. If the rate is less, early payments may be appropriate.

Also, playing one supplier against the other for purposes of securing better credit terms might be a good idea at times. Many businesses have found that some vendors will extend payment terms from the traditional net 30 days to 45 or 60 days. In some industries, terms of 90 to 180 days have been achieved.

VENDORS (SUPPLIERS)

Most small retailers purchase from wholesalers who in turn buy from manufacturers and/or jobbers. Manufacturing firms must buy their raw materials and components from other sources. The point to remember is that all businesses should have several sources of supplies readily available. Relying on a single vendor can be risky. What happens if the vendor goes out of business or changes marketing approaches so as not to include particular types of businesses?

In addition, it may be wise to let suppliers know that several vendors are being used. It will keep them on their toes. Again, it may be useful to play them against each other to negotiate better prices.

WARRANTIES

For competitive reasons, most businesses must give warranties that guarantee the successful performance of their products or services. Warranties, whether implied or expressed, are contracts that must be taken seriously. Broken warranties can lead to costly legal battles with disenfranchised customers, not to mention governmental agencies. In addition, the possibility of bad press must be taken into account and the loss of goodwill it will cause. When considering warranties, try to estimate the cost of making such guarantees and what means will be used to deliver what is promised.

When projecting warranties, try to do it in a novel and unique way. A new slant can do wonders to stimulate sales. For example, a couple of years ago a mail order firm decided to incorporate a unique approach to making a guarantee. The company in question told potential buyers that their checks or money orders would not be cashed for 30 days and if they were not satisfied with the product it could be returned within a month. Upon the return of the merchandise, the uncashed monies would be sent back. The favorable result of this new twist was tremendous.

Basic Business Start-Up*

Starting a new business is at best a dubious adventure in itself. It is of utmost importance to be organized from the beginning, to have a plan, to know what information is already in hand and what remains to be discovered. The value of being organized cannot be overemphasized. Certain tasks must be completed, some in a definite sequence; without organization, something is likely to be overlooked.

In the next four sections, we will examine the most basic steps to starting up four different businesses: one retail, one wholesale, one manufacturing, and one service business. Some basic steps are common to all businesses from the point where market research is completed, the type of business has been established, and the financing for the venture is in hand. Following these basic steps will

---

*This section is provided by Alicelee Riley, who is a small-business consultant located in Winchester, Virginia. She is owner of Riley Management Services.

THE RETAIL BUSINESS: "PENNY'S HOT SHOP"

Penny Reynolds, a private caterer, decided to open a sandwich shop for business people in the downtown district of her community. Several restaurants were already established, but they were either geared for full meal and high atmosphere or they were small specialty shops serving limited ethnic cuisine. Penny determined there was a market for a restaurant that would serve only sandwiches of a traditional sort, with a minimum of side dishes, and emphasis on fast service.

With business plan and financing in hand, the steps Penny took to open her shop were:

1. She looked at available rental property in the area she wanted to service. She talked with several realtors to find the best location for the best price and made a tentative agreement to rent a space that had been an ice cream parlor under previous renters.
2. She met with the building and fire inspectors from the city to determine what must be done to bring the building in line with regulations for her type of business. In addition, she needed to find out restrictions, limits on seating capacity, and other regulations that might apply.
3. Penny then met with the sanitation inspector to determine what regulations for food preparation and storage would apply.
4. Once she was sure she could afford to make the necessary improvements to the space (after consulting her business counselor and checking with local contractors), she signed a lease and arranged for utilities and telephone.
5. Penny went to city hall and applied for her business license and obtained other information she needed regarding local taxes and regulations.
6. The state government had a sales tax, so she applied for the necessary reporting forms, tax tables, and book of regulations.
7. Knowing she would have employees, Penny applied to the Internal Revenue Service for a federal employer identification number. (The federal government supplies a book of instructions and forms when the number is assigned).
8. While work was being completed on the space, Penny began negotiating with restaurant equipment dealers to provide the necessary equipment and fixtures for her shop. She ordered what was needed.

9. Next, she located food distributors and gathered information from them.
10. The actual menu was selected and she worked closely with her business counselor to plan markups on the menu items and initial stock levels.
11. Her record-keeping system (as a sole proprietorship) and other important files were established.
12. After meeting with several agents, Penny purchased a comprehensive business insurance plan that suited her needs.
13. Penny decided initially to hire one full-time and one part-time employee. She placed a request with the local state employment office and interviewed prospects. By the time her space was completed and equipment began arriving, she had her employees and they were helping with the final stages.
14. The menu and advertising handbills were designed and printed.
15. Penny and her employees did the interior decorating to create a pleasing atmosphere in the shop.
16. All food items were ordered, along with serving, storage, and cleaning supplies.
17. Penny paid for advertising on radio and in the local newspaper to announce the opening of her shop. Handbills were distributed.
18. The staff was trained and a couple of warm-up exercises were given so that opening day could go smoothly.
19. Finally, the sanitation inspector was called in one final time, after all was ready, to make sure the shop was in compliance with local codes.

Always remember, however, that extensive decision making was necessary at every step. Items such as employee compensation, advertising, budgeting, etc., required close attention. But by following this basic sequence, Penny was able to open on schedule with a minimum of difficulty.

THE WHOLESALE BUSINESS: "POTTERY CENTRAL"

Fred Jenkins was a plant nursery specialist. On a vacation trip to Mexico, he encountered a number of pottery makers who were producing decorative pots that were much less costly than undecorated domestic ones. He determined there would be a market for such pottery in the U.S. and decided to start a wholesale pottery business.

After Fred obtained the necessary financing and developed a plan of action, he went to work:

1. Since Fred's concept involved importing, he contacted the U.S. Commerce Department and Customs Service for information regarding importing, licensing, etc.
2. He met with his accountant and attorney to wade through the information because of the tax implications and the complexities of both importing and engaging in interstate trade.
3. He met with representatives of various trucking firms to learn about shipping rates and regulations.
4. Fred went shopping for warehouse-office space. As a wholesaler, Fred did not need a fancy building, but adequate space with easy access for shipping was essential. He made a tentative agreement for renting a small warehouse with an attached office just outside of town.
5. He checked with the zoning, building, and fire authorities about regulations and needed improvements.
6. Once he had consulted with local contractors, he signed a lease for the building and arranged for the improvements, utilities, and telephone.
7. He then applied for a business license, a federal employer identification number, and requested information on state and local taxes applicable to wholesaling.
8. He contacted chambers of commerce, advertising agencies, friends, and business associates for names of nurseries and florists in the region.
9. He worked closely with his business advisors to determine initial stock levels, markups, and equipment requirements. Also, he contacted the Mexican potters and placed his first orders, including packing supplies. Fred also negotiated orders with domestic potters for some of their pottery pieces to complement his imported products.
10. Next, Fred decided to hire a secretary-bookkeeper, shipping clerk, and warehouseman because he planned to spend a good deal of his time on the road visiting potential customers. He placed want ads in the newspaper and with the local employment office. It wasn't long before he interviewed prospects and chose his employees.
11. Working with his accountant, Fred set up his sole proprietor record-keeping system and inventory system, and developed

invoicing forms, billing policies, and other necessary items and procedures.

12. He met with various agents and purchased a sound business insurance plan.

13. With the help of a small advertising agency, business cards, sales literature, and company stationery were developed and printed. Other advertising approaches were explored and decisions made.

14. Once the space was ready, Fred and his employees organized the storage areas. Office equipment and furniture were then purchased.

15. The staff received training about business operation and Fred spent some of his time pre-selling several customers.

16. When the first shipments arrived, Fred sent a mass mailing to all the potential customers on his list and opened the doors for business.

Obviously, there are major differences between this wholesale business and the retail approach. Space requirements and marketing emphases differ widely. Once again, many details have been excluded, particularly regarding importing and shipping. Nevertheless, this scenario contains the basic start-up logic.

The Service Business: "Clean Sweepers"

Jim Black and John Simmons were servicemen for a woodstove firm. They observed a need for chimney sweep services in their community and decided to form a partnership to open a chimney sweep business. Together they met with an accountant and attorney to develop a business plan and a viable partnership agreement. Shortly thereafter, they met with their banker to arrange financing. Once these major preliminaries were concluded, they got down to the start-up details:

1. Jim owned several acres of property on the outskirts of town. On the property was a small barn in fairly good condition. The two men decided to use this building for their business. However, the area was zoned as residential. It was necessary for them to obtain a zoning variance through the city zoning board in order to locate their business in the barn.

2. Along with obtaining the variance, they met with the building and fire inspectors to determine what work was needed to bring the building in compliance with local codes. Arrangements were made with local contractors for the work to be completed.
3. The two men then applied for local business licenses and obtained other necessary information on state and local taxes applicable to their business.
4. They arranged for utilities and telephone service for their building.
5. Anticipating they would need to hire at least one employee, they filed for a federal employer identification number and accompanying forms and information.
6. They obtained information prices from various distributors regarding equipment and supplies. Orders were soon placed.
7. Since they would be traveling to their customers, a large van was purchased to accommodate all their equipment.
8. With the help of their business advisors, they set up a partnership record-keeping system, developed billing forms and procedures, and established a pricing structure for their services.
9. They consulted with several insurance agents and purchased a comprehensive business insurance plan.
10. They contacted the local employment agency, interviewed prospects, and hired a secretary-bookkeeper, their only other employee.
11. Working with a local ad agency, they developed business cards, stationery, and an advertising plan, which was executed right away.
12. After their equipment arrived and the final building inspections were made, they opened for business.

A service business is often one of the easiest to start, but frequently takes more intense marketing to convince the consumer that he needs the service, since it is an intangible. Depending on the cost of equipment and supplies, a service business, especially if it can be run from home, may have less overhead expense than other types of businesses. Pricing for services, however, is critical, since many people tend to undervalue their time, and therefore do not have enough income to keep the business operating. Sound advice is very important.

The Manufacturing Business: "Naturalures, Inc."

George McDonald, Ed Frye, and Paul Smith were fishing buddies. For years they had fished the waters of the region, and the problem of inexpensive and realistic lures was a frequent topic of discussion. Ed was a chemist for a gasket company. Paul was a machinist and George was a salesman. They tinkered with making their own plastic lures in Ed's workshop. Finally, they developed some fine products and decided to manufacture these lures to sell to tackle wholesalers.

After pooling their financial resources and developing a plan with the aid of their accountant, they began to build their business:

1. Before going further, they met with their attorney and accountant to prepare and file their articles of incorporation with the state. A board of directors was appointed and stock apportioned among the three stockholders.
2. Ed's workshop was too small to produce lures in quantity, so they sought a basic warehouse building that could be set up for manufacturing. They found a small location in the county industrial park and made a tentative agreement to rent.
3. They then contacted the building and fire inspectors and determined what improvements were needed to the site to bring it up to code for their type of business. The OSHA representative was contacted to determine what federal regulations affected their operation.
4. Contractors were hired to do the work. Also, a lease was signed for the building and utilities were arranged.
5. Meanwhile, since the men felt they had developed a new concept in manufacturing plastic lures, it was necessary to find out if their method could be patented and if the name "Naturalures" could qualify for trademark. Their local attorney referred them to a lawyer who specialized in patents and trademarks. He handled those transactions for them.
6. They applied for local business licenses and obtained other information on taxes and regulations affecting a manufacturing business.
7. They filed for a federal employer identification number for the corporation in anticipation of hiring several employees.
8. Working closely with their board of directors and accountant, they developed pricing and start-up production levels.
9. Suppliers for needed machinery and raw materials were found and queried for their best prices and terms. Orders were then placed.

10. Meetings with various shippers were held and packaging decisions were made as part of nailing down the details on shipping.
11. They contacted the local employment agency and hired a secretary-bookkeeper, shipping clerk, and two other individuals to assist with production.
12. They purchased a business insurance plan through a reputable agent after thorough study of various alternatives.
13. Their accountant helped them set up corporate record-keeping, inventory, production, and billing systems. All special forms were designed and printed.
14. Office equipment and furniture were ordered and installed.
15. With the help of an advertising agency, business cards, stationery, and a marketing plan were designed and developed to target the wholesale market.
16. Through local sporting goods stores, they gathered the names of major wholesalers of fishing gear and sent them samples of their lures.
17. Employees were trained, and special safety instruction was provided to all production workers, based on OSHA regulations.
18. Following a final building inspection, the production of "Naturalures" began.

Manufacturing requires certain technical knowledge very different from retailing and wholesaling. Generally, establishing a manufacturing business is more costly because of the equipment involved. Likewise, a manufacturing business can be more risky, especially if it involves developing new markets. Marketing effectiveness and quality control are critical factors in this field.

There are many factors to consider in any business venture. All these considerations may seem overwhelming to the person starting a business for the first time. Keeping overhead down, purchasing wisely, pricing competitively, and marketing effectively are important to early success. Investigating licensing regulations, building codes, and taxing regulations is critical. But as much as any of these, it is absolutely necessary for the novice entrepreneur to have a clear objective, to be motivated, to know as much about the pitfalls as he or she does about the potentials, and to stay organized. Following a logical plan and understanding the basic steps will help make the business adventure a more pleasant, fulfilling, and profitable experience.

Part II

DIRECTORY OF CAPITAL SOURCES

11

PRIVATE SOURCES OF CAPITAL

Private Capital Companies

This section contains a list of venture capital firms, small-business investment companies (SBICs), minority enterprise small-business investment companies (MESBICs), consulting firms, and other organizations specializing in small-business funding. These organizations have provided detailed information concerning their investment preferences. Chapter 6 describes the differences between these funding outlets and how they operate.

ALABAMA

Hickory Venture Group
200 West Court Square, Suite 100
Huntsville, AL 35801
205-539-1931

CONTACT: Monro Lanier
TYPE OF FIRM: Venture Capital
FUNDING PREFERENCE:
  Second-Round Funding
  Third-Round Funding
  Fourth-Round Funding
  Later-Stage Funding
  Leveraged Buyouts

INVESTMENT PREFERENCE:
  Diversified
  Communications Technology
  Computer Hardware
  Computer Software
  Manufacturing
  Medical Technology
  Retail
  Services
  Wholesale Distribution
  Franchise
GEOGRAPHIC PREFERENCE:
  Middle Atlantic
  Southeast
  Southwest

TYPES OF FUNDS:
  Equity (stock purchases)
  Loans With Equity Kickers
  Minimum: $500,000
  Maximum: $2,500,000

**Hickory Venture Capital
Corporation**
200 West Court Square, Suite 100
Huntsville, AL 35801
205-539-1931

CONTACT: John Bise
TYPE OF FIRM:
  Venture Capital
SBIC
FUNDING PREFERENCE:
  First-Round Funding
  Second-Round Funding
  Third-Round Funding
INVESTMENT PREFERENCE:
  Manufacturing
  Services
GEOGRAPHIC PREFERENCE:
  Middle Atlantic
  Southeast
  Midwest
  Southwest
TYPES OF FUNDS:
  Equity (stock purchases)
  Loans With Equity Kickers
  Minimum: $1,000,000
  Maximum: $5,000,000

ARIZONA

**First Interstate Equity
Corporation**
100 West Washington, 22nd Floor
Phoenix, AZ 85003
602-440-1307

CONTACT: Stephen W. Wallis, VP
TYPE OF FIRM: SBIC
FUNDING PREFERENCE:
  Later-Stage Funding
INVESTMENT PREFERENCE:
  Diversified
GEOGRAPHIC PREFERENCE:
  Southwest
TYPES OF FUNDS:
  Equity (stock purchases)
  Loans
  Loans With Equity Kickers
  Minimum: $250,000
  Maximum: $1,000,000

First Commerce and Loan LP
5620 North Kolb, #260
Tucson, AZ 85715

TYPE OF FIRM: SBIC
FUNDING PREFERENCE: Varies
INVESTMENT PREFERENCE:
  Diversified
GEOGRAPHIC PREFERENCE:
  Various
TYPES OF FUNDS:
  Other
  Minimum: Varies
  Maximum: Varies

Sundance Venture Partners, LP
400 East Van Buren, Suite 650
Phoenix, AZ 85004
602-252-5373

CONTACT: Gregory Anderson
TYPE OF FIRM: Venture Capital
FUNDING PREFERENCE:
  Start-Up Funding
  First-Round Funding
  Second-Round Funding
  Third-Round Funding
  Fourth-Round Funding

INVESTMENT PREFERENCE:
Diversified
GEOGRAPHIC PREFERENCE:
No Preference (U.S.A.)
TYPES OF FUNDS:
Equity (stock purchases)
Minimum: $750,000
Maximum: Not Determined

CALIFORNIA

Accel Partners
One Embarcadero Center
San Francisco, CA 94111
415-989-5656

CONTACT: James Breyer
TYPE OF FIRM: Venture Capital
FUNDING PREFERENCE:
Seed Funding
Start-Up Funding
First-Round Funding
Second-Round Funding
Third-Round Funding
Fourth-Round Funding
Later-Stage Funding
Leveraged Buyouts
INVESTMENT PREFERENCE:
Communications Technology
Computer Hardware
Computer Software
Media
Medical Technology
Services
GEOGRAPHIC PREFERENCE:
No Preference (U.S.A.)
TYPES OF FUNDS:
Equity (stock purchases)
Minimum: $250,000
Maximum: $2,000,000

Advanced Technology Ventures
1000 El Camino Real, Suite 360
Menlo Park, CA 94025
415-321-8601

CONTACT: Jos Henkens
TYPE OF FIRM: Venture Capital
FUNDING PREFERENCE:
Seed Funding
Start-Up Funding
First-Round Funding
INVESTMENT PREFERENCE:
Communications Technology
Computer Hardware
Computer Software
Medical Technology
GEOGRAPHIC PREFERENCE:
No Preference (U.S.A.)
TYPES OF FUNDS:
Equity (stock purchases)
Minimum: $230,000
Maximum: $1,000,000

BT Capital Corporation
300 South Grand Avenue
Los Angeles, CA 90071
213-620-8200
TYPE OF FIRM: SBIC
FUNDING PREFERENCE:
Second-Round Funding
Third-Round Funding
Later-Stage Funding
Leveraged Buyouts
Expansion Financing/
Recapitalization
INVESTMENT PREFERENCE:
Manufacturing
Retail
Services
Wholesale Distribution
GEOGRAPHIC PREFERENCE:
No Preference

TYPES OF FUNDS:
Equity (stock purchases)
Loans with Equity Kickers
Minimum: $5,000,000
Maximum: $20,000,000

Charter Venture Capital
525 University Avenue, Suite 1500
Palo Alto, CA 94301
415-325-6953

CONTACT: David Lundberg
TYPE OF FIRM: Venture Capital
FUNDING PREFERENCE:
Seed Funding
Start-Up Funding
First-Round Funding
Second-Round Funding
Third-Round Funding
INVESTMENT PREFERENCE:
Computer Hardware
Computer Software
Medical Technology
GEOGRAPHIC PREFERENCE:
No Preference (U.S.A.)
TYPES OF FUNDS:
Equity (stock purchases)
Minimum: $100,000
Maximum: $1,000,000

Comdisco Venture Partners
3000 Sand Hill Road
Building 1, Suite 290
Menlo Park, CA 94025
415-854-9484
FAX: 415-854-4026

CONTACT: Robert S. Winter,
General Partner
TYPE OF FIRM:
Venture Capital
Leasing

FUNDING PREFERENCE:
Start-Up Funding
First-Round Funding
Second-Round Funding
INVESTMENT PREFERENCE:
Diversified
Communications Technology
Computer Hardware
Computer Software
Medical Technology
Other High Technologies Not
Mentioned
Retail
GEOGRAPHIC PREFERENCE:
No Preference (U.S.A.)
TYPES OF FUNDS:
Equity (stock purchases)
Loans With Equity Kickers
Leasing
Accounts Receivable Financing
Minimum: Depends on Type of
Fund
Maximum: Depends on Type of
Fund

Delphi Bioventures, LP
3000 Sand Hill Road
Building 1, Suite 135
Menlo Park, CA 94025
415-854-9650

CONTACT: Erin Alley
TYPE OF FIRM: Venture Capital
FUNDING PREFERENCE:
Seed Funding
Start-Up Funding
INVESTMENT PREFERENCE:
BioMedical
GEOGRAPHIC PREFERENCE:
Western
TYPES OF FUNDS:
Equity (stock purchases)
Minimum: $500,000
Maximum: $2,500,000

Developers Equity Capital Corporation
1880 Century Park East, Suite 211
Los Angeles, CA 90067
310-277-0330

CONTACT: Larry Sade
TYPE OF FIRM: SBIC
FUNDING PREFERENCE:
None Given
INVESTMENT PREFERENCE:
Real Estate
GEOGRAPHIC PREFERENCE:
Immediate Area: California
TYPES OF FUNDS:
None Given
Minimum: $50,000
Maximum: $500,000

Dougery and White
155 Bouret Road, Suite 350
San Mateo, CA 94402
415-358-8701

CONTACT: Henry Wilder, General
Partner
TYPE OF FIRM: Venture Capital
FUNDING PREFERENCE:
Later-Stage Funding
Leveraged Buyouts
Acquisitions
INVESTMENT PREFERENCE:
Diversified
Computer Hardware
Computer Software
Medical Technology
GEOGRAPHIC PREFERENCE:
West Coast
TYPES OF FUNDS:
Equity (stock purchases)
Minimum: $250,000
Maximum: $2,000,000

Draper Associates
400 Seaport Court, #250
Redwood City, CA 94063
415-599-9000

CONTACT: Laura Bennett and
Karen Mostes
TYPE OF FIRM: Venture Capital
FUNDING PREFERENCE:
Seed Funding
Start-Up Funding
INVESTMENT PREFERENCE:
Communications Technology
Computer Software
Media
Other High Technologies Not
Mentioned
GEOGRAPHIC PREFERENCE:
No Preference (U.S.A.)
TYPES OF FUNDS:
Equity (stock purchases)
Minimum: $50,000
Maximum: $500,000

El Dorado Ventures
800 East Colorado Boulevard
Suite 530
Pasadena, CA 91101
818-793-1936

CONTACT: Tom Peterson
TYPE OF FIRM: Venture Capital
FUNDING PREFERENCE:
Seed Funding
Start-Up Funding
First-Round Funding
INVESTMENT PREFERENCE:
Communications Technology
Computer Hardware
Computer Software
Medical Technology
Other High Technologies Not
Mentioned

GEOGRAPHIC PREFERENCE:
Northwest
Far West
Southwest
TYPES OF FUNDS:
Equity (stock purchases)
Minimum: $500,000
Maximum: $4,000,000

Endeavor Capital Management
1880 Pacific Avenue, Suite 703
San Francisco, CA 94109
415-441-8986
CONTACT: Steven Carnevale
TYPE OF FIRM: Venture Capital
FUNDING PREFERENCE:
Start-Up Funding
First-Round Funding
INVESTMENT PREFERENCE:
Communications Technology
Computer Hardware
Computer Software
Manufacturing
Media
Retail
Services
Other High Technologies Not
Mentioned
GEOGRAPHIC PREFERENCE:
No Preference
TYPES OF FUNDS:
Equity (stock purchases)
Minimum: none
Maximum: $5,000,000

First SBIC of California
650 Town Center Drive, 17th Floor
Costa Mesa, CA 92626

CONTACT: Claudia Webb
TYPE OF FIRM: SBIC
FUNDING PREFERENCE:
Expansion Funding

INVESTMENT PREFERENCE:
Diversified
Manufacturing
GEOGRAPHIC PREFERENCE:
No Preference (U.S.A.)
TYPES OF FUNDS:
Minimum: $1,000,000
Maximum: $5,000,000

GC and H Partners
One Maritime Plaza, 20th Floor
San Francisco, CA 94110
415-981-5252
CONTACT: Edwin Huddleson
TYPE OF FIRM: SBIC, Individual
Investor
FUNDING PREFERENCE:
Start-Up Funding
INVESTMENT PREFERENCE:
Diversified
GEOGRAPHIC PREFERENCE:
Immediate Area in California
TYPES OF FUNDS:
Equity (stock purchases)
Minimum:
Maximum: $1,000

**Grace Ventures Corporation/Horn
Venture Partners**
20300 Stevens Creek Boulevard
Suite 330
Cupertino, CA 95014
408-725-0774

CONTACT: Christian Horn
TYPE OF FIRM: Venture Capital
FUNDING PREFERENCE:
Seed Funding
Start-Up Funding
First-Round Funding
INVESTMENT PREFERENCE:
Diversified

GEOGRAPHIC PREFERENCE:
No Preference (U.S.A.)
TYPES OF FUNDS:
Equity (stock purchases)
Minimum: $250,000
Maximum: $1,000,000

Institutional Venture Partners
3000 Sam Hill Road
Building 2, Suite 290
Menlo Park, CA 94025
415-854-5762

CONTACT: Geoffrey Jang
TYPE OF FIRM: Venture Capital
FUNDING PREFERENCE:
Seed Funding
Start-Up Funding
First-Round Funding
INVESTMENT PREFERENCE:
Communications Technology
Computer Hardware
Computer Software
Medical Technology
Retail
GEOGRAPHIC PREFERENCE:
Far West
TYPES OF FUNDS:
Equity (stock purchases)
Minimum: $1,000,000
Maximum: $2,500,000

Interven Partners
301 Arizona Avenue, Suite 306
Santa Monica, CA 90401
310-587-3550

CONTACT: David Jones
TYPE OF FIRM: Venture Capital
FUNDING PREFERENCE:
Seed Funding
Start-Up Funding
First-Round Funding

Second-Round Funding
Leveraged Buyouts
Acquisitions
INVESTMENT PREFERENCE:
Diversified
GEOGRAPHIC PREFERENCE:
Far West
Immediate Area in Southern
California
TYPES OF FUNDS:
Equity (stock purchases)
Minimum: $500,000
Maximum: $3,000,000

JAFCO American Ventures, Inc.
555 California Street
San Francisco, CA 94104
415-788-0706

CONTACT: Bill Shelander
TYPE OF FIRM: Venture Capital
FUNDING PREFERENCE:
Start-Up Funding
First-Round Funding
Second-Round Funding
Third-Round Funding
Fourth-Round Funding
INVESTMENT PREFERENCE:
Communications Technology
Computer Hardware
Computer Software
Manufacturing
Medical Technology
GEOGRAPHIC PREFERENCE:
No Preference (U.S.A.)
TYPES OF FUNDS:
Equity (stock purchases)
Minimum: $300,000
Maximum: $2,000,000

Jupiter Partners
600 Montgomery Street
San Francisco, CA 94111
415-421-9990

CONTACT: John Bryan
TYPE OF FIRM: SBIC
FUNDING PREFERENCE:
  First-Round Funding
INVESTMENT PREFERENCE:
  Diversified
  Manufacturing
GEOGRAPHIC PREFERENCE:
  No Preference (U.S.A.)
TYPES OF FUNDS:
  Equity (stock purchases)
  Minimum: $50,000
  Maximum: $100,000

Kleiner, Perkins, Caufield, and Byers
Four Embarcadero Center
Suite 3520
San Francisco, CA 94111
415-421-3110

CONTACT: Frank Caudfield
TYPE OF FIRM: Venture Capital
FUNDING PREFERENCE:
  Seed Funding
  Start-Up Funding
  First-Round Funding
INVESTMENT PREFERENCE:
  Communications Technology
  Computer Hardware
  Computer Software
  Medical Technology
GEOGRAPHIC PREFERENCE:
  Far West
TYPES OF FUNDS:
  Equity (stock purchases)
  Minimum: N/A
  Maximum: $5,000,000

Lailai Capital Company
223 East Garvey Avenue, Suite 228
Monterey Park, CA 91754
818-288-0704

CONTACT: Olivia Hsu
TYPE OF FIRM: SBIC
FUNDING PREFERENCE:
  Later-Stage Funding
  Acquisitions
INVESTMENT PREFERENCE:
  Diversified
GEOGRAPHIC PREFERENCE:
  No Preference (U.S.A.)
TYPES OF FUNDS:
  Equity (stock purchases)
  Minimum: $50,000
  Maximum: $300,000

Marwit Capital Corporation
180 Newport Center Drive
Suite 200
Newport Beach, CA 92660
714-640-6234

CONTACT: Matthew L. Witte
TYPE OF FIRM:
  Venture Capital
  SBIC
FUNDING PREFERENCE:
  Leveraged Buyouts
  Acquisitions
INVESTMENT PREFERENCE:
  Franchise
GEOGRAPHIC PREFERENCE:
  Immediate Area in California
TYPES OF FUNDS:
  Minimum: $200,000
  Maximum: Several Million

Matrix Partners
2500 Sand Hill Road, Suite 113
Menlo Park, CA 94025
415-854-3131

CONTACT: Frederick Fuegel
TYPE OF FIRM: Venture Capital

FUNDING PREFERENCE:
 Start-Up Funding
 First-Round Funding
 Second-Round Funding
 Third-Round Funding
 Leveraged Buyouts
INVESTMENT PREFERENCE:
 Communications Technology
 Computer Software
 Manufacturing
 Media
 Medical Technology
 Retail
 Services
GEOGRAPHIC PREFERENCE:
 West Coast
TYPES OF FUNDS:
 Equity (stock purchases)
 Minimum: $750,000
 Maximum: $5,000,000

Mayfield Fund
2800 Sand Hill Road
Menlo Park, CA 94025
415-854-5560

CONTACT: Michelle Malquist
TYPE OF FIRM: Venture Capital
FUNDING PREFERENCE:
 Seed Funding
 Start-Up Funding
INVESTMENT PREFERENCE:
 Computer Hardware
 Computer Software
 Other High Technologies Not
  Mentioned
GEOGRAPHIC PREFERENCE:
 No Preference (U.S.A.)
TYPES OF FUNDS:
 Equity (stock purchases)
 Minimum: Varies
 Maximum: Varies

Menlo Ventures
3000 Sand Hill Road
Menlo Park, CA 94025
415-854-8540

CONTACT: Thomas Bredt
TYPE OF FIRM: Venture Capital
FUNDING PREFERENCE:
 Seed Funding
 Start-Up Funding
 First-Round Funding
 Second-Round Funding
 Third-Round Funding
 Fourth-Round Funding
 Later-Stage Funding
 Leveraged Buyouts
INVESTMENT PREFERENCE:
 Diversified
 Communications Technology
 Computer Hardware
 Computer Software
 Manufacturing
 Medical Technology
 Services
 Other High Technologies Not
  Mentioned
GEOGRAPHIC PREFERENCES:
 No Preference (U.S.A.)
TYPES OF FUNDS:
 Equity (stock purchases)
 Minimum: $500,000
 Maximum: $5,000,000

Merrill, Pickard, Anderson, and Eyre
2480 Sand Hill Road, Suite 200
Menlo Park, CA 94025
415-854-8600

CONTACT: Andrea Ratchard
TYPE OF FIRM: SBIC
FUNDING PREFERENCE:
 Acquisitions

INVESTMENT PREFERENCE:
  Computer Hardware
  Computer Software
  Medical Technology
GEOGRAPHIC PREFERENCE:
  No Preference (U.S.A.)
TYPES OF FUNDS:
  Loans
  Minimum: Varies
  Maximum: Varies

Pacific Mezzanine Fund, LP
88 Kearny Street, Suite 1850
San Francisco, CA 94108
415-362-6776

TYPE OF FIRM: SBIC
FUNDING PREFERENCE:
  First-Round Funding
INVESTMENT PREFERENCE:
  Diversified
GEOGRAPHIC PREFERENCE:
  Immediate Area in California
TYPES OF FUNDS:
  Loans
  Minimum: Varies
  Maximum: Varies

Union Venture Corporation
445 South Ficueroa Street
Los Angeles, CA 90071
213-236-5658

CONTACT: Kathleen Burns, VP
TYPE OF FIRM:
  Venture Capital
  SBIC
FUNDING PREFERENCE:
  Third-Round Funding
  Fourth-Round Funding
  Leveraged Buyouts
INVESTMENT PREFERENCE:
  Diversified

Computer Hardware
Computer Software
GEOGRAPHIC PREFERENCE:
  No Preference (U.S.A.)
TYPES OF FUNDS:
  Equity (stock purchases)
  Minimum: $1,000
  Maximum: Not Determined

Weiss, Peck, and Greer Venture Partners, LP
555 California Street, Suite 4760
San Francisco, CA 94104
415-622-6864

CONTACT: Chris Schaepe
TYPE OF FIRM: Venture Capital
FUNDING PREFERENCE:
  Seed Funding
  Start-Up Funding
  Later-Stage Funding
INVESTMENT PREFERENCE:
  Computer Hardware
  Computer Software
  Medical Technology
  Other High Technologies Not
    Mentioned
GEOGRAPHIC PREFERENCE:
  No Preference (U.S.A.)
TYPES OF FUNDS:
  Equity (stock purchases)
  Minimum: Varies
  Maximum: Varies

COLORADO

Hill, Carman, and Washing
885 Arapanoe Avenue
Boulder, CO 80302
303-442-5151

CONTACT: John Hill

TYPE OF FIRM: Venture Capital
FUNDING PREFERENCE:
  Seed Funding
  Start-Up Funding
  First-Round Funding
INVESTMENT PREFERENCE:
  Communications Technology
  Computer Hardware
  Computer Software
  Medical Technology
  Other High Technologies Not
    Mentioned
GEOGRAPHIC PREFERENCE:
  Northwest
  Far West
  Southwest
TYPES OF FUNDS:
  Equity (stock purchases)
  Minimum: $500,000
  Maximum: $2,000,000

The Centennial Funds
1999 Broadway, Suite 2100
Denver, CO 80202
303-298-9066

CONTACT: G. Jackson
  Tankersley Jr.
TYPE OF FIRM: Venture Capital
FUNDING PREFERENCE:
  Seed Funding
INVESTMENT PREFERENCE:
  Communications Technology
  Medical Technology
GEOGRAPHIC PREFERENCE:
  Telecommunications—No
    Preference (U.S.A.)
  All Other Investments Colorado
TYPES OF FUNDS:
  Equity (stock purchases)
  Minimum:
    $2,000,000 Late-Stage Funding

$250,000 Seed/Start-Up
  Funding
Maximum: $5,000,000

CONNECTICUT

**All State Venture Capital
  Corporation**
The Bishop House
32 Elm Street, P.O. Box 1629
New Haven, CT 06506
203-787-5029

CONTACT: Ceasue Anguihlare,
  President
TYPE OF FIRM: SBIC
FUNDING PREFERENCE:
  Later-Stage Funding
INVESTMENT PREFERENCE:
  Diversified
GEOGRAPHIC PREFERENCE:
  Northeast
TYPES OF FUNDS:
  Loans with Equity Kickers
  Minimum: None
  Maximum: $200,000–$500,000

GE Investments
3003 Summer Street
Stamford, CT 06904
203-326-2300

CONTACT: Michael Mears
TYPE OF FIRM: Pension Fund
FUNDING PREFERENCE:
  Later-Stage Funding
  Leveraged Buyouts
  Acquisitions
INVESTMENT PREFERENCE:
  Diversified
GEOGRAPHIC PREFERENCE:
  No Preference (U.S.A.)

TYPES OF FUNDS:
Equity (stock purchases)
Bonds with Substantial Equity
Kickers
Minimum: $5,000,000
Maximum: $40,000,000

Oak Investment Partners
1 Gornam Island
Westport, CT 06880
203-226-8346

CONTACT: Ed Glassmeyer
TYPE OF FIRM: Venture Capital
FUNDING PREFERENCE:
Start-Up Funding
INVESTMENT PREFERENCE:
Computer Software
Medical Technology
Services
GEOGRAPHIC PREFERENCE:
No Preference (U.S.A.)
TYPES OF FUNDS:
Equity (stock purchases)
Minimum: $500,000
Maximum: $2,000,000

Oxford Bioscience Partners
1266 Main Street
Stamford, CT 06902
203-964-0592

CONTACT: Alan Walton
TYPE OF FIRM: Venture Capital
FUNDING PREFERENCE:
Seed Funding
Start-Up Funding
Later-Stage Funding
Acquisitions
INVESTMENT PREFERENCE:
Medical Technology
GEOGRAPHIC PREFERENCE:
No Preference (U.S.A.)

TYPES OF FUNDS:
Equity (stock purchases)
Minimum: $500,000
Maximum: $1,000,000

The Vista Group
36 Grove Street
New Canaan, CT 06480
203-972-3400

CONTACT: Gerald Bay
TYPE OF FIRM: Venture Capital
FUNDING PREFERENCE:
Start-Up Funding
First-Round Funding
Second-Round Funding
Later-Stage Funding
Leveraged Buyouts
INVESTMENT PREFERENCE:
Diversified
Communications Technology
Computer Hardware
Computer Software
Medical Technology
Retail
Other High Technologies Not
Mentioned
GEOGRAPHIC PREFERENCES:
No Preference (U.S.A.)
TYPES OF FUNDS:
Equity (stock purchases)
Minimum: $500,000
Maximum: $3,000,000

DISTRICT OF COLUMBIA

Allied Capital Corporation
1666 K Street NW, Suite 901
Washington, DC 20006
202-331-1112

CONTACT: Cabell Williams,
President
TYPE OF FIRM:
SBIC
MESBIC
FUNDING PREFERENCE:
Second-Round Funding
Third-Round Funding
Fourth-Round Funding
Later-Stage Funding
INVESTMENT PREFERENCE:
Diversified
GEOGRAPHIC PREFERENCE:
No Preference (U.S.A.)
TYPES OF FUNDS:
Loans
Loans with Equity Kickers
Minimum: $500,000
Maximum: $3,000,000

Economic Development Finance Corporation
1660 L Street NW, Suite 308
Washington, DC 20036
202-775-8815

CONTACT: Greg Johnson
TYPE OF FIRM: State
Development Company
FUNDING PREFERENCE:
Start-Up Funding
First-Round Funding
Second-Round Funding
Third-Round Funding
Fourth-Round Funding
Later-Stage Funding
Leveraged Buyouts
Acquisitions
INVESTMENT PREFERENCE:
Diversified
Manufacturing
GEOGRAPHIC PREFERENCE:
Immediate Area in Washington

TYPES OF FUNDS:
Loans
Bonds
Minimum: $50,000
Maximum: $500,000

Broadcast Capital Fund, Inc.
1771 N Street NW, 4th Floor
Washington, DC 20036
202-429-5393

CONTACT: John Oxendine,
President
TYPE OF FIRM: MESBIC
FUNDING PREFERENCE:
Start-Up Funding
Leveraged Buyouts
Acquisitions
INVESTMENT PREFERENCE:
Media/Broadcasting
GEOGRAPHIC PREFERENCE:
No Preference (U.S.A.)
TYPES OF FUNDS:
Loans with Equity Kickers
Minimum: $200,000
Maximum: $1,000,000

Minority Broadcast Investment Corporation
1001 Connecticut Avenue, Suite 622
Washington, DC 20036
202-293-1166

CONTACT: Juanita Thomas
TYPE OF FIRM: SBIC
FUNDING PREFERENCE:
Leveraged Buyouts
Acquisitions
INVESTMENT PREFERENCE:
Media
Broadcast Acquisitions
GEOGRAPHIC PREFERENCE:
No Preference

TYPES OF FUNDS:
  Equity (stock purchases)
  Loans
  Minimum: $100,000
  Maximum: $300,000

FLORIDA

Business Assistance Center
P.O. Box 470830
Miami, FL 33247
305-693-3550

CONTACT: Bridget Simpson
TYPE OF FIRM: Local or
  Certified Development Company
FUNDING PREFERENCE: None
  Given
INVESTMENT PREFERENCE:
  Franchise
GEOGRAPHIC PREFERENCE:
  Home State of Florida
TYPES OF FUNDS:
  Bonds
  Minimum: $5,000
  Maximum: $50,000

Florida Capital Ventures, Limited
100 West Kennedy Boulevard
Tampa, FL 33622
813-229-2294

CONTACT: Warren Miller
TYPE OF FIRM: Venture Capital
FUNDING PREFERENCE:
  Expansion
INVESTMENT PREFERENCE:
  Diversified
GEOGRAPHIC PREFERENCE:
  Immediate Area in Florida

TYPES OF FUNDS:
  Equity (stock purchases)
  Minimum: $500,000
  Maximum: $1,000,000

South Atlantic Venture Fund
614 West Bay Street
Tampa, FL 33606
813-253-2500

CONTACT: Sandra Barber
TYPE OF FIRM: Venture Capital
FUNDING PREFERENCE:
  First-Round Funding
  Second-Round Funding
  Third-Round Funding
  Fourth-Round Funding
  Later-Stage Funding
  Leveraged Buyouts
INVESTMENT PREFERENCE:
  Communications Technology
  Manufacturing
  Medical Technology
  Services
GEOGRAPHIC PREFERENCE:
  Southeast
TYPES OF FUNDS:
  Equity (stock purchases)
  Minimum: $250,000
  Maximum: $1,000,000

**Western Financial Capital
Corporation**
Presidential Circle
4000 Hollywood Boulevard
Suite 435 South
Hollywood, FL 33021
305-966-8868

CONTACT: Fredrick M. Rosemore,
  Chairman of the Board

TYPE OF FIRM: SBIC, SSBIC
(Lenders)
FUNDING PREFERENCE:
Acquisitions
INVESTMENT PREFERENCE:
Real Estate
Franchise
GEOGRAPHIC PREFERENCE:
Nationwide
TYPES OF FUNDS:
Loans
Minimum: $100,000
Maximum:
$1,000,000–$4,000,000

GEORGIA

Cordova Capital Partners, LP
3350 Cumberland Circle, Suite 970
Atlanta, GA 30339
404-951-1542

CONTACT: Ralph Wright
TYPE OF FIRM: SBIC
FUNDING PREFERENCE:
First-Round Funding
Second-Round Funding
Third-Round Funding
INVESTMENT PREFERENCE:
Diversified
Communications Technology
Manufacturing
Medical Technology
Services
Wholesale Distribution
GEOGRAPHIC PREFERENCE:
Southeast
TYPES OF FUNDS:
Equity (stock purchases)
Loans with Equity Kickers
Minimum: $1,000,000
Maximum: $3,000,000

Investors Equity, Inc.
945 East Paces Ferry Road
Suite 1735
Atlanta, GA 30339
404-897-1910

CONTACT: Stephanie Myers
TYPE OF FIRM: SBIC
FUNDING PREFERENCE:
First-Round Funding
INVESTMENT PREFERENCE:
Manufacturing
GEOGRAPHIC PREFERENCE:
Immediate Area in Atlanta
TYPES OF FUNDS:
Equity (stock purchases)
Loans
Minimum: $100,000
Maximum: $500,000

**North Riverside Capital
Corporation**
50 Technology Park
Norcross, GA 30092
404-446-5556

CONTACT: Tom Barry
TYPE OF FIRM:
Venture Capital
SBIC
FUNDING PREFERENCE:
Diversified
GEOGRAPHIC PREFERENCE:
None
TYPES OF FUNDS:
Equity (stock purchases)
Minimum: $5,000,000
Maximum: $175,000,000

ILLINOIS

Allstate Venture Capital
Allstate Plaza South, G5D
Northbrook, IL 60062
708-402-5681

CONTACT: Robert Lestina
TYPE OF FIRM: Venture Capital
FUNDING PREFERENCE:
  Seed Funding
  Start-Up Funding
  First-Round Funding
  Second-Round Funding
  Third-Round Funding
  Later-Stage Funding
  Leveraged Buyouts
INVESTMENT PREFERENCE:
  Diversified
  Manufacturing
  Media
  Retail
  Services
GEOGRAPHIC PREFERENCE:
  No Preference (U.S.A.)
TYPES OF FUNDS:
  Equity (stock purchases)
  Minimum: $500,000
  Maximum: $5,000,000

**American Agricultural Investment
Management Company, Inc.**
631 East Butterfield Road
Suite 302
Lombard, IL 60148
708-810-0040

CONTACT: H. Joseph Bourn
TYPE OF FIRM: Farmland
  Investment Advisor
FUNDING PREFERENCE:
  All Equity
INVESTMENT PREFERENCE:
  Farms
GEOGRAPHIC PREFERENCE:
  No Preference (U.S.A.)

TYPES OF FUNDS:
  Equity Fee Simple
  Minimum: $1,000,000
  Maximum: $10,000,000

Comdisco Venture Partners
6111 North River Road
Rosemont, IL 60018
708-398-3000
FAX 708-518-5465
CONTACT: Jim Labe, General
  Manager
TYPE OF FIRM:
  Venture Capital
  Leasing
FUNDING PREFERENCE:
  Start-Up Funding
  First-Round Funding
  Second-Round Funding
INVESTMENT PREFERENCE:
  Diversified
  Communications Technology
  Computer Hardware
  Computer Software
  Medical Technology
  Retail
  Other High Technologies Not
    Mentioned
GEOGRAPHIC PREFERENCE:
  No Preference (U.S.A.)
TYPES OF FUNDS:
  Equity (stock purchases)
  Loans with Equity Kickers
  Leasing
  Accounts Receivable Financing
  Minimum: Depends on Type of
    Fund
  Maximum: Depends on Type of
    Fund

Continental Illinois Venture Corporation
209 South LaSalle Street
Chicago, IL 60693
312-828-8023

CONTACT: John Willis
TYPE OF FIRM: SBIC
FUNDING PREFERENCE:
  Leveraged Buyouts
  Acquisitions
INVESTMENT PREFERENCE:
  Diversified
GEOGRAPHIC PREFERENCE:
  No Preference (U.S.A.)
TYPES OF FUNDS:
  Loans
  Minimum: $5,000
  Maximum: $100,000

Continental Illinois Venture Corporation
231 South LaSalle Street
Chicago, IL 60697
312-828-8021

CONTACT: John Willis
TYPE OF FIRM: SBIC
FUNDING PREFERENCE:
  Start-Up Funding
  First-Round Funding
  Second-Round Funding
  Third-Round Funding
  Leveraged Buyouts
INVESTMENT PREFERENCE:
  Communications Technology
  Manufacturing
  Medical Technology
  Services
  Other High Technologies Not
    Mentioned

GEOGRAPHIC PREFERENCE:
  No Preference (U.S.A.)
TYPES OF FUNDS:
  Equity (stock purchases)
  Minimum: $500,000
  Maximum: $10,000,000

Frontenac Company
208 South LaSalle Street
Suite 1900
Chicago, IL 60604
312-368-0044
CONTACT: Laird Koldyke
TYPE OF FIRM: Venture Capital
FUNDING PREFERENCE:
  Start-Up Funding
INVESTMENT PREFERENCE:
  Medical Technology
  Medical Healthcare
GEOGRAPHIC PREFERENCE:
  Midwest
TYPES OF FUNDS:
  Equity (stock purchases)
  Minimum: $500,000
  Maximum: $25,000,000

IEG Venture Management, Inc.
10 South Riverside Plaza
14th Floor
Chicago, IL 60606
312-993-7500

CONTACT: Francis Blair
TYPE OF FIRM: Venture Capital
FUNDING PREFERENCE: None
  Given
INVESTMENT PREFERENCE:
  Diversified
GEOGRAPHIC PREFERENCE:
  Midwest

TYPES OF FUNDS:
Equity (stock purchases)
Minimum: $200,000
Maximum: $500,000

**Mesirow Private Equity
Investments, Inc.**
350 North Clark Street
Chicago, IL 60610
312-670-6099

CONTACT: Michael Barrett
TYPE OF FIRM: Venture Capital
FUNDING PREFERENCE:
Start-Up Funding
First-Round Funding
Second-Round Funding
Third-Round Funding
Leveraged Buyouts
INVESTMENT PREFERENCE:
Diversified
GEOGRAPHIC PREFERENCE:
No Preference (U.S.A.)
TYPES OF FUNDS:
Equity (stock purchases)
Minimum: $1,000,000
Maximum: $3,000,000

**Mesirow Private Equity
Investments, Inc.**
350 North Clark Street
Chicago, IL 60610
312-670-6099

CONTACT: James Tyree
TYPE OF FIRM: Venture Capital
FUNDING PREFERENCE:
Later-Stage Funding
Leveraged Buyouts
Acquisitions

INVESTMENT PREFERENCE:
Diversified
Manufacturing
Medical Technology
Wholesale Distribution
Franchise
GEOGRAPHIC PREFERENCE:
No Preference (U.S.A.)
TYPES OF FUNDS:
Equity (stock purchases)
Loans with Equity Kickers
Bonds with Equity Kickers
Minimum: $1,000,000
Maximum: $10,000,000

**Sears Investment Management
Company**
55 West Monroe Street
Chicago, IL 60603
312-875-0415

CONTACT: David L. Bogetz
TYPE OF FIRM: Venture Capital
FUNDING PREFERENCE:
Third-Round Funding
Fourth-Round Funding
Later-Stage Funding
INVESTMENT PREFERENCE:
Communications Technology
Computer Software
Medical Technology
Retail
Services
GEOGRAPHIC PREFERENCE:
No Preference (U.S.A.)
TYPES OF FUNDS:
Equity (stock purchases)
Minimum: $500,000
Maximum: $3,000,000

INDIANA

Circle Ventures, Inc.
26 North Arsenal Avenue
Indianapolis, IN 46201
317-636-7242

CONTACT: Carrie Walkup
TYPE OF FIRM: SBIC
FUNDING PREFERENCE:
  Later-Stage Funding
  LeveragedBuyouts
  Acquisitions
INVESTMENT PREFERENCE:
  Diversified
GEOGRAPHIC PREFERENCE:
  Home State (Close to
    Indianapolis)
TYPES OF FUNDS:
  Equity (stock purchases)
  Loans with Equity Kickers

Middlewest Ventures
201 North Illinois Street
Suite 2240
Indianapolis, IN 46204
317-237-2320
FAX 317-237-2325

CONTACT: Thomas A. Hiatt
TYPE OF FIRM: Venture Capital
FUNDING PREFERENCE:
  Start-Up Funding
  First-Round Funding
  Second-Round Funding
  Acquisitions
INVESTMENT PREFERENCE:
  Diversified
  Alternative Energy
  Communications Technology

Computer Software
Manufacturing
Retail
Other High Technologies Not
  Mentioned
GEOGRAPHIC PREFERENCE:
  Midwest
TYPES OF FUNDS:
  Equity (stock purchases)
  Loans
  Minimum: $250,000
  Maximum: $3,000,000

IOWA

MorAmerica Capital Corporation
101 Second Street SE, Suite 800
Cedar Rapids, IA 52401
319-363-8249

CONTACT: David R. Schroder,
  President
TYPE OF FIRM: SBIC
FUNDING PREFERENCE:
  Later-Stage Funding
  Leveraged Buyouts
INVESTMENT PREFERENCE:
  Diversified
GEOGRAPHIC PREFERENCE:
  No Preference (U.S.A.)
TYPES OF FUNDS:
  Loans with Equity Kickers
  Minimum: $500,000
  Maximum: $1,000,000

**Principal Mutual Life Insurance
  Company**
711 High Street
Des Moines, IA 50392
515-283-4466

CONTACT: Jeff Fossell
TYPE OF FIRM: Insurance
  Company
FUNDING PREFERENCE:
  First-Round Funding
  Later-Stage Funding
  Public Offering
INVESTMENT PREFERENCE:
  Diversified
  Conventional Energy (oil, natural
    gas, and coal)
  Communications Technology
  Manufacturing
  Natural Resources (other than
    those mentioned)
  Wholesale Distribution
  Financial Services
GEOGRAPHIC PREFERENCE:
  No Preference (U.S.A.)
  Midwest
  Home State Iowa
TYPES OF FUNDS:
  Loans
  Bonds
  Minimum: $1,000,000
  Maximum: Varies

KANSAS

Kansas Venture Capital, Inc.
6700 Antioch Plaza, Suite 460
Overland Park, KS 66204
913-262-7117

CONTACT:
  Thomas C. Blackburn, VP
TYPE OF FIRM: SBIC
FUNDING PREFERENCE:
  Third-Round Funding
  Fourth-Round Funding
  Later-Stage Funding

Leveraged Buyouts
Acquisitions
INVESTMENT PREFERENCE:
  Manufacturing
  Wholesale Distribution
GEOGRAPHIC PREFERENCE:
  Kansas Only
TYPES OF FUNDS:
  Equity (stock purchases)
  Loans with Equity Kickers
  Minimum: $500,000
  Maximum: $2,000,000

KENTUCKY

Mountain Ventures, Inc.
P.O. Box 1738
London, KY 40743
606-864-5175

CONTACT: Brenda McDaniel
TYPE OF FIRM: SBIC
FUNDING PREFERENCE:
  Start-Up Funding
  Later-Stage Funding
INVESTMENT PREFERENCE:
  Manufacturing
GEOGRAPHIC PREFERENCE:
  Immediate Area in Kentucky
TYPES OF FUNDS:
  Equity (stock purchases)
  Minimum: $3,000
  Maximum: $100,000

LOUISIANA

**Louisiana Small Business
Development Center**
N.E. Louisiana University

College of Business Administration
Administration Building 2–57
Monroe, LA 71209
318-342-5506

CONTACT: Dr. John Bauer
        Dr. Lesa Lawrence
TYPE OF FIRM: Consulting Firm
FUNDING PREFERENCE: N/A
INVESTMENT PREFERENCE:
  N/A
GEOGRAPHIC PREFERENCE:
  Louisiana Only
TYPES OF FUNDS: N/A

SCDF Investment Corporation
1006 Surrey Street
Lafayette, LA 70502
318-232-9206

CONTACT: A.J. McKnight
TYPE OF FIRM: MESBIC
FUNDING PREFERENCE:
  Second-Round Funding
INVESTMENT PREFERENCE:
  Diversified
  Computer Software
  Manufacturing
  Services
  Wholesale distribution
  Other High Technologies Not
    Mentioned
GEOGRAPHIC PREFERENCE:
  Southeast
TYPES OF FUNDS:
  Equity (stock purchases)
  Loans
  Minimum: Varies
  Maximum: Varies

MAINE

Maine Capital Corporation
70 Center Street
Portland, ME 04101
207-772-1001

CONTACT: JoAnn Lombardi
TYPE OF FIRM: Venture Capital
FUNDING PREFERENCE:
  Start-Up Funding
  Leveraged Buyouts
  Acquisitions
INVESTMENT PREFERENCE:
  Services
  Franchise
GEOGRAPHIC PREFERENCE:
  Northern New England
TYPES OF FUNDS:
  Equity (stock purchases)
  Minimum: $250,000
  Maximum: $1,000,000

MARYLAND

Arete Ventures, Inc.
6110 Executive Boulevard, #1040
Rockville, MD 20852
301-881-2555

CONTACT: LuAnne Buonomo
TYPE OF FIRM: Venture Capital
FUNDING PREFERENCE:
  Seed Funding
  Start-Up Funding
  First-Round Funding
  Second-Round Funding
  Third-Round Funding
INVESTMENT PREFERENCE:
  Alternative Energy

Conventional Energy (oil, natural gas, and coal)
Products/Services Related to the Gas and Electric Utility Industry
GEOGRAPHIC PREFERENCE:
No Preference (U.S.A.)
TYPES OF FUNDS:
Equity (stock purchases)
Minimum: $250,000
Maximum: $2,000,000

Greater Washington Investments, Inc.
5454 Wisconsin Avenue
Chevy Chase, MD 20815
301-738-3939

CONTACT: Amy Mathias
TYPE OF FIRM: SBIC
FUNDING PREFERENCE:
Seed Funding
Start-Up Funding
First-Round Funding
Second-Round Funding
Third-Round Funding
Fourth-Round Funding
Later-Stage Funding
Leveraged Buyouts
Acquisitions
INVESTMENT PREFERENCE:
Manufacturing
GEOGRAPHIC PREFERENCE:
No Preference (U.S.A.)
TYPES OF FUNDS:
Equity (stock purchases)
Minimum: $500,000
Maximum: $1,500,000

J. Rowe Price Threshold Partnerships
100 East Pratt Street

Baltimore, MD 21202
410-547-2000

CONTACT: Kera Taylor
TYPE OF FIRM: Mutual Funds
FUNDING PREFERENCE: None Given
INVESTMENT PREFERENCE:
Diversified
Manufacturing
GEOGRAPHIC PREFERENCE:
No Preference (U.S.A.)
TYPES OF FUNDS:
Loans
Bonds
Minimum: $2,500
Maximum: None Given

Jupiter National, Inc.
39 West Montgomery Avenue
Rockville, MD 20850
301-738-3939

CONTACT: Haywood Miller
TYPE OF FIRM:
Venture Capital
SBIC
FUNDING PREFERENCE:
Second-Round Funding
Third-Round Funding
Fourth-Round Funding
Later-Stage Funding
Leveraged Buyouts
Acquisitions
INVESTMENT PREFERENCE:
Diversified
Communications Technology
Manufacturing
Medical Technology
Real Estate
Wholesale Distribution
GEOGRAPHIC PREFERENCE:
Northeast

Middle Atlantic
Southeast
TYPES OF FUNDS:
Loans with Equity Kickers
Minimum: $500,000
Maximum: $1,500,000

**Maryland Small Business
Development Financing
Authority**
Redwood Tower
217 East Redwood Street
Suite 2240
Baltimore, MD 21202
410-333-4270

CONTACT: Stanley Tucker
TYPE OF FIRM: SBIC
FUNDING PREFERENCE:
Acquisitions
INVESTMENT PREFERENCE:
Franchise
GEOGRAPHIC PREFERENCE:
Immediate Area in Maryland
TYPES OF FUNDS:
Equity (stock purchases)
Minimum: Undetermined
Maximum: Undetermined

New Enterprise Associates
1119 St. Paul Street
Baltimore, MD 21202
410-244-0115

CONTACT: Frank Bonsal Jr.
TYPE OF FIRM: Venture Capital
FUNDING PREFERENCE:
Seed Funding
Start-Up Funding
First-Round Funding
INVESTMENT PREFERENCE:
Diversified

Communications Technology
Computer Hardware
Computer Software
Medical Technology
Retail
GEOGRAPHIC PREFERENCE:
No Preference (U.S.A.)
TYPES OF FUNDS:
Equity (stock purchases)
Minimum: $300,000
Maximum: $2,000,000

Syncom Capital Corporation
8401 Colesville Road, Suite 300
Silver Spring, MD 29010
301-608-3208

CONTACT: Patricia Cox
TYPE OF FIRM: SBIC
FUNDING PREFERENCE:
Later-Stage Funding
Acquisitions
INVESTMENT PREFERENCE:
Telecommunications
GEOGRAPHIC PREFERENCE:
No Preference (U.S.A.)
TYPES OF FUNDS:
Equity (stock purchases)
Minimum: Depends on Project
Maximum: Depends on Project

MASSACHUSETTS

Advent International Corporation
101 Federal Street
Boston, MA 02110
617-951-9400

CONTACT: George Pfeil
TYPE OF FIRM: Venture Capital

FUNDING PREFERENCE:
  Seed Funding
  Start-Up Funding
  Later-Stage Funding
INVESTMENT PREFERENCE:
  Computer Hardware
  Computer Software
  Manufacturing
  Medical Technology
  Services
  Wholesale Distribution
  Franchise
GEOGRAPHIC PREFERENCE:
  No Preference (U.S.A.)
TYPES OF FUNDS:
  Equity (stock purchases)
  Minimum: Depends on the
    Industry
  Maximum: Depends on the
    Industry

Ampersand Ventures
55 William Street, Suite 240
Wellesley, MA 02181
617-239-0700

CONTACT: Beverly J. Trainor
TYPE OF FIRM: Venture Capital
FUNDING PREFERENCE:
  Seed Funding
  Start-Up Funding
  First-Round Funding
  Second-Round Funding
  Third-Round Funding
  Fourth-Round Funding
  Later-Stage Funding
  Leveraged Buyouts
  Acquisitions
INVESTMENT PREFERENCE:
  Communications Technology
  Manufacturing
  Medical Technology

Specialty Chemicals and
    Materials
GEOGRAPHIC PREFERENCE:
  No Preference (U.S.A.)
TYPES OF FUNDS:
  Equity (stock purchases)
  Minimum: $500,000
  Maximum: $5,000,000

Atlas Venture
222 Berkeley Street
Boston, MA 02116
617-859-9290
FAX 617-859-9292

CONTACT: Axel Bichara
TYPE OF FIRM: Venture Capital
FUNDING PREFERENCE:
  Start-Up Funding
  First-Round Funding
  Second-Round Funding
INVESTMENT PREFERENCE:
  Communications Technology
  Computer Software
  Media
  Life Sciences
GEOGRAPHIC PREFERENCE:
  Northeast
  Europe
TYPES OF FUNDS:
  Equity (stock purchases)
  Minimum: $750,000
  Maximum: $2,000,000

Banc Boston Venture, Inc.
100 Federal Street
Boston, MA 02110
617-434-2442

CONTACT: Frederick Fritz,
    President
TYPE OF FIRM: SBIC

FUNDING PREFERENCE:
Second-Round Funding
Third-Round Funding
Fourth-Round Funding
Later-Stage Funding
INVESTMENT PREFERENCE:
Diversified
GEOGRAPHIC PREFERENCE:
No Preference (U.S.A.)
TYPES OF FUNDS:
Equity (stock purchases)
Minimum: $250,000
Maximum: $2,000,000

Boston Capital Ventures
Old City Hall
45 School Street
Boston, MA 02108
617-227-6550

CONTACT: Charles Warden
TYPE OF FIRM: SBIC
FUNDING PREFERENCE:
Later-Stage Funding
Acquisitions
Public Offering
INVESTMENT PREFERENCE:
Communications Technology
Computer Software
Other High Technologies Not
Mentioned
Healthcare Services and Products
GEOGRAPHIC PREFERENCE:
Immediate Area of Boston
Chicago
TYPES OF FUNDS:
Minimum: $500,000
Maximum: $5,000,000

**Burr, Egan, Deleage and
Company**
1 Post Office Square, Suite 3800

Boston, MA 02109
617-482-8020

CONTACT: Craig Burr
TYPE OF FIRM: Venture Capital
FUNDING PREFERENCE:
Start-Up Funding
First-Round Funding
Second-Round Funding
Third-Round Funding
Fourth-Round Funding
Later-Stage Funding
Acquisitions
INVESTMENT PREFERENCE:
Diversified
Computer Hardware
Manufacturing
Media
GEOGRAPHIC PREFERENCE:
No Preference (U.S.A.)
TYPES OF FUNDS:
Equity (stock purchases)
Loans
Minimum: $1,500,000
Maximum: $5,000,000

Comdisco Venture Partners
One Newton Executive Park
2221 Washington Street, 3rd Floor
Newton Lower Falls, MA
02162-1417
617-244-6622
FAX 617-630-5599

CONTACT: Gregory V. Stento,
General Partner
TYPE OF FIRM:
Venture Capital
Leasing Firm
FUNDING PREFERENCE:
Start-Up Funding
First-Round Funding
Second-Round Funding

INVESTMENT PREFERENCE:
Diversified
Communications Technology
Computer Hardware
Computer Software
Medical Technology
Retail
Other High Technologies Not
Mentioned
GEOGRAPHIC PREFERENCE:
No Preference (U.S.A.)
TYPES OF FUNDS:
Equity (stock purchases)
Loans with Equity Kickers
Leasing
Accounts Receivable Financing
Minimum: Depends on the Type
of Fund
Maximum: Depends on the Type
of Fund

Fidelity Capital
82 Devonshire Street, Room #25C
Boston, MA 02109
617-728-6031

CONTACT: Neal Yanotsky
TYPE OF FIRM: Venture Capital
FUNDING PREFERENCE:
First-Round Funding
Second-Round Funding
Leveraged Buyouts
INVESTMENT PREFERENCE:
Diversified
GEOGRAPHIC PREFERENCE:
Northeast
TYPES OF FUNDS:
Equity (stock purchases)
Minimum: $1,000,000
Maximum: $5,000,000

**Greylock Management
Corporation**
One Federal Street
Boston, MA 02110
618-423-5525

CONTACT: Jennifer Goslin
TYPE OF FIRM: Venture Capital
FUNDING PREFERENCE:
Fourth-Round Funding
Later-Stage Funding
Leveraged Buyouts
Acquisitions
INVESTMENT PREFERENCE:
Communications Technology
Computer Software
Medical Technology
Other High Technologies Not
Mentioned
GEOGRAPHIC PREFERENCE:
No Preference (U.S.A.)
TYPES OF FUNDS:
Equity (stock purchases)
Minimum: $1,000,000
Maximum: Not Determined

Matrix Partners
One International Place, Suite 3250
Boston, MA 02110
617-345-6740

CONTACT: Timothy Barrows
TYPE OF FIRM: Venture Capital
FUNDING PREFERENCE:
Start-Up Funding
First-Round Funding
Second-Round Funding
Third-Round Funding
Leveraged Buyouts
INVESTMENT PREFERENCE:
Communications Technology

Computer Software
Manufacturing
Media
Medical Technology
Retail
Services
GEOGRAPHIC PREFERENCE:
Northeast
Northwest
Southwest
TYPES OF FUNDS:
Equity (stock purchases)
Minimum: $750,000
Maximum: $5,000,000

Morgan Holland Ventures
One Liberty Square
Boston, MA 02109
617-423-1765

CONTACT: Joseph T. McCullen Jr.
TYPE OF FIRM: Venture Capital
FUNDING PREFERENCE:
Seed Funding
Start-Up Funding
First-Round Funding
INVESTMENT PREFERENCE:
Communications Technology
Computer Software
Medical Technology
Technical Services
Other High Technologies Not
Mentioned
GEOGRAPHIC PREFERENCE:
No Preference (U.S.A.)
TYPES OF FUNDS:
Equity (stock purchases)
Minimum: $500,000 (depends on
the stage)

Maximum: $2,000,000
(Can put up to $6,000,000 in any
one company over a period of
time.)

Palmer Partners, LP
300 Unicorn Park Drive
Woburn, MA 01801
617-742-7825

CONTACT: Michael Fitzgerald
TYPE OF FIRM: Venture Capital
FUNDING PREFERENCE:
Seed Funding
Start-Up Funding
First-Round Funding
INVESTMENT PREFERENCE:
Diversified
GEOGRAPHIC PREFERENCE:
No Preference (U.S.A.)
TYPES OF FUNDS:
Equity (stock purchases)
Loans with Equity Kickers
Minimum: $250,000
Maximum: $1,000,000

**Pioneer Ventures Limited
Partnership**
60 State Street
Boston, MA 02109
617-742-7825

CONTACT: Christen Anderson
TYPE OF FIRM: Venture Capital
FUNDING PREFERENCE:
Start-Up Funding
First-Round Funding
Leveraged Buyouts
INVESTMENT PREFERENCE:
Diversified

GEOGRAPHIC PREFERENCE:
No Preference (U.S.A.)
TYPES OF FUNDS:
Equity (stock purchases)
Minimum: $200,000
Maximum: Expansion $500,000

Sprout Group
75 State Street, 9th Floor
Boston, MA 02109
617-342-8100

CONTACT: Larry Reeder
TYPE OF FIRM: Venture Capital
FUNDING PREFERENCE:
Seed Funding
Start-Up Funding
First-Round Funding
Second-Round Funding
Third-Round Funding
Fourth-Round Funding
Later-Stage Funding
Leveraged Buyouts
Acquisitions
INVESTMENT PREFERENCE:
Diversified
Communications Technology
Computer Hardware
Computer Software
Manufacturing
Medical Technology
Retail
Services
Wholesale Distribution
GEOGRAPHIC PREFERENCE:
No Preference (U.S.A.)
TYPES OF FUNDS:
Equity (stock purchases)
Minimum: $1,000,000
Maximum: $5,000,000

The Venture Capital Fund of New England
160 Federal Street, 23rd Floor
Boston, MA 02110
617-439-4646

CONTACT: Richard A. Farrell
TYPE OF FIRM: Venture Capital
FUNDING PREFERENCE:
Start-Up Funding
First-Round Funding
INVESTMENT PREFERENCE:
Communications Technology
Computer Hardware
Computer Software
Media
Medical Technology
GEOGRAPHIC PREFERENCE:
Northwest
TYPES OF FUNDS:
Equity (stock purchases)
Minimum: $500,000
Maximum: $1,000,000

MICHIGAN

Dearborn Capital Corporation (Subsidiary of Ford)
P.O. Box 1729
Dearborn, MI 48121
313-337-8578

CONTACT: Mike Kehres
TYPE OF FIRM: SSBIC
FUNDING PREFERENCE: None
Given
INVESTMENT PREFERENCE:
Services
Production Parts

GEOGRAPHIC PREFERENCE:
No Preference (U.S.A.)
TYPES OF FUNDS
Loans
Minimum: $100,000
Maximum: $1,000,000

TYPES OF FUNDS:
Loans
Minimum: $50,000
Maximum: $500,000

MINNESOTA

Greater Detroit Bidco, Inc.
The Penobscot Building
645 Griswold, Suite 2146
Detroit, MI 48226
313-962-4326

CONTACT: Catherine Lockhart
TYPE OF FIRM: SBIC
FUNDING PREFERENCE:
Later-Stage Funding
INVESTMENT PREFERENCE:
Franchise
GEOGRAPHIC PREFERENCE:
Immediate area of Michigan
TYPES OF FUNDS:
Loans
Maximum: $450,000

Motor Enterprises, Inc.
3044 West Grand Boulevard
Detroit, MI 48202
313-556-4273

CONTACT: James Kobus
TYPE OF FIRM: SSBIC
FUNDING PREFERENCE:
First-Round Funding
INVESTMENT PREFERENCE:
Diversified
GEOGRAPHIC PREFERENCE:
Midwest

Cherry Tree Ventures
3800 West 80th Street, Suite 1400
Minneapolis, MN 55431
612-893-9012

CONTACT: John Bergstrom
TYPE OF FIRM: Venture Capital
FUNDING PREFERENCE:
Start-Up Funding
First-Round Funding
Second-Round Funding
Leveraged Buyouts
INVESTMENT PREFERENCE:
Diversified
GEOGRAPHIC PREFERENCE:
Home State of Minnesota
TYPES OF FUNDS:
Equity (stock purchases)
Minimum: $500,000
Maximum: $1,000,000

Norwest Equity Partners
222 South Ninth Street
Minneapolis, MN 55402
612-667-1950

CONTACT: Daniel Haggerty,
President
TYPE OF FIRM: Venture Capital
FUNDING PREFERENCE:
Start-Up Funding

First-Round Funding
Second-Round Funding
Third-Round Funding
Fourth-Round Funding
Later-Stage Funding
INVESTMENT PREFERENCE:
  Diversified
  Manufacturing
  Franchise
GEOGRAPHIC PREFERENCE:
  Midwest
  Far West
  Southwest
TYPES OF FUNDS:
  Equity (stock purchases)
  Minimum: $1,000,000
  Maximum: $6,000,000

Piper Jaffray Ventures, Inc.
Piper Jaffray Tower
222 South Ninth Street
Minneapolis, MN 55402
612-342-6310

CONTACT: Buzz Benson
TYPE OF FIRM: Venture Capital
FUNDING PREFERENCE:
  Seed Funding
  Start-Up Funding
  First-Round Funding
  Leveraged Buyouts
  Public Offering
INVESTMENT PREFERENCE:
  Diversified
GEOGRAPHIC PREFERENCE:
  No Preference (U.S.A.)
TYPES OF FUNDS:
  Equity (stock purchases)
  Minimum: $250,000
  Maximum: $1,000,000

MISSISSIPPI

Sun-Delta Capital Access Center, Inc.
819 Main Street
Greenville, MS 38702
601-335-5291

CONTACT: Howard Bouttei Jr.
TYPE OF FIRM: MESBIC
FUNDING PREFERENCE:
  Start-Up Funding
  First-Round Funding
  Second-Round Funding
  Leveraged Buyouts
  Acquisitions
INVESTMENT PREFERENCE:
  Diversified
GEOGRAPHIC PREFERENCE:
  No Preference (U.S.A.)
TYPES OF FUNDS:
  Equity (stock purchases)
  Loans
  Loans with Equity Kickers
  Minimum: $25,000
  Maximum: $200,000

MISSOURI

Capital For Business, Inc.
11 South Meramec, Suite 800
St. Louis, MO 63105
314-746-7427

CONTACT: James F. O'Donnell
TYPE OF FIRM:
  Venture Capital
  SBIC

FUNDING PREFERENCE:
Third-Round Funding
Fourth-Round Funding
Later-Stage Funding
Leveraged Buyouts
Acquisitions
INVESTMENT PREFERENCE:
Manufacturing
Wholesale Distribution
GEOGRAPHIC PREFERENCE:
Midwest
Home State of Missouri
Minnesota to Texas
Pennsylvania to Utah
TYPES OF FUNDS:
Subordinate Debt with Warrants
Preferred Stock with Warrants
Minimum: $500,000
Maximum: $5,000,000

CFB Venture Fund
11 South Meramec, Suite 800
St. Louis, MO 63105
314-746-7427

CONTACT: James O'Donnell,
Chairman
TYPE OF FIRM: SBIC
FUNDING PREFERENCE:
First-Round Funding
Second-Round Funding
Later-Stage Funding
Acquisitions
INVESTMENT PREFERENCE:
Manufacturing
Medical Technology
GEOGRAPHIC PREFERENCE:
No Preference (U.S.A.)
TYPES OF FUNDS: N/A
Minimum: $300,000
Maximum: $1,000,000

**Kansas City Life Insurance
Company**
3520 Broadway
Kansas City, MO 64111
816-753-7000

CONTACT: Scott M. Stone
TYPE OF FIRM: Insurance
Company
FUNDING PREFERENCE: N/A
INVESTMENT PREFERENCE:
Diversified
GEOGRAPHIC PREFERENCE:
No Preference (U.S.A.)
TYPES OF FUNDS:
Loans
Bonds
Leasing
Minimum: $1,000,000
Maximum: $15,000,000

**United Missouri Capital
Corporation**
1010 Grand Avenue
Kansas City, MO 64111
816-860-7333

CONTACT: Noel Shull, Manager
TYPE OF FIRM: SBIC
FUNDING PREFERENCE:
Second-Round Funding
Third-Round Funding
Fourth-Round Funding
Later-Stage Funding
Acquisitions
INVESTMENT PREFERENCE:
Diversified
GEOGRAPHIC PREFERENCE:
Home State of Missouri
TYPES OF FUNDS:
Equity (stock purchases)

Loans with Equity Kickers
Minimum: $150,000
Maximum: $1,000,000 to
2,000,000

NEVADA

**Ameritas Life Insurance
Corporation**
5900 O Street
Lincoln, NE 68510
402-467-6973

CONTACT: Pat Henry
TYPE OF FIRM: Insurance
Company
FUNDING PREFERENCE:
Later-Stage Funding
INVESTMENT PREFERENCE:
Diversified
GEOGRAPHIC PREFERENCE:
None Given
TYPES OF FUNDS:
Bonds
Minimum: $1,000,000
Maximum: $5,000,000

NEW JERSEY

Accel Partners
One Palmer Square
Princeton, NJ 08542
609-683-4500

CONTACT: Donald Gooding
TYPE OF FIRM: Venture Capital
FUNDING PREFERENCE:
Seed Funding
Start-Up Funding

First-Round Funding
Second-Round Funding
Third-Round Funding
INVESTMENT PREFERENCE:
Communications Technology
Computer Software
Medical Technology
GEOGRAPHIC PREFERENCE:
No Preference (U.S.A.)
TYPES OF FUNDS:
Equity (stock purchases)
Minimum: $1,000,000
Maximum: $6,000,000

CIT Group/Venture Capital
650 CIT Drive
Livingston, NJ 07932
201-740-5429

CONTACT: Margaret Crisbacher
TYPE OF FIRM:
Venture Capital
SBIC
FUNDING PREFERENCE:
Acquisitions
INVESTMENT PREFERENCE:
Diversified
Manufacturing
Franchise
GEOGRAPHIC PREFERENCE:
No Preference
TYPES OF FUNDS:
Equity (stock purchases)
Minimum: $1,000,000
Maximum: $5,000,000

DSV Partners
221 Nassay Street
Princeton, NJ 08542
609-924-6420

CONTACT: Morton Collins
TYPE OF FIRM:
Venture Capital
SBIC
FUNDING PREFERENCE:
Seed Funding
Start-Up Funding
First-Round Funding
INVESTMENT PREFERENCE:
Computer Hardware
Computer Software
Medical Technology
GEOGRAPHIC PREFERENCE:
No Preference
TYPES OF FUNDS:
Equity (stock purchases)
Loans with Equity Kickers
Minimum: $250,000
Maximum: $1,000,000

Geocapital Partners
One Bridge Plaza
Fort Lee, NJ 07024
201-461-9292

TYPE OF FIRM: Venture Capital
FUNDING PREFERENCE:
Start-Up Funding
INVESTMENT PREFERENCE:
Computer Software
GEOGRAPHIC PREFERENCE:
No Preference
TYPES OF FUNDS:
Equity (stock purchases)
Minimum: Varies
Maximum: Varies

Tappan Zee Capital Corporation
201 Lower Notch Road
Little Falls, NJ 07424
201-256-8280

CONTACT: Jeffrey Birnberg,
President
TYPE OF FIRM:
Venture Capital
SBIC
FUNDING PREFERENCE:
Acquisitions
Collateral Loans
INVESTMENT PREFERENCE:
Real Estate
GEOGRAPHIC PREFERENCE:
No Preference
TYPES OF FUNDS:
Loans
Minimum: Varies
Maximum: Varies

NEW YORK

BT Capital Corporation
280 Park Avenue
New York, NY 10017
212-454-1903

CONTACT: Noel Urben
TYPE OF FIRM: SBIC
FUNDING PREFERENCE:
Second-Round Funding
Third-Round Funding
Later-Stage Funding
Leveraged Buyouts
Expansion Financing/
Recapitalization
INVESTMENT PREFERENCE:
Manufacturing
Retail
Services
Wholesale Distribution
GEOGRAPHIC PREFERENCE:
No Preference

TYPES OF FUNDS:
 Equity (stock purchases)
 Loans with Equity Kickers
 Minimum: $5,000,000
 Maximum: $20,000,000

**Chase Manhattan Capital
 Corporation**
One Chase Plaza, 7th Floor
New York, NY 10017
212-270-3220

CONTACT: Matt Lori
TYPE OF FIRM: SBIC
FUNDING PREFERENCE:
 Leveraged Buyouts
 Acquisitions
INVESTMENT PREFERENCE:
 Manufacturing
 Media
 Retail
GEOGRAPHIC PREFERENCE:
 No Preference
TYPES OF FUNDS:
 Equity (stock purchases)
 Minimum: $5,000,000
 Maximum: $20,000,000

**Chemical Venture Capital
 Assistance**
270 Park Avenue, 5th Floor
New York, NY 10017
212-270-3220

CONTACT: Max Liechtenstein
TYPE OF FIRM: SBIC
FUNDING PREFERENCE:
 Seed Funding
 Start-Up Funding
 Leveraged Buyouts
 Acquisitions

INVESTMENT PREFERENCE:
 Diversified
GEOGRAPHIC PREFERENCE:
 No Preference
 Other: Europe
TYPES OF FUNDS:
 Equity (stock purchases)
 Minimum: $5,000
 Maximum: $30,000

**CIBC Wood Gundy Ventures,
 Inc.**
425 Lexington Avenue, 9th Floor
New York, NY 10017

CONTACT: Candy White
TYPE OF FIRM: SBIC
FUNDING PREFERENCE: None
 Given
INVESTMENT PREFERENCE:
 Diversified
GEOGRAPHIC PREFERENCE:
 None Given
TYPES OF FUNDS:
 Equity (stock purchases)

Citicorp Venture Capital, Ltd.
399 Park Avenue, 14th Floor
Zone 4
New York, NY 10043
212-559-1127

CONTACT: Peter Gary
TYPE OF FIRM: Venture Capital
FUNDING PREFERENCE:
 Leveraged Buyouts
INVESTMENT PREFERENCE:
 Manufacturing
 Franchise
GEOGRAPHIC PREFERENCE:
 No Preference

TYPES OF FUNDS:
Loans
Minimum: $500,000
Maximum: Not Determined

CW Group
1041 3rd Avenue
New York, NY 10021
212-308-5266

CONTACT: Walter Channing Jr.,
General Partner
TYPE OF FIRM: Venture Capital
FUNDING PREFERENCE:
Seed Funding
Start-Up Funding
First-Round Funding
INVESTMENT PREFERENCE:
Medical Technology
GEOGRAPHIC PREFERENCE:
No Preference
TYPES OF FUNDS:
Equity (stock purchases)
Minimum: $100,000
Maximum: $3,000,000

Edwards Capital Company
Two Park Avenue, 20th Floor
New York, NY 10016
212-686-5449

CONTACT: Mr. Teitlebaum
TYPE OF FIRM: SBIC
FUNDING PREFERENCE:
Leveraged Buyouts
INVESTMENT PREFERENCE:
Diversified
GEOGRAPHIC PREFERENCE:
Immediate Area in New York
TYPES OF FUNDS:
Bonds with Equity Kickers

Minimum: $500,000
Maximum: $3,000,000

Endeavor Capital Management
2 Tudor City Place, Suite 2GN
New York, NY 10017
212-490-6975

CONTACT: Nancy Haar
Anthony Buffa
TYPE OF FIRM: Venture Capital
FUNDING PREFERENCE:
Start-Up Funding
First-Round Funding
INVESTMENT PREFERENCE:
Communications Technology
Computer Hardware
Computer Software
Manufacturing
Media
Retail
Services
Other High Technologies Not
Mentioned
GEOGRAPHIC PREFERENCE:
No Preference
TYPES OF FUNDS:
Equity (stock purchases)
Minimum: none
Maximum: $5,000,000

First County Capital, Inc.
135-14 Northern Boulevard
2nd Floor
Flushing, NY 11364
718-461-1778

CONTACT: Orest M. Glut
TYPE OF FIRM: MESBIC
FUNDING PREFERENCE:
Start-Up Funding

First-Round Funding
Second-Round Funding
Third-Round Funding
INVESTMENT PREFERENCE:
Diversified
Medical Technology
Retail
Services
Wholesale Distribution
GEOGRAPHIC PREFERENCE:
Northeast
TYPES OF FUNDS:
Equity (stock purchases)
Loans
Loans with Equity Kickers
Minimum: $50,000
Maximum: $300,000

First Wall Street SBIC, LP
26 Broadway, Suite 1320
New York, NY 10004
212-742-3770

CONTACT: Celeste Fierro
TYPE OF FIRM: SBIC
FUNDING PREFERENCE:
Leveraged Buyouts
Acquisitions
Collateral
INVESTMENT PREFERENCE:
Diversified
Manufacturing
GEOGRAPHIC PREFERENCE:
No Preference
TYPES OF FUNDS:
Maximum: $600,000
Three Partners: $3,000,000

Funder Capital Corporation
525 Northern Boulevard
Great Neck, NY 11021
516-466-8550

CONTACT: Howard Sommer
TYPE OF FIRM: SBIC
FUNDING PREFERENCE:
Later-Stage Funding
Leveraged Buyouts
Acquisitions
INVESTMENT PREFERENCE:
Diversified
GEOGRAPHIC PREFERENCE:
Northeast
TYPES OF FUNDS:
Loans
Loans with Equity Kickers
Minimum: $250,000
Maximum: $1,000,000

IBJS Capital Corporation
One State Street
New York, NY 10004
212-858-2827

CONTACT: Paul J. Echausse
TYPE OF FIRM: SBIC
FUNDING PREFERENCE:
Later-Stage Funding
Leveraged Buyouts
Acquisitions
Mezzanine
INVESTMENT PREFERENCE:
Diversified
GEOGRAPHIC PREFERENCE:
No Preference
TYPES OF FUNDS:
Equity (stock purchases)
Loans with Equity Kickers
Minimum: $1,000,000
Maximum: $5,000,000

InterEquity Capital Partners, LP
220 Fifth Avenue
New York, NY 10001
212-779-2022

CONTACT: Abraham Goldstein
TYPE OF FIRM: SBIC
FUNDING PREFERENCE:
  First-Round Funding
  Second-Round Funding
  Third-Round Funding
  Fourth-Round Funding
  Later-Stage Funding
  Leveraged Buyouts
  Acquisitions
  Public Offerings
INVESTMENT PREFERENCE:
  Diversified
  Communications Technology
  Computer Software
  Media
  Medical Technology
  Other High Technologies Not
    Mentioned
GEOGRAPHIC PREFERENCE:
  Northeast
  Home State of New York
TYPES OF FUNDS:
  Equity (stock purchases)
  Loans with Equity Kickers
  Minimum: $200,000
  Maximum: $3,000,000

J.H. Whitney and Company
630 5th Avenue, Suite 3200
New York, NY 10111
212-332-2400

CONTACT: Joan Mullins
TYPE OF FIRM: Venture Capital
FUNDING PREFERENCE:
  Start-Up Funding
  First-Round Funding
  Leveraged Buyouts
INVESTMENT PREFERENCE:
  Diversified
GEOGRAPHIC PREFERENCE:
  No Preference

TYPES OF FUNDS:
  Equity (stock purchases)
  Minimum: $2,000,000
  Maximum: $5,000,000

J.P. Morgan Capital Corporation
60 Wall Street
New York, NY 10260
212-648-9781

CONTACT: Marilyn Eiss
TYPE OF FIRM: Investment
  Banking
FUNDING PREFERENCE:
  Later-Stage Funding
  Leveraged Buyouts
  Acquisitions
  Turnaround Situations
INVESTMENT PREFERENCE:
  Diversified
GEOGRAPHIC PREFERENCE:
  No Preference (U.S.A.)
  Europe
  Asia
  Latin America
TYPES OF FUNDS:
  Equity (stock purchases)
  Minimum: $5,000,000
  Maximum: $50,000,000

J.P. Morgan Capital Corporation
60 Wall Street
New York, NY 10260
212-648-9781

CONTACT: Marilyn Eiss,
  Associate
TYPE OF FIRM:
  Venture Capital
  SBIC
FUNDING PREFERENCE:
  Second-Round Funding

INVESTMENT PREFERENCE:
Communications Technology
Computer Software
Media
Medical Technology
Retail
GEOGRAPHIC PREFERENCE:
No Preference (U.S.A.)
Global
TYPES OF FUNDS:
Equity (stock purchases)
Minimum: $10,000,000
Maximum: $25,000,000

KOCO Capital Company, LP
111 Radio Circle
Mount Kisco, NY 10549
914-242-2309

CONTACT: Albert G. Pastino
TYPE OF FIRM: SBIC
FUNDING PREFERENCE:
Second-Round Funding
Third-Round Funding
Fourth-Round Funding
Later-Stage Funding
Leveraged Buyouts
INVESTMENT PREFERENCE:
Diversified
GEOGRAPHIC PREFERENCE:
No Preference (U.S.A.)
TYPES OF FUNDS:
Equity (stock purchases)
Loans with Equity Kickers
Minimum: $250,000
Maximum: $1,000,000

The Lambda Funds
41 East 57th Street, 31st Floor
New York, NY 10022
212-838-0005

CONTACT: Celeste Barona
TYPE OF FIRM:
Venture Capital
SBIC
FUNDING PREFERENCE:
Second-Round Funding
Third-Round Funding
Fourth-Round Funding
Later-Stage Funding
Leveraged Buyouts
INVESTMENT PREFERENCE:
Diversified
GEOGRAPHIC PREFERENCE:
No Preference (U.S.A.)
TYPES OF FUNDS:
Equity (stock purchases)
Minimum: $500,000
Maximum: $1,000,000

**Nat West USA Capital
Corporation**
175 Water Street, 27th Floor
New York, NY 10038
212-602-1200

CONTACT: George Triebenbacher
TYPE OF FIRM: SBIC
FUNDING PREFERENCE:
Later-Stage Funding
Leveraged Buyouts
Acquisitions
INVESTMENT PREFERENCE:
Diversified
Manufacturing
GEOGRAPHIC PREFERENCE:
No Preference (U.S.A.)
TYPES OF FUNDS:
Equity (stock purchases)
Minimum: $1,000
Maximum: $5,000

New York Business Development Corporation
P.O. Box 738
Albany, NY 12201
518-463-2268

CONTACT: Robert Lazar
TYPE OF FIRM: SBIC
FUNDING PREFERENCE:
  Leveraged Buyouts
  Acquisitions
INVESTMENT PREFERENCE:
  Real Estate
  Other High Technologies Not
    Mentioned
GEOGRAPHIC PREFERENCE:
  Immediate Area in New York
    State
TYPES OF FUNDS:
  Equity (stock purchases)
  Minimum: $100,000
  Maximum: $1,000,000

Norwood Venture Corporation
1430 Broadway, Suite 1607
New York, NY 10018
212-869-5075

CONTACT: Mark Littell, President
TYPE OF FIRM: SBIC
FUNDING PREFERENCE:
  Later-Stage Funding
INVESTMENT PREFERENCE:
  Manufacturing
  Services
GEOGRAPHIC PREFERENCE:
  No Preference (U.S.A.)
TYPES OF FUNDS:
  Equity (stock purchases)
  Minimum: $200,000
  Maximum: $1,000,000

OMNY Capital II, LP
135 East 57th Street, 26th Floor
New York, NY 10022
212-909-8432

CONTACT: Robert Davidoff
TYPE OF FIRM: SBIC
FUNDING PREFERENCE:
  First-Round Funding
  Second-Round Funding
  Third-Round Funding
  Leveraged Buyouts
INVESTMENT PREFERENCE:
  Diversified
GEOGRAPHIC PREFERENCE:
  No Preference (U.S.A.)
TYPES OF FUNDS:
  Equity (stock purchases)
  Minimum: $200,000
  Maximum: $2,000,000

OMNY Capital II, LP
135 East 57th Street
New York, NY 10022
212-909-8428

CONTACT: Robert Davidoff
         Howard Davidoff
TYPE OF FIRM: SBIC
FUNDING PREFERENCE:
  First-Round Funding
  Leveraged Buyouts
  Acquisitions
INVESTMENT PREFERENCE:
  Diversified
GEOGRAPHIC PREFERENCE:
  No Preference (U.S.A.)
TYPES OF FUNDS:
  Loans with Equity Kickers
  Minimum: $250,000
  Maximum: $500,000

Sterling Commercial Capital, Inc.
175 Great Neck Road, Suite 408
Great Neck, NY 11021
516-482-7374

CONTACT: Philip Wachtler
TYPE OF FIRM: SBIC
FUNDING PREFERENCE:
  Second-Round Funding
  Third-Round Funding
  Later-Stage Funding
INVESTMENT PREFERENCE:
  Manufacturing
  Real Estate
  Retail
  Franchise
GEOGRAPHIC PREFERENCE:
  No Preference (U.S.A.)
TYPES OF FUNDS:
  Equity (stock purchases)
  Minimum: $200,000
  Maximum: $2,000,000

TLC Funding Corporation
660 White Plains Road
Tarrytown, NY 10591
914-332-5200

CONTACT: Pearl Rubin
TYPE OF FIRM: SBIC
FUNDING PREFERENCE:
  Later-Stage Funding
INVESTMENT PREFERENCE:
  Diversified
GEOGRAPHIC PREFERENCE:
  New York
  New Jersey
  Connecticut
TYPES OF FUNDS:
  Loans
  Minimum: $50,000
  Maximum: $300,000

Vega Capital Corporation
80 Business Park Drive, Suite 201
Armonk, NY 10504
914-273-1025

CONTACT: Ron Linden
TYPE OF FIRM: SBIC
FUNDING PREFERENCE:
  Second-Round Funding
  Fourth-Round Funding
  Acquisitions
INVESTMENT PREFERENCE:
  Diversified
  Manufacturing
GEOGRAPHIC PREFERENCE:
  Northeast
  Middle Atlantic
  Southeast
TYPES OF FUNDS:
  Loans
  Minimum: $100,000
  Maximum: $2,500,000

**Venture Opportunities
  Corporation**
110 East 59th Street, 29th Floor
New York, NY 10022
212-832-3737

CONTACT: Jerry March
TYPE OF FIRM: MESBIC
FUNDING PREFERENCE:
  First-Round Funding
  Second-Round Funding
  Acquisitions
INVESTMENT PREFERENCE:
  Diversified
GEOGRAPHIC PREFERENCE:
  No Preference (U.S.A.)
TYPES OF FUNDS:
  Equity (stock purchases)
  Loans

Loans with Equity Kickers
Minimum: $100,000
Maximum: $800,000

NORTH CAROLINA

Nations Banc SBIC Corporation
901 West Trade Street, Suite 1020
Charlotte, NC 28202
704-386-5000

CONTACT: Rebecca Griffin
TYPE OF FIRM: SBIC
FUNDING PREFERENCE:
    Second-Round Funding
    Third-Round Funding
    Fourth-Round Funding
INVESTMENT PREFERENCE:
    Manufacturing
GEOGRAPHIC PREFERENCE:
    Middle Atlantic
TYPES OF FUNDS:
    Equity (stock purchases)
    Minimum: $50,000
    Maximum: $200,000

NORTH DAKOTA

Bank of North Dakota
700 East Main Avenue
P.O. Box 5509
Bismarck, ND 58501
701-328-5600
TYPE OF FIRM: Commercial
    Bank
FUNDING PREFERENCE:
    Commercial Loans

INVESTMENT PREFERENCE:
    Fixed Income Treasuries
GEOGRAPHIC PREFERENCE:
    No Preference (U.S.A.)
TYPES OF FUNDS:
    Loans
    Bonds
    Minimum: $5,000,000
    Maximum: $50,000,000

OHIO

Banc One Capital Securities
10 West Broad Street, Suite 200
Columbus, OH 43271
614-248-5800

CONTACT: Michael Vogel
TYPE OF FIRM: SBIC
FUNDING PREFERENCE:
    Later-Stage Funding
INVESTMENT PREFERENCE:
    Manufacturing
GEOGRAPHIC PREFERENCE:
    Northeast
TYPES OF FUNDS:
    Equity (stock purchases)
    Minimum: $2,000,000
    Maximum: $5,000,000

Center City MESBIC, Inc.
8 North Main Street
Dayton, OH 45402
513-461-6164

CONTACT: Steve Budd, Manager
TYPE OF FIRM: MESBIC
FUNDING PREFERENCE:
    Start-Up Funding
    First-Round Funding

Second-Round Funding
Third-Round Funding
Fourth-Round Funding
Later-Stage Funding
INVESTMENT PREFERENCE:
Diversified
GEOGRAPHIC PREFERENCE:
Immediate Area in Ohio
TYPES OF FUNDS:
Equity (stock purchases)
Loans
Bonds
Minimum: $25,000
Maximum: $150,000

Clarion Capital Corporation
1801 East 9th Street
Cleveland, OH 44114
216-687-1096

CONTACT: Dan O'Neil
TYPE OF FIRM: Venture Capital
FUNDING PREFERENCE:
Later-Stage Funding
INVESTMENT PREFERENCE:
Natural Resources
High Technology
GEOGRAPHIC PREFERENCE:
No Preference (U.S.A.)
Midwest
TYPES OF FUNDS:
Loans
Minimum: $250,000
Maximum: $1,000,000

Key Equity Capital Corporation
127 Public Square, 4th Floor
Cleveland, OH 44114
216-689-5776

CONTACT: Shawn Ward
TYPE OF FIRM: SBIC

FUNDING PREFERENCE:
Later-Stage Funding
Acquisitions
INVESTMENT PREFERENCE:
Manufacturing
GEOGRAPHIC PREFERENCE:
No Preference (U.S.A.)
TYPES OF FUNDS:
Equity (stock purchases)
Minimum: $1,000,000
Maximum: $15,000,000

Key Equity Capital Corporation
127 Public Square, 6th Floor
Cleveland, OH 44114
216-689-5774

CONTACT: David Given
          Raymond Lancaster
TYPE OF FIRM: Equity Investment
FUNDING PREFERENCE:
Later-Stage Funding
Leveraged Buyouts
INVESTMENT PREFERENCE:
Manufacturing
Services
GEOGRAPHIC PREFERENCE:
No Preference (U.S.A.)
TYPES OF FUNDS:
Equity (stock purchases)
Minimum: $2,000,000
Maximum: $15,000,000

**National City Venture
Corporation and National City
Capital Corporation**
1965 East Sixth Street
Cleveland, OH 44114
216-575-2491

CONTACT: Carl E. Baldassarre, VP
    Sean P. Richardson, VP
    Todd S. McCuraig,
      Investment Officer
TYPE OF FIRM:
  Venture Capital
  NCCC
  Venture Capital Subsidiary of
    National City Corporation
    Bank NCVC
FUNDING PREFERENCE:
  First-Round Funding
  Second-Round Funding
  Third-Round Funding
  Leveraged Buyouts
INVESTMENT PREFERENCE:
  Manufacturing
  Medical Technology
  Retail
  Services
GEOGRAPHIC PREFERENCE:
  Midwest
TYPES OF FUNDS:
  Equity (stock purchases)
  Loans with Equity Kickers
  Minimum: $1,000,000
  Maximum: $5,000,000

OKLAHOMA

Davis Venture Partners
One Williams Center, Suite 2000
Tulsa, OK 74172
918-584-7272

CONTACT: Barry Davis
TYPE OF FIRM: Venture Capital
FUNDING PREFERENCE:
  First-Round Funding
  Second-Round Funding
  Third-Round Funding
  Leveraged Buyouts
  Acquisitions

INVESTMENT PREFERENCE:
  Diversified
  Communications Technology
  Manufacturing
  Medical Technology
  Natural Resources
  Wholesale Distribution
GEOGRAPHIC PREFERENCE:
  Southwest
TYPES OF FUNDS:
  Equity (stock purchases)
  Loans with Equity Kickers
  Minimum: $1,000,000
  Maximum: $3,000,000

OREGON

Capital Consultants, Inc.
2300 SW First Avenue
Portland, OR 97201
503-241-1200

CONTACT: Paul Clayson
TYPE OF FIRM:
  Investment Banking
  Investment Advisory
FUNDING PREFERENCE:
  Second-Round Funding
  Third-Round Funding
  Fourth-Round Funding
  Public Offerings
  Receivable Financing
INVESTMENT PREFERENCE:
  Diversified
  Medical Technology
  Natural Resources
  Real Estate
GEOGRAPHIC PREFERENCE:
  No Preference (U.S.A.)
  Northwest
  Far West

TYPES OF FUNDS:
Loans
Loans with Equity Kickers
Bonds
Bonds with Equity Kickers
Minimum: $500,000
Maximum: $20,000,000

Interven Partners
227 SW Pine Street, Suite 200
Portland, OR 97204
503-223-4334

CONTACT: Wayne Kingsley
TYPE OF FIRM: Venture Capital
FUNDING PREFERENCE:
Seed Funding
Start-Up Funding
First-Round Funding
Second-Round Funding
Leveraged Buyouts
Acquisitions
INVESTMENT PREFERENCE:
Diversified
GEOGRAPHIC PREFERENCE:
Immediate Area in Oregon
TYPES OF FUNDS:
Equity (stock purchases)
Minimum: $500,000
Maximum: $3,000,000

Olympic Venture Partners II
340 Oswego Pointe Drive
Suite 204
Lake Oswego, OR 97034
503-697-8766

CONTACT: Jerry Langeler
TYPE OF FIRM: Venture Capital
FUNDING PREFERENCE:
Start-Up Funding

INVESTMENT PREFERENCE:
Medical Technology
High Technology
GEOGRAPHIC PREFERENCE:
Home State of Oregon
TYPES OF FUNDS:
Equity (stock purchases)
Minimum: Varies
Maximum: Varies

PENNSYLVANIA

CIP Capital, LP
20 Valley Stream Parkway
Suite 265
Malvern, PA 19355
215-695-2066

CONTACT: Joseph M. Corr
TYPE OF FIRM: SBIC
FUNDING PREFERENCE:
First-Round Funding
Second-Round Funding
INVESTMENT PREFERENCE:
Communications Technology
Manufacturing
Medical Technology
GEOGRAPHIC PREFERENCE:
Middle Atlantic
TYPES OF FUNDS:
Equity (stock purchases)
Loans with Equity Kickers
Bonds with Equity Kickers
Minimum: $250,000
Maximum: $1,500,000

**Enterprise Venture Capital
Corporation of Pennsylvania**
111 Market Street
Johnstown, PA 15901
814-535-7597

CONTACT: Don Conie, CEO
TYPE OF FIRM: SBIC
FUNDING PREFERENCE:
  Start-Up Funding
  First-Round Funding
  Second-Round Funding
INVESTMENT PREFERENCE:
  Diversified
GEOGRAPHIC PREFERENCE:
  Immediate Area in Pennsylvania
TYPES OF FUNDS:
  Equity (stock purchases)
  Loans
  Minimum: $20,000
  Maximum: $100,000

Hillmann Medical Ventures, Inc.
Two Walnut Grove Drive, Suite 130
Horsham, PA 13044
215-443-5531

CONTACT: R. J. Brenner
TYPE OF FIRM: Venture Capital
FUNDING PREFERENCE:
  Seed Funding
  Start-Up Funding
  First-Round Funding
  Second-Round Funding
  Third-Round Funding
INVESTMENT PREFERENCE:
  Medical Technology
GEOGRAPHIC PREFERENCE:
  Northeast
  Middle Atlantic
  Southeast
  Midwest
TYPES OF FUNDS:
  Equity (stock purchases)
  Minimum: $200,000
  Maximum: $3,000,000

Philadelphia Ventures
200 South Broad Street
Philadelphia, PA 19102
215-732-4445

CONTACT: Eric Aguiar
TYPE OF FIRM: Venture Capital
FUNDING PREFERENCE:
  Seed Funding
  Start-Up Funding
  First-Round Funding
  Second-Round Funding
  Third-Round Funding
INVESTMENT PREFERENCE:
  Diversified
  Communications Technology
  Computer Hardware
  Computer Software
  Manufacturing
  Retail
  Services
GEOGRAPHIC PREFERENCE:
  No Preference (U.S.A.)
TYPES OF FUNDS:
  Equity (stock purchases)
  Minimum: $750,000
  Maximum: $2,000,000

Point Venture Partners
2970 VSX Towers
Pittsburgh, PA 15219
412-261-1966

CONTACT: Monica L. Price,
  Office Manager
TYPE OF FIRM: Venture Capital
FUNDING PREFERENCE:
  Second-Round Funding
  Third-Round Funding
  Later-Stage Funding
INVESTMENT PREFERENCE:
  Diversified

GEOGRAPHIC PREFERENCE:
  Middle Atlantic
TYPES OF FUNDS:
  Equity (stock purchases)
  Minimum: $500,000
  Maximum: $2,000,000

RHODE ISLAND

Moneta Capital Corporation
99 Wayland Avenue
Providence, RI 02906
401-454-7500

CONTACT: Mr. Joseph Longo Jr.
TYPE OF FIRM: SBIC
INVESTMENT PREFERENCE:
  Real Estate
GEOGRAPHIC PREFERENCE:
  Immediate Area in Rhode Island
TYPES OF FUNDS:
  Loans
  Minimum: $100,000
  Maximum: $5,000,000

Wallace Capital Corporation
170 Westminster Street
Providence, RI 02903
401-273-9191

CONTACT: Lloyd Granoff
TYPE OF FIRM: SBIC
FUNDING PREFERENCE:
  Leveraged Buyouts
  Acquisitions
INVESTMENT PREFERENCE:
  Diversified
GEOGRAPHIC PREFERENCE:
  Northeast
TYPES OF FUNDS:
  Loans

Loans with Equity Kickers
Minimum: $100,000
Maximum: $1,000,000

SOUTH CAROLINA

Charleston Capital Corporation
Yaschik Development Company
111 Church Street
P.O. Box 328
Charleston, SC 29402
803-723-6464
FAX 803-723-1228

CONTACT: Henry Yaschik
TYPE OF FIRM:
  SBIC
  Investment Banking
  Local or Certified Development
    Company
  Individual Investor
FUNDING PREFERENCE:
  First-Round Funding
  Second-Round Funding
INVESTMENT PREFERENCE:
  Diversified
  Real Estate
GEOGRAPHIC PREFERENCE:
  Southeast
  Home State of South Carolina
  Immediate Area in Charleston
TYPES OF FUNDS:
  Loans
  Minimum: None
  Maximum: $20,000,000

The Frank L. Roddey
Small Business Development
  Center of South Carolina
Hipp Building, 6th Floor

College of Business Administration
University of South Carolina
Columbia, SC 29208
803-777-4907
FAX 803-777-4403

CONTACT: John M. Lenti, State
Director
TYPE OF FIRM: Consulting Firm
GEOGRAPHIC PREFERENCE:
Home State of South Carolina

TENNESSEE

Valley Capital Corporation
Krystal Building, Suite 212
100 West Martin Luther King
Boulevard
Chattanooga, TN 37402
615-265-1557

CONTACT: Lamar Partridge,
President
TYPE OF FIRM: MESBIC
FUNDING PREFERENCE:
Second-Round Funding
Leveraged Buyouts
Acquisitions
INVESTMENT PREFERENCE:
Diversified
GEOGRAPHIC PREFERENCE:
Southeast
TYPES OF FUNDS:
Loans
Loans with Equity Kickers
Minimum: $50,000
Maximum: $150,000

**West Tennessee Venture Capital
Corporation**
5 North Third Street
Memphis, TN 38103
901-522-9237

CONTACT: Frank Banks
TYPE OF FIRM: MESBIC
FUNDING PREFERENCE:
Later-Stage Funding
Expansion Funding
INVESTMENT PREFERENCE:
None
GEOGRAPHIC PREFERENCE:
Immediate Area of Tennessee
and Mississippi
TYPES OF FUNDS:
Loans
Loans with Equity Kickers
Minimum: $50,000
Maximum: $250,000

TEXAS

Alliance Financial of Houston
Management Company for MESBIC
Financing Corporation of
Houston
Greater Houston Small Business
Equity Fund, Inc.
401 Studewood, Suite 200
Houston, TX 77007
713-869-8595

CONTACT: Attilio F. Galli
William Berry
TYPE OF FIRM:
Venture Capital
MESBIC
FUNDING PREFERENCE:
First-Round Funding
Second-Round Funding
Third-Round Funding
Fourth-Round Funding
Later-Stage Funding
Acquisitions
INVESTMENT PREFERENCE:
Diversified

GEOGRAPHIC PREFERENCE:
  Immediate Area: Houston SMSA
TYPES OF FUNDS:
  Equity (stock purchases)
  Loans
  Loans with Equity Kickers
  Bonds
  Bonds with Equity Kickers
  Minimum: $50,000
  Maximum: $500,000

AMT Capital, Limited
8204 Elmbroo Drive, Suite 101
Dallas, TX 75247
214-905-9760

CONTACT: Debbie VanNote, VP
TYPE OF FIRM:
  Venture Capital
  SBIC
FUNDING PREFERENCE:
  First-Round Funding
  Second-Round Funding
  Expansion Funding
INVESTMENT PREFERENCE:
  Manufacturing
  Chemicals
GEOGRAPHIC PREFERENCE:
  No Preference (U.S.A.)
TYPES OF FUNDS:
  Equity (stock purchases)
  Debt
  Minimum: $100,000
  Maximum: $500,000

Austin Ventures
114 West 7th Street, Suite 1300
Austin, TX 78701
512-479-0055

CONTACT: Claudia Chidester,
  Director of Research

TYPE OF FIRM: Venture Capital
FUNDING PREFERENCE:
  Start-Up Funding
  First-Round Funding
  Second-Round Funding
  Third-Round Funding
  Fourth-Round Funding
  Later-Stage Funding
  Leveraged Buyouts
INVESTMENT PREFERENCE:
  Diversified
  Communications Technology
  Computer Hardware
  Computer Software
  Manufacturing
  Media
  Other High Technologies Not
    Mentioned
  Retail
  Services
GEOGRAPHIC PREFERENCE:
  Southwest
  Home State of Texas
TYPES OF FUNDS:
  Equity (stock purchases)
  Minimum: $1,000,000
  Maximum: $8,000,000

**Banc One Capital Partners
  Corporation**
300 Crescent Court, Suite 1600
Dallas, TX 75201
214-979-4360

CONTACT: Judy Murtlant
TYPE OF FIRM: SBIC
FUNDING PREFERENCE:
  Later-Stage Funding
INVESTMENT PREFERENCE:
  Manufacturing
GEOGRAPHIC PREFERENCE:
  Midwest

TYPES OF FUNDS:
  Equity (stock purchases)
  Minimum: $2,000,000
  Maximum: $5,000,000

Capital Southwest Corporation
12900 Preston Road, Suite 700
Dallas, TX 75230
214-233-8242

CONTACT: Scott Colliem
TYPE OF FIRM: Venture Capital
FUNDING PREFERENCE:
  First-Round Funding
  Second-Round Funding
  Third-Round Funding
  Fourth-Round Funding
  Later-Stage Funding
  Leveraged Buyouts
INVESTMENT PREFERENCE:
  Communications Technology
  Manufacturing
  Medical Technology
  Other High Technology
  Retail
  Services
GEOGRAPHIC PREFERENCE:
  No Preference (U.S.A.)
TYPES OF FUNDS:
  Equity (stock purchases)
  Bonds with Equity Kickers
  Minimum: $1,000,000
  Maximum: $4,000,000

The Catalyst Group
3 Riverway, Suite 770
Houston, TX 77056
713-623-8133

CONTACT: Richard Herrman
TYPE OF FIRM: SBI Partnership

FUNDING PREFERENCE:
  Second-Round Funding
  Third-Round Funding
INVESTMENT PREFERENCE:
  Diversified
GEOGRAPHIC PREFERENCE:
  Southwest
TYPES OF FUNDS:
  Loans with Equity Kickers
  Minimum: $500,000
  Maximum: $5,000,000

The Centennial Funds
Five Post Oak Park, Suite 1650
Houston, TX 77027
713-627-9200

CONTACT: David C. Hull Jr.
TYPE OF FIRM: Venture Capital
FUNDING PREFERENCE:
  Seed Funding
INVESTMENT PREFERENCE:
  Communications Technology
  Medical Technology
GEOGRAPHIC PREFERENCE:
  Telecommunications—anywhere
    in the U.S.
  All Other Investments—Colorado
    or Texas
TYPES OF FUNDS:
  Equity (stock purchases)
  Minimum: $2,000,000 Later-
    Stage Funding
  $250,000 Seed/Start-Up
    Funding
  Maximum: $5,000,000

Cureton and Company, Inc.
1200 Travis, Suite 2050
Houston, TX 77002
713-658-9806

CONTACT: Charles Armbrust
TYPE OF FIRM: Venture Capital
FUNDING PREFERENCE:
  Seed Funding
  Start-Up Funding
  First-Round Funding
INVESTMENT PREFERENCE:
  Diversified
  Communications Technology
  Manufacturing
  Medical Technology
GEOGRAPHIC PREFERENCE:
  Texas
TYPES OF FUNDS:
  Equity (stock purchases)
  Minimum: $500,000
  Maximum: $5,000,000

Cureton and Company, Inc.
1100 Louisiana, Suite 3250
Houston, TX 77002
713-658-9806

CONTACT: Bob Antonoff
TYPE OF FIRM:
  Venture Capital
  Investment Banking
FUNDING PREFERENCE:
  First-Round Funding
  Second-Round Funding
  Third-Round Funding
  Leveraged Buyouts
  Acquisitions
INVESTMENT PREFERENCE:
  Communications Technology
  Computer Hardware
  Computer Software
  Manufacturing
  Medical Technology
  Services
  Wholesale Distribution

GEOGRAPHIC PREFERENCE:
  Texas and
  bordering states
TYPES OF FUNDS:
  Equity (stock purchases)
  Minimum: $1,000,000
  Maximum: $10,000,000

MESBIC Financial Corporation of Houston
401 Studewood, Suite 200
Houston, TX 77007
713-869-8595

CONTACT: Attilio Galli, President
TYPE OF FIRM: MESBIC
FUNDING PREFERENCE:
  First-Round Funding
  Second-Round Funding
INVESTMENT PREFERENCE:
  Diversified
GEOGRAPHIC PREFERENCE:
  Southwest
TYPES OF FUNDS:
  Loans with Equity Kickers
  Minimum: $100,000
  Maximum: $500,000

Pro Med Capital, Inc.
17772 Preston Road
Dallas, TX 75252
214-380-0044

CONTACT: Mr. Rosemount
TYPE OF FIRM: SBIC
INVESTMENT PREFERENCE:
  Franchise
GEOGRAPHIC PREFERENCE:
  National

TYPES OF FUNDS: N/A
Minimum: $50,000
Maximum: $1,000,000

Sevin Rosen Funds
13455 Noel Road, Suite 1670
Dallas, TX 75240
214-702-1100

CONTACT: C. Chris Apple, Chief
Financial Officer
TYPE OF FIRM: Venture Capital
FUNDING PREFERENCE:
Start-Up Funding
First-Round Funding
INVESTMENT PREFERENCE:
Communications Technology
Computer Hardware
Computer Software
Medical Technology
Other High Technology
GEOGRAPHIC PREFERENCE:
No Preference (U.S.A.)
TYPES OF FUNDS:
Equity (stock purchases)
Minimum: $500,000
Maximum: $5,000,000

UTAH

**First Security Business
Investment Corporation**
79 South Main Street, Suite 1300
Salt Lake City, UT 84111
801-246-5737

CONTACT: Butch Alder
TYPE OF FIRM: SBIC
FUNDING PREFERENCE:
Second-Round Funding
Third-Round Funding
Later-Stage Funding
Leveraged Buyouts
Acquisitions
INVESTMENT PREFERENCE:
Diversified
GEOGRAPHIC PREFERENCE:
Rocky Mountain States
TYPES OF FUNDS:
Loans with Equity Kickers
Minimum: $300,000
Maximum: $1,000,000

VERMONT

Green Mountain Capital, LP
RR1 Box 1503
Waterbury, VT 05672
802-299-8981

CONTACT: Michael Sweatman
TYPE OF FIRM: SBIC
FUNDING PREFERENCE:
Second-Round Funding
Third-Round Funding
Fourth-Round Funding
Bridge Finance
INVESTMENT PREFERENCE:
Diversified
GEOGRAPHIC PREFERENCE:
Immediate Area of Vermont and
New Hampshire
TYPES OF FUNDS:
Loans with Equity Kickers
Minimum: $200,000
Maximum: $500,000

VIRGINIA

Walnut Capital Corporation
8000 Tower Crescent Drive
Suite 1070

Vienna, VA 22182
703-448-3771

CONTACT: Shea Cordell
TYPE OF FIRM:
  Venture Capital
  SBIC
FUNDING PREFERENCE:
  Start-Up Funding
INVESTMENT PREFERENCE:
  Computer Hardware
  Computer Software
  Medical Technology
  Other High Technologies
GEOGRAPHIC PREFERENCE:
  No Preference (U.S.A.)
TYPES OF FUNDS:
  Equity (stock purchases)
  Minimum: $500,000
  Maximum: $1,500,000

Olympic Venture Partners II
2420 Carillon Point
Kirkland, WA 98033
206-889-9192

CONTACT: Charles P. Waite Jr.
TYPE OF FIRM: Venture Capital
FUNDING PREFERENCE:
  Start-Up Funding
INVESTMENT PREFERENCE:
  Communications Technology
  Computer Hardware
  Computer Software
  Medical Technology
GEOGRAPHIC PREFERENCE:
  Northwest
TYPES OF FUNDS:
  Equity (stock purchases)
  Minimum: $1,000,000
  Maximum: $2,000,000

WASHINGTON

Cable and Howse Ventures
777 108th Avenue NE, Suite 2300
Bellevue, WA 98004
206-646-3030

CONTACT: Jane Marks
TYPE OF FIRM: Venture Capital
FUNDING PREFERENCE:
  Start-Up Funding
INVESTMENT PREFERENCE:
  Life Sciences
GEOGRAPHIC PREFERENCE:
  Northwest
TYPES OF FUNDS:
  Equity (stock purchases)
  Minimum: Not Determined
  Maximum: Not Determined

Sirach Capital Management, Inc.
3323 One Union Square
Seattle, WA 98101
206-624-3800

TYPE OF FIRM: Investment
  Advisor
FUNDING PREFERENCE:
  None Given
INVESTMENT PREFERENCE:
  Diversified
GEOGRAPHIC PREFERENCE:
  No Preference (U.S.A.)
TYPES OF FUNDS:
  Equity (stock purchases)
  Bonds
  Minimum: $15,000,000
  Maximum: None

WEST VIRGINIA

Fourth Venture Investment Group, Inc.
208 Capitol Street, Suite 300
Charleston, WV 25301
304-344-1794

CONTACT: Tony Mazelon
TYPE OF FIRM:
  Venture Capital
  SBIC
FUNDING PREFERENCE:
  First-Round Funding
  Second-Round Funding
  Third-Round Funding
INVESTMENT PREFERENCE:
  Diversified
  Manufacturing
  Media
GEOGRAPHIC PREFERENCE:
  Northeast
  Middle Atlantic
  Southeast
  West Virginia
TYPES OF FUNDS:
  Equity (stock purchases)
  Loans
  Loans with Equity Kickers
  Minimum: $250,000
  Maximum: $500,000

WISCONSIN

Capital Investments, Inc.
744 North Fourth Street, Suite 540
Milwaukee, WI 53020
414-273-6560

CONTACT: Steven C. Rippl
TYPE OF FIRM: SBIC
FUNDING PREFERENCE:
  Later-Stage Funding
INVESTMENT PREFERENCE:
  Diversified
GEOGRAPHIC PREFERENCE:
  Midwest
TYPES OF FUNDS:
  Loans with Equity Kickers
  Minimum: $500,000
  Maximum: $1,000,000

Future Value Ventures, Inc.
330 East Kilburn Avenue, Suite 711
Milwaukee, WI 53202
414-278-0377

CONTACT: William Beckett,
  President
TYPE OF FIRM: MESBIC
FUNDING PREFERENCE:
  Start-Up Funding
  First-Round Funding
  Leveraged Buyouts
  Acquisitions
INVESTMENT PREFERENCE:
  Diversified
GEOGRAPHIC PREFERENCE:
  No Preference
  Midwest
TYPES OF FUNDS:
  Loans with Equity Kickers
  Minimum: $100,000
  Maximum: $300,000

M & I Venture Corporation
770 North Wates Street
Milwaukee, WI 53202
414-765-7910

CONTACT: Gregory J. Myers
TYPE OF FIRM:
  Venture Capital
  SBIC
FUNDING PREFERENCE:
  Second-Round Funding
  Leveraged Buyouts
  Acquisitions
INVESTMENT PREFERENCE:
  Communications Technology
  Manufacturing

Medical Technology
Other High Technologies
Specialty Chemicals and Plastics
  Manufacturing
GEOGRAPHIC PREFERENCE:
Midwest
Wisconsin
TYPES OF FUNDS:
Equity (stock purchases)
Minimum: $1,000,000
Maximum: $50,000,000

Underwriting Firms

Underwriting firms assist growth-oriented companies that seek funds for expansion purposes or start-up. Some of these funding organizations specialize in small businesses and are listed here. They will help an enterprise sell equity ownership or debt in order to raise funds if the proposition in question has merit in their opinion. Underwriting companies were discussed in Chapter 6.

Adwest
Hartford, CT
203-241-2177

A.S. Goldmen & Company
New York, NY
212-742-8500

Comprehensive Capital
West Berry, NY
516-832-8600

Cruttenden & Company
Irvine, CA
714-757-5700

Dain Bosworth
Minneapolis, MN
612-371-2800

GKN Securities
New York, NY
212-509-3800

John G. Kinnard & Company
Minneapolis, MN
612-370-2700

JW Charles/CSG
Orlando, FL
407-338-2600

Laidlaw Equities
New York, NY
212-949-5400

Network 1 Financial
Red Bank, NJ
908-758-9001

Nomura Securities
New York, NY
212-667-9300

Reich & Company
New York, NY
212-527-2900

Paragon Capital
New York, NY
212-742-1500

Whale Securities
New York, NY
212-484-2000

12

GOVERNMENT SOURCES OF CAPITAL

State Funding Programs

State governments have realized the importance of a viable business sector to their respective economies. Consequently, many states maintain funding programs, varying in depth and effectiveness, directed to the small-business community. Below are the names and addresses of these programs.

ALABAMA

Mr. Kent Rose, Director of Purchasing
Department of Finance
Division of Purchases and Stores
11 South Union Street, Room 200
Montgomery, AL 36130
(205) 242-7250

**Mr. Roger McKean,
Small Business Representative**
Department of Finance
Division of Purchases and Stores
11 South Union Street, Room 200
Montgomery, AL 36130
(205) 242-7256

Mr. James Allen Jr., Chief of Staff
Southern Development Council

671 South Perry Street, Suite 500
Montgomery, AL 36104
(205) 264-5441

Mr. Fred Braswell, Director
Alabama Development Office
State Capitol
401 Adams Avenue
Montgomery, AL 36130
(205) 242-0400

ALASKA

Mr. Greg Winegar, Loan Manager
Division of Investments
Department of Commerce and
  Economic Development
P.O. Box D

Juneau, AK 99811
(907) 465-2510

Mr. Bob Richardson, Loan Manager
Division of Investments
Department of Commerce and
Economic Development
3601 C Street, Suite 778
Anchorage, AK 99503
(907) 582-3779

Mr. Bert Wagnon, Executive Director
Alaska Industrial Development and
Export Authority
480 W. Tudor Road
Anchorage, AK 99503
(907) 561-8050

ARIZONA

Mr. Charles Deaton, Director
Business Development/National
Marketing
Commerce and Economic
Development Commission
3800 North Central, Suite 1500
Phoenix, AZ 85012
(602) 280-1328

Ms. Patty Duff
Business Finance
Arizona Department of Commerce
3800 North Central, 15th Floor
Phoenix, AZ 85012
(602) 280-1341

Ms. Patty Duff, Executive Director
Arizona Enterprise Development
Corporation
3800 North Central, 15th Floor
Phoenix, AZ 85012
(602) 280-1341

ARKANSAS

Mr. Sam Walls, Executive Director
Arkansas Capital Corporation
800 Pyramid Place
221 West Second Street
Little Rock, AR 72201
(501) 374-9247

Mr. Chuck Myers, Research Program Manager
Arkansas Science and Technology
Authority
100 Main Street, Suite 450
Little Rock, AR 72201
(501) 324-9006

Ms. Anita Millard, Fiscal Officer
Arkansas Science and Technology
Authority
100 Main Street, Suite 450
Little Rock, AR 72201
(501) 371-3554

Mr. James T. Benham
Vice President, Finance
Arkansas Science and Technology
Authority
100 Main Street, Suite 450
Little Rock, AR 72201
(501) 324-9006

CALIFORNIA

Ms. Annette L. Porini, Executive Director
California Pollution Control
Financing Authority
P.O. Box 942809
Sacramento, CA 94209
(916) 445-9597

Ms. Annette Porini, Acting Director
Alternative Energy Source
Financing Authority
P.O. Box 942809
Sacramento, CA 94209
(916) 445-9597

Ms. Alice Flissinger, Chief
Office of Small and Minority
Business
Department of General Services
1808 14th Street, Room 100
Sacramento, CA 95814
(916) 322-5060

Mr. William Harper, Executive Director
Office of Small Business
Department of Commerce
801 K Street, Suite 1600
Sacramento, CA 95814
(916) 324-1295

Mr. Gregory Mignano, Executive Director
California State World Trade
Commission
801 K Street
Sacramento, CA 95814
(916) 324-5511
Fax: (916) 324-5791

Ms. Irene L. Fisher, Director
California Export Finance Office
107 South Broadway, Suite 8039
Los Angeles, CA 90012
(213) 897-3997
Fax: (213) 897-0915

Ms. Janet Turner, Director
Office of Business Development
Department of Commerce
801 K Street, Suite 1600
Sacramento, CA 95814
(916) 322-3502

Mr. Lance Barnett, Director
Office of Economic Research
Department of Commerce
801 K Street, Suite 1600
Sacramento, CA 95814
(916) 322-3562

Mr. John Paulus
Deputy Superintendent of Banks
State Banking Department
111 Pine Street, Suite 1100
San Francisco, CA 94111
(415) 557-8686

Mr. Paul Cormier, President
State Assistance Fund for
Enterprise
Business and Industrial
Development Corporation
145 Wikiup Drive
Santa Rosa, CA 95403
(707) 577-8621

COLORADO

Ms. Colleen Schwarz, Director
Commercial Program Division
Colorado Housing and Finance
Authority
1981 Blake Street
Denver, CO 80202
(303) 297-2432
Fax: (303) 297-2615

Mr. Jim Rubingh, Secretary
Colorado Agricultural Development
Authority
700 Kipling Street, Suite 4000
Lakewood, CO 80215
(303) 239-4114
Fax: (303) 239-4125

Statewide

Mr. John Burger, Executive Director
Community Economic Development
Company of Colorado
1111 Osage Street, Suite 110
Denver, CO 80204
(303) 893-8989
Fax: (303) 892-8398

City and County of Denver

Mr. Dick Jones, Economic Development Specialist
Denver Urban Economic
Development Corporation
303 West Colfax Avenue
Suite 1025
Denver, CO 80204
(303) 575-5540

CONNECTICUT

Mr. Eric Ott, Director
Connecticut Innovations, Inc.
845 Brook Street
Rocky Hill, CT 06067
(203) 258-4305

Mr. A. Searle Field, Executive Director
Connecticut Development Authority
217 Washington Street
Hartford, CT 06016
(203) 522-3730

DELAWARE

Mr. James P. Lisa, Director of Business Finance
Delaware Development Office
99 Kings Highway

P.O. Box 1401
Dover, DE 19903
(302) 739-4271

DISTRICT OF COLUMBIA

Ms. Pamela Vaughn-Cooke-Henry, Chief
Financial Services Division
Office of Business and Economic
Development
717 14th Street NW, 10th Floor
Washington, DC 20005
(202) 727-6600

Mr. Lloyd Arrington, Acting President
District of Columbia Economic
Development Finance
Corporation
1660 L Street NW, Suite 308
Washington, DC 20036
(202) 775-8815

FLORIDA

Ms. Judy R. Jones, Executive Director
Florida Black Business Investment
Board
519 East Park Avenue
Tallahassee, FL 32301
(904) 487-4850

Mr. Ray Iannuci, Executive Director
Florida High Technology and
Industry Council
111 Collins Building, Room 128
107 West Gaines Street
Tallahassee, FL 32399
(904) 487-3136

Supervisor
Business Finance Section
Bureau of Business Assistance
Florida Department of Commerce
443 Collins Building
107 West Gaines Street
Tallahassee, FL 32399
(904) 487-0463

Ms. Doreen Shishido, Chief
Financial Assistance Branch
Department of Business, Economic
Development, and Tourism
Grosvenor Center, Mauka Tower
737 Bishop Street, Suite 1900
Honolulu, HI 96813
(808) 586-2577

IDAHO

GEORGIA

**Mr. Michael Cassidy, Small
Business Innovation Research
Manager**
Advanced Technology Development
Center
Georgia Institute of Technology
430 10th Street NW
Atlanta, GA 30318
(404) 894-3575

Mr. Bob Stevens, Special Assistant
Community Programs Section
Community and Economic
Development Section
Georgia Department of Community
Affairs
1200 Equitable Building
100 Peachtree Street
Atlanta, GA 30303
(404) 656-3872

Ms. Renee LeMoyne, Coordinator
SBIR Support Services
Idaho Small Business Development
Center
Boise State University
1910 University Drive
Boise, ID 83725
(208) 385-3870

Mr. Jay Engstrom, Administrator
Economic Development Division
Idaho Department of Commerce
700 West State Street
Boise, ID 83720
(208) 334-2470

ILLINOIS

**Mr. Sanford Morganstein,
Manager**
Division of Industry Development
Illinois Department of Commerce
and Community Affairs
100 West Randolph Street
Chicago, IL 60601
(312) 814-5246

HAWAII

**Mr. Toshio Nakamoto,
Administrator**
Agricultural Loan Division
Department of Agriculture
P.O. Box 22159
Honolulu, HI 96823
(808) 973-9460

Mr. Richard LeGrand, Manager
Loan Administration Division
Illinois Department of Commerce
and Community Affairs
620 East Adams
Springfield, IL 62701
(217) 524-4615

INDIANA

Mr. William B. Glennon
Indiana Business Modernization and
 Technology Corporation
One North Capitol Avenue, Suite
 925
Indianapolis, IN 46204
(317) 635-3058

**Ms. Peggy Boehm, Executive
 Director**
Indiana Development Finance
 Authority
One North Capitol Avenue
Suite 320
Indianapolis, IN 46204
(317) 233-4332

Mr. Robert S. Fryer, Manager
Marketing and Outreach Promotions
Indiana Business Modernization and
 Technology Corporation
One North Capitol Avenue
Suite 925
Indianapolis, IN 46204
(317) 635-3058

**Ms. Jean Wojtowicz, Executive
 Director**
Indiana Statewide Certified
 Development Corporation
8440 Woodfield Crossing, Suite 315
Indianapolis, IN 46240
(317) 469-6166

IOWA

**Mr. Daniel Dittemore, Deputy
 Director**
Wallace Technology Transfer
 Foundation
317 Sixth Avenue, Suite 840
Des Moines, IA 50309
(515) 243-1487

**Mr. Ted Chapler, Executive
 Director**
Iowa Finance Authority
100 East Grand Avenue, Suite 250
Des Moines, IA 50309
(515) 242-4990

**Ms. Lynn Muehlenthaler Bedford,
 Treasury Investment Officer**
State Treasurer's Office
Hoover Building
Des Moines, IA 50319
(515) 281-3287

**Mr. Don Albertson, Executive
 Vice President**
Iowa Business Development Credit
 Corporation
901 Insurance Exchange Building
505 Fifth AvenueDes Moines, IA
 50309
(515) 282-2164

Ms. Donna Lowery
Targeted Small Business Financial
 Assistance Program
200 East Grand Avenue
Des Moines, IA 50309
(515) 242-4813

**Ms. Kathy Beery, Division
 Administrator**
Community and Rural Development
Iowa Department of Economic
 Development
200 East Grand Avenue
Des Moines, IA 50309
(515) 242-4807

**Ms. Mary Kay Baker, Finance
 Specialist**
Iowa Department of Economic
 Development
200 East Grand Avenue
Des Moines, IA 50309
(515) 242-4839

**Mr. Kenneth Boyd, CEBA
Program Administrator**
Bureau of Business Finance
Iowa Department of Economic
  Development
200 East Grand Avenue
Des Moines, IA 50309
(515) 242-4810

Mr. Lane Palmer, Chief
Bureau of Community Financing
Iowa Department of Economic
  Development
200 East Grand Avenue
Des Moines, IA 50309
(515) 242-4837

Mr. Michael Fastenau
Bureau of Business Finance
Iowa Department of Economic
  Development
200 East Grand Avenue
Des Moines, IA 50309
(515) 242-4831

Mr. Burt Powley, SELF Manager
Bureau of Business Finance
Iowa Department of Economic
  Development
200 East Grand Avenue
Des Moines, IA 50309
(515) 242-4793

Mr. Gregg Barcus, President
Iowa Product Development
  Corporation
200 East Grand Avenue
Des Moines, IA 50309
(515) 242-4860

**Mr. Don Albertson, Executive
  Vice President**
Iowa Business Growth Company
901 Insurance Exchange Building
505 Fifth Avenue
Des Moines, IA 50309
(515) 282-2164

KANSAS

Mr. Kevin Carr, Vice President
Kansas Technology Enterprise
  Corporation
112 SW 6th Street, Suite 400
Topeka, KS 66603
(913) 296-5272

**Mr. Rex E. Wiggins, President
Mr. Thomas C. Blackburn,
  Vice President
Mr. Marshall D. Parker,
  Vice President**
Overland Park Office
6700 Antioch Plaza, Suite 460
Overland Park, KS 66204
(913) 262-7117

Mr. W. M. F. Caton, President
Kansas Development Finance
  Authority
400 SW 8th Street, Suite 100
Topeka, KS 66603
(913) 296-6747

Mr. David Ross
Kansas Partnership Fund
Division of Community
  Development
Kansas Department of Commerce
400 SW 8th Street, 5th Floor
Topeka, KS 66603
(913) 296-3485

Mr. Steve Kelly
Kansas Venture Capital Program
Division of Existing Industry
  Development
Kansas Department of Commerce
400 SW 8th Street, 5th Floor
Topeka, KS 66603
(913) 296-5298

Mr. Antonio Augusto, Director
Office of Minority Business
Division of Existing Industry
  Development
Kansas Department of Commerce
400 SW 8th Street, 5th Floor
Topeka, KS 66603
(913) 296-5298

Mr. Leo Vogel
Division of Purchases
Department of Administration
900 SW Jackson, 1st Floor
Topeka, KS 66612
(913) 296-2376

KENTUCKY

Mr. Jeff Noel, Executive Director
Kentucky Development Finance
  Authority
2400 Capital Plaza Tower
Frankfort, KY 40601
(502) 564-4554

Ms. Theresa Middleton, President
Commonwealth Small Business
  Development Corporation
2400 Capital Plaza Tower
Frankfort, KY 40601
(502) 564-4320

**Ms. Theresa Middleton, Small
  Business Branch Manager**
Kentucky Development Finance
  Authority
2400 Capital Plaza Tower
Frankfort, KY 40601
(502) 564-4554

**Mr. R. Stephen Jones, Executive
  Director**
Kentucky Rural Economic
  Development Authority
2400 Capital Plaza Tower

Frankfort, KY 40601
(502) 564-7670

**Ms. Sheila White, Program
  Coordinator**
Division of Small Business
2300 Capital Plaza Tower
Frankfort, KY 40601
(502) 564-7140

Ms. Marilyn Eaton
Kentucky Infrastructure Authority
Finance and Administration Cabinet
Room 075, New Capitol Annex
Frankfort, KY 40601
(502) 564-2090

Ms. Beth Hilliard
Finance and Administration Cabinet
Room 301, New Capitol Annex
Frankfort, KY 40601
(502) 564-2924

**Ms. Lisa Payne, Financial and
  Investment Program Analyst**
Office for Financial Management
  and Economic Analysis
Kentucky Agricultural Finance
  Corporation
261 New Capitol Annex
Frankfort, KY 40601
(502) 564-2924

LOUISIANA

**Mr. Tracy J. Mandart Jr.,
  Executive Director**
Louisiana Development Finance
  Corporation
P.O. Box 94185
Baton Rouge, LA 70804
(504) 342-5675

MAINE

Mr. David Markovchick, Director of Business Development
Finance Authority of Maine
83 Western Avenue
P.O. Box 949
Augusta, ME 04332
(207) 623-3263

Mr. Charles Spies, Director of Natural Resources
Finance Authority of Maine
83 Western Avenue
P.O. Box 949
Augusta, ME 04332
(207) 623-3263

Mr. Carl Flora, Deputy Commissioner
Department of Agriculture, Food, and Rural Resources
State House Station #28
Augusta, ME 04333
(207) 623-3263

Mr. Samuel Shapiro
State House of Maine
State House Station #39
Augusta, ME 04333
(207) 289-2771

MARYLAND

Mr. Stanley W. Tucker, Executive Director
Maryland Small Business Financing Authority
Redwood Towers, 22nd Floor
217 East Redwood Street
Baltimore, MD 21202
(410) 333-4270

Mr. James Peiffer, Assistant Secretary
Division of Business Development
Maryland Department of Economic and Employment Development
Redwood Towers, 10th Floor
217 East Redwood Street
Baltimore, MD 21202
(410) 333-6985

Mr. Len Elenowitz
Department of Economic and Employment Development
Division of Business Resources
Office of Technology Development
217 East Redwood Street
Baltimore, MD 21202
(410) 333-6975

MASSACHUSETTS

Mr. Kenneth J. Smith, President
Massachusetts Business Development Corporation
One Liberty Square
Boston, MA 02109
(617) 350-8877

Mr. John F. Hodgman, President
Massachusetts Technology Development Corporation
131 State Street, Suite 215
Boston, MA 02109
(617) 723-4920

Mr. Joseph D. Blair, Executive Director
Massachusetts Industrial Finance Authority
75 Federal Street
Boston, MA 02110
(617) 451-2477

Mr. Milton Benjamin, President
Communities and Development
  Finance Corporation
10 Post Office Square, Suite 1090
Boston, MA 02109
(617) 482-9141

MICHIGAN

Mr. Paul E. Rice, Administrator
Alternative Investments Division
Department of Treasury
Treasury Building
Lansing, MI 48922
(517) 373-4330

**Mr. Mark Morante, Acting
  Director of Operations**
Capital Resources Group
Michigan Department of Commerce
P.O. Box 30234
Lansing, MI 48909
(517) 373-7550

**Ms. Karen Ammarman, Program
  Manager**
Capital Access Program
Capital Resources Group
Michigan Department of Commerce
P.O. Box 30234
Lansing, MI 48909
(517) 373-7551

**Mr. James Paquet, Program
  Manager**
BIDCO Investment Program
P.O. Box 30234
Lansing, MI 48909
(517) 373-7551

**Mr. Lawrence Schrauben,
  Manager**
Public Finance Division

Michigan Department of Commerce
P.O. Box 30234
Lansing, MI 48909
(517) 373-6213

MINNESOTA

**Mr. George Crolick, Jr.,
  Executive Director**
Minnesota Trade Office
Minnesota Department of Trade and
  Economic Development
1000 Minnesota World Trade Center
30 East Seventh Street
St. Paul, MN 55101
(612) 297-4227

MISSISSIPPI

Mr. Bill Barry, Director
Mississippi Business Finance
  Corporation
Mississippi Department of
  Economic and Community
  Development
P.O. Box 849
Jackson, MS 39205
(601) 359-3552

MISSOURI

Mr. Mike Downing, Manager
Finance Program
Missouri Department of Economic
  Development
Truman State Office Building
P.O. Box 118
Jefferson City, MO 65102
(314) 751-0717

Mr. Dale Angel, Executive Director
Missouri Agricultural and Small
  Business Development Authority
P.O. Box 630
Jefferson City, MO 65102
(314) 751-2129

Mr. Ken Lueckenotte, Executive Director
Rural Missouri, Inc.
1014 Northeast Drive
Jefferson City, MO 65101
(314) 635-0136

Mr. Tom Barry, Coordinator
High Technology Program
Missouri Department of Economic
  Development
Truman State Office Building
P.O. Box 118
Jefferson City, MO 65102
(314) 751-3906

Ms. Alice Lusk, Assistant Director
Enterprise Development Division
Mississippi Department of
  Economic and Community
  Development
P.O. Box 849
Jackson, MS 39205
(601) 359-3179

MONTANA

Ms. Robyn Young, Chief Executive Officer
Montana Community Development
  Finance Corporation
P.O. Box 916
Helena, MT 59624
(406) 442-3261
Fax: (406) 443-0429

Mr. Robert M. Pancich, Assistant Investment Officer
Board of Investments
Capitol Station
Helena, MT 59620
(406) 442-1970
Fax: (406) 449-6579

Ms. Delrene Rasmussen
(406) 444-4153
Mr. Jim Burns
(406) 444-4127
Mr. Gary Faulkner
(406) 444-4780
Mr. Gary Morehouse
(406) 444-2787
Business Division
Department of Commerce
1424 Ninth Avenue
Helena, MT 59620
Fax: (406) 444-2808

Mr. Al Jones
(406) 245-9989
(SBDC/Billings)

NEBRASKA

Mr. Alan Eastman, Program Director
Nebraska Economic Development
  Corporation (NEDCO)
2631 O Street
Lincoln, NE 68510
(402) 475-2795

Mr. Larry Bare, Executive Director
Nebraska Investment Finance
  Authority
1033 O Street, Suite 218
Lincoln, NE 68508
(402) 434-3900

Mr. Steve Buttress, C.E.D.,
Director
Nebraska Department of Economic
  Development
P.O. Box 94666
301 Centennial Mall South
Lincoln, NE 68509
(402) 471-3747
(800) 426-6505

NEVADA

Ms. Jolene B. Rose, Deputy
Director
Department of Commerce
1665 Hot Springs Road
Carson City, NV 89710
(702) 687-4250

Mr. Harry H. Weinberg, President
Nevada State Development
  Corporation
350 South Center Street, Suite 310
Reno, NV 89501
(702) 323-3625

NEW HAMPSHIRE

Mr. Jeffrey Pollock
New Hampshire Business
  Development Corporation
1001 Elm Street
Manchester, NH 03103
(603) 623-5500

Mr. B. J. Hulen, Acting Director
Venture Capital Network, Inc.
MIT Enterprise Forum of
  Cambridge, Inc.
201 Vassar Street
Cambridge, NH 02139

(617) 253-7163
Fax: (617) 258-7264

Ms. Dawn Wivell, Trade
Specialist
New Hampshire Department of
  Resources and Economic
  Development
P.O. Box 856
Concord, NH 03302
(603) 271-2591

Mr. William Pillsbury, Director
Office of Business and Industrial
  Development
172 Pembroke Road
Concord, NH 03302
(603) 271-2591
Fax: (603) 271-2629

NEW JERSEY

Mr. Joseph Montemarano,
Associate Director
New Jersey Commission on Science
  and Technology
20 West State Street, CN 832
Trenton, NJ 08625
(609) 984-1671

Mr. Eugene J. Bukowski,
Secretary
Corporation for Business Assistance
  in New Jersey
Capital Place One, CN 990
200 South Warren Street
Trenton, NJ 08625
(609) 633-7737

Mr. Eugene J. Bukowski, Director
of Finance
New Jersey Economic Development
  Authority

Capital Place One, CN 990
200 South Warren Street
Trenton, NJ 08625
(609) 292-0187

Bond Financing

**Mr. Frank T. Mancini, Jr.,
Director of Bond Finance**
New Jersey Economic Development
  Authority
Capital Place One, CN 990
200 South Warren Street
Trenton, NJ 08625
(609) 292-0192

NEW MEXICO

**Mr. Jim Greenwood, Executive
Director**
Los Alamos Economic
  Development Corporation
P.O. Box 715
Los Alamos, NM 87544
(505) 662-0001

**Ms. Irene Catanach,
Administrative Officer**
New Mexico Business Development
  Corporation
6001 Marbel NE, Suite 6
Albuquerque, NM 87110
(505) 268-1316

Mr. Stanley G. Lane, Director
Economic Development Division
Joseph Montoya Building
1100 St. Francis Drive
Santa Fe, NM 87503
(505) 827-0380

NEW YORK

**Mr. Heyward Davenport, Deputy
Commissioner**
Minority and Women's Business
  Division
1515 Broadway, 51st Floor
New York, NY 10036
(212) 827-6180

Mr. Owen Goldfarb
New York Science and Technology
  Foundation
99 Washington Avenue, Suite 1730
Albany, NY 12210
(518) 473-9746

**Mr. Graham Jones, Executive
Director**
New York State Science and
  Technology Foundation
99 Washington Avenue, Suite 1730
Albany, NY 12210
(518) 474-4349

**Mr. Robert W. Lazar, President
and Chief Executive Officer**
New York Business Development
  Corporation
41 State Street
Albany, NY 12207
(518) 463-2268

**Mr. Gerald Demers, Senior Loan
Officer**
Empire State Certified
  Development Corporation
41 State Street
Albany, NY 12205
(518) 463-2268

**Ms. Audrey Bynoe, Acting
President**
Job Development Authority
605 Third Avenue

New York, NY 10158
(212) 818-1700

Ms. Roberta Boatti, Director
Special Programs
New York Job Development
   Authority
605 Third Avenue
New York, NY 10158
(212) 818-1700

**Mr. Manual Saenz, Deputy
   Commissioner**
Division for Small Business
New York State Department of
   Economic Development
1515 Broadway, 51st Floor
New York, NY 10036
(212) 827-6140

**Mr. Vincent Tese, Chairman and
   Chief Executive Officer**
New York State Urban Development
   Corporation
1515 Broadway, 52nd Floor
New York, NY 10036
(212) 930-0200

NORTH CAROLINA

Mr. Charles W. Moore, Director
Business License Information
   Office
301 West Jones Street
Raleigh, NC 27611
(919) 733-0641
(800) 228-8443 (in state)

NORTH DAKOTA

Mr. Jerry Rustand, Chairman
Agricultural Products Utilization
   Commission

State Capitol Building
600 Boulevard Avenue
Bismarck, ND 58501
(701) 224-4760

Mr. David Nelson, Vice President
Capital Dimensions, Inc.
400 East Broadway Avenue
Suite 420
Bismarck, ND 58501
(701) 222-0995

**Mr. Kevin Cooper, SBIR
   Coordinator**
Center for Innovation and Business
   Development
University of North Dakota
Box 8103, University Station
Grand Forks, ND 58202
(701) 777-3132
Fax: (701) 777-2339

**Mr. Warren Litten, Executive
   Director**
Fargo Cass County Economic
   Development Corporation
417 Main Avenue
Fargo, ND 58103
(701) 237-6132
Fax: (701) 235-6706

Mr. Mitchell D. Bohn, Director
Department of Economic
   Development and Finance
1833 East Bismarck Expressway
Bismarck, ND 58504
(701) 224-2810

**Mr. Eric Hardmeyer, Commercial
   Loan Officer**
Bank of North Dakota
700 East Main Avenue, Box 5509
Bismarck, ND 58502
(701) 224-5674
(800) 472-2166, Ext. 5674

OHIO

**Ms. Carolyn Seward, Credit
    Manager/Loan Officer**
Ohio Department of Development
P.O. Box 1001
Columbus, OH 43266
(614) 644-7708
(800) 848-1300

**Mr. Philip G. Shotwell, Executive
    Director**
Minority Development Financing
    Commission
Ohio Department of Development
P.O. Box 1001
Columbus, OH 43266
(614) 644-7708
(800) 848-1300

OKLAHOMA

Ms. Sherilyn S. Stickley, Director
Technology Development
Oklahoma Center for the
    Advancement of Science and
    Technology (OCAST)
205 NW 63rd Street, Suite 305
Oklahoma City, OK 73116
(405) 848-2633

**Ms. Claudette Henry, State
    Treasurer**
State Treasurer's Office
State Capitol, Room 217
Oklahoma City, OK 73105
(405) 521-3191

**Mr. Carl Clark, Executive Vice
    President**
Oklahoma Development Finance
    Authority
205 NW 63rd Street, Suite 270
Oklahoma City, OK 73116
(405) 848-9761

**Mr. Glen Robards, Director of
    Programs**
Department of Commerce
State Capitol, Room 210
Oklahoma City, OK 73105
(405) 521-3370

OREGON

**Mr. Mike Shadbolt, Small
    Business Program Manager**
Office of Small Business
    Assistance
Oregon Economic Development
    Department
775 Summer Street NE
Salem, OR 97310
(503) 373-1241
(800) 233-3306 (in-state)

**Mr. Mark D. Huston, Manager
Mr. Barrett MacDougal, Senior
    Finance Officer**
Business Finance Section
Oregon Economic Development
    Department
775 Summer Street NE
Salem, OR 97310
(503) 373-1240, Ext. 371

PENNSYLVANIA

Ms. Emily White, Acting Director
Office of Enterprise Development
Pennsylvania Department of
    Commerce
401 Forum Building
Harrisburg, PA 17120
(717) 783-8950

Ms. Lisa Marshall, Director
Pennsylvania Economic
    Development Financing Authority

Department of Commerce
466 Forum Building
Harrisburg, PA 17120
(717) 783-1109

Mr. Aqil Sabur, Director
Pennsylvania Minority Business
  Development Authority
Department of Commerce
461 Forum Building
Harrisburg, PA 17120
(717) 783-1127

**Ms. Anne Brennan, Project
  Analyst**
Revenue Bond and Mortgage
  Program
Department of Commerce
466 Forum Building
Harrisburg, PA 17120
(717) 783-1108

**Ms. Patricia Habersberger,
  Administrator**
Pennsylvania Capital Loan Fund
Department of Commerce
493 Forum Building
Harrisburg, PA 17120
(717) 783-1768

**Mr. Joseph Burke, Acting
  Director**
Office of International Development
Department of Commerce
486 Forum Building
Harrisburg, PA 17120
(717) 787-7190

**Mr. Robert W. Coy, Executive
  Director**
Ben Franklin Partnership
Pennsylvania Department of
  Commerce
352 Forum Building
Harrisburg, PA 17120
(717) 787-4147

**Mr. Gerald Kapp, Executive
  Director**
Pennsylvania Industrial
  Development Authority
Department of Commerce
480 Forum Building
Harrisburg, PA 17120
(717) 787-6245

PUERTO RICO

**Mr. Alfredo Salazar Jr.,
  Administrator**
Economic Development
  Administration
GPO Box 2350
San Juan, PR 00936
(809) 758-4747

**Diego F. Loinaz, Executive
  Director**
Corporation for Technological
  Transformation
P.O. Box 41249, Minillas Station
San Juan, PR 00940
(809) 722-7000

Mr. Ramon Peña
Banco de Desarrollo Economico
  Para Puerto Rico
P.O. Box 5009
Hato Rey, PR 00919
(809) 766-4300

**Mr. Hiram Melendez, Senior Vice
  President**
Government Development Bank for
  Puerto Rico
GPO Box 42001
San Juan, PR 00940
(809) 722-2525

RHODE ISLAND

**Ms. Claudia E. Terra, Executive
    Director**
Rhode Island Partnership for
    Science and Technology
7 Jackson Walkway
Providence, RI 02903
(401) 277-2601

**Mr. Robert E. Donovan,
    Administrator**
Small Business Loan Fund
Rhode Island Department of
    Economic Development
7 Jackson Walkway
Providence, RI 02903
(401) 277-2601
Fax: (401) 277-2102

**Mr. Earl F. Queenan, Associate
    Director**
Rhode Island Department of
    Economic Development
7 Jackson Walkway
Providence, RI 02903
(401) 277-2601
Fax: (401) 277-2102

**Mr. William J. Parsons, Associate
    Director**
Business Development Division
Rhode Island Department of
    Economic Development
7 Jackson Walkway
Providence, RI 02903
(401) 277-2601
Fax: (401) 277-2102

SOUTH CAROLINA

Mrs. Grace McKown, President
Enterprise Development, Inc., of
    South Carolina
P.O. Box 1149

Columbia, SC 29202
(803) 737-0888

**Ms. Theresa Singleton,
    Supervisory Loan Specialist**
Finance Division
U.S. Small Business Administration
1835 Assembly Street, Room 358
Columbia, SC 29201
(803) 253-3121

Mr. Richard Bannon, President
Palmetto Seed Capital Corporation
1330 Lady Street, Suite 607
Columbia, SC 29201
(803) 779-5759

Mr. Meriwether Jones
Enterprise Development
P.O. Box 1149
Columbia, SC 29202
(803) 737-0888

Private Investor Network
Economic Enterprise Institute
University of South Carolina at
    Aiken
171 University Parkway
Aiken, SC 29801
(803) 648-6851

**Mr. Mark Williams, Associate
    Manager**
The Existing Business and Industry
    Services Department
South Carolina State Development
    Board
P.O. Box 927
Columbia, SC 29202
(803) 737-0400
(800) 922-6684 (in-state)

**Ms. Brenda Lee, Small Farm
    Manager**
South Carolina Department of
    Agriculture
P.O. Box 11280

Columbia, SC 29211
(803) 734-2200

Mr. Elliott Franks, Director
South Carolina Jobs—Economic
  Development Authority
1201 Main Street
AT&T Capital Center, Suite 1750
Columbia, SC 29201
(803) 737-0079

Mr. Cleve Thomas, Director
Rural Improvement—Small and
  Minority Business Assistance
Edgar A. Brown Building
1205 Pendleton Street, Room 441
Columbia, SC 29201
(803) 734-0562

SOUTH DAKOTA

Mr. Norm Lingle
Governor's Office of Economic
  Development
711 East Wells Avenue
Pierre, SD 57501
(605) 773-5032

Statewide

**Mr. Sandy Weeldryer, Staff
  Coordinator**
South Dakota Development
  Corporation
711 East Wells Avenue
Pierre, SD 57501
(605) 773-5032

Mr. Troy Jones
Economic Development Finance
  Authority
Governor's Office of Economic
  Development
711 East Wells Avenue
Pierre, SD 57501
(605) 773-5032

**Governor's Office of Economic
  Development**
711 East Wells Avenue
Pierre, SD 57501
(605) 773-5032
(800) 872-6190

TENNESSEE

**Mr. David Weber, Small Business
  Consultant**
Small Business Office
Department of Economic and
  Community Development
7th Floor, Rachel Jackson Building
320 6th Avenue North
Nashville, TN 37243
(615) 741-2626

**Ms. Ruth Reinhardt, Executive
  Director**
Tennessee Child Care Loan
  Guarantee Corporation
6th Floor, Rachel Jackson Building
320 6th Avenue North
Nashville, TN 37243
(615) 741-4046

Dr. David Patterson, President
Tennessee Technology Foundation
P.O. Box 23184
Knoxville, TN 37933
(615) 694-6772

TEXAS

**Mr. Lindsey Dingmore, Deputy
  Assistant Commissioner for
  Intergovernmental Affairs**
Texas Department of Agriculture
P.O. Box 12408
Austin, TX 78711
(512) 463-7427

Mr. Reagan Houston, Director
Business Finance Division
Texas Department of Commerce
816 Congress Avenue
P.O. Box 12728
Austin, TX 78711
(512) 320-9634

UTAH

Dr. Richard E. Turley, Executive Director
Utah Technology Finance Corporation
419 Wakara Way, Suite 215
Salt Lake City, UT 84111
(801) 583-8832
Fax: (801) 583-5902

Mr. Scott Davis, President
Deseret Certified Development Company
7050 Union Park Center, Suite 570
Midvale, UT 84047
(801) 566-1163
Fax: (801) 566-1632

VERMONT

Mr. William E. Kenerson, Commissioner
Department of Economic Development
109 State Street
Montpelier, VT 05602
(802) 828-3221

Mr. Robert E. Fletcher, Manager
Vermont Industrial Development Authority
56 East State Street
Montpelier, VT 05602
(802) 223-7226

VIRGIN ISLANDS

Mr. Rhudel A. George, Director
Small Business Development Agency
P.O. Box 6400
St. Thomas, VI 00601
(809) 774-8784

Mr. Rhudel A. George, Director
Small Business Development Agency
1131 King Street, Suite #301
Christiansted
St. Croix, VI 00820
(809) 773-2161

VIRGINIA

Mr. David V. O'Donnell, Director
Office of Small Business and Financial Services
Virginia Department of Economic Development
P.O. Box 798
Richmond, VA 23206
(804) 371-8100

Ms. Cynthia H. Arrington
Financial Services Representative
Virginia Small Business Financing Authority
P.O. Box 798
Richmond, VA 23206
(804) 371-8254

Dr. Clinton V. Turner, Commissioner
Department of Agriculture and Consumer Services
1100 Bank Street, Suite 210
Richmond, VA 23219
(804) 786-3501

Honorable A. Lynwood Holton, President
Center for Innovative Technology
2214 Rockhill Road, Suite 600
13783 Park Center Road
Herndon, VA 22070
(703) 689-3000

WEST VIRGINIA

Mr. David Warner, President
West Virginia Certified
Development Corporation
1900 Washington Street E
Building 6, Room 525
Charleston, WV 25305
(304) 348-3650

WASHINGTON

Mr. Kenneth L. Keach, President
Small Business Export Finance
Assistance Center
2001 6th Avenue, Suite 1700
Seattle, WA 98121
(206) 464-7123

Mr. Bill Davison, Community Programmer
Department of Community Development
9th and Columbia Building
Olympia, WA 98504
(206) 753-4900

Mr. Jonathan Hayes, Bond Program Administrator
Department of Trade and Economic Development
2001 6th Avenue, Suite 2700
Seattle, WA 98121
(206) 464-7350

Mr. Brian Teller, Business Ombudsman
Business Assistance Center
Department of Trade and Economic Development
919 Lakeridge Way SW, Suite A
Olympia, WA 98502
(206) 586-3021

WISCONSIN

Mr. Paul Eble, President
Wisconsin Community Capital, Inc.
1 South Pinckney, Suite 500
Madison, WI 53703
(608) 256-3441

Mr. John Giegel, Executive Director
Wisconsin Business Development
Finance Corporation
3 South Pinckney Street
Suite GL3
P.O. Box 2717
Madison, WI 53701
(608) 258-8830

Mr. Richard Longabaugh, Director
Economic Development Group
Wisconsin Housing and Economic
Development Authority
1 South Pinckney Street, Suite 500
Madison, WI 53703
(608) 266-7884

Mr. Philip Albert, Director
Office of Development Finance
Wisconsin Department of Development
123 West Washington Avenue
P.O. Box 7970
Madison, WI 53707
(608) 266-7099

**Mr. Todd A. Boehm,
Development Finance Specialist**
Office of Development Finance
Wisconsin Department of
Development
123 West Washington Avenue
P.O. Box 7970
Madison, WI 53707
(608) 266-7099

**Ms. Carboline Gabber,
Technology Development
Finance Specialist**
Office of Development Finance
Wisconsin Department of
Development
123 West Washington Avenue
P.O. Box 7970
Madison, WI 53707
(608) 267-9383

WYOMING

**Mr. Glenn Shaffer, Deputy State
Treasurer**
Office of the State Treasurer

State Capitol Building
Cheyenne, WY 82002
(307) 777-7408

**Mr. Scott Weaver, Executive
Director**
Wyoming Industrial Development
Corporation
P.O. Box 3599
Casper, WY 82602
(307) 234-5351

**Mr. John Sedgwick, Block Grant
Manager**
Division of Economic and
Community Development
Herschler Building, 2nd Floor West
Cheyenne, WY 82002
(307) 777-7284

**Mr. Rusty Smith, Financial
Analyst**
Division of Economic and
Community Development
Herschler Building, 2nd Floor West
Cheyenne, WY 82002
(307) 777-7284

Federal Funding Programs

This section contains information on U.S. Government funding programs directed to small businesses. These sources represent an expansion of programs mentioned in Chapter 6.

AGRICULTURAL STABILIZATION AND CONSERVATION SERVICE

COTTON PRODUCTION STABILIZATION
(Cotton Direct Payments)

Objectives: To assure adequate production for domestic and foreign demand for fiber, to protect income for farmers, to take into account federal costs, to enhance the competitiveness of U.S. cotton for domestic mill use and export, and to conserve our natural resources.

Types of Assistance: Direct Payments with Unrestricted Use.

Range and Average of Financial Assistance: Up to $250,000 per person. As of January 11, 1994, the average deficiency payment per product for the 1992 upland cotton crop was $10,333 and an estimated $6,399 for the 1993 crop. Cotton, feed grain, wheat, and rice deficiency and diversion payments, in total, may not exceed $50,000 to any one person for the 1991 through 1997 crop years. The total of any (1) gains realized by repaying a loan at a level lower than the original loan level; (2) deficiency payments for wheat or feed grains attributable to a reduction in the statutory loan level; and (3) loan deficiency payments may not exceed $75,000 per person for each of the 1991 through 1997 crops. The total payment limitation, which includes inventory reduction payments and payments representing compensation for resource adjustment (other than diversion payments and cost-share assistance) or public access for recreation, combined with the above mentioned payments, is $250,000 per person for each of the 1991 through 1997 crops.

Contact Office: Deputy Administrator, Policy Analysis,
Agricultural Stabilization and Conservation Service,
P.O. Box 2415, U.S. Department of Agriculture, Washington, DC 20013.
Telephone: (202) 720-6734. Use the same number for FTS.

DAIRY INDEMNITY PROGRAM

Objectives: To protect dairy farmers and manufacturers of dairy products who, through no fault of their own, are directed to remove their milk or dairy products from commercial markets because of contamination from pesticides which have been approved for use by the federal government. Dairy farmers can also be indemnified because of contamination with chemicals or toxic substances, nuclear radiation, or fallout.

Types of Assistance: Direct Payments with Unrestricted Use.

Range and Average of Financial Assistance: $88 to $95,000; $40,000.

Contact Office: Emergency Operations and Livestock Program Division,
Agricultural Stabilization and Conservation Service,
Department of Agriculture, P.O. Box 2415, Washington, DC 20013.
Telephone: (202) 720-7673. Use the same number for FTS.

Emergency Conservation Program
(ECP)

Objectives: To enable farmers to perform emergency conservation measures to control wind erosion on farmlands, or to rehabilitate farmlands damaged by wind erosion, floods, hurricanes, or other natural disasters and to carry out emergency water conservation or water enhancing measures during periods of severe drought.

Types of Assistance: Direct Payments for Specified Use.

Range and Average of Financial Assistance: $50 to $64,000; $1,780.

Contact Office: Agricultural Stabilization and Conservation Service, Department of Agriculture, P.O. Box 2415, Washington, DC 20013. Telephone: (202) 720-6221. Use the same number for FTS.

Feed Grain Production Stabilization
(Feed Grain Direct Payments)

Objectives: To assure adequate production for domestic and foreign demand, to protect income for farmers, to take into account federal costs, to enhance the competitiveness of United States exports, to combat inflation, to conserve our natural resources, and to comply with statutory requirements.

Types of Assistance: Direct Payments with Unrestricted Use.

Range and Average of Financial Assistance: Up to $250,000 per person. As of January 11, 1994, the average deficiency payment per producer for the 1992 feed grain crop was $5,196 and an estimated $2,765 for the 1993 crop. Cotton, feed grain, wheat, and rice deficiency and diversion payment in total may not exceed $50,000 to any one person for the 1991 through 1997 crop years. The total of any (1) gains realized by repaying a loan at a level lower than the original loan level; (2) deficiency payments for wheat or feed grains attributable to a reduction in the statutory loan level; and (3) loan deficiency payments may not exceed $75,000 per person for each of the 1991 through 1997 crops. The total payment limitation, which includes inventory reduction payments and payments representing compensation for resource adjustment (other than diversion payments and cost-share assistance) or public access for recreation, combined with the above mentioned payments, is $250,000 per person for each of the 1991 through 1995 crops.

Contact Office: Deputy Administrator, Policy Analysis,
Agricultural Stabilization and Conservation Service,
Department of Agriculture, P. O. Box 2415, Washington, DC 20013.
Telephone: (202) 720-4418. Use the same number for FTS.

DEPARTMENT OF AGRICULTURE
RURAL DEVELOPMENT ADMINISTRATION

BUSINESS AND INDUSTRIAL LOANS

Objectives: To assist public, private, or cooperative organizations (profit or nonprofit), Indian tribes, or individuals in rural areas to obtain quality loans for the purpose of improving developing, or financing business, industry, and employment and improving the economic and environmental climate in rural communities including pollution abatement and control.

Types of Assistance: Guaranteed/Insured Loans.

Range and Average of Financial Assistance: $65,000 to $7,500,000; $1,030,928 (average size) for B&I guaranteed loans.

Contact Office: Administrator, Rural Development Administration, Department of Agriculture, Washington, DC 20250-0700. Telephone: (202) 690-4730. Use the same number for FTS.

MARITIME ADMINISTRATION

FEDERAL SHIP FINANCING GUARANTEES
(Title XI)

Objectives: To provide competitive financing through the issuance of guarantees of debt issued for the purpose of financing or refinancing the construction, reconstruction, or reconditioning of vessels built in United States shipyards and guarantee obligation, for advanced shipbuilding technology and modern shipbuilding technology of a general shipyard facility located in the United States to stimulate commercial ship construction for domestic and export sales, encourage shipyard modernization, and support increased productivity.

Types of Assistance: Guaranteed/Insured Loans.

Range and Average of Financial Assistance: Historically projects have ranged from approximately $2 million to several hundred million. (Average is not entered, because it would not be typical of the breadth of the program.)

Contact Office: Associate Administrator for Maritime Aids, Maritime Administration, Department of Transportation, Washington, DC 20590. Telephone: (202) 366-0364.

OPERATING—DIFFERENTIAL SUBSIDIES
(ODS)

Objectives: To promote development and maintenance of the U.S. Merchant Marine by granting financial aid to equalize cost of operating a U.S. flag ship with cost of operating a competitive foreign flag ship.

Types of Assistance: Direct Payments for Specified Use.

Range and Average of Financial Assistance: Depending upon the type of service vessel and trade, the per day subsidy payments per ship normally range from about $8,000 to $14,200 with $10,000 as an average.

Contact Office: Associate Administrator for Maritime Aids, Maritime Administration, Department of Transportation, 400 Seventh Street SW, Washington, DC 20590. Telephone: (202) 366-0364.

CAPITAL CONSTRUCTION FUND
(CCF)

Objectives: To provide for replacement vessels, additional vessels, or reconstructed vessels, built and documented under the laws of the United States for operation in the United States foreign, Great Lakes, or noncontiguous domestic trades.

Types of Assistance: Direct Payments for Specified Use.

Range and Average of Financial Assistance: Applicant receives tax benefits for depositing assets in accordance with the program.

Contact Office: Associate Administrator for Maritime Aids, Maritime Administration, Department of Transportation, Washington, DC 20590. Telephone: (202) 366-0364.

NATIONAL OCEANIC AND ATMOSPHERIC ADMINISTRATION

FISHERMEN'S CONTINGENCY FUND
(Title IV)

Objectives: To compensate U.S. commercial fishermen for damage/loss of fishing gear and 50 percent of resulting economic loss due to oil- and gas-related activities in any area of the Outer Continental Shelf.

Types of Assistance: Direct Payments with Unrestricted Use.

Range and Average of Financial Assistance: Range $500 to $25,[ ]
$6,000.

Contact Office: Chief, Financial Services Division, National Marine Fisheries Service, 1335 East-West Highway, Silver Spring, MD 20910. Telephone: (301) 713-2396. Use the same number for FTS.

FISHING VESSEL AND GEAR DAMAGE COMPENSATION FUND

Objectives: To compensate U.S. fishermen for the loss, damage, or destruction of their vessels by foreign fishing vessels and their gear by any vessel.

Types of Assistance: Direct Payments with Unrestricted Use.

Range and Average of Financial Assistance: $600 to $150,000; $7,350.

Contact Office: Chief, Financial Services Division, Attn: National Marine Fisheries Service, Department of Commerce, 1335 East-West Highway, Silver Spring, MD 20910. Telephone: (301) 713-2396. Use the same number for FTS.

NATIONAL SCIENCE FOUNDATION
Science and Technology Centers

Objectives: To provide mechanisms to exploit opportunities in science and technology where the complexity of the research problems or the resources needed to solve them require the advantages of scale, duration, facilities, or collaborative relationships that can best be provided by campus-based research grants. The research supported is basic in character.

Types of Assistance: Project Grants.

Range and Average of Financial Assistance: $750,000 to $4,705,000; $2,051,000.

Contact Office: Director, Office of Science and Technology Infrastructure, National Science Foundation, 4201 Wilson Boulevard, Arlington, VA 22230. Telephone: (703) 306-1040.

OVERSEAS PRIVATE INVESTMENT CORPORATION

FOREIGN INVESTMENT FINANCING

Objectives: To provide financing for projects sponsored by eligible U.S. investors in friendly developing countries throughout the world, thereby assisting development goals and improving U.S. competitiveness, creating increasing U.S. exports. Direct loans are reserved for s or cooperatives.

uaranteed/Insured Loans; Direct Loans.

Financial Assistance: $10,000,000 to $75,000,000 , out may go as high as $200,000,000; $20,000,000. ___,000 to $6,000,000 for direct loans; $2,300,000.

Contact Office: Information Officer, Overseas Private Investment Corporation, 1100 New York Avenue NW, Washington, DC 20527. Telephone: (202) 336-8799. For program information by teleFax: (202) 336-8700.

SMALL BUSINESS ADMINISTRATION

ECONOMIC INJURY DISASTER LOANS
(EIDL)

Objectives: To assist business concerns suffering economic injury as a result of certain presidential, SBA, and/or secretary of agriculture declared disasters.

Types of Assistance: Direct Loans; Guaranteed/Insured Loans (including Immediate Participation Loans).

Range and Average of Financial Assistance: Direct loans: Up to $1,500,000; $50,725.

Contact Office: Office of Disaster Assistance, Small Business Administration, 409 3rd Street SW, Washington, DC 20416. Telephone: (202) 205-6734. Use the same number for FTS.

LOANS FOR SMALL BUSINESSES
(Direct Loan Program, Low-Income/High-Unemployed Areas)

Objectives: To provide direct loans to small businesses owned by low-income persons or located in any area having a high percentage of unemployment, or having a high percentage of low income individuals. (Guaranteed Loans, including Immediate Participation Loans are provided under program 59.012).

Types of Assistance: Direct Loans; Advisory Services and Counseling.

Range and Average of Financial Assistance: Direct Loans: Up to $150,000; $67,694.

Contact Office: Director, Loan Policy and Procedures Branch, Small Business Administration, 409 Third Street SW, Washington, DC 20416. Telephone: (202) 205-6570. Use the same number for FTS.

WHEAT PRODUCTION STABILIZATION
(Wheat Direct Payments)

Objectives: To assure adequate production for domestic and foreign demand, to protect income for farmers, to take into account federal costs, to enhance the competitiveness of United States exports, to combat inflation, to conserve our natural resources, and to comply with statutory requirements.

Types of Assistance: Direct Payments with Unrestricted Use.

Range and Average of Financial Assistance: Up to $250,000 per person. As of January 11, 1994, the average deficiency payment per producer for the 1992 crop was $2,776 and an estimated $3,629 for the 1993 crop. Cotton, feed grain, wheat and rice deficiency and diversion payments, in total, may not exceed $50,000 to any one person for the 1991 through 1997 crop years. The total of any (1) gains realized by repaying a loan at a level lower than the original loan level; (2) deficiency payments for wheat or feed grains attributable to a reduction in the statutory loan level; and (3) loan deficiency payments may not exceed $75,000 per person for each of the 1991 through 1997 crops. The total payment limitation, which includes inventory reduction payments and payments representing compensation for resource adjustment (other than diversion payments and cost-share assistance) or public access for recreation, combined with the above mentioned payments, is $250,000 per person for each of the 1991 through 1997 crops.

Contact Office: Deputy Administrator, Policy Analysis, Agricultural Stabilization and Conservation Service, Department of Agriculture, P.O. Box 2415, Washington, DC 20013. Telephone: (202) 720-4418. Use the same number for FTS.

NATIONAL WOOL ACT PAYMENTS
(Wool and Mohair Price Support Payments)

Objectives: To encourage continued domestic production of wool at prices fair to both producers and consumers in a manner which will assure a viable domestic wool industry in the future. The National Wool Act is being phased out during the 1994 and 1995 marketing years. Payments to producers will be reduced by 25 percent and 50 percent, respectively for 1994 and 1995 marketings. As of December 31, 1995, the National Wool

Act expires. During the phase-out period, recourse loans will be made available to wool and mohair producers.

Types of Assistance: Direct Payments with Unrestricted Use.

Range and Average of Financial Assistance: Wool–$1 to $200,000; Mohair–$1 to $200,000. In fiscal year 1993, the average wool payment was $1,400 and the average mohair payment was $5,300. In fiscal years 1992 and 1993 the respective maximum per pound sales value on which wool and mohair payments were made was 4 times the 1991 and 1992 calendar year national average market price received for wool and mohair, respectively. Separate payment limits will be in effect for 1992 through 1995 as follows: $175,000 for 1992 marketings, $150,000 for 1993 marketings, $125,000 for 1994 marketings, and $100,000 for 1995 marketings. Support payments for wool and mohair do not count against the payment limit in effect for wheat, feed grains, rice, upland cotton, and ELS cotton.

Contact Office: Deputy Administrator, Policy Analysis, Agricultural Stabilization and Conservation Service, Department of Agriculture, P.O. Box 2415, Washington, DC 20013-2415. Telephone: (202) 720-6734. Use the same number for FTS.

WATER BANK PROGRAM

Objectives: To conserve surface waters, preserve and improve the nation's wetlands, increase migratory waterfowl habitat in nesting, breeding, and feeding areas in the U.S., and secure environmental benefits for the nation.

Types of Assistance: Direct Payments for Specified Use.

Range and Average of Financial Assistance: From $7 to $75 per acre; $13.00.

Contact Office: Agricultural Stabilization and Conservation Service, Department of Agriculture, P.O. Box 2415, Washington, DC 20013. Telephone: (202) 720-6221. Use the same number for FTS.

AGRICULTURAL CONSERVATION PROGRAM
(ACP)

Objectives: Control of erosion and sedimentation, encourage voluntary compliance with federal and state requirements to solve point and nonpoint source pollution, improve water quality, encourage energy conservation measures, and assure a continued supply of necessary food and fiber for a strong and healthy people and economy. The program will be directed toward the solution of critical soil, water, energy, woodland, and pollution abatement problems on farms and ranches.

Types of Assistance: Direct Payments for Specified Use.

Range and Average of Financial Assistance: $3 to $3,500; $990. Pooling agreement $50 to $10,000; $1,600.

Contact Office: Agricultural Stabilization and Conservation Service, Department of Agriculture, P.O. Box 2415, Washington, DC 20013. Telephone: (202) 720-6221. Use the same number for FTS.

FORESTRY INCENTIVES PROGRAM
(FIP)

Objectives: To bring private non-industrial forest and land under intensified managements, to increase timber production, to assure adequate supplies of timber, and to enhance other forest resources through a combination of public and private investments on the most productive sites on eligible individual or consolidated ownerships of efficient size and operation.

Types of Assistance: Direct Payments for Specified Use.

Range and Average of Financial Assistance: $50 to $10,000 per year; $1,600.

Contact Office: Agricultural Stabilization and Conservation Service, Department of Agriculture, P.O. Box 2415, Washington, DC 20013. Telephone: (202) 720-6221. Use the same number for FTS.

RICE PRODUCTION STABILIZATION
(Rice Direct Payments)

Objectives: To assure adequate production for domestic and foreign demand, to protect income for farmers, to take into account federal costs, to enhance the competitiveness of U.S. exports, and to conserve our natural resources.

Types of Assistance: Direct Payments with Unrestricted Use.

Range and Average of Financial Assistance: Up to $250,000 per person. As of January 11, 1994, the average deficiency payment per producer for the 1992 crop was $20,116 and an estimated $10,750 for the 1993 crop. Cotton, feed grain, wheat, and rice deficiency and diversion payments, in total, may not exceed $50,000 to any one person for the 1991 through 1997 crop years. The total of any (1) gains realized by repaying a loan at a level lower than the original loa2n level; (2) deficiency payments for wheat or feed grains attributable to a reduction in the statutory loan level; and (3) loan deficiency payments may not exceed $75,000 per person for each of the 1991 through 1997 crops. The total payment limitation, which includes inventory reduction payments and payments representing compensation for resource adjustment (other than diversion payments and cost-share assistance) or public access for recreation, combined with the above mentioned payments, is $250,000 per person for each of the 1991 through 1997 crops.

Contact Office: Deputy Administrator, Policy Analysis, Agricultural Stabilization and Conservation Service, Department of Agriculture, P.O. Box 2415, Washington, DC 20013. Telephone: (202) 720-6734. Use the same number for FTS.

RURAL CLEAN WATER PROGRAM
(RCWP)

Objectives: (1) To achieve improved water quality in the most cost-effective manner possible in keeping with the provisions of adequate supplies of food, fiber, and a quality environment, and (2) to develop and test programs, policies, and procedures for the control of agricultural nonpoint source pollution.

Types of Assistance: Direct Payments for Specified Use.

Range and Average of Financial Assistance: Maximum payment limited to $50,000 per individual for life of contract.

Contact Office: Agricultural Stabilization and Conservation Service, Department of Agriculture, P.O. Box 2415, Washington, DC 20013. Telephone: (202) 720-6221. Use the same number for FTS.

CONSERVATION RESERVE PROGRAM
(CRP)

Objectives: To protect the nation's long-term capability to produce food and fiber; to reduce soil erosion; to reduce sedimentation; to improve water quality; to create a better habitat for fish and wildlife; to curb production of some surplus commodities; and to provide some needed income support for farmers.

Types of Assistance: Direct Payments for Specified Use.

Range and Average of Financial Assistance: $50 to $50,000; $5,324.

Contact Office: Agricultural Stabilization and Conservation Service, Department of Agriculture, P.O. Box 2415, Washington, DC 20013. Telephone: (202) 720-6221. Use the same number for FTS.

COMMODITY LOANS AND PURCHASES

Objectives: To improve and stabilize farm income, to assist in bringing about a better balance between supply and demand of the commodities, and to assist farmers in the orderly marketing of their crops.

Types of Assistance: Direct Payments with Unrestricted Use; Direct Loans.

Range and Average of Financial Assistance: Direct payments (Purchases): Range not available. Loans: $50 to $76,000,000; $24,288.

Contact Office: Cotton, Grain, and Rice Price Support Division; Agricultural Stabilization and Conservation Service, Department of Agriculture, P.O. Box 2415, Washington, DC 20013. Telephone: (202) 720-7641. Use the same number for FTS.

GRAIN RESERVE PROGRAM

(Farmer-Held and -Owned Grain Reserve)

Objectives: To insulate sufficient quantities of grain from the market to increase price to farmers. To improve and stabilize farm income and to assist farmers in the orderly marketing of their crops.

Types of Assistance: Direct Payments with Unrestricted Use.

Range and Average of Financial Assistance: $1 to $122,863; $2,661.

Contact Office: Cotton, Grain, and Rice Price Support Division, Agricultural Stabilization and Conservation Service, Department of Agriculture, P.O. Box 2415, Washington, DC 20013. Telephone: (202) 720-9886. Use the same number for FTS.

DEPARTMENT OF ENERGY

ENERGY-RELATED INVENTIONS

Objectives: To encourage innovation in developing non-nuclear energy technology by providing assistance to individual and small business companies in the development of promising energy-related inventions.

Types of Assistance: Project Grants; Use of Property, Facilities, and Equipment; Advisory Services and Counseling; Dissemination of Technical Information.

Range and Average of Financial Assistance: Past awards average $83,000.

Contact Office: George Lewett, Director, Office of Technology Evaluation and Assessment, National Institute of Standards and Technology, Gaithersburg, MD 20899. Telephone: (301) 975-5500. Use the same number for FTS. Terry Levinson, Inventions and Innovation Division, Energy-Related Inventions Programs (EE-521), Department of Energy, 1000 Independence Avenue SW, Washington, DC 20585. Telephone: (202) 586-1479. Use the same number for FTS.

Nuclear Waste Disposal Siting
(Consultation and Cooperation Financial Assistance)

Objectives: To provide for the siting development, and operation of a repository and monitored retrievable storage facility for the disposal of high level radioactive waste and spent nuclear fuel.

Types of Assistance: Direct Payments for Specified Use; Project Grants (Cooperative Agreements).

Range and Average of Financial Assistance: $40,000 to $5,000,000 depending on program phase.

Contact Office: Office of Civilian Radioactive Waste Management. Contact: Jerome D. Saltzman. Telephone: (202) 586-2277. Use the same number for FTS.

Renewable Energy Research and Development
(Renewable Energy)

Objectives: To conduct balanced research and development efforts in the following energy technologies; solar buildings, photovoltaics, solar thermal, biomass, alcohol fuels, urban waste, wind, and geothermal. Grants will be offered to develop and transfer various renewable energy technologies to the non-federal sector.

Types of Assistance: Project Grants.

Range and Average of Financial Assistance: From $10,000 to $100,000.

Contact Office: Office of Management and Resources, Department of Energy, Washington, DC 20585. Contact: Fred Glatstein. Telephone: (202) 586-9262. Use the same number for FTS.

Management and Technical Assistance
for Minority Business Enterprises
(M&TA for MBEs)

Objectives: (1) To support increased participation of minority and women-owned and operated business enterprises (MBEs); (2) to develop energy-related minority business assistance programs and public/private partnerships to provide technical assistance to MBEs; (3) to transfer applicable technology from national federal laboratories to MBEs; and (4) to increase DOE's high technology research and development contracting activities.

Types of Assistance: Advisory Services and Counseling.

Range and Average of Financial Assistance: Not applicable.

Contact Office: Office of Minority Economic Impact, ED-1, Office of Economic Impact and Diversity, Department of Energy, Forrestal Building, Room 5B-110, Washington, DC 20585. Contact: Sterling Nichols. Telephone: (202) 586-1594. Use the same number for FTS.

DEPARTMENT OF THE INTERIOR
BUREAU OF INDIAN AFFAIRS

INDIAN LOANS—ECONOMIC DEVELOPMENT
(Indian Credit Program)

Objectives: To provide assistance to Indians, Alaska Natives, tribes, and Indian organizations to obtain financing from private and governmental sources which serve other citizens. When otherwise unavailable, financial assistance through the Bureau is provided eligible applicants for any purpose that will promote the economic development of a Federal Indian Reservation.

Types of Assistance: Direct Loans; Guaranteed/Insured Loans; Provision of Specialized Services.

Range and Average of Financial Assistance: $1,000 to over $1,000,000; $100,000.

Contact Office: Director, Office of Trust and Economic Development, Bureau of Indian Affairs, 1849 and C Street NW, Room 2528, Washington, DC 20240. Contact: Ernie Clark. Telephone: (202) 219-5274. Use the same number for FTS.

ECONOMIC DEVELOPMENT ADMINISTRATION

SPECIAL ECONOMIC DEVELOPMENT AND ADJUSTMENT ASSISTANCE
PROGRAM—SUDDEN AND SEVERE ECONOMIC DISLOCATION AND
LONG-TERM ECONOMIC DETERIORATION
(SSED and LTED)

Objectives: To assist state and local areas develop and/or implement strategies designed to address adjustment problems resulting from sudden and severe economic dislocation such as plant closings, military base closures, and defense contract cutbacks, and natural disasters (SSED), or from long-term economic deterioration in the area's economy (LTED).

Types of Assistance: Project Grants.

Range and Average of Financial Assistance: No specific minimum or maximum.

Contact Office: David F. Witschi, Director, Economic Adjustment Division, Economic Development Administration, Room H7327, Herbert C. Hoover Building, Department of Commerce, Washington, DC 20230. Telephone: (202) 482-2659. Use the same number for FTS.

FARMERS HOME ADMINISTRATION

EMERGENCY LOANS

Objectives: To assist established (owner or tenant) family farmers, ranchers, and aquaculture operators with loans to cover losses resulting from major and/or natural disasters, which can be used for annual farm operating expenses, and for other essential needs necessary to return disaster victims' farming operations to a financially sound basis in order that they will be able to return to private sources of credit as soon as possible.

Types of Assistance: Direct Loans.

Range and Average of Financial Assistance: $500 to $500,000; $66,200.

Contact Office: Administrator, Farmers Home Administration, Department of Agriculture, Washington, DC. Telephone: (202) 720-1632. Use the same number for FTS.

FARM OPERATING LOANS

Objectives: To enable operators of not larger than family farms through the extension of credit and supervisory assistance, to make efficient use of their land, labor, and other resources.

Types of Assistance: Direct Loans; Guaranteed/Insured Loans.

Uses and Use Restrictions: Loan funds may be used to: (1) Purchase livestock, poultry, fur-bearing, and other farm animals, fish, and bees; (2) purchase farm, forestry, recreation, or nonfarm enterprise equipment; (3) provide general operating expenses for farming activities.

Range and Average of Financial Assistance: Insured loans up to $200,000; guaranteed loans up to $400,000; Insured average loan size est. $41,400 and guaranteed average loan size est. $103,500 for fiscal year 1994.

Contact Office: Director, Farmer Programs Loan Making Division, Farmers Home Administration, Department of Agriculture, Washington, DC 20250. Telephone: (202) 720-1632. Use the same number for FTS.

FARM OWNERSHIP LOANS

Objectives: To assist eligible farmers, ranchers, and aquaculture operators, including farming cooperatives, corporations, partnerships, and joint operations, through the extension of credit and supervisory assistance to: become owner-operators of not larger than family farms; make efficient use of the land, labor, and other resources; carry on sound and successful farming operations; and enable farm families to have a reasonable standard of living.

Types of Assistance: Direct Loans; Guaranteed/Insured Loans.

Range and Average of Financial Assistance: Maximum insured $200,000, maximum guaranteed $300,000. Average insured $89,500, guaranteed $163,000.

Contact Office: Administrator, Farmers Home Administration, Department of Agriculture, Washington, DC 20250. Telephone: (202) 720-1632. Use the same number for FTS.

SOIL AND WATER LOANS
(SW Loans)

Objectives: To facilitate improvement, protection, and proper use of farm-land by providing adequate financing and supervisory assistance for soil conservation, water resource development, conservation and use, forestation, drainage of farmland, the establishment and improvement of permanent pasture, the development of pollution abatement and control facilities on farms, development of energy conserving measures, and other related conservation measures.

Types of Assistance: Direct Loans; Guaranteed/Insured Loans.

Range and Average of Financial Assistance: $4,000 to $300,000; $18,200.

Contact Office: Administrator, Farmers Home Administration, Department of Agriculture, Washington, DC 20250. Telephone: (202) 720-1632. Use the same number for FTS.

INDIAN TRIBES AND TRIBAL CORPORATION LOANS

Objectives: To enable federally recognized Indian tribes and tribal corporations to acquire land within tribal reservations and Alaskan communities.

Types of Assistance: Direct Loans; Guaranteed/Insured Loans.

Range and Average of Financial Assistance: $450,000 to $2,000,000; $859,000.

Contact Office: Director, Farmer Programs Loan Making Division, Community Facilities Division, Farmers Home Administration, Department of Agriculture, Washington, DC 20250. Telephone: (202) 720-1632. Use the same number for FTS.

Rural Rental Housing Loans

Objectives: To provide economically designed and constructed rental and cooperative housing and related facilities suited for rural residents.

Types of Assistance: Direct Loans.

Range and Average of Financial Assistance: Initial insured loans to individuals, $60,000 to $450,000; $250,000. Initial insured loans to organizations, $75,000 to $2,000,000; $950,000.

Contact Office: Director, Multi-Family Housing Processing Division, Farmers Home Administration, Department of Agriculture, Washington, DC 20250. Telephone: (202) 720-1604. Use the same number for FTS.

13

CERTIFIED DEVELOPMENT COMPANIES

Certified development companies (CDCs) specialize in providing capital to small firms located within specific local or regional areas. They generally prefer asset-based lending deals. CDCs were mentioned in Chapter 6.

Region I (Connecticut, Massachusetts, Maine, New Hampshire, Rhode Island, Vermont)
Region II (New Jersey, New York, Puerto Rico)
Region III (Delaware, District of Columbia, Maryland, Pennsylvania, Virginia, West Virginia)
Region IV (Alabama, Florida, Georgia, Kentucky, Mississippi, North Caroline, Ssouth Carolina, Tennessee)
Region V (Illinois, Indiana, Michigan, Minnesota, Ohio, Wisconsin)
Region VI (Arkansas, Louisiana, New Mexico, Oklahoma, Texas)
Region VII (Iowa, Kansas, Missouri, Nebraska)
Region VIII (Colorado, Montana, North Dakota, South Dakota, Utah, Wyoming)
Region IX (Arizona, California, Guam, Hawaii, Nevada)
Region X (Alaska, Idaho, Orregon, Washington)

Region I

Androscoggin Valley Council of Governments
Contact: Bryce Johnston
125 Manley Road
Auburn, ME 04210
(207) 783-9186
SBA Office: Augusta
Area of Operation: Androscoggin, Franklin, and Oxford counties

Bay Colony Development Corporation
Contact: David King
Watermill Center
800 South Street, 4th Floor
Waltham, MA 02154
(617) 891-3594
SBA Office: Boston
Area of Operation: Statewide except Dukes and Nantucket counties

Boston Local Development Corporation
Contact: John Dineen, Esquire
43 Hawkins Street
Boston, MA 02111
(617) 635-3342
SBA Office: Boston
Area of Operation: Boston

Brattleboro Development Credit Corporation
Contact: Al Moulton
5 Grove Street
P.O. Box 1177
Brattleboro, VT 05301
(802) 257-7731
SBA Office: Montpelier
Area of Operation: Windham and Windsor counties

Bridgeport Economic Development Corporation
Contact: Roy O'Neil
10 Middle Street, 14th Floor
Bridgeport, CT 06604-4229
(203) 355-3800
SBA Office: Hartford
Area of Operation: Bridgeport

Central Vermont Economic Development Corporation
Contact: Donald C. Rowan
P.O. Box 1439
Montpelier, VT 05601
(802) 223-4654
SBA Office: Montpelier
Area of Operation: Washington County; part of northern Orange County

Coastal Enterprises, Inc.
Contact: Ronald L. Phillips
P.O. Box 268 Middle Street
Wiscasset, ME 04578
(207) 882-7552

SBA Office: Augusta
Area of Operation: Cumberland, Knox, Lincoln, Sagadahoc, and York
  counties

Concord Regional Development Corporation
Contact: Niel Cannon
P.O. Box 664
Concord, NH 03301
(603) 228-1872
SBA Office: Concord
Area of Operation: Belknap, Grafton, Merrimack, and Sullivan counties

Connecticut Business Development Corporation
Contact: Vincent Pellegrino
845 Brook Street
Rocky Hill, CT 06067
(203) 258-7855
SBA Office: Hartford
Area of Operation: Statewide

East Boston Local Development Corporation
Contact: Salvatore Colombo
72 Marginal Street
6th Floor
East Boston, MA 02128
(617) 569-7174
SBA Office: Boston
Area of Operation: East Boston, Chelsea, Revere, and Winthrop

Eastern Maine Development Corporation
Contact: Charles Rowndy
One Cumberland Place
P.O. Box 2579, Suite 300
Bangor, ME 04401
(207) 942-6389
SBA Office: Augusta
Area of Operation: Hancock, Kennebec, Knox, Penobscot, Piscataquis,
  Somerset, Waldo, and Washington counties

Granite State Economic Development Corporation
Contact: Alan Abraham
126 Daniel Street
P.O. Box 1491
Portsmouth, NH 03801
(603) 436-0009
SBA Office: Concord
Area of Operation: Statewide

Greater Hartford Business Development Center
Contact: Warren Leuteritz
c/o HEDCO
15 Lewis Street
Hartford, CT 06103
(203) 527-1301
SBA Office: Hartford
Area of Operation: Hartford County

Housatonic Industrial Development Corporation
Contact: Charles E. Wrinn
57 North Street, Suite 407
Danbury, CT 06810
(203) 743-0306
SBA Office: Hartford
Area of Operation: West of Connecticut River

Lewiston Development Corporation
Contact: Stephen A. Heavener
37 Park Street
P.O. Box 1188
Lewiston, ME 04243
(207) 784-0161
SBA Office: Augusta
Area of Operation: Lewiston

Lynn Capital Investment Corporation
Contact: Peter M. DeVeau
One Market Street, Suite 4
Lynn, MA 01901
(617) 592-2361
SBA Office: Boston
Area of Operation: Lynn

Massachusetts Certified Development Corporation
Contact: Elizabeth C. DiSabatino
One Liberty Square
Boston, MA 02109
(617) 350-8877
SBA Office: Boston
Area of Operation: Statewide

New Haven Community Investment Corporation, LDC
Contact: Faron Lawrence
770 Chapel Street, #B31
New Haven, CT 06510
(203) 787-6023

SBA Office: Hartford
Area of Operation: New Haven County

North Central Massachusetts Development Corporation
Contact: Mark A. Goldstein
110 Erdman Way
Leominster, MA 01453
(508) 840-4300
SBA Office: Boston
Area of Operation: Cities and towns in northern Worcester County;
  western Middlesex County

Northeastern Massachusetts Economic Development Company
Contact: John A. Wells
28½ Peabody Square
Peabody, MA 01960
(508) 531-0454
SBA Office: Boston
Area of Operation: Essex County; portion of eastern Middlesex County

Northern Community Investment Corporation
Contact: Carl J. Garbelotti
20 Main Street
St. Johnsbury, VT 05819
(802) 748-5101
SBA Office: Montpelier
Area of Operation: Caledonia, Essex, and Orleans counties in Vermont;
  Coos, Carroll, and Grafton counties in New Hampshire

Northern Maine Development Commission
Contact: Duane Walton
2 Main Street
P.O. Box 779
Caribou, ME 04736
(207) 498-8736
SBA Office: Augusta
Area of Operation: Aroostook County; 19 unorganized townships in
  Piscataquis County; 6 communities in Penobscot County; and one
  community in Washington County

Ocean State Business Development Authority
Contact: Henry A. Violet
155 South Main Street, Suite 301
Providence, RI 02903
(401) 454-4560
SBA Office: Providence
Area of Operation: Providence, Kent, Washington, and Newport counties

Pittsfield Economic Revitalization Corporation
Contact: Kenneth E. Walto
70 Allen Street
Pittsfield, MA 01201
(413) 499-9371
SBA Office: Boston
Area of Operation: Berkshire County

Riverside Development Corporation
Contact: Richard Courchesne
70 Lyman Street
Holyoke, MA 01040
(413) 533-7102
SBA Office: Boston
Area of Operation: Holyoke

South Eastern Economic Development Corporation
Contact: Maria Gooch
88 Broadway
Taunton, MA 02780
(508) 822-1020
SBA Office: Boston
Area of Operation: Barnstable, Bristol, Dukes, Nantucket, and Plymouth
    counties

South Shore Economic Development Corporation
Contact: Tricia Fell
36 Miller Stile Road
Quincy, MA 02169
(617) 479-1111
SBA Office: Boston
Area of Operation: Plymouth and Norfolk counties

Vermont 503 Corporation
Contact: Thomas A. Porter
56 East State Street
Montpelier, VT 05602
(802) 479-7066
SBA Office: Montpelier
Area of Operation: Statewide

Western Massachusetts Small Business Assistance
Contact: Bob Reavey
1350 Main Street, 3rd Floor
Springfield, MA 01103
(413) 787-1553
SBA Office: Boston
Area of Operation: Hampden, Hampshire, and Franklin counties

Worcester Business Development Corporation
Contact: William E. Purcell
33 Waldo Street
Worcester, MA 01608
(617) 753-2924
SBA Office: Boston
Area of Operation: Worcester County and its contiguous areas

Region II

Adirondack Economic Development Corporation
Contact: Ernest S. Hohmeyer
30 Main Street
Saranac Lake, NY 12983
(518) 891-2020
SBA Office: Syracuse
Area of Operation: Clinton, Essex, and Franklin counties

Advancer Local Development Corporation
Contact: Luz Celenia Castellano
403 Del Parque Street, #352
Suite 202
Santurce, PR 00912
(809) 721-6797
SBA Office: Hato Rey
Area of Operation: Island of Puerto Rico, except for Las Marias
   Municipality

Albany Local Development Corporation
Contact: George Leveille
City Hall, 4th Floor
Albany, NY 12207
(518) 434-5133
SBA Office: Syracuse
Area of Operation: Albany

Buffalo Enterprise Development Corporation
Contact: Dick Velez
300 Pearl Street
Olympic Towers, Suite 452
Buffalo, NY 14202
(716) 842-3020
SBA Office: Buffalo
Area of Operation: Buffalo

Burlington County 503 Development Corporation
Contact: George Fekete
49 Rancocas Road
Mt. Holly, NJ 08060
SBA Office: Newark
Area of Operation: Burlington County

Caciques Development Corporation
Contact: Robert Hughes
P.O. Box 1626
Orocovis, PR 00720
(809) 876-2520
SBA Office: Hato Rey
Area of Operation: Orocovis

Chautauqua Region Industrial Development Corporation
Contact: Paul W. Sandberg
200 Harrison Street
Jamestown, NY 14701
(716) 664-3262
SBA Office: Buffalo
Area of Operation: Chautauqua County

Corporation for Business Assistance in New Jersey
Contact: Eugene Bukowski
Capital Place One, Suite 600-CN991
200 South Warren Street
Trenton, NJ 08625
(609) 633-7737
SBA Office: Newark
Area of Operation: Statewide

Corporacion para el Fomento Economico de la Ciudad Capital
Contact: Robert Ramirez, Jr.
Municipal Building, 15th Floor
Chardon Avenue, P.O.Box 1791
Hato Rey, PR 00919
(809) 756-5080
SBA Office: Hato Rey
Area of Operation: San Juan Municipality

Economic Development Corporation of Essex County
Contact: Ellsworth Salisbury
443 Northfield Avenue
West Orange, NJ 07052
(201) 731-2772
SBA Office: Newark
Area of Operation: Essex County

Empire State Certified Development Corporation
Contact: Robert Lazar
41 State Street
P.O. Box 738
Albany, NY 12207
(518) 463-2268
SBA Office: Syracuse
Area of Operation: Statewide

Greater Syracuse Business Development Corporation
Contact: Richard Arciero
572 South Salina Street
Syracuse, NY 13202
(315) 470-1800
SBA Office: Syracuse
Area of Operation: Onondaga County

Hudson Development Corporation
Contact: Lynda Davidson
444 Warren Street
Hudson, NY 12534
(518) 828-3373
SBA Office: New York
Area of Operation: Columbia County

La Marketing Development Corporation
Contact: Julio C. Morillo-Limardo
P.O. Box 3824
San Juan, PR 00919
(809) 783-1646
SBA Office: Hato Rey
Area of Operation: The Commonwealth of Puerto Rico except Vieques and
  Culebra municipalities

Long Island Development Corporation
Contact: Roslyn Goldmacher
255 Glen Cove Road
Carle Place, NY 11514
(516) 741-5690
SBA Office: New York
Area of Operation: Nassau and Suffolk counties and environs

Middlesex County Certified Local Development Company
Contact: Angel Guikoff
303 George Street, Suite 304
New Brunswick, NJ 08901
(908) 745-4005
SBA Office: Newark
Area of Operation: Middlesex County

Mohawk Valley Certified Development Corporation
Contact; Michael Reese
26 West Main Street
P.O. Box 69
Mohawk, NY 13407
(315) 866-4671
SBA Office: Syracuse
Area of Operation: Oneida, Herkimer, Fulton, Montgomery, and Schoharie
    counties

Monroe County Industrial Development Corporation
Contact: Judy Seil
1 West Main Street, #600
Rochester, NY 14614
(716) 428-5260
SBA Office: Syracuse
Area of Operation: Monroe County

N. F. C. Development Corporation
Contact: Sam Ferraro
745 Main Street
Niagara Falls, NY 14302
(716) 286-4472
SBA Office: Buffalo
Area of Operation: Niagara Falls

North Puerto Rico Local Development Company, Incorporated
Contact: Jose A. Franceschini
Mercantile Plaza, Suite 801
Hato Rey, PR 00918
(809) 754-7474
SBA Office: Hato Rey
Area of Operation: Puerto Rico

Operation Oswego County, Incorporated
Contact: L. Michael Treadwell
East 2nd and Schuyler Streets
P.O. Box 4067
Oswego, NY 13126
(315) 343-1545
SBA Office: Syracuse
Area of Operation: Oswego County

Port Jervis Development Corporation
Contact: Sally T. Martinez
14-20 Hammond Street
P.O. Box 3105

Port Jervis, NY 12771
(914) 856-8358
SBA Office: New York
Area of Operation: Orange County

Rochester Economic Development Corporation
Contact: Charlie Andrus
30 Church Street
Rochester, NY 14614
(716) 428-6808
SBA Office: Syracuse
Area of Operation: Rochester

Syracuse Economic Development Corporation
Contact: Michael F. Rosanio
233 City Hall
Syracuse, NY 13202
(315) 473-2870
SBA Office: Syracuse
Area of Operation: Syracuse

Tier Information and Enterprises Resources
Contact: Richard McCormick
46 South Washington Street
Binghamton, NY 13903
(607) 724-1327
SBA Office: Syracuse
Area of Operation: Broome, Chenango, Cortland, Delaware, Otsego,
  Schoharie, Tioga, and Tompkins counties

Trenton Business Assistance Corporation
Contact: Arthur H. Anderson, III
319 East State Street
City Hall Annex
Trenton, NJ 08608
(609) 989-3507
SBA Office: Newark
Area of Operation: Trenton

Union County Economic Development Corporation
Contact: Ralph S. Klopper
399 Westfield Avenue
Elizabeth, NJ 07208
(201) 527-1166
SBA Office: Newark
Area of Operation: Union County

Region III

4-C Certified Development Company
Contact: John Hunt
214 Main Street
Oak Hill, WV 25901
(304) 465-0585
SBA Office: Clarksburg
Area of Operation: Fayette, Nicholas, Raleigh, and Summers counties

Allentown Economic Development Corporation
Contact: Ms. Janice Gubich
801 Hamilton Mall, Suite 200
Allentown, PA 18101
(215) 435-8890
SBA Office: Philadelphia
Area of Operation: Lehigh County

Altoona Enterprises, Incorporated
Contact: Robert A. Halloran
1212 Twelfth Avenue
Altoona, PA 16601
(814) 944-6113
SBA Office: Pittsburgh
Area of Operation: Blair and Bedford counties

BEDCO Development Corporation
Contact: Carolyn Boozer
Charles Center South, Suite 1600
36 South Charles Street
Baltimore, MD 21201
(301) 837-9305
SBA Office: Baltimore
Area of Operation: Baltimore

Community Development Corporation of Butler County
Contact: George B. Howley
100 North Main Street
P.O. Box 1082
Butler, PA 16003
(412) 283-1961
SBA Office: Pittsburgh
Area of Operation: Butler County

Crater Development Company
Contact: James McClure
1964 Wakefield Street

P.O. Box 1808
Petersburg, VA 23805
(804) 861-1668
SBA Office: Richmond
Area of Operation: Colonial Heights, Emporia, Hopewell, and Petersburg;
Chesterfield, Dinwiddie, Greensville, Prince George, Surry, and Sussex
counties

Cumberland-Allegany County Industrial Foundation
Contact: John Kirby
1 Commerce Drive
Cumberland, MD 21502
(301) 777-5968
SBA Office: Baltimore
Area of Operation: Cumberland-Allegany County

Delaware Development Corporation
Contact: Gary Smith
99 Kings Highway
P.O. Box 1401
Dover, DE 19903
(302) 739-4271
SBA Office: Philadelphia
Area of Operation: Statewide

James River Certified Development Corporation
Contact: Frederick Minton
1111 East Main Street, 18th Floor
P.O. Box 27025
Richmond, VA 23261
(804) 788-6966
SBA Office: Ricmond
Area of Operation: Richmond; Charles City, Goochland, Hanover, Henrico,
James City, New Kent, Powhatan, and York counties

**Johnstown Area Regional Industries Certified
Development Corporation**
Contact: Richard M. Uzelac
551 Main Street
East Building, Suite 203
Johnstown, PA 15901
(814) 535-8675
SBA Office: Pittsburgh
Area of Operation: Cambria and Somerset counties

Keystone Small Business Assistance Corporation
Contact: John Hoishik

311 North Broad Street
P.O. Box 407
Lansdale, PA 19446
(215) 368-4880
SBA Office: Philadelphia
Area of Operation: Bucks and Montgomery counties

Lake County Development Corporation
Contact: Deborah Doyle
123 South Mecklenburg Avenue
P.O. Box 150
South Hill, VA 23970
(804) 447-7101
SBA Office: Richmond
Area of Operation: Brunswick, Mecklenburg, and Halifax counties; South
   Hill and South Boston

MetroAction
Contact: John Walsh
222 Mulberry Street
Scranton, PA 18501
(717) 342-7713
SBA Office: Wilkes-Barre
Area of Operation: Lackawanna, Luzerne, and Monroe counties

Mid-Atlantic Certified Development Company
Contact: Robert Klepper
2 Hopkins Plaza, 9th Floor
Baltimore, MD 21201
(410) 539-2449
SBA Office: Baltimore
Area of Operation: Statewide except Allegany County and Baltimore

New Castle County Economic Development Corporation
Contact: Ted Lambert
536 First Federal Plaza
704 King Street
Wilmington, DE 19801
(302) 656-5050
SBA Office: Philadelphia
Area of Operation: New Castle County

New River Valley Development Corporation
Contact: Wayne Carpenter
1612 Wadsworth Street
P.O. Box 3726
Radford, VA 24143

(703) 639-9314
SBA Office: Richmond
Area of Operation: New River Valley Planning District; Radford; Floyd,
   Giles, Montgomery, and Pulaski counties

OVIBDC CDC, Incorporated
Contact: Terry Burkhart
12th and Chapline Streets
P.O. Box 1029
Wheeling, WV 26003
(304) 232-7722
SBA Office: Clarksburg
Area of Operation: Ohio, Marshall, and Wetzel counties

PIDC Local Development Corporation
Contact: William Hankowsky
2600 Centre Square West
1500 Market Street
Philadelphia, PA 19109
(215) 496-8020
SBA Office: Philadelphia
Area of Operation: Philadelphia and Philadelphia County

Pittsburgh Countywide Corporation, Incorporated
Contact: Steven Mahaven
437 Grant Street
Frick Building, Suite 1220
Pittsburgh, PA 15219
(412) 471-1030
SBA Office: Pittsburgh
Area of Operation: Allegheny, Armstrong, Beaver, Butler, Fayette, Greene,
   Indiana, Washington, and Westmoreland counties

Pocono Northeast Enterprise Development Corporation
Contact: Len Ziolkowski
1151 Oak Street
Pittston, PA 18640
(717) 655-5587
SBA Office: Philadelphia
Area of Operation: Carbon, Lackawanna, Luzerne, Monroe, Pike,
   Schuylkill, and Wayne counties

Portsmouth Certified Development Corporation
Contact: Philip Tuning
801 Crawford Street
Portsmouth, VA 23704
(804) 393-8989

SBA Office: Richmond
Area of Operation: City of Portsmouth

Prince George's County Financial Services Corporation
Contact: Joseph R. Timer
9200 Basil Court, Suite 200
Landover, MD 20785
(301) 386-5600
SBA Office: District of Columbia
Area of Operation: Prince George's County

Quaker State Business Finance Corporation
Contact: Ira P. Lutsky
Jefferson House, Suite C 921
3900 City Line Avenue
Philadelphia, PA 19131
(215) 871-3770
SBA Office: Philadelphia
Area of Operation: Philadelphia, Montgomery, Bucks, Delaware, and
    Chester counties

Rappahannock Economic Development Corporation
Contact: Kathy Beard
904 Princess Anne Street
P.O. Box 863
Fredericksburg, VA 22401
(703) 373-2897
SBA Office: Richmond
Area of Operation: Caroline, King George, Stafford, and Spotsylvania
    counties; Fredericksburg

SEDA-COG Local Development Corporation
Contact: Jerry Bohinski
R.D. #1
Lewisburg, PA 17837
(717) 524-4491
SBA Office: Philadelphia
Area of Operation: Adams, Centre, Clinton, Columbia, Cumberland,
    Dauphin, Franklin, Juniata, Lancaster, Lebanon, Lycoming, Mifflin,
    Montour, Northumberland, Perry, Snyder, Union, and York counties

South Eastern Economic Development Company of Pennsylvania
Contact: Garry Smith
        Lisa Taylor
750 Pottstown Pike
Exton, PA 19341
(215) 363-6110

SBA Office: Philadelphia
Area of Operation: Chester County

Uniform Region Nine Certified Development Company
Contact: Mr. Dale Massie
614 Eleventh Street
Franklin, PA 16323
(814) 437-3024
SBA Office: Pittsburgh
Area of Operation: Clarion, Crawford, Erie, Forest, Lawrence, Mercer,
Venango, and Warren counties

Urban Business Development Corporation
Contact: Thomas Marino
201 Granby Street, Suite 1000
Norfolk, VA 23510
(804) 623-2691
SBA Office: Richmond
Area of Operation: Norfolk, Virginia Beach, and Chesapeake

Urban Local Development Corporation c/o PCDC
Contact: John Lenahan
1315 Walnut, 6th Floor
Philadelphia, PA 19107
(215) 790-2200
SBA Office: Philadelphia
Area of Operation: Philadelphia County

Virginia Asset Financing Corporation
Contact: Kathleen Strawhacker
12020 Sunrise Valley Drive
Suite 260
Reston, VA 22091
(703) 476-0504
SBA Office: District of Columbia
Area of Operation: Alexandria, Arlington, Clarke, Fairfax, Falls Church,
Frederick, Loudoun, Manassas, Manassas Park, Page, Prince William,
Shenandoah, Warren, and Winchester

Virginia Economic Development Corporation
Contact: James Skove
413 East Market Street, Suite 102
Charlottesville, VA 22901
(804) 972-1720
SBA Office: Richmond
Area of Operation: Albemarle, Fluvanna, Greene, Louisa, and Nelson
counties; Charlottesville

Washington, DC Local Development Corporation
Contact: John Ford
1201 Pennsylvania Avenue, 4th Floor
Washington, DC 20004
(202) 626-6890
SBA Office: District of Columbia
Area of Operation: Washington, DC

Wilmington Local Development Corporation
Contact: Ted Nutter
605 A Market Street Mall
Wilmington, DE 19801
(302) 571-9087
SBA Office: Wilmington
Area of Operation: Wilmington Citywide

West Virginia Certified Development Corporation
Contact: Timothy A. Bailey
State Capitol Complex
Building 6, Room 525
Charleston, WV 25305
(304) 558-3691
SBA Office: Clarksburg
Area of Operation: Statewide

Region IV

Advancement, Inc.
Contact: Robert Herring
711 North Cedar Street
Lumberton, NC 28358
(919) 738-4851
SBA Office: Charlotte
Area of Operation: Anson, Bladen, Columbus, Harnett, Hoke, Moore, Richmond, Robeson, Sampson, and Scotland

Alabama Community Development Corporation
Contact: Ms. Diana Roehrig
Number 3 Office Park Circle
Suite 300
Mountain Brook, AL 35223
(205) 870-3360
SBA Office: Birmingham
Area of Operation: Statewide except Sumter, Choctaw, and Washington counties

Albemarle Development Authority
Contact: Jane Miller
512 South Church Street
P.O. Box 646
Hertford, NC 27944
(919) 426-5755
SBA Office: Charlotte
Area of Operation: Camden, Chowan, Currituck, Dare, Gates, Hyde,
   Pasquotank, Perquimans, Tyrrell, and Washington counties

Appalachian Development Corporation
Contact: Robert M. Strother
P.O. Box 6668
50 Grand Avenue
Greenville, SC 29606
(803) 242-9733
SBA Office: Columbia
Area of Operation: Anderson, Cherokee, Greenville, Oconee, Pickens, and
   Spartanburg counties

Areawide Development Corporation
Contact: Don Woods
5616 Kingston Pike
P.O. Box 19806
Knoxville, TN 37919
(615) 588-7972
SBA Office: Nashville
Area of Operation: Scott, Campbell, Claiborne, Anderson, Union,
   Morgan, Roane, Loudon, Monroe, Blount, Knox, Grainger Hamblen,
   Jefferson, Cocke, and Sevier

Asheville-Buncombe Development Corporation
Contact: Robert C. Kendrich
P.O. Box 1010
Asheville, NC 28802
(704) 258-0317
SBA Office: Charlotte
Area of Operation: Buncombe County and its municipalities

Atlanta Local Development Company
Contact: Walter R. Huntley, Jr.
230 Peachtree Street NW, Suite 1650
Atlanta, GA 30303
(404) 658-7000
SBA Office: Atlanta
Area of Operation: Atlanta

Barren River Development Council
Contact: Jack Eversole
740 East 10th Street
Bowling Green, KY 42102
(502) 781-2381
SBA Office: Louisville
Area of Operation: Allen, Barren, Butler, Edmonson, Hart, Logan, Metcalfe, Monroe, Simpson, and Warren counties; southern central Kentucky

Birmingham City Wide Local Development Company
Contact: Mike Vance
North 20th Street
Birmingham, AL 35203
(205) 254-2799
SBA Office: Birmingham
Area of Operation: Birmingham Citywide; Jefferson and Shelby counties

Buffalo Trace Area Development District
Contact: Robert Money
327 West Second Street
Maysville, KY 41056
(605) 564-6894
SBA Office: Louisville
Area of Operation: Bracken, Fleming, Lewis, Mason, and Robertson counties

Business Development Corporation of Northeast Florida, Incorporated
Contact: Patricia A. Ferm
9143 Phillips Highway, Suite 350
Jacksonville, FL 32256
SBA Office: Jacksonville
Area of Operation: Nassau, Baker, Clay, St. Johns, Flagler, Putnam, and Duval counties except for Jacksonville

Business Growth Corporation of Georgia
Contact: Vicki M. Schoen
4000 Cumberland Parkway, Suite 1200A
Atlanta, GA 30339
(404) 434-0273
SBA Office: Atlanta
Area of Operation: Statewide

Capital Economic Development Corporation
Contact: Kelley Ferrante
805 New Bern Avenue

P.O. Box 1443
Raleigh, NC 27610
(919) 832-4524
SBA Office: Charlotte
Area of Operation: Durham, Wake, and Orange counties

Catawba Regional Development Corporation
Contact: Elaine Fairman
P.O. Box 862
Rock Hill, SC 29730
(803) 324-3161
SBA Office: Columbia
Area of Operation: Chester, Lancaster, Union, and York counties

Central Mississippi Development Company
Contact: Thelman Larry Anderson
1170 Lakeland Drive
Jackson, MS 39216
(601) 981-1625
SBA Office: Jackson
Area of Operation: Copiah, Hinds, Madison, Rankin, Simpson, Warren,
   and Yazoo counties

Centralina Development Corporation
Contact: Paul K. Herringshaw
P.O. Box 35008
Charlotte, NC 28235
(704) 372-2416
SBA Office: Charlotte
Area of Operation: Cabarrus, Gaston, Iredell, Lincoln, Mecklenburg,
   Rowan, Stanley, and Union counties

**Certified Development Company of Northeast
Georgia, Incorporated**
Contact: Chris McGahee
305 Research Drive
Athens, GA 30610
(404) 369-5650
SBA Office: Atlanta
Area of Operation: Barrow, Clarke, Elbert, Greene, Jackson, Madison,
   Morgan, Oconee, Oglethorpe, and Walton counties

Certified Development Corporation of South Carolina
Contact: Vern F. Amick
P.O. Box 21823
Columbia, SC 29221
(803) 798-4064

SBA Office: Columbia
Area of Operation: Statewide

Charleston Citywide Local Development Corporation
Contact: Sharon A. Brennan
496 King Street
Charleston, SC 29403
(803) 724-3796
SBA Office: Columbia
Area of Operation: Charleston

Charlotte Certified Development Corporation
Contact: Fred Miller
City Hall, 600 East 4th Street, 5th Floor
Charlotte, NC 28202
(704) 336-2114
SBA Office: Charlotte
Area of Operation: Mecklenburg County

City of Spartanburg Development Corporation
Contact: Tim Kuether
145 Broad Street
P.O. Box 1749
Spartanburg, SC 29304
(803) 596-2108
SBA Office: Columbia
Area of Operation: Spartanburg

Coastal Area District Development Authority
Contact: Vernon D. Martin, Executive Director
1313 Newcastle Street, 2nd Floor
Brunswick, GA 31520
(912) 261-2500
SBA Office: Atlanta
Area of Operation: Effingham, Chatham, Bryan, Long, Liberty, McIntosh,
    Glynn, and Camden except Savannah City

Commonwealth Small Business Development Corporation
Contact: Theresa Middleton
2400 Capital Plaza Tower
Frankfort, KY 40601
(502) 564-4554
SBA Office: Louisville
Area of Operation: Statewide

CSRA Local Development Corporation
Contact: Randy Griffin
2123 Wrightsboro Road

P.O. Box 2800
Augusta, GA 30904
(706) 737-1823
SBA Office: Atlanta
Area of Operation: Burke, Columbia, Emanuel, Glascock, Jefferson, Jenkins, Lincoln, McDuffie, Richmond, Screven, Taliaferro, Warren, Wilkes, Johnson, Washington, and Hancock counties

Cumberland Area Investment Corporation
Contact: Freda Wakefield
1225 Burgess Falls Road
Cookeville, TN 38501
(615) 432-4115
SBA Office: Nashville
Area of Operation: Cannon, Clay, Cumberland, DeKalb, Fentress, Jackson, Macon, Overton, Pickett, Putman, Smith, Van Buren, Warren, and White counties

Development Corporation of Middle Georgia
Contact: Clayton Black
600 Grand Building
Mulberry Street
Macon, GA 31201
(912) 751-6160
SBA Office: Atlanta
Area of Operation: Bibb, Crawford, Houston, Jones, Monroe, Peach, and Twigg counties

Economic Development Corporation of Fulton County
Contact: Ed Nelson
141 Pryor Street, Suite 5001
Atlanta, GA 30303
(404) 730-8076
SBA Office: Atlanta
Area of Operation: Fulton County

Economic Development Corporation of East Kentucky
Contact: Avalon Haight
3000 Louisa Street
Catlettsburg, KY 41129
(606) 739-5191
SBA Office: Louisville
Area of Operation: Boyd, Elliott, Greenup, Carter, and Lawrence counties

Financial Services Corporation of Southeast Georgia
Contact: Kenneth Hayes
3395 Harris Road
Waycross, GA 31501

(912) 285-6097
SBA Office: Atlanta
Area of Operation: Atkinson, Bacon, Brantley, Charlton, Clinch, Coffee,
    Pierce, and Ware counties

First Tennessee Economic Development Corporation
Contact: Stephen B. Holt
207 North Boone Street, Suite 800
Johnson City, TN 37604
(615) 928-0224
SBA Office: Nashville
Area of Operation: Carter, Greene, Hancock, Hawkins, Johnson, Sullivan,
    Unicoi, and Washington counties

Florida Business Development Corporation
Contact: Jerry Abraham
6801 Lake Worth Road, Room 209
Lake Worth, FL 33469
(407) 433-0233
SBA Office: Miami
Area of Operation: Dade, Broward, Palm Beach, St. Lucie, Martin, Indian
    River, Brevard, Osceola, Orange, Polk, Pinellas, and Manatee

Florida First Capital Finance Corporation
Contact: Danny Warren
107 West Gaines Street, Room 443
Collins Building
Tallahassee, FL 32399
(904) 487-0466
SBA Office: Jacksonville
Area of Operation: Statewide

Georgia Mountains Regional Economic Development Corporation
Contact: Sam Dayton
P.O. Box 1720
Gainesville, GA 30503
(404) 532-6541
SBA Office: Atlanta
Area of Operation: Banks, Dawson, Forsyth, Franklin, Habersham, Hall,
    Hart, Lumpkin, Rabun, Stephens, Towns, Union, and White counties

Greater Mobile Development Corporation
Contact: Teresa Jacobs
One St. Louis Centre, Suite 1001
Mobile, AL 36602
(205) 661-9051
SBA Office: Birmingham
Area of Operation: Mobile County

Gulf-Certco, Inc.
Contact: La Nelle C. Johnson
P.O. Box 59
#218 Downtown Building
Gulfport, MS 39502
(601) 864-5657
SBA Office: Jackson
Area of Operation: Gulfport and 10 miles outside city limits

Heart of Georgia Area Development Corporation
Contact: Nicky Cabero
501 Oak Street
Eastman, GA 31023
(912) 374-4771
SBA Office: Atlanta
Area of Operation: Bleckley, Dodge, Laurens, Montgomery, Pulaski, Talfair, Treutlen, Wheeler, and Wilcox counties

Intercounty Development
Contact: Jack Kendree
Horry-Georgetown Technical College
Highway 501, P.O. Box 1288
Conway, SC 29526
(803) 347-4604
SBA Office: Columbia
Area of Operation: Georgetown, Williamsburg, and Horry counties

Jacksonville Economic Development Company
Contact: James Taylor
Florida Theatre Building, Suite 500
128 East Forsyth Street
Jacksonville, FL 32206
(904) 630-1458
SBA Office: Jacksonville
Area of Operation: Jacksonville citywide; Duval County

Lowcountry Regional Development Corporation
Contact: Thomas McTeer
P.O. Box 98
I-95 at Point South
Yemassee, SC 29945
(803) 726-5536
SBA Office: Columbia
Area of Operation: Lowcountry region including Beaufort, Colleton, Hampton, and Jasper counties

Lower Savannah Regional Development Corporation
Contact: Donna Scotten

2748 Wagner Road, 302 North
P.O. Box 850
Aiken, SC 29801
(803) 649-7985
SBA Office: Columbia
Area of Operation: Aiken, Calhoun, Orangeburg, Bamberg, Barnwell, and
Allendale counties

Memphis Area Investment Corporation
Contact: Linda Burrell
157 Poplar Avenue, B150
Memphis, TN 38103
(901) 576-4610
SBA Office: Nashville
Area of Operation: Fayette, Lauderdale, Shelby, and Tipton counties

Metropolitan Capital Access Corporation
Contact: Randall McKenzie
200 Brown & Williamson Tower
401 South 4th Avenue
Louisville, KY 40202
(502) 625-3051
SBA Office: Louisville
Area of Operation: Jefferson County

Mid-Carolina Regional Development Authority
Contact: Roger Sheats
130 Gillespie Street
P.O. Drawer 1510
Fayetteville, NC 28302
(919) 323-4191
SBA Office: Charlotte
Area of Operation: Chatham, Cumberland, Harnett, Lee, and Sampson
counties

Mid-Cumberland Area Development Corporation
Contact: Douglas A. Remke
211 Union Street, #233
Stalman Building, 7th Floor
Nashville, TN 37201
(615) 862-8855
SBA Office: Nashville
Area of Operation: Cheatham, Davidson, Dickson, Houston, Humphreys,
Montgomery, Robertson, Rutherford, Stewart, Sumner, Trousdale,
Williamson, and Wilson

Mid-East Certified Development Corporation
Contact: Thomas Coombs

P.O. Box 1787
Washington, NC 27889
(919) 946-1038
SBA Office: Charlotte
Area of Operation: Beaufort, Bertie, Martin, and Hertford counties

Middle Flint Area Development Corporation
Contact: Bobby Lowe
P.O. Box 6
Ellaville, GA 31806
(912) 937-2561
SBA Office: Atlanta
Area of Operation: Crisp, Dooly, Macon, Marion, Schley, Sumter, Taylor,
    and Webster counties

Mississippi Business Finance Corporation
Contact: Vernon Sith
1201 Walter Sillers Building
P.O. Box 849
Jackson, MS 39205
(601) 359-6710
SBA Office: Jackson
Area of Operation: Statewide

Neuse River Development Authority
Contact: Robert Quinn
P.O. Box 1717
233 O'Marks Square
New Bern, NC 28563
(919) 638-6724
SBA Office: Charlotte
Area of Operation: Carteret, Craven, Duplin, Greene, Johnston, Jones,
    Lenoir, Onslow, Pamlico, and Wayne counties

North Central Florida Areawide Development Company
Contact: Ms. Conchi Ossa
2009 NW 67th Place
Gainesville, FL 32606
(904) 336-2199
SBA Office: Jacksonville
Area of Operation: Alachua, Bradford, Columbia, Dixie, Gilchrist,
    Hamilton, Lafayette, Madison, Suwannee, Taylor, and Union counties

North Georgia Certified Development Company
Contact: Gloria Hausser
503 West Waugh Street
Dalton, GA 30720
(404) 226-1110

SBA Office: Atlanta
Area of Operation: Cherokee, Fannin, Gilmer, Murray, Pickens, and
   Whitfield counties

**Northeast Mississippi Economic Development
Company, Incorporated**
Contact: Thomas M. Coleman
P.O. Box 600
Booneville, MS 38829
(601) 728-6228
SBA Office: Jackson
Area of Operation: Alcorn, Benton, Marshall, Prentiss, Tippah, and
   Tishomingo counties

Northern Kentucky Area Development District
Contact: Morag Adton
16 Spiral Drive
Florence, KY 41022
(606) 283-1885
SBA Office: Louisville
Area of Operation: Kenton, Campbell, Boone, Carroll, Gallatin, Grant,
   Owen, and Pendleton counties

Northwest Piedmont Development Corporation
Contact: Denice Allen
280 South Liberty Street
Winston–Salem, NC 27101
(919) 722-9348
SBA Office: Charlotte
Area of Operation: Davie, Forsyth, Stokes, Surry, and Yadkin counties

Pee Dee Regional Development Corporation
Contact: Phillip C. Goff
P.O. Box 5719
U.S. Highway 52
Florence, SC 29502
(803) 669-3139
SBA Office: Columbia
Area of Operation: Chesterfield, Darlington, Dillon, Florence, Marion,
   and Marlboro counties

Pennyrile Area Development District
Contact: Dan Bozarth
609 Hammond Plaza
Ft. Campbell Boulevard
Hopkinsville, KY 42240
(502) 886-9484

SBA Office: Louisville
Area of Operation: Caldwell, Christian, Crittenden, Hopkins, Livingston, Lyon, Muhlenberg, Todd, and Trigg counties

Pitt County Development Commission Certified Development Company
Contact: John D. Chaffee
111 South Washington Street
Greenville, NC 27835
(919) 758-0802
SBA Office: Charlotte
Area of Operation: Pitt County

Purchase Area Development District
Contact: Henry Hodges
P.O. Box 588
Highway 45 North
Mayfield, KY 42066
(502) 247-7175
SBA Office: Louisville
Area of Operation: Ballard, Calloway, Carlisle, Fulton, Graves, Hickman, Marshall, and McCracken counties

Region C Development Corporation
Contact: Ed Ghent
101 West Court Street
P.O. Box 841
Rutherfordton, NC 28139
(704) 652-3535
SBA Office: Charlotte
Area of Operation: Cleveland, McDowell, Polk, and Rutherford counties

Region D Certified Development Corporation
Contact: Rick Herndon
P.O. Box 1820
Furman Road
Executive Arts Building, Suite 11
Boone, NC 28607
(704) 265-5437
SBA Office: Charlotte
Area of Operation: Alleghany, Ashe, Avery, Mitchell, Watauga, Wilkes, and Yancey

Region E Development Corporation
Contact: James E. Chandler
317 First Avenue NW
Hickory, NC 28601

(704) 322-9191
SBA Office: Charlotte
Area of Operation: Alexander, Burke, Caldwell, and Catawba counties

Region K Certified Development Company
Contact: Tommy Marrow
238 Orange Street
P.O. Box 709
Henderson, NC 27536
(919) 492-2538
SBA Office: Charlotte
Area of Operation: Granville, Franklin, Person, Vance, and Warren
  counties

Santee–Lynches Regional Development Corporation
Contact: Dave Mueller
115 North Harvin Street, 4th Floor
P.O. Box 1837
Sumter, SC 29150
(803) 775-7381
SBA Office: Columbia
Area of Operation: Clarendon, Kershaw, Lee, and Sumter counties

Savannah Certified Development Corporation
Contact: Tony O'Reilly
31 West Congress Street, Suite 100
Savannah, GA 31401
(912) 232-4700
SBA Office: Atlanta
Area of Operation: Chatham County

Self-Help Ventures Fund
Contact: Jim Overton
409 East Chapel Hill Street
Durham, NC 27701
(919) 683-3016
SBA Office: Charlotte
Area of Operation: Statewide

Smokey Mountain Development Corporation
Contact: Thomas Fouts
100 Industrial Park Drive
Waynesville, NC 28786
(704) 452-1967
SBA Office: Charlotte
Area of Operation: Madison, Haywood, Graham, Cherokee, Clay, Macon,
  Jackson, Transylvania, Henderson, and Swain counties

South Central Tennessee Business Development Corporation
Contact: Doug Williams
P.O. Box 1346
815 South Main Street
Columbia, TN 38402
(615) 381-2041
SBA Office: Nashville
Area of Operation: Bedford, Coffee, Franklin, Giles, Hickman, Lawrence, Lewis, Lincoln, Marshall, Maury, Moore, Perry, and Wayne counties

South Georgia Area Development Corporation
Contact: Don Chancey
327 W. Savannah Avenue
P.O. Box 1223
Valdosta, GA 31601
(912) 333-5277
SBA Office: Atlanta
Area of Operation: Ben Hill, Berrien, Brooks, Cook, Echols, Irwin, Lanier, Lowndes, Tift, and Turner counties

Southeast Local Development Corporation
Contact: Tom McAutey
25 Cherokee Boulevard
P.O. Box 4757
Chattanooga, TN 37405
(615) 266-5781
SBA Office: Nashville
Area of Operation: 60-mile radius from Hamilton County Courthouse

Southern Development Council
Contact: James B.Allen, Jr.
401 Adams Avenue, Suite 680
Montgomery, AL 36130
(205) 264-5441
SBA Office: Birmingham
Area of Operation: Statewide

Southern Mississippi Economic Development Company
Contact: C. J. Tennant
1020 32nd Avenue
Gulfport, MS 39501
(601) 868-2312
SBA Office: Jackson
Area of Operation: Covington, Forrest, George, Greene, Hancock, Harrison, Jackson, Jefferson Davis, Jones, Lamar, Marion, Pearl River, Perry, Stone, and Wayne counties

Sowega Economic Development Corporation
Contact: Roborett Murrah, Jr.
30 East Broad Street
P.O. Box 346
Camilla, GA 31730
(912) 336-5617
SBA Office: Atlanta
Area of Operation: Baker, Calhoun, Colquitt, Decatur, Dougherty, Early, Grady, Lee, Miller, Mitchell, Seminole, Terrell, Thomas, and Worth counties

St. Petersburg Certified Development Company
Contact: Timothy McDowell
P.O. Box 2842
St. Petersburg, FL 33731
(813) 892-5108
SBA Office: Miami
Area of Operation: St. Petersburg

Tampa-Bay Economic Development Corporation
Contact: George Unanue
306 East Jackson Street, 7th Floor
Tampa, FL 33601
(813) 223-2311
SBA Office: Miami
Area of Operation: Hillsborough County

Three Rivers Local Development Company
Contact: Vernon R. Kelley III
P.O. Drawer B
Pontotoc, MS 38863
(601) 489-2435
SBA Office: Jackson
Area of Operation: 41 northern Mississippi counties

Troup County Local Development Corporation
Contact: Alesia Nixon
900 Dallis Street
P.O. Box 1107
LaGrange, GA 30241
(404) 884-4605
SBA Office: Atlanta
Area of Operation: Troup County

United Local Development Corporation
Contact: John Holliday
c/o Bank of Mississippi

One MS Plaza, P.O. Box 789
Tupelo, MS 38801
(601) 842-7140
SBA Office: Jackson
Area of Operation: Alcorn, Lee, Prentiss, Desoto, Itawamba, Monroe,
  Pontotoc, Union, Chichasaw, and Calhoun counties

Uptown Columbus
Contact: Shelley Montgomery
1001 Front Avenue
P.O. Box 1237
Columbus, GA 31902
(706) 571-6057
SBA Office: Atlanta
Area of Operation: Columbus

Urban County Community Development Corporation
200 East Main Street
Lexington, KY 40507
(606) 258-3100
SBA Office: Louisville
Area of Operation: Fayette County

Wilmington Industrial Development
Contact: Wayne Zeigler
508 Market Street
P.O. Box 1698
Wilmington, NC 28401
(919) 763-8414
SBA Office: Charlotte
Area of Operation: Wilmington; New Hanover, Pender, and Brunswick
  counties

Region V

Ashtabula County 503 Corporation
Contact: Duane Feher
25 West Jefferson Street
Jefferson, OH 44047
(216) 570-2040
SBA Office: Cleveland
Area of Operation: Ashtabula County

Brown County Development Corporation
Contact: Dennis Sreneski
835 Potts Avenue

Green Bay, WI 54304
(414) 499-6444
SBA Office: Madison
Area of Operation: Brown County

Business Development Corporation of South Bend, Mishawaka,
  St. Joseph County
Contact: Donald Inks
1200 County-City Building
City of South Bend, Department of Development
South Bend, IN 46601
(219) 235-9278
SBA Office: Indianapolis
Area of Operation: St. Joseph County

CANDO City-Wide Development Corporation
Contact: Ted Wysocki
343 South Dearborn Street, Suite 910
Chicago, IL 60604
(312) 939-7171
SBA Office: Chicago
Area of Operation: Chicago

Cascade CDC
Contact: Deborah Victory
One Cascade Plaza, 8th Floor
Akron, OH 44308
(216) 376-5550
SBA Office: Cleveland
Area of Operation: Ashland, Holmes, Portage, Medina, Summit, and
  Wayne counties

Central Minnesota Development Company
Contact: Kristin Wood
P.O. Box 33346
Coon Rapids, MN 55433
(612) 755-2304
SBA Office: Minneapolis
Area of Operation: City of Coon Rapids; Anoka County

1Step, Inc.
Contact: Dave Scaife
2415 14th Avenue South
Escanaba, MI 49829
(906) 786-9234
SBA Office: Detroit
Area of Operation: Alger, Schoolcraft, Marquette, Delta, Dickinson, and
  Menominee counties

Certified Development Company of Butler County
Contact: Daniel E. Walsh
130 High Street
Hamilton, OH 45011
(513) 887-3000
SBA Office: Columbus
Area of Operation: Butler County

Certified Development Corporation of Warren County
Contact: Bernard F. Eichholz
22 East 5th Street
Franklyn, OH 45005
(513) 748-1041
SBA Office: Columbus
Area of Operation: Warren County

Certified Economic Development Foundation
Contact: Charles Krupp
300 Monroe NW
Grand Rapids, MI 49503
(616) 456-3167
SBA Office: Detroit
Area of Operation: Kent County

Cincinnati Local Development Company
Contact: Gloria Simmons
805 Central Avenue, 7th Floor
Suite 710
Cincinnati, OH 45202
(513) 352-1958
SBA Office: Columbus
Area of Operation: Cincinnati

Citywide Small Business Development Corporation
Contact: Robert Murray, Jr.
8 North Main Street
Dayton, OH 45402
(513) 226-0457
SBA Office: Columbus
Area of Operation: Dayton and its environs

Clark County Development Corporation
Contact: John M. Harris
300 East Auburn Avenue
Springfield, OH 45505
(513) 322-8685
SBA Office: Columbus
Area of Operation: Clark County

Cleveland Area Development Finance Corporation
Contact: Gerald H. Meyer
200 Tower City Center
50 Public Square
Cleveland, OH 44113
(216) 241-1166
SBA Office: Cleveland
Area of Operation: Cuyahoga, Lake, Geauga, Lorain, Medina, Portage, and Summit counties

Cleveland Citywide Development Corporation
Contact: George V. Voinovich
601 Lakeside, Room 210
Cleveland, OH 44114
(216) 664-2406
SBA Office: Cleveland
Area of Operation: Cleveland

Columbus Countywide Development Corporation
Contact: Mark Barbash
941 Chatham Lane, Suite 207
Columbus, OH 43221
(614) 645-6171
SBA Office: Columbus
Area of Operation: Delaware, Fairfield, Fayette, Franklin, Licking, Madison, Perry, Pickaway, and Union counties

Community Development Corporation of Fort Wayne
Contact: Linda Doeden
Department of Economic Development
840 City-County Building
Fort Wayne, IN 46802
(219) 427-1127
SBA Office: Indianapolis
Area of Operation: Allen County

County Corp Development
Contact: Marlene J. Flagel
1600 Miami Valley Tower
40 West 4th Street
Dayton, OH 45402
(513) 225-6328
SBA Office: Columbus
Area of Operation: Darke, Miami, Montgomery, and Preble counties

Detroit Economic Growth Corporation Development Company
Contact: Joe Vassallo
John W. Maden Building, Suite 1500

151 West Jefferson
Detroit, MI 48226
(313) 963-2940
SBA Office: Detroit
Area of Operation: Detroit

East Central Michigan Development Corporation
Contact: Harold A. Steinke
3535 State Street
Saginaw, MI 48602
(517) 797-0800
SBA Office: Detroit
Area of Operation: Arenac, Bay, Clare, Gladwin, Gratiot, Huron, Iosco, Isabella, Midland, Ogemaw, and Roscommon

Eau Claire County Development Corporation
Contact: Brenda Blanchard
505 Dewey Street South, Suite 101
Eau Claire, WI 54701-3707
(715) 834-0070
SBA Office: Madison
Area of Operation: Eau Claire County

Forward Development Corporation
Contact: Mark Sullivan
1101 Beach Street
Flint, MI 48502
(313) 257-3010
SBA Office: Detroit
Area of Operation: Genesee County

Greater Gratiot Development, Incorporated
Contact: Donald C. Schurr
136 South Main
Ithaca, MI 48847
(517) 875-2083
SBA Office: Detroit
Area of Operation: Gratiot County

Greater Metropolitan Chicago Development
Contact: Howard Mullin
2725 Alison Street
Wilmette, IL 60091
(708) 251-2756
SBA Office: Chicago
Area of Operation: Cook, Lake, McHenry, Kane, DuPage, Kendall, Will, and Grundy counties

Greater Muskegon Industrial Fund
Contact: Ronald Keur
349 West Webster Avenue
Muskegon, MI 49440
(616) 726-4848
SBA Office: Detroit
Area of Operation: Muskegon County

Greater North-Pulaski Local Development Corporation
Contact: James S. Lemonides
4054 West North Avenue
Chicago, IL 60639
(312) 384-7074
SBA Office: Chicago
Area of Operation: Chicago Avenue South, Belmont Avenue North, Western Avenue East, and Cicero Avenue West

Greater Northwest Regional Development Corporation
Contact: Richard J. Beldin
2200 Dendrincos Drive
Traverse City, MI 49684
(616) 929-5010
SBA Office: Detroit
Area of Operation: Antrim, Benzie, Charlevoix, Emmet, Grand Traverse, Kalkaska, Leelanau, Manistee, Missaukee, and Wexford counties

Growth Finance Corporation
Contact: Lora Swenson
330 Oak Street
West Building 115
Big Rapids, MI 49307
(616) 592-3553
SBA Office: Detroit
Area of Operation: Allegan, Ionia, Kent, Lake, Mason, Mecosta, Montcalm, Newaygo, and Osceola counties

Hamilton County Development Company
Contact: David K. Main
1776 Mentor Avenue
Cincinnati, OH 45212
(513) 632-8292
SBA Office: Columbus
Area of Operation: Hamilton County except for Cincinnati

Hammond Development Corporation
Contact: Mark McLaughlin
Office of Economic Development

649 Conkey Street
Hammond, IN 46324
(219) 853-6399
SBA Office: Indianapolis
Area of Operation: Hammond

Illinois Business Financial Services
Contact: Floyd Barlow, Jr.
331 Fulton Street, Suite 405
Peoria, IL 61602
(309) 674-7437
SBA Office: Springfield
Area of Operation: Peoria, Tazewell, and Woodford counties

Illinois Small Business Growth Corporation
Contact: Douglas Kinley
403 East Adams Street
Springfield, IL 62701
(217) 522-2772
SBA Office: Springfield
Area of Operation: Statewide

Indiana Statewide Certified Development Corporation
Contact: Jean Wojtowicz
8440 Woodfield Crossing Boulevard
Suite 315
Indianapolis, IN 46240
(317) 469-6166
SBA Office: Indianapolis
Area of Operation: Statewide

Jackson Local Development Company
Contact: Duane Miller
City Hall, Eighth Floor
161 West Michigan
Jackson, MI 49201
(517) 788-4187
SBA Office: Detroit
Area of Operation: Jackson County

Kenosha Area Development Corporation
Contact: Cecilia Lucas
5455 Sheridan Road, Suite 101
Kenosha, WI 53140
(414) 654-7134
SBA Office: Madison
Area of Operation: Countywide

Lake County Economic Development Corporation
Contact: Margo Nelson
18 North County Street
Waukegan, IL 60085
(708) 360-6350
SBA Office: Chicago
Area of Operation: Lake County

Lake County Small Business Assistance Corporation
Contact: Lawrence Kramer
Camelot Building
Lakeland Community College
Mentor, OH 44060
(216) 951-1290
SBA Office: Cleveland
Area of Operation: Lake County

Lapeer Development Corporation
Contact: Patricia Crawford-Lucas
449 McCormick Drive
Lapeer, MI 48446
(313) 667-0080
SBA Office: Detroit
Area of Operation: Lapeer County

Lucas County Improvement Corporation
Contact: James Holzemer
218 Huron Street
Toledo, OH 43404
(419) 245-4500
SBA Office: Cleveland
Area of Operation: Lucas County

Madison Development Corporation
Contact: David Scholtens
550 West Washington Avenue
Madison, WI 53703
(608) 256-2799
SBA Office: Madison
Area of Operation: Dane County

Mahoning Valley Economic Development Corporation
Contact: Joe Burkey
4319 Belmont Avenue
Youngstown, OH 44505
(216) 759-3668
SBA Office: Cleveland
Area of Operation: Mahoning, Columbiana, and Trumbull counties

Mentor Economic Assistance Corporation
Contact: Elaine Lane
8500 Civic Center Boulevard
Mentor, OH 44060
(216) 255-1864
SBA Office: Cleveland
Area of Operation: Mentor

Metropolitan Milwaukee Enterprise Corporation
Contact: Evelyn Beale
809 North Broadway
P.O. Box 324
Milwaukee, WI 53201
(414) 223-5812
SBA Office: Madison
Area of Operation: Milwaukee, Ozaukee, Washington, and Waukesha
counties

Metropolitan Growth & Development Corporation
Contact: Marjorie Whittemore
600 Randolph, Room 323
Wayne County Building
Detroit, MI 48152
(313) 224-0750
SBA Office: Detroit
Area of Operation: Wayne County

Metro Small Business Assistance Corporation
Contact: Deborah Lutz
306 Civic Center Complex
1 NW Martin Luther King Boulevard
Evansville, IN 47708
(812) 426-5857
SBA Office: Indianapolis
Area of Operation: Posey, Gibson, and Vanderburgh counties

Michigan Certified Development Corporation
Contact: Larry Schrauben
525 West Ottawa Street
Law Building, Third Floor
Lansing, MI 48933
(517) 373-6378
SBA Office: Detroit
Area of Operation: Statewide

Mid City Pioneer Corporation
Contact: Jane Eaton
310 North Alabama Street, Suite 250

Indianapolis, IN 46204
(317) 236-6241
SBA Office: Indianapolis
Area of Operation: Boone, Hancock, Hendricks, Johnson, Marion,
    Morgan, and Shelby counties

Minneapolis Economic Development Company
Contact: Gary Whepley
105 5th Avenue South, Suite 600
Minneapolis, MN 55401
(612) 673-5176
SBA Office: Minneapolis
Area of Operation: Hennepin County

Minnesota Business Finance
Contact: Paul Moe
500 Metro Square
121 7th Place East
St. Paul, MN 55101
(612) 370-0231
SBA Office: Minneapolis
Area of Operation: Statewide

Northeast Michigan Development Company
Contact: Janis Kellogg
123 West Main Street
P.O. Box 457
Gaylord, MI 49735
(517) 732-3551
SBA Office: Detroit
Area of Operation: Alcona, Alpena, Cheboygan, Crawford, Montmorency,
    Oscoda, Otsego, and Presque Isle counties

Northwest Indiana Business Development Corporation
Contact: Arthur Pena
4525 Indianapolis Boulevard
East Chicago, IN 46312
(219) 398-1600
SBA Office: Indianapolis
Area of Operation: Lake County

Northwest Indiana Regional Development Corporation
Contact: Dennis Henson
6100 Southport Road
Portage, IN 46368
Area of Operation: Jaspor, Lake, LaPorte, Newton, Portor, Pulaski, and
    Storke counties

Oakland County Local Development Company
Contact: Cheryl Gault
1200 North Telegraph Road
Pontiac, MI 48341
(313) 858-0732
SBA Office: Detroit
Area of Operation: Oakland County

Ohio Statewide Development Corporation
Contact: Bruce Lagner
P.O. Box 1001
30 East Broad Street
Columbus, OH 43266
(614) 466-5043
SBA Office: Columbus
Area of Operation: Statewide

Ottawa County Development Company
Contact: Louis Hallacy
7 East 8th Street
P.O. Box 1888
Holland, MI 49422
(616) 392-2389
SBA Office: Detroit
Area of Operation: Ottawa County

Prairieland Economic Development Corporation
Contact: Randy Jorgenson
2524 Broadway Avenue
P.O. Box 265
Slayton, MN 56172
(507) 836-8549
SBA Office: Minneapolis
Area of Operation: Cottonwood, Jackson, Lincoln, Lyon, Murray, Nobles,
Pipestone, Redwood, and Rock counties

Racine County Business Development Corporation
Contact: Leonard Ziolkowski
4701 Washington Avenue, #215
Racine, WI 53406
(414) 638-0234
SBA Office: Madison
Area of Operation: Racine County

Red Cedar Certified Development Corporation
Contact: Roger Hamlin
201 UP&LA Building

East Lansing, MI 48826
(517) 337-2853
SBA Office: Detroit
Area of Operation: East Lansing/Meridian Township

Region Nine Development Corporation
Contact: Gina Feehan
410 South Fifth Street
P.O. Box 3367
Mankato, MN 56001
(507) 387-5643
SBA Office: Minneapolis
Area of Operation: Blue Earth, Brown, Faribault, Le Sueur, Martin,
  Nicollet, Sibley, Waseca, and Watonwan counties

Rockford Local Development Corporation
Contact: Sanders W. Howse, Jr.
515 North Court Street
Rockford, IL 61103
(815) 987-8127
SBA Office: Chicago
Area of Operation: Rockford

Saint Paul/Metro East Development Corporation
Contact: Connie Hilis
25 West Fourth Street
St. Paul, MN 55102
(612) 228-3306
SBA Office: Minneapolis
Area of Operation: Dakota, Ramsey, and Washington counties

The Small Business Finance Alliance
Contact: Debbie Groeteka
203 West Main Street
Collinsville, IL 62234
(618) 344-4080
SBA Office: Springfield
Area of Operation: Bond, Clinton, Madison, Monroe, St. Clair, Randolph,
  and Washington counties

Somercor 504, Inc.
Contact: Karen Lennon
Two East 8th Street
Chicago, IL 60605
(312) 360-3163
SBA Office: Chicago
Area of Operation: Cook, Dupage, Lake Kane, McHenry, and Will
  counties

South Central Illinois Regional Planning and Development Committee
Contact: Fred Walker
120 DelMar Avenue, Suite A
Salem, IL 62881
(618) 548-4234
SBA Office: Springfield
Area of Operation: Effingham, Fayette, and Marion counties; also cities of
  Centralia and Wamac

South Towns Business Growth Corporation
Contact: Chris Cochrane
Governors State University
University Park, IL 60466
(708) 534-4924
SBA Office: Chicago
Area of Operation: South Suburban Cook and Eastern Will counties

Southeastern Minnesota 504 Development
Contact: Dwayne Lee
220 South Broadway, Suite 100
Rochester, MN 55904
(507) 288-6442
SBA Office: Minneapolis
Area of Operation: Dodge, Fillmore, Freeborn, Goodhue, Hosuton,
  Mower, Olmsted, Rice, Wabasha, Winona counties; Blooming Prairie

Stark Development Board Finance Corporation
Contact: Roland L. Theriault
800 Savannah Avenue, NE
Canton, OH 44704
(216) 453-5900
SBA Office: Cleveland
Area of Operation: Stark County

Twin Cities-Metro Certified Development Company
Contact: Robert Heck
Four Seasons Professional Building
4200 Lancaster Lane, Suite 1200
Plymouth, MN 55441
(612) 551-1825
SBA Office: Minneapolis
Area of Operation: Carver, Dakota, Hennepin, Tamsey, Scott, and
  Washington counties

Warren Redevelopment and Planning Corporation
Contact: Janice E. Scott
106 East Market Street, #705
Warren, OH 44481

(216) 841-2566
SBA Office: Cleveland
Area of Operation: Warren and Trumbull counties

Western Wisconsin Development Corporation
Contact: Bob Ahlin
100 Digital Drive
Turtle Lake, WI 54009
(415) 986-4310
SBA Office: Madison
Area of Operation: Barron, Bayfield, Burnett, Chippewa, Dunne, Polk,
    Rusk, St. Croix, Sawyer, and Washburn counties

Wisconsin Business Development Finance Corporation
Contact: John Giegel
P.O. Box 2717
Madison, WI 53701
(608) 258-8830
SBA Office: Madison
Area of Operation: Statewide

Xenia-Greene County Small Business Development Company
Contact: Joy L. Wright
61 Greene Street
Xenia, OH 45385
(513) 372-0444
SBA Office: Columbus
Area of Operation: Greene County

Region VI

Ark-La-Tex Investment & Development Corporation
Contact: M. D. LeCompte
P.O. Box 37005
Shreveport, LA 71133
(318) 632-2086
SBA Office: New Orleans
Area of Operation: Bienville, Bossier, Caddo, Claiborne, DeSoto, Lincoln,
    Natchitoches, Red River, Sabine, and Webster parishes

Ark-Tex Regional Development Company
Contact: Stephen O. Harris
P.O. Box 1967
Texarkana, TX 75504
(903) 832-8636

SBA Office: Dallas
Area of Operation: Bowie, Cass, Delta, Franklin, Hopkins, Red River, Lamar, Morris, and Titus counties in Texas; Miller County in Arkansas

Arkansas Certified Development Corporation
Contact: Sam Walls
221 West Second Street, Suite 800
Little Rock, AR 72116
(501) 374-8841
SBA Office: Little Rock
Area of Operation: Statewide

Big Country Development Corporation
Contact: Rick Womble
1025 East North 10th Street
P.O. Box 3195
Abilene, TX 79604
(915) 672-8544
SBA Office: Lubbock
Area of Operation: Brown, Callahan, Coleman, Comanche, Eastland, Fisher, Haskell, Jones, Kent, Know, Mitchell, Nolan, Runnels, Scurry, Shackelford, Stephens, Stonewall, Taylor, and Throckmortan counties

Brenham Industrial Foundation
Contact: Richard O'Malley
314 South Austin
Brenham, TX 77833
(409) 836-8927
SBA Office: Houston
Area of Operation: Brenham and 2 miles beyond city limits

Brownsville Local Development Company, Incorporated
Contact: Ken Medders
P.O. Box 911
Brownsville, TX 78520
(512) 548-6157
SBA Office: Lower Rio Grande Valley
Area of Operation: Brownsville and environs

Bryan-College Station Certified Development Company
Contact: Dennis H. Goehring
2706 Finfeather Street
Bryan, TX 77801
(409) 775-3699
SBA Office: Houston
Area of Operation: Brazos County

Capital Certified Development Corporation
Contact: Colleen Rowland
410 East Fifth Street
Austin, TX 78701
(512) 320-9649
SBA Office: San Antonio
Area of Operation: Statewide

Caprock Business Finance Corporation
Contact: Tim Pierce
P.O. Box 3730
1328 58th Street
Lubbock, TX 79452
(806) 762-8721
SBA Office: Lubbock
Area of Operation: Baily, Cochran, Crosby, Dickens, Floyd, Garza, Hale,
    Hockley, King, Lamb, Lubbock, Lynn, Motley, Terry, and Yoakum

Cen-Tex Certified Development Corporation
Contact: Randy Cosson
3700 Lake Austin Boulevard
Austin, TX 78703
(512) 469-6853
SBA Office: San Antonio
Area of Operation: 43 central Texas counties

Central Arkansas Certified Development Corporation
Contact: Charles Cummings
112 NE Front Street
P.O. Box 187
Lonoke, AR 72086
(501) 374-6976
SBA Office: Little Rock
Area of Operation: Saline, Faulkner, Pulaski, Lonoke, Prairie, and Monroe
    counties

Central Texas Certified Development Company
Contact: Bruce Gaines
P.O. Box 154118
Waco, TX 76715
(817) 799-0259
SBA Office: Dallas
Area of Operation: Bell, Bosque, Coryell, Falls, Hamilton, Hill,
    Freestone, Limestone, McLennan, Milam, Navarro, Somervell, and
    Robertson counties

Dallas Business Finance Corporation
Contact: James R. Reid
1501 Beaumont
Dallas, TX 75215
(214) 428-7332
SBA Office: Dallas
Area of Operation: Dallas

Deep East Texas Regional Certified Development Corporation
Contact: Russell Phillips
274 East Larmor Street
Jasper, TX 75951
(409) 384-5704
SBA Office: Houston
Area of Operation: Angelina, Houston, Jasper, Nacogdoches, Newton,
  Polk, Sabine, San Augustine, San Jacinto, Shelby, Trinity, and Tyler
  counties

East Arkansas Planning & Development District
Contact: Dolores Harrelson
1801 Stadium Boulevard
P.O. Box 1403
Jonesboro, AR 72403
(501) 932-3957
SBA Office: Little Rock
Area of Operation: Clay, Craighead, Crittenden, Cross, Greene, Lawrance,
  Lee, Mississippi, Phillips, Poinsette, Randolph, and St. Francis counties

East Texas Regional Development Company
Contact: Wayne Smith
3800 Stone Road
Kilgore, TX 75662
(214) 984-8641
SBA Office: Dallas
Area of Operation: Anderson, Camp, Cherokee, Gregg, Harrison,
  Henderson, Marion, Panola, Rains, Rusk, Smith, Upshur, Van Zandt,
  and Wood counties

Enchantment Land Certified Development Company
Contact: Peter Froning
625 Silver SW, Suite 315
Albuquerque, NM 87102
(505) 843-9232
SBA Office: Albuquerque
Area of Operation: Statewide

Fort Worth Economic Development Corporation
Contact: Claude Bailey
410 West 4th Street
Fort Worth, TX 76102
(817) 336-6420
SBA Office: Dallas
Area of Operation: Fort Worth; Erath, Denton, Ellis, Hood, Kaufman,
   Palo Pinto, Dallas, Tarrant, Wise, Parker, and Johnson counties
   excluding Dallas and Garland

Garland Local Development Corporation
Contact: Harry Swanson
2734 West Kingsley Road, Suite J4
Garland, TX 75041
(214) 271-9993
SBA Office: Dallas
Area of Operation: Garland, Mesquite, Plano, and Richardson; and a
   section of northeast Dallas

Houston-Galveston Area Local Development Corporation
Contact: Richard A. Wiltz
3555 Timmons Lane, Suite 500
Houston, TX 77027
(713) 627-3200
SBA Office: Houston
Area of Operation: Austin, Brazoria, Chambers, Colorado, Fort Bend,
   Galveston, Harris, Liberty, Matagorda, Montgomery, Walker, Waller,
   and Wharton counties

JEDCO Development Corporation
Contact: M. Carol Ward
3330 North Causeway Boulevard
Suite 430
Metairie, LA 70002
(504) 830-4860
SBA Office: New Orleans
Area of Operation: Jefferson Parish

Kisatchie-Delta Regional Planning and Development District
Contact: Lawrence Jeansonne
5212 Rue Verdun Street
P.O. Box 12248
Alexandria, LA 71315
(318) 487-5454
SBA Office: New Orleans
Area of Operation: Avoyelles, Catahoula, Concordia Grant, La Salle,
   Rapides, Vernon, and Winn parishes

Louisiana Capital Certified Development Company, Inc.
Contact: Al Hodge
2014 West Pinhook Road, No. 100
P.O. Box 3802
Lafayette, LA 70502
(318) 234-2977
SBA Office: New Orleans
Area of Operation: Lafayette Parish

Lower Rio Grande Valley Certified Development Corporation
Contact: Kenneth N. Jones, Jr.
4900 North 23rd Street
McAllen, TX 78504
(512) 682-1109
SBA Office: Lower Rio Grande Valley
Area of Operation: Cameron, Hidalgo, and Willacy counties

Metro Area Development Corporation
Contact: Richard L. Hess
708 NE 42nd Street
Oklahoma City, OK 73105
(405) 424-5181
SBA Office: Oklahoma City
Area of Operation: Canadian, Cleveland, and Oklahoma counties

New Orleans Regional Business Development Loan Corporation
Contact: Kevin E. Williams
301 Camp Street, Suite 210
New Orleans, LA 70130
(504) 524-6172
SBA Office: New Orleans
Area of Operation: Assumption, Jefferson, Lafourche, Orleans,
    Plaquemines, St. Bernard, St. Charles, St. James, St. John the Baptist,
    St. Tammany, Tangipahoa, Terrebonne, and Washington parishes

North Texas Certified Development Corporation
Contact: Lewis Donaghey
106 North Hamilton Street, Room 101A
Trenton, TX 75490
(708) 989-2720
SBA Office: Dallas
Area of Operation: Grayson, Ranes, Fannin, Hunt, Collin, Cooke, and
    Rockwall counties

North Texas Regional Development Corporation
Contact: Dennis Wilde
4309 Jacksboro Highway

The Galaxy Center, #200
Wichita Falls, TX 76307
(817) 322-5281
SBA Office: Dallas
Area of Operation: Archer, Baylor, Childress, Clay, Cottle, Foard,
   Hardeman, Jack, Montague, Wichita, Wilbarger, and Young counties

Northeast Louisiana Industries
Contact: Gerald E. McDonald
Route 3, Box 182
Monroe, LA 71203
(318) 345-0878
SBA Office: New Orleans
Area of Operation: Ouachita, Union, Morehouse, Richland, Caldwell,
   Jackson, Franklin, Tensas, East Carroll, West Carroll, and Madison
   parishes

Northwest Arkansas Certified Development Company
Contact: Donald Raney
1313 Highway 62-65
P.O. Box 190
Harrison, AR 72601
(501) 741-8009
SBA Office: Little Rock
Area of Operation: Benton, Carroll, Boone, Baxter, Marion, Washington,
   Madison, Newton, and Searcy counties

Rural Enterprises
Contact: Sherry Harlin
422 Cessna Street
Durant, OK 74702
(405) 924-5094
SBA Office: Oklahoma City
Area of Operation: Atoka, Bryan, Carter, Choctaw, Coal, Creek, Garvin,
   Love, Haskell, Hughes, Johnston, Latimer, LeFlore, McCurtain, Logan,
   Lincoln, Marshall, Murray, Payne, Pottawatomie, Okfuskee, Pittsburg,
   Pontotoc, Pushmataha, and Seminole counties

S-Tex Asset Financing Corporation
Contact: Bryan Beverly
539 North Carancahua
Corpus Christi, TX 78401
(512) 880-6204
SBA Office:
Area of Operation: The 44 south Texas counties served by Central Power &
   Light Company

San Antonio Local Development Corporation
Contact: Mike Mendoza
P.O. Box 830505
San Antonio, TX 78283
(512) 299-8080
SBA Office: San Antonio
Area of Operation: Gillespie, Kerr, Kendall, Comal, Guadalupe, Bandera, Bexar, Medina, Wilson, Karnes, Atascosa, and Frio counties

Small Business Capital Corporation
Contact: Peggy Smith
616 South Boston
Tulsa, OK 74119
(918) 585-1201
SBA Office: Oklahoma City
Area of Operation: Osage, Tulsa, Creek, and Washington counties

Southeast Texas Economic Development Foundation
Contact: James M. Stokes
450 Bowie
P.O. Box 3150
Beaumont, TX 77704
(409) 838-6581
SBA Office: Houston
Area of Operation: Jefferson and Orange counties

Southwest Arkansas Regional Development Corporation
Contact: Marvin Flincher
600 Bessie Street
P.O. Box 767
Magnolia, AR 71753
(501) 234-4039
Area of Operation: Little Rock
Area of Operation: Calhoun, Columbia, Dallas, Hempstead, Howard, Lafayette, Little River, Miller, Nevada, Quachita, Sevier, and Union counties

SWODA Development Corporation
Contact: Gary Gorshing
P.O. Box 562
Burns Flat, OK 73624
(405) 562-4886
SBA Office: Oklahoma City
Area of Operation: Beckham, Custer, Greer, Harmon, Jackson, Kiowa, Roger Mills, and Washita counties

Texas Certified Development Company
Contact: Ernest Perales
909 Northeast Loop 410, Suite 300
San Antonio, TX 78209
(512) 841-5668
SBA Office: San Antonio
Area of Operation: Area under jurisdiction of SBA's San Antonio and
    Harlingen District Offices; the Corpus Christi Branch Office and
    Burleson County under the jurisdiction of the Houston D.O.

Texas Panhandle Regional Development Corporation
Contact: Perna N. Strickland
P.O. Box 9257
Amarillo, TX 79105
(806) 372-3381
SBA Office: Lubbock
Area of Operation: Armstrong, Briscoe, Carson, Castro, Collingsworth,
    Deaf, Smith, Dallam, Donley, Gray, Hall, Hansford, Hutchinson,
    Hartley, Hemphill, Lipscomb, Moore, Ochiltree, Randall, Oldham,
    Parmer, Potter, Robts, Sherman, Swisher, and Wheeler counties

Tulsa Economic Development Corporation
Contact: Jayne Ann Topper
130 North Greenwood
Tulsa, OK 74120
(918) 585-8332
SBA Office: Oklahoma City
Area of Operation: Tulsa Citywide

Upper Rio Grande Development Company
Contact: Louie Alfaro
1014 North Stanton Street, Suite 100
El Paso, TX 79902
(915) 533-1875
SBA Office: El Paso
Area of Operation: El Paso, Hudspeth, Culberson, Jeff Davis, Presidio,
    and Brewster counties

Verd-Ark-Ca Development Corporation
Contact: L. V. Watkins
600 Emporia, Suite A
Muskogee, OK 74401
(918) 683-4634
SBA Office: Oklahoma City
Area of Operation: Adair, Cherokee, McIntosh, Muskogee, Okmulgee,
    Wagoner, Rogers, Mayes, Haskell, Sequoyah, Nowata, Le Flore, Craig,
    Washington, Ottawa, Delaware, and Tulsa counties

West Central Arkansas Planning and Development District
Contact: Patricia Heusel
ABT Towers, Suite 502
P.O. Box 1558
Hot Springs, AR 71901
(501) 624-1036
SBA Office: Little Rock
Area of Operation: Johnson, Pope, Conway, Yell, Perry, Montgomery, Garland, Hot Springs, Pike, and Clark counties

Western Arkansas Planning and Development District
Contact: John Guthrie
P.O. Box 2067
1109 South 16th Street
Fort Smith, AR 72901
(501) 785-2651
SBA Office: Little Rock
Area of Operation: Crawford, Franklin, Sebastian, Logan, Scott, and Polk counties

White River Planning & Development District, Incorporated
Contact: Van C. Thomas
Highway 25 North
P.O. Box 2396
Batesville, AR 72501
(501) 793-5233
SBA Office: Little Rock
Area of Operation: Cleburne, Fulton, Independence, Izard, Jackson, Sharp, Stone, Van Buren, White, and Woodruff counties

Region VII

Avenue Area Inc.
Contact: Thomas M. Overby
753 State Avenue, #106
Kansas City, KS 66101
(913) 371-0065
SBA Office: Kansas City
Area of Operation: Downtown Kansas City; Wyandotte County

Bi-State Business Finance Corporation
Contact: Gary Vallem
1504 Third Avenue
Rock Island, IL 61201
(309) 793-1181

SBA Office: Cedar Rapids
Area of Operation: Scott and Muscatine counties in Iowa; Henry, Mercer, and Rock Island counties in Illinois

Big Lakes Certified Development Company
Contact: Betty Nelson
431 Houston Street
Manhattan, KS 66502
(913) 776-0417
SBA Office: Wichita
Area of Operation: Clay, Geary, Marshall, Pottawatomie, and Riley counties

Black Hawk County Economic Development Committee
Contact: Don Wade
8 West Fourth Street
Waterloo, IA 50701
(319) 232-1156
SBA Office: Cedar Rapids
Area of Operation: Blackhawk County

Business Finance Corporation of St. Louis County
Contact: Richard Palank
121 South Meramec, Suite 412
St. Louis, MO 63105
(314) 889-7663
SBA Office: St. Louis
Area of Operation: St. Louis County

Central Ozarks Development
Contact: James R. Dickerson
c/o Meramec Regional Planning Committee
101 West Tenth Street
Rolla, MO 65401
(314) 346-5692
SBA Office: St. Louis
Area of Operation: Camden, Laclede, Pulaski, Miller, and Morgan counties

Citywide Development Corporation of Kansas City, Kansas
Contact: J. Ray Barmby
701 North 7th Street, 7th Floor
Kansas City, KS 66101
(913) 321-4406
SBA Office: Kansas City
Area of Operation: Kansas City

Clay County Development Corporation
Contact: Bill Conroy
2900 Rockcreek Parkway, Suite 510
North Kansas City, MO 64117
(816) 472-5775
SBA Office: Kansas City
Area of Operation: Clay County

Corporation for Economic Development in Des Moines
Contact: Harley L. Thornton
The Armory Building
East 1st & Des Moines Street
Des Moines, IA 50309
(515) 283-4161
SBA Office: Des Moines
Area of Operation: Des Moines

Crawford County Industrial Development Corporation
Contact: Russ Ahrenholtz
1305 Broadway
Denison, IA 51442
(712) 263-5621
SBA Office: Des Moines
Area of Operation: Crawford County

E.C.I.A. Business Growth
Contact: Jerry Schroeder
330 Nesler Center, Suite 330
P.O. Box 1140
Dubuque, IA 52001
(319) 556-4166
SBA Office: Cedar Rapids
Area of Operation: Cedar, Clinton, Delaware, Dubuque, and Jackson
  counties

Eastern Kansas Economic Development
Contact: Dr. Bartlett Finney
ESU Campus
P.O. Box 4046
Emporia, KS 66801
(316) 342-7041
SBA Office: Wichita
Area of Operation: Chase, Clay, Coffey, Franklin, Geary, Lyon, Marshall,
  Morris, Osage, Pottawatomie, Riley, and Wabaunsee counties

Economic Development Corporation of Jefferson County, MO
Contact: Patrick Lamping
P.O. Box 623
Hillsboro, MO 63050
(314) 789-4594
SBA Office: St. Louis
Area of Operation: Jefferson County

EDC Loan Corporation
Contact: Bill Sproull
10 Petticoat Lane, Suite 250
Kansas City, MO 64106
(816) 221-0636
SBA Office: Kansas City
Area of Operation: Kansas City

Enterprise Development Corporation
Contact: Michael Crist
1015 East Broadway, Suite 210
P.O. Box 566
Columbia, MO 65201
(314) 875-8117
SBA Office: St. Louis
Area of Operation: Audrain, Boone, Callaway, Cole, Cooper, Montgomery,
    and Randolph counties

Four Rivers Development
Contact: John R. Cyr
108 East Main Street
Beloit, KS 67420
(913) 738-2210
SBA Office: Wichita
Area of Operation: Jewell, Republic, Washington, Mitchell, Cloud,
    Lincoln, Ottawa, Ellsworth, Dickinson, and Saline counties

Great Plains Development
Contact: Ronald D. Nicholas
100 Military Plaza, Suite 214
P.O. Box 1116
Dodge City, KS 67801
(316) 227-6406
SBA Office: Wichita
Area of Operation: Greeley, Wichita, Scott, Lane, Ness, Hamilton,
    Kearny, Finney, Hodgeman, Stanton, Grant, Haskell, Gray, Ford,
    Mortan, Stevens, Seward, Meade, Clark, Barber, Comanche, Kiowa,
    Pratt, Stafford, Edwards, Barton, Rush, and Pawnee counties

Green Hills Rural Development
Contact: Michael R. Johns
909 Main Street
Trenton, MO 64683
(816) 359-5086
SBA Office: Kansas City
Area of Operation: Caldwell, Davies, Grundy, Harrison, Linn, Livingston, Mercer, Putnam, Sullivan, Chariton, and Carroll counties

Iowa Business Growth Company
Contact: Don J. Albertsen
505 5th Avenue
Des Moines, IA 50309
(515) 282-2164
SBA Office: Des Moines
Area of Operation: Statewide

Johnson County Certified Development Company
Contact: David Long
Oak Park Bank Building
11111 West 95th Street, Suite 210
Overland Park, KS 66210
(913) 599-1717
SBA Office: Kansas City
Area of Operation: Johnson County

Leavenworth Area Economic Development Corporation
Contact: Gene Miller
518 Shawnee
P.O. Box 151
Leavenworth, KS 66048
(913) 682-6579
SBA Office: Kansas City
Area of Operation: Leavenworth County

Lee's Summit Economic Development Council
Contact: Andrew M. Filla
600 Miller Street
P.O. Box 710
Lee's Summit, MO 64063
(816) 525-6617
SBA Office: Kansas City
Area of Operation: City of Lee's Summit

McPherson County Small Business Development Association
Contact: David O'Dell

222 East Kansas Avenue
McPherson, KS 67460
(316) 241-3927
SBA Office: Wichita
Area of Operation: McPherson County

Meramec Regional Development Corporation
Contact: Jean Hentzel
101 West Tenth Street
Rolla, MO 65401
(314) 364-2993
SBA Office: Kansas City
Area of Operation: Philps, Dent, Crawford, Washington, Gasconade, and
   Maries counties

Mid-America, Inc.
Contact: Nancy LeGrande
1501 South Joplin
Pittsburg, KS 66762
(316) 231-8267
SBA Office: Kansas City
Area of Operation: Allen, Anderson, Bourbon, Cherokee, Crawford,
   Labette, Linn, Neosho, Miami, Montgomery, Wilson, and Woodson
   counties

Mo-Kan Development
Contact: David Laurie
1302 Faraon Street
St. Joseph, MO 64501
(816) 233-3144
SBA Office: Kansas City
Area of Operation: Andrew, Buchanan, Clinton, and Dekalb counties in
   Missouri; Atchison, Brown, and Doniphan counties in Kansas

Nebraska Economic Development Corporation
Contact: Al Goodwin
2631 O Street
Lincoln, NB 68510
(402) 346-2300
SBA Office: Omaha
Area of Operation: Statewide

Northeast Missouri Certified Development Company
Contact: David B. Shoush
326 East Jefferson
P.O. Box 246
Memphis, MO 63555

(816) 465-7281
SBA Office: Kansas City
Area of Operation: Adair, Clark, Knox, Schuyler, and Scotland counties

Pioneer Country Development
Contact: Ned Webb
317 North Pomeroy Avenue
Box 248
Hill City, KS 67642
(913) 674-3488
SBA Office: Wichita
Area of Operation: Cheyenne, Decatur, Ellis, Gove, Graham, Logan,
    Norton, Osborne, Phillips, Rawlins, Rooks, Russell, Sherman,
    Sheridan, Smith, Thomas, Trego, and Wallace counties

Platte County Industrial Development Commission
Contact: Mary O. Olson
7505 NW Tiffany Springs Parkway
Kansas City, MO 64153
(816) 891-8770
SBA Office: Kansas City
Area of Operation: Platte County

Rural Missouri, Inc.
Contact: Ken Lueckenotte
1014 Northeast Drive
Jefferson City, MO 65109
(314) 635-0136
SBA Office: St. Louis
Area of Operation: Statewide

Siouxland Economic Development Corporation
Contact: Kenneth Beekley
400 Orpheum Electric Building
Sioux City, IA 51101
(712) 279-6430
SBA Office: Des Moines
Area of Operation: Woodbury, Plymouth, Cherokee, Ida, Monona, and
    Sioux counties in Iowa; Dakota County in Nebraska; Union and Clay
    counties in South Dakota

**South Central Kansas Economic Development
    District, Incorporated**
Contact: Jack Alumbaugh
151 North Volutsia
Wichita, KS 67214
(316) 683-4422

SBA Office: Wichita
Area of Operation: Butler, Chautauqua, Cowley, Elk, Greenwood, Harper, Harvey, Kingman, Marion, McPherson, Reno, Rice, Sedgqick, and Sumners counties

St. Charles County Economic Development Council
Contact: Marsha Knudtson
5988 Mid Rivers Mall Drive, Suite 200
Saint Peters, MO 63304
(314) 441-6881
SBA Office: St. Louis
Area of Operation: Franklin, Lincoln, St. Charles, and Warren counties

St. Louis Local Development Company
Contact: Larry Bushong
330 North 15th, 3rd Floor
St. Louis, MO 63103
(314) 622-3400
SBA Office: St. Louis
Area of Operation: St. Louis

Topeka/Shawnee County Development Corporation
Contact: J. Richard Pratt
515 South Kansas Avenue, Suite 405
c/o Community & Economic Development
Topeka, KS 66603
(913) 295-3711
SBA Office: Kansas City
Area of Operation: Shawnee County

Wakarusa Valley Development, Inc.
Contact: David L. Ross
734 Vermont Street, Suite 104
Lawrence, KS 66044
(913) 749-2371
SBA Office: Kansas City
Area of Operation: Douglas County

Region VIII

Community Economic Development Company of Colorado
Contact: John Burger
1111 Osage Street, Suite 110
Denver, CO 80204
(303) 893-8989

SBA Office: Denver
Area of Operation: Statewide

Denver Urban Economic Development Corporation
Contact: Dick Jones
3003 Arapahoe Street
Denver, CO 80205
(303) 296-5570
SBA Office: Denver
Area of Operation: Denver Countywide; Boulder, Adams, Arapahoe,
Jefferson, and Douglas counties

**Greater Salt Lake Business District DBA Deseret Certified
Development Company**
Contact: Scott Davis
7050 Union Park Center, Suite 570
Midvale, UT 84047
(801) 566-1163
SBA Office: Salt Lake City
Area of Operation: Statewide Utah; Uinta, Lincoln, Sublette, Sweetwater,
and Teton counties in western Wyoming

Economic Development Corporation of Yellowstone County
Contact: Jeff Leuthold
490 North 31st
Billings, MT 59101
(406) 245-0415
SBA Office: Helena
Area of Operation: Yellowstone County

Fargo-Cass Economic Development Corporation
Contact: John Kramer
417 Main Avenue
Fargo, ND 58103
(701) 237-6132
SBA Office: Fargo
Area of Operation: Statewide

First District Development Company
Contact: Roger Clark
124 First Avenue, NW
P.O. Box 1207
Watertown, SD 57201
(605) 886-7225
SBA Office: Sioux Falls
Area of Operation: Brookings, Clark, Codington, Deuel, Grant, Hamlin,
Kingsbury, Lake, Miner, and Moody counties

Front Range Regional Economic Development Corporation
Contact: Rudolph Bianchi
P.O. Box 1059
Broomfield, CO 80038
(303) 466-2808
SBA Office: Denver
Area of Operation: Adams, Arapahoe, Boulder, Denver, Douglas,
    Jefferson, Larimer, Morgan, and Weld counties

Frontier Certified Development Company
Contact: Diane Johnston
232 East Second Street, Suite 300
P.O. Box 3599
Casper, WY 82602
(307) 234-5352
SBA Office: Casper
Area of Operation: Statewide

Montana Community Finance Corporation
Contact: Robyn Young
P.O. Box 916
555 Fuller Avenue
Helena, MT 59624
(406) 443-3261
SBA Office: Helena
Area of Operation: Statewide

Northern Hills Community Development
Contact: Craig W. Johnson
P.O. Box 677
2885 Dickson Drive
Spearfish, SD 57785
(605) 642-7106
SBA Office: Sioux Falls
Area of Operation: Butte, Custer, Fall River, Lawrence, Meade, and
    Pennington counties

Pikes Peak Regional Development Corporation
Contact: Doug Adams
228 North Cascade Avenue, Suite 208
Colorado Spring, CO 80903
(719) 471-2044
SBA Office: Denver
Area of Operation: El Paso County

SCEDD Development Company
Contact: Gil Baca
212 West 13th Street

Pueblo, CO 81002
(719) 545-8680
SBA Office: Denver
Area of Operation: Alamosa, Baca, Bent, Chaffee, Conejos, Costilla,
    Crowley, Custer, Fremont, Huerfano, Kiowa, Lake, Las Animas,
    Mineral, Otero, Prowers, Pueblo, Rio Grande, and Saguache counties

South Dakota Development Corporation
Contact: Jesse Jensen
        Troy Jones
Capital Lake Plaza
Pierre, SD 57501
(605) 773-5032
SBA Office: Sioux Falls
Area of Operation: Statewide

Weber Capital Development Corporation
Contact: Robert Richards
2404 Washington Boulevard, Suite 1100
Ogden, UT 84401
(801) 627-1333
SBA Office: Salt Lake City
Area of Operation: Weber County

Region IX

Amador Economic Development Corporation
Contact: Ron Mittelbrunn
P.O. Box 1077
Jackson, CA 95642
(209) 223-0351
SBA Office: Sacramento
Area of Operation: Amador County

Antelope Valley Local Development Corporation
Contact: Vern Lawson
104 East Avenue K4, Suite A
Lancaster, CA 93534
(805) 945-7711
SBA Office: Los Angeles
Area of Operation: Antelope Valley, Northern Los Angeles County;
    Communities of Lancaster and Palmdale

Arcata Economic Development Corporation
Contact: Cindy Copple
100 Ericson Court, Suite 100
Arcata, CA 95521

(707) 822-4616
SBA Office: San Francisco
Area of Operation: Humboldt and Del Norte counties

Arizona Enterprise Development Corporation
Contact: Patty Duff
Arizona Department of Commerce
3800 North Central Avenue, #1500
Phoenix, AZ 85012
(602) 280-1341
SBA Office: Phoenix
Area of Operation: Statewide

Arvin Development Corporation
Contact: Jack R. Schulze
200 Campus Drive, Box 546
Arvin, CA 93203
(805) 861-2041
SBA Office: Fresno
Area of Operation: Kern County

Bay Area Business Development Company
Contact: Robert Hayden
150 4th Street, Suite 220
San Francisco, CA 94105
(510) 541-4616
SBA Office: San Francisco
Area of Operation: San Francisco, Marin, Sonoma, Napa, Solano, Contra
    Costa, Alameda, Santa Clara, and San Mateo counties

Bay Area Employment Development Company
Contact: James R. Baird
1801 Oakland Boulevard, Suite 300
Walnut Creek, CA 94596
(510) 926-1020
SBA Office: San Francisco
Area of Operation: San Francisco, San Mateo, Santa Clara, Alameda,
    Contra Costa, Solani, Napa, Sonoma, and Marin counties

Business Development Finance Corporation
Contact: Gary Molenda
345 East Toole Street
Tucson, AZ 85701
(602) 623-3377
SBA Office: Phoenix
Area of Operation: Cochise, Graham, Greenlee, Pina, Pinal, and Santa
    Cruz counties; Chandler, Mesa, and Tempe in Maricopa County

Butte County Overall Economic Development
Contact: Marc Nemanic
1166 East Lassen
P.O. Box 6250
Chico, CA 95927
(916) 893-8732
SBA Office: Sacramento
Area of Operation: Butte County

California Statewide Certified Development Corporation
Contact: Barbara Vohryzek
129 C Street
Davis, CA 95616
(916) 756-9310
SBA Office: San Francisco
Area of Operation: Statewide

CDC Small Business Finance Corporation
Contact: Arthur Goodman
5353 Mission Center Road, Suite 218
San Diego, CA 92108
(619) 291-3594
SBA Office: San Diego
Area of Operation: Imperial, San Diego, and Orange counties

Central Coast Development Corporation
Contact: Tom Martin
100 Civic Center Plaza
Lompoc, CA 93436
(805) 736-1445
SBA Office: Los Angeles
Area of Operation: San Luis Obispo, Santa Barbara, and Ventura counties

Commercial Industrial Development Company
Contact: Lois C. Cyr
1101 Airport Road, #D
Imperial, CA 92251
(619) 355-1025
SBA Office: San Diego
Area of Operation: Imperial County

Crown Development Corporation of Kings County
Contact: Bill Lindsteadt
1222 West Lacey Boulevard, Suite 101
Hanford, CA 93230
(209) 582-4326
SBA Office: Fresno
Area of Operation: Kings County

Economic Development Corporation of Monterey County
Contact: Virginia Cooper
340 El Camino Real South 22
Salinas, CA 93901
(408) 754-6807
SBA Office: Fresno
Area of Operation: Monterey County

Economic Development Corporation of Shasta County
Contact: Bruce Daniels
737 Auditorium Drive, Suite D
Redding, CA 96001
(916) 225-5300
SBA Office: San Francisco
Area of Operation: Shasta, Trinity, Siskiyou, and Modoc counties

Economic Development Foundation of Sacramento
Contact: Frank Dinsmore
7509 Madison Avenue, Suite 1111
Citrus Heights, CA 95610
(916) 962-3669
SBA Office: Sacramento
Area of Operation: Alameda, Contra Costa, El Dorado, Fresno, Marin,
    Mendocino, Napa, Nevada, Placer, Sacramento, San Benito, San
    Francisco, San Mateo, San Joaquin, Santa Clara, Santa Cruz, Sierra,
    Solano, Sonoma, Sutter, Yolo, and Yuba counties

Enterprise Funding Corporation
Contact: Nick Landis
3350 Shelby Street, Suite 200
Ontario, CA 91761
(714) 989-1485
SBA Office: Los Angeles
Area of Operation: San Bernardino County

Fresno Certified Development Corporation
Contact: Robert Garcia
2300 Tulare Street, Suite 235
Fresno, CA 93721
(209) 485-5302
SBA Office: Fresno
Area of Operation: Fresno County

Greater Sacramento Certified Development Corporation
Contact: Ray Sebastian
10301 Placer Lane, Suite 200
Sacramento, CA 95827

(916) 369-1582
SBA Office: Sacramento
Area of Operation: Sacramento, El Dorado, Placer, and Yolo counties

HEDCO Local Development Corporation
Contact: Dexter J. Taniguchi
222 South Vineyard Street, Penthouse 1
Honolulu, HI 96813
(808) 521-6502
SBA Office: Honolulu
Area of Operation: Statewide, American Samoa

La Habra Local Development Company
Contact: A. Edward Evans
Civic Center
P.O. Box 337
La Habra, CA 90633
(310) 905-9741
SBA Office: Santa Ana
Area of Operation: Orange and Los Angeles counties

Long Beach Area Certified Development Corporation
Contact: Regina Grant Peterson
11 Golden Shore, Suite 630
Long Beach, CA 90802
(310) 983-7450
SBA Office: Los Angeles
Area of Operation: Southern Los Angeles County

Los Angeles County Small Business Development Corporation
Contact: Raymond K. Saikaida
2525 Corporate Place
Monterey Park, CA 91754
(213) 260-2204
SBA Office: Los Angeles
Area of Operation: Los Angeles County

Los Angeles LDC
Contact: Wilfred Marshall
200 North Spring Street, Suite 2008
Los Angeles, CA 90012
(213) 485-6154
SBA Office: Los Angeles
Area of Operation: Los Angeles

Los Medanos Fund, A Local Development Company
Contact: Thomas LaFleur

501 Railroad Avenue
Pittsburg, CA 94565
(510) 439-1056
SBA Office: San Francisco
Area of Operation: Pittsburg; Alameda, Contra Costa, Marin, Napa, San
  Francisco, San Mateo, Santa Clara, Solano, and Sonoma counties

Mid State Development Corporation
Contact: Jason Bingham
515 Truxtun Avenue
Bakersfield, CA 93301
(805) 322-4241
SBA Office: Fresno
Area of Operation: Kern County

Nevada State Development Corporation
Contact: Harry H. Weinberg
350 South Center, Suite 310
Reno, NV 89501
(702) 323-3625
SBA Office: Las Vegas
Area of Operation: Statewide

New Ventures Capital Development Company
Contact: Charles Stevenson
626 South Ninth Street
Las Vegas, NV 89101
(702) 382-9102
SBA Office: Las Vegas
Area of Operation: Clark County

Oakland Certified Development Corporation
Contact: Floyd Hicks
Dufwin Towers
519 17th Street, Suite 111
Oakland, CA 94612
(510) 763-4297
SBA Office: San Francisco
Area of Operation: Oakland

Phoenix Local Development Corporation
Contact: Jill E. Triwush
34 West Monroe, Suite 901
Phoenix, AZ 85003
(602) 495-6495
SBA Office: Phoenix
Area of Operation: Phoenix

Riverside County Economic Development Corporation
Contact: Brian P. Thiebeux
3499 Tenth Street
P.O. Box 413
Riverside, CA 92502
(714) 788-9811
SBA Office: San Diego
Area of Operation: Riverside County

Santa Ana Economic Development Corporation
Contact: Patricia Nunn
901 East Santa Ana Boulevard, Suite 106
Santa Ana, CA 92701
(714) 647-1143
SBA Office: Santa Ana
Area of Operation: Orange County

Small Business Development Corporation
Contact: Simon Sanchez
Calvo Insurance Building, Suite 204
115 Chalan Santo Papa
Agana, GU 96910
(617) 472-8083
SBA Office: Honolulu
Area of Operation: Territory of Guam

Southern Nevada Certified Development Corporation
Contact: Thomas J. Gutherie
2770 South Maryland Parkway, #216
Las Vegas, NV 89109
(702) 732-3998
SBA Office: Las Vegas
Area of Operation: Mineral, Esmeralda, Nye, Lincoln, Lyon, Douglas,
   White Pine, and Clark counties

Stanislaus County Economic Development Corporation
Contact: William Carney
1012 Eleventh Street, Suite 201
Modesto, CA 95354
SBA Office: Fresno
Area of Operation: Stanislaus County

Tracy/San Joaquin County Certified Development Corporation
Contact: Roger Birdsall
815 North Hunter Street
Stockton, CA 95320
(209) 468-2266

SBA Office: Sacramento
Area of Operation: San Joaquin County

Tulare County Economic Development Corporation
Contact: Mary J. Gonsalues
2380 West Whitendale Avenue
P.O. Box 5033
Visalia, CA 93278
(209) 627-0766
SBA Office: Fresno
Area of Operation: Tulare County

Region X

C.C.D. Business Development Corporation
Contact: Peter Graff
744 Rose Street SE
Roseburg, OR 97470
(503) 672-6728
SBA Office: Portland
Area of Operation: Oregon Statewide except Wallowa County

Cascades West Financial Services
Contact: Debbie Wright
105 High Street
Corvallis, OR 97333
(503) 757-6854
SBA Office: Portland
Area of Operation: Benten, Lane, Lincoln, Linn, Marion, Polk, and
    Yamhill counties

Clearwater Economic Development Association
Contact: Bob Wood
6th Avenue North, 1626B
Lewiston, ID 83501
(208) 746-0015
SBA Office: Spokane
Area of Operation: Clearwater, Idaho, Latah, Lewis, and Nez Perce
    counties in Idaho; Asotin, Garfield, and Whitman counties in
    Washington

East-Central Idaho Development Company
Contact: David Ogden
310 North 2nd East
P.O. Box 330

Rexburg, ID 83440
(208) 356-4524
SBA Office: Boise
Area of Operation: Bonneville, Butte, Clark, Custer, Fremont, Jefferson,
Lemhi, Madison, and Teton counties

Eastern Idaho Development Corporation
Contact: Paul Cox
1651 Alvin Ricken Drive
Pocatello, ID 83201
(208) 234-7541
SBA Office: Boise
Area of Operation: Bannock, Power, Bear Lake, Bingham, Caribou,
Franklin, and Oneida counties

Evergreen Community Development Association
Contact: Robert Wisniewski
2015 Smith Tower
Seattle, WA 98104
(206) 622-3731
SBA Office: Seattle
Area of Operation: Washington statewide; Clackamas, Columbia, Clatsop,
Multnomah, Washington, Hood River, Wasco, and Tillamook counties in
Oregon

Greater Eastern Oregon Development Corporation
Contact: Jim Rowan
17 SW Frazier, Suite 20
P.O. Box 1041
Pendleton, OR 97801
(503) 276-6745
SBA Office: Portland
Area of Operation: Gilliam, Grant, Morrow, Umatilla, Wheeler, Union,
Baker, and Wallowa counties

Greater Spokane Business Development Association
Contact: Tony Rund
West 808 Spokane Fall Boulevard
Spokane, WA 99201
(509) 625-6325
SBA Office: Spokane
Area of Operation: Statewide except Pacific County

Northwest Small Business Finance Corporation
700 NE Multnomah, Suite 400
Portland, OR 97232

(503) 232-7796
SBA Office: Portland
Area of Operation: Multnomah, Clackamas, and Washington counties

Oregon Certified Business Development Corporation
Contact: Richard G. Mackay
1135 West Highland
P.O. Box 575
Redmond, OR 97756
(503) 548-8163
SBA Office: Portland
Area of Operation: Crook, Deschutes, Harney, Jefferson, Klamath, Lake, and Malheur counties

Panhandle Area Council
Contact: Deborah Holmberg
11100 Airport Drive
Hayden, ID 83835
(208) 772-0584
SBA Office: Spokane
Area of Operation: Benewah, Bonner, Boundary, Kootenai, Shoshone counties

Railbelt Community Development Corporation
Contact: Elaine Hollier
619 Warehouse Avenue, Suite 256
Anchorage, AK 99501
(907) 277-5161
SBA Office: Anchorage
Area of Operation: Statewide except First Judicial District (southeast Alaska)

Region IV Development Corporation
Contact: Van Petterson
1300 Kimberly Road
P.O. Box 1844
Twin Falls, ID 83303
(208) 736-3065
SBA Office: Boise
Area of Operation: Blaine, Camas, Cassia, Gooding, Jerome, Lincoln, Minidoka, and Twin Falls counties

Southeastern Washington Development Association
Contact: Conrad Tobin
901 North Colorado Street
Kennewick, WA 99336
(509) 735-1000

SBA Office: Spokane
Area of Operation: Benton, Franklin, Grant, Adams, Yakima, and Walla
  Walla counties

Treasure Valley Certified Development Corporation
Contact: Dave Palumbo
10624 West Executive Drive
Boise, ID 83704
(208) 322-7033
SBA Office: Boise
Area of Operation: Ada, Adams, Boise, Canyon, Elmore, Gem, Owyhee,
  Payette, Valley, and Washington counties in Idaho; Harney and Malheur
  counties in Oregon

14
BANKS SPECIALIZING IN SBA FINANCING PROGRAMS

CLP/PLP PARTICIPANTS LIST

Updated 6-27-94

REGION I (42 CLP / 13 PLP)

Connecticut (4/1)

Hamden	LaFayette American Bank and Trust
Hartford	First National Bank of Hartford
Hartford	Mechanics Savings Bank
New Haven	Founders Bank

Maine (2/1)

Augusta	Key Bank of Central Maine
Portland	Fleet Bank of Maine

Massachusetts (9/5)

Boston	Massachusetts Business Development Corporation
Danvers	Danvers Savings Bank
Fitchburg	Safety Fund National Bank
Framingham	Shawmut Bank of Boston
Hyannis	Cape Cod Bank and Trust Company
Rockland	Rockland Trust Company
Waltham	Bank of Boston
Worcester	Commerce Bank and Trust Company
Worcester	Flagship Bank & Trust Company

New Hampshire (11/1)

Berlin	The Berlin City Bank
Concord	Concord Savings Bank

Dover	Southeast Bank for Savings
Keene	CFX Bank
Keene	Granite Bank
Manchester	Bank of New Hampshire
Manchester	First NH Bank
Manchester	New Dartmouth Bank
Nashua	Fleet Bank–NH
Nashua	N.F.S. Savings Bank
Peterborough	Peterborough Savings Bank

Rhode Island (4/0)

Providence	The Citizens Trust Company
Providence	Fleet National Bank
Providence	Home Loan and Investment Association
Providence	Rhode Island Hospital Trust National Bank

Vermont (12/5)

Barre	Granite Savings Bank & Trust
Brattleboro	First Vermont Bank & Trust
Brattleboro	Vermont National Bank
Burlington	Chittenden Bank
Burlington	The Howard Bank
Burlington	The Merchant's Bank
Charlotte	The Money Store Investment Corporation
Manchester Ctr	Factory Point National Bank
Morrisville	Union Bank
Northfield	Northfield Savings Bank
Rutland	Green Mountain Bank
St. Albans	Franklin Lamoille Bank

CLP/PLP PARTICIPANTS LIST

Updated 3-22-94

REGION II (46 CLP / 17 PLP)

New Jersey (13/5)

Annandale	First Community Bank
Burlington	First Fidelity Bank, NA South Jersey
Flemington	Prestige State Bank
Hackensack	United Jersey Bank
Jackson	Garden State Bank

North Brunswick	Farrington Bank
North Plainfield	Rock Bank
Somerset	New Era Bank
Union	The Money Store of New York
Wayne	The Ramapo Bank
Hasbrouch	Bank of New York (National Community Division)
West Trenton	New Jersey National Bank

New York (32/10)

Albany	Fleet Bank of New York
Albany	Key Bank, NA
Albany	New York Business Development Corporation
Bath	The Bath National Bank
Buffalo	Fleet Bank of New York
Buffalo	Manufacturers and Traders Trust Company
Buffalo	Marine Midland Bank
Canandaigua	The Canandaigua National Bank and Trust Company
Cortland	First National Bank of Cortland
Dewitt	Community Bank, NA
Elmira	Chemung Canal Trust Company
Geneva	The National Bank of Geneva
Glens Falls	Glens Falls National Bank and Trust Company
Islandia	Long Island Commercial Bank
Ithaca	Thompkins County Trust Company
Melville	The Bank of New York
Melville	Fleet Bank
Newburgh	Key Bank of New York
New York City	Chase Manhattan Bank, NA
New York City	Chemical Community Development Incorporated
New York City	Citibank, NA
New York City	National Westminster Bank
New York City	Republic National Bank
Norwich	The National Bank and Trust Company of Norwich
Rochester	Chase Lincoln First Bank, NA
Rosslyn Heights	The Money Store Investment Corporation
South Hampton	The Bank of the Hamptons
Syracuse	Marine Midland Bank
Syracuse	OnBank & Trust Company
Uniondale	European American Bank
Warsaw	Wyoming County Bank
Williamsville	ITT Small Business Finance Corporation

Puerto Rico (2/1)

Hato Rey	Banco Santander Puerto Rico
San Juan	Banco Popular de Puerto Rico

CLP/PLP PARTICIPANTS LIST

Updated 4-28-94

REGION III (44 CLP / 16 PLP)

Delaware (3/1)

Newark	Delaware Trust Company
Wilmington	Mellon Bank (DE), NA
Wilmington	Wilmington Trust Company

District of Columbia (Washington, DC SMSA) (2/1)

Washington, DC	Adams National Bank
Washington, DC	Allied Lending Corporation

Maryland (7/3)

Baltimore	First National Bank of Maryland
Baltimore	Maryland National Bank
Baltimore	Provident Bank of Maryland
Baltimore	Signet Bank
Greenbelt	Suburban Bank of Maryland
Owings Mills	Key Federal Savings Bank
Union, NJ	The Money Store Investment Corporation

Pennsylvania (23/9)

Bethlehem	Lehigh Valley Bank
Erie	Integra National Bank (North)
Erie	Mellon Bank (North)
Erie	PNC Bank (Northwest)
Ft. Washington	The Money Store Investment
Harrisburg	Mellon Bank (Commonwealth Region), NA
Harrisburg	Pennsylvania National Bank
Hermitage	First National Bank of Pennsylvania
Horsham	Frankford Bank
Laceyville	Grange National Bank of Wyoming County
Morrisville	Bucks County Bank & Trust Company

Philadelphia	Corestate Bank, NA
Philadelphia	Mellon Bank, NA / Mellon PSFS
Pittsburgh	Integra Bank/Pittsburgh
Pittsburgh	Mellon Bank, NA
Pittsburgh	PNC Bank
Pittston	Commonwealth Bank, A Division of Meridian Bank
Reading	Meridian Bank
Scranton	PNC Bank, Northeast PA
Souderton	Union National Bank
State College	Mellon Bank (Central)
Unionville	Integra National Bank (South)
Wilkes Barre	Mellon Bank

Virginia (6/1)

Reston	Patriot National Bank of Reston
Richmond	Crestar
Richmond	The Money Store Investment Corporation
Richmond	NationsBank of Virginia, NA
Virginia Beach	Commerce Bank
Washington, DC	Allied Lending Corporation

West Virginia (4/1)

Clarksburg	Bank One, West Virginia
Huntington	The First Huntington National Bank
Morgantown	One Valley Bank of Morgantown, Incorporated
Wheeling	Wheeling National Bank

CLP/PLP PARTICIPANTS LIST

Updated 7-12-94

REGION IV (99 CLP / 12 PLP)

Alabama (15/0)

Anniston	SouthTrust Bank of Calhoun County
Birmingham	AmSouth Bank, NA
Birmingham	Central Bank of the South
Birmingham	First Commercial Bank
Birmingham	SouthTrust Bank of Alabama–Birmingham, NA
Dothan	Southland Bancorporation

Dothan   SouthTrust Bank of Dothan
Florence   First National Bank of Florence
Guntersville   The Home Bank
Huntsville   SouthTrust Bank of Huntsville
Montgomery   First Montgomery Bank
Montgomery   SouthTrust Bank, NA
Opelika   Farmers National Bank
Opp   SouthTrust Bank of Covington County
Selma   Peoples Bank & Trust Company

Florida (21/1)

Boca Raton   First United Bank
Clearwater   Citizens Bank of Clearwater
Fernandina Beach   First Coast Community Bank
Ft. Walton Beach   First National Bank and Trust
Jacksonville   Community Savings Bank
Jacksonville   First Guaranty ᴅank & Trust Company
Longwood   Liberty National Bank
Miami   International Bank of Miami
Miami   Sun Bank/Miami, NA
Naples   BancFlorida A F.S.B.
No. Miami Beach   First Western SBLC, Inc.
Panama City   Emergent Business Capital, Inc.
Panama City   First National Bank
Port Charlotte   Charlotte State Bank
Sarasota   Enterprise National Bank of Sarasota
St. Petersburg   United Bank of Pinellas
Tampa   NationsBank
Tampa   Southern Commerce Bank
West Palm Beach   Barnett Bank of Palm Beach
Elizabethton, TN   Citizens Bank
Glenn Allen, VA   The Money Store Investment Corporation

Georgia (21.6)

Atlanta   The Business Development Corporation of Georgia
Atlanta   Commercial Bank of Georgia
Atlanta   Fidelity National Bank
Atlanta   Georgia Bankers Bank
Atlanta   HomeBanc, F.S.B.
Atlanta   Metro Bank
Atlanta   NationsBank of Georgia
Atlanta   The Summit National Bank

Augusta	Bankers First Savings & Loan Association
Byron	Middle Georgia Bank
Cordele	First State Bank & Trust
Fort Valley	First South Bank
Macon	First South Bank
Marietta	The Chattahoochee Bank
Morristown	AT&T Small Business Lending Corporation
Morrow	Southern Crescent Bank
Norcross	First Capital Bank Norcross
Savannah	The Coastal Bank
Snellville	Eastside Bank & Trust
Woodstock	First National Bank of Cherokee
Glenn Allen, VA	The Money Store Investment Corporation

Kentucky (7/0)

Florence	The Fifth Third Bank
Lexington	Bank One, Lexington
Louisville	PNC Bank–Kentucky
Louisville	National City Bank
Mount Sterling	Exchange Bank of Kentucky
Murray	Peoples Bank of Murray
Pikeville	Pikeville National Bank & Trust Company

Mississipi (10/1)

Batesville	Batesville Security Bank
Biloxi	The Jefferson Bank
Grenada	Sunburst Bank
Gulfport	Hancock Bank
Jackson	Deposit Guaranty National Bank
Jackson	Trustmark National Bank
McComb	Pike County National Bank
Picayune	First National Bank of Picayune
Starkville	National Bank of Commerce of Mississippi
Tupelo	Bank of Mississippi

North Carolina (9/1)

Charlotte	First Union National Bank of North Carolina
Charlotte	NationsBank of North Carolina
Durham	Central Carolina Bank & Trust Company
Lumberton	Southern National Bank of North Carolina
Rocky Mount	Centura Bank

Whiteville	United Carolina Bank
Wilson	Branch Banking & Trust Company
Winston-Salem	Wachovia Bank & Trust Company, NA
Glen Allen, VA	The Money Store Investment Corporation

South Carolina (5/3)

Columbia	Business Development Corporation of South Carolina
Columbia	Emergent Business Capital, Inc.
Columbia	First Citizens Bank
Columbia	NationsBank
Lexington	The Lexington State Bank

Tennessee (11/0)

Brentwood	Brentwood National Bank
Chattanooga	American National Bank & Trust Company
Chattanooga	Volunteer Bank and Trust Company
Columbia	First Farmers & Merchants National Bank
Elizabethton	Citizens Bank
Knoxville	Third National Bank of East Tennessee
Memphis	Union Planters National Bank
Memphis	United American Bank
Nashville	First American National Bank, NA
Nashville	NationsBank of Tennessee
Nashville	Third National Bank

CLP/PLP PARTICIPANTS LIST

Updated 7-6-94

REGION V (98 CLP / 27 PLP)

Illinois (29/6)

Aurora	Merchants Bank of Aurora
Aurora	Old Second National Bank of Aurora
Bellwood	The Bank of Bellwood
Chicago	Albany Bank and Trust Company, NA
Chicago	First National Bank of Chicago
Chicago	Foster Bank
Chicago	Harris Trust & Savings Bank
Chicago	ITT Small Business Finance Corporation

Chicago	The Money Store Investment Corporation
Chicago	South Central Bank & Trust
Chicago	The South Shore Bank of Chicago
Danville	Palmer American National Bank
Elgin	Union National Bank & Trust of Elgin
Fairview Heights	Central Bank
Homewood	Bank of Homewood
La Grange	Bank One, Chicago
Maywood	Maywood–Proviso State Bank
Naperville	First Colonial Bank of DuPage County
Naperville	Firstar Bank West, NA
Norridge	Plaza Bank
O'Fallon	First Bank of Illinois
Parkridge	NBD Park Ridge Bank
Pekin	First State Bank of Pekin
Rockford	Bank One, Rockford
Springfield	First of American Bank
Springfield	Bank One, Springfield
Urbana	Busey First National Bank
Urbana	Central Illinois Bank
West Frankfort	Banterra Bank of West Frankfort

Indiana (10/0)

Covington	Bank of Western Indiana
Evansville	Citizens National Bank of Evansville
Fort Wayne	NBD Summit Bank
Indianapolis	Bank One Indianapolis
Indianapolis	Huntington National Bank of Indiana
Indianapolis	NBD Bank, Indiana
LaPorte	First Citizens Bank, NA
South Bend	First Source Bank of South Bend
South Bend	Society National Bank
Whiting	Centier Bank

Michigan (10/3)

Detroit	Comerica Bank
Flint	Citizens Commercial and Savings Bank
Grand Rapids	United Bank of Michigan
Kalamazoo	First of America Bank–Michigan, NA
Kalamazoo	Old Kent Bank–Southwest
Lansing	Michigan National Bank

Midland	Chemical Bank & Trust Company
Owosso	Key State Bank
Traverse City	The Empire National Bank of Traverse City
Traverse City	Old Kent Bank–Traverse City

Minnesota (7/4)

Bloomington	Firstar Bank of Minnesota, NA
Edina	First Bank National Association
Minneapolis	Norwest Bank, Minnesota, NA
St. Cloud	First American Bank, NA
St. Cloud	Zapp Bank
West St. Paul	Signal Bank, Inc.
Young America	State Bank of Young America

Ohio (18/5)

Akron	First National Bank of Akron
Cincinnati	North Side Bank and Trust Company
Cincinnati	PNC Bank, Cincinnati
Cleveland	American National Bank
Cleveland	Society National Bank
Columbus	Bank One, Columbus, NA
Columbus	The Huntington National Bank
Columbus	National City Bank of Columbus
Columbus	Society Bank
Dayton	Bank One, Dayton, NA
Dayton	National City Bank
Dayton	Society Bank–Dayton area
Dublin	The Money Store Investment Company
Elyria	PremierBank and Trust
Lorain	Lorain National Bank
Piqua	The Fifth Third Bank of Western Ohio
Toledo	Mid American National Bank and Trust Company
Toledo	National City Bank, Northwest

Wisconsin (24/9)

Appleton	Firstar Bank, Appleton
Appleton	Valley Bank
Eau Claire	Firstar Bank Eau Claire
Eau Claire	M & I Community State Bank, Eua Claire
Fond du Lac	Firstar of Fond du Lac
Green Bay	Associated Bank, Green Bay

Green Bay	Firstar Bank, Green Bay
Green Bay	Norwest Bank
Madison	Bank One, Madison
Madison	Firststar Bank of Madison
Madison	M & I Madison Bank
Madison	Valley Bank Madison
Manitowoc	Associated Bank Lakeshore, NA
Manitowoc	First National Bank of Manitowoc
Menomonee	Associated Bank of Menomonee Falls
Milwaukee	Bank One, Milwaukee
Milwaukee	Firstar Bank of Milwaukee
Milwaukee	Marshall and Iisley Bank of Milwaukee
Neenah	Associated Bank, NA
Oshkosh	Firstar Bank Oshkosh, NA
Sheboygan	Firstar Bank Sheboygan
Sturgeon Bay	Baylake Bank
Wausau	M & I First American National Bank
West Bend	Bank One, West Bend

CLP/PLP PARTICIPANTS LIST

Updated 7-7-94

REGION VI (188 CLP / 20 PLP)

Arkansas (24/0)

Arkadelphia	Elk Horn Bank & Trust
Batesville	Worthen National Bank
Bentonville	Firstbank
Camden	Worthen National Bank of Camden
Conway	First National Bank of Conway
El Dorado	First Financial Bank
El Dorado	First National Bank of El Dorado
Fayetteville	McIlroy Bank & Trust
Fayetteville	Worthen National Bank of NW Arkansas
Fort Smith	City National Bank of Fort Smith
Fort Smith	Merchants National Bank
Hot Springs	Worthern National Bank of Hot Springs
Jonesboro	Citizens Bank of Jonesboro
Kenner	Metro Bank
Little Rock	Arkansas Capital Corporation

Little Rock	First Commercial Bank, NA
Little Rock	Metropolitan National Bank
Little Rock	Worthen National Bank of Arkansas
Mongolia	First National Bank Mongolia
North Little Rock	National Bank of Arkansas
North Little Rock	The Twin City Bank
Pine Bluff	Simmons First National Bank
Rogers	First National Bank
Russellville	Worthen National Bank of Russellville

Louisiana (20/0)

Abbeville	Gulf Coast Bank
Baton Rouge	City National Bank
Baton Rouge	Guaranty Bank and Trust Company
Baton Rouge	Premier Bank, NA
Eunice	Tri-Parish Bank
Lafayette	First National Bank
Kenner	Metro Bank
Metairie	Hibernia National Bank in Jefferson Parish
Metairie	Jefferson Guaranty Bank
Metairie	Omni Bank
Monroe	Central Bank
Monroe	First American Bank
Morgan City	First National in Saint Mary Parish
New Orleans	First National Bank of Commerce
New Orleans	Gulf Coast Bank and Trust Company
New Orleans	Whitney National Bank
Plattenville	Bayoulands Bank
Port Allen	Bank of West Baton Rouge
Ruston	Ruston State Bank
Shreveport	Commercial National Bank

New Mexico (16/3)

Albuquerque	Bank of America Nevada
Albuquerque	The First National Bank of Albuquerque
Albuquerque	Sunwest Bank of Albuquerque
Albuquerque	United New Mexico Bank at Albuquerque
Belen	First National Bank of Belen
Carlsbad	Western Commerce Bank
Clovis	Sunwest Bank
Clovis	Western Bank of Clovis

Hobbs	Lea County State Bank
Las Cruces	Bank of the Rio Grande, NA
Las Cruces	Citizens Bank of Las Cruces
Las Cruces	United New Mexico Bank at Las Cruces
Las Cruces	Western Bank
Santa Fe	Bank of Santa Fe
Taos	First State Bank of Taos
Tucumcari	The First National Bank of Tucumcari

Oklahoma (11/3)

Oklahoma City	BancFirst
Oklahoma City	Bank of Oklahoma, NA
Oklahoma City	Boatman's First National Bank
Oklahoma City	Rockwell Bank, N.A.
Ponca City	Pioneer Bank & Trust
Poteay	Central National Bank
Stillwater	Stillwater National Bank and Trust Company
Tonkawa	First National Bank of Tonkawa
Tulsa	Bank IV Oklahoma, NA of Tulsa
Tulsa	Boatman's First National Bank
Tulsa	Woodland Bank

Texas (117/14)

Abilene	Security State Bank
Amarillo	The First National Bank of Amarillo
Arlington	Bank One, Texas MidCities
Austin	Cattlemen's State Bank
Austin	Hill County Bank
Austin	Horizon Savings Association
Austin	Liberty National Bank
Austin	Texas Bank
Austin	Texas Commerce Bank
Baytown	Citizens Bank and Trust Company
Beaumont	Parkdale Bank
Bellaire	Park National Bank
Brownsville	International Bank of Commerce, NA
Brownsville	Mercantile Bank, NA
Brownsville	Texas Commerce Bank–Brownsville
Bryan	Victoria Bank & Trust
Carrollton	Compass Bank
College Station	Commerce National Bank

Converse	Converse National Bank
Corpus Christi	American National Bank
Corpus Christi	Bank of Corpus Christi
Corpus Christi	Citizens State Bank
Corpus Christi	First Commerce Bank
Corpus Christi	Frost National Bank
Dallas	Abrams Centre National Bank
Dallas	Bank One Texas, NA
Dallas	Comerica Bank–Texas
Dallas	Equitable Bank
Dallas	First Texas Bank
Dallas	First Western SBLC, Inc.
Dallas	Gateway National Bank
Dallas	Heller First Capital Corporation
Dallas	Independence Funding Corporation, Limited (IFC)
Dallas	The Money Store Investment Corporation
Dallas	Texas Commerce Bank
El Paso	Bank of the West
El Paso	The Bank of El Paso
El Paso	Montwood National Bank
El Paso	Sunwest Bank of El Paso
El Paso	Texas Commerce Bank of El Paso, NA
Fort Worth	Bank of North Texas
Galveston	Bank of Galveston
Garland	Central Bank
Garland	Security Bank
Harlingen	Harlingen National Bank
Harlingen	The Harlingen State Bank
Houston	Allied Lending Corporation
Houston	Bank One, Texas
Houston	Charter National Bank–Houston
Houston	Comerica Bank–Texas
Houston	Enterprise Bank
Houston	First Bank Houston
Houston	First Interstate Bank
Houston	First Western SBLC
Houston	Great Southwest Bank, F.S.B.
Houston	Houston Independent Bank
Houston	Independence Bank
Houston	Langham Creek National Bank
Houston	Lockwood National Bank
Houston	Metrobank, NA

Houston	The Money Store Investment Corporation
Houston	NationsBank
Houston	OmniBank, NA
Houston	Park National Bank
Houston	QuestStar Bank
Houston	Southwest Bank of Texas
Houston	Sunbelt National Bank
Houston	Texas Capitak Bank, NA
Houston	Texas Commerce Bank
Houston	Texas Guaranty Bank
Hutto	Hutto State Bank
Irving	Bank of America, NV
Irving	Bank of the West
Irving	Irving National Bank
Katy	Community Bank
Katy	First Bank
Kilgore	Kilgore First National Bank
Lampasas	First National Bank of Lampasas
LaPorte	Bayshore National Bank of LaPorte
Laredo	South Texas National Bank
League City	League City Bank and Trust
Longview	Longview Bank and Trust Company
Los Fresnos	First Bank Los Fresnos
Lubbock	American State Bank
Lubbock	First National Bank at Lubbock
Lubbock	Lubbock National Bank
Lubbock	Plains National Bank
Mansfield	Overton Bank and Trust, NA
McAllen	Inter National Bank of McAllen
McAllen	Texas State Bank
Midland	Midland American Bank
Midland	Texas National Bank of Midland
Missouri City	First National Bank of Missouri City
Navasoto	First Bank
Odessa	First State Bank of Odessa
Odessa	Texas Bank
Pharr	Lone Star National Bank
Plainview	First National Bank of Plainview
Plano	Plano Bank & Trust
San Angelo	Texas Commerce Bank
San Antonio	Bank of America Nevada
San Antonio	Bank One, Texas, NA

San Antonio	First Western SBLC
San Antonio	Frost National Bank / Corpus Christi
San Antonio	Heller First Capital Corp.
San Antonio	ITT Small Business Finance Corporation
San Antonio	The Money Store Investment Corporation
San Antonio	Nationsbank of Texas, NA
San Antonio	Plaza Bank
San Antonio	Security National Bank
Seguin	First Commercial Bank
Sonora	First National Bank of Sonora
Sundown	Sundown State Bank
Temple	First National Bank of Temple
Tomball	Texas National Bank
Weatherford	Texas Bank, Weatherford
Wolfforth	American Bank of Commerce

CLP/PLP PARTICIPANTS LIST

Updated 6-27-94

REGION VII (64 CLP / 13 PLP)

Iowa (18/4)

Ames	Firstar Bank Ames
Cedar Rapids	Firstar Bank Cedar Rapids
Davenport	Norwest Bank Iowa, NA
Des Moines	Bankers Trust Company
Des Moines	Boatmen's National Bank of Des Moines
Des Moines	Brenton National Bank of Des Moines
Des Moines	Firstar Bank Des Moines
Des Moines	Hawkeye Bank & Trust of Des Moines
Des Moines	Norwest Bank Des Moines, NA
Dubuque	Dubuque Bank and Trust Company
Fort Dodge	Norwest Bank Iowa, NA
Iowa City	Iowa State Bank and Trust Company
Maquoketa	Maquoketa State Bank
Marion	Farmers State Bank
Newton	Hawkeye Bank of Jasper County
Sioux Center	American State Bank
Spencer	Boatman's National Bank of Northwest Iowa
Storm Lake	Commercial Trust and Savings Bank
West Des Moines	West Des Moines State Bank

Kansas (20/3)

Dodge City	Fidelity State Bank & Trust Company
Dodge City	First National Bank and Trust Company in Dodge City
Great Bend	Farmers Bank & Trust
Hayes	Emprise Bank, NA
Haysville	Intrust Bank
Hutchinson	Emprise Bank, NA
Kansas City	Guaranty Bank & Trust
Liberal	First National Bank of Liberal
Merriam	United Kansas Bank and Trust
Newton	Midland National Bank
Neodesha	First National Bank of Neodesha
Olathe	Bank IV Olathe
Olathe	First National Bank
Overland Park	Metcalf State Bank
Overland Park	UMB Overland Park Bank
Ulysses	Grant County State Bank
Wichita	American National Bank
Wichita	Bank IV Wichita
Wichita	Emergent Business Capital, Inc.
Wichita	Intrust Bank

Missouri (19/3)

Brentwood	Magna Bank of Missouri
Carthage	Boatman's Bank of Carthage
Clayton	The Money Store Investment Corporation
Columbia	Capital Bank of Columbia
Independence	Standard Bank and Trust Company
Jefferson City	The Central Trust Bank
Joplin	Mercantile Bank and Trust Company of Joplin
Kansas City	Bannister Bank & Trust
Kansas City	Boatmen's First National Bank of Kansas City
Kansas City	United Missouri Bank of Kansas City, NA
Springfield	The Boatmen's National Bank of Southern Missouri
Springfield	Citizens National Bank of Springfield
Springfield	Commerce Bank of Springfield
Springfield	First City National Bank
Springfield	Mercantile Bank of Springfield
St. Louis	ITT Small Business Finance Corporation
St. Louis	Mercantile Bank, St. Louis, NA

St. Louis — United Missouri Bank of St. Louis, NA
Washington — Bank of Washington

Nebraska (7/3)

Lincoln — FirsTier Bank, NA
Lincoln — National Bank of Commerce
Lincoln — Union Bank and Trust Company
Omaha — Douglas County Bank & Trust
Lincoln — FirsTier Bank, NA
Omaha — First National Bank of Omaha
Omaha — Norwest Bank Nebraska, NA

CLP/PLP PARTICIPANTS LIST

Updated 6-2-94

REGION VIII (70 CLP / 14 PLP)

Colorado (13/1)

Alamosa — The First National Bank in Alamosa
Aurora — Aurora National Bank
Aurora — The Money Store Investment Corporation
Denver — Key Bank of Colorado
Denver — Colorado National Bank
Denver — First Commercial Bank, NA dba
    First Commercial Capital Corporation
Denver — ITT Small Business Finance Corporation
Denver — Norwest Bank Denver
Denver — Vectra Bank
Durango — Durango National Bank
Hotchkiss — The First State Bank of Hotchkiss
Lakewood — Bank One, Denver, NA
Montrose — Norwest Bank Montrose, NA

Montana (18/6)

Bigfork — Flathead Bank of Bigfork
Billings — First Interstate Bank
Billings — Norwest Bank Billings
Billings — Yellowstone Bank
Bozeman — First Security Bank of Bozeman

Bozeman	Montana Bank of Bozeman
Great Falls	Norwest Bank Great Falls
Helena	Mountain West Bank
Helena	Valley Bank of Helena
Kalispell	Norwest Bank Kalispell, NA
Kalispell	Valley Bank of Kalispell
Livingston	First National Park Bank
Missoula	First Interstate Bank
Missoula	First Security Bank of Missoula
Missoula	Montana Bank of South Missoula
Polson	First Citizens Bank
Sidney	Richland Bank and Trust
Whitefish	Mountain Bank

North Dakota (12/0)

Bismark	United Bank of Bismark
Dickinson	Liberty National Bank and Trust
Fargo	First Community Bank
Fargo	State Bank of Fargo
Grand Forks	Community National Bank
Grand Forks	First American Bank Valley
Grand Forks	First National Bank in Grand Forks
Mandan	First Southwest Bank of Mandan
Minot	First American Bank West
Minot	First Western Bank of Minot
West Fargo	First National Bank North Dakota
Williston	American State Bank and Trust Company

South Dakota (17/2)

Belle Fourche	Pioneer Bank and Trust
Brookings	First National Bank in Brookings
Burke	First Fidelity Bank
Custer	First Western Bank
Huron	Farmers & Merchants Bank
Milbank	Dakota State Bank
Philip	First National Bank
Pierre	American State Bank
Pierre	BankWest, NA
Pierre	First National Bank
Rapid City	Rushmore State Bank
Sioux Falls	First Bank of South Dakota, NA

Sioux Falls	First National Bank in Sioux Falls
Sioux Falls	Marquette Bank of South Dakota, NA
Sioux Falls	Norwest Bank Sioux Falls, NA
Sioux Falls	Western Bank
Yankton	First Dakota National Bank

Utah (7/4)

Ogden	Bank of Utah
Salt Lake City	Bank One
Salt Lake City	Brighton Bank
Salt Lake City	First Security Bank
Salt Lake City	Guardian State Bank
Salt Lake City	Key Bank
Salt Lake City	Zions First National Bank, NA

Wyoming (3/1)

Casper	Hilltop National Bank
Cheyenne	Norwest Bank Wyoming
Cheyenne	Key Bank

CLP/PLP PARTICIPANTS LIST

Updated 7-11-94

REGION IX (72 CLP / 34 PLP)

Arizona (6/1)

Phoenix	Bank One, Arizona
Phoenix	First Interstate Bank of Arizona, NA
Phoenix	ITT Small Business Finance Corporation
Phoenix	M & I Thunderbird Bank
Phoenix	Republic National Bank
Tempe	Rio Salado Bank

California (59/29)

Anaheim	Landmark Bank
Auburn	The Bank of Commerce, NA
Bakersfield	San Joaquin Bank
Cameron Park	Western Sierra National Bank

Carlsbad	Capital Bank of Carlsbad
Chula Vista	Pacific Commerce Bank
Concord	Tracy Federal Bank
Coronado	Bank of Coronado
Cupertino	Cupertino National Bank
El Centro	Valley Independent Bank
Encinitas	San Dieguito National Bank
Escondido	First Pacific National Bank
Escondido	North County Bank
Eureka	U.S. Bank of California
Fallbrook	Fallbrook National Bank
Fresno	Bank of Fresno
Fresno	Regency Bank
Hemet	Valley Merchants Bank
Huntington Beach	Liberty National Bank
Inglewood	Imperial Bank
Laguna Hills	Bank of Yorba Linda
LaPalma	Frontier Bank
Los Angeles	Hanmi Bank
Los Angeles	National Bank of California
Los Angeles	Wilshire State Bank
Modesto	Modesto Banking Company
Modesto	Pacific Valley National Bank
Monterey	Monterey County Bank
Ontario	Western Community Bank
Orange	Orange National Bank
Rancho Cordova	Bank of America Community Development Bank
Redding	North Valley Bank
Rosemead	General Bank
Sacramento	The Money Store Investment Corporation
Sacramento	Sacramento Commercial Bank
Sacramento	Sacramento First National Bank
Salinas	First National Bank of Central California
San Clemente	Mariners Bank
San Diego	Bank of Commerce
San Diego	Bank of Southern California
San Diego	ITT Small Business Finance Corporation
San Diego	Rancho Santa Fe National Bank
San Diego	San Diego Trust & Savings Bank
San Diego	Union Bank
San Francisco	Commercial Bank of San Francisco
San Francisco	Heller First Capital
San Jose	California Business Bank

San Jose	Comerica Bank
San Jose	San Jose National Bank
San Leandro	Bay Bank of Commerce
San Luis Obispo	First Bank of San Luis Obispo
Santa Cruz	Coast Commercial Bank
Santa Rosa	National Bank of Redwoods
Santa Rosa	Sonoma National Bank
Sherman Oaks	American Pacific State Bank
Truckee	Truckee River Bank
Tustin	Eldorado Bank
Van Nuys	Industrial Bank
West Covina	California State Bank

Hawaii (4/1)

Honolulu	Bank of Hawaii
Honolulu	Central Pacific Bank
Honolulu	City Bank
Honolulu	First Hawaiian Bank

Nevada (3/2)

Las Vegas	Bank of America Nevada
Las Vegas	First Interstate Bank of Nevada, NA
Las Vegas	Nevada State Bank

CLP/PLP PARTICIPANTS LIST

Updated 4-12-94

REGION X (36 CLP / 19 PLP)

Alaska (5/0)

Anchorage	First National Bank of Anchorage
Anchorage	Key Bank of Alaska
Anchorage	National Bank of Alaska
Anchorage	Northrim Bank
Fairbanks	Denali State Bank

Idaho (4/3)

Boise	American Bank of Commerce
Boise	First Security Bank of Idaho
Boise	Key Bank of Idaho
Boise	West One Bank

Oregon (6/5)

Eugene	Pacific Continental Bank
Medford	Western Bank
Portland	First Interstate Bank of Oregon, NA
Portland	Key Bank of Oregon
Portland	The Money Store Investment Corporation
Portland	U.S. National Bank of Oregon

Washington (21/11)

Bellevue	The Money Store Investment Corporation
Chelan	North Cascades National Bank
Duvall	Valley Community Bank
Everett	American First National Bank
Everett	Frontier Bank
Ferndale	Whatcom State Bank
Kennewick	American National Bank
Lacey	First Community Bank of Washington
Lynnwood	City Bank
Olympia	Centennial Bank
Seattle	First Interstate Bank of Washington, NA
Seattle	Key Bank of Washington
Seattle	Pacific Northwest Bank
Seattle	Seattle–First National Bank
Seattle	US Bank of Washington
Seattle	West One Bank Washington
Snohomish	First Heritage Bank
Spokane	Washington Trust Bank
Tacoma	North Pacific Bank
Tukwila	National Bank of Tukwila
Yakima	Pioneer National Bank

15

VENTURE CAPITAL NETWORKS

This chapter consists of a list of venture capital networks, which are membership organizations that operate as informal funding facilitators. They bring entrepreneur and investor together in group meetings. The entrepreneur will pitch his or her deal in front of the funding outlets. These networks do not have their own capital for investment purposes and they will not negotiate deals.

Venture capital networks are noted for assisting firms in the seed and/or start-up phase of financing.

ALABAMA

Birmingham Venture Club
Patricia Tucker Fox
P.O. Box 10127
Birmingham, AL 35202
205-895-6407

ALASKA

Alaska Venture Capital Club
Walter F. Fournier
613 East 22nd Avenue
Anchorage, AK 99503
907-277-7474

ARIZONA

Enterprise Network Incorporated
Michael LaFlam

P.O. Box 15210
Phoenix, AZ 85060-5210
602-952-8116

CALIFORNIA

Sacramento Valley V.C. Forum
D. James Sabra
P.O. Box 15364
Sacramento, CA 95851
916-455-0480

COLORADO

MIT Enterprise Forum of Colorado
President
4940 East Evans, Suite 115
Denver, CO 80222
303-757-7303

CONNECTICUT

Connecticut MIT Venture Forum
John C. Linderman, Esq., Chair
266 Pearl Street
Hartford, CT 06102
203-549-5290

DELAWARE

Delaware Entrepreneurs Forum
Helga Russell
30 East Swedesford
Malbern, NJ 19388
312-652-4247

DISTRICT OF COLUMBIA

**Baltimore/Washington/MIT
Enterprise Forum**
Robert Snyder
51 Monroe Street, Suite 1701
Rockville, MD 20850
301-762-6325 Fax: 301-762-9417

FLORIDA

**World Venture Capital Center at
Miami**
Charlotte Gallogly
One World Trade Plaza
80 SW 8th Street, Suite 1800
Miami, FL 33130
305-579-0064

HAWAII

**Hawaii Venture Capital
Association**
Louis Cuschighao
P.O. Box 1602
Kailua, HI 96734
808-587-3829

IDAHO

**Treasure Valley Venture Capital
Forum**
Jim Lyons
c/o Broise State University
1910 University Drive
Boise, ID 83725
208-385-1640

ILLINOIS

Chicago/MIT/Venture Forum
Bruce P. Golden, Esq., Co-Chair
Fishman & Merrick
30 North LaSalle Street, Suite 3500
Chicago, IL 60602
312-726-1223 Fax: 312-726-2649

INDIANA

Venture Club of Indiana
Bob Engle
P.O. Box 40872
Indianapolis, IN 46204
317-253-1244

IOWA

Venture Network of Iowa
Peggy Russell
601 Locust, Suite 100
Des Moines, IA 50309
515-286-4997

KANSAS

Centre for Creative Capital
Perry Bemus
1330 East First Street
Wichita, KS 67214
316-262-1123

KENTUCKY

**Louisville Venture Forum
  Incorporated**
Tonya York
One Riverfront Plaza
Louisville, KY 40202
502-625-0000

LOUISIANA

**Greater Baton Rouge Venture
  Capital Forum**
J. David Wansley
564 Laurel Street
P.O. Box 3217
Baton Rouge, LA 70821
504-381-7125

MAINE

Maine Capital Network
Karen Lazareth
Finance Authority of Maine
P.O. Box 949
Augusta, ME 04332
207-623-3263

MARYLAND

**Baltimore-Maryland Venture
  Group**
John Ver Steeg
P.O. Box 965
Bowie, MD 20715
301-369-4900

**Baltimore/Washington/MIT
  Enterprise Forum**
Robert Snyder, Chair
51 Monroe Street, Suite 1701
Rockville, MD 20850
301-762-6325
Fax: 301-762-2417

MASSACHUSETTS

**Cambridge/MIT Enterprise
  Forum**
Barry Unger
Boston University, Room M6
808 Commonwealth Avenue
Boston, MA 02215
617-353-3016 Fax: 617-353-6328

MICHIGAN

**West Michigan Business/Finance
  Network**
Raymond DeWinkle
17 Fountain NW
Grand Rapids, MI 49503
616-542-0682

MINNESOTA

Entrepreneurs Network
Norman Stoehr
1433 Utica Avenue South, Suite 70
Minneapolis, MN 55416
612-542-0682

MISSISSIPPI

Biloxi Venture Capital Club
Mr. & Mrs. Doyle Moody
c/o Coast Properties
P.O. Box 8008
Biloxi, MS 39535
601-388-5055

MISSOURI

**Missouri Venture Forum,
  Incorporated**
Judith E. Meador
7536 Forsyth, Suite 314
St, Louis, MO 63105
314-432-7440

MONTANA

Montana Private Capital Network
Carl Bear
1632 West Main
Bozeman, MT 59715
406-587-1231

NEBRASKA

Nebraska Venture Group
Mary l. Woita, c/o University of
  Nebraska
Northeast Business Development
  Center
1313 Farnham-on-the-Mall
Omaha, NE 68182-0248
402-554-8381

NEW HAMPSHIRE

**Venture Capital Network, Inc.
  (Database)**
Helen Goodman
P.O. Box 882
Durham, NH 03824
603-743-3993

NEW JERSEY

Bergan County Venture Club
John R. Lieberman
14 Bergen Street
Hackensack, NJ 07601
201-488-8445

NEW MEXICO

**Venture Capital Club of New
  Mexico**
Bill Royal
538 Camino del Monte Sol
Sana Fe, NM 87501
505-984-2905

NEW YORK

New York/MIT Enterprise Forum
Stephen C. Ho, Chair
The Chase Manhattan Bank
One Chase Manhattan Plaza
William Street
New York, NY 10081
212-552-3652 Fax: 212-422-1792

NORTH CAROLINA

Investors Network
Raymond Marker
P.O. Box 9881
Greensboro, NC 27429
919-854-8009

NORTH DAKOTA

Minndak Seed Capital Club
Bruce Gjovig
Box 8103, University Station
Grand Forks, ND 58202
701-777-3132

OHIO

**Greater Cincinnati Venture
  Association**
Don Feldman
c/o The Provident Bank
One East Fourth Street, 5th Floor
Cincinnati, OH 45202
513-579-2806

OKLAHOMA

Okahoma Venture Forum,
Alva Hayes
2501 North Blackwell Drive
Oklahoma City, OK 73016
405-528-8751

OREGON

Oregon/MIT/Venture Forum
William S. Manne, Esq., Chair
Sussman, Shank, Wapnick, Caplan
  & Stiles
1111 Security Pacific Plaza
1001 SW Fifth Avenue
Portland, OR 97204
503-227-1111 Fax: 503-248-0130

PENNSYLVANIA

**Venture Investment Forum of
  Central PA**
Beverly Lesher
1660 South Cameron Street
Harrisburg, PA 17104
717-234-3274EP

PUERTO RICO

Puerto Rico Venture Capital Club
Danola A. Morales, President
P.O. Box 2284
Hato Rey, PR 00910
809-787-9040

RHODE ISLAND

**Venture Capital Club of
  Providence**
Ernie Baptista
c/o Lauderdale Investment Company
144 Westminster Street
Providence, RI 02903
401-272-4700

SOUTH DAKOTA

**Eastern South Dakota V.C.
  Forum**
Don Greenfield
c/o SD Business Research Bureau
University of South Dakota

414 East Clark Street
Vermillion, SD 57069
605-677-5272

TENNESSEE

Seed Capital Network
Dr. Robert Gaston
8095 Kingston Pike, Suite 12
Knoxville, TN 37932
615-693-2091

TEXAS

Southwest Venture Forum
Louis Adams
SMU Box 333
Dallas, TX 75275
214-692-3027 Fax: 214-692-4099

UTAH

Moountain West Venture Group
Sharon Western
P.O. Box 210
Salt Lake City, UT 84144
801-531-8900

VERMONT

Vermont Venture Capital Club
H. Kenneth Merritt, Jr.
110 Main Street
P.O. Box 5839
Burlington, VT 05402
802-658-7830 Fax: 802-658-0989

VIRGINIA

Virginia Ventures Corporation

Stan Maupin
1407 Huguenot Road
Richmond, VA 23113
804-379-2034 Fax: 804-794-6090

WASHINGTON

Northwest/MIT Enterprise Forum
Joseph P. Whitford, Chair
Foster Pepper & Shelfman
1111 Third Avenue
Seattle, WA 98101
206-447-4400 Fax: 206-447-9700

WEST VIRGINIA

**West Virginia Venture Capital
   Club**
Paul Brant

204½ West Maple Avenue
Fayetteville, WV 25840
304-574-3036

WISCONSIN

**Wisconsin Venture Network,
   Incorporated**
Annabel Havlicek
1645 West Blue Mound Road
Suite 350
Brookfield, WI 53005
414-278-7070

APPENDIXES

APPENDIX A

This section lists several firms that have key business ratio studies available for specified industries (see pp. 34–35 for explanation)

Dun & Bradstreet
One Diamond Hill Road
Murray Hill, NJ 07974

Retailing
Auto and home supplies
Children's and infants' wear stores
Clothing and furnishings, men's and boys'
Department stores
Discount stores
Discount stores, leased departments
Family clothing stores
Furniture stores
Gasoline service stations
Grocery stores
Hardware stores
Household appliance stores
Jewelry stores
Lumber and other building materials dealers
Miscellaneous general merchandise stores
Motor vehicle dealers
Paint, glass, and wallpaper stores
Radio and television stores
Retail nurseries, lawn and garden supply dealers
Shoe stores
Variety stores
Women's ready-to-wear stores

Wholesaling
Air-conditioning and refrigeration equipment and supplies
Automotive equipment
Beer, wine, and alcoholic beverages
Chemicals and allied products
Clothing and accessories, women's and children's
Clothing and furnishings, men's and boys'
Commercial machines and equipment
Confectionery
Dairy products
Drugs, drug proprietaries, and sundries
Electrical appliances, TV and radio sets
Electrical apparatus and equipment
Electronic parts and equipment
Farm machinery and equipment
Footwear
Fresh fruits and vegetables
Furniture and home furnishings
Groceries, general line
Hardware
Industrial machinery and equipment
Lumber and construction materials
Meats and meat products
Metals and minerals
Paints, varnishes, and supplies
Paper and its products
Petroleum and petroleum products
Piece goods
Plumbing and heating equipment and supplies
Poultry and poultry products
Scrap and waste materials
Tires and tubes
Tobacco and its products

Manufacturing and Construction
Agricultural chemicals
Airplane parts and accessories
Bakery products
Blast furnaces, steel works, and rolling mills
Blouses and waists

Books, publishing and printing
Broad woven fabrics, cotton
Canned and preserved fruits and vegetables
Commercial printing except lithographic
Communication equipment
Concrete, gypsum, and plaster products
Confectionery and related products
Construction, mining, and handling machinery and equipment
Converted paper and paperboard products
Cutlery, hand tools, and general hardware
Dairy products
Dresses
Drugs
Electric lighting and wiring equipment
Electric transmission and distribution equipment
Electrical industrial apparatus
Electrical work
Electronic components and accessories
Engineering, laboratory, and scientific instruments
Fabricated structural metal products
Farm machinery and equipment
Footwear
Fur goods
General building contractors
General industrial machinery and equipment
Grain mill products
Heating and plumbing equipment
Heavy construction, except highway and street
Hosiery
Household appliances
Industrial

Dun & Bradstreet also has studies available on the *cost of doing business* for the following industries:

Retailing
Apparel and accessories
Automotive dealers
Building materials, hardware, and farm equipment
Drug and proprietary stores

Eating and drinking places
Food stores
Furniture and home furnishings
Gasoline service stations
General merchandise
Liquor stores

Wholesaling
Alcoholic beverages
Drugs
Dry goods
Electrical goods
Farm products
Groceries
Hardware, plumbing and heating equipment
Lumber and construction materials
Machinery
Metals and minerals
Motor vehicles
Paper and its products
Petroleum and its products

Manufacturing
Apparel
Chemicals and allied products
Electrical supplies and equipment
Fabricated metal products
Food products (bakery products, beverage industries, canned goods, dairy products, grain mill products, meats and sugar)
Furniture and fixtures
Leather and its products
Lumber and wood products
Machinery
Motor vehicles and equipment
Ordnance, except guided missiles
Paper and allied products
Petroleum refining
Primary metal industries
Printing and publishing
Rubber and miscellaneous plastics products

Scientific industries
Stone, clay, and glass products
Textile mill products
Tobacco
Transportation equipment

Services, Transportation and Communication
Advertising
Air transportation
Automobile parking, repair, and service
Business services
Electrical companies and systems
Hotels
Medical services
Motion picture production
Motion picture theaters
Personal services
Pipeline transportation
Radio and television broadcasting
Railroad transportation
Repair services
Telephone and telegraph services
Trucking and warehousing
Water supply and other sanitary services
Water transportation

Finance, Insurance, and Real Estate

Agriculture and Mining

Robert Morris Associates
1650 Market Street
One Liberty Place, Suite 2300
Philadelphia, PA 19103
(215) 851-9100

Manufacturing
Advertising displays and devices
Apparel and other finished fabric products:
  Canvas products

Children's clothing
Curtains and draperies
Men's, youths', and boys' suits, coats, and overcoats
Women's dresses
Women's suits, skirts, sportswear, and coats
Women's undergarments and sleepwear
Beverages:
    Flavoring extracts and syrups
    Malt liquors
    Wines, distilled liquor, and liqueurs
Caskets and burial supplies
Chemicals and allied products:
    Drugs and medicines
    Fertilizers
    Industrial chemicals
    Paint, varnish, and lacquer
    Perfumes, cosmetics, and other toilet preparations
    Plastic materials and synthetic resins
    Soap, detergents, and cleaning preparations
Food and kindred products:
    Bread and other bakery products
    Candy and dried fruits and vegetables
    Dairy products
    Flour and other grain mill products
    Frozen fruits, fruit juices, vegetables, and specialties
    Meat packing
    Prepared feed for animals and poultry
    Vegetable oils
Furniture and fixtures:
    Mattresses and bedsprings
    Metal household furniture
    Store, office, bar and restaurant fixtures
    Wood furniture—except upholstered
    Wood furniture—upholstered
Jewelry, precious metals
House furnishings
Leather and leather products:
    Footwear
    Furs
    Hats

Men's and boys' sport clothing
Men's work clothing
Men's, youths', and boys' separate trousers
Men's, youths', and boys' shorts, collars, and nightwear
Luggage and special leather products
Tanning, currying, and finishing
Lumber and wood products:
Millwork
Prefabricated wooden buildings and structural members
Sawmills and planing mills
Veneer, plywood, and hardwood
Wooden boxes and containers
Machinery, equipment, and supplies—electrical:
Air-conditioning
Electronic components and accessories
Equipment for public utilities and industrial use
Machinery, except electrical equipment:
Ball and roller bearings
Construction and mining machinery and equipment
Farm machinery and equipment
General industrial machinery and equipment
Industrial and commercial refrigeration equipment and complete
air-conditioning units
Machine shops—jobbing and repair
Machine tools and metal working equipment
Measuring, analyzing, and controlling instruments
Oil field machinery and equipment
Special dies and tools, die sets, jigs, and fixtures
Special industry machinery
Metal industries—primary:
Iron and steel forgings
Iron and steel foundries
Non-ferrous foundries
Metal products—fabricated, except ordnance, machinery, and trans-
portation equipment:
Coating, engraving, and allied services
Cutlery, hand tools, and general hardware
Enameled iron, metal sanitary ware, and plumbing supplies
Fabricated plate ware
Fabricated structural steel

Heating equipment, except electric
Metal cans
Metal doors, sash, frames, molding, and trim
Metal stampings
Miscellaneous fabricated wire products
Miscellaneous non-ferrous fabricated products
Screw machine products, bolts, nuts, screws, rivets, and washers
Sheet metal work
Valves and pipe fittings, except plumbers' brass goods
Paper and allied products:
Envelopes, stationery, and paper bags
Paperboard containers and boxes
Pulp, paper, and paperboard
Printing, publishing, and allied industries:
Book printing
Bookbinding and miscellaneous related work
Books: publishing
Commercial printing, lithographic
Newspapers: publishing and printing
Periodicals
Typesetting
Rubber and miscellaneous plastics products:
Miscellaneous plastics products
Rubber footwear and fabricated rubber products
Stone, clay, and glass products:
Brick and structural clay tile
Concrete brick, block, and other products
Minerals and earths, ground or otherwise treated
Pressed and blown glass and glassware
Ready-mixed concrete
Textile mill products:
Broad woven fabric—cotton, silk, and synthetic
Broad woven fabric—woolens and worsteds
Dyeing and finishing
Hosiery—anklets—children's, men's, and boys'
Hosiery—women's—full fashioned and seamless
Knitting—cloth, outerwear, and underwear
Narrow fabrics and other smallwares
Yard—cotton, silk, and synthetic

Toys, amusement, sporting and athletic goods:
  Games and toys, except dolls and children's vehicles
  Sporting and athletic goods
Transportation equipment:
  Aircraft parts, except electric
  Motor vehicle parts and accessories
  Motor vehicles
  Ship and boat building and repairing

Wholesaling
Automotive equipment and supplies:
  Automobiles and other motor vehicles
  Automotive equipment
  Tire and tubes
Beauty and barber supplies and equipment
Drugs, drug proprietaries, and druggists' sundries
Electrical equipment:
  Electrical supplies and apparatus
  Electronic parts and supplies
  Radios, refrigerators, and electrical appliances
Flowers and florists' supplies
Food, beverages, and tobacco:
  Coffee, tea, and spices
  Confectionery
  Dairy products and poultry
  Fish and seafoods
  Frozen foods
  Fruits and vegetables
  General groceries
  Grains
  Meats and meat products
  Tobacco and tobacco products
  Tobacco leaf
  Wine, liquor, and beer
Furniture and home furnishings:
  Floor coverings
  Furniture
General merchandise

Iron, steel, hardware, and related products:
  Air-conditioning and refrigeration equipment and supplies
  Hardware and paints
  Metal products
  Metal scrap
  Plumbing and heating equipment and supplies
  Steel warehousing
Lumber, building materials, and coal:
  Building materials
  Coal and coke
  Lumber and millwork
Machinery and equipment:
  Agricultural equipment
  Heavy commercial and industrial machinery and equipment
  Laundry and dry cleaning equipment and supplies
  Mill supplies
  Professional equipment and supplies
  Restaurant and hotel supplies, fixtures, and equipment
  Transportation equipment and supplies, except motor vehicles
Paper and paper products:
  Printing and writing paper
  Wrapping or coarse paper and products
Petroleum products:
  Fuel oil
  Petroleum products
Scrap and waste materials:
  Textile waste
Sporting goods and toys
Textile products and apparel:
  Dry goods
  Footwear
  Furs
  Men's and boys' clothing
  Women's and children's clothing
  Wool

Retailing
Aircraft
Apparel and accessories:

Family clothing stores
Furs
Infants' clothing
Men's and boys' clothing
Shoes
Women's ready-to-wear
Boat dealers
Books and office supplies:
Books and stationery
Office supplies and equipment
Building materials and hardware:
Building materials
Hardware stores
Heating and plumbing equipment dealers
Lumber
Paint, glass, and wallpaper stores
Cameras and photographic supplies
Department stores and general merchandise:
Department stores
Dry goods and general merchandise
Drugs
Farm and garden equipment and supplies:
Cut flowers and growing plants
Farm equipment
Feed and seed—farm and garden supply
Food and beverages:
Dairy products and milk dealers
Groceries and meats
Restaurants
Fuel and ice dealers:
Fuel, except fuel oil
Fuel oil dealers
Furniture, home furnishings, and equipment:
Floor coverings
Furniture
Household appliances
Radio, TV, and record players
Jewelry
Liquor

Luggage and gifts
Motor vehicle dealers:
  Autos—new and used
  Gasoline service stations
  Mobile homes
  Motorcycles
  Tires, batteries, and accessories
  Trucks—new and used
Musical instruments and supplies
Road machinery equipment
Sporting goods
Vending machine operators, merchandise

Services
Advertising agencies
Auto repair shops
Auto and truck rental and leasing
Bowling alleys
Cable television
Car washing
Commercial research and development laboratories
Data processing
Direct mail advertising
Engineering and architectural services
Farm products warehousing
Funeral directors
Insurance agents and brokers
Intercity bus lines
Janitorial services
Laundries and dry cleaners
Linen supply
Local trucking
Local trucking—without storage
Long distance trucking
Motels, hotels, and tourist courts
Nursing homes
Outdoor advertising
Photographic studios
Radio broadcasting

Real estate holding companies
Refrigerated warehousing, except food lockers
Refuse systems
Telephone communications
Transportation on rivers and canals
Travel agencies
Television stations
Water utility companies

Contractors (Not Classified Elsewhere)
Beef cattle raisers
Bituminous coal mining
Bottlers—soft drinks
Commercial feed lots
Construction, sand and gravel
Crude petroleum and natural gas mining
Horticultural services
Poultry, except broiler chickens
Seed companies (vegetable and garden)

National Cash Register Company
1700 South Patterson Boulevard
Dayton, OH 45479
513-445-5000

Apparel stores
Appliance and radio dealers
Automobile dealers
Auto parts dealers
Beauty shops
Bookstores
Building material dealers
Cocktail lounges
Department stores
Dry cleaners
Feed stores
Furniture stores
Florists
Garages
Food stores
Gift, novelty, and souvenir stores
Hardware stores
Hotels
Jewelry stores
Laundries
Liquor stores
Mass merchandising stores
Meat markets
Menswear stores
Motels and motor inns
Music stores
Novelty stores
Nursery and garden supply stores
Photographic studio and supply stores
Professional services

Repair services
Restaurants
Service stations
Shoe stores (family)

Sporting goods stores
Supermarkets
Transportation and service
Variety stores

Trade Associations

Associations that have published
ratio studies in the past include the following:

**American Association of
Advertising Agencies**
666 Third Avenue, 13th Floor
New York, NY 10017
212-682-2500

American Camping Association
5000 State Road, 67 North
Martinsville, IN 46151
317-342-8456

**American Forest and Paper
Association**
1250 Connecticut Avenue
Washington, DC 20036
202-463-2455

American Meat Institute
P.O. Box 3556
Washington, DC 20007
202-841-2400

**American Society of Association
Executives**
1575 Eye Street NW
Washington, DC 20005
202-626-2723

American Supply Association
222 Merchandise Mart, Suite 1360

Chicago, IL 60654
312-464-0090

**American Wholesale Marketers
Association**
1128 16th Street
Washington, DC 20036
202-463-2124

Apparel Retailers of America
2011 Eye Street NW, Suite 250
Washington, DC 20006
202-347-1932

**Bowling Proprietors Association of
America**
615 Six Flags Drive
Arlington, TX 76011
817-649-5105

**Building Owners and Managers
Association, International**
1201 New York Avenue NW
Suite 300
Washington, DC 20005
202-408-2662

Door and Hardware Institute
14170 Newbrook Drive
Chantilly, VA 22021
703-222-2010

Florists Transworld Delivery
Association, Interflora
29200 Northwestern Highway
Southfield, MI 48076
810-355-5300

Food Marketing Institute
800 Connecticut Avenue NW
Suite 500
Washington, DC 20006
202-452-8444

Foodservice Equipment
Distributors Association
332 South Michigan Avenue
Chicago, IL 60604
312-427-9605

Independent Insurance Agents of
America
127 South Peyton
Alexandria, VA 22314
703-683-4422

Institute of Management Account
(IMA)
Ten Paragon Drive
Montvale, NJ 07645
201-573-9000

International Hardware
Distributors Association
401 North Michigan Avenue
Chicago, IL 60611
312-644-6610

Kitchen Cabinet Manufacturers
Association
1899 Preston White Drive
Reston, VA 22091
703-264-1690

Material Handling Equipment
Distributors Association
201 Route 45
Vernon Hills, IL 60061
312-680-3500

Measurement, Control, and
Automation Association
225 Reinekers Lane, Suite 625
Alexandria, VA 22314
703-836-1360

Mechanical Contractors
Association of America
1385 Piccard Drive
Rockville, MD 20850
301-869-5800

Motor and Equipment
Manufacturers Association
10 Laboratory Drive
Research Triangle Park, NC 27709
919-549-4800

National American Wholesale
Grocers Association
201 Park Washington Court
Falls Church, VA 20046
703-532-9400

National Art Materials Trade
Association
178 Lakeview Drive, Box 739
Clifton, NJ 07015
201-546-6400

National Association of Electrical
Distributors
45 Danbury Road
Wilton, CT 06897
203-834-1908

National Association of Furniture
   Manufacturers
P.O. Box HP-7
High Point, NC 27261
919-884-5000

National Association of Music
   Merchants, Inc.
5140 Avenida Encinas
Carlsbad, CA 92008
619-438-8001

National Association of Plastics
   Distributors
4707 College Boulevard, Suite 105
Leawood, KS 66211
913-345-1005

National Association of Retail
   Dealers of America
10 East 22nd Street
Lombard, IL 60148
312-953-8950

National Beer Wholesalers
   Association of America
1100 South Washington
Alexandria, VA 22314
703-683-4300

National Confectioners
   Association of the U.S.
7900 West Park Drive
McLean, VA 22102
703-790-5750

National Consumer Finance
   Association
919 18th Street NW
Washington, DC 20006
202-296-5544

National Decorating Products
   Association
1050 North Lindbergh Blvd.
St. Louis, MO 63132
314-991-3470

National Electrical Contractors
   Association
3 Bethesda Metro Center
Suite 1100
Bethesda, MD 20814
301-657-3110

National Electrical Manufacturers
   Association
2101 L Street NW
Washington, DC 20037
202-457-8400

National Grocers Association
1825 Samuel Morse Drive
Suite 820
Reston, VA 22090
703-437-5300

National Home Furnishings
   Association
P.O. Box 2396
High Point, NC 27261
919-883-1650

National Lumber and Building
   Material Dealers Assoc.
40 Ivy Street SE
Washington, DC 20036
202-547-2230

National Office Products
   Association
301 North Fairfax Street
Alexandria, VA 22314
703-549-9040

National Paint and Coatings
  Association
1500 Rhode Island Avenue NW
Washington, DC 20005
202-462-6272

National Paper Box Association
1201 East Abingdon Drive
Alexandria, VA 22314
703-684-2212

National Paper Trade Association
111 Great Neck Road
Great Neck, NY 11021
516-829-3070

National Parking Association
1112 16th Street NW, Suite 2000
Washington, DC 20036
202-296-4336

National Restaurant Association
1200 17th Street, N.W.
Washington, DC 20036
202-331-5900

National Retail Federation
701 Pennsylvania Avenue NW
Washington, DC 20004
202-783-7971

National Retail Hardware
  Association
5822 West 74th Street
Indianapolis, IN 46278
317-290-0338

National Shoe Retailers
  Association
9861 Broken Land
Columbia, MD 21046
410-381-8282

National Soft Drink Association
1101 16th Street NW
Washington, DC 20036
202-436-6732

National Sporting Goods
  Association
1699 Wall Street
Mt. Prospect, IL 60056
312-439-4000

National Tire Dealers and
  Retailers
1250 Eye Street NW, Suite 400
Washington, DC 20005
202-789-2300

National Wholesale Druggists
  Association
1821 Michael Farady Drive
Reston, VA 22090
703-787-0000

North American Equipment
  Dealers Association
10877 Watson Road
St. Louis, MO 63127
314-821-7220

North American Heating and Air-
  Conditioning Wholesalers
  Association
P.O. Box 16790
Columbus, OH 43216
614-488-1835

North American Wholesale
  Lumbers Association
3601 Algonquin Road
Rolling Meadows, IL 60008
708-870-7470

**Northeastern Retail Lumberman's
Association**
339 East Avenue
Rochester, NY 15604
716-325-1626

Optical Laboratories Association
P.O. Box 2000
Merrifield, VA 22116
703-359-2830

**Painting and Decorating
Contractors of America**
3913 Old Lee Highway
Fairfax, VA 22050
703-359-0826

Petroleum Equipment Institute
Box 2380
Tulsa, OK 74101
918-494-9696

Printing Industries of America
100 Daingerfield Road
Alexandria, VA 22314
703-519-8100

Shoe Service Institute of America
5024 Campbell Boulevard

Baltimore, MD 21236
410-931-8100

Society of the Plastics Industry
1275 K Street NW
Washington, DC 20005
202-371-5200

**Textile Care Allied Trades
Association**
546 Valley Road
Upper Montclair, NJ 07043
201-744-0090

**United Fresh Fruits and
Vegetables Association**
727 North Washington Street
Alexandria, VA 22314
703-836-7745

Urban Land Institute
625 Indiana Avenue NW, Suite 400
Washington, DC 20004
202-624-7000

**Wine and Spirit Wholesalers of
America**
1023 15th Street NW
Washington, DC 20005
202-371-9792

APPENDIX B

STATE AND LOCAL SOURCES OF ASSISTANCE

ALABAMA

U.S. Department of Commerce
US&FCS District Office
Berry Building, 3rd Floor
2015 2nd Avenue North
Birmingtham, AL 35203
(205) 731-1331; fax (205) 731-0076

U.S. Small Business Administration
2121 8th Avenue North, Suite 200
Birmingham, AL 35203
(205) 731-1344; fax (205) 731-1404

Alabama Development Office
International Development Office
135 South Union Street
(Mailing address: c/o State Capitol)
Montgomery, AL 36130
(205) 263-0048; fax (205) 265-5078

Alabama International Trade Center
University of Alabama, Tuscaloosa
P.O. Box 870396
Tuscaloosa, AL 35487
(205) 348-7621; fax (205) 348-6974

North Alabama International Trade Association
Madison County Courthouse
7th Floor
Huntsville, AL 35801
(205) 532-3505; fax (205) 532-3704

Department of Planning and Economic Development
Madison County Courthouse,
7th Floor
Huntsville, AL 35801
(205) 532-3505; fax (205) 532-3704

Center for International Trade & Commerce
250 North Water Street, Suite 131
Mobile, AL 36602
(205) 433-1151; fax (205) 438-2711

Alabama World Trade Association
International Trade Center
250 North Water Street, Suite 131
Mobile, AL 36602
(205) 433-3174; fax (205) 438-2711

Alabama Export Council
2015 2nd Avenue North, Room 302
Birmingham, AL 35203
(205) 731-1331

Birmingham Area Chamber of Commerce
International Department
P.O. Box 10127
Birmingham, AL 35202
(205) 323-5461; fax (205) 324-2320

ALASKA

U.S. Department of Commerce
US&FCS District Office
World Trade Center
4201 Tudor Center Drive, Suite 319
Anchorage, AK 99508
(907) 271-6237; fax (907) 271-6242

U.S. Small Business Administration
222 West 8th Avenue, #67
Anchorage, AK 99513
(907) 271-4022; fax (907) 271-4545

Alaska Department of Commerce and Economic Development
International Trade Division
3601 C Street, Suite 798
Anchorage, AK 99503
(907) 561-5585; fax (907) 561-4557

World Trade Center Alaska/ Anchorage
World Trade Center
4201 Tudor Center Drive, Suite 320
Anchorage, AK 99508
(907) 561-1516; fax (907) 561-1541

Alaska Center for International Business
World Trade Center
4201 Tudor Center Drive, Suite 120
Anchorage, AK 99508
(907) 561-2322; fax (907) 561-1541

Alaska State Chamber of Commerce—Juneau
310 Second Street

Juneau, AK 99801
(907) 586-2322; fax (907) 586-3744

Alaska State Chamber of Commerce—Anchorage
801 B Street, Suite 405
Anchorage, AK 99501
(907) 278-2722; fax (907) 278-6643

Anchorage Chamber of Commerce
437 E Street, Suite 300
Anchorage, AK 99501
(907) 272-2401; fax (907) 272-4117

Fairbanks Chamber of Commerce
First National Center
100 Cushman Street
Fairbanks, AK 99707
(907) 452-1105

ARIZONA

U.S. Department of Commerce
US&FCS District Office
Federal Building & U.S. Courthouse
230 North Firth Avenue, Room 3412
Phoenix, AZ 85025
(602) 379-3285; fax (602) 379-4324

U.S. Small Business Administration
Central and One Thomas, Suite 800
2828 North Central Avenue
Phoenix, AZ 85004
(602) 379-3732

U.S. Small Business Administration
300 West Congress, Box FB33
Tucson, AZ 85701
(602) 670-6715

Arizona Department of Commerce
International Trade and Investment Division
3800 North Central Avenue
Suite 1500
Phoenix, AZ 85012
(602) 280-1371

Foreign Trade Zone Number 48
7800 South Nogales Highway
Tucson, AZ 85706
(602) 741-1940

Arizona World Trade Association
34 West Monroe, Suite 900
Phoenix, AZ 85003
(602) 254-5521

ARKANSAS

U.S. Department of Commerce
US&FCS District Office
Room 811, Savers Building
320 West Capitol
Little Rock, AR 72201
(501) 324-5794; fax (501) 324-7380

U.S. Small Business Administration
Little Rock Field Office
Savers Building, Room 600
320 West Capitol
Little Rock, AR 72201
(501) 324-5871

Marketing Division
Arkansas Industrial Development Commission
1 Capitol Mall
Little Rock, AR 72201
(501) 682-7690; fax (501) 682-7691

The World Trade Club
c/o Marketing Division

Arkansas Industrial Development Commission
1 Capitol Mall
Little Rock, AR 72201
(501) 682-7690

Export Finance Office
Arkansas Development Finance Authority
100 South Main
Little Rock, AR 72201
(501) 682-5909

Arkansas International Center
University of Arkansas at Little Rock
2801 South University
Little Rock, AR 72204
(501) 569-3282

Mid-South International Trade Association
P.O. Box 888
100 South Main, Room 438
Little Rock, AR 72201
(501) 374-1957; fax (501) 375-8317

Arkansas Small Business Development Center
100 South Main, Suite 401
Little Rock, AR 72201
(501) 324-9043

CALIFORNIA

U.S. Department of Commerce
US&FCS District Office
11000 Wilshire Boulevard
Suite 9200
Los Angeles, CA 90024
(213) 575-7104; fax (213) 575-7220

U.S. Department of Commerce
US&FCS District Office
250 Montgomery Street, 14th Floor

San Francisco, CA 94104
(415) 705-2300; fax (415) 705-2299

U.S. Department of Commerce
US&FCS District Office
6363 Greenwich Drive, Suite 145
San Diego, CA 92122
(619) 557-5395; fax (619) 557-6176

U.S. Department of Commerce
US&FCS Branch Office
116-A West 4th Street, Suite #1
Santa Ana, CA 92701
(714) 836-2461; fax (714) 836-2330

U.S. Department of Commerce
Bureau of Export Administration
5201 Great America Parkway
Suite 226
Santa Clara, CA 95050
(408) 748-7450; fax (408) 748-7470

**U.S. Small Business
Administration**
2719 North Air Fresno Drive
Fresno, CA 93727
(209) 487-5189

**U.S. Small Business
Administration**
330 North Brand Boulevard
Suite 190
Glendale, CA 91203-2304
(213) 688-2956; fax (213) 894-5665

**U.S. Small Business
Administration**
660 J Street, Room 215
Sacramento, CA 95814-2413
(916) 551-1445

**U.S. Small Business
Administration**
880 Front Street, Room 4-S-29
San Diego, CA 92188
(619) 557-7252

**U.S. Small Business
Administration (Regional
Office)**
71 Stevenson Street, 20th Floor
San Francisco, CA 94105
(415) 744-6418

**U.S. Small Business
Administration (District Office)**
211 Main Street, 4th Floor
San Francisco, CA 94105
(415) 744-6801

**U.S. Small Business
Administration**
901 West Civic Center Drive
Suite 160
Santa Ana, CA 92703
(714) 836-2494; fax (714) 836-2528

**California State World Trade
Commission**
1121 L Street, Suite 310
Sacramento, CA 95814
(916) 324-5511; fax (916) 324-5791

**California State World Trade
Commission**
Office of Export Development
One World Trade Center, Suite 990
Long Beach, CA 90831
(213) 590-5965; fax (213) 590-5958

California Export Finance Office
425 Market Street, Suite 2838
San Francisco, CA 94105
(415) 557-9812; fax (415) 557-7770

California Export Finance Office
107 South Broadway, Suite 8039
Los Angeles, CA 90012
(213) 620-2433; fax (213) 620-6102

**California Chamber of
Commerce,**
International Trade Department

1201 K Street, 12th Floor
P.O. Box 1736
Sacramento, CA 95812
(916) 444-6670

**California Council for
International Trade**
700 Montgomery Street, Suite 305
San Francisco, CA 94111
(415) 788-4127

**California Department of Food
and Agriculture**
Agriculture Export Program
1220 N Street, Room 104
Sacramento, CA 95814
(916) 322-4339; fax (916) 324-1681

**Economic Development
Corporation of Los Angeles
County**
6922 Hollywood Boulevard
Suite 415
Los Angeles, CA 90028
(213) 462-5111; fax (213) 462-2228

**Long Beach Area Chamber of
Commerce**
International Business Association
One World Trade Center, Suite 350
Long Beach, CA 90853
(213) 436-1251; fax (213) 436-7088

**Century City Chamber of
Commerce**
International Business Council
1801 Century Park East, Suite 300
Century City, CA 90067
(213) 553-4062

**Los Angeles Area Chamber of
Commerce**
International Commerce Division
404 South Bixel Street
Los Angeles, CA 90017
(213) 629-0602; fax (213) 629-0708

San Diego Chamber of Commerce
402 West Broadway, Suite 1000
San Diego, CA 92101
(619) 232-0124

**San Francisco Chamber of
Commerce**
San Francisco World Trade
Association
465 California Street, 9th Floor
San Francisco, CA 94104
(415) 392-4511

**The Greater Los Angeles World
Trade Center Association**
One World Trade Center, Suite 295
Long Beach, CA 90831
(213) 495-7070; fax (213) 495-7071

**Citrus College Center for
International Trade
Development**
363 South Park Avenue, Suite 105
Pomona, CA 91766
(714) 629-2223; fax (714) 622-4217

**Riverside Community College
Center for International Trade
Development**
1760 Chicago Avenue, Building K
Riverside, CA 92507
(714) 276-3400

**Custom Brokers & Freight
Forwarders Association**
303 World Trade Center
San Francisco, CA 94111
(415) 536-2233

**Export Managers Association of
California**
124 East Olympic Boulevard
Suite 517
Los Angeles, CA 90015
(213) 749-8698

**Foreign Trade Association of
Southern California**
350 South Figueroa Street, #226
Los Angeles, CA 90071
(213) 627-0634

**International Marketing
Association of Orange County**
Cal State Fullerton
Marketing Department
Fullerton, CA 92634
(714) 773-2223

**Santa Clara Valley World Trade
Association**
P.O. Box 611208
San Jose, CA 95161
(408) 998-7000

**Valley International Trade
Association**
(San Fernando Valley)
1323 Carmelina Avenue, Suite 214
Los Angeles, CA 90025
(213) 207-1802

**World Trade Association of
Orange County**
1 Park Plaza, Suite 150
Irvine, CA 92714
(714) 549-8151

**World Trade Association of San
Diego**
6363 Greenwich Drive, Suite 140
San Diego, CA 92122
(619) 453-4605

**San Mateo County Economic
Development Association**
951 Mariners Island Boulevard
Suite 200
San Mateo, CA 94404
(415) 345-8300; fax (415) 345-6896

**San Jose Center for International
Trade and Development**
50 West San Fernando Street

Suite 900
San Jose, CA 95113
(408) 277-4060; fax (408) 277-3615

**Santa Clara Chamber of
Commerce**
P.O. Box 387
Santa Clara, CA 95052
(408) 970-9825; fax (408) 970-8864

COLORADO

U.S. Department of Commerce
US&FCS District Office
World Trade Center Denver
1625 Broadway, Suite 680
Denver, CO 80202
(303) 844-3246; fax (303) 844-5651

**U.S. Small Business
Administration**
U.S. Customhouse, Room 454
721 19th Street
Denver, CO 80202
(303) 844-3984

**International Trade Office of
Colorado**
Governor's Office of Economic
Development
World Trade Center Denver
1625 Broadway, Suite 680
Denver, CO 80202
(303) 892-3850

**Colorado Department of
Agriculture, Markets Division**
700 Kipling
Lakewood, CO 80215
(303) 239-4114

**Colorado International Capital
Corporation**
1981 Blake Street
Denver, CO 80202
(303) 297-2605
(800) 877-2432

Rocky Mountain World Trade Center Association
World Trade Center Denver
1625 Broadway, Suite 680
Denver, CO 80202
(303) 592-5760

Greater Denver Chamber of Commerce
1445 Market Street
Denver, CO 80202
(303) 534-8500

Colorado Springs Chamber of Commerce
P.O. Drawer B
Colorado Springs, CO 80901
(719) 635-1551

International Business Association of the Rockies
10200 West 44th Avenue, Suite 304
Wheat Ridge, CO 80033
(303) 422-7905

Export Legal Assistance Network
(Federal Bar Association/U.S.
Small Business Administration/
U.S. Department of Commerce)
(303) 922-7687Federal Bar
Association
(303) 844-3984
Small Business Administration
(303) 844-3246
Department of Commerce
Note: The above network is an agreement that allows a small firm to receive an initial, free consultation with an attorney to discuss legal issues and concerns relating to international trade.

CONNECTICUT

U.S. Department of Commerce
US&FCS District Office
Federal Building, Room 610-B

450 Main Street
Hartford, CT 06103
(203) 240-3530; fax (203) 844-5651

U.S. Small Business Administration
33 Main Street
Hartford, CT 06106
(203) 240-4670

International Division
Department of Economic
Development
865 Brook Street
Hartford, CT 06067-3405
(203) 258-4256

DELAWARE

U.S. Department of Commerce
US&FCS District Office
*See listing for US&FCS,
Philadelphia, Pennsylvania*

U.S. Small Business Administration
920 King Street, Room 412
Wilmington, DE 19801
(302) 573-6295

Delaware Development Office
Box 1401
Dover, DE 19903
(302) 736-4271; fax (302) 736-5749

Delaware Department of Agriculture
2320 South DuPont Highway
Dover, DE 19901
(302) 736-4811; fax (302) 697-6287

Delaware State Chamber of Commerce
One Commerce Center, Suite 200
Wilmington, DE 19801
(302) 655-7221

Delaware-Eastern Pennsylvania Export Council
475 Allendale Road, Suite 202
King of Prussia, PA 19406
(215) 962-4980; fax (215) 951-7959

World Trade Center Institute
Dupont Building, Suite 1022
Wilmington, DE 19899
(302) 656-7905; fax (302) 656-2145

DISTRICT OF COLUMBIA

U.S. Department of Commerce
US&FCS Branch Office
*See listing for US&FCS,
Gaithersburg, MD*

World Trade Center, Washington, DC
1101 King Street, Suite 700
Alexandria, VA 22314
(703) 684-6630

Office of International Business
Government of the District of
Columbia
1250 Eye Street NW, Suite 1003
Washington, DC 20005
(202) 727-1576

Washington/Baltimore Regional Association
1129 20th Street, NW, Suite 202
Washington DC 20036
(202) 861-0400

FLORIDA

U.S. Department of Commerce
US&FCS District Office
Federal Building, Suite 224
51 SW First Avenue
Miami, FL 33130
(305) 536-5267; fax (305) 536-4765

U.S. Department of Commerce
US&FCS Branch Office
c/o Clearwater Chamber of
Commerce
128 North Osceola Avenue
Clearwater, FL 34615
(813) 461-0011; fax (813) 449-2889

U.S. Department of Commerce
US&FCS Branch Office
c/o University of Central Florida
RM 346, CEBA II
Orlando, FL 32816
(407) 648-6235

U.S. Department of Commerce
US&FCS Branch Office
Collins Building, Rm 401
107 West Gaines Street
Tallahassee, FL 32304
(904) 488-6469; fax (904) 487-1407

U.S. Small Business Administration
7825 Bay Meadows Way, Suite 100-B
Jacksonville, FL 32256-7504
(904) 443-1900; fax (904) 443-1980

U.S. Small Business Administration
1320 South Dixie Highway, Suite 501
Coral Gables, FL 33146
(305) 536-5521; fax (305) 536-5058

U.S. Small Business Administration
501 East Polk Street, Suite 104
Tampa, FL 33602
(813) 228-2594; fax (813) 228-2111

Division of International Trade and Development
Florida Department of Commerce
Collins Building, Room 366
Tallahassee, FL 32399-2000
(904) 488-6124; fax (904) 487-1407

Tampa Bay International Trade Council
P.O. Box 420
Tampa, FL 33601
(813) 228-7777; fax (813) 223-7899

World Trade Center Miami
One World Trade Plaza, Suite 1800
80 SW 8th Street
Miami, FL 33130
(305) 579-0064; fax (305) 536-7701

Office for Latin American Trade
Florida Department of Commerce
2701 LeJeune Road, Suite 330
Coral Gables, FL 33134
(305) 442-6921; fax (305) 442-6931

GEORGIA

U.S. Department of Commerce
US&FCS District Office
Plaza Square North
4360 Chamblee Dunwoody Road
Suite 310
Atlanta, GA 30341
(404) 452-9101; fax (404) 452-9105

U.S. Department of Commerce
US&FCS District Office
Room A-107
120 Barnard Street
Savannah, GA 31401
(912) 944-4204; fax (912) 944-4241

U.S. Small Business Administration
1720 Peachtree Road NW
6th Floor
Atlanta, GA 30309
(404) 347-4749; fax (404) 347-4745

U.S. Small Business Administration
52 North Main Street, Room 225
Statesboro, GA 30458
(912) 489-8719

Department of Industry, Trade and Tourism
Suite 1100
285 Peachtree Center Avenue
Atlanta, GA 30303
(404) 656-3545; fax (404) 656-3567

International Trade Division
Division of Marketing
Department of Agriculture
19 Martin Luther King Jr. Drive
Room 330
Atlanta, GA 30334
(404) 656-3740; fax (404) 656-9380

HAWAII

U.S. Department of Commerce
US&FCS District Office
40 Ala Moana Boulevard
P. O. Box 50026
Honolulu, HI 96850
(808) 541-1782; fax (808) 541-3435

U.S. Small Business Administration
2213 Federal Building
300 Ala Moana Boulevard
Box 50207
Honolulu, HI 96850
(808) 541-2987

Department of Business, Economic Development, & Tourism
Business Development and
  Marketing Division
P.O. Box 2359
Honolulu, HI 96804
(808) 548-7719

Chamber of Commerce of Hawaii
World Trade Association
735 Bishop Street
Honolulu, HI 96813
(808) 531-4111

Economic Development Corporation of Honolulu
1001 Bishop Street, Suite 735
Honolulu, HI 96813
(808) 545-4533
Also served by the Honolulu
District Office.

AMERICAN SAMOA

Office of Development Planning
Territory of American Samoa
Pago Pago, American Samoa 96799
(684) 633-5155; fax (684) 633-4195

GUAM

Department of Commerce
Territory of Guam
590 South Marine Drive
Tamuning, Guam 96911
(671) 646-5841; fax (671) 646-7242

Guam Chamber of Commerce
P.O. Box 283
Agana, Guam 96910
(671) 472-6311; fax (671) 472-6202

COMMONWEALTH OF THE NORTHERN MARIANA ISLANDS

Department of Commerce & Labor
Commonwealth of the Northern
Mariana Islands
Saipan, MP 96950
(670) 322-8711; fax (670) 322-4008

Saipan Chamber of Commerce
P.O. Box 806
Saipan, MP 96950
(670) 234-6132; fax (670) 234-7151

IDAHO

U.S. Department of Commerce
US&FCS Branch Office
2nd Floor, Joe R. Williams
Building
700 West State Street
Boise, ID 83720
(202) 334-3857; fax (202) 334-2783

U.S. Small Business Administration
1020 Main Street, Suite 290
Boise, ID 83702
(208) 334-1696

Idaho Department of Commerce
International Business Division
700 West State Street, 2nd Floor
Boise, ID 83720
(208) 334-2470; fax (208) 334-2783

Department of Agriculture
International Marketing Division
2270 Old Penitentiary Road
P.O. Box 790
Boise, ID 83701
(208) 334-2227; fax (208) 334-2170

District Export Council
*See Boise US&FCS Branch
Office listing*

World Trade Committee
Boise Area Chamber of Commerce
P.O. Box 2368
Boise, ID 83701
(208) 344-5515

ILLINOIS

U.S. Department of Commerce
US&FCS District Office
55 East Monroe Street, Room 1406
Chicago, IL 60603
(312) 353-4450; fax (312) 886-8025

U.S. Department of Commerce
US&FCS Branch Office
IIT—Rice Campus
201 East Loop Drive
Wheaton, IL 60187
(708) 353-4332

U.S. Department of Commerce
US&FCS Branch Office
P.O. Box 1747
515 North Court Street
Rockford, IL 61110
(815) 363-4347; fax (815) 987-8122

U.S. Small Business
  Administration
Business Development Office
500 West Madison, Suite 1250
Chicago, IL 60606
(708) 353-4578

U.S. Small Business
  Administration/SCORE
500 West Madison, Suite 1250
Chicago, IL 60606
(312) 353-4528

U.S. Small Business
  Administration
511 West Capitol, Suite 302
Springfield, IL 62704
(217) 492-4416

International Business Division
Illinois Department of Commerce
  & Community Affairs
100 West Randolph Street
Suite 3-400
Chicago, IL 60601
(312) 814-7166

Illinois Department of Agriculture
1010 Jorie Boulevard, Room 20
Oak Brook, IL 60521
(708) 990-8256

Illinois Department of Agriculture
Division of Marketing and
  Promotion
State Fairgrounds
P.O. Box 19281
Springfield, IL 62794
(217) 782-6675

Automotive Exporters Council
463 North Harlem Avenue
Oak Park, IL 60303
(708) 524-1880

Carnets
U.S. Council for International
  Business
1930 Thoreau Drive, Suite 101
Schaumburg, IL 60173
(708) 490-9696

Central Illinois Exporters
  Association
302 East John Street, Suite 202
Champaign, IL 61820
(217) 333-1465

Chicago Association of Commerce
  and Industry
World Trade Division
200 North LaSalle Street
Chicago, IL 60616
(312) 580-6928

Chicago Convention and Tourism
  Bureau
McCormick Place on the Lake
Chicago, IL 60616
(312) 567-8500

Chicago Council on Foreign
  Relations
116 South Michigan Avenue
10th Floor
Chicago, IL 60603
(312) 726-3860

Chicago Midwest Credit Management Associations
315 South Northwest Highway
Park Ridge, IL 60068
(708) 696-3000

City of Chicago
Economic Development Commission
1503 Merchandise Mart
Chicago, IL 60654
(312) 744-2622

City of Chicago
Department of Economic Development
International Division
24 East Congress Parkway, 7th Floor
Chicago, IL 60605
(312) 408-7485

Customs Brokers and Foreign Freight Forwarders Association of Chicago
P.O. Box 66584/AMF O'Hare
Chicago, IL 60666
(708) 678-5400

Foreign Credit Insurance Association
19 South LaSalle Street, Suite 902
Chicago, IL 60603
(312) 641-1915

Foreign Trade Zones
U.S. Customs Service
Warehouse Desk
610 South Canal Street
Chicago, IL 60607
(312) 353-5822

Illinois District Export Council
55 East Monroe Street, Room 1406
Chicago, IL 60603
(312) 353-4450

Illinois Export Council
321 North Clark Street, Suite 550
Chicago, IL 60610
(312) 793-4982

Illinois Export Development Authority
321 North Clark Street, Suite 550
Chicago, IL 60610
(312) 793-4995

Illinois International Port District
3600 East 95th Street
Chicago, IL 60617
(312) 646-4400

Illinois Manufacturers' Association
209 West Jackson Boulevard
Suite 700
Chicago, IL 60606
(312) 922-6575

Illinois State Chamber of Commerce
International Trade Division
20 North Wacker Drive, Suite 1960
Chicago, IL 60606
(312) 372-7373

Illinois World Trade Center Association
321 North Clark Street, Suite 550
Chicago, IL 60610
(312) 793-4982

International Trade Association of Greater Chicago
P.O. Box 454
Elk Grove Village, IL 60009
(708) 980-4109

International Trade Club of Chicago
203 North Wabash, Suite 1102
Chicago, IL 60601
(312) 368-9197

International Visitors Center
520 North Michigan Avenue
Suite 522
Chicago, IL 60611
(312) 645-1836

Library of International Relations
77 South Wacker Drive
Chicago, IL 60606
(312) 567-5234

Mid-America International Agri-Trade Council (MIATCO)
820 Davis Street, Suite 212
Evanston, IL 60201
(708) 866-7300

Overseas Sales & Marketing Association of America
P.O. Box 37
Lake Bluff, IL 60044
(708) 234-1760

World Trade Council of Northern Illinois
515 North Court Street
Rockford, IL 61103
(815) 987-8128

INDIANA

U.S. Department of Commerce
US&FCS District Office
One North Capitol, Suite 520
Indianapolis, IN 46204-2227
(317) 226-6214; fax (317) 226-6139

U.S. Small Business Administration
429 North Pennsylvania Street
Suite 100
Indianapolis, IN 46204
(317) 226-7272

Indiana District Export Council
One North Capitol, Suite 520

Indianapolis, IN 46204
(317) 226-6214; fax (317) 226-6139

Indiana Department of Commerce
International Trade Division
One North Capitol, Suite 700
Indianapolis, IN 46204-2248
(317) 232-3527

Indiana Chamber of Commerce
One North Capitol, Suite 200
Indianapolis, IN 46204-2248
(317) 264-3100

World Trade Committee
Fort Wayne Chamber of Commerce
826 Ewing Street
Fort Wayne, IN 46802
(219) 424-1435

World Trade Club of Indiana, Inc.
One North Capitol, Suite 200
Indianapolis, IN 46204-2248
(317) 264-3100

Tri-State World Trade Council
Old Post Office Place
100 NW 2nd Street, Suite 202
Evansville, IN 47708
(812) 425-8147

Michiana World Trade Club
P.O. Box 1715-A
South Bend, IN 46634
(219) 289-7323

Forum for International Professional Services
One North Capitol, Suite 200
Indianapolis, IN 46204-2248
(317) 264-3100

Indiana-ASEAN Council, Inc.
One American Square, Box 82017
Indianapolis, IN 46282
(317) 685-1341

IOWA

U.S. Department of Commerce
US&FCS District Office
817 Federal Building
210 Walnut Street
Des Moines, IA 50309
(515) 284-4222; fax (515) 284-4021

U.S. Department of Commerce
US&FCS Branch Office
424 First Avenue NE
Cedar Rapids, IA 52401
(319) 362-8418; fax (319) 398-5228

U.S. Small Business Administration
373 Collins Road NE
Cedar Rapids, IA 52402
(319) 393-8630; fax (319) 393-7585

U.S. Small Business Administration
749 Federal Building
210 Walnut Street
Des Moines, IA 50309
(515) 284-4422; fax (515) 284-4572

Iowa Department of Economic Development
Bureau of International Marketing
200 East Grand Boulevard
Des Moines, IA 50309
(515) 242-4743; fax (515) 242-4749

Iowa Department of Agriculture and Land Stewardship
International Trade Bureau
Wallace Building
Des Moines, IA 50319
(515) 281-5993; fax (515) 242-5015

Northeast Iowa Small Business Development Center
770 Town Clock Plaza
Dubuque, IA 52001
(319) 588-3350; fax (319) 557-1591

Siouxland International Trade Association
Sioux City Chamber of Commerce
101 Pierce Street
Sioux City, IA 51101
(712) 255-7903; fax (712) 258-7578

Iowa-Illinois International Trade Association
Davenport Chamber of Commerce
112 East Third Street
Davenport, IA 52801
(319) 322-1706; fax (319) 322-2251

Internaional Trade Bureau
Cedar Rapids Area Chamber of Commerce
424 First Avenue NE
Cedar Rapids, IA 52401
(319) 398-5317; fax (319) 398-5228

International Traders of Iowa
P.O. Box 897
Des Moines, IA 50309
(515) 245-5284; fax (515) 245-5286

Northeast Iowa International Trade Council
Regional Economic Development Center
Hawkeye Institute of Technology
1501 East Orange Street
Waterloo, IA 50704
(319) 296-2320; fax (319) 296-2874

Top of Iowa Trade Forum
Regional Economic Development Center
North Iowa Community College
500 College Drive
Mason City, IA 50401
(515) 421-4353; fax (515) 424-2011

KANSAS

U.S. Department of Commerce
US&FCS Branch Office

151 North Volutsia
Wichita, KS 67214
(316) 269-6160; fax (316) 262-5652

**U.S. Small Business
Administration**
110 East Waterman Street
Wichita, KS 67202
(316) 269-6571

Kansas Department of Commerce
400 SW 8th, Suite 500
Topeka, KS 66603-3957
(913) 296-4027

International Trade Council
P.O. Box 1588
Manhattan, KS 66502
(913) 539-6799

Kansas District Export Council
c/o Sunflower Manufacturing
  Company
Box 628
Beloit, KS 67420
(913) 738-2261

World Trade Council of Wichita
Wichita State University
Barton School of Business,
MBMT-IB
Campus Box 88
Wichita, KS 67208
(316) 689-3176

KENTUCKY

U.S. Department of Commerce
US&FCS District Office
U.S. Post Office & Courthouse
  Building
Room 636-B
601 West Broadway
Louisville, KY 40202
(502) 582-5066; fax (502) 582-6573

**U.S. Small Business
Administration**
600 Federal Place, Room 188
Louisville, KY 40201
(502) 582-5971

Office of International Marketing
Kentucky Cabinet for Economic
Development
Capitol Plaza Tower, 24th Floor
Frankfort, KY 40601
(502) 564-2170

**Louisville/Jefferson County Office
for Economic Development**
200 Brown & Williamson Tower
401 South Fourth Avenue
Louisville, KY 40202
(502) 625-3051

Kentucky District Export Council
601 West Broadway, Room 636-B
Louisville, KY 40202
(502) 582-5066

**Kentuckiana World Commerce
Council**
P.O. Box 58456
Louisville, KY 40258
(502) 583-5551

**Bluegrass International Trade
Association**
P.O. Box 24074
Lexington, KY 40524
(606) 272-6656

**Northern Kentucky International
Trade Association**
7505 Sussex Drive
Florence, KY 41042
(606) 283-1885; fax (606) 283-8178

Kentucky World Trade Center
410 West Vine Street, Suite 290
Lexington, KY 40507
(606) 258-3139; fax (606) 233-0658

University of Louisville
School of Business
Louisville, KY 40292

University of Kentucky
Patterson School of Diplomacy
Lexington, KY 40506

LOUISIANA

U.S. Department of Commerce
US&FCS District Office
432 World Trade Center
2 Canal Street
New Orleans, LA 70130
(504) 589-6546; fax (504) 586-2337

**U.S. Small Business
Administration**
1661 Canal Street, Suite 2000
New Orleans, LA 70114
(504) 589-6685

Office of Commerce and Industry
Louisiana Department of Economic
Development
P.O. Box 94185
Baton Rouge, LA 70804
(504) 342-9232; fax (504) 342-5389

**Chamber of Commerce/New
Orleans and the River Region**
301 Camp Street
New Orleans, LA 70130
(504) 527-6900

**International Business Council of
North Louisiana**
c/o Shreveport Chamber of
Commerce
P.O. Box 20074
Shreveport, LA 71120
(318) 667-2510

International Trade Center
(Small Business Administration
Office)

University of New Orleans -
Lakefront Campus
New Orleans, LA 70148
(504) 286-6978

**World Trade Center of New
Orleans**
Executive Offices, Suite 2900
2 Canal Street
New Orleans, LA 70130
(504) 529-1601; fax (504) 529-1691

**Le Centre International de
Lafayette**
P.O. Box 4017-C
Lafayette, LA 70502
(318) 268-5474

**Small Business Development
Center**
Northeast Louisiana University
Monroe, LA 71209
(318) 342-1224

MAINE

U.S. Department of Commerce
US&FCS Branch Office
77 Sewall Street
Augusta, ME 04330
(207) 622-8249; fax (207) 626-9156

**U.S. Small Business
Administration**
40 Western Avenue, Room 512
Augusta, ME 04333
(207) 622-8378

State Development Office
State House, Station 59
Augusta, ME 04333
(207) 289-2656

MARYLAND

U.S. Department of Commerce
US&FCS District Office

413 U.S. Customhouse
40 South Gay Street
Baltimore, MD 21202
(301) 962-3560; fax (301) 962-7813

U.S. Department of Commerce
US&FCS Branch Office
c/o National Institute for Standards
and Technology
Building 411
Gaithersburg, MD 20899
(301) 962-3560; fax (301) 962-7813

**U.S. Small Business
Administration**
Equitable Building
10 North Calvert Street
Baltimore, MD 21202
(301) 962-2235

Maryland International Division
World Trade Center
401 East Pratt Street
7th Floor
Baltimore, MD 21202
(301) 333-4295

**Maryland Chamber and Economic
Growth Associates**
111 South Calvert Street, Suite 2220
Baltimore, MD 21202
(301) 837-6068

**Maryland Chamber and Economic
Growth Associates**
275 West Street, Suite 400
Annapolis, MD 21401

**Foundation for Manufacturing
Excellence, Inc.**
Catonsville Community College
800 South Rolling Road
Baltimore, MD 21228
(301) 455-4919

**Eastern Baltimore Area Chamber
of Commerce**
2 Dunmanway

Dunkirk Building, Suite 238
Dundalk, MD 21222
(301) 282-9100

Greater Baltimore Committee
Legg Mason Tower
111 South Calvert Street, Suite 1500
Baltimore, MD 21202
(301) 727-2820

Office of Economic Development
Anne Arundel County
Arundel Center
Annapolis, MD 21401
(301) 280-1122

Office of Economic Development
Prince George's County
9200 Basil Court, Suite 200
Landover, MD 20785
(301) 386-5600

**Baltimore County Economic
Development Commission**
400 Washington Avenue
Courthouse Mezzanine
Towson, MD 21204
(301) 887-8000

Office of Economic Development
Montgomery County
Executive Office Building
101 Monroe Street, Suite 1500
Rockville, MD 20850
(301) 762-6325

**Howard County Office of
Economic Development**
3430 Court House Drive
Ellicott City, MD 21043
(301) 313-2900

World Trade Center Institute
401 East Pratt Street, Suite 1355
Baltimore, MD 21202
(301) 516-0022

Montgomery County High-Tech Council, Incorporation
51 Monroe Street, Suite 1701
Rockville, MD 20850
(301) 762-6325

Maryland Small Business Development Center
(Central Maryland)
1414 Key Highway
Baltimore, MD 21230
(301) 234-0505

International Visitors Center
The World Trade Center, Suite 1353
Baltimore, MD 21202
(301) 837-7150

Washington/Baltimore Regional Association
1129 20th Street NW, Suite 202
Washington, DC 20036
(202) 861-0400

MASSACHUSETTS

U.S. Department of Commerce
US&FCS District Office
World Trade Center, Suite 307
Boston, MA 02110
(617) 568-8563; fax (617) 565-8530

U.S. Small Business Administration
155 Federal Street, 9th Floor
Boston, MA 02110
(617) 451-2047

U.S. Small Business Administration
1550 Main Street
Springfield, MA 01103
(413) 785-0268

Massachusetts Department of Commerce & Development
Office of Economic Affairs
100 Cambridge Street, 13th Floor
Boston, MA 02202
(617) 727-3206

Office of International Trade
100 Cambridge Street, Suite 902
Boston, MA 02202
(617) 367-1830

Massachusetts Department of Food and Agriculture
100 Cambridge Street
Boston, MA 02202
(617) 727-3018

Massachusetts Port Authority (MASSPORT)
Foreign Trade Unit
World Trade Center, Suite 321
Boston, MA 02210
(617) 439-5560

International Business Center of New England
World Trade Center, Suite 323
Boston, MA 02210
(617) 439-5280

Smaller Business Association of New England, Incorporated
69 Hickory Drive
Waltham, MA 02254
(617) 890-9070

Associated Industries of Massachusetts
441 Stuart Street, 5th Floor
Boston, MA 02116
(617) 262-1180

Metro South Chamber of Commerce
60 School Street
Brockton, MA 02401
(508) 586-0500

Central Berkshire Chamber of Commerce
60 West Street
Pittsfield, MA 01201
(413) 499-4000

Chamber of Commerce of the Attleboro Area
42 Union Street
Attleboro, MA 02703
(508) 222-0801

Fall River Area Chamber of Commerce
P.O. Box 1871
200 Pocasset Street
Fall River, MA 02722
(508) 676-8226

Greater Boston Chamber of Commerce
600 Atlantic Avenue
Boston, MA 02110
(617) 227-4500

North Central Massachusetts Chamber of Commerce
110 Erdman Way
Leominster, MA 01453
(508) 840-4300

Greater Gardner Chamber of Commerce
55 Lake Street
Gardner, MA 01440
(508) 632-1780

Greater Lawrence Chamber of Commerce
264 Essex Street
Lawrence, MA 01840
(508) 686-0900

Greater Springfield Chamber of Commerce
1350 Main Street, Third Floor
Springfield, MA 01103
(413) 787-1542

New Bedford Area Chamber of Commerce
P.O. Box G-827
794 Purchase Street
New Bedford, MA 02742
(508) 999-5231

North Suburban Chamber of Commerce
7 Alfred Street
Woburn, MA 01801
(617) 933-3499

Metro West Chamber of Commerce
1671 Worcester Street, Suite 201
Framingham, MA 01701
(508) 879-5600

South Shore Chamber of Commerce
36 Miller Stile Road
Quincy, MA 02169
(617) 479-1111

Waltham/West Suburban Chamber of Commerce
500 Main Street
Waltham, MA 02154
(617) 894-4700

Watertown Chamber of Commerce
101 Walnut Street
P.O. Box 45
Watertown, MA 02272-0045
(617) 926-1017

Worcester Area Chamber of Commerce
33 Waldo Street
Worcester, MA 01608
(508) 753-2924

MICHIGAN

U.S. Department of Commerce
US&FCS District Office

1140 McNamara Building
Detroit, MI 48226
(313) 226-3650; fax (313) 226-3657

U.S. Department of Commerce
US&FCS Branch Office
300 Monroe Avenue NW
Room 406A
Grand Rapids, MI 49503
(616) 456-2411; fax (616) 456-2695

**U.S. Small Business
Administration**
515 McNamara Building
Detroit, MI 48226
(313) 226-6075; fax (313) 226-4769

**U.S. Small Business
Administration**
300 South Front
Marquette, MI 49855
(906) 225-1108; fax (906) 225-1109

**Office of International
Development**
Michigan Department of Commerce
Law Building, 5th Floor
Lansing, MI 48909
(517) 373-6390; fax (517) 335-2521

**Michigan Export Development
Authority**
Michigan Department of Commerce
Law Building, 5th Floor
Lansing, MI 48909
(517) 373-6390; fax (517) 335-2521

**Michigan Department of
Agriculture**
Office of International Trade
P.O. Box 30017
Lansing, MI 48909
(517) 373-1054; fax (517) 335-2521

City of Detroit
Community & Economic
Development Department

150 Michigan Avenue
Detroit, MI 48226
(313) 224-6533; fax (313) 224-4579

**Detroit/Wayne County Port
Authority**
174 Clark Street
Detroit, MI 48209
(313) 841-6700; fax (313) 841-6705

**Michigan State Chamber of
Commerce**
Small Business Programs
200 North Washington Square
Suite 400
Lansing, MI 48933
(517) 371-2100; fax (517) 371-7224

**Ann Arbor Chamber of
Commerce**
211 East Huron, Suite 1
Ann Arbor, MI 48104
(313) 665-4433; fax (313) 995-7283

**Greater Detroit Chamber of
Commerce**
600 West Lafayette Boulevard
Detroit, MI 48226
(313) 964-4000; (313) 964-0531

**Downriver Community
Conference**
15100 Northline
Southgate, MI 48195
(313) 283-8933; fax (313) 281-3418

Flint Area Chamber of Commerce
708 Root
Flint, MI 49503
(313) 232-7101; fax (313) 233-7437

**Greater Grand Rapids Chamber
of Commerce**
17 Fountain Street NW
Grand Rapids, MI 49503
(616) 459-7221; fax (616) 771-0318

Kalamazoo Chamber of
Commerce
128 North Kalamazoo Mall
Kalamazoo, MI 49007
(616) 381-4000; fax (616) 343-0430

Macomb County Chamber of
Commerce
10 North Avenue
P.O. Box 855
Mt. Clemens, MI 48043
(313) 463-1528

Muskegon Area Chamber of
Commerce
1065 Fourth Street
Muskegon, MI 49441
(616) 722-3751

Greater Port Huron-Marysville
Chamber of Commerce
920 Pine Grove Avenue
Port Huron, MI 48060
(313) 985-7101

Greater Saginaw Chamber of
Commerce
901 South Washington
Saginaw, MI 48606
(517) 752-7161; fax (517) 752-9055

Cornerstone Alliance
P.O. Box 428
Kenton Harbor, MI 49023
(616) 925-0044; fax (616) 925-4471

Detroit Customhouse Brokers &
Foreign Freight Forwarders
Association
1237-45 First National Building
Detroit, MI 48226
(313) 961-4130

Michigan Manufacturers
Association
124 East Kalamazoo

Lansing, MI 48933
(517) 372-5900; fax (517) 372-3322

Business & Institutional Furniture
Manufacturers Association
2335 Burton SE
Grand Rapids, MI 49506
(616) 243-1681; fax (616) 243-1011

Michigan District Export Council
c/o Arthur Anderson & Company
400 Renaissance Center, Suite 2500
Detroit, MI 48243
(313) 568-9210

Kalamazoo International Trade
Council (KITCO)
128 North Kalamazoo Mall
Kalamazoo, MI 49007
(616) 382-5966

Central Business District
Association
700 Penobscot Building
Detroit, MI 48226
(313) 961-1403; fax (313) 961-9547

President's Export Council
c/o ASC, Inc.
One Sunroof Center
Southgate, MI 48195
(313) 285-4911; fax (313) 246-0500

Port Huron Trade Center
511 Fort Street, Suite 530
Port Huron, MI 48060
(313) 982-3510

World Trade Center
150 West Jefferson Avenue
Detroit, MI 48226
(313) 965-6500; fax (313) 965-1525

International Business Centers
Michigan State University
6 Kellogg Center

East Lansing, MI 48824
(517) 353-4336; fax (517) 336-1009

West Michigan World Trade Association
17 Fountain Street NW
Grand Rapids, MI 49503
(616) 771-0319; fax (616) 771-0318

World Trade Club of Detroit
600 West Lafayette Boulevard
Detroit, MI 48226
(313) 964-4000; fax (313) 964-0531

MINNESOTA

U.S. Department of Commerce
US&FCS District Office
110 South 4th Street, Room 108
Minneapolis, MN 55401
(612) 348-1632; fax (612) 348-1650

U.S. Small Business Administration
100 North 6th Street, Suite 610C
Minneapolis, MN 55403
(612) 370-2324; fax (612) 370-2303

Minnesota Export Finance Authority
30 East 7th Street, Suite 1000
St. Paul, MN 55101
(612) 297-4659; fax (612) 296-3555

Minnesota Trade Office
30 East 7th Street, Suite 1000
St. Paul, MN 55101
(612) 297-4222; fax (612) 296-3555

Minnesota World Trade Center Corporation
30 East 7th Street, Suite 400
St. Paul, MN 55101
(612) 297-1580; fax (612) 297-4812

Minnesota World Trade Association
P.O. Box 24341
Apple Valley, MN 55124
(612) 441-9261

MISSISSIPPI

U.S. Department of Commerce
US&FCS District Office
300 Woodrow Wilson Boulevard
Suite 328
Jackson, MS 39213
(601) 965-4388; fax (601) 965-5386

U.S. Small Business Administration
101 West Capitol Street, Suite 400
Jackson, MS 39201
(601) 965-4378

U.S. Small Business Administraion
One Hancock Plaza, Suite 1001
Gulfport, MS 39501
(601) 863-4449

Mississippi Department of Economic and Community Development
P.O. Box 849
Jackson, MS 39205
(601) 359-3552

Mississippi Department of Agriculture and Commerce
P.O. Box 1609
Jackson, MS 39205
(601) 961-4725

International Trade Club of Mississippi, Inc.
P.O. Box 16673
Jackson, MS 39236
(601) 366-0331

MISSOURI

U.S. Department of Commerce
US&FCS District Office
7911 Forsyth Boulevard, Suite 610
St. Louis, MO 63105
(314) 425-3302; fax (314) 425-3381

U.S. Department of Commerce
US&FCS District Office
601 East 12th Street, Room 635
Kansas City, MO 64106
(816) 426-3141; fax (816) 426-3140

**U.S. Small Business
Administration**
1103 Grand Avenue, 6th Floor
Kansas City, MO 64106
(816) 374-6760

**U.S. Small Business
Administration**
620 South Glenstone, Suite 110
Springfield, MO 65802
(417) 864-7670

**U.S. Small Business
Administration**
815 Olive Street, Second Floor
St. Louis, MO 63101
(314) 539-6600

Export Development Office
Missouri Department of Economic
Development
P.O. Box 118
Jefferson City, MO 65102
(314) 751-4855

**Missouri Department of
Agriculture**
International Marketing Division
P.O. Box 630
Jefferson City, MO 65102
(314) 751-5611

Missouri District Export Council
7911 Forsyth Boulevard, Suite 610
St. Louis, MO 63105
(314) 425-3306

**Mid America District Export
Council (MADEC)**
601 East 121th Street, Room 635
Kansas City, MO 64106
(816) 426-3141

**International Trade Club of
Greater Kansas City**
920 Main Street, Suite 600
Kansas City, MO 64105
(816) 221-1462

**World Trade Club of St. Louis,
Incorporated**
135 North Meramec Avenue, Fifth
Floor
St. Louis, MO 63105
(314) 725-9605

MONTANA

U.S. Department of Commerce
US&FCS Branch Office
2nd Floor, Joe R. Williams
Building
700 West State Street
Boise, ID 83720
(208) 334-3857; fax (208) 334-2783

**U.S. Small Business
Administration**
301 South Park, Room 528
Helena, MT 59626-0054
(406) 449-5381

**U.S. Small Business
Administration**
2525 Fourth Avenue North
2nd Floor
Billings, MT 59101
(406) 657-6567

Department of Commerce
International Trade Division
1424 Ninth Avenue
Helena, MT 59620-0401
(406) 444-3923

NEBRASKA

U.S. Department of Commerce
US&FCS District Office
11133 O Street
Omaha, NE 68137
(402) 221-3664; fax (402) 221-3668

**U.S. Small Business
Administration**
11145 Mill Valley Road
Omaha, NE 68154
(402) 221-3604

International Division
Nebraska Department of Economic
Development
P.O. Box 94666
301 Centennial Mall South
Lincoln, NE 68509
(402) 471-3111

Omaha Chamber of Commerce
International Affairs
1301 Harney Street
Omaha, NE 68102
(402) 346-5000

**Midwest International Trade
Association**
P.O. Box 37402
Omaha, NE 68137
(402) 221-3664

NEVADA

U.S. Department of Commerce
US&FCS District Office
1755 East Plumb Lane, Room 152

Reno, NV 89502
(702) 784-5203; fax (702) 784-5343

**U.S. Small Business
Administration**
301 East Stewart Street
Las Vegas, NV 89125
(702) 385-6611

**U.S. Small Business
Administration**
50 South Virginia Street, Room 238
Reno, NV 89505
(702) 388-5268

**Commission on Economic
Development**
Capitol Complex
Carson City, NV 89710
(702) 687-4325

**Economic Development Authority
of Western Nevada**
5190 Neil Road, Suite 111
Reno, NV 89502
(702) 829-3700

Latin Chamber of Commerce
P.O. Box 7534
Las Vegas, NV 89125-2534
(702) 385-7367

Nevada Development Authority
3900 Paradise Road, Suite 155
Las Vegas, NV 89109
(702) 791-0000

Nevada District Export Council
1755 East Plumb Lane, Suite 152
Reno, NV 84502
(702) 784-5305

NEW HAMPSHIRE

U.S. Department of Commerce
US&FCS District Office

See listing for US&FCS Boston, MA

U.S. Small Business Administration
55 Pleasant Street, Room 211
Concord, NH 03301
(603) 244-4041

New Hampshire Department of Resources & Economic Development
Office of Industrial Development
172 Pembroke Street
P.O. Box 856
Concord, NH 03301
(603) 271-2591

NEW JERSEY

U.S. Department of Commerce
US&FCS District Office
3131 Princeton Pike
Building 6, Suite 100
Trenton, NJ 08648
(609) 989-2100; fax (609) 989-2395

U.S. Department of Commerce
US&FCS District Office
c/o Bergen Community College
368 Paramus Road
Paramus, NJ 07632
(201) 447-9624

U.S. Small Business Administration
60 Park Place, 4th Floor
Newark, NJ 07102
(201) 645-6065

World Trade Association of New Jersey
c/o Schering-Plough International
27 Commerce Drive
Cranford, NJ 07016
(908) 709-2632

New Jersey Division of International Trade
Department of Commerce & Economic Development
153 Halsey Street
Newark, NJ 07102
(201) 648-3518

New Jersey Small Business Development Center— International Trade (NJSBDC)
Rutgers, the State University
Graduate School of Management
180 University Avenue
Newark, NJ 07102
(201) 648-5950

Raritan Valley Community College
International Education Program
P.O. Box 3300
Somerville, NJ 08876
(908) 526-1200, ext. 312

NEW MEXICO

U.S. Department of Commerce
US&FCS Branch Office
625 Silver SW, 3rd Floor
Albuquerque, NM 87102
(505) 766-2070, fax (505) 766-1057

U.S. Small Business Administration
625 Silver SW, 3rd Floor
Albuquerque, NM 87102
(505) 766-1879; fax (505) 766-1057

Trade Division
State of New Mexico
Economic Development and Tourism Department
1100 St. Francis Drive
Joseph M. Montoya Building
Santa Fe, NM 87503
(505) 827-0307; fax (505) 827-0263

New Mexico Department of Agriculture
Marketing and Development
Division
Box 30005, Dept. 5600
Las Cruces, NM 88003
(505) 646-4929; fax (505) 646-3303

New Mexico Small Business Development Center Network
P.O. Box 4187
Santa Fe, NM 87502
(505) 438-1362; fax (505) 438-1237

New Mexico International Trade Council
P.O. Box 25381
Albuquerque, NM 87125
(505) 821-2318; fax (505) 821-2318

Greater Albuquerque Chamber of Commerce
International Trade Committee
P.O. Box 25100
Albuquerque, NM 87125
(505) 764-3700; fax (505) 247-9140

Albuquerque Hispano Chamber of Commerce
International Trade Committee
1600 Lomas Street NW
Albuquerque, New Mexico 87104
(505) 842-9003; fax (505) 764-9003

NEW YORK

U.S. Department of Commerce
US&FCS District Office
1312 Federal Building
111 West Huron Street
Buffalo, NY 14202
(716) 848-4191; fax (716) 846-5290

U.S. Department of Commerce
US&FCS Branch Office
111 East Avenue, Suite 220

Rochester, NY 14604
(716) 263-6480; fax (716) 325-6505

U.S. Department of Commerce
US&FCS District Office
Federal Office Building, Room 3718
26 Federal Plaza
New York, NY 10278
(212) 264-0600; fax (212) 264-1356

U.S. Department of Commerce
US&FCS Associate Office
216 C.E.D.C.
Jamestown Community College
Jamestown, NY 14701
(716) 665-6066

U.S. Small Business Administration
26 Federal Plaza, Room 3100
New York, NY 10278
(212) 264-4355

U.S. Small Business Administration
35 Pinelawn Road, Room 102E
Melville, NY 11747
(516) 454-0750

U.S. Small Business Administration
100 South Clinton Street, Room 1071
P.O. Box 7317
Syracuse, NY 13260-7317
(315) 423-5383

U.S. Small Business Administration
111 West Huron Street, Room 1311
Buffalo, NY 14202
(716) 846-4301

U.S. Small Business Administration
333 East Water Street

Elmira, NY 14901
(607) 734-8130

**U.S. Small Business
Administration**
445 Broadway, Room 2368
Albany, NY 12207
(518) 472-6300

**U.S. Small Business
Administration**
100 State Street, Room 601
Rochester, NY 14614
(716) 263-6700

International Division
New York State Department of
Economic Development
1515 Broadway, 51st Floor
New York, NY 10036
(212) 827-6100

International Division
New York State Department of
Economic Development
111 East Avenue, Suite 220
Rochester, NY 14604
(716) 325-1944

International Division
New York State Department of
Economic Development
16 Hawley Street
Binghamton, NY 13901
(607) 773-7813

International Division
New York State Department of
Commerce
333 East Washington Street
Syracuse, NY 13202
(315) 428-4097

**Canada-United States Trade
Center**
State University of New York at
Buffalo

130 Wilkeson Quadrangle
Buffalo, NY 14261
(716) 636-2299

**Southern Tier World Commerce
Association**
c/o School of Management
State University of New York at
Binghampton
P.O. Box 6000
Binghamton, NY 13902-6000
(607) 777-2342

**American Association of
Exporters and Importers**
11 West 42nd Street
New York, NY 10036
(212) 944-2230

**Foreign Credit Insurance
Association**
40 Rector Street, 51st Floor
New York, NY 10006
(212) 306-5000

**National Association of Export
Companies**
747 Middle Neck Road
Great Neck, NY 11024
(516) 487-0700

World Trade Institute
One World Trade Center
New York, NY 10048
(212) 466-4044

**Syracuse International Trade
Council**
Greater Syracuse Chamber of
Commerce
572 South Salina Street
Syracuse, NY 13202
(315) 470-1883

**U.S. Council of the International
Chamber of Commerce**
1212 Avenue of the Americas

New York, NY 10036
(212) 354-4480

**Albany-Colonie Regional Chamber
of Commerce**
518 Broadway
Albany, NY 11207
(518) 434-1214

**Greater Buffalo Area Chamber of
Commerce**
107 Delaware Avenue
Buffalo, NY 14202
(716) 852-7100

Long Island Association
80 Hauppauge Road
Commack, NY 11725
(516) 499-4400

**International Business Council of
the Rochester Area Chamber of
Commerce**
55 St. Paul Street
Rochester, NY 14604
(716) 454-2220

**New York Chamber of Commerce
& Industry**
One Battery Park Plaza
New York, NY 10009
(212) 493-7500

Buffalo World Trade Association
P.O. Box 39
Tonawanda, NY 14150
(716) 877-1452

**Long Island Association World
Trade Club**
Legislative & Economic Affairs
80 Hauppauge Road
Commack, NY 11725
(516) 499-4400

**Mohawk Valley World Trade
Council**
P.O. Box 4126

Utica, NY 13540
(315) 826-3600

**Tappan Zee International Trade
Association**
One Blue Hill Plaza, Suite 812
Pearl River, NY 10965-1575
(914) 735-7040

Westchester County Association
World Trade Club of Westchester
235 Mamaroneck Avenue
White Plains, NY 10605
(914) 948-6444

World Trade Club of New York
28 Vesey Street, Suite 230
New York, NY 10007
(212) 435-8335

**Western New York International
Trade Council**
P.O. Box 1271
Buffalo, NY 14240
(716) 852-7160

**Western New York Economic
Development Corporation**
Liberty Building, Suite 717
424 Main Street
Buffalo, NY 14202
(716) 856-8111

NORTH CAROLINA

U.S. Department of Commerce
US&FCS District Office
324 West Market Street, Room 203
P.O. Box 1950
Greensboro, NC 27402
(919) 333-5345; fax (919) 333-5158

**U.S. Small Business
Administration**
222 South Church, Suite 300
Charlotte, NC 28202
(704) 371-6563

North Carolina Department of Economic and Community Development—International Division
430 North Salisbury Street
Raleigh, NC 27611
(919) 733-7193

North Carolina Department of Agriculture
P.O. Box 27647
Raleigh, NC 27611
(919) 733-7912

North Carolina World Trade Association
P.O. Box 28271
Raleigh, NC 27611
(919) 794-4327

Research Triangle World Trade Center
1007 Slater Road, Suite 200
Morrisville, NC 27560
(919) 549-7467

North Carolina Port Authority Headquarters
North Carolina Maritime Building
2202 Burnett Boulevard
P.O. Box 9002
Wilmington, NC 28402
(919) 763-1621
Outside North Carolina (800) 334-0682

North Carolina Small Business and Technology Development Center
4509 Creedmoor Road, Suite 201
Raleigh, NC 27612
(919) 733-4643

NORTH DAKOTA

U.S. Department of Commerce
US&FCS District Office

See listing for US&FCS Omaha, NE

U.S. Small Business Administration
657 2nd Avenue North, Room 218
Fargo, ND 58108
(701) 237-5771

International Trade Division
North Dakota Department of Economic Development and Finance
1833 East Expressway
Bismarck, ND 58504
(701) 224-2810

Fargo Chamber of Commerce
321 North 4th Street
Fargo, ND 58108
(701) 237-5678

OHIO

U.S. Department of Commerce
US&FCS District Office
9504 Federal Building
550 Main Street
Cincinnati, OH 45202
(513) 684-2844; fax (513) 684-3200

U.S. Department of Commerce
US&FCS District Office
668 Euclid Avenue, Room 600
Cleveland, Ohio 44114
(216) 522-4750; fax (216) 522-2235

U.S. Small Business Administration
1240 East 9th Street, Room 317
Cleveland, Ohio 44199
(216) 552-4180

U.S. Small Business Administration
85 Marconi Boulevard

Columbus, OH 43215
(614) 469-6860

U.S. Small Business Administration
5028 Federal Office Building
550 Main Street, Room 5028
Cincinnati, OH 45202
(513) 684-2814

International Trade Development Office
37 North High Street
Columbus, OH 43215
(614) 221-1321

State of Ohio Department of Development
International Trade Division
77 South High Street
P.O. Box 1001
Columbus, OH 43266
(614) 466-5017

Greater Cincinnati Chamber of Commerce
Export Development and World
Trade Association
441 Vine Street, 300 Carew Tower
Cincinnati, OH 45202
(513) 579-3122

Columbus Area Chamber of Commerce
Economic Development
37 North High Street
Columbus, OH 43215
(614) 221-1321

Dayton Area Chamber of Commerce
Chamber Plaza
5th and Main
Dayton, OH 45402
513-226-8256

Columbus Council on World Affairs
Two Nationwide Plaza, Suite 705
Columbus, OH 43215
(614) 249-8450

Cleveland World Trade Association
Greater Cleveland Growth
Association
200 Tower City Center
50 Public Square
Cleveland, OH 44113
(216) 621-3300

Dayton Council on World Affairs
Wright Brothers Branch
P.O. Box 9190
Dayton, OH 45409
(513) 229-2319

Miami Valley International Trade Association
P.O. Box 291945
Dayton, OH 45429
(513) 439-9465

International Business & Trade Association of Akron Regional Development Board
One Cascade Plaza, 8th Floor
Akron, OH 44308
(216) 376-5550

Toledo Area International Trade Association
Toledo Area Chamber of Commerce
218 Huron Street
Toledo, OH 43604
(419) 243-8191

Stark International Marketing
Greater Canton Chamber of
Commerce
229 Wells Avenue NW
Canton, OH 44703
(216) 456-9654

Youngstown Area Chamber of Commerce
200 Wick Building
Youngstown, OH 44503
(216) 744-2131

OKLAHOMA

U.S. Department of Commerce
US&FCS District Office
6601 Broadway Extension
Oklahoma City, OK 73116
(405) 231-5302; fax (405) 841-5245

U.S. Small Business Administration
200 NW 5th Street, Suite 670
Oklahoma City, OK 73102
(405) 231-4301

Oklahoma Department of Commerce
International Trade and Investment Division
6601 Broadway Extension
Oklahoma City, OK 73116
(405) 841-5220

Oklahoma Department of Agriculture
Market Development Division
2800 Lincoln Boulevard
Oklahoma City, OK 73105
(405) 521-3864

Oklahoma State Chamber of Commerce
4020 Lincoln Boulevard
Oklahoma City, OK 73105
(405) 424-4003

Oklahoma City Chamber of Commerce
Economic and Community Development
One Santa Fe Plaza

Oklahoma City, OK 73102
(405) 278-8900

Oklahoma District Export Council
6601 Broadway Extension
Oklahoma City, OK 73116
(405) 231-5302

Metropolitan Tulsa Chamber of Commerce
Economic Development Division
616 South Boston Avenue
Tulsa, OK 74119
(918) 585-1201

Oklahoma City International Trade Associaion
P.O. Box 1936
Oklahoma City, OK 73101
(405) 943-9590

Tulsa World Trade Association
616 South Boston Avenue
Tulsa, OK 74119
(918) 585-1201

Small Business Development Center
6420 SE 15th Street
Midwest City, OK 73110
(405) 733-7348

Center for International Trade Development
Oklahoma State University
Hall of Fame and Washington
Stillwater, OK 74078
(405) 744-7693

OREGON

U.S. Department of Commerce
US&FCS District Office
One World Trade Center
121 SW Salmon, Suite 242

Portland, OR 97204
(503) 326-3001; fax (503) 326-6351

**U.S. Small Business
Administration**
International Trade Program
One World Trade Center
121 SW Salmon, Suite 210
Portland, OR 97204
(503) 274-7482

**Department of Economic
Development**
International Trade Division
One World Trade Center
121 SW Salmon, Suite 300
Portland, OR 97204
(503) 229-5625

Oregon Department of Agriculture
One World Trade Center
121 SW Salmon, Suite 240
Portland, OR 97204
(503) 229-6734

International Trade Institute
One World Trade Center
121 SW Salmon, Suite 230
Portland, OR 97204
(503) 725-3246

World Trade Center Portland
One World Trade Center
121 SW Salmon, Suite 250
Portland, OR 97204
(503) 464-8888

**Central Oregon International
Trade Council**
2600 NW College Way
Bend, OR 97701
(503) 385-5524

**Mid-Willamette Valley Council of
Governments**
105 High Street, SE
Salem, OR 97301
(503) 588-6177

**Pacific Northwest International
Trade Association**
200 SW Market, Suite 190
Portland, OR 97201
(503) 228-4361

Portland Chamber of Commerce
221 NW End Avenue
Portland, OR 97209
(503) 228-9411

**Southern Oregon International
Trade Council**
290 NE C Street
Grants Pass, OR 97526
(503) 474-0762

**Willamette International Trade
Center**
1059 Willamette, Room 209
Eugene, OR 97401
(503) 686-0195

PENNSYLVANIA

U.S. Department of Commerce
US&FCS District Office
475 Allendale Road, Suite 202
King of Prussia, PA 19406
(215) 962-4980; fax (215) 951-7959

U.S. Department of Commerce
US&FCS District Office
2002 Federal Building
1000 Liberty Avenue
Pittsburgh, PA 15222
(412) 644-2850; fax (412) 644-4875

**Delaware-Eastern Pennsylvania
District Export Council**
475 Allendale Road, Suite 202
King of Prussia, PA 19406
(215) 962-4980; fax (215) 951-7959

**U.S. Small Business
Administration**
475 Allendale Road, Suite 201

King of Prussia, PA 19406
(215) 962-3815; fax (215) 962-3795

**U.S. Small Business
Administration Branch Office**
100 Chestnut Street, Suite 309
Harrisburg, PA 17101
(717) 782-3840

**U.S. Small Business
Administration Branch Office**
20 North Pennsylvania Avenue
Wilkes-Barre, PA 18701
(717) 826-6495

**U.S. Small Business
Administration District Office**
960 Pennsylvania Avenue, 5th Floor
Pittsburgh, PA 15222
(412) 644-2780

**Pennsylvania Department of
Commerce**
Bureau of International
Development
433 Forum Building
Harrisburg, PA 17120
(717) 783-5107

**Pennsylvania Department of
Agriculture Bureau of Markets**
2301 North Cameron Street
Harrisburg, PA 17110
(717) 783-3181; fax (717) 234-4560

**Economic Development Council
of Northwestern Pennsylvania**
1151 Oak Street
Pittston, PA 18640
(717) 655-5581; fax (717) 654-5137

**Technology Development and
Education Corporation**
4516 Henry Street
Pittsburgh, PA 15213
(412) 687-2700

**Western Pennsylvania District
Export Council**
1000 Liberty Avenue, Room 2002
Pittsburgh, PA 15222
(412) 644-2850

**American Society of International
Executives, Inc.**
15 Sentry Parkway, Suite One
Blue Bell, PA 19422
(215) 540-2295; fax (215) 540-2290

**Berks County Chamber of
Commerce**
P.O. Box 1698
645 Penn Street
Reading, PA 19603
(215) 376-6766; fax (215) 376-6769

**Delaware County Chamber of
Commerce**
602 East Baltimore Pike
Media, PA 19063
(215) 565-3677; fax (215) 565-1606

Delaware River Port Authority
World Trade Division
Bridge Plaza
Camden, NJ 08101
(215) 925-8780, ext. 2264
fax (609) 964-8106

International Business Forum
1520 Locust Street
Philadelphia, PA 19102
(215) 732-3250; fax (215) 732-3258

**Lancaster Chamber of Commerce
and Industry**
Southern Market Center
100 South Queen Street
P.O. Box 1558
Lancaster, PA 17603-1558
(717) 397-3531; fax (717) 293-3159

Lehigh University Small Business Development Center
International Trade Development Program
30 Broadway
Bethlehem, PA 18015
(215) 758-4630; fax (215) 758-5205

Montgomery County Department of Commerce
#3 Stoney Creek Office Center
151 West Marshall Road
Norristown, PA 19401
(215) 278-5950; fax (215) 278-5944

Northern Tier Regional Planning and Development Commission
507 Main Street
Towanda, PA 18848
(717) 265-9103; fax (717) 265-7585

Pennsylvania State University Small Business Development Center
Export Development Program of South Central Pennsylvania
777 West Harrisburg Pike
Middletown, PA 17057
(717) 948-6069; fax (717) 249-4468

Greater Philadelphia Chamber of Commerce
1346 Chestnut Street, Suite 800
Philadelphia, PA 19107
(215) 545-1234; fax (215) 875-6700

Philadelphia Industrial Development Corp.
123 South Broad Street, 22nd Floor
Philadelphia. Pennsylvania 19109
(215) 875-3508; fax (215) 790-1537

University of Scranton Small Business Development Center
415 North Washington Avenue
Scranton, PA 18510
(717) 961-7577; fax (717) 961-4053

SEDA-Council of Governments
Timberhaven Road, #1
Lewisburg, PA 17838
(717) 524-4491; fax (717) 524-9190

Wharton Export Network
Wharton School
University of Pennsylvania
3733 Spruce Street, 413 Vance Hall
Philadelphia, PA 19104
(215) 898-4187; fax (215) 898-1299

Wilkes College Small Business Development Center
Hollenbeck Hall
192 South Franklin Street
Wilkes-Barre, PA 18766
(717) 831-4340

Clarion University of Pennsylvania
Small Business Development Center
Still Hall, Room 102
Clarion, PA 16214
(814) 226-2060; fax (814) 226-2636

Duquesne University
Small Business Development Center
Rockwell Hall, Room 10
600 Forbes Avenue
Pittsburgh, PA 15282
(412) 434-6233; fax (412) 434-5072

Gannon University
Small Business Development Center
University Square
Erie, PA 16541
(814) 871 -7714; fax (814) 871-7383

Greater Pittsburgh World Trade Association
3 Gateway Center, 14th Floor
Pittsburgh, PA 15222
(412) 392-4500; fax (415) 392-4520

Indiana University of
Pennsylvania
Small Business Development Center
202 McElhaney Hall
Indiana, PA 15705
(412) 357-2929; fax (412) 357-5743

North Central Pennsylvania
Regional Planning and
Development Commission
P.O. Box 488
Ridgway, PA 15853
(814) 722-6901; fax (814) 722-1552

SMC/Pennsylvania Small Business
1400 South Braddock Avenue
Pittsburgh, PA 15218
(412) 371-1500; fax (412) 371-0460

Southern Alleghenies Commission
541 58th Street
Altoona, PA 16602
(814) 2S2-3595; fax (814) 949-6505

St. Francis College
Small Business Development Center
P.O. Box 600
Loretto, PA 15940
(814) 472-3200; fax (814) 472-3154

St. Vincent College
Small Business Development Center
Fraser-Purchase Road
Alfred Hall, 4th Floor
Latrobe, PA 15650
(412) 537-4572; fax (412) 537-4554

Southwestern Pennsylvania
Economic Development District
12300 Perry Highway
Wexford, PA 15090
(412) 935-6122; fax (412) 935-6888

Greater Willow Grove Chamber of
Commerce
603 North Easton Road
P.O. Box 100

Willow Grove, PA 19090
(215) 657-2227; fax (215) 657-8564

Erie Area Chamber of Commerce
1006 State Street
Erie, PA 16501
(814) 454-7191
fax (814) 459-0241

Women's International Trade
Association
P.O. Box 40004
Philadelphia, PA 19106
(215) 922-6610; fax (215) 922-0784

World Trade Association of
Philadelphia
P.O. Box 58640
Philadelphia, PA 19110
(215) 988-0711

York Area Chamber of Commerce
13 East Market Street
York, PA 17401
(717) 848-4000; fax (717) 843-8837

PUERTO RICO/U.S. VIRGIN ISLANDS

U.S. Department of Commerce
US&FCS District Office
U.S. Federal Building, Suite G-55
150 Carlos Chardon Avenue
Hato Rey, Puerto Rico 00918-1738
(809) 766-5555

U.S. Small Business
Administration
U.S. Federal Building, Suite 691
150 Carlos Chardon Avenue
Hato Rey, Puerto Rico 00918
(809) 766-5572

Puerto Rico Department of
Commerce
Box 4275
San Juan, Puerto Rico 00936
(809) 721-3290

Puerto Rico Economic Development Administration
G.P.O. Box 2350
San Juan, Puerto Rico 00936
(809) 758-4747

Puerto Rico Chamber of Commerce
Box 3789
San Juan, Puerto Rico 00904
(809) 721-6060

Puerto Rico Manufacturers Association
Box 2410
Hato Rey, Puerto Rico 00919
(809) 759-9445

Puerto Rico/Virgin Islands District Export Council
U.S. Federal Building, Suite G-55
150 Carlos Chardon Avenue
Hato Rey, Puerto Rico 00918-1738
(809) 766-5555

Virgin Islands Department of Economic Development & Agriculture
Commissioner of Commerce
P.O. Box 6400
St. Thomas, Virgin Islands 00801
(809) 774-8784

RHODE ISLAND

U.S. Department of Commerce
US&FCS Branch Office
7 Jackson Walkway
Providence, RI 02903
(401) 528-5104; fax (401) 528-5067

U.S. Small Business Administration
380 Westminster Mall
Providence, RI 02903
(401) 528-4562

Department of Economic Development
7 Jackson Walkway
Providence, RI 02903
(401) 277-2601

SOUTH CAROLINA

U.S. Department of Commerce
US&FCS District Office
1835 Assembly Street, Suite 172
Columbia, SC 29201
(803) 765-5345; fax (803) 253-3614

U.S Department of Commerce
US&FCS Branch Office
JC Long Building
9 Liberty Street
Charleston, SC 29424
(803) 724-4361

South Carolina District Export Council
1835 Assembly Street, Suite 172
Columbia, SC 29201
(803) 765-5345; fax (803) 253-3614

U.S. Small Business Administration
Strom Thurmond Federal Building
Suite 172
1835 Assembly Street, Room 358
Columbia, SC 29202
(803) 765-5376

International Division
South Carolina State Development Board
P.O. Box 927
Columbia, SC 29202
(803) 737-0400; fax (803) 737-0481

South Carolina State Ports Authority
P.O. Box 817
Charleston, SC 29402
(803) 577-8100; fax (803) 577-8616

Jobs-Economic Development
Authority
1201 Main Street, Suite 1750
Columbia, SC 29201
(803) 737-0079; fax (803) 737-0016

Charleston-Trident Chamber of
Commerce
P.O. Box 975
Charleston, SC 29402
(803) 577-2510; fax (803) 723-4853

Greater Greenville Chamber of
Commerce
P.O. Box 10048
Greenville, SC 29603
(803) 242-1050; fax (803) 282-8549

Greater Columbia Chamber of
Commerce
P.O. Box 1360
Columbia, SC 29202
(803) 733-1110; fax (803) 733-1149

Small Business Development
Center
College of Business
University of South Carolina
Columbia, SC 29208
(803) 777-5118; fax (803) 777-4403

Low Country International Trade
Association
P.O. Box 159
Charleston, SC 29402
(803) 724-3566; fax (803) 724-3400

Midlands International Trade
Association
P.O. Box 1481
Columbia, SC 29202
(803) 822-5039; fax (803) 822-5147

Pee Dee International Trade
Association (Florence)
P.O. Box 669
Hartsville, SC 29550

(803) 383-4507, ext. 42
fax (803) 332-8003

Western South Carolina
International Trade Association
P.O. Box 2081
Greenville, SC 29602-2081
(803) 574-9540; fax (803) 574-9566

SOUTH DAKOTA

U.S. Department of Commerce
US&FCS District Office
*See listing for US&FCS Omaha,
Nebraska*

U.S. Small Business
Administration
101 South Main Avenue, Suite 101
Sioux Falls, SD 57102
(605) 336-2980

South Dakota Governor's Office
of Economic Development
Export, Trade, & Marketing
Division
Capitol Lake Plaza
Pierre, SD 57501
(605) 773-5032

Rapid City Area Chamber of
Commerce
P.O. Box 747
Rapid City, SD 57709
(605) 343-1774

Sioux Falls Chamber of
Commerce
127 East 10th Street
Sioux Falls, SD 57101
(605) 336-1620

TENNESSEE

U.S. Department of Commerce
US&FCS District Office
Parkway Towers, Suite 1114
404 James Robertson Parkway
Nashville, TN 37219-1505
(615) 736-5161

U.S. Department of Commerce
US&FCS Branch Office
Falls Building, Suite 200
22 North Front Street
Memphis, TN 38103
(901) 544-4137

U.S. Department of Commerce
US&FCS Branch Office
301 East Church Avenue
Knoxville, TN 37915
(615) 549-9268

**U.S. Small Business
  Administration**
50 Vantage Way, Suite 201
Nashville, TN 37228
(615) 736-5881

Tennessee Export Office
Department of Economic &
  Community Development
7th Floor, Rachel Jackson Building
Nashville, TN 37219
(615) 741-5870

**Tennessee Department of
  Agriculture**
Ellington Agricultural Center
P.O. Box 40627, Melrose Station
Nashville, TN 37294
(615) 360-0160

**Tennessee Small Business
  Development Center**
International Trade Center
Memphis, TN 38152
(901) 678-4174

Tennessee Export Council
Suite 114, Parkway Towers
404 James Robertson Parkway
Nashville, TN 37219-1505
(615) 736-7771

World Trade Center
1001 Market Street
Chattanooga, TN 37402
(615) 752-4316

Chattanooga World Trade Council
1001 Market Street
Chattanooga, TN 37402
(615) 752-4302

**East Tennessee International
  Commerce Council**
P.O. Box 2688
Knoxville, TN 37901
(615) 637-4550

Memphis World Trade Club
P.O. Box 3577
Memphis, TN 38173-0577
(901) 345-5420

**World Affairs Council of
  Memphis**
577 University
Memphis, TN 38112
(901) 523-6764

Mid-South Exporters' Roundtable
P.O. Box 3521
Memphis, TN 38173
(901) 523-4420

**Middle Tennessee World Trade
  Council**
P.O. Box 198073
Nashville, TN 37219-8073
(615) 736-6223

TEXAS

U.S. Department of Commerce
US&FCS District Office
1100 Commerce Street, Room 7A5
Dallas, TX 75242
(214) 767-0542; fax (214) 767-8240

U.S. Department of Commerce
US&FCS District Office
2625 Federal Building
515 Rusk Street
Houston, TX 77002
(713) 229-2578; fax (713) 229-2203

U.S. Department of Commerce
US&FCS Branch Office
P.O. Box 12728
816 Congress Avenue
Austin, TX 78701
(512) 482-5939; fax (512) 320-9674

**U.S. Small Business
Administration**
300 East 8th Street, Room 520
Austin, TX 78701
(512) 482-5288

**U.S. Small Business
Administration**
7400 Blanco, Suite 20
San Antonio, TX 78216
(512) 229-4551

**U.S. Small Business
Administration**
400 Mann Street, Suite 403
Corpus Christi, TX 78401
(512) 888-3301

**U.S. Small Business
Administration**
1100 Commerce Street, Room 3C36
Dallas, TX 75242
(214) 767-0496

**U.S. Small Business
Administration**
819 Taylor Street, Room 8A32
Ft. Worth, TX 76102
(817) 334-5613

**U.S. Small Business
Administration**
222 East Van Buren Street
Room 500
Harlingen, TX 78550
(512) 427-8533

**U.S. Small Business
Administration**
505 East Traves, Room 103
Marshall, TX 75670
(903) 935-5257

U.S. Customs Service
P.O. Box 61050
DFW Airport, TX 75261
(214) 574-2170

Texas Department of Agriculture
Export Services Division
P.O. Box 12847, Capitol Station
Austin, TX 78711
(512) 463-7624

Texas Department of Commerce
Office of International Trade
P.O. Box 12728, Capitol Station
816 Congress
Austin, TX 78711
(512) 472-5059

Texas Department of Commerce
Export Finance
P.O. Box 12728, Capitol Station
816 Congress
Austin, TX 78711
(512) 320-9662

**South Texas District Export
Council**
515 Rusk Street, Room 2625

Houston, TX 77002
(713) 229-2578

North Texas District Export Council
1100 Commerce Street, Room 7A5
Dallas, TX 75242
(214) 767-0496

City of Dallas Office of International Affairs
City Hall 5EN
Dallas, TX 75201
(214) 670-3319

Foreign Credit Insurance Association
600 Travis
Suite 2860
Houston, TX 77002
(713) 227-0987

Dallas/Fort Worth Airport Board
P.O. Box DFW
DFW Airport, TX 75261
(214) 574-3079

Export Assistance Center
Greater Austin Chamber of
Commerce
P.O. Box 1967
111 Congress, Suite 10
Austin, TX 78767
(512) 322-5695

International Committee
P.O. Box 1967
Austin, TX 78767
(512) 322-5695

Austin World Affairs Council
P.O. Box 5912
Austin, TX 78763
(512) 469-0158

Port of Beaumont
P.O. Drawer 2297
Beaumont, TX 77704
(409) 835-5367

Brownsville Economic Development Council
1600 East Elizabeth
Brownsville, TX 78520
(512) 541-1183

Brownsville Minority Business Development Center
2100 Boca Chica Tower, Suite 301
Brownsville, TX 78521
(512) 546-3400

Brownsville Navigation District
P.O. Box 3070
Brownsville, TX 78523
(512) 831-4592

Cameron County Private Industry Council
285 Kings Highway
Brownsville, TX 78521
(512) 542-4351

Texas Information and Procurement Service
601 Jefferson, Suite 2330
Houston, TX 77002
(713) 752-8477

Port of Corpus Christi Authority
P.O. Box 1541
Corpus Christi, TX 78403
(512) 882-5633

Corpus Christi Area Economic Development Corp. and Corpus Christi Small Business Development Center
1201 North Shoreline
P.O. Box 640
Corpus Christi, TX 78403
(512) 883-5571

Council for South Texas Economic Progress (COSTEP)
1701 West Business Highway 83
Texas Commerce Bank, Suite 600
McAllen, TX 78501
(512) 682-1201

Greater Dallas Chamber of Commerce
1201 Elm Street, Suite 2000
Dallas, TX 75270
(214) 746-6739

Fort Worth Chamber of Commerce
777 Taylor, Suite 900
Fort Worth, TX 76102
(817) 336-2491

Port of Houston Authority
111 East Loop North
Houston, TX 77029
(713) 670-2400

International Small Business Development Center
P.O. Box 58299
Dallas, TX 75258
(214) 653-1777

International Trade Association of Dallas/Fort Worth
P.O. Box 58035
Dallas, TX 75258
(214) 748-3777

International Trade Resource Center
P.O. Box 581249
Dallas, TX 75258
(214) 653-1113

McAllen Minority Business Development Center
1701 West Business Highway 83
Suite 1023

McAllen, TX 78501
(512) 687-5224

North Harris County College
Small Business Development Center
20000 Kingwood Drive
Kingwood, TX 77339
(713) 359-1624

Port of Port Arthur
Box 1428
Port Arthur, TX 77641
(409) 983-2011

San Antonio World Trade Center
118 Broadway, Suite 600
P.O. Box 1628
San Antonio, TX 78205
(512) 978-7601

San Antonio World Trade Association
118 Broadway, Suite 640
San Antonio, TX 78205
(512) 229-9036

International Trade Center
Greater San Antonio Chamber of Commerce
P.O. Box 1628
San Antonio, TX 78296
(512) 229-2113

Greater Houston Partnership, World Trade Division
1100 Milam Building, 25th Floor
Houston, TX 77002
(713) 658-2408

U.S. Chamber of Commerce
4835 LBJ Freeway, Suite 750
Dallas, TX 75244
(214) 387-0404

Dallas Council on World Affairs
P.O. Box 58232
Dallas, TX 75258
(214) 748-5663

UTAH

U.S. Department of Commerce
US&FCS District Office
324 South State Street, Suite 105
Salt Lake City, UT 84111
(801) 524-5116; fax (801) 524-5886

U.S. Small Business Administration
125 South State Street, Room 2237
Salt Lake City, UT 84138
(314) 524-5800

Utah Economic & Industrial Development Division
324 South State Street, Suite 201
Salt Lake City, UT 84111
(801) 538-8700

Salt Lake Area Chamber of Commerce
Export Development Committee
175 East 400 South, 6th Floor
Salt Lake City, UT 84111
(801) 364-3631

World Trade Association of Utah
324 South State Street, Suite 105
Salt Lake City, UT 84111
(801) 524-5116

Salt Lake County Inland Port
2001 South State Street, Suite S-2100
Salt Lake City, UT 84109
(801) 468-3246; fax (801) 468-3684

VERMONT

U.S. Department of Commerce
US&FCS District Office
See listing for US&FCS Boston, Massachusetts

U.S. Small Business Administration
87 State Street, Room 204
Montpelier, VT 05602
(802) 229-0538

Agency of Development & Community Affairs
Pavillion Office Building
109 State Street
Montpelier, VT 05602
(802) 828-3221

VIRGINIA

U.S. Department of Commerce
US&FCS District Office
Suite 8010
400 North 8th Street
Richmond, VA 23240
(804) 771-2246; fax (804) 771-2390

U.S. Small Business Administration
P.O. Box 10126
400 North 8th Street
Richmond, VA 23240
(804) 771-2765

Virginia Department of Economic Development
2 James Center
P.O. Box 798
Richmond, VA 23206
(804) 371-8100

Virginia Department of Agriculture
Office of International Marketing
1100 Bank Street, Suite 915
Richmond, VA 23219
(804) 786-3953

Virginia Port Authority
600 World Trade Center

Norfolk, VA 23510
(804) 771-2765

Virginia Chamber of Commerce
9 South Fifth Street
Richmond, VA 23219
(804) 644-1607

Virginia District Export Council
P.O. Box 10190
Richmond, VA 23240
(804) 771-2246

International Trade Association of
Northern Virginia
P.O. Box 2982
Reston, VA 22090

Piedmont World Trade Council
P.O. Box 1374
Lynchburg, VA 24505
(804) 528-7511

WASHINGTON

U.S. Department of Commerce
US&FCS District Office
3131 Elliott Avenue, Suite 290
Seattle, WA 98121
(206) 553-5615; fax (206) 553-7253

U.S. Department of Commerce
US&FCS Branch Office
Room 625
West 808 Spokane Falls Boulevard
Spokane, WA 99201
(509) 456-2922; fax (509) 458-2224

U.S. Small Business
Administration
915 Second Avenue, Room 1792
Seattle, WA 98174
(206) 553-8405; fax (206) 553-8635

U.S. Small Business
Administration
Farm Credit Building, 10th Floor
Spokane, WA 99204
(509) 353-2424; fax (509) 353-2829

Washington State Department of
Trade and Economic
Development
2001 6th Avenue, Suite 2600
Seattle, WA 98121
(206) 464-7143; fax (206) 464-7222

Washington State Department of
Agriculture
406 General Administration
Building
Olympia, WA 98504
(206) 753-5046

Export Assistance Center of
Washington
2001 Sixth Avenue, Suite 1700
Seattle, WA 98121
(206) 464-7123

Washington State International
Trade Fair
1020 First Interstate Center
Seattle, WA 98104
(206) 682-6900; fax (206) 682-6190

Trade Development Alliance of
Greater Seattle
One Union Square, 12th Floor
Seattle, WA 98101
(206) 389-7301; fax (206) 389-7288

Inland Northwest World Trade
Council
P.O. Box 1124
Spokane, WA 99210
(509) 456-3243; fax (509) 458-2224

Spokane International Coordinating Council
City Hall, Room 650
West 808 Spokane Falls Boulevard
Spokane, WA 99201
(509) 456-3243

Washington Council on International Trade
Suite 350, Fourth and Vine Building
Seattle, WA 98121
(206) 443-3826; fax (206) 443-3828

World Affairs Council
515 Madison Street, Suite 501
Seattle, WA 98164
(206) 682-6986

World Trade Club of Seattle
P.O. Box 21488
Seattle, WA 98111
(206) 624-9586

World Trade Center
3600 Port of Tacoma Road
Tacoma, WA 98424
(206) 383-9474; fax (206) 926-0384

International Trade Institute
North Seattle Community College
9600 College Way North
Seattle, WA 98103
(206) 527-3732; fax (206) 527-3734

WEST VIRGINIA

U.S. Department of Commerce
US&FCS District Office
405 Capitol Street, Suite 809
Charleston, WV 25301
(304) 347-5123; fax (304) 347-5408

U.S. Small Business Administration
District Office
P.O. Box 1608
Clarksburg, WV 26302
(304) 623-5631; fax (304) 623-0023

U.S. Small Business Administration
Branch Office
550 Eagan Street
Charleston, WV 25301
(304) 347-5220; fax (304) 347-5350

Governor's Office of Community & Industrial Development
International Development Division
Room 517, Building #6
1900 Washington Street East
Charleston, WV 25305
(304) 348-2234; fax (304) 348-0449

Institute for International Trade Development
Marshall University
1050 Fourth Avenue
Huntington, WV 25755-2131
(304) 696-6271; fax (304) 696-6880

West Virginia Chamber of Commerce
P.O. Box 2789
Charleston, WV 25330
(304) 342-1115; fax (304) 342-1130

West Virginia Export Council
P.O. Box 26
Charleston, WV 25321
(304) 347-5123; fax (304) 347-5408

West Virginia Manufacturers Association
405 Capitol Street, Suite 503
Charleston, WV 25301
(304) 342-2123; fax (304) 342-4552

WISCONSIN

U.S. Department of Commerce
US&FCS District Office
Room 596
517 East Wisconsin Avenue
Milwaukee, WI 53202
(414) 297-3473; fax (414) 297-3470

U.S. Small Business Administration
212 East Washington Avenue
Room 213
Madison, WI 53703
(608) 264-5261

U.S. Small Business Administration
500 South Barstow Street, Room 17
Eau Claire, WI 54701
(715) 834-9012

U.S. Small Business Administration
310 West Wisconsin Avenue
Room 400
Milwaukee, WI 53203
(414) 291-3941

Wisconsin Department of Development
123 West Washington Avenue
Madison, WI 53702
(608) 266-1767

Small Business Development Center
602 State Street
Madison, WI 53703
(608) 263-7766

Milwaukwee Association of Commerce
756 North Milwaukee Street
Milwaukee, WI 53202
(414) 273-3000

Central Wisconsin World Trade Association
P.O. Box 803
Stevens Point, WI 54481
(715) 346-2728

Northeastern Wisconsin World Trade Association
213 Nicolet Boulevard
Neenah, WI 54956
(414) 722-7758

Madison World Trade Association
P.O. Box 7900
Madison, WI 53707
(608) 222-3484

Milwaukee World Trade Association
756 North Milwaukee Street
Milwaukee, WI 53202
(414) 273-3000

Western Wisconsin World Trade Association
P.O. Box 1425
Eau Claire, WI 54702
(715) 232-2311

South Central Wisconsin World Trade Association
Small Business Development Center
University of Wisconsin—
Whitewater
2000 Carlson Hall
Whitewater, WI 53190
(414) 472-3217

WYOMING

U.S. Department of Commerce
US&FCS District Office
See listing for US&FCS Denver,
Colorado

**U.S. Small Business
  Administration**
100 East B Street, Room 4001
Casper, WY 82602
(307) 261-5761

Department of Commerce
Division of Economic and
  Community Development

Herschler Building, 2nd Floor West
Cheyenne, WY 82002
(307) 777-7284

Department of Commerce
International Trade Office
Herschler Building, 2nd Floor West
Cheyenne, WY 82002
(307) 777-7519

APPENDIX C

This list of Small Business Development Centers and subcenters is arranged alphabetically by town or city within each state. The lead office—or "Lead SBDC"—for each state is marked by an asterisk. Specialized centers—such as those targeted at high technology firms, minority-owned firms, etc.—are marked by a double asterisk.

ALABAMA

Auburn University
Small Business Development
Center
College of Business
226 Thach Hall
Auburn, AL 36849
(205) 844-4220

University of Alabama at
Birmingham*
Alabama Small Business
Development Center
1717 11th Avenue South, Suite 419
Birmingham, AL 35294
(205) 934-7260

Alabama Small Business
Procurement System**
Small Business Development
Center
1717 11th Avenue South, Suite 419
Birmingham, AL 35294
(205) 934-7260

University of Alabama at
Birmingham
Small Business Development
Center
Mathematics and Criminal Justice
Building
901 South 15th Street, Room 143
Birmingham, AL 35294
(205) 934-6760

University of North Alabama
Small Business Development
Center
P.O. Box 5017
Keller Hall
Florence, AL 35632
(205) 760-4629

North East Alabama
Regional Small Business
Development Center
225 Church Street
P.O. Box 343
Huntsville, AL 35804
(205) 535-2061

479

Jacksonville State University
Small Business Development
  Center
113-B Merrill Hall
Jacksonville, AL 36265
(205) 782-5271

Livingston University
Small Business Development
  Center
Station 35
Livingston, AL 35470
(205) 652-9661, ext. 439

University of South Alabama
Small Business Development
  Center
College of Business and
  Management Studies
BMSB 101
Mobile, AL 36688
(205) 460-6004

Alabama State University
Small Business Development
  Center
915 South Jackson Street
Montgomery, AL 36195
(205) 293-4137

CALIFORNIA

Inland Empire
Small Business Development
  Center
800 North Haven Avenue, Suite 100
Ontario, CA 91764
(714) 941-7877

Eastern Los Angeles
Small Business Development
  Center
363 South Park Avenue, Suite 105
Pomona, CA 91766
(714) 629-2247

Department of Commerce*
California Small Business
  Development Center
Office of Small Business
1121 L Street, Suite 600
Sacramento, CA 95814
(916) 324-9234

Greater Sacramento
Small Business Development
  Center
1787 Tribute Road, Suite A
Sacramento, CA 95815
(916) 920-7949

Greater San Diego Chamber of
  Commerce
Small Business Development
  Center
4275 Executive Square, Suite 920
San Diego, CA 92037
(916) 450-1518

Silicon Valley, San Mateo County
Small Business Development
  Center
380 North First Street, Suite 202
San Jose, CA 95112
(408) 298-8455

San Joaquin Delta College
Small Business Development
  Center
5151 Pacific Avenue
Stockton, CA 95207
(209) 474-5089

Solano County
Small Business Development
  Center
320 Campus Lane
Suisun, CA 94585
(707) 864-3382

Northern Los Angeles
Small Business Development
Center
14540 Victory Boulevard, Suite 200
Van Nuys, CA 91411
(818) 989-4377

COLORADO

Adams State College
Small Business Development
Center
Alamosa, CO 81002
(719) 589-7372

Community College of Aurora
Small Business Development
Center
791 Chambers Road, #302
Aurora, CO 80011
(303) 360-4745

Burlington City Hall
Small Business Development
Center
480 15th Street
Burlington, CO 80807
(719) 346-9311

Pikes Peak Community College
Colorado Springs Chamber of
Commerce
Small Business Development
Center
P.O. Drawer B
Colorado Springs, CO 80901
(719) 635-1551

Colorado Northwestern
Community College
Small Business Development
Center
50 Spruce Drive
Craig, CO 81625
(303) 824-7071

Delta Montrose Vocational School
Small Business Development
Center
1765 U.S. Highway 50
Delta, CO 81416
(303) 874-7671

Community College of Denver
Small Business Development
Center
1445 Market Street
Denver, CO 80202
(303) 620-8076

Office of Business Development*
Colorado Small Business
Development Center
1625 Broadway, #1710
Denver, CO 80202
(303) 892-3840

Fort Lewis College
Small Business Development
Center
Miller Student Center, Room 108
Durango, CO 81301
(303) 247-7188

Morgan Community College
Small Business Development
Center
300 Main Street
Fort Morgan, CO 80701
(303) 867-3351

Grand Junction Business
Incubator
Small Business Development
Center
304 West Main Street
Grand Junction, CO 81505
(303) 248-7314

Greeley/Weld Chamber of
Commerce
Small Business Development
Center
1407 Eighth Avenue
Greeley, CO 80631
(303) 352-3661

Red Rocks Community College
Small Business Development
Center
13300 West Sixth Avenue
Lakewood, CO 80401
(303) 987-0710

Lamar Community College
Small Business Development
Center
2400 South Main
Lamar, CO 81052
(719) 336-8141

Arapahoe Community College
Small Business Development
Center
South Metro Denver Chamber of
Commerce
1101 West Mineral Avenue
Suite 160
Littleton, CO 80120
(303) 795-5855

Pueblo Community College
Small Business Development
Center
900 West Orman Avenue
Pueblo, CO 81004
(719) 549-3224

Trinidad State Junior College
Small Business Development
Center
600 Prospect Street
Davis Science Building
Trinidad, CO 81081
(719) 846-5645

Colorado Mountain College
Small Business Development
Center
1310 Westhaven Drive
Vail, CO 81657
(303) 476-4040
(800) 621-1647

Front Range Community College
Small Business Development
Center
3645 West 112th Avenue
Westminster, CO 80030
(303) 466-8811

CONNECTICUT

Business Regional B.C.
Small Business Development
Center
10 Middle Street, 14th Floor
Bridgeport, CT 06604
(203) 335-3800

University of Bridgeport
Small Business Development
Center
141 Linden Avenue
Bridgeport, CT 06601
(203) 576-4572

University of Connecticut
Small Business Development
Center
Administration Building, Room 313
1084 Shennecossett Road
Groton, CT 06340-6097
(203) 449-1188

Greater New Haven Chamber of
Commerce
Small Business Development
Center
195 Church Street
New Haven, CT 06506
(203) 773-0782

University of Connecticut*
Connecticut Small Business
    Development Center
School of Business Administration
Box U-41, Room 422
368 Fairfield Road
Storrs, CT 06269-2041
(203) 486-4135

Greater Waterbury Chamber of
    Commerce
Small Business Development
    Center
83 Bank Street
Waterbury, CT 06702
(203) 757-0701

University of Connecticut/MBA**
Community Accounting Aid and
    Services
Small Business Development
    Center
1800 Asylum Avenue
West Hartford, CT 06117
(203) 241-4984

DELAWARE

University of Delaware*
Delaware Small Business
    Development Center
Purnell Hall, Suite 005
Newark, DE 19716
(302) 451-2747

DISTRICT OF COLUMBIA

Gallaudet University
Small Business Development
    Center
Management Institute
800 Florida Avenue NE
Washington, DC 20002
(202) 651-5312

Howard University*
Metropolitan Washington
Small Business Development
    Center
2600 Sixth Street NW
Washington, DC 20059
(202) 806-1550

FLORIDA

Product Innovation Center**
The Progress Center
Small Business Development
    Center
#1 Progress Boulevard, Box 7
Alachua, FL 32615
(904) 462-3942

Seminole Community College
Small Business Development
    Center
P.O. Box 150784
Altamonte Springs, FL 32715-0784
(407) 843-7001

Florida Atlantic University
Small Business Development
    Center
Building T-9
P.O. Box 3091
Boca Raton, FL 33431
(407) 367-2273

Florida Atlantic University**
Energy Conservation Assistance
    Program
Small Business Development
    Center
Building T-9
P.O. Box 3091
Boca Raton, FL 33431
(407) 367-2273

Florida Atlantic University**
Office of International Trade
Small Business Development
Center
Building T-9
P.O. Box 3091
Boca Raton, FL 33431
(407) 367-2271

Small Business Development
Center
1519 Clearlake Road
Cocoa, FL 32922
(407) 951-1060, ext. 2045

Small Business Development
Center
46 SW First Avenue
Dania, FL 33304
(305) 987-0100

Stetson University
Small Business Development
Center
School of Business Administration
P.O. Box 8417
Deland, FL 32720
(407) 822-7326

Florida Atlantic University
Commercial Campus
Small Business Development
Center
1515 West Commercial Boulevard
Room 11
Fort Lauderdale, FL 33309
(305) 771-6520

University of South Florida
Small Business Development
Center
Sabel Hall, Rooms 219 and 220
8111 College Parkway
Fort Myers, FL 33907
(813) 489-4140

Indian River Community College
Small Business Development
Center
3209 Virginia Avenue, #114
Fort Pierce, FL 34981
(305) 468-4756

Small Business Development
Center
414 Mary Esther Cutoff
Fort Walton Beach, FL 32548
(904) 244-1036

Central Florida Community
College
Small Business Development
Center
214 West University Avenue
P.O. Box 2518
Gainesville, FL 32601
(904) 377-5621

University of North Florida
Small Business Development
Center
College of Business
4567 St. John's Bluff Road South
Building 11, Room 2163
Jacksonville, FL 32216
(904) 646-2476

Brevard Community College
Small Business Development
Center
3865 North Wickham Road
Melbourne, FL 32935
(407) 254-0305

Florida International University
Small Business Development
Center
Trailer M01
Tamiami Campus
Miami, FL 33199
(305) 348-2272

Florida International University
Small Business Development
Center
NE 151 and Biscayne Boulevard
North Miami Campus
Academic Building #1, Room 350
Miami, FL 33181
(305) 940-5790

University of Central Florida
Small Business Development
Center
P.O. Box 25000
Building CEBA II
Orlando, FL 32816
(407) 823-5554

University of West Florida*
Florida Small Business
Development Center
11000 University Parkway
Pensacola, FL 32514
(904) 474-3016

Procurement Technical Assistance
Program**
Small Business Development
Center
11000 University Parkway
Building 8
Pensacola, FL 32514
(904) 474-2919

University of South Florida
Small Business Development
Center
St. Petersburg Campus
830 First Street South, Room 113
St. Petersburg, FL 33701
(813) 893-9529

Small Business Development
Center
5700 North Tamiami Trail
Sarasota, FL 33580
(813) 359-4292

Florida A&M University
Small Business Development
Center
1715-B South Gadsdey Street
Tallahassee, FL 32301
(904) 599-3407

Florida State University
Small Business Development
Center
Business Building, Room 426
College of Business
Tallahassee FL 32306
(904) 644-2053

Florida State University
(Downtown Office)
Small Business Development
Center
1605 Eastwood Office Plaza
Suite #1
Tallahassee, FL 32308
(904) 644-6524

University of South Florida
Small Business Development
Center
College of Business Administration
4202 East Fowler Avenue
BSN 3403
Tampa, FL 33620
(813) 974-4274

Small Business Development
Center
Prospect Place, Suite 123
3111 South Dixie Highway
West Palm Beach, FL 33405
(407) 837-5311

GEORGIA

Southwest Georgia Regional
Small Business Development
Center
230 South Jackson Street, Suite 333

Albany, GA 31701
(912) 430-4303

University of Georgia*
Georgia Small Business
Development Center
Chicopee Complex
1180 East Broad Street
Athens, GA 30602
(404) 542-5760

North Georgia Regional
Small Business Development
Center
Chicopee Complex
1180 East Broad Street
Athens, GA 30602
(404) 542-7436

Georgia State University
Small Business Development
Center
Box 874
University Plaza
Atlanta, GA 30303
(404) 651-3550

Augusta College
Small Business Development
Center
1180 East Broad Street
Augusta, GA 30602
(404) 737-1790

South Georgia Regional
Small Business Development
Center
1107 Fountain Lake Road
Brunswick, GA 31520
(912) 264-7343

West Central Georgia District
Small Business Development
Center
P.O. Box 2441
Columbus, GA 31902
(404) 649-7433

Decatur Area Office
Small Business Development
Center
750 Commerce Drive
Decatur, GA 30030
(404) 378-8000

Gainesville Area Office
Small Business Development
Center
Brenau College, Butler Hall
Box 4517
Gainesville, GA 30501
(404) 536-7984

Gwinnett Area Office
Small Business Development
Center
1250 Atkinson Road
Lawrenceville, GA 30246
(404) 963-4902

Central Georgia Region
Small Business Development
Center
P.O. Box 13212
Macon, GA 31209
(912) 751-6592

Kennesaw State College
Small Business Development
Center
P.O. Box 444
Marietta, GA 30061
(404) 423-6450

Clayton State College
Small Business Development
Center
P.O. Box 285
Morrow, GA 30260
(404) 961-3440

Floyd College District
Small Business Development
Center
P.O. Box 1864

Rome, GA 30163
(404) 295-6326

**Savannah District
Small Business Development
Center**
6555 Abercorn Extension
Suite 224
Savannah, GA 31405
(912) 356-2755

**Georgia Southern College
Small Business Development
Center**
Landrum Center Box 8156
Statesboro, GA 30460
(912) 681-5194

HAWAII

**University of Hawaii at Hilo*
Hawaii Small Business
Development Center**
523 West Lanikaula Street
Hilo, HI 96720
(808) 933-3515

**University of Hawaii at West
O'ahu
Small Business Development
Center**
1130 North Nimitz Highway
Suite A254
Honolulu, HI 96817
(808) 543-6695

**Maui Community College
Small Business Development
Center**
310 Kaahumanu Avenue
Kahului, HI 96732
(808) 242-7044

**Kaua'i Community College
Small Business Development
Center**

3-1901 Kaumualii Highway
Lihue, HI 96766
(808) 245-8287

IDAHO

**Boise State University*
Idaho Small Business
Development Center**
College of Business
1910 University Drive
Boise, ID 83725
(208) 385-1640
(800) 225-3815

**Idaho Small Business
Development Center**
7270 Potomac Drive
Boise, ID 83704
(208) 323-1154

**Idaho Small Business
Development Center**
1110 Airport Drive
Hayden, ID 83835
(208) 772-0587

**Idaho State University
Small Business Development
Center**
2300 North Yellowstone
Idaho Falls, ID 83401
(208) 523-1087

**Lewis-Clark State College
Idaho Small Business
Development Center**
Eighth Avenue and Sixth Street
Lewiston, ID 83501
(208) 799-2465

**Idaho State University
Small Business Development
Center**
1651 Alvin Ricken Drive
Pocatello, ID 83201
(208) 232-4921

Panhandle Area Council
Small Business Development
  Center
Sandpoint Unlimited
P.O. Box 724
Sandpoint, ID 83864
(208) 263-4073

College of Southern Idaho
Small Business Development
  Center
P.O. Box 1844
Twin Falls, ID 83303
(208) 734-9554, ext. 477

ILLINOIS

Black Hawk College
Small Business Development
  Center
207 College Avenue
Aledo, IL 61231
(309) 582-5373

Waubonsee Community College
Small Business Development
  Center
Aurora Campus
5 East Galena Boulevard
Aurora, IL 60506
(708) 892-3334, ext.141

Illinois State University
Small Business Development
  Center
c/o McClean County Chamber of
  Commerce
210 South East Street
P.O. Box 1586 (mailing address)
Bloomington, IL 61702
(309) 829-6632

Southern Illinois University at
  Carbondale
Small Business Development
  Center
Carbondale, IL 62901
(618) 536-2424

Spoon River College
Small Business Development
  Center
R.R. #1
Canton, IL 61520
(309) 647-4645, ext. 320

Kaskaskia College
Small Business Development
  Center
Shattuc Road
Centralia, IL 62801
(618) 532-2049

Parkland College
Small Business Development
  Center
2400 West Bradley Avenue
Champaign, IL 61821
(217) 351-2556

Back of the Yards Neighborhood
  Council
Small Business Development
  Center
1751 West 47th Street
Chicago, IL 60609
(312) 523-4419

Chicago Area Neighborhood
  Development Organizations
  (CANDO)
Small Business Development
  Center
343 South Dearborn Street
Suite 910
Chicago, IL 60604

Chicago State University
Small Business Development
Center
95th and King Drive
Chicago, IL 60628
(312) 995-3944

Cosmopolitan Chamber of
Commerce
Small Business Development
Center
1326 South Michigan Avenue
Chicago, IL 60605
(312) 786-0212

Daley College
Small Business Development
Center
7500 South Pulaski Road
Building 200
Chicago, IL 60652
(312) 838-0300

Eighteenth Street Development
Corporation
Small Business Development
Center
1839 South Carpenter
Chicago, IL 60608
(312) 733-2287

Greater North Pulaski Economic
Development Commission
Small Business Development
Center
4054 West North Avenue
Chicago, IL 60639
(312) 384-2262

Greater Southwest Development
Corporation
Small Business Development
Center
2358 West 63rd Street
Chicago, IL 60636
(312) 436-4448

Hyde Park-Kenwood Development
Corporation
Small Business Development
Center
5307 South Harper
Chicago, IL 60615
(312) 667-2610

Illinois International Trade
Center**
Department of Commerce and
Community Affairs
Small Business Assistance Bureau
100 West Randolph, Suite 3-400
Chicago, IL 60601
(312) 814-2092

Latin/American Chamber of
Commerce
Small Business Development
Center
2539 North Kedzie, Suite 11
Chicago, IL 60647
(312) 252-5211

The Neighborhood Institute
Small Business Development
Center
2255 East 75th Street
Chicago, IL 60649
(708) 933-2021

North River Commission
Lawrence Avenue Development
Corporation
Small Business Development
Center
4745 North Kedzie
Chicago, IL 60625
(312) 478-0202

Olive-Harvey Community College
Small Business Development
Center
10001 South Woodlann Avenue
Chicago, IL 60628
(312) 660-4839

Southeast Chicago Development
Commission
Small Business Development
Center
9204 South Commercial, #212
Chicago, IL 60617
(312) 731-8755

University Village Association
Small Business Development
Center
925 South Loomis Street
Chicago, IL 60607
(312) 243-4045

Women's Business Development
Center
Small Business Development
Center
230 North Michigan Avenue
Suite 1800
Chicago, IL 60601
(312) 853-3477

Danville Area
Small Business Development
Center
28 West North Street
Danville, IL 61832
(217) 442-7232

Richland Community College
Small Business Development
Center
One College Park
Decatur, IL 62521
(217) 875-7200

Northern Illinois University
Small Business Development
Center
Department of Management
305 East Locust
Dekalb, IL 60115
(815) 753-1403

Sauk Valley Community College
Small Business Development
Center
173 Illinois Route #2
Dixon, IL 61021-9110
(815) 288-5605

Southern Illinois University at
Edwardsville
Small Business Development
Center
Campus Box 1107
Center for Advanced Manufacturing
and Production
Edwardsville, IL 62026
(618) 692-2929

Southern Illinois University at
Edwardsville**
International Trade Center
Small Business Development
Center
Campus Box 1107
Edwardsville, IL 62026
(618) 692-2452

Elgin Community College
Small Business Development
Center
1700 Spartan Drive, Office B-15
Elgin, IL 60123
(708) 697-1000, ext. 7923

Evanston Business Investment
Corporation
Small Business Development
Center
1840 Oak Avenue
Evanston, IL 60201
(312) 866-1841

College of DuPage
Small Business Development
Center
22nd Street and Lambert Road
Glen Ellyn, IL 60137
(312) 858-2800, ext. 2771

College of DuPage**
International Trade Center
Small Business Development
Center
22nd Street Development Center
Glen Ellyn, IL 60137
(708) 858-2800, ext 3052

College of Lake County
Small Business Development
Center
19351 West Washington
Grayslake, IL 60030
(312) 223-3614

Rend Lake Community College
Small Business Development
Center
Upper Level, Student Center
Route #1
Ina, IL 62846
(618) 437-5321, ext 267

Joliet Junior College
Small Business Development
Center
Renaissance Center, Room 319
214 North Ottawa Street
Joliet, IL 60431
(815) 727-6544, ext 1313

Kankakee Community College
Small Business Development
Center
Box 888 River Road
Kankakee, IL 60901
(815) 933-0374

Blackhawk Community College
(East Campus)
Small Business Development
Center
Business Resource Assistance
Center
P.O. Box 489
Kewanee, IL 61443
(800) 798-5671, ext. 260

Lake Land College
Small Business Development
Center
South Route #45
Mattoon, IL 61938
(217) 235-3131

Mid-Metro Economic
Development Group
Small Business Development
Center
1505 West Lake Street
Melrose Park, IL 60160
(708) 343-9205

Blackhawk Community College
Small Business Development
Center
c/o Quad-Cities Chamber of
Commerce
622 19th Street
Moline, IL 61265
(309) 762-3661

Maple City Business and
Technology Center
Small Business Development
Center
620 South Main Street
Monmouth, IL 61462
(309) 734-4664

Illinois Valley Community College
Small Business Development
Center
Building 11, Route One
Oglesby, IL 61348
(815) 223-1740

Illinois Eastern Community
Colleges
Small Business Development
Center
1110 South West Street
Box 576
Olney, IL 62450
(618) 395-3011

Moraine Valley Community
College
Small Business Development
Center
Employment Training Center
10900 South 88th Avenue
Palos Hills, IL 60465
(708) 974-5468

Bradley University
Small Business Development
Center
Lovelace Hall
1501 West Bradley
Peoria, IL 61625
(309) 677-2309

Bradley University**
International Trade Center
Small Business Development
Center
Lovelace Hall
Peoria, IL 61625
(309) 677-3075

John Wood Community College
Small Business Development
Center
301 Oak
Quincy, IL 62301
(217) 228-5510

Rock Valley College
Small Business Development
Center
1220 Rock Street, Suite 180
Rockford, IL 61101
(815) 968-4087

Department of Commerce and
Community Affairs
Illinois Small Business
Development Center
620 East Adams Street, 5th Floor
Springfield, IL 62701
(217) 524-5856

Shawnee College
Small Business Development
Center
Shawnee College Road
Ullin, IL 62992
(618) 634-9618

Governors State University
Small Business Development
Center
University Park, IL 60466
(312) 534-3713

INDIANA

Greater Bloomington Chamber of
Commerce
Small Business Development
Center
116 West Sixth Street
Bloomington, IN 47404
(812) 339-8937

Columbus Enterprise
Development Center, Inc.
Small Business Development
Center
4920 North Warren Drive
Columbus, IN 47203
(812) 379-4041

Evansville Chamber of Commerce
Small Business Development
Center
SBDC Old Post Office Place
#200
100 NW 2nd Street
Evansville, IN 47708
(812) 425-7232

Forth Wayne Enterprise Center
Small Business Development
Center
1830 Wayne Trace
Fort Wayne, IN 46803
(219) 426-0040

Northlake Small Business
Development Center
504 Broadway, Suite 710
Gary, IN 46402
(219) 882-2000

Economic Development Council*
Indiana Small Business
Development Center
One North Capitol, Suite 420
Indianapolis, IN 46204
(317) 264-6871

Indiana University
Small Business Development
Center
1317 West Michriver
Indianapolis, IN 46202
(317) 274-8200

Hoosier Valley Economic
Opportunity Corporation
Small Business Development
Center
1613 East Eighth Street
P.O. Box 1567
Jeffersonville, IN 47130
(812) 288-6451

Kokomo-Howard County
Chamber of Commerce
Small Business Development
Center
P.O. Box 731
106 North Washington
Kokomo, IN 46903
(317) 457-5301

Greater Lafayette Area
Small Business Development
Center
224 Main Street
Lafayette, IN 47901
(317) 742-0095

LaPorte Small Business
Development Center
321 Lincolnway
LaPorte, IN 46350
(219) 326-7232

Madison Area Chamber of
Commerce
Small Business Development
Center
301 East Street
Madison, IN 47250
(812) 265-3127

Northwest Indiana Forum, Inc.
Small Business Development
Center
8002 Utah Street
Merrillville, IN 46410
(219) 942-3496

Muncie/Delaware County
Chamber of Commerce
Small Business Development
Center
P.O. Box 842
401 South High Street
Muncie, IN 47308
(317) 284-8144

Southern Indiana Small Business
Development Center
P.O. Box 653
1702 East Spring Street
New Albany, IN 47150
(812) 945-0054

Richmond Area Chamber of
Commerce
Small Business Development
Center
600 Promenade Street
Richmond, IN 47374
(317) 962-2887

Project Future
Small Business Development Center
300 North Michigan
South Bend, IN 46601
(219) 282-4350

Indiana State University
School of Business
Small Business Development Center
Terre Haute, IN 47809
(812) 237-3232

IOWA

Iowa State University*
Iowa Small Business Development Center
College of Business Administration
137 Lynn Avenue
Ames, IA 50010
(515) 292-6351

Iowa State University
Small Business Development Center
111 Lynn Avenue, Suite One
Ames, IA 50010
(515) 292-6355

Audubon Branch Office
Small Business Development Center
405 Washington Street
Audubon, IA 50025
(712) 563-3165

University of Northern Iowa
Small Business Development Center
Suite 5, Business Building
Cedar Falls, IA 50614
(319) 273-2696

Iowa Western Community College
Small Business Development Center
2700 College Road, Box 4C
Council Bluffs, IA 51502
(712) 325-3260

Southwestern Community College
Small Business Development Center
1501 West Townline
Creston, IA 50801
(515) 782-4161

Eastern Iowa Community College
Small Business Development Center
304 West Second Street
Davenport, IA 52801
(319) 322-4499

Drake University
Small Business Development Center
Professional and Business Development Center
Des Moines, IA 50311
(515) 271-2655

Dubuque Area Chamber of Commerce
NE Iowa Small Business Development Center
770 Town Clock Plaza
Dubuque, IA 52001
(319) 588-3350

University of Iowa Oakdale Campus
Small Business Development Center
106 Technology Innovation Center
Iowa City, IA 52242
(800) 253-7232

Kirkwood Community College
Small Business Development
Center
2901 Tenth Avenue
Marion, IA 52302
(319) 377-8256

North Iowa Area Community
College
Small Business Development
Center
500 College Drive
Mason City, IA 50401
(515) 421 -4342

Indian Hills Community College
Small Business Development
Center
525 Grandview Avenue
Ottumwa, IA 52501
(515) 683-5127

Western Iowa Tech Community
College
Small Business Development
Center
5001 E. Gordon Drive, Box 265
Sioux City, IA 51102
(712) 274-6400

Iowa Lakes Community College
Small Business Development
Center
Highway 71 North
Spencer, IA 51301
(712) 262-4213

Southeastern Community College
Small Business Development
Center
Burlington Branch Office
Drawer F
West Burlington, IA 52655
(319) 752-2731, ext. 103

KANSAS

Cowley County Community
College
Small Business Development
Center
125 South Second
Arkansas City, KS 67005
(316) 442-0430, ext. 251

Butler County Community
College
Small Business Development
Center
420 Walnut
Augusta, KS 67010
(316) 775-1124

Colby Community College
Small Business Development
Center
1255 South Range
Colby, KS 67701
(913) 462-3984, ext. 239

Dodge City Community College
Small Business Development
Center
2501 North 14th Avenue
Dodge City, KS 67801
(316) 225-1321, ext. 247

Emporia State University
Small Business Development
Center
207 Cremer Hall
Emporia, KS 66801
(316) 343-5308

Barton County Community
College
Small Business Development
Center
115 Administrative Building
Great Bend, KS 67530
(316) 792-2701, ext. 267

Fort Hays State University
Small Business Development
  Center
1301 Pine
Hays, KS 67601
(913) 628-5340

Hutchinson Community College
Small Business Development
  Center
Ninth and Walnut, #225
Hutchinson, KS 67501
(316) 665-4950

Kansas City Kansas Community
  College
Small Business Development
  Center
7250 State Avenue
Kansas City, KS 66112
(913) 334-1100, ext. 228

University of Kansas
Small Business Development
  Center
734 Vermont Street
Lawrence, KS 66054
(913) 843-8844

Seward County Community
  College
Small Business Development
  Center
1801 North Kansas
Liberal, KS 67901
(316) 624-1951, ext. 148

Kansas State University
Small Business Development
  Center
College of Business Administration
204 Calvin Hall
Manhattan, KS 66506
(913) 532-5529

Ottawa University
Small Business Development
  Center
College Avenue, Box 70
Ottawa, KS 66067
(913) 242-5200, ext. 342

Johnson County Community
  College
Small Business Development
  Center
CEC Building, Room 3051
Overland Park, KS 66210
(913) 469-3878

Pittsburg State University
Small Business Development
  Center
Shirk Hall
Pittsburg, KS 66762
(316) 231-8267

Pratt Community College
Small Business Development
  Center
Highway 61
Pratt, KS 67124
(316) 672-5641

Kansas College of Technology
Small Business Development
  Center
2409 Scanlan Avenue
Salina, KS 67402
(913) 825-0275, ext. 445

Washburn University
Small Business Development
  Center
School of Business
101 Henderson Learning Center
Topeka, KS 66621
(913) 295-6305

Wichita State University*
Kansas Small Business
Development Center
Campus Box 148
Wichita, KS 67208
(316) 689-3193

KENTUCKY

Ashland Small Business
Development Center
Boyd-Greenup County Chamber of
Commerce Building
P.O. Box 830
207 15th Street
Ashland, KY 41105
(606) 329-8011

Western Kentucky University
Bowling Green Small Business
Development Center
245 Grise Hall
Bowling Green, KY 42101
(502) 745-2901

Southeast Community College
Small Business Development
Center
Room 113, Chrisman Hall
Cumberland, KY 40823
(606) 589-4514

Elizabethtown Small Business
Development Center
238 West Dixie Highway
Elizabethtown, KY 42701
(502) 765-6737

Northern Kentucky University
Small Business Development
Center
BEP Center, Room 463
Highland Heights, KY 41076
(606) 572-6524

Hopkinsville Small Business
Development Center
300 Hammond Drive
Hopkinsville, KY 42240
(502) 886-8666

University of Kentucky*
Kentucky Small Business
Development Center
205 Business and Economics
Building
Lexington, KY 40506
(606) 257-7668

Bellarmine College
Small Business Development
Center
School of Business
2001 Newburg Road
Louisville, KY 40205
(502) 452-8282

University of Louisville**
Small Business Development
Center
Center for Entrepreneurship and
Technology
School of Business, Belknap
Campus
Louisville, KY 40292
(502) 588-7854

Morehead State University
Small Business Development
Center
207 Downing Hall
Morehead, KY 40351
(606) 783-2895

Murray State University
West Kentucky Small Business
Development Center
College of Business and Public
Affairs
Murray, KY 42071
(502) 762-2856

Owensboro Small Business
Development Center
3860 U.S. Highway 60 West
Owensboro, KY 42301
(502) 926-8085

Pikeville Small Business
Development Center
222 Hatcher Court
Pikeville, KY 41501
(606) 432-5848

Eastern Kentucky University
South Central Small Business
Development Center
107 West Mt. Vernon Street
Somerset, KY 42501
(606) 678-5520

LOUISIANA

Alexandria Small Business
Development Center
5212 Rue Verdun
Alexandria, LA 71306
(318) 487-5454

Southern University
Capital Small Business
Development Center
9613 Interline Avenue
Baton Rouge, LA 70809
(504) 922-0998

Southeastern Louisiana University
Small Business Development
Center
College of Business Administration
Box 522, SLU Station
Hammond, LA 70402
(504) 549-3831

University of Southwestern
Louisiana
Acadian Small Business
Development Center
College of Business Administration
P.O. Box 43732
Lafayette, LA 70504
(318) 265-5344

McNeese State University
Small Business Development
Center
College of Business Administration
Lake Charles, LA 70609
(318) 475-5529

Northeast Louisiana University*
Louisiana Small Business
Development Center
College of Business Administration
Room 2-57
Monroe, LA 71209
(318) 342-5506

Northeast Louisiana University
Small Business Development
Center
College of Business Administration
Monroe, LA 71209
(318) 342-1224

Northeast Louisiana University**
Louisiana Electronic Assistance
Program
College of Business Administration
Monroe, LA 71209
(318) 342-1215

Northwestern State University
Small Business Development
Center
College of Business Administration
Natchitoches, LA 71209
(318) 357-5611

Loyola University
Small Business Development
Center
College of Business Administration
Box 134
New Orleans, LA 70118
(504) 865-3475

University of New Orleans**
International Trade Center
Small Business Development
Center
368 Business Administration
New Orleans, LA 70148
(504) 286-7197

Southern University at New
Orleans
Small Business Development
Center
College of Business Administration
New Orleans, LA 70126
(504) 286-5308

University of New Orleans
Small Business Development
Center
College of Business Administration
Lakefront Campus
New Orleans, LA 70148
(504) 286-6978

Louisiana Tech University
Small Business Development
Center
College of Business Administration
Box 10318, Tech Station
Ruston, LA 71272
(318) 257-3537

Louisiana State University at
Shreveport
Small Business Development
Center
College of Business Administration
One University Place

Shreveport, LA 71102
(318) 797-5144

Nicholls State University
Small Business Development
Center
College of Business Administration
P.O. Box 2015
Thibodaux, LA 70310
(504) 448-4242

MAINE

Androscoggin Valley Council of
Governments (AVCOG)
Small Business Development
Center
125 Manley Road
Auburn, ME 04210
(207) 783-9186

Eastern Maine Development
Corporation
Small Business Development
Center
One Cumberland Place, Suite 300
Bangor, ME 04402
(207) 942-6389

Northern Maine Regional
Planning Commission
Small Business Development
Center
P.O. Box 779
Caribou, ME 04736
(207) 498-8736

University of Maine at Machias
Small Business Development
Center
Math and Science Building
Machias, ME 04654
(207) 255-3313

University of Southern Maine*
Maine Small Business
  Development Center
15 Surrenden Street
Portland, ME 04101
(207) 780-4420

Southern Maine Regional
  Planning Commission
Small Business Development
  Center
P.O. Box Q
255 Maine Street
Sanford, ME 04073
(207) 324-0316

North Kennebec Regional
  Planning Commission
Small Business Development
  Center
7 Benton Avenue
Winslow, ME 04901
(207) 873-0711

Coastal Enterprises Incorporated
Small Business Development
  Center
Water Street
Box 268
Wiscasset, ME 04578
(207) 882-7552

MARYLAND

Department of Economic and
  Employment Development*
Maryland Small Business
  Development Center
217 East Redwood Street
10th Floor
Baltimore, MD 21202
(410) 333-6996
(800) 873-7273

Central Region Small Business
  Development Center
1414 Key Highway
Suite 310, Box #9
Baltimore, MD 21230
(410) 234-0505

Montgomery College
Small Business Development
  Center
7815 Woodmount Avenue
Bethesda, MD 20814
(301) 656-7482

Western Region Small Business
  Development Center
Three Commerce Drive
Cumberland, MD 21502
(301) 724-6716

National Business League of
  Southern Maryland
Small Business Development
  Center
9200 Basil Court, Suite 210
Landover, MD 20785
(301) 772-3683

Salisbury State University
Small Business Development
  Center
1101 Camden Avenue
Salisbury, MD 21801
(800) 999-SBDC

Southern Region Small Business
  Development Center
235 Smallwood Village Shopping
  Center
Waldorf, MD 20602
(301) 932-4155
(800) 762-SBDC

MASSACHUSETTS

University of Massachusetts*
Massachusetts Small Business
Development Center
Room 205, School of Management
Amherst, MA 01003
(413) 545-6301

University of Massachusetts**
International Trade Program
Small Business Development
Center
Room 205, School of Management
Amherst, MA 01003
(413) 545-6301

University of Massachusetts**
Minority Business Assistance
Center
Small Business Development
Center
250 Stuart Street, 12th Floor
Boston, MA 02116
(617) 287-7018

Boston College
Metropolitan Boston Regional
Small Business Development
Center
96 College Road, Rahner House
Chestnut Hill, MA 02167
(617) 552-4091

Boston College
Capital Formation Service
Small Business Development
Center
96 College Road, Rahner House
Chestnut Hill, MA 02167
(617) 552-4091

Southeastern Massachusetts
University
Small Business Development
Center
200 Pocasset Street

P.O. Box 2785
Fall River, MA 02722
(508) 673-9783

Salem State College
North Shore Regional Small
Business Development Center
292 Loring Avenue, Alumni House
Salem, MA 01970
(508) 741-6639

University of Massachusetts
Western Regional Small Business
Development Center
101 State Street, Suite 424
Springfield, MA 01103
(413) 737-6712

Clark University
Central Regional Small Business
Development Center
950 Main Street
Worcester, MA 01610
(508) 793-7615

MICHIGAN

Ottawa County Economic
Development Office, Inc.
Small Business Development
Center
6676 Lake Michigan Drive
P.O. Box 539
Allendale, MI 49401
(616) 892-4120

MERRA**
Small Business Development
Center
2200 Commonwealth, Suite 230
Ann Arbor, MI 48105
(313) 930-0034

Kellogg Community College
Small Business Development
Center
450 North Avenue
Battle Creek, MI 49107
(616) 965-3023
(800) 955-4KCC

Lake Michigan Community
College
Small Business Development
Center
Corporation and Community
Development
2755 East Napier
Benton Harbor, MI 49022
(616) 927-3571, ext. 247

Ferris State College*
Small Business Development
Center
Alumni 226
Big Rapids, MI 49307
(616) 592-3553

Comercia Small Business
Development Center
8300 Van Dyke
Detroit, MI 48213
(313) 371-1680

NILAC—Marygrove College
Small Business Development
Center
8425 West McNichols
Detroit, MI 48221
(313) 345-2159

Manufacturers Reach Small
Business Development Center
1829 Pilgrim
Detroit, MI 48223
(313) 869-2120

Wayne State University*
Michigan Small Business
Development Center
2727 Second Avenue

Detroit, MI 48201
(313) 577-4848

Wayne State University
Small Business Development
Center
2727 Second Avenue
Detroit, MI 48201
(313) 577-4850

Michigan State University**
International Trade Business
Development Center
Six Kellogg Center
East Lansing, MI 48824
(517) 353-4336
(800) 852-5727

First Step, Inc.
Small Business Development
Center
2415 14th Avenue South
Escanaba, MI 49829
(906) 786-9234

Grand Rapids Community
College
Small Business Development
Center
Applied Technology Center
Grand Rapids, MI 49503
(616) 771-3600

Michigan Technological University
Small Business Development
Center
1400 Townsend Drive
Houghton, MI 49931
(906) 487-2470

Michigan Technological
University**
Forest Products Industry
Assistance Center
Small Business Development
Center
Bureau of Industrial Development
1700 College Avenue

Houghton, MI 49931
(906) 487-2470

Livingston County Small Business Development Center
404 East Grand River
Howell, MI 48843
(517) 546-4020

Kalamazoo College Small Business Development Center
Stryker Center
1327 Academy Street
Kalamazoo, MI 49007
(616) 383-8602

Handicapper Small Business Association Small Business Development Center
1900 South Cedar, Suite 112
Lansing, MI 48910
(517) 484-8440

Lansing Community College Small Business Development Center
P.O. Box 40010
Lansing, MI 48901
(517) 483-1921

Thumb Area Community Growth Alliance Small Business Development Center
3270 Wilson Street
Mariette, MI 48453
(517) 635-3561

Northern Michigan University Small Business Development Center
1009 West Ridge Street
Marquette, MI 49855
(906) 228-5571

Macomb County Small Business Development Center
115 South Groesbeck Highway
Mt. Clemens, MI 48043

Muskegon Economic Growth Alliance Small Business Development Center
349 West Webster Avenue, Room 104
Muskegon, MI 49443
(616) 722-3751

Saint Clair County Community College Small Business Development Center
323 Erie Street
Port Huron, MI 48060
(313) 984-3881, ext. 457

Saginaw Area Growth Alliance Small Business Development Center
301 East Genesse
Fourth Floor
Saginaw, MI 48607
(517) 754-8222

Downriver Small Business Development Center
15100 Northline Road
Southgate, MI 48192
(313) 281-0700

Northwestern Michigan College Small Business Development Center
1701 East Front Street
Traverse City, MI 49685
(616) 922-1719

Walsh/O.C.C. Business Enterprise Development Center
3838 Livernois Road
Troy, MI 48007-7006
(313) 689-4094

MINNESOTA

Bemidji State University
Small Business Development
Center
1500 Birchmont Drive NE
Bemidji, MN 56601
(218) 755-2750

Normandale Community College
Small Business Development
Center
9700 France Avenue South
Bloomington, MN 55431
(612) 830-6395

Brainerd Technical College
Small Business Development
Center
300 Quince Street
Brainerd, MN 56401
(218) 828-5302

University of Minnesota at Duluth
Small Business Development
Center
101 University Drive, 150 SBE
Duluth, MN 55811
(218) 726-8761

Faribault City Hall
Small Business Development
Center
208 NW First Avenue
Faribault, MN 55021
(507) 334-2222

Itasca Development Corporation
Grand Rapids Small Business
Development Center
19 Northeast Third Street
Grand Rapids, MN 55744
(218) 285-2255

Hibbing Community College
Small Business Development
Center
1515 East 25th Street

Hibbing, MN 55746
(218) 262-6700

Rainy River Community College
Small Business Development
Center
Highway 11 and 17
International Falls, MN 56649
(218) 285-2255

Mankato State University
Small Business Development
Center
Box 145
Mankato, MN 56001
(507) 389-1648

Southwest State University
Small Business Development
Center
Science and Technical Resource
Center
Marshall, MN 56258
(507) 537-7386

Minnesota Project Innovation**
Small Business Development
Center
Supercomputer Center, Suite M100
1200 Washington Avenue South
Minneapolis, MN 55415
(612) 338-3280

Moorhead State University
Small Business Development
Center
P.O. Box 303
Moorhead, MN 56563
(218) 236-2289

Pine Technical College
Small Business Development
Center
1100 Fourth Street
Pine City, MN 55063
(612) 629-7340

Hennepin Technical College
Small Business Development
   Center
1820 North Zenuim Lane
Plymouth, MN 55441
(612) 550-7153

Red Wing Technical Institute
Small Business Development
   Center
Highway 58 at Pioneer Road
Red Wing, MN 55066
(612) 388-4079

Rochester Community College
Small Business Development
   Center
Highway 14 East
851 30th Avenue SE
Rochester, MN 55904
(507) 282-2560

Dakota County Technical College
Small Business Development
   Center
1300 145th Street East
Rosemount, MN 55068
(612) 423-8262

St. Cloud University
Small Business Development
   Center
Business Resource Center
1840 East Highway 23
St. Cloud, MN 56304
(615) 255-4842

University of St. Thomas
Small Business Development
   Center
23 Empire Drive
St. Paul, MN 55103
(613) 223-8663

Department of Trade and
   Economic Development*
Minnesota Small Business
Development Center

900 American Center Building
150 East Kellogg Boulevard
St. Paul, MN 55101
(612) 297-5770

Thief River Falls Technical
   Institute
Small Business Development
   Center
Highway One East
Thief River Falls, MN 56701
(218) 681-5424

Mesabi Community College
Small Business Development
   Center
9th Avenue and West Chestnut
   Street
Virginia, MN 55792
(218) 749-7729

Wadena Technical College
Small Business Development
   Center
222 Second Street SE
Wadena, MN 56482
(218) 631-3530, ext. 371

Northeast Metro Technical College
Small Business Development
   Center
3554 White Bear Avenue
White Bear Lake, MN 55110
(612) 779-5764

Mid Minnesota Development
   Commission
Small Business Development
   Center
P.O. Box 1097
Willmar, MN 56201
(612) 235-5114

Winona State University
Small Business Development
   Center
Somsen Hall, Room 101
Winona, MN 55987
(507) 457-5088

MISSISSIPPI

Northeast Mississippi Community College
Cunningham Boulevard
Stringer Hall, 2nd Floor
Booneville, MS 38829
(601) 728-7751, ext. 317

Delta State University
Small Business Development
Center
P.O. Box 3235 DSU
Cleveland, MS 38733
(601) 846-4236

Mississippi Delta Community College
Small Business Development
Center
1656 East Union Street
Greenville, MS 38702
(601) 378-8183

Pearl River Community College
Small Business Development
Center
Route 9, Box 1325
Hattiesburg, MS 39401
(601) 544-0030

Jackson State University**
International Trade Center
Small Business Development
Center
Jackson Enterprise Center
Suite A-1
Jackson, MS 39204
(601) 968-2795

Jackson State University
Small Business Development
Center
Jackson Enterprise Center
Suite A-1
931 Highway 80 West
Jackson, MS 39204
(601) 968-2795

Mississippi Department of Economic and Community Development
Small Business Development
Center
P.O. Box 849
Jackson, MS 39205
(601) 359-3179

University of Southern Mississippi
Small Business Development
Center
USM—Gulf Park Campus
Long Beach, MS 39560
(601) 865-4544

Meridian Community College
Small Business Development
Center
5500 Highway 19 North
Meridian, MS 39307
(601) 482-7445

Mississippi State University
Small Business Development
Center
P.O. Drawer 5288
Mississippi State, MS 39762
(601) 325-8684

Copiah-Lincoln Community College
Small Business Development
Center
Natchez Campus
Natchez, MS 39120
(601) 445-5254

Hawamba Community College
Small Business Development
Center
653 Eason Boulevard
Tupelo, MS 38801
(601) 680-8515

University of Mississippi*
Mississippi Small Business
Development Center

Old Chemistry Building, Suite 216
University, MS 38677
(601) 232-5001

University of Mississippi
Small Business Development
Center
Old Chemistry Building, Suite 216
University, MS 38677
(601) 234-2120

Hinds Community College
Small Business Development
Center
1624 Highway 27
Vicksburg, MS 39180
(601) 638-0600

MISSOURI

Southern Missouri State
University
Small Business Development
Center
222 North Pacific
Cape Girardeau, MO 63701
(301) 290-5965

University of Missouri at
Columbia*
Missouri Small Business
Development Center
300 University Place
Columbia, MO 65211
(314) 882-0344

University of Missouri at
Columbia
Small Business Development
Center
1800 University Place
Columbia, MO 65211
(314) 882-7096

Mineral Area College
Small Business Development
Center
P.O. Box 100

Flat River, MO 63601
(314) 431-4593, ext. 283

University Extension**
Business and Industrial
Specialists
Small Business Development
Center
2507 Industrial Drive
Jefferson City, MO 65101
(314) 634-2824

Missouri Product Finder**
Small Business Development
Center
P.O. Box 118
301 West High, Room 720
Jefferson City, MO 65102
(314) 751-4892

Missouri Southern State College
Small Business Development
Center
107 Matthews Hall
3950 Newman Road
Joplin, MO 64801
(417) 625-9313, ext. 557

Rockhurst College
Small Business Development
Center
1100 Rockhurst Road
Kansas City, MO 64110
(816) 926-4572

Northeast Missouri State
University
Small Business Development
Center
207 East Patterson
Kirksville, MO 63501
(816) 785-4307

Northwest Missouri State
University
Small Business Development
Center
127 South Buchanan

Maryville, MO 64468
(816) 562-1701

**Three Rivers Community College
Small Business Development
Center**
3019 Fair Street
Poplar Bluff, MO 63901
(314) 686-3499

Center for Technology Transfer
Small Business Development
Center**
Room 104, Building 1
Nagogami Terrace
Rolla, MO 65401
(314) 341-4559

**University of Missouri at Rolla
Small Business Development
Center**
Engineering Management Building
Room 223
Rolla, MO 65401
(314) 341-4561

**St. Louis University
Small Business Development
Center**
3642 Lindell Boulevard
St. Louis, MO 63108
(314) 534-7232

**Southwest Missouri State
University
Small Business Development
Center**
901 South National
Springfield, MO 65804
(417) 836-5685

**Central Missouri State University
Small Business Development
Center**
Grinstead #80
Warrensburg, MO 64093
(816) 543-4402

**Central Missouri State
University**
Center for Technology
**Small Business Development
Center**
Grinstead #80
Warrensburg, MO 64093
(816) 429-4402

MONTANA

**Billings Incubator
Small Business Development
Center**
P.O. Box 7213
Billings, MT 59101
(406) 245-9989

**Gallatin Development
Corporation College
Small Business Development
Center**
321 East Main, Suite 413
Bozeman, MT 59715
(406) 587-3113

**REDI
Small Business Development
Center**
305 West Mercury, Suite 211
Butte, MT 59701
(406) 782-7333

**Dawson Community College
Small Business Development
Center**
Box 421
Glendive, MT 59330
(406) 365-2377

**High Plains Development
Authority
Small Business Development
Center**
Procurement
#2 Railroad Square Building

Great Falls, MT 59403
(406) 454-1934

Montana Department of
Commerce*
Montana Small Business
Development Center
1424 Ninth Avenue
Helena, MT 59620
(406) 444-4780

Flathead Valley Community
College
Small Business Development
Center
777 Grandview Drive
Kalispell, MT 59901
(406) 756-3833

Missoula Incubator
Small Business Development
Center
127 North Higgins, Third Floor
Missoula, MT 59802
(406) 728-9234

NEBRASKA

Chadron State College
Small Business Development
Center
Administration Building
Chadron, NE 69337
(308) 432-6282

Kearney State College, West
Campus
Small Business Development
Center
Business Development Office
Building
Kearney, NE 68849
(308) 234-8344

University of Nebraska at Lincoln
Small Business Development
Center
Suite 302, Cornhusker Bank
11th & Cornhusker Highway
Lincoln, NE 68521
(402) 472-3358
(800) 742-8800

Mid-Plains Community College
Small Business Development
Center
416 North Jeffers, Room 26
North Platte, NE 69101
(308) 534-5115

Nebraska Small Business
Development Center
University of Nebraska at Omaha
College of Business Administration
Suite 407D
Omaha, NE 68182
(402) 554-2521

University of Nebraska at
Omaha*
Nebraska Small Business
Development Center
Peter Kewit Center
1313 Farnam-on-the-Mall
Suite 132
Omaha, NE 68182
(402) 595-2381

Peru State College
Small Business Development
Center
T. J. Majors Hall, Room 248
Peru, NE 68421
(402) 872-2274
(800) 742-4412

Western Nebraska Community
College
Small Business Development
Center
Nebraska Public Power Building

1721 Broadway, Room 408
Scottsbluff, NE 69361
(308) 635-7513

Wayne State College
Small Business Development
Center
Connell Hall
Wayne, NE 68787
(402) 375-2004

NEVADA

Carson City Chamber of
Commerce
Small Business Development
Center
1900 South Carson Street, #100
Carson City, NV 89701
(702) 882-1565

Northern Nevada Community
College
Small Business Development
Center
901 Elm Street
Elko, NV 89801
(702) 738-8493

University of Nevada at Las Vegas
Small Business Development
Center
College of Business and Economics
4505 Maryland Parkway
Las Vegas, NV 89154
(702) 739-0852

University of Nevada Reno*
Nevada Small Business
  Development Center
College of Business Administration
Room 411
Reno, NV 89557-0100
(702) 784-1717

University of Nevada at Reno
Cooperative Extension Service
Small Business Development
Center
College of Agriculture
Reno, NV 89557-0016
(702) 784-1679

Tri-County Development
  Authority
Small Business Development
Center
50 West Fourth Street
Winnemucca, NV 89445
(702) 623-5777

NEW HAMPSHIRE

University of New Hampshire*
New Hampshire Small Business
  Development Center
108 McConnell Hall
Durham, NH 03824
(603) 862-2200

University of New Hampshire
Small Business Development
Center
Seacoast Subcenter
Kingman Farm
Durham, NH 03824
(603) 743-3995

Keene State College
Small Business Development
Center
Blake House
Keene, NH 03431
(603) 358-2602

North County Subcenter
Small Business Development
Center
P.O. Box 786
Littleton, NH 03561
(603) 444-1053

Merrimack Valley Subcenter
Small Business Development
Center
400 Commercial Street, Room 311
Manchester, NH 03101
(603) 625-5691

Plymouth State College
Small Business Development
Center
Small Business Development Center
Hyde Hall
Plymouth, NH 03264
(603) 536-2523

NEW JERSEY

Greater Atlantic City Chamber of
Commerce
Small Business Development
Center
1301 Atlantic Avenue
Atlantic City, NJ 08401
(609) 345-5600
(800) 252-4322

Rutgers University at Camden
Small Business Development
Center
Business and Science Building
Room 243
Camden, NJ 08102
(609) 757-6221

Brookdale Community College
Business/Management Team
Small Business Development
Center
Newman Springs Road
Lincroft, NJ 07738
(201) 842-1900, ext. 551

Rutgers University at Newark*
New Jersey Small Business
Development Center
Ackerson Hall, 3rd Floor

1800 University Street
Newark, NJ 07102
(201) 648-5950

Mercer County Community
College
Small Business Development and
Management Training Center
120 Old Trenton Road
Trenton, NJ 08690
(609) 586-4800

Kean College of New Jersey
Small Business Development
Center
East Campus, Room 242
Union, NJ 07083
(908) 527-2954

Warren County Community
College
Skylands Small Business
Development Center
Route 57 West, RD #1 Box 55A
Washington, NJ 07882
(201) 689-7613

NEW MEXICO

New Mexico State University at
Alamogordo
Small Business Development
Center
1000 Madison
Alamogordo, NM 88310
(505) 434-5272

Albuquerque Technical Vocational
Institute
Small Business Development
Center
525 Buena Vista SE
Albuquerque, NM 87106
(505) 768-0651

New Mexico State University at
Carlsbad
Small Business Development
Center
301 South Canal
P.O. Box 1090
Carlsbad, NM 88220
(505) 887-6562

Clovis Community College
Small Business Development
Center
417 Chepps Boulevard
Clovis, NM 88101
(505) 769-2811

Northern New Mexico
Community College
Small Business Development
Center
1002 North Onate Street
Espanola, NM 87532
(505) 753-7141

San Juan College
Small Business Development
Center
203 West Main, Suite 201
Farmington, NM 87401
(505) 326-4321

University of New Mexico at
Gallup
Small Business Development
Center
103 West Highway 66
P.O. Box 1395
Gallup, NM 87305
(505) 722-2220

New Mexico State University at
Grants
Small Business Development
Center
709 East Roosevelt Avenue
Grants, NM 87020
(505) 287-8221

New Mexico Junior College
Small Business Development
Center
5317 Lovington Highway
Hobbs, NM 88240
(505) 392-4510

University of New Mexico at Los
Alamos
Small Business Development
Center
901 18th Street, #18
P.O. Box 715
Los Alamos, NM 87544
(505) 662-0001

New Mexico State University at
Dona Ana
Small Business Development
Center
Box 30001, Department 3DA
3400 South Espina Street
Las Cruces, NM 88003
(505) 527-7566

University of New Mexico at
Valencia
Small Business Development
Center
280 La Entrada
Los Lunas, NM 87031
(505) 865-9596, ext. 317

Luna Vocational Technical
Institute
Luna Campus
Small Business Development
Center
P.O. Drawer K
Las Vegas, NM 88701
(505) 454-2595

Eastern New Mexico University at
Roswell
Small Business Development
Center
#57 University Avenue

P.O. Box 6000
Roswell, NM 88201
(505) 624-7133

Santa Fe Community College*
New Mexico Small Business
Development Center
South Richards Avenue
P.O. Box 4187
Santa Fe, NM 87502
(505) 438-1343

Western New Mexico University
Small Business Development
Center
Phelps Dodge Building
P.O. Box 2672
Silver City, NM 88062
(505) 538-6320

Tucumcari Area Vocational School
Small Business Development
Center
824 West Hines
P.O. Box 1143
Tucumcari, NM 88401
(505) 461-4413

NEW YORK

State University of New York
(SUNY)*
Downstate and Upstate New York
Small Business Development
Center
SUNY Plaza, S-523
Albany, NY 12246
(518) 443-5398
(800) 732-SBDC

State University of New York at
Albany
Small Business Development
Center
Draper Hall, 107
135 Western Avenue

Albany, NY 12222
(518) 442-5577

State University of New York at
Binghamton
Small Business Development
Center
P.O. Box 6000
Vestal Parkway East
Binghamton, NY 13902
(607) 777-4024

Long Island University
Small Business Development
Center
One University Plaza
Humanities Building, 7th Floor
Brooklyn, NY 11201
(718) 852-1197

State University of New York at
Buffalo
Small Business Development
Center
BA 117
1300 Elmwood Avenue
Buffalo, NY 14222
(716) 878-4030

Corning Community College
Small Business Development
Center
24-28 Denison Parkway West
Corning, NY 14830
(607) 962-9461

State University College of
Technology at Farmingdale
Small Business Development
Center
Laffin Administration Building
Room 007
Farmingdale, NY 11735
(516) 420-2765

York College/City University of New York
Small Business Development Center
Jamaica, NY 11451
(718) 262-2880

Jamestown Community College
Small Business Development Center
P.O. Box 20
Jamestown, NY 14702-0020
(716) 665-5220
(800) 522-7232

Pace University
Small Business Development Center
Pace Plaza
New York, NY 10038
(212) 346-1899

State University College at Plattsburgh
Small Business Development Center
Plattsburgh, NY 12901
(518) 564-7232

Manhattan College
Small Business Development Center
Farrell Hall
Riverdale, NY 10471
(212) 884-1880

Monroe Community College
Small Business Development Center
1000 East Henrietta Road
Rochester, NY 14623
(716) 424-5200, ext. 3030

Niagara County Community College
Small Business Development Center
3111 Saunders Settlement Road

Sanborn, NY 14132
(716) 693-1910

Ulster County Community College
Small Business Development Center
Stone Ridge, NY 12484
(914) 687-5272

State University at Stony Brook
Small Business Development Center
Harriman Hall, Room 109
Stony Brook, NY 11794
(516) 632-9070

Rockland Community College
Small Business Development Center
145 College Road
Suffern, NY 10901
(914) 356-0370

Greater Syracuse Incubator Center**
Small Business Development Center
1201 East Fayette Street
Syracuse, NY 13210
(315) 475-0083

State University Institute of Technology at Utica/Rome
Small Business Development Center
P.O. Box 3050
Utica, NY 13504
(315) 792-7546

Jefferson Community College
Small Business Development Center
Watertown, NY 13601
(315) 782-9262

NORTH CAROLINA

**Appalachian State University
Northwestern Region Small
  Business Development Center**
Walker College of Business
Boone, NC 28608
(704) 262-2095

**University of North Carolina at
  Charlotte
Southern Piedmont Region Small
  Business Development Center**
c/o The Ben Craig Center
8701 Mallard Creek Road
Charlotte, NC 28213
(704) 548-1090

**Western Carolina University
Western Region Small Business
  Development Center**
c/o Center for Improving Mountain
  Living
Cullowhee, NC 28723
(704) 227-7494

**Elizabeth City State University
Northeastern Region Small
  Business Development Center**
P.O. Box 874
Elizabeth City, NC 27909
(919) 335-3247

**Fayetteville State Continuing
  Education Center
Cape Fear Region Small Business
  Development Center**
P.O. Box 1334
Fayetteville, NC 28302
(919) 486-1727

**North Carolina A&TT State
  University
Northern Piedmont Center
  (Eastern Office)**
C.H. Moore Agricultural Research
  Center

Greensboro, NC 27411
(919) 334-7005

**Eastern Carolina University
Eastern Region Small Business
  Development Center**
Willis Building
First and Reade Streets
Greenville, NC 27834
(919) 757-6157

**University of North Carolina*
North Carolina Small Business
  Development Center**
Research Triangle Park SBDC
4509 Creedmoor Road, Suite 201
Raleigh, NC 27612
(919) 571-4154

**University of North Carolina at
  Wilmington
Southeastern Region Small
  Business Development Center**
601 South College Road
Room 131, Cameron Hall
Wilmington, NC 28403
(919) 395-3744

**Winston-Salem State University
Northern Piedmont Region Small
  Business Development Center**
P.O. Box 13025
Winston-Salem, NC 27110
(919) 750-2030

NORTH DAKOTA

**Bismarck Regional
Small Business Development
  Center**
400 East Broadway, Suite 421
Bismarck, ND 58501
(701) 223-8583

Dickinson State College
Small Business Development
Center
314 3rd Avenue West
Drawer L
Dickinson, ND 58602
(701) 227-2096

University of North Dakota*
North Dakota Small Business
Development Center
Gamble Hall, University Station
Grand Forks, ND 58202
(701) 777-3700

Grand Forks Regional
Small Business Development
Center
1407 24th Avenue South, Suite 201
Grand Forks, ND 58201
(701) 772-8502

Jamestown Area Business and
Industrial Development
Small Business Development
Center
121 First Avenue West
P.O. Box 1530
Jamestown, ND 58402
(701) 252-9243

Minot Chamber of Commerce
Small Business Development
Center
1020 20th Avenue Southwest
P.O. Box 940
Minot, ND 58702
(701) 852-8861

OHIO

Akron Regional Development
Board
Small Business Development
Center
One Cascade Plaza, 8th Floor

Akron, OH 44308
(216) 379-3170

Akron-WEGO
Small Business Development
Center
58 West Center Street
P.O. Box 544
Akron, OH 44309
(216) 535-9346

Northwest Technical College
Small Business Development
Center
State Route One, Box 246-A
Archbold, OH 43502
(419) 267-5511

Ohio University Innovation
Center**
Small Business Development
Center
1 President Street
Athens, OH 45701
(614) 593-1797

Athens Small Business
Development Center
900 East State Street
Athens, OH 45701
(614) 592-1188

WSOS Community Action
Commission, Inc.
Small Business Development
Center
P.O. Box 48
118 East Oak Street
Bowling Green, OH 43402
(419) 352-7469

Wright State University Lake
Campus
Small Business Development
Center
7600 State Route 703
Celina, OH 45822
(419) 586-2365

Chillicothe-Ross Chamber of
Commerce
Small Business Development
Center
165 South Paint Street
Chillicothe, OH 45601
(614) 772-4530

Cincinnati Small Business
Development Center
IAMS Research Park—MC189
1111 Edison Avenue
Cincinnati, OH 45216
(513) 948-2082

Clermont County Chamber of
Commerce
Small Business Development
Center
4440 Glen Este-Withamsville Road
Cincinnati, OH 45245
(513) 753-7141

Greater Cleveland Growth
Association
Small Business Development
Center
200 Tower City Center
50 Public Square
P.O. Box 94095
Cleveland, OH 44115
(216) 621-3300

Columbus Area Chamber of
Commerce
Small Business Development
Center
37 North High Street
Columbus, OH 43216
(614) 221-1321

Ohio Department of
Development*
Ohio Small Business Development
Center
30 East Broad Street
P.O. Box 1001

Columbus, OH 43226
(614) 466-2711

Coshocton Area Chamber of
Commerce
Small Business Development
Center
124 Chestnut Street
Coshocton, OH 43812
(614) 622-5411

Dayton Area Chamber of
Commerce
Small Business Development
Center
Chamber Plaza
5th and Main
Dayton, OH 45402
(513) 226-8230

Terra Technical College
Small Business Development
Center
1220 Cedar Street
Fremont, OH 43420
(419) 332-1002

Lima Technical College
Small Business Development
Center
Perry Building
545 West Market Street, Suite 305
Lima, OH 45801
(419) 229-5320

Ashtabula County Economic
Development Council, Inc.
Small Business Development
Center
36 West Walnut Street
Jefferson, OH 44047
(216) 576-9126

Logan-Hocking Chamber of
Commerce
Small Business Development
Center
11½ West Main Street

Box 838
Logan, OH 43138
(614) 385-7259

Lorain County Chamber of
Commerce
Small Business Development
Center
6100 South Broadway
Lorain, OH 44053
(216) 246-2833

Mid-Ohio Small Business
Development Center
193 North Main Street
Mansfield, OH 44902
(419) 525-1614

Marietta College
Small Business Development
Center
Marietta, OH 45750
(614) 374-4649

Marion Area Chamber of
Commerce
Small Business Development
Center
206 Prospect Street
Marion, OH 45750
(513) 382-2181

Lakeland Community College
Lake County Economic
Development Center
Small Business Development
Center
Mentor, OH 44080
(216) 951-1290

Tuscarawas Chamber of
Commerce
Small Business Development
Center
1323 Fourth Street NW
P.O. Box 232
New Philadelphia, OH 44663
(216) 343-4474

Miami University
Department of Decision Sciences
Small Business Development
Center
336 Upham Hall
Oxford, OH 45056
(513) 529-4841

Upper Valley Joint Vocational
School
Small Business Development
Center
8811 Career Drive
North Country Road 25-A
Piqua, OH 45356
(513) 779-8419

Portsmouth Area Chamber of
Commerce
Small Business Development
Center
P.O. Box 509
Portsmouth, OH 45662
(614) 353-1116

Department of Development of
the CIC of Belmont County
Small Business Development
Center
100 East Main Street
St. Clairsville, OH 43950
(614) 695-9678

Sandusky City Schools
Small Business Development
Center
407 Decatur Street
Sandusky, OH 44870
(800) 548-6507

Lawrence County Chamber of
Commerce
Small Business Development
Center
U.S. Route 52 and Solida Road
P.O. Box 488
Southpoint, OH 45680
(614) 894-3838

Greater Steubenville Chamber of Commerce
Small Business Development Center
630 Market Street
P.O. Box 278
Steubenville, OH 43952
(614) 282-6226

Toledo Area Chamber of Commerce
Small Business Development Center
218 North Huron Street
Toledo, OH 43602
(419) 243-8191

Youngstown State University
Cushwa Center
Small Business Development Center
Youngstown, OH 44555
(216) 742-3495

Zanesville Area Chamber of Commerce
Small Business Development Center
217 North Fifth Street
Zanesville, OH 43701
(614) 452-4868

OKLAHOMA

East Central University
Small Business Development Center
1036 East 10th
Ada, OK 74820
(405) 436-3190

Northwestern Oklahoma State University
Small Business Development Center
Alva, OK 73717

(405) 327-1700
(405) 327-5883

Southeastern Oklahoma State University*
Oklahoma Small Business Development Center
517 University
Durant, OK 74701
(405) 924-0277
(800) 522-6154

University of Central Oklahoma
Small Business Development Center
100 North Boulevard
Edmond, OK 73034
(405) 359-1968

Phillips University
Small Business Development Center
100 South University Avenue
Enid, OK 73701
(405) 242-7989

Langston University**
Minority Assistance Center
Small Business Development Center
P.O. Box 667
Langston, OK 73050
(405) 466-3256

American National Bank Building
Small Business Development Center
601 Southwest D, Suite 209
Lawton, OK 73501
(405) 248-4946

Rose State College**
Small Business Development Center
6420 Southeast 15th Street
Midwest City, OK 73110
(405) 733-7348

Albert Junior College
Small Business Development
Center
1507 South McKenna
Poteau, OK 74953
(918) 647-4019

Northeastern Oklahoma State
University
Small Business Development
Center
Tahlequah, OK 74464
(918) 458-0802

Tulsa State Office Building
Small Business Development
Center
440 South Houston, Suite 206
Tulsa, OK 74107
(918) 581-2502

Southwestern Oklahoma State
University
Small Business Development
Center
100 Campus Drive
Weatherford, OK 73096
(405) 744-1040

OREGON

Linn-Benton Community College
Small Business Development
Center
6500 SW Pacific Boulevard
Albany, OR 97321
(503) 967-6112

Southern Oregon State College/
Ashland
Small Business Development
Center
Regional Service Institute
Ashland, OR 97520
(503) 482-5838

Central Oregon Community
College
Small Business Development
Center
2600 NW College Way
Bend, OR 97701
(503) 385-5524

Southwestern Oregon Community
College
Small Business Development
Center
340 Central
Coos Bay, OR 97420
(503) 267-2300

Lane Community College*
Oregon Small Business
Development Center
99 West Tenth, Suite 216
Eugene, OR 97401
(503) 726-2250

Lane Community College
Small Business Development
Center
1059 Williamette Street
Eugene, OR 97401
(503) 726-2255

Rouge Community College
Small Business Development
Center
290 Northeast C Street
Grants Pass, OR 97526
(503) 474-0762

Mount Hood Community College
Small Business Development
Center
323 NE Roberts Street
Gresham, OR 97030
(503) 667-7658

Oregon Institute of Technology
Small Business Development
Center
3201 Campus Drive, South 314
Klamath Falls, OR 97601
(503) 885-1760

Eastern Oregon State College
Small Business Development
Center
Regional Services Institute
LaGrande, OR 97850
(800) 452-8639

Oregon Coast Community College
Service District
Small Business Development
Center
P.O. Box 419
4157 NW Highway 101
Lincoln City, OR 97367
(503) 994-4166

Southern Oregon State College/
Medford
Small Business Development
Center
Regional Services Institute
229 North Bartlett
Medford, OR 97501
(503) 772-3478

Clackamas Community College
Small Business Development
Center
7616 SE Harmony Road
Milwaukie, OR 97222
(503) 656-4447

Treasure Valley Community
College
Small Business Development
Center
88 SW Third Avenue
Ontario, OR 97914
(503) 889-2617

Blue Mountain Community
College
Small Business Development
Center
37 SE Dorian
Pendleton, OR 97801
(503) 276-6233

Portland Community College
Small Business Development
Center
123 NW 2nd Avenue, Suite 321
Portland, OR 97209
(503) 273-2828

Portland Community College**
Small Business International
Trade Program
121 SW Salmon Street, Suite 210
Portland, OR 97204
(503) 274-7482

Umpqua Community College
Small Business Development
Center
744 SE Rose
Roseburg, OR 97470
(503) 672-2535

Chemeketa Community College
Small Business Development
Center
365 Ferry Street SE
Salem, OR 97301
(503) 399-5181

Clatstop Community College
Small Business Development
Center
1240 South Holladay
Seaside, OR 97138
(503) 738-3347

Columbia George Community
  College
Small Business Development
  Center
212 Washington
The Dalles, OR 97058
(503) 296-1173

Tillamook Bay Community
  College
Small Business Development
  Center
401 B Main Street
Tillamook, OR 97141
(503) 842-2551

PENNSYLVANIA

Lehigh University
Small Business Development
  Center
301 Broadway, Route 230
Bethlehem, PA 18015
(215) 758-3980

Clarion University of
  Pennsylvania
Small Business Development
  Center
Dana Still Building
Clarion, PA 16214
(814) 226-2060

Gannon University
Small Business Development
  Center
Carlisle Building, 3rd Floor
Erie, PA 16541
(814) 871-7714

St. Vincent College
Small Business Development
  Center
Alfred Hall, 4th Floor
Latrobe, PA 15650
(412) 537-4572

Bucknell University
Small Business Development
  Center
126 Dana Engineering Building
Lewisburg, PA 17837
(717) 524-1249

St. Francis College
Small Business Development
  Center
Business Resource Center
Loretto, PA 15940
(814) 472-3200

Pennsylvania State University
Small Business Development
  Center
The Capital College
Crags Building, Route 230
Middletown, PA 17057
(717) 948-6069

LaSalle University
Small Business Development
  Center
19th and West Olney Avenue
Box 365
Philadelphia, PA 19141
(215) 951-1416

Temple University
Small Business Development
  Center
Room 6, Speakman Hall, 006-00
Philadelphia, PA 19122
(215) 787-7282

University of Pennsylvania*
Pennsylvania Small Business
  Development Center
The Wharton School
444 Vance Hall
3733 Spruce Street
Philadelphia, PA 19104
(215) 898-1219

University of Pennsylvania
Small Business Development
Center
The Wharton School
409 Vance Hall
Philadelphia, PA 19194
(215) 898-4861

Dequesne University
Small Business Development
Center
Rockwell Hall, Room 10
Concourse
600 Forbes Avenue
Pittsburgh, PA 15282
(412) 434-6233

University of Pittsburgh
Small Business Development
Center
Room 343 Mervis Hall
Pittsburgh, PA 15260
(412) 648-1544

University of Scranton
Small Business Development
Center
St. Thomas Hall, Room 588
Scranton, PA 18510
(717) 941-7588

Wilkes College
Small Business Development
Center
Hollenback Hall
192 South Franklin Street
Wilkes-Barre, PA 18766
(717) 824-4651, ext. 4340

PUERTO RICO

University of Puerto Rico
Humacao Small Business
Development Center
Antonio Lopez Street
Casa Roig Annex

Box 10226—CUH Station
Humacao, PR 00661
(809) 850-2500

Interamerican University
San Juan Metro II
Small Business Development
Center
One Francisco Sein Street
Casa Llompart
Box 1293
Hato Rey, PR 00919
(809) 765-2335

University of Puerto Rico*
Puerto Rico Small Business
Development Center
Mayaguez Campus
Box 5253—College Station
Mayaguez, PR 00680
(809) 834-3590

University of Puerto Rico
Small Business Development
Center
San Juan Metro I
11 Margarida Street
Box 21417—U.P.R. Station
Rio Piedras, PR 00918
(809) 763-5880
(809) 763-5933

RHODE ISLAND

University of Rhode Island
Small Business Development
Center
24 Woodward Hall
Kingston, RI 02881
(401) 792-2451

Community College of Rhode
Island
Small Business Development
Center
One Hilton Street

Providence, RI 02905
(401) 455-6042

**Downtown Providence Small
Business Development Center**
270 Weybosset Street
Providence, RI 02903
(401) 831-1330

Bryant College*
**Rhode Island Small Business
Development Center**
1150 Douglas Pike, Route 7
Smithfield, RI 02917
(401) 232-6111

**Opportunities Industrialization
Center**
**Small Business Development
Center**
One Hilton Street
South Providence, RI 02905
(401) 272-4400

SOUTH CAROLINA

**University of South Carolina at
Beaufort**
**Small Business Development
Center**
800 Carteret Street
Beaufort, SC 29902
(803) 524-7112, ext. 4143

Trident Technical College
**Small Business Development
Center**
66 Columbus Street
P.O. Box 20339
Charleston, SC 29413
(803) 727-2020

Clemson University
**Small Business Development
Center**
College of Commerce and Industry

425 Sirrine Hall
Clemson, SC 29634
(803) 656-3227

University of South Carolina*
**South Carolina Small Business
Development Center**
College of Business Administration
1710 College Street
Columbia, SC 29208
(803) 777-5118

Coastal Carolina College
**Small Business Development
Center**
School of Business Administration
Conway, SC 29527
(803) 347-2169

**Florence Darlington Technical
College**
**Small Business Development
Center**
P.O. Box 100548
Florence, SC 29501
(803) 661-8324

Greenville Technical College
**Small Business Development
Center**
Station B GHEC
Box 5616
Greenville, SC 29606
(803) 271-4259

**Upper Savannah Council of
Government**
**Small Business Development
Center**
Exchange Building
222 Phoenix Street, Suite 200
Greenwood, SC 29648
(803) 227-6110

**Aiken/North Augusta Small
Business Development Center**
Triangle Plaza, Highway 25

North Augusta, SC 29841
(803) 442-3670

South Carolina State College
Small Business Development
Center
School of Business Administration
P.O. Box 1676
Orangeburg, SC 29117
(803) 536-8445

Winthrop College
Small Business Development
Center
School of Business Administration
119 Thurman Building
Rock Hill, SC 29733
(803) 323-2283

Spartanburg Chamber of
Commerce
Small Business Development
Center
P.O. Box 1636
Spartanburg, SC 29304
(803) 594-5080

SOUTH DAKOTA

Aberdeen Small Business
Development Center
226 Citizens Building
Aberdeen, SD 57401
(605) 622-2252

Pierre Small Business
Development Center
105 South Euclid, Suite C
Pierre, SD 57501
(605) 773-5941

Rapid City Small Business
Development Center
2525 West Main, Suite 105
P.O. Box 7715

Rapid City, SD 57709
(605) 394-5311

Sioux Falls Small Business
Development Center
231 South Phillips, Room 365
Sioux Falls, SD 57101
(605) 339-3366

University of South Dakota*
South Dakota Small Business
Development Center
School of Business
414 East Clark, Patterson 115
Vermillion, SD 57069
(605) 677-5272

TENNESSEE

Tennessee Technological
University
Small Business Development
Center
College of Business Administration
P.O. Box 5023
Cookeville, TN 38505
(615) 372-3648

Dyersburg State Community
College
Small Business Development
Center
Office of Extension Services
P.O. Box 648
Dyersburg, TN 38024
(901) 286-3201

East Tennessee State University
Small Business Development
Center
College of Business
P.O. Box 23, 440A
Johnson City, TN 37614
(615) 929-5630

**Pellissippi State Technical
   Community College
Small Business Development
   Center**
Business/Industrial Services
P.O. Box 22990
Knoxville, TN 37933
(615) 694-6660

**University of Tennessee at Martin
Small Business Development
   Center**
School of Business Administration
402 Elm Street
Martin, TN 38237
(901) 587-7236

**Memphis State University*
Tennessee Small Business
   Development Center**
Memphis, TN 38152
(901) 678-2500

Memphis State University
International Trade Center
Tennessee Small Business
   Development Center**
320 South Dudley Street
Memphis, TN 38152
(901) 678-4174

**Walters State Community College
Small Business Development
   Center**
Business/Industrial Services
500 South Davy Crockett Parkway
Morristown, TN 37813
(615) 587-9722, ext. 447

**Middle Tennessee State University
Small Business Development
   Center**
School of Business
P.O. Box 487
Murfreesboro, TN 37132
(615) 898-2745

**Tennessee State University
Small Business Development
   Center**
School of Business
10th and Charlotte Avenue
Nashville, TN 37203
(615) 251-1178

TEXAS

**Abilene Christian University
Small Business Development
   Center**
College of Business Administration
ACU Station, Box 8307
Abilene, TX 79699
(915) 674-2776

**Alvin Community College
Small Business Development
   Center**
3110 Mustang Road
Alvin, TX 77511
(713) 388-4686

**West Texas State University
Small Business Development
   Center**
T. Boone Pickens School of
   Business
1800 South Washington, Suite 110
Amarillo, TX 79102
(806) 372-5151

**Trinity Valley Community College
Small Business Development
   Center**
500 South Prairieville
Athens, TX 75751
(214) 675-6230

**Texas Small Business
   Development Center**
Chamber of Commerce
221 South IH35, Suite #103

Austin, TX 78741
(512) 473-3510

Lee College
Small Business Development
Center
511 South Whiting Street
Rundell Hall
Baytown, TX 77520
(713) 425-6309

Lamar University
Small Business Development
Center
855 Florida Avenue
Beaumont, TX 77705
(409) 880-2367
(800) 722-3443

Blinn College
Small Business Development
Center
902 College Avenue
Brenham, TX 77833
(409) 830-4137

Bryan/College Station Chamber of
Commerce
Small Business Development
Center
401 South Washington
Bryan, TX 77803
(409) 823-3034

Texas Engineering Experiment
Station
Small Business Development
Center
310 Engineering Research Center
College Station, TX 77843
(409) 845-0538

Navarro Small Business
Development Center
120 North 12th Street
Corsicana, TX 75110
(903) 874-0658

Corpus Christi Chamber of
Commerce
Small Business Development
Center
1201 North Shoreline
Corpus Christi, TX 78403
(512) 882-6161

Dallas County Community
College*
Northeastern Texas Small
Business Development Center
1402 Corinth Street
Dallas, TX 75215
(214) 747-0555

International Trade Center**
Small Business Development
Center
World Trade Center, Suite #150
2050 Stemmons Freeway
P.O. Box 58299
Dallas, TX 75258
(214) 653-1777

Grayson County College
Small Business Development
Center
6101 Grayson Drive
Denison, TX 75020
(214) 465-6030
(903) 463-8654

University of Texas–Pan
American
Small Business Development
Center
1201 West University Drive
Edinburg, TX 78539
(512) 381-3361

El Paso Community College
Small Business Development
Center
103 Montana Avenue, Room 202
El Paso, TX 79902
(915) 534-3410

Tarrant County Junior College
Small Business Development
Center
Mary Owen Center
1500 Houston Street, Room 163
Fort Worth, TX 76102
(817) 877-9254

Cooke County Community
College
Small Business Development
Center
1525 West California
Gainesville, TX 76240
(817) 665-4785

Galveston College
Small Business Development
Center
4015 Avenue Q
Galveston, TX 77550
(409) 740-7380

University of Houston*
Texas Small Business
Development Center
Park 601 Jefferson, Suite 2330
Houston, TX 77002
(713) 752-8444

University of Houston**
Texas Information Procurement
Service
401 Louisiana Street, 7th Floor
Houston, TX 77002
(713) 752-8477
(800) 252-7232

University of Houston**
International Trade Center
601 Jefferson, Suite 2330
Houston, TX 77002
(713) 752-8404

University of Houston
Texas Product Development
Center
401 Louisiana, 7th Floor

Houston, TX 77002
(713) 752-8400

Central Texas Small Business
Development Center
P.O. Box 1800
Killeen, TX 76540
(817) 609-8848

Kingsville Chamber of Commerce
Small Business Development
Center
635 East King
Kingsville, TX 78363
(512) 592-6438

North Harris Montgomery
Community College District
Small Business Development
Center
Administration Building
20000 Kingwood Drive, Room 104
Kingwood, TX 77339
(713) 359-1677
(800) 443-SBDC

Brazoport College
Small Business Development
Center
500 College Drive
Lake Jackson, TX 77566
(409) 265-6131, ext. 380

Laredo Development Foundation
Small Business Development
Center
Division of Business Administration
616 Leal Street
Laredo, TX 78041
(512) 722-0563

Kilgore College
Small Business Development
Center
300 South High
Longview, TX 75601
(903) 753-2643

Texas Tech University*
Northwestern Texas Small
Business Development Center
Center for Innovation
2579 South Loop 289, Suite 210
Lubbock, TX 79423
(806) 745-1637

Angelina Chamber of Commerce
Small Business Development
Center
1615 South Chestnut
P.O. Box 1606
Lufkin, TX 75901
(409) 634-1887

Northeast/Texarkana
Small Business Development
Center
P.O. Box 1307
Mt. Pleasant, TX 75455
(214) 572-1911

University of Texas/Permian Basin
Small Business Development
Center
College of Management
4901 East University, Room 298
Odessa, TX 79762
(915) 563-0400

Paris Junior College
Small Business Development
Center
Alford Learning Center
2400 Clarksville Street
Paris, TX 75460
(903) 784-1802

Angelo State University
Small Business Development
Center
2610 West Avenue N
Campus Box 10910
San Angelo, TX 70909
(915) 942-2098

University of Texas at San
Antonio*
South Texas Border Small
Business Development Center
College of Business
San Antonio, TX 78249
(512) 224-0791

Houston Community College
Small Business Development
Center
13600 Murphy Road
Stafford, TX 77477
(713) 499-4870

Tarleton State University
Small Business Development
Center
School of Business
Box T-158
Stephenville, TX 76402
(817) 968-9330

College of the Mainland
Small Business Development
Center
8419 Emmett F. Lowry Expressway
Texas City, TX 77591
(409) 938-7578

Tyler Junior College
Small Business Development
Center
1530 South SW Loop 323
Suite 100
Tyler, TX 75701
(903) 510-2975

University of Houston
Small Business Development
Center
700 Main Center, Suite 102
Victoria, TX 77901
(512) 575-8944

McLennan Community College
Small Business Development
 Center
4601 North 19th Street, Suite A-15
Waco, TX 76708
(817) 750-3600

Wharton County Junior College
Small Business Development
 Center
Administration Building, Room 102
911 Boling Highway
Wharton, TX 77488
(409) 532-2201

Midwestern State University
Small Business Development
 Center
Division of Business Administration
3400 Taft Boulevard
Wichita Falls, TX 76308
(817) 696-6738

UTAH

Southern Utah University
Small Business Development
 Center
351 West Center
Cedar City, UT 84720
(801) 586-5401

Snow College
Small Business Development
 Center
345 West First North
Ephraim, UT 84627
(801) 283-4021

Utah State University
Small Business Development
 Center
East Campus Building
College of Business
Logan, UT 84322
(801) 750-2277

Weber State College
Small Business Development
 Center
School of Business and Economics
3750 South Harrison
Ogden, UT 84408
(801) 626-7232

College of Eastern Utah
Small Business Development
 Center
Applied Sciences
451 East 400 North
Price, UT 84501
(801) 637-1995

Brigham Young University
Small Business Development
 Center
Graduate School of Management
790 Tanner Building
Provo, UT 84602
(801) 378-4022

University of Utah*
Utah Small Business Development
 Center
102 West 500 South, Suite 315
Salt Lake City, UT 84101
(801) 851-7905

Dixie College
Small Business Development
 Center
225 South 700 East
St. George, UT 84770
(801) 673-4811, ext. 455

VERMONT

University of Vermont Extension
 Service*
Vermont Small Business
 Development Center
Morrill Hall
Burlington, VT 05405
(802) 656-4479

University of Vermont Extension
Office
Central Small Business
Development Center
RFD One, Box 2280
Morrisville, VT 05661
(802) 888-4972

University of Vermont Extension
Office
Southwestern Small Business
Development Center
Box 489
Rutland, VT 05701
(802) 773-3349

University of Vermont Extension
Office
Northeast Small Business
Development Center
HCR 31, Box 436
St. Johnsbury, VT 05819
(802) 748-5512

University of Vermont Extension
Office
Southeastern Small Business
Development Center
411 Western Avenue, Box 2430
West Brattleboro, VT 05301
(802) 257-7967

University of Vermont Extension
Office
Northwestern Small Business
Development Center
4A Laurette Drive
Winooski, VT 05404
(802) 655-9540

VIRGIN ISLANDS

University of the Virgin Islands
Small Business Development
Center
United Plaza Shopping Center
Suite #5-6, Sion Farm

St. Croix, VI 00820
(809) 778-8270

University of the Virgin Islands*
Virgin Islands Small Business
Development Center
Grand Hotel
Box 1087
St. Thomas, VI 00804
(809) 776-3206

VIRGINIA

Mountain Empire Community
College
Small Business Development
Center
Drawer 700, Route 23
Big Stone Gap, VA 24219
(703) 523-2400

Central Virginia Small Business
Development Center
700 Harris Street, Suite 207
Charlottesville, VA 22901-4553
(804) 295-8198

Northern Virginia Small Business
Development Center
4260 Chainbridge Road, Suite B-1
Fairfax, VA 22030
(703) 993-2131

Longwood College
Small Business Development
Center
Farmville, VA 23901
(804) 395-2086

James Madison University
Small Business Development
Center
College of Business Building
Room 523
Harrisonburg, VA 22807
(703) 568-6334

Lynchburg Small Business Development Center
147 Mill Ridge Road
Lynchburg, VA 25402
(804) 582-6100

Flory Small Business Development Center
10311 Sudley Manor Drive
Manassas, VA 22110
(703) 335-2500

Small Business Development Center of Hampton Roads, Incorporated
420 Bank Street
P.O. Box 327
Norfolk, VA 23501
(804) 622-6414
(804) 825-2957

Southwest Virginia Community College Small Business Development Center
P.O. Box SVCC
Richlands, VA 24641
(703) 964-7345

Capital Area Small Business Development Center
801 East Main Street, Suite 501
Richmond, VA 23219
(804) 648-7838

Blue Ridge Small Business Development Center
310 First Street, SW Mezzanine
Roanoke, VA 24011
(703) 983-0719

Commonwealth of Virginia Department of Economic Development*
Virginia Small Business Development Center
1021 East Cary Street, 11th Floor

Richmond, VA 23219
(804) 371-8258

Longwood College
Small Business Development Center
South Boston Branch
3403 Halifax Road
P.O. Box 739
South Boston, VA 24592
(804) 575-0044

WASHINGTON

Bellevue Small Business Development Center
13555 Bel-Red Road #208
Bellevue, WA 98005
(206) 643-2888

Western Washington University Small Business Development Center
College of Business and Economics
415 Parks Hall
Bellingham, WA 98225
(206) 676-3899

Edmonds Community College Small Business Development Center
917 134th Street SW
Everett, WA 98204
(206) 745-0430

Columbia Basin College Tri-Cities Small Business Development Center
901 North Colorado
Kennewick, WA 99336
(509) 735-6222

Big Bend Community College Small Business Development Center
7662 Chanute Street, Building 1500

Moses Lake, WA 98837
(509) 762-6289

Skagit Valley College
Small Business Development
Center
2405 College Way
Mt. Vernon, WA 98273
(206) 428-1282

Department of Trade and
Economic Department
Small Business Development
Center
919 Lakeridge Way, Suite A
Olympia, WA 98502
(206) 586-4854

Wenatchee Valley College
Small Business Development
Center
P.O. Box 1042
Omak, WA 98841
(509) 826-5107

Washington State University*
Washington Small Business
Development Center
College of Business and Ecomonics
441 Todd Hall
Pullman, WA 99164
(509) 35-1576

Small Business Development
Center
2001 Sixth Avenue, Suite 2608
Seattle, WA 98121
(206) 464-5450

North Seattle Community
College**
International Trade Institute
Small Business Development
Center
9600 College Way North
Seattle, WA 98103
(206) 527-3733

Small Business Development
Center
Duwamish Industrial Educational
Center
6770 East Marginal Way South
Seattle, WA 98108
(206) 764-5375

Washington State University
Spokane Small Business
Development Center
West 601 First
Spokane, WA 99204
(509) 456-2781

Small Business Development
Center
Financial Center
950 Pacific Avenue, #300
Tacoma, WA 98402
(206) 272-7232

Columbia River Economic
Development Council
Small Business Development
Center
100 East Columbia Way
Vancouver, WA 98660
(206) 694-2190

Wenatchee Valley Community
College
Small Business Development
Center
Grand Central Building
25 North Wenatchee Avenue
Wenatchee, WA 98801
(509) 662-8016

Yakima Valley Community
College
Small Business Development
Center
P.O. Box 1647
Yakima, WA 98907
(507) 575-2284

WEST VIRGINIA

**Concord College
Small Business Development
  Center**
Center for Economic Action
Box D-125
Athens, WV 24712
(304) 384-5103

**Bluefield State College
Small Business Development
  Center**
219 Rock Street
Bluefield, WV 24701
(304) 327-4107

**Governor's Office of Community
  and Industrial Development***
**West Virginia Small Business
  Development Center**
1115 Virginia Street, East
Charleston, WV 25310
(304) 348-2960

**Fairmount State College
Small Business Development
  Center**
Fairmount, WV 26554
(304) 367-4125

**Marshall University
Small Business Development
  Center**
1050 Fourth Avenue
Huntington, WV 25755
(304) 696-6789

**Potomac State College
Small Business Development
  Center**
75 Arnold Street
Keyser, WV 26726
(304) 788-3011

**West Virginia Institute of
  Technology
Small Business Development
  Center**
Engineering Building, Room 102
Montgomery, WV 25136
(304) 442-5501

**West Virginia University
Small Business Development
  Center**
P.O. Box 6025
Morgantown, WV 26506
(304) 293-5839

**West Virginia University at
  Parkersburg
Small Business Development
  Center**
Route 5, Box 167-A
Parkersburg, WV 26101
(304) 424-8277

**Shepherd College
Small Business Development
  Center**
120 North Princess Street
Shepherdstown, WV 25433
(800) 344-5231, ext. 261

**West Virginia Northern
  Community College
Small Business Development
  Center**
College Square
Wheeling, WV 26003
(304) 233-5900, ext. 206

WISCONSIN

**University of Wisconsin at Eau
  Claire
Small Business Development
  Center**
Schneider Hall, #113

Eau Claire, WI 54701
(715) 836-5811

University of Wisconsin at Green Bay
Small Business Development Center
2420 Nicolet Drive
460 Wood Hall
Green Bay, WI 54311
(414) 464-2089

University of Wisconsin at Parkside
Small Business Development Center
234 Tallent Hall
Kenosha, WI 53141
(414) 553-2189

University of Wisconsin at La Crosse
Small Business Development Center
School of Business Administration
La Crosse, WI 54601
(608) 785-8782

University of Wisconsin*
Wisconsin Small Business Development Center
432 Northlake Street, Room 423
Madison, WI 53706
(608) 263-7794

University of Wisconsin**
International Trade Program
423 North Lake Street
Madison, WI 53706
(608) 263-7810

University of Wisconsin
Small Business Development Center
905 University Avenue
Madison, WI 53715
(608) 263-0221

University of Wisconsin at Milwaukee
Small Business Development Center
929 North Sixth Street
Milwaukee, WI 53203
(414) 224-3240

University of Wisconsin at Oshkosh
Small Business Development Center
Clow Faculty Building, Room 157
Oshkosh, WI 54901
(414) 424-1541

WIS-BID (Procurement Match Program)**
W9859 Highway 16 and 60
Reeseville, WI 53579
(414) 927-5484

University of Wisconsin at Stevens Point
Small Business Development Center
012 Old Main Building
Stevens Point, WI 54481
(715) 346-2004

University of Wisconsin at Stevens Point**
Wisconsin American Indian Economic Development
Main Building
Stevens Point, WI 54481
(715) 346-2004

University of Wisconsin at Superior
Small Business Development Center
29 Sundquist Hall
Superior, WI 54880
(715) 394-8351

University of Wisconsin at
    Whitewater
Small Business Development
    Center
2000 Carlson Building
Whitewater, WI 53190
(414) 472-3217

University of Wisconsin at
    Whitewater**
Wisconsin Innovation Service
    Center
402 McCutchan Hall
Whitewater, WI 53190
(414) 472-1365

WYOMING

Casper Community College*
Wyoming Small Business
    Development Center
111 West Second Street, Suite 416
Casper, WY 82601
(307) 235-4825

Casper College
Small Business Development
    Center
350 West A Street, Suite 200
Casper, WY 82601
(307) 268-2713

Laramie County Community
    College
Small Business Development
    Center
1400 East College Drive
Cheyenne, WY 82007
(307) 778-1222

Eastern Wyoming Community
    College
Small Business Development
    Center
Douglas Branch

203 North Sixth Street
Douglas, WY 82633
(307) 358-4090

Northern Wyoming Community
    College District
Gillette Campus
Small Business Development
    Center
720 West Eighth
Gillette, WY 82716
(307) 686-0297

Central Wyoming College
Small Business Development
    Center
360 Main Street
Lander, WY 82502
(307) 332-3394
(800) 735-8394

University of Wyoming
Small Business Development
    Center
University Station Box 3275
Laramie, WY 82071
(307) 766-2363

Northwest Community College
Small Business Development
    Center
146 South Bent, #103
Powell, WV 82435
(307) 754-3746

Western Wyoming Community
    College
Small Business Development
    Center
P.O. Box 428
Rock Springs, WY 82902
(307) 382-1830

APPENDIX D

ALABAMA

Birmingham Business Assistance Network
Susan W. Matlock, Director
180 1st Avenue South
Midtown Center, Suite 333
Birmingham, AL 36233
205-250-8000

Business Innovation Center
Lynn Stacey, Director
2000 Old Bay Front Drive
Mobile, AL 36616
205-433-2224

ARIZONA

Arizona Technology Incubator
John Pope, Coordinator
Arizona State Research Institute
Post Office Box 23717
Tempe, AZ 85258
602-965-8976 Fax: 602-965-0225

ARKANSAS

Genesis Project Engineering Experiment Station
Genesis Project
Sam Pruett, Manager
University of Arkansas
Fayetteville, AR 72701
501-575-7227

Arkansas Science & Technology Authority
Chuck Myers, Research Program Manager
100 Main Street, Suite 450
Little Rock, AR 72201
501-342-9006

CALIFORNIA

Vermont Stauson Economic Development Corporation
Marva Smith Battle-Bey, Director
5918 South Vermont Avenue
Los Angeles, CA 90044
213-753-1335

San Francisco Renaissance Entrepreneurship Center
Claudia Vick, Executive Director
1453 Mission Street, 5th Floor
San Francisco, CA 94103
415-863-5337

COLORADO

Boulder Technology Incubator
Robert J. Calcaterra, Executive Director
1727 Conestoga Street
Boulder, CO 80301
303-449-3323 Fax: 303-441-2487

Colorado BioVenture Center
Lewis T. Kontnik, Executive
  Director
860 Clermont Avenue, Suite 101
Denver, CO 80220
303-320-5651 Fax: 303-320-4965

CONNECTICUT

**Southeast Area Technology
  Development Center**
Theodore S. Montgomery,
  Executive Director
1084 Shennesccett Road
U-Conn Avery Point
Groton, CT 06340
203-445-3415

Hartford Graduate Center
Michael Darchek
275 Windor Street
Hartford, CT 06120
203-528-2400

DELAWARE

**Business Open Incubator Project
New Castle County Economic
  Development Corporation**
Darrell Minott, Esq.
704 King Street, First Federal
  Plaza, Suite 536
Wilmington, DE 19801
302-636-5050

Silverside Carr Executive Center
Jordan Fern, Manager
2502 Silverside Road
Wilmington, DE 19809
302-792-1100

DISTRICT OF COLUMBIA

Dunlop Building Incubator
  (proposed)
Gregory Johnson
2321 4th Street NE

Washington, DC 20018
202-727-6600

Gem Building Incubator
Kenilworth Industrial Park
Chris LoPiano and Steve Morales
1235 Kenilworth Avenue NE
Washington, DC 20019
202-396-1200

FLORIDA

**Biomedical Research and
  Innovation Center**
Murray H. Dubbin, Chairman
444 Brickell Avenue, Suite 650
Miami, FL 33131
305-373-3606

University of Florida
Donald R. Price, Vice President
Gainesville, FL 32511
904-462-4040

GEORGIA

**Albany Business and Technology
  Center**
Johnny Hamilton, Manager
230 South Jackson Street
Albany, GA 31701
912-430-3999

**Advanced Technology
  Development Center**
Georgia Institute of Technology
C. Michael Cassidy, Assistant
  Director
430 10th Street NW, Suite N116
Atlanta, GA 30318
404-894-3575

HAWAII

**Kaimuki Technology Enterprise
  Center**
William M. Bass, Executive
  Director

1103 Ninth Avenue
Honolulu, HI 96816
808-625-5293 Fax: 808-625-6363

Manoa Innovation Center
William M. Bass, Executive
    Director
300 Kahelu Avenue, Suite 35
Mililani, HI 86789
808-625-5293 Fax: 808-625-6363

IDAHO

Business Innovation Center
Jim Deffenbaugh, Director
11100 Airport Drive
Hayden Lake, ID 83835
208-772-0584 Fax: 208-772-6196

**Idaho Innovation Center,
    Incorporated**
Joe Pehrson, Manager
2300 North Yellowstone
Idaho Falls, ID 83401
208-523-1026 Fax: 208-523-1049

ILLINOIS

Business and Technology Center
Dennis L. McConaha, Manager
701 Devonshire Drive
Champaign, IL 61820
217-398-5759

**Chicago Park Technology
    Corporation**
David Livingston, President and
    CEO
2201 West Campbell Park Drive
Chicago, IL 60612
312-829-7252

INDIANA

**Indiana Institute for New
    Business Ventures**
David C. Clegg, President

One North Capital Avenue
Suite 1275
Indianapolis IN 46204
317-264-2820 Fax: 317-264-2806

Fort Wayne Enterprise Center
Roy W. Hossier
1830 Wayne Trace
Fort Wayne, IN 46803
219-426-5700

IOWA

**Technology Innovation Center
    University of Iowa**
Bruce Wheaton, Director
#109 Oakdale Campus
Iowa City, IA 52242
319-335-4063

Sioux City Chamber Foundation
Del White
101 Pierce Street
Sioux City, IA 51101
712-255-7903

KANSAS

Enterprise Place
Perry Bemis, Director
1330 East First Street
Wichita, KS 67214

Kansas Entrepreneurial Center
John Walters, President
1640 Fairchild Avenue
Manhattan, KS 66502
913-537-0110

KENTUCKY

Ashland Business Center
Lillian Rigsby, Manager
1401 Winchester Avenue, 4th Floor
Ashland, KY 41101
606-324-3690

The Innovation Center
Marty E. Blubaugh, Director
225 Third Street
Bowling Green, KY 42101
502-782-5511

LOUISIANA

Louisiana BTC-Louisiana State University
Charles D'Agostino, Executive Director
South Stadium Drive
Baton Rouge, LA 70803-6110
504-334-5555

Arts Council of New Orleans, Arts Incubator
Shirley Trusty Corey, Executive Director
821 Gravzer Street, Suite 600
New Orleans, LA 70112
504-523-1465 Fax: 504-529-2430

MAINE

Bangor International Enterprise Development Center
Ken Gibb, Director, Community and Economic Development
73 Harlow Street
Bangor, ME 04401
207-945-4400

Brunswick Incubator
Peter Wellin, Director
14 Main Street—Fort Andross
Brunswick, ME 04011
207-729-7970

MARYLAND

Baltimore Medical Incubator, Baltimore Economic Development Corporation
Dave Paulson

36 South Charles Street, Suite 24
Baltimore, MD 21201
301-837-9305

Crossroads Venture Center
Robin Douglas, Director
3 Commerce Drive, Suite 100
Cumberland, MD 21502
301-777-0800

MASSACHUSETTS

Wadsworth Village
Frederick R. Schaeffer, Manager
130 Centre Street
Danvers, MA 01923
617-777-4602

Massachusetts Biotechnology Research Park
Raymond L. Quinlan, Executive Director
373 Plantation Street
Worcester, MA 01605
508-755-2230

MICHIGAN

Metropolitan Center for High Technology
Charles W. Henderson
2727 Second Avenue
Detroit, MI 48201
313-963-0616

Madison Square Co-Operative
Noah Seifullah
1155 Madison SE
Grand Rapids, MI 49507
616-245-2563

MINNESOTA

Itaska Development Corporation
Joseph Wood

501 Second Avenue NW
Grand Rapids, MN 55744
218-327-2241

Franklin Avenue Business Center
Manager
1433 East Franklin Avenue
Minneapolis, MN 55404
612-870-7555

MISSISSIPPI

**Gulf Coast Business Technology
Center**
Adele Lyons, Manager
1636 Popps Ferry Road
Biloxi, MS 39532
601-392-9741

Canton Small Business Incubator
Jo Ann Gorden, Manager
P.O. Box 1016
Canton, MS 39046
601-859-1307

MISSOURI

Center for Business Innovation
Robert Sherwood, President
4747 Troost Avenue
Kansas City, MO 64110
815-561-8567

St. Louis Technology Center
Gene Boesch, Managing Director
9666 Olive Boulevard, Suite 305
St. Louis, MO 63132
314-432-4204

MONTANA

Butte Development Center
Jim Kambich, Director
305 West Mercury
Butte, MT 59701
406-723-4061

**HAEDCO Business Development
Center**
Rose Leavitt, President
P.O. Box 221
Helena, MT 59624
406-442-6882

NEBRASKA

**Lincoln Business Innovation
Center**
Kay Davis, Executive Director
100 North 12th, #303
Lincoln, NE 68508
402-477-4476

Business and Technology Center
James Thele, Manager
2505 North 24th Street
Omaha, NE 68110
402-346-8262

NEVADA

Nanho Office Center
Nancy Van Dyke, Owner/Director
3838 Raymert Drive
Las Vegas, NV 89121
702-454-0601 Fax: 702-456-9255

The Home Office
Tom Weir, Administrator
3305 Spring Mountain Road, #60
Las Vegas, NV 89102
702-873-5700 Fax: 702-362-1657

NEW HAMPSHIRE

Thayer Innovation Incubator
Carl Long
Dartmouth College
Hanover, NH 03755
603-646-2851

The Incubator to Launch Your Innovation
Roan Venture, Incorporated
Richard J. Ash, President
1155 Elm Street
Manchester, NH 03101
603-644-6110

NEW JERSEY

Hoboken Business Incubator City of Hoboken
Jean Forest, Principal Planner
Hoboken, NJ 07030
201-420-2198

South New Jersey Technical Consortium
Thomas Ward, Director of Operations
Ohey & Esterbrook, Building 14
Cherry Hill, NJ 08003-4001
609-424-4450

NEW MEXICO

Small Business Development Center
Roy Miller, Coordinator
Clovis Community College
417 Schepps Boulevard
Clovis, NM 88101
505-769-4136

Small Business Development Center
Don Leach, Coordinator

New Mexico Junior College
5317 Lovington Highway
Hobbs, NM 88240
505-392-4510

NEW YORK

University at Buffalo Foundation, Inc.
Baird Research Park

Dale M. Landi, Vice President
Box 590
Buffalo, NY 14221
716-636-3321

190 Willow Avenue Industrial Incubator
Public Development Corporation
Frank Napolitano, Development Manager
161 Willow Avenue
New York, NY 10038
212-619-5000

NORTH CAROLINA

Triangle Entrepreneurial Development Center
Julie Williams
3261 Atlantic Avenue, Suite 200
Raleigh, NC 27604
919-876-5928 Fax: 919-876-5934

F. Roger Page Business and Technology Development Center
Steve Johnson
1001 South Marshall Street, Box 45
Winston-Salem, NC 27101
919-777-2600

NORTH DAKOTA

Roosevelt-Custer Regional Council
Roy Jilek, Director
Pulver Hall
Dickinson, ND 58601
701-227-1241 Fax: 701-227-2002

Lake Agassiz Regional Council
Irv Rustad, Director
417 Main Avenue
Fargo, ND 58103
701-235-7885 Fax: 701-235-6706

OHIO

Akron-Summit Industrial Incubator
Michael Lehere, Manager

100 Lincoln Street
Akron, OH 44308
216-353-7918

**Edison Technology Incubator,
Enterprise Development, Inc**
Diann Rucki, Director
11000 Cedar Avenue
Cleveland, OH 44106
216-229-9445

OKLAHOMA

Entrepot
Dick Rubin, Owner-Manager
Suite 400, 5110 South Yale
Tulsa, OK 74135
918-496-8228

**Northeast Oklahoma Business
  Resource Center**
Janetta Chapple, Project
  Administrator
15000 NE 4th
Oklahoma City, OK 73117
405-235-1415

OREGON

**Oregon Technology Center
  Incubator c/o KCEDA**
Craig Rovzar, Executive Vice
  President
P.O. Box 1777
Klamath Falls, OR 97601
503-882-9600

Cascade Business Center Corp.
Tom Hampson, Executive Director
4134 North Vancouver
Portland, OR 97217
503-284-3830

PENNSYLVANIA

Incubator Business Services, Inc.
William Roberts
99 South Cameron Street

Harrisburg, PA 17101
717-257-1360

**Philadelphia Business and
  Technology Center**
Marjorie Ogilvie
5070 Parkside Avenue
Philadelphia, PA 19131
215-877-1404

PUERTO RICO

Producir, Inc.
Dr. Antonio Pantoja
P.O. Box 1660
Canovanas, PR 00629
809-876-7150

**Asociacion de Pequeños
  Agricultores Del Rabanel, Inc.**
Francisco Figueroa Laracunte
Box 849
Cidra, PR 00639
809-745-6415

RHODE ISLAND

Para-Search
Marie D'Amico
222 Jefferson Boulevard
Warwick, RI 02888
401-732-2490

**Ecco Place Business Incubator
  and Manufacturing Center**
Rev. Virgil A. Wood, Manager
645 Elmwood Avenue
Providence, RI 02907
401-461-4321

SOUTH CAROLINA

Business and Technology Center
Jerome Clemons, Director
701 East Bay Street
Charleston, SC 29403
803-722-1219

North Augusta Business and Technology Center
David Vipperman, Center Director
802 East Martintown Road
North Augusta, SC 29841
803-329-9700 Fax: 803-329-9798

SOUTH DAKOTA

Center for Innovation, Technology and Enterprise
Dr. Sam Gingerich, Director
Northern State University
South Jay Street
Aberdeen, SD 57401
605-622-2258

Brookings Economic Development Center
Thomas O. Manzer, Manager
2308 Sixth Street
P.O. Box 431
Brookings, SD 57006
605-692-6125

TENNESSEE

Business Development Center
Joe Schultz, Manager
100 Cherokee Boulevard
Chattanooga, TN 37405
615-265-0991/756-2121

Knox County Government Fairview Incubation Center
Melissa Zeigler, Director
400 Main, Room 603
City/County Building
Knoxville, TN 37902
615-521-2000

TEXAS

Entrepreneurial Development Center
C. Dean Kring, Director of Research

8845 Long Point Road
Houston, TX 77055
713-932-7495 Fax: 713-932-7498

Dallas County Community College District Business Incubation Center
Mark Keith
1402 Corinth Street
Dallas, TX 75215
214-565-5851 Fax: 214-565-5817

UTAH

Technology Transfer Cooperative
G. Richard Hill, Technology Transfer Administrator
Weber State University
Ogden, UT 84408-4001
801-626-7313 Fax: 801-626-7878

University of Utah Research Park
Charles Evans, Director
505 Wakara Way
Salt Lake City, UT 84108
801-581-8133 Fax: 801-581-7195

VERMONT

Chace Mill Associates
Tom Anderson, Manager
One Mill Street
Burlington, VT 05401
802-658-1698

Newport Incubator
Forest Buckland, Job Zone Coordinator
RFD #1, Box 125G
Newport, VT 05885
802-334-5861

VIRGINIA

Lynchburg Business Development Center
Georgeann Snead, Manager

147 Mill Ridge Road
Lynchburg, VA 24502
804-582-6100

**Richmond Technology and
Enterprise Center**
Taylor Cousins, Director
403 East Grace Street
Richmond, VA 23219
804-648-7838

WASHINGTON

**Port Kennewick Development
Building**
Port of Kennewick
Sue Watkins, Manager
One Clover Island
Kennewick, WA 99336
509-545-2293

**Evergreen CDA Incubator—
Thurston Company**
Evergreen CDA
Mary Jean Ryan
2122 Smith Tower
Seattle, WA 98104
206-622-3731

WEST VIRGINIA

Mid Ohio Valley Development
Manager
P.O. Box 247
1200 Grand Central Avenue
Parkerburg, WV 26101

Charleston Enterprise Center
Howard Johnson, Manager
1116 Smith Street
Charleston, WV 25301
304-340-4250

WISCONSIN

Laboratory Associated Businesses
Phil Derse, Vice President
1202 Ann Street
Madison, WI 53713
608-251-3005

**Community Enterprise of Greater
Milwaukee**
Bill Lock, Director
3118 North Teutonia Avenue
Milwaukee, WI 53206
414-265-5055/2346

WYOMING

Enterprise Center
Laramie County Community
College
Patrice Gaspen, Director
1400 East College Drive
Cheyenne, WY 82001
307-635-5853

Small Business Incubator
Small Business Development Center
Jay Neilsen, Director
P.O. Box 1028
Douglas, WY 82633
307-358-4090

APPENDIX E

SMALL BUSINESS ASSOCIATIONS

American Business Women's Association
P.O. Box 8728
9100 Ward Parkway
Kansas City, MO 64114
(816) 361-6621

American Federation of Small Business
407 South Dearborn Street
Chicago, IL 60605
(312) 427-0207

Center for Family Business
P.O. Box 24268
Cleveland, OH 44124
(216) 442-0800

Commercial Finance Association
225 West 34th Street
New York, NY 10122
(212) 594-3490

Conference of American Small Business Organizations
407 South Dearborn Street
Chicago, IL 60605
(312) 427-0207

Continental Association of Resolute Employers
511 C Street NE

Washington, DC 20002
(202) 546-4609

International Council for Small Business
3674 Lindell Boulevard
St. Louis University
St. Louis, MO 63108
(314) 658-3896

National Association for the College Industry
P.O. Box 14460
Chicago, IL 60614
(312) 472-8116

National Association of Investment Companies
1111 14th Street NW, Suite 700
Washington, DC 20005
(202) 289-4336

National Association of the Self-Employed
P.O. Box 612067
Dallas, TX 75261
(800) 551-4446

National Association of Small Business Investment Companies
1199 North Fairfax Street
Suite 200

546

Alexandria, VA 22314
(703) 683-1601

National Association of Women Business Owners
1010 Wayne Avenue, Suite 900
Silver Springs, MD 20910
(301) 608-2596

National Business League
1511 K Street NW, Suite 432
Washington, DC 20005
(202) 737-4430

National Family Business Council
1640 West Kennedy Road
Lake Forest, IL 60045
(708) 295-1040

National Federation of Independent Business
53 Century Boulevard, Suite 300
Nashville, TN 37214
(615) 872-5800

National Small Business United
1155 15th Street NW, Suite 710
Washington, DC 20005
(202) 293-8830

National Venture Capital Association
1655 North Fort Myer Drive
Suite 700
Arlington, VA 22209
(703) 351-5269

Service Corps of Retired Executives Association
c/o Small Business Administration
409 3rd Street SW, Suite 5900
Washington, DC 20024
(202) 205-6762

Small Business Foundation of America
1155 15th Street
Washington, DC 20005
(202) 273-1103

Small Business Legislative Council
1156 15th Street NW, Suite 510
Washington, DC 20005
(202) 639-8500

Smaller Business Association of New England
204 Second Avenue
Waltham, MA 02154
(617) 890-9070

Support Service Alliance
P.O. Box 130
Schoharie, NY 12157
(800) 322-3920

United States Chamber of Commerce
1615 H Street NW
Washington, DC 20062
(202) 659-6000

APPENDIX F*

What follows is a detailed outline of the contents of a venture investment agreement. The main sections of a typical agreement are briefly described and many of the terms that might appear in each section are noted. However, not all of the terms listed will appear in an investment agreement. Venture capital investors select terms from among those listed (and some not listed) to best serve their needs in a particular venture-investment situation.

1. Description of the Investment

This section of the agreement defines the basic terms of the investment. It includes descriptions of the:

a. Amount and type of investment.
b. Securities to be issued.
c. Guarantees, collateral subordination, and payment schedules associated with any notes.
d. Conditions of closing: time, place, method of payment.

When investment instruments are involved that carry warrants, or debt conversion privileges, the agreement will completely describe them. This description will include the:

a. Time limits on the exercise of the warrant or conversion of the debt.
b. Price and any price changes that vary with the time of exercise.
c. Transferability of the instruments.
d. Registration rights on stock acquired by the investor.
e. Dilution resulting from exercise of warrants or debt conversion.
f. Rights and protections surviving after conversion, exercise, or redemption.

---

*Reprinted with the permission of Jeffry A. Timmons and Paul T. Babson, from their book *New Venture Creation* (Homewood, Ill.: Richard D. Irwin, Inc.) pp. 599–602.

2. Preconditions to Closing

This section covers what the venture must do or what ancillary agreements and documents must be submitted to the investor before the investment can be closed. These agreements and documents may include:

a. Corporate documents; e.g., by-laws, articles of incorporation, resolutions authorizing sale of securities, tax status certificates, list of stockholders, and directors.
b. Audited financial statements
c. Any agreements for simultaneous additional financing from another source or for lines of credit.
d. Ancillary agreements; e.g., employment contracts, stock option agreements, key man insurance policies, and stock repurchase agreements.
e. Copies of any leases or supply contracts.

3. Representations and Warranties by the Venture

This section contains legally binding statements made by the venture's officers that describe its condition on or before the closing date of the investment agreement. The venture's management will warrant:

a. That it is a duly organized corporation in good standing.
b. That its action in entering into an agreement is authorized by its directors, allowed by its by-laws and charter, legally binding upon the corporation, and not in breach of any other agreements.
c. If a private placement, that the securities being issued are exempt from registration under the Securities Act of 1933 as amended, under state securities law, and that registration is not required under the Securities Exchange Act of 1934.
d. That the capitalization, shares, options, directors, and shareholders of the company are as described (either in the agreement or an exhibit) .
e. That no trade secrets or patents will be used in the business that are not owned free and clear or if rights to use them have not been acquired.
f. That no conflicts of interest exist in their entering the agreement.
g. That all material facts and representations in the agreement and exhibits are true as of the date of closing (includes accuracy of business plan and financials) .
h. That the venture will fulfill its part of the agreement so long as all conditions are met.
i. That any patents, trademarks, or copyrights owned and/or used by the company are described.

j. That the principal assets and liabilities of the company are as described in attached exhibits.

k. That there are no undisclosed obligations, litigations, or agreements of the venture of a material nature not already known to all parties.

l. That any prior-year income statements and balance sheets are accurate as presented and have been audited. And that there have been no adverse changes since the last audited statements.

m. That the venture is current on all tax payments and returns.

4. Representations and Warranties by the Investor

This section contains any legally binding representations made by the investor. They are much smaller in number than those made by the company. The investor may warrant:

a. If a corporation, that it is duly organized and in good standing.

b. If a corporation, that its action in entering into an agreement with the venture is authorized by its directors, allowed by its by-laws and charter, legally binding upon the corporation, and not in breach of any existing agreements.

c. If a private placement, that the stock being acquired is for investment and not with a view to or for sale in connection with any distribution.

d. The performance of his or her part of the contract if all conditions are met.

5. Affirmative Covenants

In addition to the above representations and warranties, the company in which the investor invests usually has a list of affirmative covenants with which it must comply. These could include agreeing to:

a. Pay taxes, fees, duties, and other assessments promptly.

b. File all appropriate government or agency reports.

c. Pay debt principal and interest.

d. Maintain corporate existence.

e. Maintain appropriate books of accounts and keep a specified auditing firm on retainer.

f. Allow access to these records to all directors and representatives of the investor.

g. Provide the investor with periodic income statements and balance sheets.

h. Preserve and provide for the investor's stock registration rights as described in the agreement.

i. Maintain appropriate insurance, including key man life insurance with the company named as beneficiary.
j. Maintain minimum net worth, working capital, or net assets levels.
k. Maintain the number of investor board seats prescribed in the agreement.
l. Hold prescribed number of directors' meetings.
m. Comply with all applicable laws.
n. Maintain corporate properties in good condition.
o. Notify the investor of any events of default of the investment agreement within a prescribed period of time.
p. Use the investment proceeds substantially in accordance with a business plan that is an exhibit to the agreement.

6. Negative Covenants

These covenants define what a venture must not do, or must not do without prior investor approval; such approval not to be unreasonably withheld. A venture usually agrees not to do such things as:

a. Merge, consolidate with, acquire, or invest in any form of organization.
b. Amend or violate the venture's charter or by-laws.
c. Distribute, sell, redeem, or divide stock except as provided for in the agreement.
d. Sell, lease, or dispose of assets whose value exceeds a specified amount.
e. Purchase assets whose value exceeds specified amount.
f. Pay dividends.
g. Violate any working capital or net worth restrictions described in the investment agreement.
h. Advance to, loan to, or invest in individuals, organizations, or firms except as described in the investment agreement.
i. Create subsidiaries.
j. Liquidate the corporation.
k. Institute bankruptcy proceedings.
l. Pay compensation to its management other than as provided for in the agreement.
m. Change the basic nature of the business for which the firm was organized.
n. Borrow money except as provided for in the agreement.
o. Dilute the investors without giving them the right of first refusal on new issues of stock.

7. Conditions of Default

This section describes those events that constitute a breach of the investment agreement if not corrected within a specified time and under which an investor can exercise specific remedies. Events that constitute default may include:

a. Failure to comply with the affirmative or negative covenants of the agreement.
b. Falsification of representations and warranties made in the investment agreement.
c. Insolvency or reorganization of the venture.
d. Failure to pay interest or principal due on debentures.

8. Remedies

This section describes the actions available to an investor in the event a condition of default occurs. Remedies depend on the form an investment takes. For a common stock investment the remedies could be:

a. Forfeiture to the investor of any stock of the venture's principals that was held in escrow.
b. The investor receiving voting control through a right to vote some or all of the stock of the venture's principals.
c. The right of the investor to "put" his stock to the company at a predetermined price.

For a debenture, the remedies might be:

a. The full amount of the note becoming due and payable on demand.
b. Forfeiture of any collateral used to secure the debt.

In the case of a preferred stock investment, the remedy can be special voting rights (e.g., the right to vote the entrepreneurs' stock) to obtain control of the board of directors.

9. Other Conditions

A number of other clauses that cover a diverse group of issues often appear in investment agreements. Some of the more common issues covered are:

a. Who will bear the costs of closing the agreement; this is often borne by the company.
b. Who will bear the costs of registration of the investors' stock; again, the investors like this to be borne by the company for the first such registration.
c. Right of first refusal for the investor on subsequent company financings.

APPENDIX G

The Small Business Innovation Research (SBIR) Program is a highly competitive three-phase award system that provides qualified small business concerns with opportunities to propose innovative ideas that meet the specific research and R&D needs of the federal government.

Phase 1 is to evaluate the scientific technical merit and feasibility of an idea. Awards of up to $50,000 with a period of performance of up to six months are involved in this phase.

Phase II is to expand on the results of and further pursue the development of Phase I. Awards of up to $500,000 with a period of performance normally not to exceed two years are involved in this phase.

Phase III is for the commercialization of the results of Phase II & requires the use of private or non-SBIR federal funding. *No SBIR funds are expended in this phase.*

The only way a small-business concern can obtain SBIR funding is to successfully compete for an SBIR award.

While stimulating technological innovation, the SBIR Program is designed to:

- Assist the federal agencies participating in the program to meet their respective research and R&D needs, and
- Provide qualified small-business concerns with opportunities to compete for a greater share of federal R&D awards.

The following agencies of the federal government participate in the SBIR Program:

Department of Agriculture
Department of Commerce

553

Department of Defense
Department of Education
Department of Energy
Department of Health & Human Services
Department of Transportation
Environmental Protection Agency
National Aeronautics & Space Administration
National Science Foundation
Nuclear Regulatory Commission

Each of these federal agencies:

• Designates topics upon which SBIR proposals will be sought
• Releases at least one SBIR solicitation annually
• Receives and evaluate SBIR proposals
• Awards SBIR funding agreements competitively that are based on technical and scientific merit and cost effectiveness as well as meeting the agency's needs and requirements.

For the next several years, it is anticipated total Phase I and Phase II SBIR awards will average approximately $500 million annually.

The Small Business Innovation Development Act of 1982 designated SBA as the agency for program implementation, governing program policy, monitoring, analysis, and annual reporting of government-wide activities of SBIR to Congress.

To assist small-business firms, SBA publishes the SBIR Pre-Solicitation Announcement. This quarterly publication describes SBIR in detail and contains pertinent facts on current and upcoming SBIR solicitations.

For more information on the SBIR Program, contact:

U.S. Small Business Adminstration
Office of Innovation, Research & Technology
409 Third Street SW
Washington, DC 20416
(202) 205-7777

APPENDIX H

ASSESSING A PRODUCT'S EXPORT POTENTIAL

There are several ways to gauge the overseas market potential of products and services. (For ease of reading, products are mentioned more than services in this guide, but much of the discussion applies to both). One of the most important ways is to assess the product's success in domestic markets. If a company succeeds at selling in the U.S. market, there is a good chance that it will also be successful in markets abroad, wherever similar needs and conditions exist.

In markets that differ significantly from the U.S. market, some products may have limited potential. Those differences may be climate and environmental factors, social and cultural factors, local availability of raw materials or product alternatives, lower wage costs, lower purchasing power, the availability of foreign exchange (hard currencies like the dollar, the British pound, and the Japanese yen), government import controls, and many other factors. If a product is successful in the United States, one strategy for export success may be a careful analysis of why it sells here, followed by a selection of similar markets abroad. In this way, little or no product modification is required.

If a product is not new or unique, low-cost market research may already be available to help assess its overseas market potential. In addition, international trade statistics (available in many local libraries) can give a preliminary indication of overseas markets for a particular product by showing where similar or related products are already being sold in significant quantities. One of the best sources for U.S. export-import statistics is the National Trade Data Bank

*This section is excerpted from *A Basic Guide to Exporting,* published by the U.S. Department of Commerce, 1992.

555

(NTDB), which can be accessed at many U.S. Department of Commerce district offices across the country.

If a product is unique or has important features that are hard to duplicate abroad, chances are good for finding an export market. For a unique product, competition may be nonexistent or very slight, while demand may be quite high.

Finally, even if U.S. sales of a product are now declining, sizeable export markets may exist, especially if the product once did well in the United States but is now losing market share to more technically advanced products. Countries that are less developed than the United States may not need state-of-the-art technology and may be unable to afford the most sophisticated and expensive products. Such markets may instead have a surprisingly healthy demand for U.S. products that are older or that are considered obsolete by U.S. market standards.

Making the Export Decision

Once a company determines it has exportable products, it must still consider other factors, such as the following:

- What does the company want to gain from exporting?
- Is exporting consistent with other company goals?
- What demands will exporting place on the company's key re-sources—management and personnel, production capacity, and finance—and how will these demands be met?
- Are the expected benefits worth the costs, or would company resources be better used for developing new domestic business?

The Value of Planning

Many companies begin export activities haphazardly, without care-fully screening markets or options for market entry. While these companies may or may not have a measure of success, they may overlook better export opportunities. In the event that early export efforts are unsuccessful because of poor planning, the company may even be misled into abandoning exporting altogether. Formulating an export strategy based on good information and proper assessment increases the chance that the best options will be chosen, that resources will be used ffectively, and that efforts will consequently be carried through to cor pletion.

The purposes of the export plan are, first, to assemble facts, constraints, and goals and, second, to create an action statement that takes all of these into account. The statement includes specific objectives, it sets forth time schedules for implementation, and it marks milestones so that the degree of success can be measured and help motivate personnel.

The first draft of the export plan may be quite short and simple, but it should become more detailed and complete as the planners learn more about exporting and their company's competitive position. At least the following ten questions should ultimately be addressed:

1. What products are selected for export development? What modifications, if any, must be made to adapt them for overseas markets?
2. What countries are targeted for sales development?
3. In each country, what is the basic customer profile? What marketing and distribution channels should be used to reach customers?
4. What special challenges pertain to each market (competition, cultural differences, import controls, etc.), and what strategy will be used to address them?
5. How will the product's export sales price be determined?
6. What specific operational steps must be taken and when?
7. What will be the time frame for implementing each element of the plan?
8. What personnel and company resources will dedicated to exporting?
9. What will be the cost in time and money for each element?
10. How will results be evaluated and used to modify the plan?

One key to developing a successful plan is the participation of all personnel who will be involved in the exporting process. All aspects of an export plan should be agreed upon by those who will ultimately execute them.

A clearly written marketing strategy offers six immediate benefits:

1. Because written plans display their strengths and weaknesses more readily, they are of great help in formulating and polishing an export strategy.
2. Written plans are not as easily forgotten, overlooked, or ignored by those charged with executing them. If deviation from the original plan occurs, it is likely to be due to a deliberate choice to do so.

3. Written plans are easier to communicate to others and are less likely to be misunderstood.
4. Written plans allocate responsibilities and provide for an evaluation of results.
5. Written plans can be of help in seeking financing. They indicate to lenders a serious approach to the export venture.
6. Written plans give management a clear understanding of what will be required and thus help to ensure a commitment to exporting. In fact, a written plan signals that the decision to export has already been made.

This last advantage is especially noteworthy. Building an international business takes time; it is usually months, sometimes even several years, before an exporting company begins to see a return on its investment of time and money. By committing to the specifics of a written plan, top management can make sure that the firm will finish what it begins and that the hopes that prompted its export efforts will be fulfilled.

The Planning Process and the Result

A crucial first step in planning is to develop broad consensus among key management on the company's goals, objectives, capabilities, and constraints.

The first time an export plan is developed, it should be kept simple. It need be only a few pages long, since important market data and planning elements may not yet be available. The initial planning effort itself gradually generates more information and insight that can be incorporated into more sophisticated planning documents later.

From the start, the plan should be viewed and written as a management tool, not as a static document. For instance, objectives in the plan should be compared with actual results as a measure of the success of different strategies. Furthermore, the company should not hesitate to modify the plan and make it more specific as new information and experience are gained.

A detailed plan is recommended for companies that intend to export directly. Companies choosing indirect export methods may require much simpler plans.

Approaches to Exporting

The way a company chooses to export its products can have a significant effect on its export plan and specific marketing strategies. The basic distinction among approaches to exporting relates to a company's level of involvement in the export process. There are at least four approaches, which may be used alone or in combination:

1. Passively filling orders from domestic buyers who then export the product. These sales are indistinguishable from other domestic sales as far as the original seller is concerned. Someone else has decided that the product in question meets foreign demand. That party takes all the risk and handles all of the exporting details, in some cases without even the awareness of the original seller. (Many companies take a stronger interest in exporting when they discover that their product is already being sold overseas.)
2. Seeking out domestic buyers who represent foreign end users or customers. Many U.S. and foreign corporations, general contractors, foreign trading companies, foreign government agencies, foreign distributors and retailers, and others in the United States purchase for export. These buyers are a large market for a wide variety of goods and services. In this case a company may know its product is being exported, but it is still the buyer who assumes the risk and handles the details of exporting.
3. Exporting indirectly through intermediaries. With this approach, a company engages the services of an intermediary firm capable of finding foreign markets and buyers for its products. Export management companies (EMCs), export trading companies (ETCs), international trade consultants, and other intermediaries can give the exporter access to well-established expertise and trade contacts. Yet, the exporter can still retain considerable control over the process and can realize some of the other benefits of exporting, such as learning more about foreign competitors, new technologies, and other market opportunities.
4. Exporting directly. This approach is the most ambitious and difficult, since the exporter personally handles every aspect of the exporting process from market research and planning to foreign distribution and collections. Consequently, a significant commitment of management time and attention is required to achieve good results. However, this approach may also be the best way to achieve

maximum profits and long-term growth. With appropriate help and guidance from the Department of Commerce, state trade offices, freight forwarders, international banks, and another service groups, even small or medium-sized firms, can export directly if they are able to commit enough staff time to the effort. For those who cannot make the commitment, the services of an EMC, ETC, trade consultant, or another qualified intermediary are indispensable.

Approaches 1 and 2 represent a substantial proportion of U.S. sales, perhaps as much as 30 percent of U.S. exports. They do not, however, involve the firm in the export process. Consequently, this guide concentrates on approaches 3 and 4. (There is no single source or special channel for identifying domestic buyers for overseas markets. In general, they may be found through the same means that U.S. buyers are found, for example, trade shows, mailing lists, industry directories, and trade associations.)

If the nature of the company's goals and resources makes an indirect method of exporting the best choice, little further planning may be needed. In such a case, the main task is to find a suitable intermediary firm that can then handle most export details. Firms that are new to exporting or are unable to commit staff and funds to more complex export activities may find indirect methods of exporting more appropriate.

Using an EMC or other intermediary, however, does not exclude all possibility of direct exporting for the firm. For example, a U.S. company may try exporting directly to such "easy" nearby markets as Canada, Mexico, or the Bahamas while letting its EMC handle more ambitious sales to Egypt or Japan. An exporter may also choose to gradually increase its level of direct exporting later, after experience has been gained and sales volume appears to justify added investment.

For more information on different approaches to exporting and their advantages and disadvantages, you may want to consult appropriate advisors. The next chapter presents information on a variety of organizations that can provide this type of help—in many cases, at no cost.

Management Issues Involved in the Export Decision

Management objectives

*   What are the company's reasons for pursuing export markets? Are they solid objectives (e.g., increasing sales volume or developing a broader,

more stable customer base) or are they frivolous (e.g., the owner wants an excuse to travel)?

- How committed is top management to an export? Is exporting viewed as a quick fix for a slump in domestic sales? Will the company neglect its export customers if domestic sales pick up?
- What are management's expectations for the export effort? How quickly does management expect export operations to become self-sustaining? What level of return on investment is expected from the export program?

Experience

- With what countries has business already been conducted, or from what countries have inquires already been received?
- Which product lines are mentioned most often?
- Are any domestic customers buying the product for sale or shipment overseas? If so, to what countries?
- Is the trend of sales and inquiries up or down?
- Who are the main domestic and foreign competitors?
- What general and specific lessons have been learned from past export attempts or experiences?

Management and personnel

- What in-house international expertise does the firm have (international sales experience, language capabilities, etc)?
- Who will be responsible for the export department's organization and staff?
- How much senior management time (a) should be allocated and (b) could be allocated?
- What organizational structure is required to ensure that export sales are adequately serviced?
- Who will follow through after the planning is done?

Production capacity

- How is the present capacity being used?
- Will filling export orders hurt domestic sales?
- What will be the cost of additional production?
- Are there fluctuations in the annual work load? When? Why?
- What minimum order quantity is required?
- What would be required to design and package products specifically for export?

Financial capacity

- What amount of capital can be committed to export production and marketing?
- What level of export department operating costs can be supported?
- How are the initial expenses of export efforts to be allocated?
- What other new development plans are in the works that may compete with export plans?
- By what date must an export effort pay for itself?

Sample Outline for an Export Plan

Table of Contents

Executive Summary (one or two pages maximum)
Introduction: Why This Company Should Export

Part I–Export Policy Commitment Statement

Part II–Situation/Background Analysis

- Product or Service
- Operations
- Personnel and Export Organization
- Resources of the Firm
- Industry Structure, Competition, and Demand

Part III–Marketing Component

- Identifying Evaluating, and Selecting Target Markets
- Product Selection and Pricing
- Distribution Methods
- Terms and Conditions
- Internal Organization and Procedures
- Sales Goals: Profit and Loss Forecasts

Part IV–Tactics: Action Steps

- Primary Target Countries
- Secondary Target Countries
- Indirect Marketing Efforts

Part V–Export Budget

- Pro Forma Financial Statements

Part VI–Implementation Schedule

- Follow-up
- Periodic Operational and Management Review (Measuring Results Against Plan)

Addenda: Background Data on Target Countries and Market

- Basic Market Statistics: Historical and Projected
- Background Facts
- Competitive Environment

Export Advice

For companies making initial plans to export or to export in new areas, considerable advice and assistance are available at little or no cost. It is easy, through lack of experience, to overestimate the problems involved in exporting or to get embroiled in difficulties that can be avoided. For these and other good reasons, it is important to get expert counseling and assistance from the beginning.

This section gives a brief overview of sources of assistance available through federal, state, and local government agencies and in the private sector. Information on where to find these organizations can be found in the appendixes.

Some readers may feel overwhelmed at first by the number of sources of advice available. Although it is not necessary to go to all of these resources, it is valuable to know at least a little about each of them and to get to know several personally. Each individual or organization contacted can contribute different perspectives based on different experience and skills.

While having many sources to choose from can be advantageous, deciding where to begin can also be difficult. Some advice from experienced exporters may be helpful in this regard. Recognizing this point, President George Bush created the Trade Promotion Coordination Committee (TPCC) and charged it with harnessing all the resources of the federal government to serve American exporting business. The TPCC conducts export conferences, coordinates trade events and missions that cross-cut federal agencies, and operates an export information center that can help exporters find the right federal program to suit their needs (telephone 1-800-USA-TRADE).

In general, however, the best place to start is the nearest U.S. Department of Commerce district office, which can not only provide export counseling in its own right but also direct companies toward other government and private sector export services.

Department of Commerce

The scope of services provided by the Department of Commerce to exporters is vast, but it is often overlooked by many companies. Most of the information and programs of interest to U.S. exporters are concentrated in the department's International Trade Administration (ITA), of which the subdivision called the U.S. and Foreign Commercial Service (US&FCS) maintains a network of international trade specialists in the United States and commercial officers in foreign cities to help American companies do business abroad. By contacting the nearest Department of Commerce district office, the U.S. exporter can tap into all assistance programs available from ITA and all trade information gathered by U.S. embassies and consulates worldwide. The following sections detail the kinds of assistance offered.

Export Assistance Available in the United States

Department of Commerce District Offices

Sixty-eight Department of Commerce district and branch offices in cities throughout the United States and Puerto Rico provide information and professional export counseling to business people. Each district office is headed by a director and supported by trade specialists and other staff. Branch offices usually consist of one trade specialist. These professionals can counsel companies on the steps involved in exporting, help them assess the export potential of their products, target markets, and locate and check out potential overseas partners. In fact, because Commerce has a worldwide network of international business experts, district offices can answer almost any question exporters are likely to ask—or put them in touch with someone who can.

Each district office can offer information about

- International trade opportunities abroad
- Foreign markets for U.S. products and services
- Services to locate and evaluate overseas buyers and representatives

- Financial aid to exporters
- International trade exhibitions
- Export documentation requirements
- Foreign economic statistics
- U.S. export licensing and foreign nation import requirements
- Export seminars and conferences

Most district offices also maintain business libraries containing Commerce's latest reports as well as other publications of interest to U.S. exporters. Important data bases, such as the NTDB, are also available through many district offices that provide trade leads, foreign business contacts, in-depth country market research, export-import trade statistics, and other valuable information.

DISTRICT EXPORT COUNCILS

Besides the immediate services of its district offices, the Department of Commerce gives the exporter direct contact with seasoned exporters experienced in all phases of export trade. The district offices work closely with 51 district export councils (DECs) comprising nearly 1,800 business and trade experts who volunteer to help U.S. firms develop solid export strategies.

These DECs assist in may of the workshops and seminars on exporting arranged by the district offices (see below) or sponsor their own. DEC members may also provide direct, personal counseling to less experienced exporters, suggesting marketing strategies, trade contacts, and ways to maximize success in overseas markets.

Assistance from DECs may be obtained through the Department of Commerce district offices with which they are affiliated.

EXPORT SEMINARS AND EDUCATIONAL PROGRAMMING

In addition to individual counseling sessions, an effective method of informing local business communities of the various aspects of international trade is through the conference and seminar program. Each year, Commerce district offices conduct approximately 5,000 conferences, seminars, and workshops on topics such as export documentation and licensing procedures, country-specific market opportunities, export trading companies, and U.S. trade promotion and trade policy initiatives. The seminars are usually held in conjunction with DECs, local chambers of commerce, state agencies, and world trade clubs. For information on scheduled seminars across the country, or for educational programming assistance, contact the nearest district office.

ASSISTANCE AVAILABLE FROM DEPARTMENT OF COMMERCE SPECIALISTS IN WASHINGTON, DC

Among the most valuable resources available to U.S. exporters are the hundreds of trade specialists, expert in various areas of international business, that the Department of Commerce has assembled in its Washington headquarters.

Country counseling. Every country in the world is assigned a country desk officer. These desk officers, in Commerce's International Economic Policy (IEP) area, look at the needs of an individual U.S. firm wishing to sell in a particular country, taking into account that country's overall economy, trade policies, political situation, and other relevant factors. Each desk officer collects up-to-date information on the country's trade regulations, tariffs and value-added taxes, business practices, economic and political developments, trade data and trends, market size and growth, and so on. Desk officers also participate in preparing Commerce's country-specific market research reports, such as Foreign Economic Trends and Overseas Business Reports, available from the U.S. Government Printing Office and through the NTDB. The value of IEP's market data may be gauged from the fact that this agency develops much of the country-specific background for negotiating positions of the U.S. trade representative.

Products and service sector counseling. Complementing IEP's country desks are the industry desk officers of Commerce's Trade Development area. They are grouped in units (with telephone numbers):

- Aerospace, 202-377-2835
- Automotive Affairs and Consumer Goods, 202-377-0823
- Basic Industries, 202-377-0614
- Capital Goods and International Construction, 202-377-5023
- Science and Electronics, 202-377-3548
- Services, 202-377-5261
- Textiles and Apparel, 202-377-3737.

The industry desk officers participate in preparing reports on the competitive strength of selected U.S. industries in domestic and international markets for the publication *U.S. Industrial Outlook* (available from the U.S. Government Printing Office). They also promote exports for their industry sectors through marketing seminars, trade missions and trade fairs, foreign buyer groups, business counseling, and information on market opportunities.

Export counseling and international market analysis. The Market Analysis Division provides U.S. firms with assistance in market research efforts and export counseling on market research. Many of the research reports described in this chapter are planned and prepared by the Office of Product Development and Distribution, Market Analysis Division (202-377-5037).

Major projects. For major projects abroad, the International Construction unit works with American planning, engineering, and construction firms to win bid contracts. The Major Projects Reference Room in Commerce's Washington headquarters keeps detailed project documents on multilateral development bank and U.S. foreign assistance projects. Companies able to bid on major overseas projects can reach the Major Projects Reference Room at 202-377-4876.

The Office of Telecommunications (202-377-4466) has major projects information exclusively for that sector.

Other assistance. Rounding out the Trade Development area is a unit that cuts across industry sector issues. Trade Information and Analysis gathers, analyzes, and disseminates trade and investment data for use in trade promotion and policy formulation. it also includes specialists in technical areas of international trade finance, such as countertrade and barter, foreign sales corporations, export financing, and the activities of multilateral development banks. For more information, contact the nearest Department of Commerce district office.

Export Marketing Information and Assistance Available Overseas

US&FCS OVERSEAS POSTS

Much of the information about trends and actual trade leads in foreign countries is gathered on site by the commercial officers of the US&FCS. About half of the approximately 186 US&FCS American officers working in 67 countries (with 127 offices) have been hired from the private sector, many with international trade experience. All understand firsthand the problems encountered by U.S. companies in their efforts to trade abroad. U.S.-based regional directors for the US&FCS can be contacted at the following telephone numbers:

- Africa, Near East, and South Asia, 202-377-4836.
- East Asia and Pacific, 202-377-8422.
- Europe, 202-377-1599.
- Western Hemisphere, 202-377-2736.
- Fax (Europe and Western Hemisphere), 202-377-3159.
- Fax (all others), 202-377-5179.

In addition, a valued asset of the US&FCS is a group of about 525 foreign nationals, usually natives of the foreign country, who are employed in the U.S. embassy or consulate and bring with them a wealth of personal understanding of local market conditions and business practices. The US&FCS staff overseas provides a range of services to help companies sell abroad: background information on foreign companies, agency-finding services, market research, business counseling, assistance in making appointments with key buyers and government officials, and representations on behalf of companies adversely affected by trade barriers.

U.S. exporters usually tap into these services by contacting the Department of Commerce district office in their state. While exporters are strongly urged to contact their district office before going overseas, U.S. business travelers abroad can also contact U.S. embassies and consulates directly for help during their trips. District offices can provide business travel facilitation assistance before departure by arranging advance appointments with embassy personnel, market briefings, and other assistance in cities to be visited.

US&FCS posts also cooperate with overseas representatives of individual states. Almost all 50 states have such representation in overseas markets, and their efforts are closely coordinated with the resources of the US&FCS.

Other Commerce Export Services

Besides ITA, a number of other Department of Commerce agencies offer export services.

EXPORT ADMINISTRATION

The undersecretary for export administration is responsible for U.S. export controls. Assistance in complying with export controls can be obtained directly from local district offices or from the Exporter Counseling Division with the Bureau of Export Administration (BXA) Office of Export Licensing in Washington, DC (202-377-4811). BXA also has four field offices that specialize in counseling on export controls and regulations: the Western Regional Office (714-660-0144), the Northern California Branch Office (408-748-7450), the Portland Branch Office (503-326-5159), and the Eastern Regional Office (603-834-6300).

TRADE ADJUSTMENT ASSISTANCE

Trade Adjustment Assistance, part of Commerce's Economic Development Administration, helps firms that have been adversely affected by imported products to adjust to international competition. Companies eligible for trade adjustment assistance may receive technical consulting to upgrade operations such as product engineering, marketing, information systems, export promotion, and energy management. The federal government may assume up to 75 percent of the cost of these services. For more information call 202-377-3373.

TRAVEL AND TOURISM

The U.S. Travel and Tourism Administration (USTTA) promotes U.S. export earnings through trade in tourism. USTTA stimulates foreign demand, helps to remove barriers, increases the number of small and medium-sized travel businesses participating in the export market, provides timely data, and forms marketing partnerships with private industry and with state and local governments.

To maintain its programs in international markets, USTTA has offices in Toronto, Montreal, Vancouver, Mexico City, Tokyo, London, Paris, Amsterdam, Milan, Frankfurt, Sydney, and (serving South America) Miami.

Travel development activities in countries without direct USTTA representation are carried out under the direction of USTTA regional directors, who cooperate with Visit USA committees composed of representative from the U.S. and foreign travel industry in those countries, and also with the US&FCS. For more information, U.S. destinations and suppliers of tourism services interested in the overseas promotion of travel to the United States should call 202-377-4003.

Foreign Requirements for U.S. Products and Services

For information about foreign standards and certification systems, write National Center for Standards and Certificates Information, National Institute for Standards and Technology (NIST), Administration Building, A629, Gaithersburg, MD 20899; telephone 301-975-4040, 4038, or 4036. NIST maintains a General Agreement on Tariffs and Trade (GATT) hotline (301-975-4041) with a recording that reports on the latest notifications of proposed foreign regulations that may affect trade. Exporters can also get information from the nongovernmental American National Standards Institute (212-354-3300).

Minority Business Development Agency (MBDA)

The MBDA identifies minority business enterprises (MBEs) in selected industries to increase their awareness of their relative size and product advantages and to aggressively take them through the advanced stages of market development.

Through an interagency agreement with the ITA, MBDA provides information on market and product needs worldwide. MBDA and ITA coordinate MBE participation in Matchmaker and other trade delegations.

MBDA provides counseling through the Minority Business Development Center network to help MBEs prepare international marketing plans and promotional materials and to identify financial resources.

For general export information, the field organizations of both MBDA and ITA provide information kits and information on local seminars. Contact Minority Business Development Agency, Office of Program Development, U.S. Department of Commerce, Washington, DC 20230; telephone 202-377-3237.

Foreign Metric Regulations

The Office of Metric Programs (202-377-0944) provides exporters with guidance and assistance on matters relating to U.S. transition to the metric system. It can also give referrals to metric contacts in state governments.

FISHERY PRODUCTS EXPORTS

The National Oceanic and Atmospheric Administration (NOAA) assists seafood exporters by facilitating access to foreign markets. NOAA's National Marine Fisheries Service provides inspection services for fishery exports and issues official U.S. government certification attesting to the findings. Contact Office of Trade and Industry Service, Room 6490, 1335 East-West Highway, Silver Spring, MD 20910. Telephone numbers are as follows: Trade Matters, 301-427-2379 or 2383; Export Inspection, 301-427-2355; and Fisheries Promotion, 301-427-2379.

BUREAU OF THE CENSUS

The Bureau of the Census is the primary source of trade statistics that break down the quantity and dollar value of U.S. exports and imports by commodity (product) and country. Commerce district offices can help retrieve Census export statistics for exporters who want to identify potential export markets for their products. Firms interested in more extensive statistical data can contact the Bureau of the Census at 301-763-5140.

Census data can also provide authoritative guidance on questions concerning shippers' export declarations. Call 301-763-5310.

Department of State

The Department of State has a diverse staff capable of providing U.S. exporters with trade contacts. These staff members include bureau commercial coordinators, country desk officers, policy officers in the functional bureaus (such as the Bureau of Economic and Business Affairs), and all U.S. embassies and consular posts abroad. While the Department of Commerce's US&FCS is present in 67 countries, the Department of State provides commercial services in 84 embassies and numerous consular posts. Their addresses and telephone numbers are published in the directory titled *Key Officers of Foreign Service Posts,* available from the U.S. Government Printing Office (202-783-3238).

The ambassador takes the lead in promoting U.S. trade and investment interests in every U.S. embassy. All members of U.S. diplomatic missions abroad have the following continuing obligations:

- To ascertain the views of the American business sector on foreign policy issues that affects its interests, in order to ensure that those views are fully considered in the development of policy.
- To seek to ensure that the ground rules for conducting international trade are fair and nondiscriminatory.
- To be responsive when U.S. firms seek assistance, providing them with professional advice and analysis as well as assistance in making and developing contacts abroad.
- To vigorously encourage and promote the export of U.S. goods, services, and agricultural commodities and represent the interests of U.S. business to foreign governments where appropriate.
- To assist U.S. business in settling investment disputes with foreign governments amicably and, in cases of expropriation or similar action, to obtain prompt, adequate, and effective compensation.

Bureau of Economic and Business Affairs

The Bureau of Economic and Business Affairs has primary responsibility within the Department of State for (1) formulating and implementing polices regarding foreign economic matters, trade promotion, and business services of an international nature and (2) coordinating regional economic policy with other bureaus. The bureau is divided functionally as follows: Planning and Economic Analysis Staff; Office of Commercial, Legislative, and Public Affairs; Trade and Commercial Affairs (including textiles and food policy); International Finance and Development (including investment and business practices); Transportation (including aviation and maritime affairs); International Energy and Resources Policy; International Energy and Resources Policy; and International Trade Controls. For more information, contact Commercial Coordinator, Bureau of Economic and Business Affairs; telephone 202-647-1942.

Regional Bureaus

Regional bureaus, each under the direction of an assistant secretary of stage, are responsible for U.S. foreign affairs activities in specific major regions of the world. Bureau commercial coordinators can be reached on the following telephone numbers:

- Bureau of African Affairs, 202-647-3503.
- Bureau of East Asian and Pacific Affairs, 202-647-2006.
- Bureau of Near Eastern and South Asian Affairs, 202-647-4835.
- Bureau of European and Canadian Affairs, 202-647-2395.
- Bureau of International Communications and Information Policy, 202-647-5832.

Country desk offices maintain day-to-day contact with overseas diplomatic posts and provide country-specific economic and political analysis and commercial counseling to U.S. business.

Cooperation Between State and Commerce

The Departments of State and Commerce provide many services to U.S. business jointly. Firms interested in establishing a market for their products or expanding sales abroad should first seek assistance from their nearest Department of Commerce district office, which can tap into the worldwide network of State and Commerce officials serving in U.S. missions abroad and in Washington.

Small Business Administration

Through its 107 field offices in cities throughout the United States, the U.S. Small Business Administration (SBA) provides counseling to potential and current small business exporters. These no-cost services include the following:

- **Legal advice.** Through an arrangement with the Federal Bar Association (FBA), exporters may receive initial export legal assistance. Under this program, qualified attorneys from the International Law Council of the FBA, working through SBA field offices, provide free initial consultations to small companies on the legal aspects of exporting.
- **Export training.** SBA field offices cosponsor export training programs with the Department of Commerce, other federal agencies, and various private sector international trade organizations. These programs are conducted by experienced international traders.

- **Small Business Institute and small-business development centers.** Through the Small Business Institute advanced business students from more than 500 colleges and universities provide in-depth, long-term counseling under faculty supervision to small businesses. Additional export counseling and assistance are offered through small-business development centers, which are located in some colleges and universities. Students in these two programs provide technical help by developing an export marketing feasibility study and analysis for their client firms.
- **Export counseling.** Export counseling services are also furnished to potential and current small business exporters by executives and professional consultants. Members of the Service Corps of Retired Executives, with practical experience in international trade, help small firms evaluate their export potential and strengthen their domestic operations by identifying financial, managerial, or technical problems. These advisors also can help small firms develop and implement basic export marketing plans, which show where and how to sell goods abroad.

For information on any of the programs funded by SBA, contact the nearest SBA field office (see Appendix B).

Department of Agriculture

The U.S. Department of Agriculture (USDA) export promotion efforts are centered in the Foreign Agricultural Service (FAS), whose marketing programs are discussed in Chapter 7. However, other USDA agencies also offer services to U.S. exporters of agricultural products: the Economic Research Service, the Office of Transportation, the Animal and Plant Health Inspection Service, and the Federal Grain Inspection Service. A wide variety of other valuable programs is offered, such as promotion of U.S. farm products in foreign markets; services of commodity and marketing specialists in Washington, DC; trade fair exhibits; publications and information services; and financing programs. For more information on programs contact the director of the High-Value Product Services Division, Foreign Agricultural Service, U.S. Department of Agriculture, Washington, DC 20250; telephone 202-447-6343.

State Governments

State economic development agencies, departments of commerce, and other departments of state governments often provide valuable assistance to exporters. State export development programs are growing rapidly. In many areas, county and city economic development agencies also have export assistance programs. The aid offered by these groups typically includes the following;

* **Export education**–helping exporters analyze export potential and orienting them to export techniques and strategies. This help may take the form of group seminars or individual counseling sessions.
* **Trade missions**–organizing trips abroad enabling exporters to call on potential foreign customers.
* **Trade shows**–organizing and sponsoring exhibitions of state-produced goods and services in overseas markets.

Appendix B lists the agencies in each state responsible for export assistance to local firms. Also included are the names of other government and private organizations, with their telephone numbers and addresses. Readers interested in the role played by state development agencies in promoting and supporting exports may also wish to contact the National Association of State Development Agencies, 444 North Capitol Street, Suite 611, Washington, DC 20001; telephone 202-624-5411.

To determine if a particular county or city has local export assistance programs, contact the appropriate economic development agency. Appendix B includes contact information for several major cities.

Commercial Banks

More than 300 U.S. banks have international banking departments with specialists familiar with specific foreign countries and various types of commodities and transactions. These large banks, located in major U.S. cities, maintain correspondent relationships with smaller banks throughout the country. Larger banks also maintain correspondent relationships with banks in most foreign countries or operate their own overseas branches, providing a direct channel to foreign customers.

International banking specialists are generally well informed about export matters, even in areas that fall outside the usual limits of international banking. If they are unable to provide direct guidance or assistance, they may be able to refer inquirers to other specialists who can. Banks frequently provide consultation and guidance free of charge to their clients, since they derive income primarily from loans to the exporter and from fees for special services. Many banks also have publication available to help exporters. These materials often cover particular countries and their business practices and can be a valuable tool for initial familiarization with foreign industry. Finally, large banks frequently conduct seminar and workshops on letters of credit, documentary collections, and other banking subjects of concern to exporters.

Among the many services a commercial bank may perform for its clients are the following;

- Exchange of currencies.
- Assistance in financing exports.
- Collection of foreign invoices, drafts, letters of credit, and other foreign receivables.
- Transfer of funds to other countries.
- Letters of introduction and letters of credit for travelers.
- Credit information on potential representative or buyers overseas.
- Credit assistance to the exporter's foreign buyers.

Export Intermediaries

Export intermediaries are of many different types, ranging from giant international companies, many foreign owned, to highly specialized, small operations. They provide a multitude of services, such as performing market research, appointing overseas distributors or commission representatives, exhibiting a client's products at international trade shows, advertising, shipping, and arranging documentation. In short, the intermediary can often take full responsibility for the export end of the business, relieving the manufacturer of all the details except filling orders.

Intermediaries may work simultaneously for a number of exporters on the basis of commissions, salary, or retainer plus commission. Some take title to the goods they handle, buying and selling in their own right. Products of a trading company's clients are often related, although the items usually are non-competitive. One advantage of using an intermediary is that it can immediately make available marketing resources that a smaller firm would need years to develop on its own. Many export intermediaries also finance sales and extend credit, facilitating prompt payment to the exporter. Ask your state or local field office at the U.S. Department of Commerce for a list of export intermediaries. (See Appendix B for addresses and phone numbers.)

World Trade Centers and International Trade Clubs

Local or regional world trade centers and international trade clubs are composed of area business people who represent firms engaged in international trade and shipping, banks, forwarders, customs brokers, government agencies, and other service organizations involved in world trade. These organizations conduct educational programs on international business and organize promotional events to stimulate interest in world trade. Some 80 world trade centers or affiliated associations are located in major trading cities throughout the world.

By participating in a local association, a company can receive valuable and timely advice on world markets and opportunities from business people who are already knowledgeable on virtually any facet of international business. Another important advantage of membership in a local world trade club is the availability of benefits—such as services, discounts, and contacts—in affiliated clubs from foreign countries.

Chambers of Commerce and Trade Associations

Many local chambers of commerce and major trade associations in the United States provide sophisticated and extensive services for members interested in exporting. Among these services are the following:

- Conducting export seminars, workshops, and roundtables.
- Providing certificates of origin.
- Developing trade promotion programs, including overseas missions, mailings, and event planning.

- Organizing U.S. pavilions in foreign trade shows.
- Providing contacts with foreign companies and distributors.
- Relaying export sales leads and other opportunities to members.
- Organizing transportation routings and shipment consolidations.
- Hosting visiting trade missions from other countries.
- Conducting international activities at domestic trade shows.

In addition, some industry associations can supply detailed information on market demand for products in selected countries or refer members to export management companies. Most trade associations play an active role in lobbying for U.S. trade policies beneficial to their industries.

Industry trade associations typically collect and maintain files on international trade news and trends affecting manufactures. Often they publish articles and newsletters that include government research.

American Chambers of Commerce Abroad

A valuable and reliable source of market information in any foreign country is the local chapter of the American chamber of commerce. These organizations are knowledgeable about local trade opportunities, actual and potential competition, periods of maximum trade activity, and similar considerations.

American chambers of commerce abroad usually handle inquires from any U.S. business. Detailed service, however, is ordinarily provided free of charge only for members of affiliated organizations. some chambers have a set schedule of charges for services rendered to nonmembers. For contact information on American chambers in major foreign markets, write WCCD, P.O. Box 1029, Loveland, CO, 80539.

International Trade Consultants and Other Advisors

International trade consultants can advise and assist a manufacturer on all aspects of foreign marketing. Trade consultants do not normally deal specifically with one product, although they may advise on product adaptation to a foreign market. They research domestic and foreign regulations and also assess commercial and political risk. They conduct foreign market research and establish contacts with foreign government agencies and other necessary resources, such as advertising companies, product service facilities, and local attorneys.

These consultants can locate and qualify foreign joint venture partners as well as conduct feasibility studies for the sale of manufacturing rights, the location and construction of manufacturing facilities, and the establishment of foreign branches. After sales agreements are completed, trade consultants can also ensure that follow-through is smooth and that any problems that arise are dealt with effectively.

Trade consultants usually specialize by subject matter and by global area or country. For example, firms may specialize in high-technology exports to the Far East. Their consultants can advise on which agents or distributors are likely to be successful, what kinds of promotion are needed, who the competitors are, and how to deal with them. They are also knowledgeable about foreign government regulations, contract laws, and taxation. Some firms may be more specialized than others; for example, some may be thoroughly knowledgeable on legal aspects and taxation and less knowledgeable on marketing strategies.

Many large accounting firms, law firms, and specialized marketing firms provide international trade consulting services. When selecting a consulting firm, the exporter should pay particular attention to the experience and knowledge of the consultant who is in charge of its project. To find an appropriate firm, advice should be sought from other exporters and some of the other resources listed in this chapter, such as the Department of Commerce district office or local chamber of commerce.

Consultants are of greatest value to a firm that knows exactly what it wants. For this reason, and because private consultants are expensive, it pays to take full advantage of publicly funded sources of advice before hiring a consultant.

APPENDIX I

National Venture Capital Association
1655 North Fort Myer Drive
Suite 700
Arlington, VA 22209
(703) 351-5269

Western Association of Venture Capitalists
3000 Sand Hill Road
Building 1, Suite 190
Menlo Park, CA 94025
(415) 854-1322

A.D.S. Financial
524 Camino del Monte Sol
Santa Fe, NM 87501
(505) 983-1769

APPENDIX J

ASSOCIATIONS REPRESENTING SMALL BUSINESS
INVESTMENT COMPANIES

National Association of Small Business Investment Companies
1199 North Fairfax Street
Suite 200
Alexandria, VA 22314
(703) 683-1601

National Association of Investment Companies
1111 14th Street NW
Suite 700
Washington, DC 20005
(202) 289-4336

APPENDIX K

ASSOCIATIONS REPRESENTING COMMERCIAL FINANCE COMPANIES

Commercial Finance Association
225 West 34th Street
Suite 1815
New York, NY 10122
(212) 594-3490

American Association of Equipment Lessors
1300 North 17th Street
Suite 1010
Arlington, VA 22209
(703) 527-8655

INDEX